THE ECONOMIC ADVISORY COUNCIL
1930–1939

THE ECONOMIC ADVISORY COUNCIL 1930-1939

A STUDY IN ECONOMIC ADVICE DURING DEPRESSION AND RECOVERY

SUSAN HOWSON

WOLFSON COLLEGE, CAMBRIDGE

DONALD WINCH

UNIVERSITY OF SUSSEX

CAMBRIDGE UNIVERSITY PRESS

CAMBRIDGE

LONDON · NEW YORK · MELBOURNE

Published by the Syndics of the Cambridge University Press
The Pitt Building, Trumpington Street, Cambridge CB2 1RP
Bentley House, 200 Euston Road, London NW1 2DB
32 East 57th Street, New York, NY 10022, USA
296 Beaconsfield Parade, Middle Park, Melbourne 3206, Australia

First published 1977

Printed in Great Britain
at the
University Printing House, Cambridge

Library of Congress Cataloguing in Publication Data
Howson, Susan, 1945-
The Economic Advisory Council, 1930-1939.
Bibliography: p.
Includes index.
1. Great Britain. Economic Advisory Council.
2. Great Britain – Economic conditions – 1918-1945.
3. Depressions – 1930. I. Winch, Donald, joint author. II. Title.
HC256.2.H65   338.941   75-38187
ISBN 0 521 21138 7

CONTENTS

CONTENTS

ACKNOWLEDGEMENTS

We should like to acknowledge the help we have received from a number of people who have read and commented on earlier drafts of parts of this study. Our chief debts in this respect are to Donald Moggridge, Lord Kahn, Sir Austin Robinson, Ian Drummond, Mark Blaug, Jacques Melitz, and Don Patinkin. We are particularly grateful to Donald Moggridge, who encouraged us to undertake the project in the first place.

We should also like to thank Lord Kahn for allowing us to use the Keynes Papers and to reproduce the complete text of a letter from Keynes to MacDonald in 1931, David Marquand for allowing us access to the MacDonald Papers in his possession, and Lady Henderson for allowing us to cite documents in the Henderson Papers at Nuffield College, Oxford. Transcripts of Crown-copyright records in the Public Record Office appear by permission of the Controller of Her Majesty's Stationery Office. We are grateful to Dr W. H. Janeway for permission to cite his unpublished University of Cambridge Ph.D. dissertation, 'The Economic Policy of the Second Labour Government, 1929–31' (© William Hall Janeway 1971), and to Dr D. E. Pitfield for permission to cite his University of Stirling Ph.D. thesis, 'Labour Migration and the Regional Problem in Britain, 1920–1939' (1973). Sir Austin Robinson and Lord Kahn have kindly allowed us to use information which they gave us in conversations and letters about the Economic Advisory Council, and Donald Moggridge has allowed us to read and quote from the forthcoming second world war volumes of *The Collected Writings of John Maynard Keynes*.

We would also like to acknowledge the sponsorship of the Royal Economic Society and the financial assistance of the Social Science Research Council and the Political Science Fund of the University of Cambridge. During the latter stages of the preparation of this book one of the authors, Donald Winch, had the good fortune to be resident at the Institute for Advanced Study in Princeton. Our thanks are also due to Coral George and Catharine Rhubart for their typing.

Numbers in the text refer to Notes (pp. 382–404)
which are primarily source notes.

CHAPTER 1

INTRODUCTION

One of the dominant themes of twentieth-century political and economic history has been the assumption by the state not merely of an increasingly wide range of social and economic obligations but of explicit responsibilities in the field of economic management. Connected with this have been changes in the machinery of government, the most significant of which have been the creation of special organs of economic appraisal and advice. There has also been a succession of attempts to establish regular means of collaboration between government and the representatives of industry on matters of economic policy. Since the second world war the official employment of economists in government in this country has become commonplace; and it is no accident that all the important early milestones in the history of economic management in the post-Keynesian sense of the term – the main ones being the creation of the Central Economic Information Service within the Cabinet Office in 1939, the Kingsley Wood budget of 1941, and the White Paper on Employment Policy of 1944 – belong to the second world war. These developments also have an interesting pre-history which belongs to the inter-war period, and the Economic Advisory Council, the subject of this volume, played an important part in that pre-history.

The Economic Advisory Council was established by the second Labour Government in January 1930, and was widely regarded as the brainchild of the Prime Minister, Ramsay MacDonald. According to the Labour Party's election manifesto it was to be the Prime Minister's 'eyes and ears on economic questions'. More formally, but no less ambitiously, it was intended to advise the government on all matters of economic policy and to 'make continuous study of developments in trade and industry and in the use of national and imperial resources, of the effect of legislation and fiscal policy at home and abroad, and of all aspects of national, imperial and international economy with a bearing on the prosperity of the country'.[1] The Council was in fact the first attempt in Britain to recruit economists into government service on a full-time basis, and to create a mechanism whereby the government could call upon a wide range of outside experts for advice on a regular and formal basis.

The Council came into existence at a particularly difficult period in the political and economic history of Britain. When the minority Labour Government took office in 1929 it was pledged 'to deal immediately and practically' with the problem of chronic unemployment from which Britain had suffered throughout the 1920s. Not long after taking office, however, the government found itself faced with a severe intensification of unemployment as a result of the world-wide depression. Later, in 1931, it was overtaken by an international financial crisis which led to a split within the Cabinet over measures to deal with the crisis, the replacement of the Labour Government by a National Government under the leadership of MacDonald in August, and the abandonment of the gold standard in September.

Although individual members of the Council continued to give advice throughout the crisis period, the Council itself was in abeyance over the summer of 1931, and was never revived in the same form again. Partly, no doubt, as a result of the association of the Council with Ramsay MacDonald and the dramatic events which led to the break-up of the Labour Government, the verdict passed on the experiment so far by most historians has been one of failure.[2] The Council certainly did not live up to the claims made on its behalf when it was first created; and it cannot be said to have exercised a major influence, for good or ill, on the policies actually pursued by the government which brought it into being. But the precise nature of the failure of the original Council idea cannot be established by reference to the events and personalities of the unfortunate Labour Government alone. It should be seen against a wider background of hopes and experience throughout the 1920s which led many to advocate the creation of some kind of economic advisory body as an essential part of the machinery of government. Chapter 2 of this study attempts to provide this wider perspective, while Chapters 3 and 4 deal with the role of the Council in the policy-making machinery of the government against the background of world depression which conditioned its work and eventually led to its demise.

Another, more serious, defect in comment on the Economic Advisory Council by both contemporaries and historians has been a tendency to overlook or underestimate the accomplishments of its more modest successor, the Committee on Economic Information, which carried on many of the essential functions of the Economic Advisory Council throughout the 1930s.* It has rightly been said of this Committee that 'it was the first body at the centre of the government consisting preponderantly of economists and concerned exclusively with economic advice'.[3] As such, it served as an essential stepping-stone towards the more ambitious advisory system devised during the early stages of the second world war, when it was transformed first into Stamp's Survey of War Plans and then, via the Central Economic Information Service, into the Economic Section of the Cabinet

---

* A. J. P. Taylor manages to deal with the Committee in one sentence: '[The Council] remained theoretically in existence and even circulated some papers' (*English History 1914–1945*, p. 409n).

Office. Here again, though, the verdict passed by one of its members leans towards failure. Sir Arthur Salter wrote:

All the relevant information was at our disposal. We were able over a great range of controversial questions to make unanimous recommendations which would, if adopted, have profoundly changed the policy of the time. In retrospect they can, I think, be seen to have anticipated much that later became orthodox in Whitehall as elsewhere. But in fact we had little practical effect. Our reports were secret and could be and were rejected and ignored by any department which disliked them, without explanation in public, or even in private to ourselves.[4]

The purpose of Chapter 5 of this study is to provide an account of the work of the Committee on Economic Information by tracing its influence on those Treasury and Cabinet deliberations which form part of the history of economic management in this period. The study concludes with a chapter principally devoted to an evaluation of the successes and failures of the Economic Advisory Council in the light of the foregoing material. It is one of the main conclusions that the influence of the Committee on Economic Information on official attitudes and policies during the 1930s, as represented by the verdicts cited above, has been seriously undervalued.

Any account of bodies like the Council and the Committee must be more than a study in administrative history; it must deal with the economic situation faced by those being advised, and the possibilities thought to be available. One of the virtues of the reports produced by the Council is that they provide a clear picture of the situation as seen by contemporaries concerned with the formation and implementation of economic policies. Since we believe that the influence of the reports on policy-makers, notably in the Treasury after 1932, was by no means negligible, we hope that this study will throw light on the history of economic policy in the 1930s. Moreover, since the Council and later the Committee provided a forum and one of the channels through which the views of a number of leading economists – notably John Maynard Keynes – were made available to ministers and civil servants during a crucial period in the history of economics, we also hope that the material presented here will be of interest to historians of economic thought, and to those generally concerned with the application of social scientific expertise in government. The events and deliberations described here provide the relevant policy background to the writing of *The General Theory of Employment, Interest and Money*.

In common with some other recent studies, ours relies heavily on the wealth of official material now available at the Public Record Office.* Indeed, this study was undertaken in the belief that a selection of the con-

---

* Here we have in mind D. E. Moggridge, *The Return to Gold, 1925* (1969) and *British Monetary Policy 1924–1931* (1972); I. M. Drummond, *British Economic Policy and the Empire, 1919–1939* (1972) and *Imperial Economic Policy 1917–1939* (1974); W. H. Janeway, 'The Economic Policy of the Second Labour Government, 1929–31', unpublished Cambridge Ph.D. thesis, 1971; and S. K. Howson, *Domestic Monetary Management in Britain, 1919–38* (1975).

fidential reports and memoranda written by economists for the Economic Advisory Council would be of sufficient interest to warrant its being made more readily and widely available. Its present form is the result of finding that publication of the documents would have to accompanied by more than a brief editorial introduction.*

* Another consequence of the weight of relevant material among the government records is that we have had to concentrate on this evidence. For an account of economic policy in the inter-war years based on other evidence, see Donald Winch, *Economics and Policy: A Historical Study* (1969; revised paperback edn, 1972), Chs. 4–10.

CHAPTER 2

ORIGINS AND BACKGROUND

As it finally emerged the Economic Advisory Council represented a compromise between two ideas which were first articulated during the latter half of the first world war as part of the general interest in 'reconstruction'. The first of these ideas found expression in arguments for establishing what later became known as an economic general staff within the machinery of government, consisting of economists and statisticians acting as a regular organ of economic intelligence and advice. The second idea was more diffuse in character: it was advocated in several different guises during the inter-war period, but can be clearly recognised in its most influential form as a case for creating a national council composed mainly of employers' and trade union representatives drawn together in a deliberative assembly which could also serve as an advisory channel to the government on all matters affecting industrial relations as well as the wider issues of industrial and economic policy. While the former idea was largely administrative and technocratic in inspiration, though not, of course, without political significance, the latter entailed a combination of technocratic and representative elements.

Post-war reconstruction and the Committee of Civil Research

There is a long history of involvement by economists in the processes of official policy-making in Britain which goes back to the first half of the nineteenth century. For the most part this took the form of *ad hoc* advice given by economists acting as members of, or expert witnesses before, Royal Commissions and parliamentary select committees; it did not extend to full-time employment of economists *as such* within government until the Economic Advisory Council was established. Before the first world war there was an optional paper on political economy in the Civil Service Commissioners' examinations, but as Sir John Anderson pointed out,

Up to the beginning of the first European War, the idea of employing professional economists in the business of government in any sphere seemed hardly to have occurred to anyone. It was, of course, only to a very limited extent that government and government departments had until then found occasion to concern themselves with economic problems. To the extent that they did, they produced their own experts.[1]

In this way a number of senior civil servants achieved prominence as internal economic and financial experts. This was true, for example, of Sir Hubert

Llewellyn Smith and Sir Sydney Chapman at the Board of Trade. The Treasury produced a succession of such figures, the leading examples before and after the war being Sir John Bradbury, Sir Basil Blackett, Sir Otto Niemeyer, Sir Frederick Leith-Ross, Sir Richard Hopkins (originally with the Board of Inland Revenue), Sir Frederick Phillips, and Sir Ralph Hawtrey. Hawtrey had entered the civil service on an ordinary basis before the war, and from 1919 onwards was Director of Financial Enquiries at the Treasury. During this period he published numerous works on economic theory, and was appointed Professor at the Royal Institute of International Affairs upon his retirement in 1944. He had earlier been Visiting Professor at Harvard in 1928–9.

During the war a number of economists and statisticians entered government service on a temporary basis. The most distinguished of these was John Maynard Keynes, who began his career as a civil servant at the India Office (1906–9) and served on the Royal Commission on Indian Finance and Currency in 1913 under the chairmanship of Austen Chamberlain. It was partly through Chamberlain that Keynes was drafted into the Treasury in 1914, where he came to take charge of a division concerned with external finance and subsequently became the principal Treasury adviser at the Peace Conference at Versailles. He resigned in 1919 in disagreement over the reparations question and the general peace terms.[2] Keynes later featured prominently as a member of the Economic Advisory Council alongside Josiah Stamp, another economist who began his career as a civil servant, though in the humble capacity of boy clerk. By the time Stamp left the civil service in 1919 to enter business, he had become Assistant Secretary at the Board of Trade, and was soon to be acknowledged one of the country's leading experts on taxation and the statistical problems connected with national income estimates.[3] According to Sir John Anderson, who was Stamp's official chief at the Board of Inland Revenue,

the proof that [Stamp] gave of the need for expert advice on economic problems, together with a realisation of the inconvenience and danger . . . of undue dependence on one man, even of the stupendous energy and resource of Stamp, must have stimulated consideration of possible alternative methods of organisation, particularly at a time when the progressive extension of Government activity in the economic field was seen to be inevitable.[4]

Other economists in war-time government service and later members of the Economic Advisory Council were Hubert Henderson (Secretary of the Cotton Control Board) and Arthur Salter (Director of Ship Requisitioning).

With the greatly expanded role of the state in coordinating and directing the national productive effort during the war came an increased awareness of the need to strengthen the machinery of economic intelligence at the departmental, if not Cabinet, level. The earliest effort in this direction was the establishment of a General Economic Department inside the Board of Trade in 1917. The prime mover was Llewellyn Smith, then Permanent

Secretary to the Board, whose aim, as he later explained to the Haldane Committee on the Machinery of Government, was to establish a body which would 'anticipate, watch and suggest means of dealing with, important questions and movements likely to arise in commerce and industry, and which from their generality or novelty did not fall within the scope of any specialised Department'.[5] It was to be staffed by civil service secondments and temporary appointments of students with degrees in economics. The Haldane Committee had been set up by the Ministry of Reconstruction; the report which it produced in 1918 commented favourably on the Board of Trade experiment, while making a general recommendation 'that in the sphere of civil government the duty of investigation and thought, as a preliminary to action, might with great advantage be more definitely recognised'. It also noted with favour the existence of the Medical Research Council and the establishment of the Department of Scientific and Industrial Research in 1916 under the direction of the Lord President of the Council; it considered the latter body might provide a model for a specialised research organisation concerned with economic questions, though it also recommended that every existing department should make provision for research, and envisaged the possible need for a separate Department of Intelligence and Research to work on problems outside the range of the other departments.[6]

The origins, therefore, of the case for an economic general staff, at the departmental level at least, can be traced back to the reconstruction movement which flourished briefly towards the end of the war; and its fate during the first half of the 1920s follows that of the movement generally. The mood of optimism concerning the possibilities of economic planning and national cooperation which prevailed at the end of the war soon evaporated in the face of pressures for dismantling war-time economic control.[7] The desire to return to pre-war methods of doing business was accompanied by an almost obsessive concern with ways of reducing government expenditure, particularly on administration, symbolised by the appointment of the powerful Geddes Committee on National Expenditure in 1921. Little or no action was taken to implement the findings of the Haldane Committee, and by 1922 the embryonic developments within the Board of Trade had fallen victims to the Geddes axe, leaving as their only residue the post of Chief Economic Adviser to the Government, a post which Llewellyn Smith occupied after his retirement as Permanent Secretary.[8] The main duties of this post in the 1920s and 1930s were connected with international and inter-imperial matters, preparatory work for international conferences, and attendance as British delegate on such bodies as the committees of the Economic Organisation of the League of Nations.[9] The next holder of the post, from 1930 to 1932, was Sir Sydney Chapman, also previously Permanent Secretary to the Board of Trade. His successor was a Treasury official, Sir Frederick Leith-Ross, who continued to carry out the original functions as delegate to various standing international committees, but retained many of his Treasury duties connected with international finance. He was also involved in the work of the Economic Advisory Council. Leith-Ross regarded his title as a misnomer, and his attitude is perhaps best summed up by his comment that while some ministers took the title literally and asked his advice on domestic economic problems, 'happily, [such requests] were not frequent'.[10]

The case for employing economic experts within government has usually gone hand in hand with arguments for improving the collection and presentation of official statistics. In November 1919 a petition on this subject organised by a committee of the Royal Statistical Society and signed by an impressive list of statisticians and economists was presented to the Prime Minister. It drew attention to various major defects in the collection of official statistics and urged the need for a central statistical office to be established with adequate funds to supervise and coordinate the statistical work of all the departments with economic responsibilities. It pointed out that no general information on wages had been made available since the 1906 census; that home production figures were incomplete; that no figures existed on household consumption of food and clothing; and that the census returns on population had never been amalgamated with figures of national production and wages. Finally, the petition requested that a Royal Commission be appointed to consider this range of questions. The belated official response came in 1921 in the form of a report by a committee under the chairmanship of Sir Alfred Watson which denied the need for a Royal Commission or any general supervision of the collection of statistics; the committee also questioned the value, especially at a time when economy in public expenditure was at a premium, of extra-departmental data, such as that on national income and wealth, which had no direct relevance to the needs of day-to-day administration. As a concession to the petition, however, the committee recommended that an inter-departmental consultative committee should be set up to advise the Cabinet and the departments on statistical matters.[11]

The second idea to emerge in the immediate post-war period, and to figure later in the minds of some proponents of the Economic Advisory Council, was that of establishing some form of representative national industrial council.* One of the more influential committees set up by the Ministry of Reconstruction was that which sat under the chairmanship of J. H. Whitley to consider remedies for industrial unrest. The recommendations of this

---

* The idea has an earlier history which can be traced back to the Industrial Union society of the 1890s, a National Federation proposal of 1900, and an actual Industrial Council set up by the government in 1911 on the advice of Sir Charles Macara. On this, and for a detailed history of the episode considered in the text, see E. Halévy, 'The Policy of Social Peace in England', in *The Era of Tyrannies* (English edn, 1967); and R. Charles, *The Development of Industrial Relations in Britain 1911–39* (1973), pp. 36–74, 229–59.

committee in favour of sponsoring an elaborate network of joint industrial councils at the national, district, and works level were, of course, intended as a means of reducing conflict between capital and labour on an industry-by-industry basis; and the limited successes of 'Whitleyism' were achieved in specific industries which offered propitious circumstances for joint consultation. For a brief interlude after the war there was also considerable interest in the possibility of establishing a single national body which could be placed, albeit somewhat precariously, at the apex of the Whitley industrial relations pyramid. The interest focussed on the proceedings of the National Industrial Conference attended by eight hundred representatives drawn from both sides of industry which had its first meeting in February 1919. The conference was called into being by the Prime Minister, Lloyd George, and presided over by the Minister of Labour, Sir Robert Horne. A Provisional Joint Committee consisting of thirty representatives from each side of industry was charged with a brief to produce reports on wages, hours of work, unemployment, and all the major current sources of disagreement between unions, employers, and the government. One of the chief recommendations of this body was that a permanent elected National Industrial Council should be established which would meet bi-annually to consider industrial questions. Between meetings a standing committee under the chairmanship of the Minister of Labour would carry on the functions of the council, which were to intervene in industrial disputes where normal conciliation procedures had failed, and to act as the official consultative body to the government on all legislative matters affecting industry.

For a time high hopes centred on this proposal; and the whole report of the Provisional Joint Committee was adopted unanimously at the second meeting of the National Industrial Conference held in April. It subsequently became clear, however, that the government was mainly interested in using the conference as a temporary peace-making device, and had no intention of implementing the recommendations of the report of the Provisional Joint Committee. As a result, the trade union representatives resigned and the whole conference was finally disbanded in 1921. In spite of this failure the episode provided a precedent which some felt worth recalling later in the decade, particularly when reinforced by the more positive experience of the Mond–Turner talks held in 1928-9.[12]

The first signs of a revival of interest in questions of economic inquiry and intelligence came during the election campaign at the end of 1923. This election was fought by the Conservatives on the single issue of tariff protection as a means of reducing unemployment, and economic issues remained well to the fore throughout the campaign. There was a considerable measure of bi-partisan support for the publication of more and better information on industrial and economic matters.[13] For Labour supporters there was an added interest derived from an assumption that all such disclosures would support their case against the existing economic system, and furnish the necessary information for a plan of attack by any Labour government. Not long after the election, when Ramsay MacDonald had formed his first minority government, Clifford Allen, Treasurer and Chairman of the Independent Labour Party, spoke to Tom Jones, then Deputy Secretary to the Cabinet, about the marvellous opportunity now available for creating an economic general staff whose task it would be to draw up 'an economic Doomsday Book' showing 'precisely how the great industries are in fact now being run, their finances, markets, etc.'[14]

Whatever political attractions may have attached to the idea of establishing an economic general staff or council, it was chiefly from those with war-time administrative experience that most of the constructive proposals were to come. At the end of 1923 William Beveridge was one of the first to advocate the creation of an economic general staff at the Cabinet level along the lines of the Committee of Imperial Defence. It may also be significant that he did so in articles which appeared in *The Nation & Athenaeum*, a Liberal journal edited by Hubert Henderson under the control of a company chaired by Keynes. Beveridge argued that 'modern governments are faced with problems in the field of economic science as technical as those raised by war in the field of military and naval science'. This required a body that would stand above the existing departments, which were mainly concerned with day-to-day administration and staffed by civil servants with inadequate training in economics. It should be headed by 'a person of high authority in the science of economics, and of corresponding authority in the public service'.*

Haldane's acceptance of the post of Lord Chancellor in the Labour Government provided the first opportunity to implement some of the proposals contained in his report on the machinery of government. By 1924, however, in common with Beveridge's, Haldane's views had shifted away from an organisation along the lines of the Department of Scientific and Industrial Research towards a more flexible advisory body modelled on the Committee of Imperial Defence. He was supported in this by Lord Esher, one of the architects of that committee, whose scheme for a Coordinating Committee on Civil Affairs was submitted to the Cabinet together with memoranda prepared by Sir Warren Fisher for the Treasury and Sir Richard Hopkins for the Board of Inland Revenue. From Tom Jones's account of this episode it seems that the civil servants applied most of their efforts to ensuring that any new body would not encroach on the work of existing departments. Neither Maurice Hankey, Secretary to the Cabinet, nor Tom Jones himself was keen on the idea; and Hopkins's memorandum was

---

* *Nation*, 29 December 1923 and 5 January 1924. Beveridge had served with the Board of Trade before the war, and with the Ministries of Munitions and Food during the war; he also served on one of the sub-committees of the Ministry of Reconstruction, and appeared as a witness before the Haldane Committee. When the E.A.C. was formed he became one of its earliest defenders (*Times*, 14 February 1930).

practically confined to statistics, and is much narrower, therefore, than the scheme which Haldane and Esher have in mind'.[15]

By June a compromise had been reached and was embodied in a Treasury memorandum entitled 'Foresight and Co-ordination in Economic Enquiry' which was considered by the Cabinet and approved with minor modifications on 22 July 1924.[16] Tom Jones was to be the Secretary to the Committee of Economic Inquiry, as it was now called, and a list of proposed members was compiled for Cabinet approval. In spite of the advanced nature of these preparations the Prime Minister took no action before the government fell in October. Haldane later claimed that this was due to MacDonald's lack of interest in administrative matters, but in view of later events it seems more likely to have been due to the pressure of other business.

The Treasury memorandum spoke of the need 'for an organisation under the ultimate direction of the Prime Minister and the Cabinet charged with the duty of giving connected forethought from a central standpoint to the development of economic and statistical research in relation, more especially, to problems of an inter-departmental character, or in pursuit of knowledge in spheres not within the orbit of any single Minister'. In summary the objects of the committee were stated to be:

(a) To ensure that national problems were actually being faced and thought out in advance on a basis of fact;
(b) To assist the Government of the day with an organisation – stable but not rigid – for exploring the problems in which it is interested, without the need of improvising co-ordination; and
(c) To utilise to the greatest advantage the existing facilities of the Government Departments under conditions most likely to command the ready co-operation of their officials.[17]

To the modern reader, the striking feature of the memorandum is the almost compulsive emphasis on statistical information. In his covering note MacDonald, after stressing the analogies with the Committee of Imperial Defence, described the function of the committee as being 'to examine, from the point of view of ascertained and ascertainable economic data, proposals of policy, potential as well as actual'. The memorandum itself refers to the importance of compiling accurate and impartial statistics as a means of keeping the public informed and reducing the area of needless public controversy, and remarks that 'it has been said, with much force, that in this age most political and social problems are at bottom economic, and most economic problems are at bottom statistical'. This emphasis probably reflects Hopkins's contribution, as well as some of the themes arising out of the election.[18] It may also have something to do with the general state of opinion on economic questions.[19]

The Conservative Government took up the Treasury memorandum in the following year, with Lord Balfour, Lord President of the Council, making most of the running.[20] The result was the establishment of the

Committee of Civil Research. Although the committee carried out useful scientific work,[21] Balfour's leadership gave a special character to the committee. As a result, it was felt by 1929 that the committee was incapable, without substantial modification, of fulfilling the hopes of those interested in establishing an economic general staff.

In common with Haldane and Esher, Balfour had considerable experience of the Committee of Imperial Defence. Moreover, his main interests lay in the application of scientific research to the problems of industry and government.[22] As Lord President he became responsible for the Department of Scientific and Industrial Research and the associated research councils –a task which he had performed for the coalition government between 1919 and 1921. By 1925, however, a new influence made itself felt in the form of a report by a Parliamentary Commission on the administration and economic development of Britain's East African dependencies. This report was highly critical of existing policies; it also emphasised the importance of applying science and technology to the development of the agricultural resources of the colonies, and the need to devote more medical research and resources to the control of tropical diseases. Prior to the publication of the report Balfour had received a memorandum from the secretaries of the Department of Scientific and Industrial Research, the Medical Research Council, and the Development Commission urging the case for an Imperial Development Council. He responded enthusiastically to this new impetus, and it figured strongly in Cabinet discussions of the future role of the Committee of Civil Research. The Cabinet agreed 'that the scope of the enquiries of the Committee should cover the Empire as a whole in so far as it is under the direct control of the British Government, and also extend to the Dominions in so far as the latter might desire to associate themselves with it, but that there was no advantage in introducing the word Imperial into the title'.[23]

From its inception, therefore, the committee acquired an 'imperial' and scientific bias which had not been nearly so marked in the earlier discussions by the Labour Government.* The inquiries undertaken by the sub-committees through which the committee chiefly operated reflected this bias. With one or two important exceptions they were posed by ministries such as the Colonial Office or the Ministry of Agriculture and Fisheries, or alternatively by the Department for Scientific and Industrial Research, the Medical Research Council, and the British Association for the Advancement of Science. The committee also became one of the main channels for the funds which the Empire Marketing Board had at its disposal for supporting agricultural and pest-control projects in the colonies. On all such matters the committee was working with the grain in the sense that it was sponsoring research of a high technical, but relatively low political, content, and was not invading or threatening to invade territories marked out by the estab-

* Though colonial development was mentioned as one of the possible fields of inquiry (T. Jones, *Whitehall Diary*, Vol. I, p. 282).

lished departments. In fact, of course, it undertook projects which the departments themselves could not or did not wish to tackle. For such tasks the flexibility of the arrangements, and the fact that its permanent staff consisted only of a Secretary (Tom Jones) and an Assistant Secretary (A. F. Hemming), was a positive advantage.

In the light of this it is interesting to examine what happened in the small number of cases where the committee conducted inquiries into domestic economic issues. The first of these was a sub-committee on Overseas Loans which met in 1925 with a brief 'to examine the question of our capacity to meet the demands for credit at home and abroad, having particular regard for the requirements of Empire development and the maintenance of our export trade'.* Although this inquiry had political overtones, it was in many respects a continuation of work done in the previous year by the important Treasury committee under Lord Bradbury's chairmanship which had recommended return to gold at the pre-war parity. After the return to gold the Bank of England, with Treasury support, continued to exercise restraint over foreign lending in order to protect the reserves without raising Bank rate. Control over colonial issues and loans to the Dominions proved more difficult to achieve, and a draft telegram to Dominion Governors-General asking for cooperation in reducing demands on London led to conflict between the Chancellor of the Exchequer, Churchill, and the Colonial Secretary, L. S. Amery, who was anxious to protect imperial economic ties. In his account of this episode Moggridge conjectured that one of the conditions exacted by Amery in return for not raising the issue in the Cabinet, and for acquiescing in the dispatch of the telegrams, was a Committee of Civil Research inquiry into the general question of control over foreign and imperial lending.[24] In October the sub-committee's report recommended that the policy of embargo on foreign loans be discontinued; in future over-lending should be dealt with by more normal gold standard mechanisms, notably by raising Bank rate.[25] Churchill announced the end of the embargo on 3 November 1925, though this did not prevent the use of moral suasion to restrict foreign lending during the latter half of the 1920s. It seems clear that the inter-departmental character of the Committee of Civil Research made it convenient for use in a situation in which there was a disagreement between ministers to be resolved with the least publicity. Even so, the Treasury, according to Tom Jones, was 'not very enthusiastic about this inquiry'; Niemeyer initially tried to prevent its taking place, presumably on the grounds that any inquiry into the delicate matters controlled by the Bank of England was undesirable.[26] Moreover, the sub-committee would not let the committee see the minutes of its discussion,

* Cab. 58/1, C.C.R. 1st meeting, 18 June 1925. The members of the sub-committee were Lord Bradbury (ex-Treasury), Montagu Norman (Governor of the Bank of England), Otto Niemeyer (Treasury), S. J. Chapman (Board of Trade), H. Lambert (Crown Agent for the Colonies), C. H. Kisch (India Office), with J. Stamp as the only non-official member.

and omitted from its report the precise date recommended for ending the embargo 'in view of the exceptional need for secrecy'.[27]

Perhaps a more important example of an ostensibly economic inquiry undertaken by the committee was that into the iron and steel industry which began in 1925 and continued intermittently for the next three years. This arose out of a legitimate request by the industry for an inquiry by the Board of Trade under the Safeguarding of Industry Act of 1921. The problem posed by such a request was an awkward one for a government committed to using the safeguarding apparatus but pledged not to grant any request for a safeguarding duty which might act as a wedge for a general system of tariff protection. Moreover, the Cabinet was itself deeply divided over the merits of protection and free trade, with Amery and Churchill acting, once more, as the main adversaries. In the case of a key industry like iron and steel any safeguarding inquiry would raise the broader tariff question; but in order to reject the industry's request for an inquiry some alternative was necessary. Churchill, the leading free-trader in the Cabinet, suggested the cumbersome procedure of a Royal Commission, but the Cabinet agreed to the suggestion by the President of the Board of Trade, Cunliffe-Lister, of using the Committee of Civil Research instead.[28]

The sub-committee appointed was a weighty one, with the Prime Minister, Baldwin, choosing for the first and practically the only time to exercise his prerogative of chairing Committee of Civil Research meetings.* From the large amount of evidence taken, the members no doubt learnt a great deal about the problems of an important industry suffering from heavy unemployment; but at the end of three years they produced no report and made no recommendations to the Cabinet. The main result was political, and followed the original motive, namely to buy time while placating the industry. A similar conclusion applies to the inquiry undertaken in 1927 into unemployment in the coal industry, though the issue was narrower and less overtly political. Here a number of minor recommendations emerged, but after issuing an interim report the sub-committee failed to meet again.

The committee itself had little more than formal existence, and even on this level depended a great deal on the enthusiasm of Lord Balfour, who died in 1928. Confidentiality of its proceedings concealed little from the general public that was of great interest; the main committee merely gave general approval to sub-committee reports before passing them on to the relevant body. One of the main difficulties of the committee as a device for tackling controversial economic problems was, in Tom Jones's words,

---

* The other members were the Chancellor of the Exchequer, the President of the Board of Trade, the Colonial Secretary, and several heads of departments, including Hopkins, Fisher, and Chapman. The two most prominent outside members were the industrialists Sir Alfred Mond and Sir Hugo Hirst, though representatives of the industry attended for consultative purposes. There was some discussion in the Cabinet as to whether outsiders should be selected 'on political grounds or on account of their technical qualifications' (Cab. 23/50, Cabinet 31(25)2, 26 June 1925).

that 'emphasis was laid on the importance, especially when the experiment was critically regarded, of taking all possible steps to secure the co-operation of the Departments and to avoid the appointment of a large staff'.[29] There was suspicion and hostility within the Treasury to the new body, though other departments seem to have been more favourably disposed, particularly when the committee was first formed, possibly because they hoped that it might be a way of by-passing the Treasury.[30] There is some evidence that Tom Jones would have liked the committee to take on more fundamental questions in the economic field; but in the case, for example, of 'unemployment as a more or less permanent problem for the next ten years', it was possible to point to the existence of the Balfour Committee on Industry and Trade which sat from 1924 to 1929.[31] In any case it is difficult to see how a body which operated in a purely *ad hoc* way, and possessed no permanent staff with economic qualifications, could have undertaken any continuous study of economic problems. Tom Jones's list of subjects which had been put forward at one time or another for investigation by the Committee of Civil Research is miscellaneous, but with a bias towards statistical inquiry.* It avoids most of the central policy questions which any economist would consider important, especially those connected with the gold standard and monetary policy.†

Still less did the Committee of Civil Research satisfy the proponents of a representative industrial or economic council. The history of this idea in the second half of the 1920s is intimately bound up with the history of industrial relations, and more particularly with the work of two outstanding trade union leaders, Walter Citrine and Ernest Bevin, both of whom later served on the Economic Advisory Council. Between them these two men were chiefly responsible for strengthening and remodelling the General Council

* Prem. 1/70, 'The Committee of Civil Research': the amount and distribution of the national income; changes in the volume and profitability of the main industries in the country; the economic aspects of Empire unity; Empire cooperation in fundamental scientific research; family allowances; the bulk purchase of imports, e.g. wheat; a National register; cooperation and profit-sharing; preparation of a new Doomsday Book, showing distribution of land, houses, ownership, husbandry, etc.; the inter-relation of preventive measures against disease in farm stock and human beings.

† Keynes's list of inquiries that should have been undertaken during the period was rather different: the reactions on British industry of currency disturbances abroad; the effect on British trade of tariffs and policies of national self-sufficiency abroad; the return to the gold standard; the effects of unrestricted foreign investment and the possibility of controlling the rate and kind of foreign lending; credit and industry (including all the questions to be examined by the Committee on Finance and Industry); the housing problem; the effect of the rating system on industry and on housing; the unemployment problem; the state of agriculture; the staple export trades; the obstacles to the rationalisation of industry and the means of overcoming them – taken industry by industry; the special problems of the coal industry; the bearing of the prospective rate of population growth on education programmes, housing, pensions, etc.; the social and business consequences of a high level of direct taxation; the reactions of hours, wages and conditions of labour abroad on similar conditions at home; trade union restrictions; the public concern; the direction of investment (Prem. 1/70, P.M.C. 10, Keynes, 'Economic General Staff', 10 December 1929).

of the Trades Union Congress along lines that made it capable of acting as a coordinating body for the trade union movement, and a force to be reckoned with in all negotiations at the national level with employers' organisations and the government. In so doing, they gave the General Council an articulate voice on a wide range of national economic issues which had previously been thought to lie outside the purview of the movement.[32] Citrine and Bevin also became the chief architects and spokesmen for the policy of cooperation with the employers' organisations which resulted in the Mond–Turner talks of 1928–9 – a policy which they successfully defended against charges of 'class collaboration' at the T.U.C. annual conference in 1928. The response to the General Council's initiative in proposing machinery for joint conference between the two sides of industry came from an *ad hoc* grouping of industrialists under the leadership of Sir Alfred Mond rather than from the official employers' organisations. Moreover, unlike the ill-fated National Industrial Conference of 1919, the talks owed little to government initiative.[33] After the General Strike a heightened interest in methods of achieving industrial peace was understandable: what makes the Mond–Turner talks interesting, however, is the fact that a considerable measure of agreement was achieved on questions other than industrial relations, such as rationalisation and the gold standard.

Bevin and Citrine were both influenced by Keynes's attack on the decision to return to gold in 1925 at the pre-war parity.[34] Indeed, this was one of the main reasons why they considered it essential for the General Council to be able to sustain a general position on economic policy, and why the creation of the Economic Committee of the General Council for this purpose after 1928 was an important innovation. Mond too had criticised the original decision to return to gold.[35] During the talks common ground was established in opposition to a monetary policy which appeared to operate in the interests of the City rather than those of industry. One of the recommendations which bore fruit not long after the talks had petered out was for a thorough official inquiry into the relationship of finance and industry: this was the Macmillan Committee set up in 1929 by the Labour Government. There was also agreement on the need for a properly constituted National Industrial Council capable of voicing the opinions of those with practical knowledge of industry on economic policy. Although very little came of this proposal, it was a sign of recognition that industrial relations and economic policy questions could no longer be kept in separate compartments, and of the growing feeling that the representatives of both sides of industry had a right to be regularly consulted on policies which affected the economic life of the nation.

The second Labour Government and the formation of the Council

By 1929, when the next general election was held, economic problems had occupied the forefront of political debate for nearly a decade. Unemployment, concentrated in the staple export industries, had remained stubbornly around the 10 per cent mark throughout the period, and by the second half of the 1920s any hope that this might be due simply to post-war maladjustments had evaporated. It was widely recognised that Britain faced special problems of a structural character resulting from the long-term decline in competitive power of her basic export industries, notably coal, iron and steel, cotton, and shipbuilding. 'Rationalisation' was the compendium word used to describe solutions to the problems of these industries which entailed elimination of excess capacity and reduction of costs through reorganisation into larger production and marketing units. The role of the state in sponsoring rationalisation, and in arresting the process of decline by means of various expedients ranging from export promotion, through tariff truces, up to a full-blooded system of protective tariffs, had become a major area of policy debate. By the end of the period there was also growing support for the minority view that in addition to structural difficulties the British economy was suffering from deflationary pressures arising out of the decision to return to gold at pre-war parity. To those who held this view one of the main policy questions was to determine how far reflationary schemes of public investment could operate within the constraints posed by the gold standard, by the large volume of government debt contracted at high war-time rates of interest, and by a budgetary position made weaker as a result of the post-war growth of expenditure on 'non-productive' social services, which included the rising cost of propping up the unemployment insurance system.[36]

The election campaign provided an opportunity for each of the three main parties to rehearse the merits of all the leading diagnoses and remedies which had emerged in public discussion during the preceding years. Several of the economists who were later to become members of the Economic Advisory Council played a part by writing some of the election material. Thus R. H. Tawney was one of the authors of the Labour manifesto, while G. D. H. Cole, in addition to being a candidate, wrote *How to Conquer Unemployment: Labour's Reply to Lloyd George*. As the title of this pamphlet suggests, most of the running was made by the Liberals, whose main proposal for dealing with unemployment was an ambitious loan-financed programme of public expenditure controlled by a Board of National Investment, directed towards a wholesale renewal of the nation's capital, particularly in roads, housing, docks, electricity, agriculture, and telephones. The inspiration and rationale of this programme derived from the Liberal 'Yellow Book' on *Britain's Industrial Future* which had been produced in the previous year by a distinguished group of experts under the chairmanship of Walter

Layton. This group included Keynes and Henderson, who combined to write a defence of the Liberal programme entitled *Can Lloyd George Do It?* in 1929. The Conservatives' response was to issue a White Paper defending the government's record on public spending, making use of a Treasury memorandum which cast doubt on the economic validity of loan-financed public works as a method of increasing employment.[37] This 'Treasury view' drew a further attack from Keynes in the pages of *The Nation*.[38]

In support of its other proposals the Liberal 'Yellow Book' made a strong case for creating an economic general staff along lines advocated earlier by Beveridge. The authors pointed out that in spite of the dominance of economic problems of a novel and technical character, the Cabinet still did not have at its disposal expert appraisal and advice on such matters, and could therefore neither anticipate nor take the initiative when formulating economic policy decisions. An economic general staff armed with considerable prestige and resources was essential to the modern state. Its Chief should occupy a position of comparable power and importance to that held by the First Sea Lord or the Chief of the Imperial General Staff in time of war. The other members of the staff should be the Permanent Secretaries of the Treasury, the Board of Trade, and the Ministries of Labour, Health, and Agriculture. The secretariat 'should be very few in number, the best experts available, and well remunerated by Civil Service standards'; it should have the power to request information from other departments and the resources 'to finance special enquiries at home or abroad, by individuals outside the Civil Service'. Coupled with this was a proposal to establish within the Cabinet a Committee of Economic Policy to which all questions of economic policy should be referred in the first instance; the Chief of the Economic General Staff would then act as secretary to this 'inner ring of the Cabinet'.[39] The 'Yellow Book' also discussed the case for establishing a large national industrial council representative of industry as a whole. The members of the group were divided on the merits of such a body but agreed in recommending that a small Council of Industry should be attached to a new Ministry of Industry with a brief to keep all wage and industrial relations questions under constant review, and to give preliminary consideration and advice on all legislation affecting 'the organisation and well-being of industry'.[40]

The first Labour Government had, as we have seen, taken steps to set up a body capable of advising the Cabinet on economic questions. In 1929 the Labour Party pursued this idea further with a pledge 'to create permanent machinery through which scientific knowledge and technical skill may be mobilised for improving the organisation of industry, increasing economic efficiency, and raising the standard of life throughout the whole community'. It would establish a 'National Economic Committee' to 'serve the Government and the public as a barometer of economic change'.[41] After forming his second minority government in June, however, Ramsay MacDonald waited for six months before acting on this pledge. It seems that MacDonald found it necessary to revive the idea as a result of marked signs of dissatisfaction with the machinery to deal with unemployment which his government had created on taking office, and a sharp deterioration in the economic situation which threatened to aggravate the difficulties already experienced in trying to redeem the Labour Party's 'unqualified pledge' to deal with the unemployment problem.

On taking office as Lord Privy Seal, J. H. Thomas had special responsibility for coordinating government unemployment policies. To assist him he had a team of three junior ministers, George Lansbury (First Commissioner of Works), Tom Johnston (Under-Secretary of State for Scotland), and Sir Oswald Mosley (Chancellor of the Duchy of Lancaster), and an inter-departmental Committee on Unemployment, consisting initially of a number of senior civil servants, but subsequently augmented to include the three junior ministers, Sir Sydney Chapman, and Tom Jones.* Making use of this machinery the government got off to a busy but fairly conventional start. Thomas announced a trunk road-building programme, increased borrowing powers for railways and public utilities, and a colonial development scheme. He also made it clear that the government had no intention of infringing orthodox canons of investing only in projects which were remunerative in a commercial sense, as 'no useful purpose would be served by adopting extravagant and indefensible proposals'.[42] At the end of the summer he made a much publicised but not very successful trip to Canada in an effort to sell British goods. By the time he returned in the autumn very little definite progress or change of direction had occurred as a result of the return of a Labour government. Inquiries were still on foot with a view to implementing pledges to reduce the size of the work-force by raising the school-leaving age and improving retirement pensions. In spite of changes designed to ease conditions for local authority spending supported by the Unemployment Grants Committee, the wheels were turning slowly, and the government was handicapped in its dealings with the local authorities by its unwillingness to do anything which might undermine their autonomy. Ironically, one of the most practical early steps taken by the government – the first of several – was to increase the borrowing powers of the Unemployment Insurance Fund to meet the claims of those on 'transitional benefit'. On a related matter the Minister of Labour, Margaret Bondfield, was running into trouble with Labour and trade union supporters as a result of difficulties in finding a formula which would enable her to abolish the controversial 'genuinely seeking work' clause. As its contribution to the problem of rationalisation the government was using the Committee of

---

* The minutes and memoranda of this committee (the D.U.(29) Committee) are in Cab. 27/389 and 390. The committee met only occasionally after July 1929, but remained in existence until May 1930. A similar inter-departmental committee had been in operation under the Conservative Government since 1928 (T. Jones, *Whitehall Diary*, Vol. II, pp. 155-6, 187-8; Cab. 27/378, Minutes and memoranda of D.U.(28) Committee).

Civil Research to conduct inquiries into the iron and steel and cotton industries, and preparing legislation for the reorganisation of the coal industry.[43]

Dissatisfaction with the machinery and policies of the government during its first months of office was brought to a head by Mosley, whose first attempt to influence the direction being taken came in September in the form of proposals that the government should assume direct control of an enlarged road-building programme, thereby taking the matter out of the hands of local authorities. Mosley 'emphasized the necessity for a body working directly under the head of the Government and giving continuous consideration to long-term development and reconstruction proposals'.[44] The government had already used the Committee of Civil Research to carry out its inquiries into the iron and steel and cotton industries; and the special Cabinet Committee set up to consider the matter discussed the possibility of using the same machinery to accommodate Mosley's ideas.[*] It may have been as a result of this that on the next day the Prime Minister asked Tom Jones to supply an account of the objects and achievements of the Committee of Civil Research.[†] MacDonald also convened a series of luncheon meetings to discuss remedies for the immediate industrial situation and ways of improving the information and advice on economic policy available to the government. It was from these meetings attended by a number of prominent economists, businessmen, and trade unionists, that the Economic Advisory Council emerged.[‡]

The economists, Henry Clay, Keynes, G. D. H. Cole, Stamp, J. A. Hobson, and W. Layton, were naturally in favour of creating an economic general staff, the first three submitting detailed proposals on the subject. Clay pointed out that the existing method of conducting investigations into economic policy questions, namely by means of Royal Commissions or committees of inquiry, suffered from several drawbacks:

(1) it works too slowly and is set in motion only after an emergency has arisen
(2) there is no continuity of personnel or organisation and therefore no cumulative result from successive enquiries in connected fields

[*] The committee was the N.S. (29) Committee which at two meetings in November 1929 rejected Mosley's proposals largely on the basis of the Ministry of Transport's arguments (Cab. 27/387, Minutes and memoranda of N.S. (29) Committee).

[†] Prem. 1/70, Tom Jones to MacDonald, 'The Committee of Civil Research', 29 November 1929. A month later Tom Jones described the establishment of the E.A.C. as 'a device for saving [J. H. Thomas's] face' (*Whitehall Diary*, Vol. II, p. 229). On the other hand, Tom Jones, in his covering letter to MacDonald on 29 November suggested that 'The Committee would have the further advantage of enlisting the co-operation of persons of all political parties and spreading the area of criticism now concentrated on the Lord Privy Seal' (Prem. 1/70, Jones to MacDonald, 29 November 1929). MacDonald had spoken to Jones about 'big developments [he had] in mind in connection with the C.C.R.' as early as June, and again in August, 1929 (*Whitehall Diary*, Vol. II, pp. 190, 204).

[‡] Those present at the first meeting, on 22 November 1929, were MacDonald, Lord Weir, Sir Andrew Duncan, Warren Fisher, J. M. Keynes, W. Layton, G. D. H. Cole, Professor Henry Clay, Tom Jones. At the second meeting, on 9 December, there were also Sir Josiah Stamp, Sir Kenneth Stewart, J. H. Thomas, J. A. Hobson, W. M. Citrine and Colonel David Carnegie. Snowden joined this company at the final meeting on 16 December.

(3) it is not integrated with the structure of administration, so that the enquiries are not always as relevant to current needs or as practical in their results as might be hoped.[45]

To this Keynes added the criticism that the reports usually 'represent a compromise between different interests and opinions, rather than a strictly expert analysis based solely on scientific and technical grounds'.

Keynes outlined a fairly elaborate plan of the duties of an economic general staff. Its functions would be to engage in a continuous study of current problems, to coordinate and advise on the collection of official statistics, to propose policy solutions, and to supply expert secretarial assistance to other official bodies. He suggested that the staff of this economic secretariat could be less than a dozen to begin with, and that to facilitate interchange with the academic world they need not be given permanent civil service status. The staff should be supplemented by a permanent panel of economists and others – 'a Scientific Committee' – whose task would be to provide confidential and impartial advice on specific questions. Although the role of the economic general staff would be purely advisory, Keynes argued along the lines of the Liberal 'Yellow Book' that its Chief should be accorded sufficient status to ensure that the Cabinet paid close attention to the advice. The importance which he attached to this proposal went far beyond that of its being an administrative device entailing official recognition of his own discipline; his memorandum on the subject ended on a high note:

a move along these lines would indeed be an act of statesmanship, the importance of which cannot easily be exaggerated. For it would mark a transition in our conception of the functions and purposes of the State, and a first measure towards the deliberate and purposive guidance of the evolution of our economic life. It would be a recognition of the enormous part to be played in this by the scientific spirit as distinct from the sterility of the purely party attitude, which is never more out of place than in relation to complex matters of fact and interpretation involving technical difficulty. It would mean the beginning of ways of doing and thinking about political problems which are probably necessary for the efficient working of modern democracy. For it would be an essay in the art of combining representative institutions and the voice of public opinion with the utilisation by Governments of the best technical advice in spheres, where such advice can never, and should not, have the last word or the power, but must be a necessary ingredient in the decisions of those entrusted by the country with the last word and with the power.[46]

In some respects Cole's conception of the duties of an economic general staff was even more ambitious than Keynes's; it was certainly more *dirigiste* in tone. He wanted the staff to prepare as well as coordinate statistics provided by the departments; and to employ 'field investigators' to gather material in particular industries and locations. While the new body would mainly be advisory, it should also make inquiries on its own initiative, and occasionally, where appropriate, publish its findings. Cole thought that members of the staff should be more akin to salaried commissioners than civil servants, and clearly saw one of their duties as supplying practical plans for the reorganisation of industry.[47]

By the end of the second meeting there was fairly general agreement on the need to recruit a small nucleus of economists which would be attached to the Prime Minister's office. Sir Maurice Hankey, however, opposed this innocuous proposal; he thought the scheme entailed 'feckless duplication of work already done quite efficiently by departments'.[48] On the basis of his experience as Secretary to the Committee of Imperial Defence, he maintained that the appointment of a panel of experts attached to the Prime Minister would antagonise and weaken the sense of responsibility of those departments which would have to implement policies. The only form of an economic general staff acceptable to Hankey was one composed of the permanent heads of all the departments with economic responsibilities – who might or might not wish to call upon the advice of outside experts. The Prime Minister marked on his copy of Hankey's memorandum 'most useful criticism'.[49]

The Treasury, as represented by its Permanent Secretary, Sir Warren Fisher, did not favour giving economists civil service status.

The Public would not be impressed by an 'Economic General Staff' which resolved itself into a mere addition of half a dozen more 'bureaucrats', and in so far as fundamental economic research with a view to more 'scientific' government is the aim, it is clear that this can best be promoted by enlisting the co-operation of the most eminent Economists in the country, untrammelled and unhampered and entitled to have their economic conclusions made available for the information of this, and indeed any other, country.

Accordingly, Fisher favoured the establishment of an independent Council of Economic Research along the lines of the Medical Research Council and the Department of Scientific and Industrial Research.[50]

The chief protagonists of the idea of a representative council at the discussions were Hobson, Layton, and Citrine. In its most radical form, advocated by Hobson, the proposal involved the creation of a permanent National Industrial Council composed of representatives from the employers and trade unions, together with government appointees, acting with a large degree of autonomy but with well-defined powers. According to Hobson such a body was essential if the conclusions reached by the expert members of an economic general staff were to influence 'the general business public, both employers and employed'; and if the reconstruction of industry was to be undertaken with a full knowledge of the effects on costs, employment, and prices in other industries.[51] Layton agreed that 'the case for such an organisation includes the advantage that Industrial leaders would constantly be compelled to consider not merely the situation of their own industries, but also the industrial interests of the nation as a whole'; one of its functions would be to bring pressure on industrialists and trade unions to reorganise and abandon restrictive practices. But he was aware of the twin dangers that a council without well-defined powers and duties could turn into an acrimonious talking-shop, while a council which shared responsibility for economic policy with the government could create 'a sort of diarchy in government which is foreign to British ideas'. As a compromise, therefore, Layton returned to the Liberal 'Yellow Book' proposals in recommending the establishment of a smaller Council of Industry to which 'all proposals for putting statutory sanction behind wage agreements' would be referred, and which would pronounce upon 'proposals to give sanction to price and other agreements of trade associations'.[52] What seems to have been in mind, therefore, was a body that would act partly as policeman-cum-arbitrator on industrial relations questions, and partly as a lever to achieve industrial reorganisation through a mixture of consent and public pressure. In view of the fact that Keynes was one of the authors of the 'Yellow Book', while Cole had been secretary to the Provisional Joint Committee of the ill-fated National Industrial Conference of 1919, it seems worth pointing out that Keynes did not speak up for the representative council idea, and Cole actually opposed the creation of a large representative body at this stage.*

If the economists were luke-warm about the council idea, the same cannot be said of some of the politicians present at the discussions. MacDonald responded eagerly, if somewhat vaguely, by proclaiming: 'I want Labour, Capital, and Economics to unite in operating an administrative organ to spur on our industries. It could be an epitome of the country's effort.'[53] He was obviously attracted by the possibility of combining investigation, inspiration, and leverage on recalcitrant industries in need of reorganisation, though he was understandably perturbed by Layton's suggestion that the council should act as 'an outside body bringing pressure on the Government through its influence on public opinion'.[54] J. H. Thomas also responded enthusiastically to some aspects of the council idea; he saw it chiefly as a means of overcoming 'the individualistic attitude of Capital and Labour', and agreed with MacDonald that if such a body had existed when the government had first taken power their task would have been much easier. He seems to have thought that 'it would have stopped many of our impossible Election promises'.[55] The council idea had, of course, immediate political attractions to MacDonald as Prime Minister of a minority government in an unstable three-party Parliament. MacDonald invited and received advice from many quarters, and given the entrenched position of the Treasury and the orthodoxy on matters of economic policy of Philip Snowden, the Chancellor of the Exchequer, he may have been attracted by the idea of a counterweight to the Treasury in the Prime Minister's Office.[56] But it is important to recognise that the ideas which went into the making of the Economic Advisory Council were neither simply quirks of MacDonald's

* On the announcement of the E.A.C. Cole wrote a welcoming note for the *New Statesman* (8 February 1930) – 'it may evidently become a very important body indeed' – which seems to indicate that he did not at that stage regard the Council as being too large; see p. 39 below for the change in his views on this subject.

administrative style, nor a straightforward product of a three-party situation in which 'above-party' solutions were at a premium. It arose out of the experience of a wide spectrum of serious observers of the economic scene throughout the 1920s.

Inevitably, what emerged from these discussions as the Economic Advisory Council was a scaled-down mixture of what had been advocated by one person or another. The idea of a large representative body similar to the National Industrial Council of 1919, or the French and German councils, was abandoned. So was the Liberal proposal championed by Layton for a smaller Council of Industry. But MacDonald apparently wanted something more than an economic general staff. During the discussions he referred to this as the 'thinking part' of the scheme; he also wanted 'an Advisory Committee to keep [the thinking part] in contact with the other job, namely, that of moving people in the field into action'. What he obtained was a body of which he was chairman consisting of (a) the Chancellor of the Exchequer, the Lord Privy Seal, President of the Board of Trade, and the Minister of Agriculture; (b) such other ministers as he might wish to summon; and (c) such other persons chosen 'in virtue of their special knowledge and experience of industry and economics'.[57]

On 15 February 1930 he announced the following list of fifteen names qualifying under (c): Sir Arthur Balfour, Ernest Bevin, W. R. Blair, Sir John Cadman, Walter Citrine, G. D. H. Cole, Ernest Debenham, Sir Andrew Duncan, Sir Daniel Hall, Sir William Hardy, J. M. Keynes, Sir Alfred Lewis, Sir William McLintock, Sir Josiah Stamp, and R. H. Tawney. Roughly speaking this amounted to seven industrialists (including two bankers), two trade union officials, two scientists, three economists, and a historian. The Council was to meet regularly, and was empowered to appoint standing or other committees to conduct special inquiries; it was to take over the functions of the Committee of Civil Research and draw up a list of other persons who might be called on to assist the Council. Stress was laid on the advisory nature of the new body's duties: 'it will interfere in no way with the functions of or responsibilities of Ministers or of the Departments over which they preside and it will have no administrative or executive powers'.

More important from some points of view was the staff or secretariat. The new body took over the Secretary (Tom Jones) and Assistant Secretary (A. F. Hemming) of the Committee of Civil Research. Tom Jones's memorandum on an 'economic general staff' suggested 'two economists of standing, as full-time Civil Servants, with perhaps one or two promising junior economists', one of whom should be a statistician. Jones suggested that since Henry Clay might not be available, as he was probably taking a post at the Bank of England, H. D. Henderson should be offered one of the senior posts.[58] He, or MacDonald, apparently had Cole in mind for the other senior post; but a few days later Jones expressed doubts as to Cole's willingness to work as a member of a team, and on the grounds of his well-known commitment to the Labour Party.[59] No similar qualms seem to have been registered about Henderson, in spite of his connections with the Liberal Party, possibly because of the strength of the support coming from Hopkins and Keynes.* Keynes also helped to persuade Henderson to overcome his 'considerable misgivings . . . and . . . distinct reluctance to become a muzzled Civil Servant'. Henderson accepted the job when persuaded that he 'really would be at the centre of things and not in a sort of Hawtrey backwater'.†

Tom Jones also consulted Keynes about the other appointments. Keynes did not favour Jones's suggestions of P. A. Sloan or Alan Loveday (later Director of Economic Intelligence at the League of Nations), though Loveday was in fact offered the second senior post in February.[60] For one of the junior posts Keynes strongly recommended Austin Robinson. Colin Clark, an Oxford pupil of Cole's, was recommended by Cole, and Keynes, who knew him only by reputation, agreed that he 'sounds rather good'.[61] A large number of other names was canvassed for the junior posts, but adverse public comment on the cost of the staff may have kept down the number of economists employed. Besides Henderson only H. V. Hodson and Colin Clark were appointed, and Piers Debenham (son of Ernest Debenham) was taken on in an unpaid capacity.‡ 'Treasury control' also kept down the cost: the Treasury refused to buy an adding machine for Colin Clark and allowed the Council staff to use the Treasury library rather than supplying it with back numbers of economic journals.§ The total cost of the staff, including clerks, was £6,500 p.a.[62]

Before the conversations which preceded the establishment of the Economic Advisory Council had taken place, the government's economic strategy had

---

* Prem. 1/70, Jones to Macdonald, 18 December 1929. There was, however, some adverse comment in the I.L.P. weekly *New Leader* (24 January) on Henderson's appointment; and on 21 February, while welcoming the general composition of the Council, it commented that Henderson 'is a good critical mind, but deeply political and not very constructive'. Earlier (7 February) it had suggested the appointment of one of the four following socialist economists: E. M. H. Lloyd, R. H. Tawney, M. H. Dobb and G. L. Schwartz.

† Keynes Papers NS/12, Henderson to Keynes, 3 January 1930. In consequence Henderson turned down the offer of a chair at the London School of Economics, which went to Hayek instead.

‡ Among those considered or approached were John Hilton (then a statistician with the Ministry of Labour and shortly afterwards Professor of Industrial Relations in Cambridge), K. Lindsay (a temporary civil servant with the Overseas Settlement Department), D. H. Robertson, J. W. F. Rowe and J. Wedgwood (Prem. 1/70, Jones to MacDonald, 18 December 1929; Keynes Papers L/30, MacDonald to Keynes, 17 March 1930; Jones, *Whitehall Diary*, Vol. II, pp. 244–5; and information from Sir Austin Robinson). Questions were asked in Parliament on 6 February, particularly with reference to the duplication of services provided by the Chief Economic Adviser at a salary of £3,000 p.a. When the list of Council members appeared, *The Times* queried the need for another body to replace the C.C.R. (13 February 1930).

§ T. 162/472/E23399, correspondence between Colin Clark, T. Jones, and various junior Treasury officials, May 1930. Given the tradition of Treasury control, the development of national income estimates in 1940 was no doubt facilitated by the fact that Richard Stone brought his own machine. On the development of national income estimates, see below, p. 151.

been called in question by some of its supporters at the Labour Party's annual conference in Brighton in October. On this occasion the criticism focussed on the rise in Bank rate to $6\frac{1}{2}$ per cent on 20 September in response to the outflow of funds associated with the final stages of the New York stock market boom.[63] The leading critic at the conference was Ernest Bevin, who maintained that '1% on the Bank Rate means 250,000 increase in unemployment in six months'. J. H. Thomas gave a floundering answer to Bevin's attack, but on the following day the Chancellor of the Exchequer, Philip Snowden, made a speech on the subject which he had discussed with the Governor of the Bank of England, Montagu Norman, beforehand. Snowden defended the independence of the Bank and explained the powerlessness of the Treasury to control Bank rate. At the same time he claimed that the increase in Bank rate would not affect employment. He did, however, make one important concession at the end of his speech, namely that he intended to institute a thorough investigation of 'all aspects of banking, financial and credit policy, particularly to find out what . . . are the effects of the present policy upon industry, and to put forward suggestions for improving these relations'.[64] This was established on 5 November as the Committee on Finance and Industry under the chairmanship of Lord Macmillan, with Bevin and Keynes as two of its most important members.* The committee hearings provided another major arena for Keynes to rehearse his views on the causes of and remedies for Britain's problems. In this respect the Macmillan Committee was similar to the Economic Advisory Council, though since the two bodies operated in parallel with one another, the existence of the Macmillan Committee could be cited as a reason why the important issues of monetary policy should not be discussed by the Council.[65]

The Macmillan Committee also provided an opportunity for the Bank of England and the Treasury to state their views on economic policy. The Deputy Governor of the Bank, Sir Ernest Harvey, stated that the Bank's policy was 'to maintain a credit position which will afford reasonable assurance of the convertibility of the currency into gold in all circumstances, and within the limits imposed by that objective to adjust the price and volume of credit to the requirements of industry and trade'. Its principal weapon was Bank rate, which was varied in response to the 'state of the Bank's reserves, the condition of the money market . . . and . . . the position and trend of the foreign exchanges'. Hence, the overriding objective was the maintenance of the gold standard. Norman tried to justify the relegation of domestic considerations to second place on the grounds that Bank rate policy had little effect on economic activity, but in response to Keynes's persistent questioning he reluctantly admitted it might affect employment. He did,

---

* The other members were Sir Thomas Allen, Lord Bradbury, R. H. Brand, Professor T. E. Gregory, L. B. Lee, C. Lubbock, R. McKenna, J. T. Walton Newbold, Sir Walter Raine, J. Frater Taylor, and A. A. G. Tulloch.

however, maintain that many of Britain's difficulties were due to structural problems and took a large personal hand in trying to promote rationalisation in particular industries.[66]

The Treasury's attitude to economic policy was more clearly influenced by theoretical considerations. This was partly, but not entirely, due to the presence in the Treasury of Hawtrey, who provided theoretical justifications for Treasury policy when needed. Hawtrey provided the strongest rationale for the 'Treasury view' in an *Economica* article in 1925; but the presuppositions of the theory are evident in many Treasury memoranda of the 1920s. The basic theory was the quantity theory of money, whereby the supply of money determined the general level of prices in the long run, and the 'real' forces of productivity and thrift determined the levels of income and employment. Adherence to the gold standard was desirable because it necessitated control of the supply of money and hence the prevention of domestically generated inflation. The trade cycle was largely a monetary phenomenon and should, therefore, be treated by monetary measures. Cheap and plentiful money was the classic remedy for depression, but since interest rates tended to fall in such times anyway, government policy should be to assist these 'natural' forces; it should certainly not go so far as to jeopardise maintenance of the gold standard. Public expenditure would tend to increase employment only insofar as it was financed by creating credit; hence there was no need for such expenditure. Furthermore, it could be positively harmful if it absorbed savings that would otherwise be invested in private industry.

In his evidence to the Macmillan Committee, Hopkins used many of Hawtrey's ideas: for example, Hawtrey's belief in the importance of short-term interest rates in determining economic activity to justify the issue in November 1929 of long-term government debt at a high interest rate. He also attempted, with some difficulty, to claim that public works which were both productive and non-competitive with private industry for funds were acceptable, while others which gave more employment but yielded a lower rate of return were not. Hopkins also argued that there was a need for rationalisation schemes to restore the competitive position of the older industries, and he supported the Bank's efforts to encourage the private provision of finance for such schemes.[67]

The 'Treasury view' was as useful to the Labour Government in rebutting criticism of existing government policy as it had been to the Conservatives.[68] As Hopkins made clear in his Macmillan evidence, however, this did not mean that the Treasury adhered rigidly to the view. Nonetheless, given that one important test of the feasibility of a scheme was its effect on public opinion, the 'Treasury view' did act as a brake on the Labour Government's policy as the depression deepened and fears of the effects of lack of public confidence grew.[69]

By the time that the precise form of the Council had been settled, but before the Council had begun to operate in earnest, the government found itself under pressure from Mosley once more. In a long memorandum giving details of the much bolder line of attack on unemployment which he felt the government should be pursuing, Mosley criticised the lack of coordinated thinking and action on economic policy. He wanted to see an executive committee of the Cabinet set up under the Prime Minister, and served by a series of standing committees headed by ministers; a secretariat of civil servants; a staff of economists; and an advisory panel of businessmen and representatives of other parties. He divided his proposals into long- and short-term schemes. Into the former category fell projects for industrial and agricultural reorganisation; these had a clear bias away from the export trades towards the reconstruction and development of industries producing for a home market protected by strategic import controls and bulk purchase agreements. The financing of these rationalisation schemes was to be taken out of the hands of the commercial banks, and placed under the direct control of a government agency. The short-term policies included raising the school-leaving age, a retirement pension scheme, and a speeded-up and enlarged loan-financed public works programme, to be concentrated chiefly on a national roads scheme.[70]

The Cabinet appointed a special committee under Snowden to consider the Mosley memorandum. Snowden was duly armed with a critical Treasury memorandum which eventually formed the basis for the committee's negative report to the Cabinet on 1 May. The report rejected Mosley's long- and short-term proposals, and upheld the Treasury view. On the question of machinery the report was equally negative. Mosley's suggestion that responsibility for implementing public works policies should be taken away from the local authorities was rejected: it would only clog the machinery of central government and undermine 'our democratic system of local government', replacing it with 'a bureaucratic system on the continental model'. Mosley's proposals for drastic changes in the central policy-making machinery, it was held, would 'cut at the root of the individual responsibilities of Ministers, the special responsibility of the Chancellor of the Exchequer in the sphere of finance, and the collective responsibility of the Cabinet to Parliament'. In any event the government had just set up the Economic Advisory Council,

a body which has been formed after exhaustive enquiry for this object on lines devised by the Prime Minister and consistent with the maintenance of Ministerial responsibility and the ordered conduct of Government affairs. This body is capable of development to any size that is found by experience to be expedient, and Sir Oswald Mosley is merely beating the air in asking for more. Indeed his almost disdainful dismissal of this Council and its purpose can be attributed only to confusion of thinking or ignorance.[71]

Mosley's memorandum did not die immediately. In a last effort to achieve reconciliation, the Prime Minister called a series of ministerial conferences which included Mosley and the other members of Thomas's team.* During the third of these conferences, on 20 May, Mosley resigned, having rehearsed all the issues once more with no greater success from his point of view.[72] During the subsequent dramatic debate within the Parliamentary Labour Party MacDonald announced that he intended to give 'personal and complete attention to the unemployment problem'.[73] MacDonald had already moved in this direction, partly as a result of the initial meetings of the Economic Advisory Council, and partly as a result of the ministerial conferences. During the fifth of these conferences, on 3 June, new machinery for dealing with unemployment was formally proposed and accepted later by the Cabinet on 4 June. On the following day J. H. Thomas went to the Dominions Office and Vernon Hartshorn became Lord Privy Seal. In place of Thomas's 'team' there was now a panel of ministers served by a secretariat under Sir John Anderson consisting of senior civil servants, with Hubert Henderson acting as a link with the Economic Advisory Council. The Prime Minister outlined the duties of this panel on 16 June. Owing to the failures of the previous machinery 'it had been decided to restore responsibility to the Departments'. The panel would first meet weekly, and later fortnightly, to formulate policy; it would receive departmental reports 'and see that all was being done that could reasonably be expected by the Departments'. Although financial policy was reserved to the Macmillan Committee at the moment, the panel might have to become involved; but the primary task would be 'to devise programmes of work which would result in absorbing men and women'.[74]

The Economic Advisory Council was, therefore, a part of the elaborate machinery set up by the Labour Government to tackle the problem of unemployment. The changes in the machinery during the first half of 1930 reflected not merely Mosley's dissatisfaction with his senior colleagues' policies, but also the increasing dimensions of the unemployment problem due to the world slump.

* Lansbury, who had been a member of Snowden's committee, dissented from some of its conclusions. The Cabinet referred the Committee's report and Lansbury's memorandum to the conference of Ministers. (Cab. 24/211, C.P. 145(30), Memorandum by First Commissioner of Works; Cab. 23/64, Cabinet 26(30)2, 8 May 1930.)

CHAPTER 3

THE COUNCIL AND THE SLUMP

The Council was in full operation when the world depression first began to make an obvious impression on the British economy. It held its first meeting on 17 February 1930 and met regularly at 10 Downing Street up to the thirteenth meeting on 16 April 1931. This chapter is concerned with the proceedings of the Council and its role in the policy-making machinery of the government up to the beginning of the 1931 financial crisis, which, as it turned out, settled the fate of the Council as well as that of the second Labour Government. During its comparatively brief life the Council set on foot and considered the results of many special inquiries, a list of which is in Appendix I; here we concentrate on those reports and discussions most relevant to the central issues of economic policy.

When the Labour Government took office, unemployment, though still above the million mark, was lower than it had been a year earlier. During the summer of 1929 and well into the autumn it was still possible to assume that the government was faced with problems which had to a large extent been peculiar to Britain throughout the post-war period.* In retrospect, however, there were already signs of an international collapse of commodity prices due to overproduction in the primary-producing countries, and of increasing strain on the world's financial system. The latter was due to the gold sterilisation policies of France and the United States and the drastic cutback in American foreign lending which accompanied the New York stock market boom. Deflationary effects of the impending world slump made themselves felt in Britain early in 1929 when exports fell as a result of the decline in the incomes of British customers in the primary-producing countries.[1] Moreover, the cutback in American foreign lending which took place after mid-1928 had a severe effect on debtor countries, which included many primary-producers, as well as placing the main European financial centres under considerable pressure. One result was a tightening of British monetary policy from mid-1928 onwards, reaching a climax in the raising of Bank rate to $6\frac{1}{2}$ per cent in September 1929.[2]

The Wall Street collapse in October brought immediate relief to London and other centres from the strains of the previous fifteen months. The Bank

---

* This was, for example, the assumption made by the Macmillan Committee when it was established in November 1929 (Committee on Finance and Industry, *Report* (1931), Cmd. 3897, paras. 12–15).

of England gradually reduced Bank rate from $6\frac{1}{2}$ per cent to 3 per cent by May 1930. Similar steps toward cheap money were taken in the United States; these led to a revival in foreign lending in the first half of 1930, but one that was insufficient to overcome the gathering momentum of world depression. International commodity prices continued to fall, and unemployment in Britain continued to rise as a result of the erosion of export markets. Consequently, hopes of an early revival in prices and production, and of a continuance of American foreign investment, began to fade in the summer of 1930. Furthermore, in these conditions sterling was persistently weak, so that although the Bank of England may have wanted to pursue an easier monetary policy, it was constrained by its determination to remain on the gold standard. For a year after May 1930 it made no further moves towards cheap money.

The Treasury also wanted to see lower interest rates, both to stimulate economic activity and to enable it to convert £2000m 5 per cent War Loan 1929–47 to a lower interest rate; but its immediate preoccupation was balancing the 1930 budget.[3] The depression brought declining revenues and increased expenditure, especially on unemployment relief, and particularly after the spring of 1930, when the normal seasonal improvement in employment failed to materialise. Snowden was also more committed to 'sound finance' than his predecessor, Churchill, had been. For as he said in a letter to Churchill in January 1930: 'The difference between us does not lie in a nice calculation of figures. It lies in differing conceptions of sound finance . . . A well-balanced budget is not a luxury which is to be avoided; it is a necessity which is to be provided for.'[4] As a convinced free-trader he also wished to repeal the few protective duties Britain had. As a result of the financial stringency that the worsening economic situation imposed on the Exchequer, he did not repeal the McKenna and silk duties and the food taxes in his 1930 budget, though the safeguarding duties were allowed to lapse. In this budget he increased income tax, super tax, estate duties, and the beer duty, and, to make up for Churchill's apparent laxity over the sinking fund, the provision for debt redemption. Even so, Snowden found it necessary to depart somewhat from his principles by using paper transfers from Treasury capital accounts to balance the budget, a practice he had consistently criticised Churchill for adopting. Nevertheless, the budget signalled a clear commitment to orthodoxy.[5]

The government's commitment to orthodoxy became clearer and stronger as the year wore on. The additional difficulties created by the world depression tended to drive a wedge between policies designed to deal with Britain's special and long-standing problems, and policies considered feasible in the light of external constraints; they could, therefore, be used to encourage greater caution and justify lack of action.[6] Keynes, on the other hand, pointed out to the Economic Advisory Council that 'it does not mean that we should abandon the attempt to cure our local disorders, or take refuge in the international problem which is superimposed on them as an excuse for doing nothing about the former'.[7]

Earlier, at the Prime Minister's luncheons in December 1929, Keynes had suggested a number of ways in which the government could overcome a mood 'of business pessimism and lethargy' that MacDonald detected. He proposed that the government should make a series of public pronouncements to the effect that 'it is now practicable to attack the problems of the future in a new spirit of optimism and energy'. To encourage this the government should undertake not to make changes in the safeguarding duties or to enter into new commitments involving taxation. The Governor of the Bank of England should declare 'that in his view the apparent termination of the epoch of dear money in the United States has entirely altered the situation so far as concerns the risks of allowing a general easing of credit conditions in this country', and that in consequence the Bank would stand ready to furnish capital for rationalisation schemes. This could be supported by similar statements from the clearing banks, issue houses, and building societies. Other public and semi-public bodies such as the railway companies, the Central Electricity Board, the Road Board, the proposed London Traffic Board, and the local authorities should all declare their intention to accelerate existing investment programmes, while the trade unions and the Federation of British Industry should state 'that they will be content during 1930 with the status quo in wages and will observe a truce in regard to Labour Disputes'.[8] But Keynes's suggestion did not meet with approval. Although Lord Weir complained that 'there is nothing inspiring to the basic producer in the present Government's programme of legislation', his priorities were quite different from Keynes's. He thought that the 'first thing is to get all Ministers to feel and to say that the producer is now to be recognised as the man to save the situation; that the Government cannot do it'. The criterion for all public schemes of road or rail development should be whether they would reduce costs in productive industry.[9] Snowden sided with Weir, judging Keynes's suggestions to be 'far less practicable'; he also used the opportunity of this discussion to ridicule J. H. Thomas's current road and rail programmes.[10]

A mood of would-be optimism created by lower interest rates hung over the early meetings of the Economic Advisory Council and persisted through the spring of 1930. Henderson's April 1930 assessment of the economic outlook reflected that mood. 'World-wide depression has been superimposed on our special national difficulties', and 'the fall in the prices of primary products during the last four months is of a most formidable character', threatening British exports to producers of these commodities. Nevertheless, 'when we look further ahead, the outlook is far more hopeful', mainly because of the prospect of cheap money.* The mood did not survive the summer.

---

* Cab. 58/145, E.A.C. (E.O.) 4, Henderson, 'The Economic Outlook', 3 April 1930. Henderson prepared this for the Committee on Economic Outlook, who incorporated it in its report

The early meetings and reports

The early meetings of the Council were devoted to general discussion of the economic situation and to decisions as to which subjects merited further inquiry by specialist sub-committees.[11] In the latter respect the Council got off to a brisk start. The Prime Minister had invited government departments 'faced with major economic problems to submit suggestions for the consideration of the Council', and a miscellany of topics emerged. At its first meeting the Council appointed three committees. J. H. Thomas suggested an urgent examination of the form and presentation of the unemployment statistics, because he felt that the existing method of presentation 'affected British business interests adversely by creating a wholly misleading impression among foreign customers'. The Prime Minister himself came up with the idea of a committee on empire trade.

[He] hoped that it would be possible for the Council to assist the government in the preparation of a national policy for consideration at the Imperial Conference [due to meet on 30 September 1930]. He had in mind a scientific investigation of the nature of Empire trade, the actual effect of tariff preferences and the future trade relations between this country and the Dominions, having regard to the position of Great Britain vis-à-vis the continent of Europe, and to the proposals that had been suggested by the French for a European Zollverein.

The third inquiry and the one more immediately relevant to the problem of unemployment was suggested by Keynes, who 'thought it was desirable that the Council should look ahead at the more fundamental economic problems with which the country was faced. The view was held in some quarters that the underlying economic situation of the present day was very serious, and it would, in his opinion, be advantageous to attempt a diagnosis of the situation in order to prepare plans for action should the situation unhappily grow worse.' Accordingly, a Committee on Economic Outlook, 1930, was set up 'to supervise the preparation of a memorandum indicating the principal heads of the investigation (excluding those connected with currency) which should be embraced in a diagnosis of the underlying economic situation'.

Other subjects raised at this opening meeting, on two of which the Council later appointed committees, were the education and supply of biologists, the prospects of the sugar-beet industry, and agricultural policy. Sir Arthur Balfour suggested empire migration as a valuable topic because 'the partial closure of this method of reducing unemployment was very serious and merited close investigation'. Cadman raised the problem of 'the high cost of marketing and distribution in many materials', as he thought that 'its solution, like that of many other present economic problems, was intimately

(reprinted below). Henderson had earlier sent a shorter version to MacDonald (Keynes Papers EA/1, Henderson to Keynes, and Henderson, 'The Economic Outlook', 12 March 1930).

bound up with an accurate understanding of costing systems'. The only subject raised at this meeting that the Council decided *not* to investigate further was whether the government needed to devise reserve powers to prevent American control of British industries.

The membership of the Committee on Economic Outlook, 1930, was balanced between two economists, Keynes (chairman) and Cole, two businessmen, Sir Arthur Balfour and Sir John Cadman, with a trade unionist, Citrine, added for good measure. Before the committee met the Council agreed at its second meeting to accept Tawney's suggestion to drop the exclusion of currency matters from the committee's terms of reference, where this was understood to entail 'inquiry into the desirability of more extensive State action for the purpose of increasing employment by capital expenditure by loan or otherwise'. On this question there was, as MacDonald later remarked, 'a real cleavage of opinion in the public world',[12] which was faithfully reflected in the reports of the Committee on Economic Outlook.

The first report of this committee reached the Council at its third meeting, in April; it took the form of a short note signed by Keynes, Cole, and Cadman covering a memorandum on the current economic situation by Henderson. Neither Balfour nor Citrine had been able to attend the committee's meetings, and Cadman took the opportunity of the Council meeting to dissociate himself from the report he had signed, saying that he did not agree with Henderson's diagnosis, or with the suggestion of the covering memorandum that 'state-aided home development' was a possible remedy for unemployment. Snowden sent a memorandum to the Council which effectively forbade any discussion of monetary policy or public works on the grounds that the Macmillan Committee was dealing with these.[13] Speaking as a member of both committees Keynes pointed out that the Macmillan Report would not be available for a long time, and that Snowden's ban was inconsistent with the Council's earlier decision to accept Tawney's suggestion.* He also urged the Council not to expect or require 'absolute unanimity on controversial questions'. While accepting this point the Council asked the committee to meet again 'on the understanding that every effort would be made to obtain agreement on the maximum common ground'. The second report, produced the following month, revealed that agreement was unobtainable. Keynes and Cole resubmitted their first statement without significant change, while Balfour and Cadman produced a report of their own. Bevin, who had replaced Citrine on the committee because of Citrine's illness, refused to sign either of the reports.

In their report the economists stated bluntly that the policy choices before the government were 'tariffs, bounties, import control and the like,

---

* It was also inconsistent with the position adopted by Snowden at the first Council meeting when he stated that 'a large programme financed by a Government loan of many millions had been suggested in some quarters [by Mosley?], and he thought it would be useful if the Council considered whether such a programme would be of aid to industry in reducing its costs of production'. Presumably he lost interest once the question was posed in a less orthodox form.

on the one hand, and a programme of productive and useful home development on the other'. Rationalisation of the export trades, though desirable in itself, was not an alternative because it would not improve employment in the short run. Questions requiring further investigation were:

(I) Is there room for a material reduction of marketing and distribution costs on consumable commodities? . . .
(II) Have the abnormalities of the present time any important bearing on the issue of Free Trade, treating this issue in a broad sense so as to cover proposals for tariffs, subsidies, Import Boards, inter-imperial arrangements, etc.?
(III) Would a very large plan of State-aided home development materially reduce unemployment? . . .
(IV) Is a long period of cheap money of vital importance? If so, what are the best means of securing this?

The businessmen on the other hand '[did] not believe the situation [was] capable of solution by direct action of the State'. The only effective solution was wage and cost reductions, and the only action that should be taken was 'an urgent inquiry . . . into the effect upon unemployment and migration of increased expenditure on social services'.[14]

At the Council's fourth meeting in May, Keynes underlined once more the gravity of the employment situation and pointed out that as far as employment was concerned home investment and exports were on an equal footing. Snowden, however, endorsed the businessmen's view of the necessity for rationalisation; he also maintained a rearguard action on the subject of further inquiry by the Council into the effects of public works policies.* In response to Bevin's fears about the effect of rationalisation on employment, Snowden cited the expansion of 1840 to 1863 [sic] as a period in which there had been 'a more rapid transformation of methods of production than was going on today'. But Bevin was not to be fobbed off with bland historical allusions: with the support of the Minister of Labour he obtained agreement that he should submit a memorandum on the effect of rationalisation on employment – though he was not given much satisfaction by the Council when he presented it.† The Council concluded its discussion of the committee's reports by agreeing that 'the questions raised . . . should remain . . . on the agenda'.

At the March and April meetings the Council also discussed at some length the question of a Channel tunnel. The Channel Tunnel Committee of the Committee of Civil Research, set up by Baldwin in April 1929, had provided a 'carefully balanced statement of the advantages and disadvantages'

---

* At the suggestion of Keynes, Snowden agreed to ask Lord Macmillan if his committee would be willing to submit an interim report to the E.A.C. on public works; he reported later that Lord Macmillan thought this 'impracticable' and 'would strongly deprecate the institution of a separate inquiry' (Cab. 58/2, E.A.C. 5th meeting, 6 June 1930).

† At the sixth Council meeting, MacDonald said the question was being studied by Bondfield and Attlee and could not, therefore, be usefully discussed by the Council. (On these studies, see below, p. 44). MacDonald did, however, later appoint an E.A.C. Committee on Problems of Rationalisation (below, p. 83).

in its report of March 1930. Although it reached the broad conclusion that 'the construction of a channel tunnel, by creating new traffic and thus increasing trade would be of economic advantage to this country', it hedged this with many qualifications, and one member, Lord Ebbisham, dissented and was 'opposed to the scheme on economic grounds'. MacDonald therefore asked the Council to set up a committee to advise on whether the government should consent to the construction of the tunnel by private enterprise and whether the government should assist in the financing of construction if it appeared that sufficient private funds would not be forth-coming. The committee, which included Duncan, Cadman, Bevin, Keynes, and Lewis, replied in the negative to the second question and in the affirma-tive to the first, but only 'on the clear understanding that if private enterprise commences the operation and fails to carry the venture through, they cannot call upon His Majesty's Government for a subsidy or for financial support'. The Council and the Cabinet agreed.[15] It seems that MacDonald and Keynes both favoured a Channel tunnel in principle. MacDonald told the Cabinet that 'as a supporter' of the idea, he was 'disappointed to find how many elements of doubt and uncertainty exist, and how lukewarm is the support to the project from trade and industry', while he told Keynes that 'if I were quite clear that the project would really be in the national interest, I should nationalise it from the beginning'. In the report of the Channel Tunnel Policy Committee, Keynes criticised the Channel Tunnel Committee for failing to take into account many relevant factors.[16]

At these early meetings the Council appointed committees on agricul-tural policy, marketing and distribution, revision of the cost-of-living index number, and empire migration. It also asked the staff to examine the effect on employment, under optimistic assumptions, of expansion in the export trades.* These were the only kinds of inquiry which, it seems, could be accepted at this stage in the light of the division of opinion revealed by the Committee on Economic Outlook.

In saying this there is no intention of discounting the value of some of

* Colin Clark prepared a note on 'Export Trade in Relation to Unemployment' with the help of A. W. Flux of the Board of Trade. The conclusion reached was that the effect of a rise in exports by £100,000,000 at 1929 prices, being an increase of some 13.7 per cent, would lead to a rise in employment of between 385,000 and 450,000. No estimate was given of the secondary effects of this increase in employment on the following grounds: 'It will be seen at once that any crude calculation, such as assuming a further rise in employment owing to the spending in the home market of any given proportion of the earnings of the re-employed workers in the export trades, would lead to assuming an infinite series of beneficial reper-cussions. This clearly cannot represent the case, nor on the other hand can we categorically deny the possibility of beneficial repercussions. The limiting factors, however, are obscure and economic theory cannot state the possibilities with precision' (Cab. 58/10, E.A.C. (H) 91; B.T. 70/27/S825/30, 'Export Trade in Relation to Unemployment, Note prepared by the Staff of the E.A.C. in consultation with the Statistical Department of the Board of Trade'). This neatly summarises the state of knowledge on such matters prior to R. F. Kahn's formula-tion of the multiplier principle, hints of which figured in the Committee of Economists' discussion in August 1930 (below pp. 48–9, 59).

these early Economic Advisory Council inquiries of an economic or statistical nature. The reports on unemployment statistics and the revision of the cost-of-living index number, for example, reached useful conclusions on the collection and presentation of official statistics which were later acted upon by the National Government. In both cases the delay was due to the delicate political issues involved in introducing modifications in the form of presentation and computation of these key statistics at a time when unemployment was rising, and when so many wage agreements might be disturbed.* Similarly, the Committee on Marketing and Distribution, whose report was never discussed by the Council, mounted within the time available a major study of the economics of retailing and of the service industries. If published at the time it would certainly have taken its place among the more useful pieces of applied economic research produced in this period.

The reports on empire trade and empire migration helped to bring home to the government the realities of the economic situation. The report on empire trade was based on a memorandum written by the committee's secretaries, Henderson and A. E. Overton (of the Board of Trade), after the committee's first meeting. It took a sober and realistic view of the prospects of fostering inter-imperial trade. Any initiatives in this field would have to be based on a recognition that the Dominions wished to develop their own manufacturing industries, that trade with the 'outside world' was important to all parts of the Empire, especially to Great Britain, and that no action should be taken which 'could be regarded as exploitation of the Colonies

* The report on unemployment statistics recommended that the unemployment returns should be published monthly and in more detail than the current weekly returns. An appendix put forward Bevin's suggestion that charts showing unemployment in relation to the state of trade should be published along with the unemployment figures. The Council passed the report on to the Cabinet on 10 April; the Cabinet on 15 April approved the recommendations and asked Miss Bondfield to agree a date for bringing them into operation with the leaders of the Opposition. The change in the unemployment statistics was not in fact made until the end of 1931; in the meantime, however, Bevin's charts were published periodically in the Ministry of Labour Gazette. (Cab. 58/146, Minutes, memoranda and report of Committee on Unemployment Statistics, 26 March–7 April 1930; Cab. 58/2, E.A.C. 3rd and 4th meetings, 10 April and 8 May 1930; Cab. 23/63, Cabinet 23(30)6, 15 April 1930; T. 175/39, T. Jones to Grigg, 15 April, John Hilton to Hawtrey, 29 April, Hawtrey to Hopkins, 30 April, and Hopkins to Grigg, 1 May 1930; Cab. 23/64, Cabinet 30(30)8, 28 May 1930; Cab. 23/69, Cabinet 93(31)1, 16 December 1931). The Committee on Revision of the Cost-of-Living Index Number reported in January 1931, recommending that a new cost-of-living index number should be established as soon as practicable. The Committee consulted the T.U.C., who were in favour, and the National Confederation of Employers' Organisations, who were not. The Labour Cabinet, on several occasions, therefore, decided that the time was inopportune for the revision of the index number. (Cab. 58/147, Minutes, memoranda and report of Committee on Revision of Cost-of-Living Index Number, July 1930–January 1931; Cab. 58/2, E.A.C. 11th meeting, 12 February 1931; Cab. 23/66, Cabinets 14(31)7, 19(31)13, 21(31)8, 13 February, 25 and 31 March 1931; Cab. 23/67, Cabinet 40(31)19, 30 July 1931). Five years later, when the National Government's Minister of Labour raised the question of revision of the index number, he suggested, and the Cabinet agreed, that the government should act on the basis of the E.A.C. committee's report. (Cab. 23/83, Cabinets 2(36)6, 4(36)6, 11(36)8, 22 January, 5 and 26 February 1936).

and Protectorates in the interests of the United Kingdom'. While there were certain areas in which trading relationships would be fostered, the committee thought the forthcoming Imperial Conference was 'an inappropriate medium for any detailed negotiations about Imperial preferences'. The effect of existing tariff preferences was almost impossible to measure. The cautious final conclusion may also be of some historic interest:

> Our general view is that an Empire policy which led to the creation of fresh barriers to trade with Europe would be disadvantageous to this country. But it would be a mistake to assume at this stage that a European Union must necessarily be prejudicial to our interests. Difficult though it might prove to be in practice, our policy should be to maintain harmonious trade relations, both with Europe and the Dominions, and not to merge our identity or surrender our freedom of action in relation to either group.

The Cabinet discussed the report on 17 September along with a brief by an inter-departmental committee on Economic Questions at the Imperial Conference. This also discouraged British initiatives at the conference, and suggested the government should propose the setting up of an Imperial Economic Secretariat analogous to the economic side of the League of Nations Secretariat. The Cabinet asked the President of the Board of Trade to prepare a memorandum on the subject, which it later 'accept[ed] . . . as the basis of the Government's policy', though only to be proposed if 'the course of events in the Imperial Conference should render this desirable'.*

The report on empire migration dealt with a subject which was close to the hearts of some members of the Labour Government, notably George Lansbury, who had visions of resettling large numbers of coal-miners as wheat-farmers in Australia. J. H. Thomas's Canadian trip was partly a migration mission. But the depressed economic conditions which made migration so desirable to Britain made it undesirable to the Dominions; in 1930 Canada and Australia stopped all migration assistance. The Committee on Empire Migration in its interim report pointed out that 'the economic difficulties of the present time . . . are such as to render impracticable any immediate extension of migration'. The most that could usefully be done would be to increase the proportion of aid to migrants provided by the British Government relative to that provided by the receiving country. At the same time the Treasury and the Ministry of Labour agreed that the existing 50:50 arrangement should be retained, and the Cabinet accepted the departments' recommendation. When the Imperial Conference met, it agreed that migration was now a dead issue. A few months later the final report of the Committee on Empire Migration concluded that the economic value to Great

---

* Cab. 58/149, Minutes, memoranda and report of Committee on Empire Trade 1930, 4 March–12 June 1930; Cab. 23/65, Cabinets 52(30)1 and 53(30)1, 17 and 25 September 1930; Cab. 24/215, C.P. 304(30), 'Imperial Trade Policy and Imperial Economic Machinery being prepared for Imperial Conference 1930', and C.P. 313(30), 'Imperial Economic Machinery, Memorandum by President of Board of Trade', 11 and 23 September 1930. On the conference, see Drummond, *Imperial Economic Policy 1917–1939*, pp. 145–62.

Britain of emigration was negligible in the long run; it would be significant only in the short run when it was in fact impracticable.[17]

The report of the Committee on Agricultural Policy became entangled in the prolonged controversy within the Cabinet over agricultural protection. Although the Cabinet decided in March 1930 that 'no proposal that involved either a crude subsidy or protective tariffs could be considered', it argued over home wheat quotas and import boards until June 1931. The main antagonists were Snowden, who eventually won the battle, and Addison, who became Minister of Agriculture and Fisheries in June 1930. When the Economic Advisory Council's Committee on Agricultural Policy reported that it could not recommend 'a policy which would place agriculture on a peculiar footing and extend to it state assistance which is denied to other depressed basic industries', Snowden used the report to attack Addison's proposals.[18] In the Council Keynes criticised the report of the Committee on Agricultural Policy for not touching upon the two most important issues, namely the long-run trend of agricultural prices and the future prospects of British agriculture.[19]

In general, however, the Council and its committees tended to focus more closely and rapidly on economic questions than its predecessor the Committee of Civil Research had ever done. Henderson's monthly reports to the Prime Minister were also an important innovation.[20] But this did not mean that the aims built into the original Council idea were being fulfilled.

The Prime Minister's questions

After only four meetings of the Council there were clear signs of dissatisfaction with the way in which it was operating. By this time there was a steady flow of reports to consider; and since the Council had taken over the functions of the Committee of Civil Research, a number of reports on scientific and technological subjects also required its attention, perfunctory though it was for the most part.* There seems to have been a growing feeling that the agenda was overcrowded, and that the size and composition of the Council prevented continuous and constructive discussion of the main policy questions. The Labour members of the Council, Bevin, Tawney, Cole, and Citrine, were particularly dissatisfied, since they felt they were not being given a proper chance to carry out an advisory role.† As a result the Council reviewed its procedures at its sixth meeting in June. Complaints

---

* For example, during the first five meetings the subjects of the education and supply of biologists, tsetse-fly investigations, agricultural research organisations, and irrigation research appeared on the agenda.

† Tom Jones told MacDonald in June that Tawney and Cole had complained that 'the presence of Ministers cramped their style and that they would propose that Ministers should be absent from the discussion, at any rate during the initial stages'. In July all four Labour members, under Bevin's leadership, made their views known to MacDonald in a private meeting (T. Jones, *Whitehall Diary*, Vol. II, pp. 267, 270; and Bullock, *Life of Bevin*, Vol. I, p. 438).

were made about the burden of detail, the difficulties of doing justice to the matters raised, and the lack of time devoted to systematic analysis and follow-up. The Council was roughly divided between those who accepted a 'scientific' and critical role, and those who wanted the body to take more initiative, plan ahead, and generally become 'an engine of action'. Neither Keynes nor Henderson made any strong complaints about the Council at this stage: Keynes thought 'it should be allowed to evolve naturally'. No genuine consensus on procedural remedies emerged from the discussion, though certain miscellaneous items were subsequently removed from the agenda.

There was, however, one important by-product of these procedural discussions. Acting on a suggestion of Henderson's, the Prime Minister circulated a list of questions at the June meeting, requesting members' views in writing in time for consideration at the next meeting.[21] The object was, in MacDonald's words, 'to enable the Council to concentrate on large questions of public policy'.[22] The questions were:

1. What in your view are the chief causes of our present industrial position?
2. What, in your view, should be the trade policy adopted by His Majesty's Government to restore trade?
3. How, in your view, can the Home market be developed, and thus put people in a position to earn a living and to command effective power to consume?
4. How, in your view, can the volume of exports be increased?
5. What, in your opinion, would be the framework of a definite Imperial trade policy as regards markets, tariffs, organisation for the supply and purchase of bulk produce like wheat, etc.?[23]

Keynes commented that the first question was a 'highly complicated issue requiring thorough investigation and elucidation'. Although Balfour flatly contradicted this by stating that 'it would be possible to state quite briefly what were the chief causes of the present industrial position',* Keynes's view prevailed, and he persuaded MacDonald to set up a small committee of economists to go into the matter in detail. MacDonald announced at the beginning of the seventh Council meeting that since 'there were a number of fundamental points of a purely economic character connected with the present situation on which there was not at present agreement and on which it was desirable to obtain an authoritative expression of opinion', he had decided to appoint a committee under Keynes's chairmanship consisting of Professors Pigou and Robbins, Sir Josiah Stamp, and H. D. Henderson; its brief was 'to review the present economic condition of Great Britain, to examine the causes which are responsible for it, and to indicate the conditions of recovery'. The mere establishment of this committee marked a small but significant victory for the economists' point of view. It headed off extensive discussion of policy issues on which the lines

---

* Having presided over the Committee on Industry and Trade for five years, Balfour may have thought the exercise did not need repeating.

of disagreement were already well established; and it was an attempt to ensure that future discussions of the short-term policy alternatives would revolve around a report produced solely by economists.

At the seventh meeting the Council had before them the individual replies to the Prime Minister's questions, which Henderson prefaced by remarks on the economic outlook which were far more gloomy and alarmist than his prognosis in April.

The question before us now is not merely one of restoring our economic life to a more healthy condition than that of recent years, but of averting a new danger, viz. the danger that our economic system, with its vitality already lowered by long-continued post-war misfortunes, may fail to come through the present world crisis without suffering irreparable injury ... So far from our British difficulties having been aggravated during recent years by unfavourable world trade conditions, the truth, it is now clear, is rather that the full extent of those difficulties has been concealed by the fact that we have been passing through a favourable phase of the trade cycle.

This consideration has an important bearing on many questions of social and economic policy ... There is, I suggest, a very real danger that higher taxation, combined with a growing distrust of the soundness of our financial position, may suffice to delay recovery in Great Britain after recovery has commenced in the outside world, and may further serve to maintain a high level of interest rates for British Government loans. Latent in the background there is the less likely but more formidable possibility that distrust might go so far during the next year or two as to develop into a real alarm as to the stability of the British pound and a prolonged period of industrial confusion.

If there is anything in these apprehensions, the governing principle of policy for the immediate future must be to do everything possible to avert such dangers, and to do nothing to increase them; and this test must be applied to all proposals that are put forward.[24]

The discussion opened with an exchange between Snowden and Keynes on the international financial situation. On what he chose to call the 'theoretical questions' involving currency, Snowden noted that there had recently been 'a significant change in the attitude of businessmen to economic theories'; they no longer considered monetary difficulties as of 'paramount importance'. According to Snowden, 'there was no evidence of any deficiency of gold supply or of credit, and ... the root of the problem lay rather in the lack of equilibrium in the production of particular commodities'. Keynes did not agree that the gold sterilisation policies of the United States and France over the previous two years could be dismissed so easily; he felt that re-entry of America into the business of foreign investment could be 'the first step towards the recovery of the British position'.

The discussion was incomplete and inconclusive, and illustrated the ease with which the Council could be sidetracked. After agreeing that Henderson should prepare a revised summary of the replies to the Prime Minister's questions, separating controversial proposals from those on which there was agreement, the Council passed on to other matters. The first of these was the future of British trade in China, and the feasibility of a British loan under existing political conditions; this merited a committee chaired by the President of the Board of Trade. This was followed by a rambling discussion of domestic agricultural protection in the light of a warning from Keynes about the possibility of a further dramatic fall in world wheat prices. But the question which drew most attention and agreement was the misleading character and damaging effect of the unemployment returns. They included many people who would not previously have been called unemployed, and the whole system was open to abuses which, according to Snowden, were giving rose to 'a widespread feeling of indignation in the public mind'. The Council decided to appoint a committee under Cole's chairmanship 'to examine the figures of unemployment benefit and their significance, to indicate the abuses which have grown up in that system and to submit recommendations for their removal'.

The Council did not in fact ever discuss the summaries of the replies to the Prime Minister's questions, partly no doubt because of the existence of the Committee of Economists, and partly because Henderson's revised summary revealed so little agreement among members on remedies.

Two remedies alone were mentioned generally and on the whole with approval.
(1) The acceleration of 'Rationalisation'. In one Memorandum the use of compulsion for this purpose was advocated.
(2) A partial exclusion of foreign goods from the home market. The importance attached to this varied considerably; as also did the methods suggested for carrying it into effect. The latter included –
  (a) a general tariff, imposed primarily for the sake of revenue;
  (b) an expansion of safeguarding, particularly to Iron and Steel;
  (c) bulk purchase through import boards (this suggestion was expressly condemned in some of the memoranda);
  (d) import prohibitions.
There was fairly general agreement that agriculture should be assisted by some such measures as the above.[25]

There was a continuation of the discussion of the unemployment insurance scheme at the Council's eighth meeting in September. The Prime Minister had asked the Council to consider whether it would be possible to use the money currently spent on transitional benefit to stimulate industrial activity and employment. For example, would some practicable scheme along these lines be preferable to extending the insurance scheme to agriculture? After all, was it not widely accepted that payment by the Treasury of 'transitional benefit' to workers whose contributions were exhausted could not be regarded as part of the normal insurance scheme? There was general agreement that the insurance principle had broken down for a large number of workers receiving benefit. Cole, for example, expressed the view that 'the employed person's contribution had ceased to be insurance and was now in effect only a tax on employed persons'. Bevin was more cautious: was the government intending to revert to a system of strict insurance? 'If there was to be an overhaul of the system it must be a complete one. Only if the Government were prepared to take responsibility for transitional benefit and to separate it from the Unemployment Insurance Fund, would he be prepared to discuss how best it could be spent.' He was not willing to allow the government to shuffle off the problem on to the Poor Law, though the Minister of Labour pointed out that certain categories of the unemployed would be better off under the Poor Law.[26]

As far as the positive use of funds was concerned the discussion mainly turned on the feasibility of subsidies to wages, subsidies to interest on new capital, and subsidies to keep prices down. While Balfour and Lewis were sceptical about such policies, Stamp, Cole, and Keynes were willing at least to consider the possibilities. For this meeting Keynes had prepared a statement on the present economic situation which began on an optimistic note.

As I have been something of a Cassandra hitherto, I should like to record my opinion that an upward reaction may be due shortly. Commodity prices may, I think, touch their lowest point sometime this month ... I do not think we need expect a large further increase [in unemployment] apart from [seasonal] causes. I should be inclined to predict that this figure will not at any time exceed 2,500,000.*

Keynes's view of unemployment benefit was that it provided a measure of the subsidy to employment which the government could pay and yet still be in pocket. 'If it was assumed that the value of the output of an employed man was £3 a week and that unemployment pay was £1, a subsidy of 33% would be profitable to the Government provided that it was only paid for additional employment.' He acknowledged that some of the money would be wasted on existing employment, and that even if one could differentiate between new and existing employed there was a danger of subsidising the less efficient firms. Nevertheless, there was still a good case for subsidies where 'the new output was likely to be high in relation to old output'. This case for subsidies to new employment could be extended to tariffs. 'Where the elasticity of home supply is great – which is the case wherever there is surplus capacity – the subsidy or net cost of the tariff may more than pay for itself out of the dole earned, even though it applies to the existing output as well as to the new output'.[27]

The Prime Minister's questions to the Economic Advisory Council were one of a number of steps taken by MacDonald in the summer of 1930. These included the ministerial conferences in May and the establishment of the Ministerial Panel on Unemployment in June. At these conferences MacDonald backed the Minister of Transport, Herbert Morrison, in squeezing additional funds out of the Treasury to expand the trunk-road programme, and then, to cope with the local authorities' slowness to take up grants, he called a conference in London of local authority representatives

---

* Cab. 58/11, E.A.C. (H) 121, 'The Present Economic Position', 8 September 1930. His optimism was not because 'much progress has been made towards remedying the fundamental causes of the slump but because a slump of this kind always has an inherent tendency to be overdone'. This belief was based on the analysis of his *Treatise on Money*, Vol. I (*Collected Writings*, Vol. v), Chs. 19, 20.

on 17 June. As a result of the complaints voiced at this conference the panel decided to ease the conditions for making grants in such a way that all authorities became eligible for the maximum rate of grant. In addition a Public Works Facilities Bill was introduced in July to simplify the procedure for acquiring land for local authority projects. Extra funds amounting to £500,000 were set aside for grants to local authorities mounting employment schemes in 'necessitous areas'. The immediate object of these measures was to increase the volume of work available over the coming winter.[28]

At an early meeting of the panel, MacDonald 'indicated a desire to go outside the scope of existing programmes and arrangements and to consider large scale projects involving possibly large expenditure and direct government action'. He therefore asked Sir John Anderson, the head of the panel's secretariat of officials, to re-examine the Mosley memorandum in the light of the grave unemployment prospects, and to ask the departments 'to supply in the shortest possible time projected schemes of work'. At the same time the Cabinet asked Attlee, Mosley's successor as Chancellor of the Duchy of Lancaster, to 'make an immediate and intensive study of what is wrong with British industry and what steps ought to be taken to provide a remedy', and gave him the assistance of the Economic Advisory Council staff for this purpose. There were also conversations between the government and the Liberal leaders in the summer of 1930.[29]

The departmental heads could find few projects which could be justified as both economically useful and employment-creating, and hence little scope for new government initiatives. Furthermore, the Treasury and Sir John Anderson were by now concerned about the worsening financial situation. When Snowden acquiesced in Morrison's road programmes, Hopkins remarked: 'If expenditure goes further we shall clearly find the Exchequer unable to stand the racket and a Road loan – Sir Oswald Mosley's expedient! – will be the outcome. This is sheer borrowing for current expenditure and a long step down the hill.' Sir John Anderson told MacDonald that 'it is open to serious question whether expenditure which might have been regarded as justifiable in January, is justifiable or possible, in July'.[30] The Treasury officials were particularly concerned to avoid large-scale borrowing, because they believed that low interest rates were the best remedy for depression and feared that large government debt issues would raise interest rates.[31]

Attlee, in his memorandum on 'The Problems of British Industry', moved towards solutions outlined by Mosley earlier, proposing more 'deliberate decision by the Government as to what is the right basis for the economic life of this country'. Planning of rationalisation and the location of new industrial development should be undertaken by a Ministry of Industry, rather than left to such private bodies as the Bankers' Industrial Development Company. In reply the Treasury defended departmental autonomy, and was sceptical as to whether any government agency was equipped to take on the business of financing new industries. If the new planning body was intended to make profits, then it would have to be more efficient than private enterprise: if not, then the taxpayer would have to make good the losses. The Treasury also disapproved of Attlee's suggestion that domestic stability could be ensured by the use of import boards and bulk purchase agreements. Attlee's proposals would not improve the existing private machinery for channelling funds into industry; they would simply distribute public money without imposing effective conditions, and this would mean 'undermining the basic principle of our present industrial system, which is that industries that cannot pay their way must go under'.[32]

Increasing concern with the budget situation meant increasing concern about unemployment benefit payments. In October the Liberals published their pamphlet *How to Tackle Unemployment*. Although rejecting deflation as an active policy, it attributed the continuance of high unemployment partly to the fact that 'we are seeking to ensure to the nation a standard of life higher than our present relative national effort and efficiency justify'. It suggested that the government should call together industrial representatives in an effort to get them to reduce costs by 10 per cent, possibly on the basis of an Economic Advisory Council report. To give a lead to industry the government should also set up a new Geddes committee to achieve economies in government spending. It mentioned reform of abuses in the unemployment insurance scheme with a view to restoring the insurance principle, but in view of the existence of a three-party committee on the subject did not deal with this thoroughly.* The Economic Advisory Council committee under Cole reported in November. Given the many abuses of the unemployment insurance scheme, the committee thought there was 'a strong case for the complete re-casting' of the scheme. The principles on which the new scheme should be based included 'absolute separation of the finance of that part of the scheme which can be properly treated as insurance from that which cannot', and 'application of radically different conditions' for benefits under the two parts. This meant in particular a strict means test for transitional benefit. The Cabinet did not discuss this report until January 1931, by which time it had decided to appoint a Royal Commission on Unemployment Insurance under the chairmanship of Holman Gregory. Its terms of reference were to suggest ways of making the scheme self-supporting, and to devise arrangements outside the scheme for those who had run out of benefit.[33]

One other topic the government was particularly concerned with in the second half of 1930 was promoting rationalisation of industries such as iron

---

* Its authorship was given as Lloyd George, Lord Lothian and Seebohm Rowntree. Experts mentioned in the preface were Sir Alan Pim, Professor G. C. Allen, and Sir William Wallace. See also G. C. Allen, 'Advice from Economists – Forty-five Years Ago', *Three Banks Review*, June 1975.

and steel and cotton. The apparent need to go slow with public works schemes because of the budget position strengthened the emphasis on rationalisation.[34] The committees on the iron and steel and cotton industries both completed their reports at the end of May 1930. Keynes found the iron and steel report 'an extraordinarily depressing document': he wondered if Henderson 'became a conservative under . . . [its] influence . . . [as that] would be quite natural'. It regarded the formation of 'large regional amalgamations' as essential to the recovery of the industry, but rejected a safeguarding tariff to help the process along because it feared that the industry would be less inclined to rationalise if it enjoyed the benefits of a tariff. It also accepted Montagu Norman's assurance that adequate finance for rationalisation schemes would be forthcoming from the City. Norman, who gave evidence to the committee, was by this time much involved with rationalisation: after several specific interventions in and after 1926, he had formed the Securities Management Trust in November 1929, and the Bankers' Industrial Development Company in April 1930.[35]

After considerable discussion the Cabinet decided against publication of the iron and steel report. In the meantime MacDonald chaired a conference of government officials and representatives of the steel industry, the Bankers' Industrial Development Company, and the Economic Advisory Council; he then asked J. H. Thomas and Horace Wilson to 'prepare a concrete scheme'. But discussions with the industry were hampered by the industry's desire for a tariff and the government's insistence that this could not be considered. At the end of July, Larke and Pugh (for the industry) and Bruce-Gardner (Norman's adviser) agreed to draft a 'definite scheme'. Once this was ready in February 1931, discussions with the industry were resumed, only to founder again on the protection issue. Further delay resulted from the government's proposals for a large public utility company and consultation with the Liberals, to both of which Norman and Bruce-Gardner objected. The Labour Government's involvement in rationalisation of the iron and steel industry came to an end when Norman became preoccupied with the international financial crisis in May 1931.[36]

The report on the cotton industry was along similar lines to that on iron and steel. Since protection was not at issue in traditionally free-trade Lancashire, the report was published. Although, thanks to the industry's 'traditionalism', there was no battle over safeguarding, the same traditionalism meant that progress towards rationalisation was even more limited than in the iron and steel industry – in spite of the precedent set by earlier moves in that direction.[37]

The Committee of Economists

While the official initiatives were being taken in the summer of 1930 the Committee of Economists was attempting to produce – in the words Keynes used in his letter to MacDonald proposing the committee – 'an agreed diagnosis of our present problems, and a reasoned list of possible remedies'. Although the letter stressed diagnosis rather than remedies, there is little doubt that Keynes hoped to be able to secure a high degree of consensus on remedies as well. Pigou proved nearer the mark when he said that 'we shall be genii if we get an agreed report out of a reference like that'.[38] Nevertheless, this must have been the first occasion that an official body consisting entirely of economists was entrusted with such a far-ranging brief. Of the many reports produced under the auspices of the Economic Advisory Council the one submitted by this committee has certainly aroused most comment so far, though the course of the discussion leading up to the report has not been dealt with fully before.[39] For these reasons it seems worth tracing the genesis and subsequent history of the report in some detail.

In his original letter to MacDonald, Keynes admitted that the committee would be an experiment. Economists, he claimed, have a language and a method of analysing problems which though unfamiliar to businessmen 'enables them to understand one another fairly quickly'. The results could be made intelligible to everyone, and would therefore be available for criticism.

But the process of preliminary debate and of arriving at the conclusions cannot be successfully carried on . . . by a mixed body. It may be that Economics is not enough of a science to be able to produce useful fruits. But I think it might be given a trial, and that we might assume for a moment, if only as a hypothesis, that it can be treated like any other science, and ask for qualified scientists in the subject to say their say.

Keynes's selection of 'qualified scientists' originally included Professor Henry Clay and D. H. Robertson as well as those who actually served on the committee. He commended the list to MacDonald on the following grounds:

I have selected [them] as being people, all of whom are well accustomed to the most up-to-date academic methods and ways of discussing these problems, are essentially reasonable and good members of a committee, and happen to have given already a good deal of time and thought to the problem which would be set them.

Even without Clay and Robertson the committee was a strong one, and well primed for its purpose. Keynes had just put the finishing touches to his about-to-be-published *A Treatise on Money*, the book which provided the analytical framework for the diagnoses and remedies which he had been canvassing for the past year or so. He had given an extended exposition of this framework in his private evidence to the members of the Macmillan Committee; it featured in a long letter of advice written to the Governor of the Bank of England in May; and it provided the basis for his answers to the Prime Minister's questions on the state of trade in July. Pigou and Stamp had also given evidence before the Macmillan Committee. In fact Pigou stated initially that there was little he wished to add to his Macmillan evidence, which, together with that of Stamp, D. H. Robertson, and A. L.

Bowley, was among the first documents circulated to the Committee of Economists.[40] Robbins, the youngest member of the group at thirty-two, had not appeared before the Macmillan Committee; but he had assisted Sir William Beveridge in producing the second edition of his book on *Unemployment: A Problem of Industry*, and made a thorough study of trade-cycle theories, particularly the monetary over-investment theories associated with the names of von Mises and Hayek.

Keynes's main hopes of producing an agreed diagnosis rested explicitly on the assumption of a common language, and implicitly perhaps on confidence in his powers of persuading his fellow economists to accept the diagnostic framework of his *Treatise*. In his letter to the Governor of the Bank of England in May, after giving a brief account of one of his main theoretical propositions to the effect that business losses and unemployment followed 'inevitably and mathematically' from the inequality of savings and total investment, he had said that it was 'very important that a competent decision should be reached whether it is true or false. I can only say that I am ready to have my head chopped off if it is false!'[41] The Committee of Economists was obviously seen by Keynes as an appropriate body to make this 'competent decision'. From the outset, therefore, an attempt was made to tackle the brief on a fundamental theoretical level.

Most of the members of the committee knew something about Keynes's *Treatise* position prior to the meetings of the committee. Pigou had received and commented on galley proofs of the *Treatise* in 1929;* he had also crossed swords with Keynes on a number of related issues when he appeared before the Macmillan Committee. Henderson was specifically mentioned in the preface of the *Treatise* as someone who had helped Keynes, and the two men were, of course, in close contact with one another throughout this period on Economic Advisory Council business. Stamp too, as a member of the Council, was familiar with the general line of Keynes's thinking. Although Robbins was more of an outsider, he was probably aware of some features of Keynes's position at this time; he received a copy of proofs of the *Treatise* when the committee began its meetings.

The person most closely acquainted with the details of Keynes's argument was undoubtedly Richard Kahn, whom Keynes recruited from Cambridge to act as joint secretary to the committee alongside A. F. Hemming. As Keynes made clear in the preface to the *Treatise*, he considered himself indebted to Kahn for his help 'in the gradual evolution of the book into its final form and in the avoidance of errors'.† In the summer of 1930 Kahn

---

* *Collected Writings*, Vol. XIII, pp. 118, 135, 138. At this stage Pigou's comments were apparently oral or in the margins of the proofs. He took part in the post-publication discussions (ibid. pp. 202, 211–18) and reviewed the book in *The Nation & Athenaeum*, 24 January 1931.

† Some idea of the role played by Kahn in relation to the *Treatise* and in the transition towards the *General Theory* can now be gauged from *Collected Writings*, Vol. XIII, pp. 120–6, 203–7, 218, 237–8, 273–5, 412–14, 634–7, and from Moggridge's reconstruction of events on pp. 337–43.

had begun the work on the relationship between primary and secondary employment which was to result in the publication of his famous mutiplier article the following year. This article was of major help to Keynes in his shift from the *Treatise* emphasis on price levels towards the focus of the *General Theory* on output and employment levels. An early version of Kahn's multiplier idea, together with an attempt to measure the relationship between primary and secondary employment, was circulated to the Committee of Economists.[42] Keynes tried to use the idea to argue for public works in the report, but Pigou's and Henderson's objections ensured that there was no sign of this in the final product.[43]

Kahn's first contribution to the committee's proceedings came in the form of a list of draft heads for discussion which was circulated to members at Keynes's suggestion before the first meeting, on 10 September.[44] This shows clear marks of the influence of the *Treatise* and hints at Kahn's own developing interest in the question of primary and secondary employment under conditions where the supply schedules of output were likely to be highly elastic. Kahn's questions attempted to distinguish between the fall in real efficiency wages necessary to reduce unemployment under normal conditions, and that required under conditions of world slump and excess capacity. If unemployment was still likely to be high after excess capacity had been eliminated and the slump had passed, did this not indicate that it would be 'preferable to grapple with [unemployment] forthwith as a long period problem rather than to apply temporary palliatives which serve merely to postpone the day of reckoning'? If on the other hand the problem was likely to be short-lived did this not strengthen the case for alternative short-term remedies such as tariffs? There might even be a good case for tariffs as a long-term measure if reduction in money rather than real wages was thought to be the 'intractable element'. Some 'special' remedies (i.e. those not involving wage reductions) were objected to on the grounds of their effect in raising prices: was this the result of the remedies themselves or a minor by-product of increased output, and therefore likely to occur with any 'ordinary revival of trade'? What was the likely volume of secondary employment generated by any increase in primary employment due to tariffs or public investment? Were they in fact likely to be of the same order, and how should the related effects on prices and the foreign balance be included in the reckoning? Of the 'special' remedies, tariffs would minimise the unfavourable side-effects on the foreign balance, whereas cheap money and public investment would not. Loan-financed public investment could be carried out without reducing rates of interest, and might be combined with tariffs to reduce the side-effects. How far would such remedies require amenable behaviour on the part of the banking system? Would they retard the normal processes of improving efficiency? Kahn also listed a number of other questions concerning taxes, the budgetary situation, and international action.

Kahn's document served as the agenda for the committee's first discussion of its line of approach, but during the second meeting, held on the following day, the committee decided to proceed on the basis of members' replies to a much shorter, and ostensibly less ambitious, questionnaire drawn up by Keynes. This ran as follows:

I

In what way would (a) British employment
                (b) British prices
                (c) British real wages
be affected by (i) an increase of investment
                (a) in the world at large
                (b) in Great Britain
      (ii) a tariff
      (iii) a reduction of British money wages
                (a) all round
                (b) in the relatively highly paid industries?

II

How much too high (in order or magnitude) are
                (a) real wages
                (b) money wages at the existing level of world prices?
What is your estimate of the increase
                (a) of real wages
                (b) of productivity per head since 1910–14?
If your estimate of the excess of real wages is greater than your estimate of the increase in real wages per unit of productivity, how do you explain this?[45]

When the committee met again two weeks later for a weekend session at Stamp's home at Shortlands in Kent on 26–28 September, they had before them each member's written answers to these questions. This marks the opening of the real proceedings, which were to develop rapidly in the next three weeks or so under pressure from the Prime Minister to produce the report by 20 October so that it could be considered by the government before Parliament assembled on the 28th. After four meetings in London, the committee held another weekend session on 18–19 October at King's College, Cambridge. Controversy resulted in two more meetings in London, but the committee finally managed to complete its report by 24 October.

Although the final report did contain an agreed diagnosis, and a majority of the committee endorsed some of Keynes's policy proposals, the outcome fell short of Keynes's hopes. The agreement reached did not result from whole-hearted acceptance of Keynes's theoretical framework, and was often based on uneasy compromise between points of view that remained deeply divided on fundamental questions of analysis and terminology. Such divisions were more serious than the usual kinds of disagreements (which also figured in the report) over remedies and the weight to be attached to particular pieces of empirical evidence, where political and other value-judgments were inevitably brought into play. In order to understand the nature of the underlying divisions over both theory and policy it is necessary to consider the main features of Keynes's *Treatise* position and the response which it evoked from Robbins, Henderson, and Pigou. Stamp played a fairly passive role throughout the proceedings; he was not interested in theoretical questions *per se*, and tended to defer to Keynes's authority on such matters.[46]

By virtue of his *Tract on Monetary Reform* (1923), and his contributions to the gold standard debate, Keynes had established himself as the leading exponent of a monetary interpretation of Britain's economic difficulties. Throughout the latter half of the 1920s he was a consistent opponent of deflationary monetary policies, and became one of the chief advocates of loan-financed public works. But over this period the theoretical rationale underwent considerable refinement as a result of Keynes's abandonment of the purely monetary approach of the *Tract* in favour of one couched in terms of the relationship between savings and investment, which attempted to bring 'real' and monetary variables into closer relationship.[47] As in the *Tract*, though, one of Keynes's chief concerns was with the possibilities of conflict between the conditions required for internal and external stability. He also retained his earlier interest in short-run analysis, though in the *Treatise* this interest became focussed primarily on the problems of moving from one equilibrium position to another in a world of large-scale change but reduced flexibility.

From an insular British point of view the essence of the *Treatise* position can be approached as an elaboration of the special problems faced by a nation prevented from achieving domestic equilibrium at full employment by gold standard constraints which precluded action to reduce the long-term rate of interest to a level consonant with the expectations of domestic investors.[48] It is important to underline the fact that Keynes depicted this dilemma as occurring within an international context; in spite of his criticisms of the gold standard, and his espousal of what many regarded as insular solutions, Keynes's theoretical system was essentially an 'open' one. According to the *Treatise* explanation of post-war maladies, the root of world problems lay in the height and stickiness of long-term rates of interest. A combination of circumstances, chiefly the large volume of international government borrowing and the general climate of tight money associated with the return to the gold standard, had kept post-war interest rates at a level which was too high in relation to profit expectations, particularly in older countries such as Britain. The United States, with its greater buoyancy, had not suffered from this problem until 1928–9, when speculation had driven rates above what could be borne by 'genuine' borrowers. For Keynes the world slump was not simply a dramatic departure from a normal state of affairs, but a product of these post-war strains, as well as being a possible means of finding release from them. Hence his view of the slump as 'the death struggle of the high rates of interest established by the war, and the re-birth of the low rates which prevailed before 1914'.[49]

Under the gold standard, or indeed any international standard, the system of fixed exchange rates imposed constraints and burdens. After debating seriously whether an international standard was necessary or desirable, Keynes came out in its favour and was not prepared to advocate departure from the gold standard or devaluation until it became inevitable. But if exchange rates were 'given' then so to a large extent was the rate of interest. Keynes normally assumed that any individual country's attempt to depart from the rate of interest determined by world conditions would either be constrained by capital outflow and loss of reserves, or require the application of special expedients. This did not mean that powerful nations acting singly, and more so if they acted in concert, could not influence the situation. Since Keynes believed that the international slump was to a large extent the outcome of mistaken monetary policies and artificialities in the situation, he could be quite optimistic about the possibilities of achieving rapid results from international cooperation. Throughout the slump and even during the financial crisis of 1931, he advocated bold action by the Bank of England to exercise leadership in bringing down the long-term rate of interest by 'open market operations à outrance'. Chances of quick success would, of course, be greatly improved if Paris and New York could be induced to work for the same goal. He was particularly hopeful of collaboration with the Federal Reserve Board, and if Paris continued to be greedy in demanding gold he advocated borrowing from New York in order to 'feed the French with it to the teeth'.[50] However, Keynes did not regard international remedies as the only ones available, and he refused to regard the international problem as a reason for adopting only 'safe' solutions at home.

According to the *Treatise* position, since the war Britain's membership of the international system had imposed special burdens of adjustment, which chiefly manifested themselves as business losses and unemployment. Keynes used his new savings and investment apparatus to show why this was so. The deflationary situation from which Britain had suffered throughout the 1920s was due to an excess of voluntary savings over what would be invested at home at prevailing world rates of interest, coupled with limitations posed by the state of the foreign balance on the capacity of foreign investment to absorb the excess savings. The level of 'efficiency wages' entered into the system as one of the chief influences on costs of production relative to those abroad, and hence, via the foreign balance, on the capacity to lend abroad without putting the exchange rate under pressure. While the capacity of foreign investment to absorb domestic savings was determined by the surplus of exports over imports, the amount of foreign lending depended on the rate of interest on foreign loans when compared with the rate of return on new investment at home. This was an acute problem for an old country like Britain because the rate of return on capital at home was lower than elsewhere.

Our dilemma in recent years, as I see it, is that if we raise the rate of interest sufficiently to keep our foreign lending down to the amount of our favourable balance, we raise it too high for domestic enterprise. The consequence is that our savings can neither get abroad in the form of exports, nor be used at home for new developments here, with the result that unemployment and business losses ensue and the excess savings are in effect used up in financing the costs of unemployment and the other losses.[51]

The formal conditions for the existence of full employment equilibrium in an open economy would be fulfilled when 'the rate of interest is such that the amount of foreign lending at that rate is exactly equal to the amount of the favourable foreign balance, as determined by comparative money-costs of production at home and abroad, and also such that the amount of home investment at that rate is also equal to the excess of the country's savings over the amount of the foreign lending'.[52]

The problems created by a clash between the conditions for external and internal equilibrium were partly questions of sheer magnitude and partly matters involving responsiveness to small changes in the key variables. Britain's difficulties lay in the volume of her savings relative to the size of her foreign balance, and in the insensitivity of the foreign balance to small downward changes in money costs of production, which were in any case difficult to achieve. The problem was magnified by the overvaluation of sterling since 1925, as well as by the tariffs imposed by other countries. In fact Britain suffered from a peculiarly bad combination of circumstances.

If . . . there is a high degree of mobility of foreign lending, a low degree of mobility of home wage-rates, inelasticity in the demand-schedule for our country's exports and a high elasticity in the demand for borrowing for home investment, then the transition from one position of internal equilibrium to another required by the necessity for preserving external equilibrium may be difficult, dilatory and painful.[53]

Keynes believed that other commentators had underestimated the extent to which novel but enduring features of the post-war situation had not only made the possibility of conflict between external and internal stability more likely, but made the adjustment from one state of equilibrium to another more difficult, more socially divisive, and more costly in terms of lost income and wealth. Furthermore, while a tight monetary policy dictated by considerations of external stability was only too capable of producing profit deflation and unemployment, it was 'singularly ill-adapted' to the aim of producing an income deflation, or a lower level of money earnings and prices, in a world of strong trade unions and other inflexibilities.[54] Much of his thinking on policy was conditioned by his urgent search for a course between the Scylla of high and sticky long-term rates of interest determined by international conditions, and the Charybdis of downward inflexibility of wage costs.

For a country in Britain's position the *Treatise* analysis furnished dual criteria for judging policy measures: 'Nothing is any good which does not either increase our favourable balance or find an increased outlet for our savings at home'. In his attempt to counter what he described as the negative 'grin and bear it' school of thought, personified by Snowden, he was willing to support almost all the active remedies being canvassed in 1930 which met one or other of these criteria. In his answers to the Prime Minister's questions in July he said that 'the peculiarity of my position lies, perhaps, in the fact that I am in favour of practically all the remedies which have been suggested in any quarter. Some of them are better than others. But nearly all of them seem to me to tend in the right direction.' He commended with varying degrees of warmness as 'means to increase our favourable foreign balance' rationalisation, reduced aggregate taxation, reduced efficiency-wages, tariffs, import boards, and international reflationary action. As 'means to increase the outlet for our savings at home' he supported public investment, subsidies to private investment, discrimination in favour of home investment, an embargo on foreign loans, and budget economies designed to foster business confidence.*

Several negative policy conclusions also followed from his savings and investment analysis. Since high rates of interest were not evidence of a deficiency in the supply of savings relative to the demand for savings for investment purposes, thrift and economy campaigns were the very opposite of what was needed.[55] On the other hand, although reductions in the level of total savings would have the desired effect in reducing deflationary pressure on the economy, such a policy was a 'council of despair' because the savings could have been used to finance additions to the community's capital stock.[56] He was in favour, however, of temporary suspension of the sinking fund.† A related argument concerned the negative savings resulting from financing the dole out of borrowing. Keynes pointed out that under the right conditions an increase in the rate of the dole, in common with other unproductive expenditure similarly financed, would have the effect of reducing unemployment; the objection was simply, but crucially, that it had a less beneficial effect on 'the rate of accumulation of our capital wealth' than other expedients which had the same effect on unemployment.[57]

Another negative conclusion to emerge from the *Treatise* position concerned the controversial question of wage reductions as a remedy for unemployment. When drawing attention in 1925 to the deflationary implications of return to gold at the pre-war parity, Keynes had contended that

---

* 'The State of Trade'. He made the same point and suggested ten different sorts of remedies in his private evidence to the Macmillan Committee in February and March 1930 (Keynes Papers and T. 200/4).

† He advocated this as early as 1924 (Committee on National Debt and Taxation (Colwyn Committee), *Minutes of Evidence* (1927), Q. 4023). He returned to the idea in 1930 in a letter to Henderson (Keynes Papers EA/1, 6 June) and in his own answers to his Questionnaire for the Committee of Economists (Cab. 58/150, E.A.C. (E) 15, and *Collected Writings*, Vol. XIII, p. 196).

it would result in an overvaluation of sterling of around 10 per cent, and that this in turn would require reducing prices and wages in the export industries by the same amount. He called the theory 'that wages should be settled by economic pressure, otherwise called "hard facts"', the 'theory of the economic Juggernaut', contrasting it unfavourably with a theory which holds 'that wages should be fixed by reference to what is "fair" and "reasonable" as between classes'. At this time his main objection to wage-cuts was solely on grounds of equity: since there was no way of reducing incomes and prices generally, the decision to return to gold involved singling out a vulnerable group of workers. But he did not rule out the possibility of achieving a fair and economically desirable result from a national treaty to reduce all incomes simultaneously.[58] By the time he reached the *Treatise* position the argument about the effect of wage reductions was more sophisticated. Keynes's attitude to the moral aspects of such a policy had not changed: if anything it had hardened as a result of his examination of the ineffectiveness and harmful side-effects of monetary policy as a way of reducing prices and wages. As a member of the Macmillan Committee he was also impressed by public opposition to the policy of general wage-cuts: 'The unwillingness of employers and associations of employers, who have appeared before the Macmillan Committee to recommend this solution has been truly remarkable. In order to test this feeling, I have often in examination pressed them to fall back on this recommendation and almost always without success.'[59]

He acknowledged, however, that wage-cuts could have beneficial effects. A reduction of money wages, or an undertaking by trade unions to increase efficiency without demanding commensurate increases in pay, could have a favourable effect on profit expectations and hence domestic investment; and it would also improve the foreign balance over the long period, provided that elasticities of demand were favourable and other nations did not follow suit. It certainly could not be ruled out of account, and Keynes kept returning to the question.

The almost complete rigidity of our wage-rates since 1929, in spite of the great reduction of all other price levels, is very striking to the imagination. The fact that, in spite of all adverse circumstances, we have been increasing real wages faster than ever before in our history, has undoubtedly much aggravated our other difficulties. We have been going ahead – by force of circumstances rather than by any deliberate decision – rather faster than is wise.[60]

He frequently urged restraint on trade unions and pointed out that specific wage-reductions in the sheltered trades were in the interests of the workers themselves. During the Council's discussion of the Economists' report he committed himself to 'a theoretical case for, say, a 10% cut in wages and salaries accompanied by an extra 2/- income tax on other sources of income'.[61] Earlier he had raised doubts as to whether it was not preferable to raise working-class living standards by means of taxes and public welfare expenditure, rather than via higher wages, which reduced profits, encouraged capital outflow, and led to reduced output and employment.[62] In June 1930 he told Henderson that

> it may be that wages are so much too high, and there is so little chance of the facts catching up to the existing level of wages, that it is short-sighted to play for time and try to avoid, so far as is possible, the waste of wealth meanwhile. One ought, rather, to concentrate in an assault on wages. This is the view which I have hitherto been rejecting and still on the whole, I think, reject.[63]

Although at this stage in Keynes's thinking wage-reductions were more than a mere theoretical possibility, he provided a number of reasons why wage-cuts were not likely to be a very effective line of attack in his private evidence to the Macmillan Committee.[64] To the Committee of Economists he proposed a tariff-bounty scheme, which he commended as a fairer and more effective way of reducing real wages without the attendant disadvantages of achieving the same result by mounting a direct attack on money wages.[65]

The advocacy of loan-financed public works as a solution to unemployment was by no means unique to Keynes among economists at this time, though his journalistic writings and his contribution (with Henderson) to the Liberal campaign literature made him the most prominent advocate of this type of solution in Britain, particularly in 1929 and 1930. At this time Keynes's case for public works followed from his *Treatise* analysis of the special problems of a nation constrained by the gold standard from making full use of monetary policy to bring down long-term rates of interest. With the incorporation of Kahn's multiplier into Keynes's thinking, however, the case for public works took a different form.[66] But in 1930 Keynes's basic case for public works did not turn on his ability, or lack of it, to state the precise relationship between primary and secondary employment. It followed directly from his view that an excess of saving over total investment inevitably ran to waste in the form of business losses and unemployment. This provided sufficient reason for maintaining that the prevailing market rate of interest should not be allowed to determine the level of either public or private investment, and certainly for rejecting the orthodox Treasury view that loan-financed public works should satisfy ordinary commercial criteria. Moreover, public works should be seen as part of the package of policy alternatives then being pressed by Keynes.

Although Keynes continued to advocate public works policies throughout 1930, there are signs that he was beginning to recognise the practical difficulties of organising schemes which would be large enough for the job in hand. Thus in May he wrote to the Governor of the Bank of England saying that he was 'appalled by the difficulties of absorbing our surplus savings at anything like the present rate of interest'. He estimated that even the most drastic reorganisation of the iron and steel industry at a cost of £50m would only absorb surplus savings on a non-recurrent basis for about fifty days.

The same was true of other rationalisation schemes, as well as housing, transport, and public utilities. He saw the main task of the Bank as creating a favourable monetary climate through efforts to bring down rates of interest both abroad and at home. He proposed various technical measures designed to reduce the spread between long- and short-term rates, as well as devices such as widening the gap between gold buying and selling prices which would give the Bank greater scope for influencing and insulating the domestic monetary position. Taking a bolder tack, he also advocated the use of subsidies and tax allowances to reduce rates of interest to home investors, private and public, and coupled this with a proposal to discriminate against foreign investment through the tax system and via a partial embargo on foreign loans.[67]

Keynes would, on occasion, speak of ways of increasing the domestic outlet for savings and reducing the pressure to lend abroad as though they were interchangeable. When he also advocated measures to improve the foreign balance, this apparent eclecticism could give rise to misunderstandings. For as Robbins commented, it seems to be 'a very perilous balance of probabilities which enables one at once to suggest that capital export is undesirable, and, at the same time to recommend measures which would facilitate its accomplishment'.[68] The logic of Keynes's analysis gave him an interest in any remedy which raised total investment, whether domestic or foreign; but the realities of Britain's weakened foreign trade and exchange position biassed him in favour of domestic investment.

Robbins's real target was Keynes's apostasy on the question of free trade. In February 1930 the emphasis of Keynes's private policy advice had begun to shift towards a revenue tariff. If the object was to reduce unemployment by improving the foreign balance, rather than improving the employment situation in existing export industries *per se*, then, as Keynes pointed out, it was just as effective and probably much easier to reduce imports. Although in July he said that he had 'become reluctantly convinced' of the need for protection, he acknowledged that tariffs alone were not a panacea, and that 'the theoretical case for protection is in the case of Great Britain much stronger than the practical case'. He admitted the force of all the usual political and moral counter-arguments, and stated that he would have preferred to get through the next ten years without recourse to tariffs. But according to the *Treatise* position, the equilibrium conditions required by free trade – notably wage flexibility – were no longer present. Like 'sound finance', free trade was one of those principles other nations had forsaken but which Britain continued to adhere to at considerable cost to herself. The pursuit of such long-run policies was 'a grand thing in its way – unless, like the operation of systems at Monte Carlo, one has not the resources to last through the short run'. Keynes also believed that the gains from international specialisation in manufactured goods were no longer sufficiently large to compensate for the loss of stability involved in a world where

British money wages were no longer capable of being driven down to meet the conditions of external equilibrium, especially during an international slump. A uniform tariff of 10 per cent on manufactured imports had other virtues too: it could make a contribution to the budget problem; it was 'the only form of taxation which will positively cheer people up'; and it would turn the terms of trade in Britain's favour.★

It was the problems associated with the alternative of general money wage reductions that mainly conditioned Keynes's growing support for a tariff. He estimated in September 1930 that a reduction in money wages of between 5 per cent and 20 per cent would be necessary to offset the effects of the slump. The benefits of such a policy would take several years to show themselves in the form of higher exports and employment, always assuming that other nations did not follow suit. A uniform tariff of 10 per cent on all goods coupled with an equivalent bounty on all exports would have the same effect as a devaluation, since it was equivalent to a reduction in money costs of 10 per cent, but would be much fairer than an attempt to achieve the same result by attacking money wages alone, especially those in the unsheltered industries. The whole scheme could be put into effect by a simple piece of legislation, and would not involve 'a sort of civil war or guerilla warfare carried on, industry by industry, all over the country'.[69]

In his answers to his own questionnaire Keynes rehearsed some of the relevant parts of the *Treatise* analysis, making use of the concept of an equilibrium level of real wages which would rule at full employment when all firms were earning normal returns. In a closed system it would be justifiable to speak of unemployment in terms of whether real wages were above equilibrium, but in an open system the equilibrium level of real wages could be seriously affected by shifts in the terms of trade with the outside world, uncompensated by reductions in money wages per unit of output at home. Keynes defined 'equilibrium terms of trade' as those which would obtain when 'the level of money-wages at home relatively to money-wages abroad is such that the amount of the foreign balance (i.e. of foreign investment) *plus* the amount of home investment at the rate of interest set by world conditions (i.e. which just prevents gold movements) is at least equal to the amount of home savings'. The policy problem resolved itself, therefore, into one of whether real wages should be brought down directly, or whether, as Keynes preferred, the various measures he was advancing should be used to shift the equilibrium terms of trade in Britain's favour.[70]

★ Cab. 58/11, E.A.C. (H) 106, 'The State of Trade'. Keynes first admitted he was coming round to protection to the Macmillan Committee on 28 February 1930. He was more definite when he opened a discussion at the Tuesday Club on 9 April 1930 on 'Are the Presuppositions of Free Trade satisfied today?' Robbins was a guest at the Tuesday Club that night so he already knew of Keynes's 'conversion' by August. (Unpublished Minutes of Committee on Finance and Industry, and Keynes's notes for his speech, in Keynes Papers, and Minute book of Tuesday Club). Keynes did not come out publicly in favour of tariffs until March 1931 (below, p. 79).

Keynes also attempted to incorporate the early results of Kahn's work on primary and secondary employment. Since it was not necessary to the *Treatise* analysis, Keynes simply used it at this stage to give some idea of the magnitudes involved in an expansionary programme, and to emphasise that the 'inflationary' effects on domestic prices of increases in employment would arise out of any scheme for increasing employment. Even so, Kahn's findings gave rise to controversy between Kahn, Pigou, and Keynes on the validity of the exercise.[71]

The questions in part II of Keynes's questionnaire succeeded in eliciting a set of estimates of the changes in real wages and productivity per head since the war, but Robbins, Henderson, and Pigou raised doubts as to the value of attempts to state by how much real or money wages were too high under existing world conditions.* Keynes suffered less from doubts about making informed 'guesstimates' on such matters. Although he was sensitive to the problems of index-number construction, having worked on them extensively for the *Treatise*, as a monetary theorist he was perhaps more at home with the use of aggregated measures of price and wage levels. Robbins, however, did not feel that statistics of wage and productivity movements enabled him 'to give a straight answer to the quantitative question how far are real or money wages out of equilibrium'. To him the concept of equilibrium implied an optimal allocation rather than an average. The very existence of unemployment might justify the assumption that present rates were wrong, but it did not warrant any conclusion that they were uniformly wrong unless it was further assumed that the labour force was mobile or already optimally distributed between employments. In other words, the average level of wages was merely the statistical result of a given distribution of labour, whether in equilibrium or not, rather than a causal influence on its distribution. From this it followed only that 'when labour is badly distributed the average will presumably be lower than when it is better distributed', and it was impossible to derive any useful conclusion from 'a hypothetical disparity from a fictitious average'. Hence he considered that 'it is not high wages but rigid wages which are the main condition of disequilibrium. Given the rigidity wages may be too high, but it is the rigidity not the height which is causally effective.' This had the advantage that 'theoretical purity' and 'practical argument' were, for once, in harmony. Rigidities due to restrictive practices and abuses in the unemployment insurance scheme were manifest, whereas average levels were highly disputable. By removing these rigidities the unemployed (i.e. 'those who are precluded from selling their labour at prices which will command a buyer') would benefit and 'the average earnings of the total labour force would be increased'.

* The estimates are in each member's reply to the questionnaire (Cab. 58/150, E.A.C. (E) 9, 12–15). Keynes also circulated two supplementary notes on the estimates (Cab. 58/151, E.A.C. (E) 18 and 19, Keynes, 'Real Wages compared with physical productivity per head' and 'The relation between a given change in money wages and the associated changes in real wages', 25 September 1930).

Pigou expressed similar, though less fundamental, doubts. Any answer entailing assumptions about the 'economic real wage' would have to differ as between industries. Such scruples did not prevent him, however, from supplying an estimate of the 'elasticity of the general real demand for labour' as being somewhere in the neighbourhood of one. Henderson's objection was somewhat different again. Even if the existence of unemployment was taken to signify that wages were at present too high, this provided 'no justification for regarding the maximum volume of employment as the only objective of policy'. There was also the question of rates of labour transference and industrial expansion to consider, as well as the glaring disparities between wages in the sheltered and unsheltered trades. Nevertheless, he felt that at current world prices money wages were 'decidedly too high to permit any industrial expansion', and that if British money wages remained unchanged 'we should, as a nation, go progressively downhill'. Like Robbins, he also placed considerable emphasis on the effects of the unemployment insurance scheme in generating unemployment and perpetuating wage disparities.

The answers to the first part of the questionnaire revealed far more basic differences in theoretical standpoint. These are most obvious in the case of Robbins, who had made it clear from the outset that he intended to take an independent line by producing a separate list of topics for discussion to set beside Kahn's. He also suggested that the committee would benefit from evidence on the British situation taken from such prominent Continental authorities as Hayek, Röpke, and Ohlin.* It was from the first two of these economists, and ultimately from Wicksell and von Mises, that Robbins derived his framework of analysis. He was unwilling to be bowled over by 'the complexity and great aesthetic beauty of the theorems propounded by Mr. Keynes'. If, as he felt, 'many of our deliberations are going to turn upon the validity and the quantitative assumptions of what may be called the interest theory of fluctuation' then guidance from the Continent, where 'the broad notions are familiar to those who walk in the paths of Wicksell and Mises and the habit of judging events in these terms is more widely diffused', would be valuable to the committee. A day's conversation with Hayek might be 'more helpful at this stage than many days spent elucidating our private differences'.[72] This was not the result of arrogance on the part of the youngest member of the committee, but of viewing the problem from a theoretical standpoint which needed to be defended at length because, as Robbins pointed out at the time, 'I cannot expect that my colleagues are as well acquainted with my general background as I am with theirs.'[73]

---

* Cab. 58/150, E.A.C. (E) 4, 5 September 1930; Keynes Papers EA/1, Robbins to Keynes, 31 August 1930. Earlier he hinted that Keynes's proposed timetable would not allow enough time 'to cogitate ultimate differences of opinion – if such exist' (Keynes Papers EA/1, Robbins to Keynes, 16 August).

Keynes in the *Treatise* employed the Wicksellian distinction between the 'natural' rate of interest, determined by long-term 'real' factors, and the money or market rate of interest prevailing at any given time. The Austrian version of Wicksell's theory made use of the same terminology, but the savings and investment analysis behind the two theories was radically different. According to Robbins's position, the problems of the slump could only be approached via an understanding of the 'real' disproportionalities produced by the preceding boom, which was defined as a period in which there was overinvestment in fixed capital. The boom was the outcome of a situation in which the money rate of interest was *below* the 'natural' rate of interest, thereby causing a cumulative upward movement of prices and investment in fixed capital. Collapse could be due to a variety of factors but the slump would bear the marks of the preceding boom, and viable remedies would have to take this into account. Indeed, since the slump was a period in which mistaken investments were written off and prices were brought down to a more realistic level, the slump could be said, under ideal conditions, to be *the* remedy for the structural deficiencies created by the boom.

According to Keynes's diagnosis, however, money rates of interest had been kept *above* the natural rate for several years in Britain, and since 1928 in the United States, by various circumstances chiefly connected with the gold standard. If Keynes was right, then, in Robbins's words, 'the problem now facing us is to restore confidence and set in motion the normal machinery of investment'; the difficulties were chiefly 'vertical' in character, and since 'monetary influences have precipitated a fall from a "natural" level of prosperity', a policy of reducing money rates of interest could rapidly produce recovery. But 'the whole picture undergoes a kaleidoscopic transformation' if the original assumption about the natural rate is questioned; and this is what Robbins set out to do. Suppose that since the war the natural rate was relatively high as a result of population increase, technical change, and the need to make up for the rundown of fixed capital during the war. The boom in America could be explained in this way, and the slump could be attributed to the sudden rise in money rates as a result of speculation and gold difficulties.* Under these circumstances, on top of the 'vertical' difficulties would be others of a 'horizontal' variety. Recovery would not be 'a mere question of readjusting the money streams and returning to prosperity at the old levels'. It followed from this diagnosis that hopes of speedy recovery could not be justified, and that attempts to lower money rates of interest either nationally or internationally 'would merely secure an artificial prosperity in the immediate future at the expense of sowing the seeds of disproportionalities and depression later on'. Similar considerations

---

* Robbins squared the existence of boom with a stable or falling price level in America by speaking of 'the failure of prices to fall as rapidly as would be warranted by growing productivity': this would cause 'disproportionate development' quite as much as a positive rise in prices.

applied to any increase in investment which did not come through 'normal' channels. The best solution was to allow the curative forces of the slump to write off mistaken investments, and to increase the supply of voluntary savings by reducing the pressure on consumption.

At this point it may be helpful to quote Robbins's later reflections on this mode of analysis.

> ... as an explanation of what was going on in the early thirties, I now think it was misleading. Whatever the genetic factors of the pre-1929 boom, their *sequelae*, in the sense of inappropriate investments fostered by wrong expectations, were completely swamped by vast deflationary forces sweeping away all those elements of constancy in the situation which might have provided a framework for an explanation in my terms ... Assuming that the original diagnosis of excessive financial ease and mistaken real investment was correct – which is certainly not a settled matter – to treat what developed subsequently in a way which I then thought was valid was as unsuitable as denying blankets and stimulants to a drunk who has fallen into an icy pond, on the ground that his original trouble was overheating.[74]

Given this wide divergence between Keynes and Robbins over diagnosis, it is hardly surprising that they failed to agree on solutions. For Robbins wage rigidities were an active causal influence on the employment situation, while Keynes felt they were merely a factor which made matters worse at a time when the general price level was falling. Any inflexible system was bound to suffer when external demand conditions were changing rapidly, but Robbins believed that unemployment was merely one aspect of a set of disproportionalities produced by the failure of the economic system to adjust to changes in the pattern, rather than the level, of demand. For Robbins it was not an issue as to whether a general wage reduction would improve matters; his main concern was that 'no artificial support should be given by governments to resistance to such reductions where the state of the market notifies them'. Whereas Keynes made the absence of wage flexibility almost a 'given', Robbins believed that since it was the source of so many of Britain's problems a committee of economists ought not to bow to political expediency on this matter. The report should highlight the effect of unemployment insurance on employment 'via the rigidity of wage rates and the general support it gives to resistance of the forces of change'; it should also emphasise the other rigidities in the price system due to monopolies and trade union restrictive practices which prevented productivity rising in line with real wages. The issue was one of 'whether having organised our whole system of production on the price basis we are going to admit the principle that the prices of the various kinds of labour must never be allowed to fluctuate in the downward direction'. Robbins did point out, however, that measures for reducing the burden of war debt had become 'not only morally obligatory but politically absolutely essential if refusal to countenance rigidity elsewhere is to be justified'.

Robbins's analysis ruled out such 'artificial' methods of stimulating investment as cheap money or discrimination against foreign lending, but it did not make him an opponent of public-works policies, only a sceptic as to their value unless they met certain conservative conditions; chiefly that they should only be undertaken if there was a 'clear opening' for the work, and if they could be 'carried out with speed'. It would also have to be clear that they would not 'create as big a problem of unemployment when the demobilisation period arrives as they arose to solve in the first instance'. He did not at this stage stress budgetary constraints, being in fact in favour of 'relaxing the austerity of our Sinking Fund policy'. But given Robbins's theoretical beliefs, it was impossible for him to adopt an expansionist attitude. He was also unable to acquiesce or compromise over the tariff issue, where moral and political considerations were more strongly involved.

Robbins's wholesale rejection of Keynes's position came before the committee at the weekend session at Stamp's home. After this meeting Keynes prepared a draft report; at the next two meetings the committee agreed that Pigou and Henderson should rewrite various sections and that Robbins should prepare a draft statement 'setting out the matters on which he was in disagreement with the Chairman's Draft'. Keynes responded to this statement by recasting the report and incorporating a good deal of Robbins's draft into the section dealing with the causes of the world depression. Robbins had circulated a note on the unsatisfactory state of the discussions, which he described as 'theoretical wrangling', but 'in view of the changes adopted . . . he did not press for discussion of his paper'.[75] Three days later, at the second weekend meeting in Cambridge, 'at the conclusion of the discussion on tariffs, Professor Robbins indicated that he would probably be unable to sign the report prepared by his colleagues'. He reiterated this at the next meeting, at the end of which Keynes agreed to ask Hankey, the Secretary of the Cabinet, if there was a precedent for a minority report by a single member. By this time feelings were running high on both sides.[76] Robbins left the next and final meeting when Keynes reported that Hankey had been unable to find a precedent. After some negotiation Hemming and Henderson managed to persuade Keynes and Robbins to accept the inclusion of a statement by Robbins at the end of the report but preceding the statistical appendix.[77]

The older members of the committee were more concerned with consensus: they were content to have their differences of opinion over tariffs recorded in a few paragraphs within the report (paras. 74, 92, 97, 106) and in the conclusions. In order not to damage the chances of useful economic policies being adopted, they were prepared to minimise their disagreements over matters of economic theory. This is clear from the policy debates of the next few years, when Keynes, Pigou, and Stamp often joined forces to press for reflationary policies.* The theoretical differences were, however,

* For instance, Macgregor, Pigou, Keynes, Layton, Salter, and Stamp to *The Times*, 17 October 1932; Keynes to *The Times*, 28 July 1933. Robbins continued to advocate the maintenance of free trade and deflation in and out of Whitehall (Robbins, *Autobiography*, pp. 152-3; below,

important to the discussions which took place within the Committee of Economists.

Pigou's oblique opposition to Keynes took the form of an unwillingness to discuss the committee's brief in any terms other than those which he had become accustomed to using in his writings over the previous few years. Pigou was, of course, the senior academic on the committee and had behind him a long record of concern with the problem of unemployment.* There was no direct antagonism between the two men but there does seem to have been a distinct coolness, attributable perhaps to a clash of personal and intellectual styles. Pigou had been a member of both the Cunliffe and Bradbury Committees which had recommended the return to gold at pre-war parity. Keynes criticised not only this decision but also the advice on which it was based, and during the Macmillan Committee hearings he subjected Pigou to lengthy cross-examination on the subject. When he came to write the *General Theory* Keynes chose to attack Pigou's *Theory of Unemployment* (1933) as a prime example of the kind of 'classical' thinking which he wished to undermine. Nevertheless, they were fellow Cambridge economists, sharing a common master in Alfred Marshall, and they frequently found themselves on the same side on many of the crucial policy questions of the day.[78] Indeed, the large degree of common inheritance, coupled with Pigou's rather lofty and inflexible approach to matters of shared concern, may account for Keynes's peculiar annoyance.†

While recognising the existence of cyclical influences, Pigou addressed himself mainly to the long-term problem, namely explaining the quasi-permanent extra five or six per cent in post-war unemployment levels over the pre-war average. Labour immobility in the face of large-scale changes in the pattern of demand was one factor producing this situation, while the failure of aggregate demand for labour to expand *pari passu* with the level of real wages was another. It was not a question of wages being too high, but one of maladjustment between demand and price, compounded by maldistribution at existing wage relativities. Pigou believed that the excessive rise in real wages in the post-war period could be attributed to lack of movement from depressed to non-depressed industries, the unemployment insurance scheme, greater resistance to wage cuts, and the decline in prices

pp. 124–5; Robbins, 'A Reply to Mr. Keynes', *New Statesman*, 14 March 1931, and letters to the editor of the *New Statesman* on 28 March and 18 April 1931; Gregory, Plant, Hayek, and Robbins to *The Times*, 19 October 1932). Later, in the second world war, Robbins and Hayek were prepared to sink theoretical differences in the interests of the adoption of sensible wartime policies (*Collected Writings*, Vol. XXII; Robbins, *Autobiography*, Ch. 8).

* E.g. A. C. Pigou's *Unemployment* (1913) and *Industrial Fluctuations* (1927). More relevant as an indication of the line he was to take during the proceedings of the Committee of Economists are his 'Wage Policy and Unemployment', *Economic Journal*, September 1927, and his evidence to the Macmillan Committee.

† Keynes seems to have had Pigou in mind when expounding his *Treatise* position to the committee, and Pigou was the only member whose answer to Keynes's questionnaire drew a point-by-point written response from Keynes (Cab. 58/151, E.A.C. (E) 23, 'Notes by Keynes on Pigou's Memorandum (E.A.C. (E) 12)', 25 September 1930).

consequent upon the return to gold unaccompanied by equivalent reductions in money wages. The whole approach was based very much on an extension of microeconomic theory, whereby the quantity of employment was determined by the relationship between real wages and the productivity of labour. According to this view, there was a direct mechanism linking a reduction in real wages in any particular trade to the ability of employers to offer more employment. Pigou's system also allowed for certain indirect or secondary benefits to accrue as a result of the expansion of demand and output in related industries. By taking into account these repercussion effects he arrived at an optimistic estimate of the real wage elasticity of demand for labour. Since, however, according to Pigou changes in real wages could only be effected by means of changes in money wages, he acknowledged that there might be hitches in this process.

Although Pigou was willing to contemplate redistribution of the labour surplus from depressed to non-depressed industries by means of a reduction of wages in the latter, he was not prepared to advocate such a policy, or one of general wage reductions. It could be argued that Pigou's scepticism as to whether existing wage-fixing institutions could be changed in order to permit wage reductions placed him in the same camp as Keynes with regard to wage flexibility. Such a view overlooks another major general feature of Pigou's approach which placed him at odds with Keynes: this was his belief that when not considering purely cyclical movements in price levels, where psychological influences and banking policies were important, it was possible to keep 'real' and monetary factors in fairly water-tight compartments until the final stage of the analysis. According to Keynes, on the other hand, 'real wages seem . . . to come in as a by-product of the remedies which we adopt to restore equilibrium. They come in at the end of the argument rather than at the beginning.'[79]

Pigou argued that monetary 'devices' would only raise employment insofar as they affected real wages or the productivity of labour. Thus additional investment which was not the result of a fall in the rate of interest or an improvement in technology was simply a 'monetary affair', and would 'only increase employment so far as it makes prices rise more than the rate of money wages, i.e. insofar as it causes, through friction, bamboozlements and so on, the rate of real wages to fall'.[80]

From a long-term point of view, if real wages could not, or should not, be reduced, Pigou's theory suggested that the only way of increasing employment was by means of improvements in technical efficiency and industrial organisation which would raise the real demand for labour. In the short run unemployment had to be treated as an abnormal state of affairs arising out of obstructions to the normal working of the system. It was, therefore, a second-best situation in which, if the obstacles could not be removed, there was a case for using counterbalancing expedients. In 1927 Pigou had considered both wage subsidies and tariffs as possible devices for dealing with the short-term problem. Economically they could be justified as ways of increasing employment by transferring income from non-wage to wage earners; he did not support them because they might have damaging long-term consequences, and because he considered that their implementation would be bungled by the politicians.[81] This remained his position when he gave evidence to the Macmillan Committee, but he did support 'large Government expenditure on really useful public goods' as an emergency measure.[82] A few months later in the Committee of Economists he drew attention once more to the wage-subsidy idea, indicating that the deterioration in economic circumstances had led him to modify his earlier scruples on the subject. He also admitted once more that tariffs might have a beneficial effect on employment and business psychology.[83] When it came to signing the final report, however, while he endorsed a scheme for subsidising the wages of additional employees, he refused to support a tariff.*

The role played by Henderson during the committee's proceedings needs to be set against the background of his evolving relationship with Keynes after the establishment of the Council. After their collaboration in the latter half of the 1920s, a gap opened up between Henderson and Keynes on a variety of issues – a gap which widened with time and the deterioration of the economic situation. This divergence of opinion can, perhaps, be partly attributed to the differences in their official positions, with Henderson becoming increasingly associated with the problems of government seen from the inside, while Keynes remained a privileged outsider with access to a good deal of official information but retaining the freedom Henderson had lost to comment freely on public affairs in newspapers and journals.

As early as March 1930 Henderson had expressed doubts to Keynes concerning the viability of the Lloyd George schemes which they had defended the year before in *Can Lloyd George Do It?*[84] By the end of May he had come to the conclusion 'that only the most meagre results can follow from the attempt to expedite schemes of work by local authorities', which was where the government was then placing most of its hopes. He felt that the only promising field for capital expenditure lay in speeding up industrial reconstruction. He proposed, therefore, an emergency measure which entailed the creation of a special Industrial Reorganisation Fund based on the proceeds of a temporary 10 per cent import duty on manufactured goods, with rebates on goods coming from the Empire and a drawback on imports used by export industries. The fund would be used partly to reduce the deficit of the unemployment insurance fund, and partly to support rationalisation schemes already approved by the Bankers' Industrial Development Com-

---

* It should be clear from this that Pigou was not a simple-minded and fatalistic advocate of wage-cuts as a remedy for unemployment. Nevertheless, it is not difficult to see how such a misconception could arise, and why Keynes should succumb to the temptation of treating Pigou's *Theory of Unemployment* as the repository of 'classical' ideas.

pany, provided that they were of a kind which could be started quickly. The fund would be used to reduce interest costs on a sliding scale which would favour work begun in the near future. Similar offers of support could be made to public utility and railway companies; and the scheme could be associated with a similar fund for agriculture based on the proceeds of a 5 per cent duty on imported grain products. At the end of three years the fund would be wound up and the revenue tariff removed. Henderson hoped that the scheme would meet the present needs of the unemployed and the future needs of industry, while counteracting the fears of increased taxation which were depressing business confidence. Tom Jones described this scheme, involving as it did a departure from free trade principles, as 'a bombshell'; he put it before the Cabinet on 4 June but the proposals were not considered.[85]

In putting forward this tariff proposal Henderson was, of course, following the lead given by Keynes in February; but Henderson attached much greater importance to budgetary limitations on capital spending than did Keynes. This was the subject of an exchange of letters between them in May and June. Henderson no longer felt that the bulk of unemployment was of a transitional character, 'yielding to the treatment of a purely temporary stimulus'. If this was so then public works policies could no longer be justified on pump-priming grounds; they would entail a much larger and continuing annual charge on the budget. 'A capital programme may still be right; but you must contemplate the likelihood of having to continue it for many years, turning to ever less remunerative things, to parks and playing grounds on the German model, so that your charges on the Budget will steadily mount up.'[86] The cumulative effect of this on taxation, and hence on business psychology, would be quite different from a temporary programme largely devoted to remunerative projects. Henderson was also alarmed by the prospects of what he called 'insular socialism'. Although Keynes had always appreciated the danger of uneconomic wage-rates in Britain's new economic situation, had he not reacted by saying that even if wages could not be raised it was still possible to raise standards of living by increasing the social services and taxing the rich? Surely there was a point beyond which such a policy led to disaster?*

In his first reply Keynes agreed that wage-reductions operated in the same direction as a public works policy, but he hoped the latter would make them unnecessary. He agreed that it would not be practicable to charge the budget with 'a bounty on investment, or some form of differential rate of interest' over a long period, but he did not think that it would be a permanent charge, or that it need be as high as £50m per annum even in the first two years.

* Henderson was probably referring to Keynes's article on 'The Question of High Wages', *Political Quarterly*, January 1930. Henderson expressed his fears about 'the limits of insular socialism' in an article in *The Nation & Athenaeum* on 30 November 1929. The article, written before Henderson took up his position with the Council, was a warning to Snowden not to proceed too far with redistribution policies.

> Whether we can get on permanently with complete *laissez-faire* in foreign investment, and without some sort of discrimination between rates for home lending and rates for foreign lending, I am not sure. But if this proves to be a permanent problem, I should certainly not hope to solve it by making subsidies out of the Budget.

Keynes had fewer fears than Henderson concerning the psychology of the business community, mainly because he thought they would be the first to experience the benefits of a large capital programme; and if the wealth of the country was increasing 'it follows that the dangers of insular socialism would be diminished rather than increased'. If the main point of Henderson's argument was that he felt a large capital programme, though still necessary, would have to be financed from another source, then Keynes was in full agreement: 'But I should not make it a *sine qua non*. Far from it.'[87]

Henderson admitted that he was 'scared by the Budget position quite apart from whether capital programmes are pushed forward or not'; the main source of worry was the growing cost of unemployment pay, declining revenues, and the prospect of having to raise taxes to cover the deficit. This was far more important than the results of any feasible public works policy, which at present meant heavy cost to the Exchequer in order to secure only a slight increase in the volume of work undertaken by local authorities, much of which 'will be generally condemned as largely wasteful'. Unless Keynes faced up to the budgetary problem he was likely to go down in history 'as the man who persuaded the British people to ruin themselves by gambling on a greater illusion than any of those which he had helped to shatter'.[88]

Keynes agreed that the problem of unemployment pay and of alternative sources of revenue, such as that provided by the tariff, required attention by the government.

> But what chiefly divides us, I think, is what seems to me the lack of fundamental diagnosis in your present attitude. After all, the budgetary problem is largely a by-product of unemployment. To avoid an increase of taxation will not remedy unemployment, whilst a decrease of taxation is scarcely to be hoped for. The main question is, therefore, to diagnose unemployment.

For this purpose, of course, he commended his savings and investment analysis. Psychological factors and high taxation had some effect in producing the low level of domestic investment, but the fact that the rate of interest was 50 per cent higher than pre-war levels was the major influence. Similarly, while a revenue tariff, suspension of the sinking fund, and amendment of the insurance scheme would be useful measures, they would not cure unemployment; 'they would only make easier the application of other remedies and, perhaps, remove a possible further aggravation of the position'.[89]

Henderson was not convinced by this exchange. His growing opposition to Keynes's views became apparent during the proceedings of the Committee of Economists. He answered Keynes's question concerning the effect of an increase in investment on British employment by saying that it might be beneficial while it was actually taking place, but its 'ultimate effects would depend on the utility of the increased investment'. The real question was whether any given method of stimulating investment would actually lead to a *net* increase. He went on to give his own views, mainly along historical lines, on what he presciently suggested would in future be known as the 'Great Slump'. Having painted a picture of an 'uncertain and menacing background', he went on to draw some gloomy conclusions for Britain, largely on the grounds of the slow rate of growth and the burden of debt and taxation. The moral he was anxious to stress was that it would be 'utterly wrong under present circumstances to embark on anything in the nature of a gamble'. Short-term expedients could not be justified when there was no guarantee that the situation would be better in the near future, and especially when business confidence was at such low ebb and the unemployment insurance scheme was incurring debt at a rate of £30m a month. For this reason he opposed raiding the sinking fund. He was, however, willing to support tariffs for revenue, balance of payments, and protective purposes. But tariffs were not a substitute for lower wages, and if prices continued to fall both remedies would be necessary. Reform of the unemployment insurance scheme would also have to be tackled.[90]

Keynes's first draft of the section of the report dealing with ways of increasing home investment argued strongly for public works, partly on the basis of Kahn's multiplier. Henderson objected that the 'conclusions reached . . . rest upon no appeal to fact at all'. He particularly objected to the multiplier argument which ignored the 'essential tendency for new demands for capital to raise the rate of interest', and pointed out that it did not square with the *Treatise*'s stress on the importance of low interest rates for promoting investment. He asked for a 'more thorough-going, realistic discussion than we have as yet had' on the subject of investment, interest rates, and public works. At the second weekend session Henderson produced a paper on objections to public works. As a result, Keynes's draft of this section disappeared, and the secretaries, Kahn and Hemming, added Henderson's paper to the next version of the report, which they prepared after Saturday's meeting.[91]

By this time Henderson had found himself 'in such serious disagreement with [the] practical gist and tenor' of Keynes's draft report that he circulated a statement of his views which was sharply critical of the proceedings.

The broad effect produced on my mind is that the central argument of the Report is lacking in sense. It seems to me to run away, under cover of complex sophistication, from the plain moral of the situation which it diagnoses; namely, that in view of the turn which world prices have taken and the extreme slenderness of the chance of substantial recovery, in view of the fact that before the slump began our costs were not properly competitive and we were faced even then with the danger of a steady erosion of our export trade, in view of the overwhelming probability that we shall now be faced with sharper international competition at reduced prices, in view finally of the highly dangerous touch-and-go position we have reached in regard to the public finances and the public credit, we have no alternative now but to face up to the disagreeable reactionary necessity of cutting costs (including wages) in industry and cutting expenditure in public affairs, acting generally in short as Sir Otto Niemeyer advises the Australians to act,* and as any similar competent impartial outsider would certainly advise us to act.

That I say is the plain moral of the situation, as plain as a pikestaff. It is of course extremely disagreeable in itself. Furthermore, it is the moral drawn by the ordinary, conservative, unintellectual business-man; and some may find it still more disagreeable to admit that the ordinary business-man can possibly be right. But, if we allow ourselves to be swayed by such distaste we run a danger of making applicable the Duke of Wellington's description of another controversy:– 'All the clever fellows were on the one side, and all the damned fools were on the other; and, by God! all the damned fools were right'.

The draft Report, as it seems to me, after half-recognising the truth of the foregoing, runs right away from it, and proceeds to twist and wriggle and turn in a desperate attempt to evade the logic of the situation. Its practical drift is that we may with luck be able to evade the necessity for reducing costs by adopting a series of expedients of the most different kinds, which are all labelled 'Remedies for Unemployment', but some of which, whether they deserve that description or not, are in no sense remedies for but rather aggravations of the fundamental maladjustment which has got to be put right.

Henderson concluded that wage cuts and public retrenchment were now imperative. Useful public works were acceptable as a palliative, but there was no room for grandiose schemes when the budget and public credit was in disarray; they could not be described as an alternative to any of the more disagreeable policies. The committee should face up to the problem of how wages, along with other salaries and fees, could be reduced, especially when there was every likelihood of a further fall in world prices: 'It is idle to suppose that we can avert that tendency by refusing to take part in it, and building roads instead.' Devaluation might be less damaging to British credit if undertaken in concert with other nations; but 'the attempt to reduce money costs must be made first'. Henderson suspected that Keynes was in favour of dangerous policies because 'he doesn't think it would matter much if the pound should go the same way as the mark and the rouble'. The issues dividing the committee were not just technical but 'of a broad and almost temperamental nature'.[92]

---

* The Bank of England sent Niemeyer to Australia in July 1930 after the Australian Government had inquired of the British Government about a deferment of the March war debt payment and other assistance with the Australians' overseas borrowing commitments in London (C. B. Schedvin, *Australia and the Great Depression* (1970), pp. 132–5, 180–3; E. O. G. Shann and D. B. Copland, *The Crisis in Australian Finance 1929 to 1931* (1931), pp. 18–29). Needless to say, Keynes did not agree with Henderson on the Australian question, advocating devaluation instead. During the Economists' proceedings he wrote to E. C. Dyason, one of the influential group of Australian economists led by Giblin: 'I see immense advantages in looking to a change in the exchange rather than to a forcing down of wages, as the way of escape' (Keynes Papers L/30, Keynes to Dyason, 16 October 1930; see also Keynes to Giblin, 2 June 1932, Keynes Papers CO/6/1, and the article by Keynes, 25 May 1932, reprinted in Shann and Copland, *The Australian Price Structure, 1932* (1933), pp. 79–85).

Since Henderson's outburst occurred at the same time as Robbins's revolt, it will be clear that the committee was in some disarray in the final stages of producing its report. It is a tribute to Keynes's chairmanship that not only did the report get written, but that it showed so few marks of the unresolved conflicts that lay beneath its surface. The initial section on the causes of the world depression was, as we have noted, largely based on Robbins's draft. This included the section on rigidities to which he attached such paramount importance in both his diagnosis and remedies; it featured in the report mainly as diagnosis. The next section, on the fall of prices, emphasised maladjustments between money costs and prices, but made no mention of Keynes's saving and investment analysis or the rate of interest. Keynes had originally intended that the report should begin with short sections on the fall of prices, the effect of large changes in the value of money, and the special difficulties of Great Britain, with the rest of the report being devoted to remedies.* The eventual second and third sections were based on Keynes's early drafts, though modified by Henderson, who added the paragraphs on 'The disparity between the prices of primary products and manufactured goods' and revised Keynes's 'Remedies of an external character'. In the report's favour it must be said that these early sections provided a clear picture of the dangers inherent in the situation which were to materialise in the following year.

The section (v) on 'Ways of restoring elasticity to the economic structure of Great Britain' was one outcome of Robbins's and Henderson's disagreement with Keynes. Keynes's early draft briefly mentioned the problems of restrictive practices, of hindrances to mobility, and of industrial efficiency, in a section on 'Remedies for unemployment that increase ability to pay money wage rates other than by materially raising the price level'. At an early meeting the committee decided that Henderson should rewrite this section; Henderson's draft included the final report's section (vi) of 'Ways of increasing industrial efficiency'. Keynes later tried to take account of Robbins's views by strengthening the criticism of restrictive practices in section v.

In spite of all the attention paid to wage levels earlier, the section of the report dealing with wage-reductions was remarkably moderate; it certainly did not reflect Henderson's strongly expressed views on the subject. Apart from condemning rigidities, urging reform of the unemployment insurance scheme, and proposing some reduction in wages in the sheltered industries, the main emphasis was on 'the immense practical difficulties' of carrying out such policies in an equitable fashion. It was in fact a redraft by Pigou of a draft by Henderson, with a summary (para. 51) by Keynes. Pigou and Stamp wrote the next section on the proposal for wage subsidies, which was supported by Keynes, Pigou, and Stamp, but opposed by Henderson on the grounds of its openness to abuse.

* Keynes's classification of remedies was similar to that given to the Macmillan Committee in February and March.

On the subject of business confidence (section IX) the report provided little more than a list, compiled by Keynes, of various disparate remedies. The rudiments of Keynes's *Treatise* position appeared in the next section, on home investment, where his idea of discriminating against foreign lending was also endorsed. Public works policies were defended, but qualified by Henderson's views in the last three paragraphs. The section was primarily Keynes's, although Stamp rewrote the paragraph on the regulation of foreign issues and Henderson wrote the final three paragraphs on public works. Keynes wrote the bulk of the next two sections, on tariffs, devaluation, and his tariff-bounty proposal. Although Pigou's and Henderson's paragraphs of dissent (73, 97, and 106) were included, the sections reflected a good deal of Keynes's position at this time. From the space devoted to the general tariff proposal the reader would be correct in inferring that this was the one major new remedy being proposed. In addition to the revenue tariff, Keynes, Stamp, and Henderson favoured – though less strongly – imposing safe-guarding duties on iron and steel products and a serious examination of the case for protecting pig and poultry products; they also gave some support to imperial preference. Devaluation was mentioned and dismissed, though there was a hint of the need for an international effort to find an alternative to the 'currency system which is serving us so ill'. The whole of Keynes's tariff-bounty proposal was, so to speak, simply read into the record, in spite of the fact that it received the support of Stamp alone.*

The statistical appendix was the work of Colin Clark. Some of the tables appeared in the report of the Macmillan Committee, which also enjoyed the benefit of Clark's help in 1930–1. Clark himself utilised the work he had done for the two committees in his *The National Income 1924–1931*, which was published in 1932 with Keynes's active encouragement, and he used some of his statistical exercises for the Economic Advisory Council in an article in the *Economic Journal* in 1931.[93]

Given the nature of the underlying disagreements the Economists' report is a surprisingly coherent document, much more penetrating than the report of the Committee on Economic Outlook, and a good deal more to the point than much of the discussion of alternatives which took place at Council meetings. Nevertheless, in the light of the proceedings of the Committee of Economists it may be easier to understand Keynes's decision a few years later when writing the *General Theory* 'to bring to an issue the deep divergences of opinion between fellow economists which have for the time being almost destroyed the practical influence of economic theory, and will, until they are resolved, continue to do so'.[94]

---

* The attribution of the various parts of the report is based on the annotated drafts in the Keynes Papers EA/4 and the minutes of the meetings in Cab. 58/150.

Council deliberations and Cabinet decisions in the light of the Economists' report

When the report of the Committee of Economists came before the Council for the first time on 7 November, the Council decided to take it section by section, beginning with the agreed diagnosis. Interestingly enough, the first comment on the report brought Bevin and Lewis together in resenting the references to craft loyalties, restrictive practices, and 'anti-social' rings and combinations. Keynes defended the paragraph in question (12) by saying that 'the fact that such abuses existed was notorious'; he also said the committee had chiefly been concerned with 'the lack of adaptability of the British industrial system' at a time when large changes in the value of money were taking place: it had laid no great stress on rigidities when putting forward remedies. Keynes's last remark underplayed a little the report's later paragraphs on this subject (37–41), but more to the point, it passed over much of the discussion of this topic during the committee's proceedings, as well as Robbins's position. The Council dropped the subject when MacDonald pointed out that the report was not to be published, and that in fact 'it was marked most secret and to be kept under lock and key'.

Keynes then enlarged on the section dealing with the fall of prices (18–27), which was 'the main cause for the sombre character of the report'. 'What was novel was the emphasis given by the committee to the suggestion that the cyclical element may not prove to be so large as might be expected, and that though some small recovery might be anticipated in the near future, there was a real danger of a continual sagging movement over a long period.'

On the possibilities of remedying this situation by international cooperation the Council agreed that circumstances were not propitious, though Keynes thought that 'if there were a good understanding between the central banks of this country and the United States, the two countries could do much to improve the situation'. At this point Bevin and Cole raised the question of leaving the gold standard. Snowden thought this would have 'disastrous repercussions', while MacDonald was convinced that 'whatever action was taken . . . it should not be taken by the British government as such'. Keynes's view at this time was that every other remedy should be tried first, and he added that 'there was no certainty that action such as Mr. Cole suggested would, in fact, prove an adequate remedy'.

The Council moved on to discuss the section (v) on 'Ways of restoring elasticity to the economic structure of Great Britain'. There was agreement that a large representative conference on this subject would serve little purpose; it was better to deal with the problems of each industry separately. Bevin defended the record of the trade unions on acceptance of reorganisation, but argued that the government could do more through a pensions scheme to compensate those displaced. This brought the Council back to the abuses and side-effects of the unemployment insurance scheme. Leaving this controversial issue on one side (until the report of the Council's committee on this subject was available), the Council turned to the even more controversial question of reductions in money wages (section VII of the report). Bevin agreed emphatically with the paragraph (51, vi) which pointed out that if a general wage-cut became necessary it was essential 'that it should be undertaken as part of a wider scheme for resettling money incomes generally (including *rentier* incomes in particular), and not wages alone'. He received support for the principle of 'equal sacrifice' from the Prime Minister. Keynes drew attention to the tariff-bounty proposal in section XII as a possible basis for a general scheme, adding that 'there was also a theoretical case for, say, a 10% cut in wages and salaries accompanied by an extra 2/- income tax on other sources of income'. It was at this point that the Council turned briefly to the revenue tariff proposal as a more equitable way of reducing real incomes. Snowden attacked this root and branch on the grounds that being evenly spread it was bound to be regressive; it would also have most effect on the export industries where wages were low. In reply to Snowden, Keynes said his tariff-bounty scheme was intended as 'a tax upon the sheltered industries for the benefit of the unsheltered industries'; he also pointed out that *any* rise in prices, whether produced by a revenue tariff or not, would be open to the Chancellor's objections. After some desultory discussion raised by Lewis on the importance of maintaining business confidence by keeping taxes down, which elicited the statement from Snowden that 'the addition of 6d to the income tax next year might mean an increase of 500,000 in the unemployed', the Council adjourned.

At the next meeting the Council discussed the section of the Economists' report on 'Ways of increasing industrial efficiency'.* MacDonald returned to the effects of the unemployment insurance scheme in artificially swelling the numbers of unemployed and in giving an incentive to short-time working. Duncan broached the topic of rationalisation, but Keynes underlined the Economists' conclusion that while rationalisation should be encouraged 'it was not of itself likely to do much in the way of increasing employment'. MacDonald noted the adverse effect of rationalisation on what he called 'the problem of a waterlogged population concentrated in particular areas'. The government had tried to encourage new industries in such areas, within the limitations of the existing machinery and finances of local government, but he wondered if more could be done through general planning and other methods of disposing of the surplus industrial population. Although emigration was not practicable because of the world depression, and the government could not expect quick results from its agricultural

---

* The meeting opened with consternation being expressed about the leakage in the *Manchester Guardian* (9 December 1930) of some of the contents of the Economists' report. The article revealed the membership of the committee and the fact that it was divided over tariffs; it also commented that the report 'can hardly be regarded as a success by the Government, who must have expected something a little more definite'. MacDonald proposed an inquiry under the Official Secrets Act, though Keynes drew the moral that reports 'that were not essentially secret should be published'.

resettlement policies, 'he was in favour of a complete bar on Irish immigration' – though he doubted whether this could be done. Keynes regarded the planning and distributional aspects of the problem as less important than the problem of increased aggregate demand for manufactured goods.

The discussion moved on to the familiar and depressing problems of the iron and steel industry: was tariff protection necessary to secure rationalisation, or would it remove the incentive to rationalise? Could rationalisation be achieved voluntarily, or would it, as Keynes felt, be necessary 'to face the need for some measure of public control in this and probably many other industries'? The Council agreed to continue the discussion at the next meeting on the basis of a memorandum which Henderson would prepare on the possibilities of stimulating new industries in the declining areas.

When discussion resumed in February 1931 – after an excursion into such problems as the revision of the cost-of-living index number, ways of rehabilitating Chinese railways,* native dietetics, and centralised slaughtering – it was under the rather grandiose heading of 'national planning'. The Council took up the question of the southward drift of new industries together with the possibilities of using local rather than national initiative to revive the 'derelict areas'. Most members favoured the former while Attlee pressed the case for 'national assistance and direction'. Important though this topic was, it meant that discussion of the Economists' short-term tariff proposals was postponed until the next meeting of the Council in March.

At the beginning of this meeting Keynes made a lengthy statement explaining his and the committee's position on tariffs. His own views on free trade had changed as a result of 'a large intractable mass of unemployment associated with dislocations between costs and world prices ever since the post-armistice boom'. The committee had stressed a new argument for tariffs (para. 75) as a means of maintaining the level of foreign investment: this was necessary in view of the tendency to lend abroad larger sums than could be borne by the existing foreign balance. Tariffs were preferable to

* The Committee on the Chinese Situation had reported in December 1930. It believed that 'the revival and development of the trade of China would be a factor of first-rate importance in reviving British trade' and that Britain should offer financial and technical help for rebuilding China's railway system. The Cabinet agreed that negotiations with the Chinese would be desirable and passed the report on to Sir Arthur Salter, then head of the Economic and Finance Section of the League of Nations, who was at that time in China advising the Government of Chiang Kai-shek. Salter later described his mission as 'For China . . . of no value. The simple fact was . . . of course that where there is no effective and stable system of government, there can be no advanced economy.' What is significant about the proceedings of the Committee on the Chinese Situation is the importance the government attached to it, reflecting its desire to do something to increase employment which did not involve a tariff or large-scale government expenditure. The President of the Board of Trade chaired the committee, to which several government departments made representations. (Cab. 58/121, Committee on Chinese Situation, Minutes, memoranda and report, 6 October–29 December 1930; Cab. 23/66, Cabinets 6(31)6 and 15(31)5, 14 January and 25 February 1931; Salter, *Slave of the Lamp* (1967), pp. 110–11.)

wage-cuts as a means of improving this balance, though the committee was 'lukewarm' on the merits of safeguarding tariffs except for iron and steel, and pig and poultry products, where a majority thought that a *prima facie* case had been made out. There was more support for a general flat-rate tariff because it was less likely to be abused, and because of its favourable effects on the budget and business confidence. If it also kept out imports then the level of employment would rise. Speaking for himself, Keynes thought the revenue tariff would be essential if the government adopted any of the bolder plans in the report, because the initial effects on the budget and the foreign balance would be adverse. 'It would be extremely difficult to proceed with any such plans unless the budget was not only balanced but had such a margin that causes for immediate anxiety were allayed.' He also thought a tariff would enable Britain to take 'a bolder line in urging international co-operation'. At present foreigners tended to regard British initiatives as a sign of weakness.

In Snowden's absence there were no determined defenders of free trade. Keynes received the backing of Stamp and Henderson once more on the revenue tariff, and MacDonald showed himself unwilling to uphold free trade on principle:

the case in its old form for the policy of free trade had completely gone. In their own field the trade unions were entirely opposed to free competition. There was no free trade in labour, and the problem was whether by constructive co-operation this country could protect itself. The economic policy of a country must be such as to suit the circumstances of the time, and, if a policy formerly desirable was no longer appropriate, it was necessary to change it. A revenue tariff would not, however, meet the claims of the hard-hit industries such as the iron and steel industry.

Unfortunately, MacDonald's last remark steered the discussion back towards safeguarding tariffs and the problems of the iron and steel industry. On this subject Keynes backed Bevin's strong line that if protection was accorded to iron and steel the industry should be taken into public ownership – a view which Lewis and Thomas opposed. Keynes tried, unsuccessfully, to bring the discussion back to the urgent need for a revenue tariff on budgetary grounds alone.

Since by the time the Council next met, in April, the international financial situation had become more serious, there was no further discussion of the Economists' report. It had been on the agenda for five months and in this respect had vindicated some of the hopes expressed when the committee was established. Even bearing in mind the purely advisory character of the Council, however, the discussion of the report cannot be regarded as a success. The fact that the economists had not presented a united front cannot be cited as a reason for this lack of success: no reference was made to lack of unanimity by the members of the Council, though it was mentioned at Cabinet level. More to the point is the tendency of the Council to be deflected into such issues as unemployment insurance and the long-term

rationalisation problems of iron and steel, neither of which figured prominently in the Economists' report. As a result, none of the more positive
short-term remedies discussed in the report – cheap money, regulation of
foreign investment, public works, temporary wage subsidies, the tariff-
bounty proposal – were given any attention by the Council, and revenue
tariffs were not adequately discussed. How far this was due to defects
inherent in the composition and infrequency of Council meetings, and how
far it can be laid at the door of slack chairmanship by MacDonald is difficult
to say. MacDonald used the meetings to ride some of his own hobby-
horses, such as those connected with the surplus population in the declining
areas, and he might well have pressed some of the Economists' remedies if
he had been so inclined. He did not use the Council as a counterweight to
the Treasury position as represented by Snowden, in spite of the appearance
of being open-minded on certain questions.

The Cabinet discussed the report of the Committee of Economists in
December 1930. Before the report had been completed the Cabinet appointed
a committee to discuss it alongside Attlee's memorandum on unemployment
policy and one by Vernon Hartshorn. This committee, which consisted of
the Prime Minister, the Chancellor of the Exchequer, the Lord Chancellor
(Sankey) and the Home Secretary (Clynes), was 'to prepare for the use of
their colleagues a synopsis of the whole field covered by the three papers in
a form which could be used as an agenda for the Cabinet'.[95] However, on
25 September, before the Economists' report was available, the Cabinet had
a preliminary discussion of unemployment policy in the light of the rise in
the previous month's unemployment figures. This discussion showed how
little scope for positive short-term initiatives the government saw themselves
as having – which may help to explain the inconclusiveness of Council
deliberations on the Economists' report. The Cabinet agreed that 'relief
works' were already as large as they could be in existing circumstances,
that anomalies in the unemployment insurance scheme would need attention, and that 'the psychological attitude towards trade prospects [needed]
improving'. It criticised the slow progress in rationalisation, particularly in
iron and steel and cotton, and noted the fact that in the iron and steel industry
this was due to 'the desire of many of those concerned for a tariff . . . and by
their belief that by waiting they would obtain it'. Finally, 'agriculture was
advocated as one of the long-range methods of dealing with unemployment,
and proposals for the development of allotments and small holdings in
industrial districts that have become derelict owing to rationalisation . . .
evoked considerable interest'. Three weeks later, and still before the discussion of the Economists' report, the Cabinet confirmed these negative
conclusions. On public works it recognised that it had reached a limit of what
could be done, and that 'while it would be undesirable to state this publicly,
or to discourage any schemes that might come forward, it was a point which
the government would have to bear in mind'.[96]

On 6 and 19 November 1930 the Cabinet had the Economists' report before it. In view of the delays caused by the Imperial Conference it decided to set up a new committee, the Committee on Trade Policy, to consider the report together with the memoranda by Attlee and Hartshorn. The chairman was Snowden, and the members Shaw (War Secretary), Hartshorn, Graham, and Alexander (First Lord of the Admiralty). They met five times in rapid succession early in December. At the first meeting

the view was generally expressed that [the report of the Committee of Economists] was a disappointing document. There was lack of unanimity in its conclusions and while it was prolific of suggestions of a general character it contained no practical propositions to which immediate effect could be given. It touched, and no more than touched, on several very important matters which demanded exhaustive treatment.

Having delivered this summary verdict the committee went on to discuss the scope for 'international co-operation in the use of gold, the development of selling agencies in foreign markets and the establishment of the inevitable surplus of labour in the staple industries in other trades'. Shaw argued that even if Attlee's machinery for planning was introduced there would still be a large volume of unemployment as a result of the fall in world prices. This would mean that 'reductions in the real value of wages would be pressed on the Government', but could not be contemplated unless rentier incomes were also reduced. Graham agreed with the Committee of Economists in thinking that a general rise in world prices was 'the best of all means of adjusting money incomes', but he could see little prospect of this happening. The return to the gold standard in 1925 and the gold sterilisation policies of France and the United States were the basic causes of present weaknesses. Were the Chancellor of the Exchequer and the Bank of England able to hold out any prospects of domestic or international action?*

Snowden agreed that gold sterilisation 'was a serious menace to the proper functioning of the gold standard' – a view which he had denied a few months earlier. The main obstacle to improvement in the situation was the suspicion with which France and the United States greeted any British initiative. Political instability in Europe also inhibited American foreign investors. He was hoping that the good relations between the Bank of England and the Federal Reserve Board would make it possible for the Governor of the Bank to induce the Board to release £100m of gold; but he strongly deprecated any idea of government, as opposed to central bank, intervention. On rentier incomes in relation to wages, he pointed out that while real wages had been rising since 1929, 'it would be wrong to assume that there had been no falling off in the prosperity of the rentier class'. Interest rates had fallen, and 'he was looking forward in the absence of any catastrophe,

---

* The view that the world slump was largely caused by a worldwide shortage of gold in use as reserve money due to maldistribution of the gold supply (in particular, concentration in the 'hoards' of the French and U.S. monetary authorities) was widely held at this time; for examples in British government circles see pp. 80–1, 117–18 below and T. 175/57, 'Future Policy', 5 March 1932.

to bringing the long-term rate down to 4%'.* More generally, he maintained that the availability of credit posed no problem for industries with good prospects.

Snowden opened the second meeting by suggesting that 'no good would come of a discussion of the conclusions rendered by the Committee of Economists on wage reductions and tariffs'. Hartshorn thought that there was a good case for considering a safeguarding tariff for iron and steel. If re-organisation of industry and agriculture did not result in the retention of the home market, the government would have to entertain 'some modification of fiscal policy'. Snowden believed that to guarantee the home market, tariffs would have to be prohibitive, and that the main effect would be to ruin the export trade, particularly in iron and steel, which affected the costs of so many other industries. Hartshorn received some support from Attlee, who said he would support a tariff if it was the only means of keeping an industry in existence. Graham likewise thought that tariffs were undesirable but that iron and steel was a special case. The committee agreed, however, that since it was unanimous on the need for industrial reorganisation 'consideration of the tariff question need not for the present be further pursued'. Having surmounted this obstacle the committee could move on. At its remaining meetings it discussed rationalisation, electrical development, and the bacon industry; no report was prepared for the Cabinet.[97]

This was in some ways the official burial of the Economists' report, though some of the remedies in the report surfaced again in August during the Cabinet's crisis meetings, and MacDonald recirculated the report to the National Cabinet the day after Britain left the gold standard. One of the proposals in the report, the revenue tariff, was kept alive by Keynes's public campaign on the subject – obviously designed to influence the budget – which started with an article in the New Statesman on 7 March, and continued in the correspondence columns for some weeks after. Keynes sent copies of his article to MacDonald and Snowden. At that time Snowden was ill and MacDonald replied that 'it will be a fortnight or three weeks before I can see [Snowden] to exchange views on the budget'. Snowden's wife replied on the Chancellor's behalf: 'I have read your article, and will tell him the contents when he is able to listen. I dare say he will feel as sad as I do that you should think it necessary to take this line, for we are as strongly convinced that it is wrong (taking a long view) as you are that it is right.' Keynes's position on the tariff was unchanged, though more urgently expressed, as he foresaw that the only other options remaining open to the government were devaluation or an assault on wages. As he said in a letter to Alexander,

* In line with its belief in the efficacy of low interest rates as a recovery policy, and the desire to reduce the interest charge on the national debt, the Treasury was at the end of 1930 beginning to prepare plans to convert £2,000m 5 per cent War Loan 1929/47 to a 4 per cent interest rate in the second half of 1931. In May 1931 the conversion was postponed because of the onset of the international financial crisis (Howson, Domestic Monetary Management in Britain 1919–38, pp. 71–4).

'it seems to me so vitally important to consider these proposals not in isolation but in comparison with their alternatives. We are in a position in which all the courses open to us have objectionable features.'[98] Keynes's difficulty remained one of distinguishing his case for a general tariff from an attack on free trade principles *tout court*; and it was particularly galling to find his critics condemning his proposal on the grounds of its effect on the cost of living when their own alternatives involved a much more direct assault on working-class living standards.

Nevertheless, Keynes's campaign was sufficiently successful to induce Snowden's secretary to prepare ammunition for Snowden to use when he returned from his sick-bed. Fergusson asked Forber at the Board of Inland Revenue to provide a

statement of the difficulties and objections – parliamentary, administrative, and economic (i.e. inconvenience to traders etc.). The higher these can be put the better it will be from [Snowden's] point of view. He has not himself asked for anything of this sort, but a good deal will have to be done after he returns in a very short time, and from what I hear he will have to be ready to meet a good deal of pressure on this matter.

Forber's lengthy memorandum certainly complied with the terms of this request, though it was largely concerned with legislative and administrative difficulties, and assumed that the main object was to raise revenue rather than keep out imports. Snowden did not, however, need sophisticated ammunition to reject the revenue tariff. In his budget speech in April he referred to it in traditional free-trade terms as a method 'of relieving the well-to-do at the expense of the poor'.[99] In fact, Snowden's economic priorities, and hence those of the government, had already been decided on, either directly or by elimination. The political and economic events of 1931 served to push the government, however reluctantly, along its chosen path at a faster rate.

Before these events brought an end to the Council's regular meetings, the Council devoted its April 1931 meeting to a discussion of the international financial situation. By this time the staff had been reporting to the Council the 'disquieting' trends in the British balance of trade and payments for six months. Its February report had prompted some Council discussion: Citrine objected to its statement that there had been 'a definitely unfavourable change in the foreign estimation of British credit' attributable to the Treasury's evidence to the Royal Commission on Unemployment Insurance.[100] Lewis, on the other hand, pressed for 'a drastic policy of economy together with a revenue tariff' as the best way of improving foreign confidence. Bevin argued that there should be no reduction in unemployment pay unless rentier incomes from British government securities were also reduced.[101]

In April MacDonald asked Lord D'Abernon (formerly British Ambassador in Berlin) to attend the Council's meeting to give his views on the international situation. D'Abernon believed that the only solution to the current problems was central bank cooperative action to increase the supply of gold (by release from America and France) and hence to raise prices. Keynes pointed out that one alternative was all-round devaluation. This Lewis (a banker) 'looked upon with horror' because 'the position of this country largely depended on its reputation for honesty'; he agreed with Keynes that a tariff was preferable. Citrine also argued that the Council should concentrate on some of the internal remedies suggested in the Economists' report. Bevin, however, stuck to his earlier view that

The gold standard was not sacrosanct ... He could not look with equanimity upon an expanding world of commerce harnessed to a relatively diminishing quantity of a metal. Only the *rentier* classes stood to gain from the gold standard. Personally, he did not believe that it was possible to find a solution of the problem within the four walls of that policy.

Keynes responded by saying that it might become necessary to pursue that line but at the moment he favoured less dangerous expedients. He gave two reasons: firstly, 'one of our greatest industries was international banking'; secondly, any public discussion of devaluation would provoke 'an immediate confidence crisis which would be so strong as to destroy the Government'.* MacDonald sadly remarked that 'this was one of the great difficulties with which the Government was faced'.

Keynes pressed for the revenue tariff, saying that it need only be a temporary device, which would improve the balance of trade and enable Britain to take a lead in reviving international lending. MacDonald thought tariffs were unlikely to be temporary. Furthermore, such short-term expedients 'involved important departures from accepted policy ... The question before the Council was, therefore, proposals for a radical change in the whole economic system of the country. This might ultimately be found to be necessary in order to maintain the existing standard of consumption.'

* D'Abernon may have held similar views to Keynes's: later in the year Hankey discovered he was 'a violent opponent of the policy [of maintaining the value of sterling] – though unwilling to attack it during the crisis' (Hankey's diary, in S. Roskill, *Hankey: Man of Secrets*, Vol. II (1972), pp. 251–2).

CHAPTER 4

ECONOMIC ADVICE DURING THE CRISIS

The Treasury and the Bank of England were aware of the possibility of a balance-of-payments crisis from the beginning of 1931.* This determined to a large extent the policy of the second Labour Government in the last few months of its life. In January Hopkins submitted evidence on behalf of the Treasury to the Royal Commission on Unemployment Insurance which stressed the effect of an unbalanced budget on foreign confidence: 'continued state borrowing on the present vast scale without adequate provision for repayment would quickly call in question the stability of the British financial system'. This confirmed the Opposition's fears and provided ammunition for the campaign on public economy. As a result of a Conservative censure motion and a Liberal amendment on the lines of their suggestions in *How to Tackle Unemployment*, the government set up the Committee on National Expenditure under Sir George May in February to suggest ways of reducing public expenditure. The report of this committee, which consisted of five members (including the chairman) representing business interests, four of whom the Conservatives and the Liberals nominated, and two trade union representatives, was to figure prominently in the political crisis in August.

In January Snowden had warned his Cabinet colleagues in no uncertain terms that the financial situation was a 'grim one . . . As each month passes with no sign of a lifting of the world economic crisis, the financial prospect constantly and steadily deteriorates.' He stressed two reasons for balancing the budget. First, the 'steady trickle of money being transferred . . . abroad' must not be allowed to increase, for 'a flight from the pound would be fraught with the most disastrous consequences . . . to the whole economic organisation of the country'. Second, abandonment of attempts to maintain a sinking fund 'would postpone indefinitely all prospects of the conversion of the war debt to a lower interest basis, which [was] one of the few hopeful means of securing a reduction of expenditure in the future'. The Treasury was still hoping to introduce a period of sustained cheap money by converting 5 per cent War Loan, and was at this time preparing a scheme to be announced in June 1931. The European financial crisis in May caused it to postpone the scheme, which was eventually announced in June 1932.[1]

In the meantime Snowden introduced his April 1931 budget. As with his

---

* D. E. Moggridge, 'The 1931 Financial Crisis: A New View', *The Banker*, August 1970; H. Clay, *Lord Norman*, pp. 369–71. The actual deterioration of the balance of payments in 1930–1 was such that a current account surplus of £104m in 1930 turned into a deficit of £114m in 1931.

1930 budget, Snowden's principles gave way to the expediency suggested by his Treasury officials; he used the existence of the Royal Commission on Unemployment Insurance and the May Committee as an excuse for postponing expenditure reductions and increases in direct taxation.[2] One possibility that the Treasury discussed but did not act upon was a tax on rentier incomes. In January a Cabinet Committee of Thomas, Alexander, and Graham sat under Snowden to consider ways of balancing the budget; all three were in favour of all-round cuts that included the rentier. Possibly in response to this, Fisher, Hopkins, and Grigg discussed a rentier tax. They regarded the political difficulties as being 'so stupendous that it could only be carried out by agreement between Parties and the House of Commons', but 'if . . . it could be brought about, the effect on the morale of the country and its reputation abroad would be stupendous too'. They finally rejected the proposal later in the year on the basis of an Inland Revenue memorandum.[3]

In the next few months the government attempted to implement its policies within the limits which it had by now set itself. Since short-term remedies were ruled out, the government continued to worry about the encouragement of rationalisation, despite the difficulties experienced in regard to the iron and steel industries.[4] This was apparently a view that Henderson and MacDonald shared. After Henderson proposed his 'industrial reconstruction scheme' in June 1930, he prepared several memoranda for the government on the need to encourage industrial reconstruction of one form or another;[5] MacDonald for his part set up three committees on these problems in 1931.* The topics included the development of new industries, particularly in depressed areas, and government promotion of new industrial research as well as rationalisation in the older industries. The first committee MacDonald set up was an Economic Advisory Council Committee on New Industrial Development after the question of the formation of a central industrial research institute had been raised in the Panel of Ministers in March. Such an institute had earlier been proposed by the Liberals in *How to Tackle Unemployment*. This committee began to meet in April but did not report until June 1932, when it recommended no action.[6] Henderson suggested the Committee on Problems of Rationalisation as 'a subject which would repay systematic investigation of the long-distance type, which the Economic Advisory Council was designed to undertake'. MacDonald appointed it in August with Henderson as its secretary. It did not begin to meet until after the government crisis, and although it held numerous meetings, and prepared an outline of its report, it abandoned its task in June 1932.†

---

* MacDonald also appointed the Standing Committees on Economic Information and on Scientific Research in July 1931; these did not begin to meet regularly until 1932, although the Committee on Economic Information was asked to prepare a report on the balance of payments during the financial crisis.

† Cab. 58/12, E.A.C. (H) 142, Henderson, 'Suggested Inquiry into certain problems connected with rationalisation', 28 May 1931; Cab. 58/175–80, Committee on Problems of Rationalisa-

Earlier, in April, MacDonald had also appointed a Cabinet committee consisting of himself, Snowden, Thomas, Graham, and Johnston, with Colin Clark as secretary, 'to survey the trade position in the light of changes (some of them final) that had taken place in world trade since the war and the changes that were still going on'. The questions of protection and the iron and steel industry dominated the first meeting, but for the second Colin Clark produced a lengthy and interesting memorandum. This reviewed the effects of falling world prices on Britain's balance of trade, and the lag of money wages behind prices, but placed little stress on relative costs or the improvement in real wages as a cause of British difficulties. It pointed out that in spite of the loss of export markets 'we appear on the whole to be retaining our competitive position in the industries working for the home market'. Clark estimated that if all the manufactured goods imported by Britain in 1930 had been produced domestically, unemployment would have been reduced by 875,000. With the improvement in the terms of trade it was possible to think of shifting resources towards industries producing for the home market, if only because a smaller volume of exports now sufficed to purchase Britain's food and raw material imports. Clark did not think that it could be argued that the decline in exports had significantly reduced Britain's capacity to lend abroad, though he thought that the reciprocal effect of such investment on exports could be exaggerated. While he estimated that the decline in exports accounted for about 600,000 of the total unemployment (then averaging 2,300,000) it did not follow that increasing exports was the only means of reducing unemployment. Even if the pre-war position was restored, there would still be a large residue of unemployment which would have to be absorbed in new industries producing for the home market. The encouragement of these industries was 'the central feature of the economic question'.

From here on Clark's memorandum adopted elements of Keynes's *Treatise* framework to show that unused savings were running to waste when they might be absorbed in the expansion of new industries. Clark did not accept the view that unemployment was due to profits being squeezed by labour demanding 'too high a remuneration or too high a share of [the] total product of industry'. He also pointed out that the simultaneous reduction of wages, interest, and profits as a method of improving Britain's competitive position in export markets would merely be self-stultifying when applied to the home trades on which 80 per cent of the population were employed. He calculated that labour's share of national income over recent years had been constant; those who argued that real wages should be re-

tion, Minutes and memoranda, September 1931–June 1932; Henderson Papers Box 1. The committee ceased presumably because of a lack of interest by the National Government. Henderson remained involved with these questions throughout his secretaryship of the E.A.C. In 1933, for instance, he wrote a memorandum for the President of the Board of Trade on 'Increasing productivity and the demand for labour' (Henderson Papers Box 2, 12 December 1933; reprinted in *The Inter-War Years*, pp. 126–50).

duced were actually demanding an increase in the share going to profits.[7]

For the same meeting MacDonald submitted a survey of his own of the ground to be covered. The memorandum was characteristically diffuse and woolly, and seems to be an attempt to find a way forward through a mixture of protection and deflation. The committee decided to accept this rather than Clark's memorandum as its agenda; subsequent meetings concentrated on the problems of agriculture and iron and steel, and the proceedings petered out in July with an acknowledgment of 'the difficulty of achieving rapid progress in regard to any of the foregoing problems'.[8]

The crisis

The international liquidity crisis began with the failure of the Credit-Anstalt in Austria on 13 May and spread immediately to Germany. The resulting mad scramble for liquidity could not be stopped by credits from the Bank for International Settlements, the Bank of England, the Bank of France, and the Federal Reserve Bank of New York to the Reichsbank, nor by President Hoover's offer of a one-year moratorium on inter-governmental debts announced on 20 June. The crisis raged for two months on the Continent until the German banking system was forced to close on 13 July. At this point attention shifted to Britain, and during the next two weeks the Bank of England lost one-quarter of its official reserves and raised Bank rate from $2\frac{1}{2}$ per cent to $3\frac{1}{2}$ per cent on 23 July, and to $4\frac{1}{2}$ per cent on 30 July. Confidence was partially restored by the announcement of credits to the Bank of England from the Bank of France and the Federal Reserve Bank of New York on 1 August. But this was undermined by the simultaneous announcement of an increase in the fiduciary note issue, and by the publication of the report of the May Committee forecasting a budget deficit of £120m and recommending cuts in public expenditure amounting to £97m, including a 20 per cent cut in the rate of unemployment benefit. Coming as it did not long after the publication of the report of the Macmillan Committee on 13 July, which had revealed the volume of London's short-term liabilities, the effect of the May report on foreign confidence was to lead to a resumption of the gold drain. Further foreign credits became necessary if Britain was to try to remain on the gold standard.[9]

It was at this point that the crisis began for the Labour Government. While the exact timing and ferocity of the crisis could not have been predicted accurately, the government could not claim to be unaware of the international and domestic dimensions of the problem facing them. Moreover, many of the policy choices which the government might have to make if the situation deteriorated further had been fully canvassed in Economic Advisory Council discussions. At every stage of the crisis the Labour Government and its successor was provided with advice from civil servants, the banking community (domestic and international), the Opposition parties, the General Council of the Trades Union Congress, and individual members of the Economic Advisory Council. Here we are mainly concerned with the role played by the last of these groups.

During the months of May to August the Economic Advisory Council, though not its staff, was inactive. Keynes's appointment book has an entry 'E.A.C.' for 23 and 30 July; the latter is crossed through and neither meeting in fact took place. During this period and before the final stages of the crisis, the Labour Government received the report of the Macmillan Committee on 1 July, followed by the May Committee report at the end of the month. On the first of these the Cabinet decided that since the report had taken two years to produce the government had 'a good answer for not making an early announcement'. Nevertheless, it was thought that a special meeting might become necessary, and the Treasury was asked to prepare a commentary on the report.[10] Although much of the report dealt with long-term matters, the 'proposals relating to domestic monetary policy to meet the present emergency' contained many of Keynes's expansionist ideas which had already been raised at the Economic Advisory Council and – implicitly at least – rejected by the government. In spite of its criticism of the way in which the gold standard had worked since 1925, and its recognition of the need for conscious monetary management, the report came out firmly against the idea put forward by two of its members, Bevin and Thomas Allen, that Britain should abandon the gold standard unilaterally. Even the dissenters agreed with their colleagues that such a policy was difficult to carry out, and that it was easier 'to endorse a de facto devaluation'.[11] It is ironic, therefore, that the report may have contributed to the run on the pound. The government could also have derived support for the orthodox course which it had already adopted, and was soon to be forced to carry to its logical conclusion, from various reservations and memoranda of dissent supplied by R. H. Brand, Professor T. E. Gregory, and Lord Bradbury.

On the report of the May Committee, which gave decisive support in its majority report to policies which the Chancellor of the Exchequer had considered essential long before there was any question of an international liquidity crisis, the Cabinet decided to appoint a Cabinet committee, which was scheduled to meet first on 25 August, and in the meantime to publish the report.

On 2 August the Prime Minister, having retired to his home at Lossie-mouth, wrote to Keynes asking him to send anything that he might decide to write on the May Committee's report, 'as I should like very much to have your views for my guidance'.[12] At the same time the Prime Minister sought Henderson's views on the subject.

A division of opinion between Henderson and Keynes had emerged during the course of 1930 over the importance to be attached to the deterioration of the budgetary situation.[13] In February 1931, just after the parliamentary debate on economy which led to the establishment of the May Committee, Henderson returned to this question in a strongly worded letter to Keynes.

My complaint against the tenor of all your public writings or utterances in the last year or so is that in not a single one of them has there been a trace of a suggestion that the Budget situation is one which is really very serious and must be treated seriously. On the contrary, over and over again you have implied that it doesn't matter a bit, that expenditure is a thing you want to press on with, whether by the Government or by anybody else, and that the question of whether it involves a budget charge is a minor matter which is hardly worth considering. The notion that this is the right emphasis just now, the thing that most needs stressing, seems to me wildly false. The effect is to convey the impression to all people, however intelligent and open-minded, who have some appreciation of the financial difficulties, that you have gone completely crazy, and impairing all the influence you have with them, while pleasing and encouraging only those who say that you mustn't lay a finger on the dole.

Henderson's accusation was that Keynes was lending support to Lloyd George and those members of the Labour party who considered there was no budgetary problem, thereby undermining Snowden's position in 'standing for a responsible approach to the whole financial position'. Keynes's unwillingness to take the problem seriously, Henderson thought, might perhaps be cured if Keynes could be made 'Chancellor of the Exchequer in a Government where Ll. G. was Lord Privy Seal'.[14]

In his memorandum to MacDonald on 'The Economy Report' on 7 August Henderson said that he thought that the May Committee had 'laid on the dark colours very thick indeed'; that its criteria for a properly balanced budget were 'unreasonably austere', largely as a result of the inclusion of £52m for the sinking fund; and that 'no other important country' could satisfy the committee's criteria at present. He also felt that the effect of the committee's recommendation for expenditure cuts and increased taxes 'must be to aggravate the trade depression further, to reduce the public revenue still further, to plunge us still deeper into the vicious circle of deflationary consequences which it is so difficult to break through'. On the other hand, Henderson felt that the committee had probably over-estimated revenue prospects. But above all there was the 'vital' question of confidence in the pound, which the unfortunate timing of the report had helped to make the prime factor in the situation. Since Henderson believed that abandonment of the gold standard would have 'formidable and enduring' consequences, he considered that the only course open to the government was to balance the budget by a combination of 'substantial and unpopular' economies and tax increases. This could be done by going a long way in the direction indicated by the May Committee, including 'considerable cuts in unemployment benefit', but excluding the proposed cuts in the road programme.[15]

The deflationary option was also favoured by Sir Arthur Balfour, another member of the Council whose advice MacDonald sought at this time.

Balfour thought that the country could no longer postpone the policy of lowering wages and hence costs.

We have for years, with our eyes open, deliberately ignored the vast difference between our cost of production and that of other industrial competing countries. We are being bled white by national expenditure and taxation and I am more and more convinced that the situation in which we find ourselves can never be settled on Party lines. We are in a time of real National emergency and the sooner we face the fact on these lines, the better.[16]

Keynes, however, although not unwilling to recognise the effect of higher taxation and mounting expenditure on business confidence at home, did not think that such considerations should stand in the way of any of the positive initiatives he favoured. He was not opposed to efforts to remove anomalies in the unemployment insurance scheme, nor to calling for a moratorium on new expenditure commitments. But his opposition to anything that smacked of deliberate deflation is abundantly clear. Furthermore, he was not prepared to take the issue of foreign confidence seriously because he had decided that there was no future in trying to defend the existing parity. In this respect his ideas had changed since he signed the report of the Macmillan Committee in July. As his first letter to MacDonald, written on 5 August 1931, shows, he was already thinking of ways in which a positive act of devaluation could be turned to advantage:

I do not propose to publish anything about the Report of the Economy Committee, because my views are not fit for publication;– they are not even fit for circulation to the E.A.C., but I welcome very much the opportunity, in response to your letter, to tell you personally what is in my mind.

One could criticise the Committee's recommendations in detail, but I would prefer to consider them on very broad lines, because their recommendations are a quite logical outcome of a general point of view which many responsible and authoritative people hold – or have held up till recently.

The Committee's recommendations obviously represent in substance and broad effect an effort to make the existing deflation effective by bringing incomes down towards the level of prices. They are part and parcel of the policy of seeking equilibrium by *general* reductions of wages and salaries and they would indeed, if they were taken in isolation, be a most gross perversion of social justice. To select the school teachers as solitary victims is surely unthinkable. The effect, therefore, on my mind is to be hard up against a prompt and definite decision whether I am in favour to make deflation effective, or whether I prefer to seek another exit. This is the question which we now have to face, because the adoption of the Committee's recommendations as an isolated act and not as part of a much larger policy on the same lines would, I am sure, be useless.

My advice is that we do *not* attempt to make the deflation effective, because, apart from the question whether it is intrinsically desirable, I am convinced for the following reasons that an attempt made now would be both futile and disastrous:–

1. The *first* effect of adopting the proposals of the Economy Committee and analogous measures would certainly be a further decline in business profits and a substantial increase of unemployment, because economies which are not balanced by reduced taxation must necessarily reduce demand relatively to supply, – the buying power of those immediately affected would be diminished, whilst no one else's buying power would be increased. Thus there would be no initial success from adopting the policy to give us the necessary courage to persevere and take strong doses.

2. The cut in money incomes which would be required to reach equilibrium by this route would be more than those concerned would submit to. It might well be 30 per cent. Indeed, there might be no feasible cut which would be sufficient, because of the reaction of what we might do on what would be done abroad.

3. It would be impossible to obtain the public consent to such measures unless bondholders, etc., were treated in the same way. I know no practical means to ensure this or to secure even a modicum of social justice.

4. But above all – and this is the new fact within the last two months – it is now nearly *certain* that we shall go off the existing gold parity at no distant date. Whatever may have been the case some time ago, it is now too late to avoid this. We can put off the date for a time, if we are so foolish as to borrow in terms of francs and dollars and so allow a proportion of what are now sterling liabilities to be converted into franc and dollar liabilities, thus giving a preference to those of our creditors who are the quickest to sell. But when doubts as to the prosperity of a currency, such as now exist about sterling, have come into existence, the game's up; for there is no object to foreigners in keeping sterling balances if there is any appreciable doubt about their value. It is conceivable that we might have avoided this if we had been more clear-sighted. But we cannot avoid it now.

It will be for the City to give clear guidance at the present time. The Accepting Houses, who constitute the major part of the Court of the Bank of England, are many of them more or less insolvent. The Governor is probably near the end of his nervous resources. It is now a problem for the Government rather than for the City. I suggest that you should consult a Committee consisting of all living ex-Chancellors of the Exchequer, whether they believe that deflation *à outrance* is possible and are in favour of attempting it, or whether we should not at once suspend gold convertibility and then take collective thought as to the next step.

We might, I think, try to convert disaster into success. We should remember that most of the rest of the world is suffering much as we are. I should seek forthwith to win the hegemony of a new Currency Union by inviting all Empire countries to join us in adhering to a new currency unit. I believe they would all, including Canada, accept, with the possible exception of South Africa. I should further have it in mind to invite also at some stage all South America, Asia, Central Europe, Italy and Spain – indeed anyone who felt inclined to come in.

The new currency unit might be a gold unit, obtained by devaluing existing units by not less than 25 per cent. It is *vital* that the change should not be smaller than this, and preferably greater. But it would be much better that its value should not be permanently fixed in gold – at least in the first instance – but should be allowed to depend on the future behaviour of the countries still remaining on the gold standard. Do not forget that the initial effect of these measures would be more or less to destroy the export trade of these Gold Standard countries. Having thus put exchange difficulties behind us, we should then proceed to organise activity and prosperity at home and abroad along the boldest possible lines.

I believe that many people, even in the City, far more than might be expected – very likely the Governor of the Bank of England himself, for example – are now in favour of something of this sort at the bottom of their hearts. It might quite well be taken by the country as a whole, not as a disaster, but with an extraordinary sense of relief and of hope. The 'inner opinion' – what everyone believes at the bottom of his heart but never realises until the last moment – is a mighty force in this country.[17]

A week later, having changed his mind about publishing anything on the subject, Keynes sent MacDonald a copy of an article on the May Report written for the *New Statesman*. In this article he charged the committee with having ignored the deflationary repercussions of its proposals on the level of unemployment and tax yields: he estimated that the negative multiplier effects would actually involve a net reduction in the budget deficit of £50m as a result of economies of £100m. The proposals would not have the direct benefits for the balance of trade which might have followed from a reduction in wages and costs; and he did not think that any favourable effects on private investment could be expected via an improvement in business confidence. His own policy for the budget was to suspend the sinking fund, continue borrowing for unemployment pay in order to maintain incomes, and impose a revenue tariff.[18] Keynes did not mention devaluation in this article, but he referred to it in a postscript to his covering letter to MacDonald.

The impressions I have collected today persuade me that there will be a crisis within a month unless the most drastic and sensational action is taken. I believe that it is still possible for us to keep on the gold standard if we deliberately decide to do so, but in this case we should have to conform our whole policy accordingly. Personally, I should support for the time being whichever policy was made, provided the decision was accompanied by action sufficiently drastic to make it effective. But I should only *favour* the gold standard policy if it were part of a general scheme for restoring credit everywhere – which it probably would not be.*

Keynes was not very optimistic that the necessary drastic measures would be taken. The next day he wrote to Kahn: 'The foreigners are taking their money away as fast as they can. We should be off, I should say, within a month unless heroic measures are taken. Perhaps they will be, perhaps they won't. Betting slightly on.'[19]

At much the same time that MacDonald obtained the divergent views of Keynes and Henderson on the May Report, he received a letter from Snowden summoning him to London.[20] As soon as he arrived in London on 11 August, MacDonald found himself surrounded by advisers pressing for a deflationary solution. Janeway's conclusion is not too harsh: 'The question of whether to remain on gold or not was supplanted – not even by the question of how to remain on gold at the least possible cost – but by the question of how to implement one prescribed means for remaining on gold.' In advising the Prime Minister on whom he should see when he returned, Henderson had said that he was 'not sure in the circumstances that there would be much to be gained by an informal consultation with E.A.C. members as such'. Lewis and Stamp were away, Keynes and Balfour had already given their views; and these were 'the members of the Council who follow most closely the development of the economic situation'.[21] It seems unlikely that MacDonald would have been able to find time to consult anybody besides those with whom he found himself day in, day out in the next six weeks.

The Cabinet Economy Committee met as a matter of urgency on 12, 13, 17, and 18 August. Snowden presented it with an estimated deficit for

* MacDonald Papers 1/19F, Keynes to MacDonald, 12 August 1931. One person Keynes had seen that day was R. H. Brand (Keynes Papers, Appointment book for 1931).

1932–3 of £170m (rather than the May Committee's £120m), and a set of Treasury proposals for expenditure cuts which included a 10 per cent cut in the standard rate of unemployment benefit (rather than the 20 per cent suggested by the May Committee). The committee agreed to a list of economies which amounted to £78½m including a reduction of £20m on transitional benefit but excluding a cut in the rate of unemployment benefit; and a £90m increase in taxation whose details were to be left to the Treasury.[22]

The Cabinet deliberations opened with a nine-hour meeting on 19 August. It considered alternatives not included in the Cabinet Economy Committee report or that of the May Committee. Debt conversion was raised at the first meeting but not mentioned again, market conditions being definitely unfavourable. Revenue tariffs and suspension of the sinking fund had a longer run. Snowden rejected the former on principle, but although he was equally opposed to suspension of the sinking fund, the Cabinet agreed on 21 August 'that for the purpose of their present calculations the possibility of deducting £47½m in respect of the sinking fund from the gross deficiency should be taken into account'. The Cabinet the same day provisionally agreed to economies of £56m (without a cut in the rate of unemployment benefit); MacDonald said he would show this list of economies plus the sinking fund proposal to the Opposition parties and the Bank of England.[23]

The Opposition parties had been involved since 13 August, when Harvey, with Snowden's permission, had informed their leaders of the grave financial position.* On the same day the Treasury had asked the Bank to sound out New York as to the possibility of a loan to the government. Harrison, Governor of the Federal Reserve Bank of New York, had replied that he thought loans from New York and Paris of, say, £50m each would be practicable 'provided the programme of economy was adequate and received the approval of Parliament'.[24] Hence the need to consult the Opposition on any proposed economy measures. On 20 August MacDonald and Snowden had discussed the Cabinet Economy Committee's proposals with Chamberlain, Hoare, Samuel, and Maclean, on the one hand, and the General Council of the Trades Union Congress on the other. While the former regarded a cut in the standard rate of unemployment benefit as essential, the latter regarded it as intolerable.[25] The Opposition representatives also rejected the sinking fund proposals. When Snowden reported this to the Cabinet on 22 August, he justified his own determination that Britain should remain on the gold standard by the inflation which would follow suspension; it would 'reduce the standard of living of the workmen

* MacDonald Papers 1/19F, Harvey to Snowden, 6 August 1931; Clay, Lord Norman, p. 317. When Harvey made his request, Snowden remarked to MacDonald that the Opposition leaders probably already knew since Norman had seen Baldwin. He himself had seen Chamberlain. (MacDonald Papers 1/19F, Snowden to MacDonald, 7 August 1931; Snowden, An Autobiography, Vol. II: 1919–1934 (1934), p. 929; K. Feiling, The Life of Neville Chamberlain (1946), p. 190).

4-2

by 50%'. He wanted *additional* economies of £25–30m (on top of the £56m). Although the Cabinet was 'not prepared to authorise the Prime Minister to make ... [an] offer' of £20m more economies, obtained mostly by a 10 per cent cut in the rate of unemployment benefit, it did allow him to approach the Opposition representatives to see if they would be satisfied by such a proposal. The reply was that they would be satisfied if the plan was acceptable to 'the financial authorities responsible for raising the contemplated loan in New York and Paris'.[26]

The Bank therefore put the plan to Morgan's, the Treasury's agents in New York. Their answer came in a cable brought by Harvey to a Cabinet meeting on 23 August. It was 'the occasion of a break in the Cabinet . . . because it assumed – and was understood to assume – a programme of economies on which compromise or agreement was impossible'.[27] After Harvey had said that the City would support £56m economies plus the extra £20m which included the cut in unemployment benefit, the Cabinet voted: the division was eleven (including MacDonald) to nine in favour of these economies. In the words of the Cabinet minutes, 'it became clear that acceptance would involve resignation of several members; in those circumstances the Prime Minister said he would see the King and ask him to hold a conference with Baldwin, Samuel, and himself the next day'.[28]

A National Government under MacDonald was formed on 24 August. It appointed another Cabinet economy committee on 26 August, which met the next day and agreed on economies amounting to £70m, including the 10 per cent cut in unemployment benefit.[29] Two days later the government succeeded in raising loans in Paris and New York. Snowden introduced a second budget for the year on 10 September, describing it as 'the most disagreeable task I have ever been called upon to perform'. To meet a current deficit of £74½m and a prospective deficit for 1932/3 of £176m, there were economies totalling £70m for the full financial year 1932/3, an increase in direct and indirect taxation which would yield £40m in the current year and £91m in the next, and suspension of the non-contractual part of the sinking fund, which saved £20m. Snowden also introduced clauses to facilitate conversion of 5 per cent War Loan when circumstances were favourable. The economies came from cuts in the salaries of ministers, judges, Members of Parliament, teachers, the police, and the armed forces; from a 10 per cent cut in the standard rate of unemployment benefit; an increase in unemployment insurance contributions; and a reduction of the period allowed for receipt of transitional benefit. Borrowing by the Unemployment and Road Funds was to cease, and there was to be a cutback in local authority capital expenditure supported by the Treasury.[30]

Not long after the fall of the Labour Government Keynes wrote what was, for him, a peculiarly temporising article in the *New Statesman*. He felt that public opinion was not prepared for a rational debate on devaluation, yet drastic economies were necessary to preserve the existing parity. 'Consequently it is not for those who doubt the wisdom of the decision or hesitate before all it implies and symbolises to attempt to carry it out.' Although he still found the thinking behind the economy programme unacceptable, he was willing to see if an effort could be made along these lines 'without too much stress or strain, too many insolvencies or too great social injustice'.[31] When Snowden presented his budget and Economy Bill, however, Keynes attacked the 'folly and injustice' of it. He told an all-party group of M.P.s at the House of Commons on 16 September that 'the Government's programme is one of the most wrong and foolish things which Parliament has deliberately perpetrated in my lifetime'.[32] It did not touch the fundamental problem of the balance of trade; and there were in fact 'only three lines of policy to which it is worth the Cabinet's while to direct their minds', namely import controls, devaluation, and an international conference 'for giving the gold standard countries a last opportunity'. At such a conference Britain should announce that 'it cannot and will not work the international gold standard if the other creditor countries do not play the "rules of the game"'. Pending the outcome of this threat Britain should impose exchange and capital controls.[33]

Henderson took a very different line in a memorandum which he wrote for MacDonald on 27 August, as a defence against the new government's critics. He predicted that the main attack would be on 'class grounds' but that the government's policy might also be criticised as economically unsound. He may have had Keynes in mind here as well as MacDonald's embittered ex-colleagues. Henderson was concerned to emphasise the genuine gravity of having to defend the pound by deflationary means. If the pound had been allowed to go (it had still not gone) there would have been a major fall in its value in terms of foreign currencies, making a stiffer dose of economy necessary later on in order to balance the budget. There was, therefore, no choice open to the government, even though he acknowledged with less force than he had done earlier that economy measures might intensify the depression. This was now merely a partial truth amounting to a fallacy because of the overwhelming importance he attached to the confidence factor. Indeed, the best contribution that Britain could make to world recovery was to put her house in order and eliminate 'once and for all, the misgivings about sterling that exist today'. Henderson even allowed himself some moderate optimism on this matter on the grounds of the possible upturn in the business cycle. His final conclusion was exactly the opposite of the one reached by Keynes, for whereas Keynes believed that devaluation would enable Britain to lead a recovery in world prices, Henderson felt that 'nothing could be more certain than that a break in sterling would cause prices to fall further'.[34]

There was, however, one policy recommendation on which Keynes and Henderson were still in agreement, namely the revenue tariff; they both continued to argue for it to help both the budget and the balance of trade in the weeks before Britain left the gold standard. Henderson made his last pro-tariff statement on 18 September when commenting on a set of provisional balance-of-payments figures, which suggested that as compared with the previous year invisible earnings were currently far below what would be required to cover the adverse visible balance, and that the situation was continuing to deteriorate. Having rejected the prohibition of imports, the stimulation of exports by subsidies, and the restriction of exchange dealings as impractical, Henderson advocated a 10 per cent general tariff with higher rates of duty on manufactures. He also made clear, however, that if it proved impossible to hold sterling at its present parity then devaluation would 'diminish the force of the argument for tariff action as a means of redressing the balance of payments'.[35] One of MacDonald's first decisions as Prime Minister of the National Government had been to set up a Cabinet Committee on the Financial Situation, consisting of Snowden, Lord Reading (Foreign Secretary), and Neville Chamberlain (Minister of Health), to 'produce to the Cabinet . . . a statement of the actual financial position, which, assuming the present crisis is allayed, will have to be faced and to make recommendations as to what, if anything, will have to be done'. MacDonald asked the Committee on Economic Information, which he had appointed in July, to provide the Cabinet committee with balance-of-payments estimates.[36] The Cabinet committee did not discuss either Henderson's memorandum or the report on the balance of payments by the Committee on Economic Information, since on 18 September the decision to leave the gold standard was taken.

The reserve drain had not ceased with the resolution of the political crisis. On the evening of 18 September Harvey and Peacock of the Bank of England told MacDonald that the credits were nearly exhausted and that they 'did not think that we could raise enough to save the situation and if the situation could not be saved it was merely a waste of more money'. They therefore decided to give up the fight and spent most of their meeting discussing ways and means of going off the gold standard. At one point in the discussion MacDonald

observed that all the theorists would at once rush into print. Was there any way of using them? We ought to enlist every brain and it would be a case of all hands to the pumps . . . A number of names were mentioned, and it was decided that the Prime Minister should see Stamp in the morning with a view to collecting a body of persons whose names would carry confidence with the various sections of the community, who should be constituted a Council or Committee to watch and advise on the situation.[37]

The weekend was spent preparing the Gold Standard (Amendment) Bill, which was introduced and passed on Monday, 21 September, after a Cabinet meeting on Sunday night. There were also discussions in the Treasury of exchange control, in which both Stamp and Keynes participated. They both argued in favour of exchange control against Leith-Ross, who 'vigorously opposed' the idea.[38] In fact some restrictions were imposed, but only temporarily.

As the chief economist employed within government, Henderson was drawn into the weekend preparations for making the decision public. For a government which had been formed with the explicit intention of carrying through an unpopular programme to balance the budget for the purpose of keeping Britain on the gold standard, some explanation was obviously needed as to whether all the sacrifices which had been made were necessary now that the government had manifestly failed to achieve its main object. It was to this problem that Henderson addressed himself in preparing drafts for the press releases and broadcasts made by the Prime Minister and the Chancellor of the Exchequer on 20 and 21 September respectively. Henderson took the line that

> if the pound had gone when there was a big deficit in the Budget an internal inflation would have been almost inevitable . . . It is one thing to go off the gold standard with an unbalanced Budget and uncontrolled inflation; it is quite another thing to take this measure, not because of internal financial difficulties, but because of excessive withdrawals of borrowed capital.[39]

Government spokesmen made extensive use of the view expressed in this statement during the next few weeks, particularly during the election campaign held in October. Snowden used Henderson's arguments (and his words) with special force in his election address on 17 October;[40] MacDonald also played on fears of uncontrolled inflation at his election meetings.

The election preoccupied the National Cabinet for several weeks. The tariff question divided the Prime Minister and the Conservatives, who were in favour of an election, and Snowden and the Liberals, who were not. It was not until after the election that the Cabinet could return to matters of economic policy.*

The reorientation of policy after September 1931

'The suspension of the gold standard was followed by a remarkable reorientation of British economic and financial policy. Like Candide, Great Britain

* Cab. 24/223, C.P. 243(31), Memorandum by Home Secretary, 24 September 1931, and C.P. 247(31), Note by Prime Minister on a General Election, September 1931; Cab. 23/68, Cabinets 65(31)9, 66(31)1, 67(31)8, 68(31)3, 69(31)4, and 70(31)1, 28, 29, and 30 September, 1, 2, and 5 October 1931; Snowden, *An Autobiography*, Vol. II, pp. 988–91; Feiling, *Neville Chamberlain*, pp. 194–6. Keynes and Stamp were urging MacDonald *not* to hold an election. Keynes feared a banking crisis in the U.S.A. was imminent, and 'it would be too foolish to be caught . . . in the middle of a General Election fought on largely irrelevant issues'. The 'matters that ought to be occupying everyone's attention for the next six months or so are . . . the currency question, the Indian Conference, and the Disarmament Conference'. MacDonald's reaction was to invite Keynes to Sunday lunch at Chequers. (Keynes Papers L/31, Keynes to MacDonald, 30 September and 1 October, Keynes to Stamp, 30 September, Stamp to Keynes, 1 October, and MacDonald to Keynes, 1 October 1931).

resolved to accept, without rejoicing, the results of the concatenation of past events and to cultivate her garden.'[41] Economic Advisory Council members were involved in one way or another in the reorientation of economic policy, particularly the introduction of a tariff and the new monetary policy.

The tariff

The National Government's landslide victory in the October election gave the Conservatives the opportunity to introduce a tariff which they had been prevented from introducing in their previous administration (1925–9) by Baldwin's pledge of no general tariff or food taxes, and by the presence of Churchill, a free trader, at the Exchequer. While in opposition in 1929–31 the Conservative Party had set up a research department at Neville Chamberlain's instigation, and from March 1931 under his chairmanship. Again on Chamberlain's initiative, and with the assistance of the new research department, a sub-committee of the shadow cabinet under Cunliffe-Lister prepared a complete plan which, in the words of L. S. Amery, a member of the committee, was 'ready to be rushed through Parliament at a moment's notice'.[42] When Chamberlain became Chancellor of the Exchequer in November his 'primary object' was to impose a tariff without breaking up the government over the issue.[43] His first move was to remind his Cabinet colleagues on 10 November that the Board of Trade had forecast an adverse balance of trade for 1931 of £86m; he added that 'information as to subsequent months did not improve the prospect'. The Cabinet agreed to obtain additional information and to consider the subject further; it also agreed that MacDonald should recirculate the Committee on Economic Information's report on the balance of payments.*

This report provided estimates based on Board of Trade figures and then discussed the likely effects on the balance of payments of the depreciation of sterling. On the subject of policy the committee thought it 'vital for the solvency of our trade balance that sterling should remain for the time being substantially below parity, and . . . [a depreciation of] 25 per cent. would not be excessive'.† It also played down the tariff question; this reflected the views of both Keynes and Henderson. A week after the suspension of the gold standard Keynes had publicly withdrawn his support for a tariff in a letter to *The Times*, maintaining that 'the immediate question for attention is not

---

* Cab. 23/69, Cabinet 74(31)3, 10 November 1931. Other E.A.C. reports prepared for the Labour Government were recirculated at this time, namely the reports of the Committee of Economists, on Iron and Steel, and on Empire Migration.

† Cab. 58/30, C.E.I., 1st Report, 25 September 1931; reprinted below. Henderson may have felt that 25 per cent was excessive; he told the Treasury on 6 October that 15–20 per cent was quite enough (below, p. 102). Keynes had advocated – though the report did not – exchange controls and summoning an international conference (Cab. 58/18, E.A.C. (E) 4, 'The Balance of International Payments, Draft Report, Draft Concluding Paragraphs prepared by Mr. J. M. Keynes', 21 September 1931).

a tariff but the currency question'. Henderson stressed the irrelevance of tariffs in a series of letters and memoranda to MacDonald.*

The Cabinet merely 'took note' of this report on 18 November, but the issue of a general tariff arose again early in December. By this time the Abnormal Importations and Horticultural Imports Acts had been passed, the free traders within the Cabinet having acquiesced on the grounds that the Acts were temporary. On 7 December MacDonald produced a list of outstanding policy questions, which included fiscal policy. He noted that this would 'present us with the greatest difficulties of our co-operation', and suggested that Henderson be asked to supply information on 'the problems of our trade' from 'the pigeonholes of the Economic Advisory Council'. A Cabinet committee should then consider this and other information from the Board of Trade. In the same memorandum MacDonald, presumably feeling a need to justify the existence of the Economic Advisory Council to his new colleagues, also defended his use of committees of outside experts on the grounds that 'the departmental mind, although admirably expert within Whitehall conditions, is not always fully alive to outside feeling'. He considered that the danger of such committees assuming executive functions had been adequately guarded against in the previous two years.44 After discussion of MacDonald's list the Cabinet appointed a Committee on the Balance of Trade under Chamberlain to 'report on subjects arising out of the memoranda . . . including remedies for an adverse balance if there was such an adverse balance'.45 This committee was the vehicle by which the National Cabinet was brought to accept a tariff policy.

The committee's report advocated a 10 per cent general tariff and the establishment of an Import Duties Advisory Committee as the machinery for imposing higher selective duties.† This proposal differed from the plan worked out by the Conservative Party's research department because of the need to make concessions to the free traders on the committee. Runciman, the President of the Board of Trade and a Liberal who had been converted to protection, acted as a bridge between the two groups on the committee by suggesting to Chamberlain that he should use Keynes's idea of a 10 per

* *Times*, 28 September 1931, reprinted in *Essays in Persuasion* (*Collected Writings*, Vol. IX), pp. 243–4. Keynes later made his practical proposals clear to the Prime Minister, the Cabinet, and the Treasury in 'Notes on the Currency Question' (below, pp. 101, 103). Prem. 1/97, Henderson to MacDonald, 26 September 1931; Cab. 58/169, 'The Problems arising from the suspension of gold payments', 24 and 25 September 1931, and MacDonald Papers 1/180, 'Notes on the Balance of Payments', 21 January 1932. A later version of the last appears in Henderson, *The Inter-War Years and Other Papers*, pp. 89–90. Keynes much approved of this memorandum and sent it to the Bank of England (Keynes Papers, Keynes to Henderson, 17 February 1932).

† Cab. 27/467, Cabinet Committee on Balance of Trade, Minutes, memoranda and report. There is some evidence to suggest Chamberlain was genuinely concerned about the balance-of-payments position (Feiling, *Neville Chamberlain*, p. 195; Drummond, *Imperial Economic Policy 1917–1939*, p. 177n). Drummond points out that a tariff and a floating exchange rate are inconsistent policies given the likely joint effects on employment and the trade balance (pp. 177–9).

cent revenue tariff as the basis of legislation.[46] When Chamberlain invoked Keynes in support of the revenue tariff, however, Phillips of the Treasury pointed out that Keynes was no longer in favour of this policy.[47] Samuel thought that Keynes should be asked to give evidence to the committee, but Chamberlain turned this down, allowing Samuel only to 'consult . . . economists on particular points provided [he] made it clear that the inquiry was purely personal'.[48] This conformed with the advice offered by Chamberlain's secretary, Fergusson, who suggested that 'once economists are let loose on a topic of this kind, they are sure to disagree and your committee will be side-tracked into academic discussions'.[49]

Samuel consulted Layton, Stamp, and Keynes, and recorded their views in a memorandum of dissent to the committee's report. According to Samuel, Stamp

favour[ed] an all-round tariff, but mainly with the object of 'redistributing incomes'. It should only be temporary, and he holds strongly that it should be on imports of every class, with no exceptions.

Mr. Keynes is 'not now worrying about the Balance of Trade'. In his opinion the Government need take no special action in regard to it. He had been in favour of an all-round tariff, but the currency depreciation is doing what he wanted to do by that means, and better. Circumstances might, however, arise in the future which would change the situation and make some restriction advisable. If so, it would be better effected by a system of licences. And it is possible that budgetary or political conditions might be found to require a tariff for revenue.[50]

In his memorandum of dissent Snowden objected to the economic assumptions of the report, particularly to the fact that capital movements had been ignored. He also complained, with some justice, that the Board of Trade memoranda supplied to the committee were 'tendentious in their character and clearly aimed at supporting the case for tariffs'.[51]

Despite the disagreement within the committee and the Cabinet, the committee's tariff proposals provided the basis for the Import Duties Bill which Chamberlain introduced on 4 February. This was only possible without the resignation of the four dissenting ministers by the use of an unprecedented expedient, suggested by Chamberlain, whereby the four concerned were allowed to record their dissent and subsequently to speak against the Bill in Parliament.[52] The Import Duties Act imposed a general 10 per cent duty on all goods except basic foodstuffs, raw materials, and goods already subject to duty; it also provided for an independent advisory committee to recommend higher duties for specific products.

Chamberlain regarded the tariff as a potential weapon to promote rationalisation in such industries as iron and steel and cotton.[53] His efforts in this direction did not, however, meet with a great deal of success. He first asked the Import Duties Advisory Committee to consider a tariff on iron and steel. The committee immediately recommended a temporary duty of $33\frac{1}{3}$ per cent for three months, informing the industry that 'provided the industry was prepared to carry through a satisfactory scheme of reorganisation, it was their intention to recommend ... such a measure of protection as was necessary to make that scheme effective and in the meantime to continue the existing temporary duty'. Although after a second three months' temporary duty the industry had still not come up with any scheme, the committee, with the government's agreement, offered to extend the duty for two years. Early in 1933 the National Committee of the industry put up what was, in its own words, 'a scheme for establishing the machinery whereby a reorganisation may be carried out rather than a scheme of reorganisation itself'. Chamberlain publicly welcomed this in a White Paper, but the industry's general reaction was apathetic. Once the National Committee and the Import Duties Committee had persuaded the industry to accept the scheme in 1934, the government made the tariff permanent. It would therefore be difficult to maintain that the tariff 'weapon' had been effective in promoting rationalisation. As the Import Duties Committee pointed out, 'the threat of withdrawing protection would not greatly alarm the leaders of the industry for they appreciate the political difficulty of plunging it again into serious depression'.[54]

In 1935 the tariff was a more effective weapon in bargaining with the Continental Iron and Steel Cartel,* but this was hardly rationalisation. Although the tariff undoubtedly encouraged investment in the steel industry (particularly after the tariff was made permanent), this was not a consequence of government-sponsored rationalisation. Furthermore, other factors were at work in promoting recovery in the industry during the 1930s, notably the rapid growth of the motor industry and rearmament.[55]

In the cotton industry progress was even slower; its problems of surplus capacity, of numerous small firms in different sections of the industry, and poor long-term prospects, were more acute than in the iron and steel industry. A 1934 rationalisation scheme for the spinning section of the industry required lengthy negotiations between the Board of Trade and the industry's representatives, as well as an Act of Parliament, before it could come into operation in late 1936. Even so, like the iron and steel scheme, it was 'only a prelude ... to consideration by the industry of other measures'.[56] Not until 1937, when prospects brightened briefly, were proposals for the whole cotton industry framed. Again lengthy negotiations followed and an Act of Parliament was required to overcome opposition within the industry, which increased in the first half of 1938 when demand had fallen off once more. Soon after the Act was passed war broke out.[57]

Thus, the National Government's efforts to promote rationalisation in the iron and steel and cotton industries met with little more success than the efforts of its predecessor. Indeed, the experience with the tariff bore out the fears of the Economic Advisory Council committee on the iron and steel industry in 1930.[58] Nor can the steps taken in these industries be regarded

* It was more rapidly effective than the government had anticipated (T. 160/951/F 14140/1, Waterfield to Fergusson and Chancellor, 'Iron and Steel Duties', 20 April 1935).

as innovations in economic management. The advances toward modern economic management made under the National Government lay more in the macroeconomic field of monetary and financial policy. As we shall see in the rest of this chapter and its successor, the initiatives in these matters came from civil servants. We shall also see that it was through them that the economists serving on the Economic Advisory Council and the Committee on Economic Information made their views known in Whitehall and had an indirect influence on the policies pursued.

The new monetary policy

As soon as Britain left the gold standard, MacDonald, acting on his desire to 'enlist every brain',[59] appointed an Advisory Committee on Financial Questions which included several Economic Advisory Council members. This committee met regularly until March 1932, but by the time it produced a report on sterling policy, the Treasury had formed its own view about the future management of sterling. Henderson and Keynes, however, were involved in the Treasury's discussions.

The Prime Minister's Advisory Committee initially consisted of Brand, Layton, McKenna, Lord Macmillan, Stamp, and Henderson (secretary). Salter joined at the end of September, Keynes in November. Since the Prime Minister had asked for 'something in the nature of an agenda of the financial problems from both the domestic and the international standpoint', the first meeting of the committee was devoted to general discussion.[60] There are no minutes of the next two meetings, but Henderson recorded their drift in a letter to the Prime Minister and in a memorandum for the committee. He told MacDonald that differences of opinion had delayed production of a report, but the committee was 'unanimous in holding that it would be a great mistake if the Bank of England were to make it their aim to return to the gold standard at the old parity as soon as circumstances permit it'. To prevent the Bank from undertaking such a commitment, the committee urged the Cabinet to make an early decision to tell the Bank not to do so. Henderson also said that he and some other members of the committee thought that since sterling was depreciated, the government should not impose a tariff: the effects of one had already been achieved, and any additional attack on foreign exporters might provoke retaliation.[61]

The committee's opposition to an early return to gold was reiterated in Henderson's memorandum and at the committee's meeting on 29 September which MacDonald attended. The memorandum mentioned a difference of opinion over whether 'we should aim at ultimately restoring the pound to a gold basis with a new and lower parity, or at securing the adoption of a standard of value of a type designed to keep the purchasing power of money over commodities stable'. The latter would allow other countries which had 'suffered like ourselves from the instability of the price level in recent years' to opt for a link with sterling rather than with gold. Henderson stressed, however, that this difference of opinion had 'no material bearing on any question of immediate policy, since we are agreed that for the time being we should pursue a waiting policy and allow sterling to settle at whatever level circumstances suggest is most appropriate'. As far as international action was concerned the committee suggested an international conference to explore the questions of price stabilisation, war debts, and reparations. With respect to immediate problems there was some dispute over exchange controls and tariffs, but general agreement that pegging the exchanges within fairly wide limits was 'worth considering'.[62] At the 29 September meeting the committee, after pointing out that the question of long-term policy was now a matter for the government rather than the Bank, told MacDonald that the Bank should 'as a provisional policy endeavour to keep sterling within certain limits, by buying sterling at the lower limit and buying foreign currencies at the higher'; the government should invite the Bank to state its view on the limits within which sterling should be held.[63]

At the 26 November meeting Keynes arrived with MacDonald, who had made him a member of the committee and circulated his 'Notes on the Currency Question' to the committee and to some members of the Cabinet. The committee did not, however, discuss the memorandum at any length, unlike the Treasury, for whom the memorandum had originally been written.[64]

In January MacDonald asked the committee 'whether they thought the time had come when a deliberate policy should be pursued with regard to the pound sterling, and if so what kind of policy they suggested'. The committee agreed to 'meet together to thrash the matter out and prepare a statement of their views'.[65] A draft statement went to the Prime Minister in February, recommending that Bank rate should be lowered from the 6 per cent in force since Britain left gold. The committee was still opposed to a return to gold at the old parity, and favoured consolidation of the sterling area, though not by formal discussion at the forthcoming Ottawa Imperial Economic Conference.[66] Differences of opinion over other matters persisted: Henderson disliked the idea of keeping the pound down, whereas the others thought that sterling should not be allowed to rise until world prices had risen substantially.[67] As the final report shows, Henderson did not succeed in convincing his fellow committee members.[68]

In the meantime, in line with the Advisory Committee's suggestion of a waiting policy, MacDonald had told ministers on 10 November that they should not attempt to state when the pound could be stabilised or when an international conference on the monetary situation could be arranged. Ministers 'would be on safe ground if they confined themselves to the immediate need of balancing the Budget and maintaining the value of the pound sterling'.[69] The government sought the views of the Governor of the Bank early in December and then asked the Treasury for a memorandum on the currency question.

By this time the Treasury had been discussing the currency question for several weeks. Although before the suspension of the gold standard the senior Treasury officials had been firm believers in making strenuous efforts to maintain the gold standard, afterwards they immediately began to consider alternatives to the gold standard and the question of an appropriate exchange rate for sterling.* In line with this they asked Hawtrey, Henderson, and Keynes for their views.

Henderson apparently first became involved by being asked by Hopkins to comment on Hawtrey's case for pegging the pound initially at $3.40 and then raising (or lowering) it *pari passu* with the world price level. Hawtrey chose $3.40, a 30 per cent devaluation of the pound, on the assumption that there was 'tolerable' equilibrium between wages and prices in 1925, while world prices had fallen approximately 30 per cent since then. Henderson objected to the notion of an equilibrium exchange rate on which this argument was based. He also objected to as large a devaluation as 30 per cent because of its effect on the cost of living and hence on wages. His own 'unscientific and judgmatic' approach stressed that the fall of the pound was 'pre-eminently a disturbing factor' in the world economy. Since he also 'could not believe that it would be healthy for the exporting industries to have an immoderate bounty', he favoured depreciation of 15–20 per cent, which 'seems to me as much in the way of a windfall as it is ever good for anyone to get, and as much in the way of a disturbance as a strained world economic system can cope with'.[70]

Early in October Leith-Ross wrote to both Henderson and Keynes. He referred to the view, whose wide acceptance he attributed to Keynes, that if France and America observed 'the rules of the game' the international gold standard would work properly, and asked the two economists for a statement of the practical measures that should now be taken.[71] Henderson replied on 16 October with a memorandum which he admitted was 'not very helpful' on the question of what France and America could be asked to do, but did give his views on a stabilisation policy. He was against any stabilisation of the pound at a definite parity and suggested an interim policy of pegging the pound at $3.90 by means of Keynes's *Tract on Monetary Reform* scheme of variable selling prices for gold announced from time to time by the Bank of England and altered in response to gold flows. The advantages of such a policy would be a fair measure of exchange stability and a free hand as to future policy: the options of an eventual return to gold and of a currency managed so as to stabilise the price level would be left open.[72]

Henderson gave several reasons in his memoranda for favouring a current exchange rate of $3.90:

Howson, *Domestic Monetary Management in Britain 1919–38*, pp. 82–6 and Appendix 4. Such questions had not been considered when the decision to return to the gold standard at pre-war parity in 1925 had been taken (Moggridge, *The Return to Gold, 1925* and *British Monetary Policy 1924–1931*, Ch. 3).

(1) A lower value of the pound would lessen the improvement in the balance of payments (reckoned in gold prices) by reducing revenue from exports (in the short run) and from fixed-interest investments abroad.

(2) A low pound would cause inflation, by substantially raising, in turn, import prices, the cost of living, and wages. He estimated that a 30 per cent depreciation would raise the cost of living by 10 per cent.

(3) A low value of the pound might adversely affect confidence and therefore induce withdrawals by foreign holders of sterling.

(4) Any substantial depreciation of the pound would depress gold (i.e. world) prices and aggravate financial insolvency abroad.

Keynes sent his 'Notes on the Currency Question' to Leith-Ross on 20 November. He suggested an Imperial Currency Conference in order to form an Empire sterling standard which other countries might later join. There were three ways in which this standard could be managed:

(1) By carrying on as at present, allowing frequent moderate fluctuations in the exchange around $3.85 (the current level) with the Bank stepping in secretly to prevent extreme fluctuations;

(2) By deciding upon a new parity and returning to a strict gold standard at that parity;

(3) By fixing sterling within broad limits in terms of a price standard.

In favour of (1) and against (2) were the many uncertainties in the present situation: no definite step should be taken until the reparations problem had been solved. The memorandum argued for (3) along the lines of the *Treatise on Money* and the *Tract on Monetary Reform*.[73]

In deciding the present and future value of sterling, four criteria were available:

(1) prevention of inflation, which would indicate a present rate of $3.75–$4;

(2) reduction of the burden of the national debt ($3);

(3) maximising the benefit to the balance of payments ($3.50–$3.75);

(4) raising the prices of agricultural products and raw materials to at least their 1929 level so as to restore prosperity in the primary-producing countries and hence increase Britain's trade. This was particularly to be recommended if a sterling area was to be formed; it would require a present exchange rate of $3.40 to $3.50, and a future policy of managing sterling on the basis of an index of prices of the main internationally traded raw commodities.

The last of these criteria was Keynes's recommendation.[74]

Henderson wrote to Keynes about the memorandum 'agree[ing] of course with your old "Tract on Monetary Reform" proposal for variable gold prices', but 'perturbed lest you may prejudice the consideration of something that is possible by mixing it up . . . with something that is quite impossible', namely the price-index standard of value. He also thought the bottom of a severe slump was not the time to start a policy of price stabilisation; and he repeated his contention that 'we must be content . . . with the immediate object of restoring a satisfactory competitive position relatively to other producers, and I feel certain in my bones that 15 to 20 per cent is fully enough for this'.[75]

Keynes's memorandum provoked considerable comment in the Treasury. Hopkins wrote a long memorandum on Keynes's views, and when the Cabinet asked the Chancellor of the Exchequer for a Treasury memorandum, the Treasury decided to use Hopkins's memorandum as the basis for it.[76] Although Hopkins initially doubted the feasibility of pegging the exchange rate Phillips was less sceptical. Phillips was also more willing to consider the possibility that Britain might never return to the gold standard. Once Phillips, Hopkins, and Waley began to redraft Hopkins's memorandum, a significant shift of view towards management of sterling appeared.[77] Although Hopkins and Phillips agreed with Henderson's objection to Keynes's scheme that the bottom of a world slump was not the best time to put it into operation, they were in favour, as Henderson was not, of managing sterling with prices as the criterion. Where they differed from Keynes was in wishing to see a substantial rise in world prices before letting the pound rise, rather than committing themselves to such a course of action as soon as prices began to rise.

Between them, Hawtrey, Henderson, and Keynes raised a series of issues which the Treasury officials might, and did, take into account when deciding on the desirable value of sterling. In a January draft of the Treasury memorandum Hopkins adopted Henderson's arguments (and his words) to argue for an exchange rate of $3.60–3.70. In the final draft, however, although Phillips pointed out the advantages of a high value ($3.90) for the pound, he went on to the 'more theoretical . . . but for all that . . . extremely strong' and 'decisive' arguments for $3.40. These were that:

(1) The Treasury wanted to raise wholesale prices.
(2) The burden of the debt would be lower.
(3) The Treasury wanted to help exporters, and while the present state of world trade might prevent much increase of exports, depreciation was the best method of assistance available.

In future, if world prices continued to decline, the authorities might have to lower the pound further; they should not raise the exchange rate unless and until sterling prices had risen to at least 25 per cent above the September 1931 level.[78] Thus the Treasury wanted a low exchange rate in order to encourage a rise in domestic prices; they also wanted cheap money for the same reason.[79]

In these discussions an attempt to return to the gold standard was never seriously considered; Leith-Ross was the only senior Treasury official in favour of this policy and partly for this reason played only a minor role in the discussions. The Cabinet originally appointed a committee to discuss the Treasury memorandum, but owing to the disappearance of its records, it is not known whether the committee discussed either the Treasury memorandum or the Prime Minister's Advisory Committee's report on sterling policy, which was circulated at the same time. The government obviously accepted the Treasury memorandum as official policy since the Treasury proceeded to put its ideas into practice by establishing the Exchange Equalisation Account in the April 1932 budget and announcing the conversion of 5 per cent War Loan in June 1932. Bank rate was lowered to 2 per cent on the day the conversion was announced, where it remained until the outbreak of the second world war. This reduction was the last of a series which began on 18 February.[80]

By the spring of 1932 the fall of the Labour Government and the departure from the gold standard had resulted in a new framework of economic policy. Firstly, Britain now had a tariff, to which were soon to be added the Ottawa arrangements for imperial preference.[81] Secondly, and far more important, was the new monetary régime under which the Treasury was committed to managing the pound, both internally and externally, so as to promote British prosperity. In this new setting the Committee on Economic Information began its work.

CHAPTER 5

THE COMMITTEE ON
ECONOMIC INFORMATION 1932–9

The bottom of the depression was reached in 1932. Recovery began in the autumn when the housing boom, which was the most conspicuous feature of Britain's recovery, got under way. The recovery period lasted for five years; in late 1937 the American recession of that year spread to Britain, but its effects were soon countered by rearmament expenditure, which began to exert a substantial impact on the economy in 1938. How far the post-gold-standard policy changes in 1931 and 1932 were responsible for recovery has been a subject of debate ever since. Although the depreciation of sterling arrested the decline, it did not result in a significant rise in exports; the staple export trades remained depressed for most of the 1930s. Depreciation and the tariff substantially reduced imports but the big fall came late in 1932, *after* the beginning of recovery. A small post-'devaluation' burst of activity in the iron and steel and textile trades soon petered out. Although investment in iron and steel was encouraged by the tariff, most of the large post-tariff increases came in 1934 when the tariff was made permanent. In the meantime housebuilding had risen by 70 per cent, and the strongest explanation for recovery is that the introduction of cheap money set off the housing boom, and once employment began to rise in 1933, other factors, such as increased investment in the newer industries, operated to reinforce the expansion of output and employment.[1]

Although the role of cheap money in recovery has been a matter of dispute, that of budgetary policy has not. The British government, unlike its counterparts in Sweden and, under Roosevelt's 'New Deal', the United States, did not resort to deficit budgeting or loan-financed public works.[2] In spite of a great deal of pressure from economists and others, Britain publicly maintained an orthodox position on the budgetary issue throughout the 1930s. Campaigns for an expansionary policy were launched in *The Times* in 1933 and 1937. Keynes's contribution to the first of these was 'The Means to Prosperity'; in both campaigns he and other Economic Advisory Council members played a leading role. At the end of 1934 Lloyd George launched his 'New Deal', calling for an increase in public expenditure and other measures such as agricultural development. In each case the government felt obliged to prepare a reply in the form of either a statement in the House of Commons or, in the case of Lloyd George's proposals, a substantial document prepared by a special Cabinet committee. But there was no apparent change in policy. This gap between the government's attitude and the economists' views has led most writers on the period to conclude that the economists' contribution to policy-making in the 1930s was negligible – a verdict which has been extended to the activities of the Economic Advisory Council in this period.

The Economic Advisory *Council* did not survive the 1931 crisis. It met once in January 1932, when MacDonald suggested that since its discussions had been 'sometimes rather diffuse' and ineffective, the Council should meet less frequently, leaving more of its work to committees. In the previous couple of years the work of the committees had been 'of the greatest value' to the government, especially the report on the balance of payments by the Committee on Economic Information.[3] As it subsequently turned out, this Committee* effectively replaced the defunct Council, which was given an official burial in 1938.[4] The Committee began to meet regularly in March 1932 and continued to do so until the outbreak of the second world war when it was transformed first into Stamp's Survey of War Plans and then into what became the Economic Section of the Cabinet Office.

The Economic Advisory Council's claims as an influence on economic policy and as the forerunner of future development rest on the work of the Committee on Economic Information. Unlike its parent body, it had a modest brief 'to supervise the preparation of monthly reports to the Economic Advisory Council on the economic situation and to advise as to the continuous study of economic development'; it was intended initially to complement the advisory function of the Council.[5] At the time of its establishment, in July 1931, its members were Stamp (chairman), Citrine, Cole, Keynes, Lewis, and Henderson (secretary). In January 1932 it was enlarged to include Sir Arthur Salter and Sir Ernest Simon, with Sir Sydney Chapman, Chief Economic Adviser to the Government, attending meetings.[6] Thereafter membership was more or less constant. Chapman attended only the first meeting in 1932, but his successor, Leith-Ross, attended throughout 1932-9. Phillips joined in October 1935; and both Treasury officials took an active part in the proceedings. Henderson remained a member of the Committee after his resignation as Secretary of the Economic Advisory Council in May 1934, when Hemming and Debenham became the Committee's secretaries, with Debenham taking over Henderson's job of writing the reports. Dennis Robertson joined early in 1936, having previously served on the Sub-Committee on the Trend of Unemployment. Simon resigned in May 1936;† Citrine attended only a few meetings in 1932-3.

After a meeting to discuss procedure the Committee began to prepare the first of its regular (but not monthly) 'Surveys of the Economic Situation' in March 1932. In these surveys the intention was to 'draw . . . attention to

---

* To distinguish the Committee on Economic Information from the several other committees mentioned in this chapter, 'Committee' referring to it is capitalised.

† Salter says that Simon broke the rule of secrecy imposed on the C.E.I. by mentioning an opinion of the Committee when on a deputation to a minister from an organisation which he represented (*Slave of the Lamp*, p. 87).

salient features of the period under review and to the tendencies of the immediate future'. The method of procedure was for the Committee to hold a meeting to decide what topics it would discuss in the next report and then for Henderson (Debenham after May 1934) to prepare a draft report for consideration at further meetings. It was agreed that reports would be written 'on the basis that each member acquiesced in what was stated rather than necessarily approved of the exact wording adopted'.[7]

This may account for the striking fact that the Committee's twenty-seven reports maintained a consistent viewpoint which theoretical disagreements between the economists did not disturb. The reports usually comprised a brief factual survey of the situation and a set of policy proposals for dealing with the authorities' current problems. For the first three years the reports reflected the common concern of Keynes, Henderson, Salter, and Stamp that the government should actively promote recovery at home and abroad by means of cheap money, public works, and international monetary measures designed to give debtor countries relief from the pressures which had led them to adopt beggar-my-neighbour trade policies.[8] They also reflected Keynes's current theoretical preoccupation, the preparation of his *General Theory of Employment, Interest and Money*, which was published in February 1936. Most of the reports 'bore the impress of Keynes',[9] even during Keynes's absence through illness in 1937. By this time the Committee was concentrating on advocating Keynesian measures, particularly the maintenance of low long-term interest rates and counter-cyclical public works, to combat the U.K. recession which in 1935 they had forecast would begin two or three years later. The international outlook remained unsettled, however, and many of the reports of 1936 and 1937 discussed international economic problems. On top of these came the problems posed by rearmament and preparations for war, which formed the subjects of the last two reports. This was partly at the request of the government, who had also sought the Committee's advice earlier on other issues such as commercial policy. The focus of attention in the following pages will be on the effects in Whitehall of the advice tendered on these various topics.

The documentary evidence is primarily the memoranda to be found in the papers of Hopkins, Phillips, and Leith-Ross. All three wrote commentaries on the reports for each other and for the Chancellor, to whose attention they also drew other relevant memoranda. These other memoranda had usually been prepared as part of the normal process of economic policy-making in the Treasury; they consisted of briefs for the Chancellor to use in Cabinet discussion, suggestions for replies to press and parliamentary criticisms, papers arising from budget preparations or debt management, and longer statements of Treasury policy for circulation to the Cabinet or inter-departmental committees.[10] These officials also argued among themselves about policy issues, particularly about those new problems thrown up by changing circumstances. The outcome was often the recommendation of a novel solution, usually devised by Phillips. Although the government's continued adherence to an orthodox line on budgetary policy served to convince the members of the Committee on Economic Information that their advice had been ignored, the major conclusion of this chapter is that by 1937 the macroeconomic position which we associate with Keynes's *General Theory* had altered the thinking of the most important policy-making civil servants in the Treasury. These men were prepared to rethink the *theoretical* basis of the policies which they had so far pursued, and to adjust their policy recommendations to ministers accordingly. Sir Austin Robinson, who was involved in the war-time transformation of the Committee on Economic Information into the Economic Section of the Cabinet Office, believes the Committee's importance was that 'the Treasury was effectively prevented from living in a private Ivory Tower of its own. It had to defend its policies with a jury of very competent and potentially vocal outside critics, and if it could not defend them it had to change them'.[11] This development also provides an explanation for the apparent rapidity with which Britain moved over to being a highly managed economy on Keynesian lines after 1939.

The Committee on Economic Information and the cheap money policy 1932-5

The Treasury's cheap money policy involved (i) the establishment of low long-term interest rates by the conversion of 5 per cent War Loan, (ii) the management of sterling by the Exchange Equalisation Account, and (iii) the embargo on overseas loans, imposed initially for the purposes of the conversion scheme but maintained for the rest of the 1930s. The Committee on Economic Information approved wholeheartedly of the first two elements of the Treasury's policy, and consistently stressed the importance of maintaining low long-term interest rates. However, in 1934 the Committee began to press for a relaxation of the embargo in order to promote exports, and in 1935 it tentatively advocated exchange stabilisation for the same purpose.

The Committee's Second Report, its first survey of the economic situation, dated 8 March 1932, described at some length the marked deterioration in the state of the world economy since Britain's departure from the gold standard, and the beggar-my-neighbour policies which this had provoked. It dealt more briefly with Britain's economic position, which in that setting 'could hardly be expected . . . [to] be satisfactory'. Against the effects of a post-'devaluation' spurt in some export trades, notably iron and steel and textiles, had to be set not only the continuing decline in world trade but also the deflationary effects of the economy policy and high interest rates. The Committee noted, however, three more hopeful signs: first, the growing strength of sterling, which opened out the prospects of cheaper money in the

U.K., a recovery of the exchange rate,* and revival of Britain's power to lend abroad; second, the reflationary measures in the U.S.A., namely the establishment of the Reconstruction Finance Corporation and the passing of the Glass–Steagall Act; third, the flooding of France with gold. The Committee concluded the report with a recommendation in favour of cheap money, which it thought could outweigh the deflationary factors.†

When the conversion scheme was announced the Committee welcomed it heartily, seeing it and the Lausanne Agreement on Reparations as the outstanding events of recent months and the 'most hopeful development[s] since the depression began'. It added to its report of July 1932 a memorandum by Keynes entitled 'A Note on the Conversion Scheme in relation to the Rate of Interest', in which he congratulated the authorities on the conversion scheme and argued for a further reduction in the long-term interest rate. Keynes urged maintenance of a lower rate by means of a policy of supplying the market with securities of different types and maturities in order to satisfy its psychologically based preferences. Leith-Ross circulated this memorandum and drafts of the report's comments on Lausanne and the conversion to his Treasury colleagues.‡

During the winter of 1932–3 the Committee concentrated on trying, unsuccessfully, to persuade the government to back up the cheap money policy with a more expansionary budgetary policy. It regarded the housing boom, then getting under way, as a consequence of low interest rates and cheap money and as a reason for increasing efforts to promote recovery. Housebuilding, especially the building of working-class houses, should be encouraged by low interest rates and other more direct methods.[12]

By the second half of 1933 'practically every economic signpost in this country point[ed] to a slow but steady and sustained recovery'.[13] This was brought home to the Cabinet in October by the Committee's Ninth Report, which Chamberlain commended to his colleagues. The report concluded that 'The economic outlook for Great Britain seems to us more hopeful than it has been at any time since the depression began.' The President of the Board of Trade agreed with this on the basis of his department's own investigations, and Chamberlain suggested that his colleagues should read the whole of the second part of the report.§ In this the Committee

* This might help to raise world prices, and the adverse effect on the U.K. economy would not be serious if there was cheap money.
† The Committee noted in its 3rd Report, of May 1932, that the improvement in the export trades was short-lived.
‡ The bulk of this report (the 4th) advocated Henderson's plan for an international note issue, on which see below, pp. 114–21. Some of the report, but not its Appendix, is reprinted below. Keynes published his memorandum in the *Economic Journal* in September 1932, as 'A Note on the Long-term Rate of Interest in relation to the Conversion Scheme', and he sent an offprint to Hopkins. This and copies of the C.E.I. drafts and Keynes's memorandum are in T. 175/93. On the place of the memorandum in the evolution of Keynes's ideas, see Moggridge and Howson, 'Keynes on Monetary Policy, 1910–46', *Oxford Economic Papers*, July 1974.
§ Cab. 23/77, Cabinet 61 (33) 10, 8 November 1933. The Board of Trade submitted regular reports to the Cabinet on the state of trade in particular industries, based on reports from

argued that recovery was 'the fruits of the systematic pursuit of a policy of cheap money during the past year and a half'. Investment was interest-elastic, and increased production of capital goods was essential to recovery.

The easier terms on which capital can be borrowed serves to offset the diminished profitability of capital enterprise, and, as soon accordingly as the conviction becomes established that constructional costs have touched their lowest point, the demand for constructional goods begins to revive . . . The movement towards lower interest rates [in Great Britain] . . . has made industrial and commercial concerns less anxious to keep their resources liquid, and has given them confidence that new capital can be obtained when required on reasonable terms.

The Committee regarded the housing boom, and the accompanying increase in the purchase and production of consumer durables, as the most important factors in Britain's recovery.[14]

The Treasury shared this belief in the effectiveness of monetary policy and attributed the housing boom and hence recovery to cheap money.[15] Since the Treasury officials shared the Committee's fears that a decline in housebuilding would precipitate another slump, they were also anxious to maintain cheap money throughout the later stages of recovery.* They also agreed with the Committee's recommendation of relaxing the embargo on overseas loans.

At the beginning of 1934, after the devaluation of the American dollar and with the continuing unpromising outlook on the Continent, the prospects for Britain's overseas trade were not encouraging. The Committee pointed out that continuance of recovery depended on further domestic expansion, but that such a recovery could not be expected to reduce unemployment below 1,500,000. It was, therefore, 'a vital interest of this country that there should be a revival of world trade'. Although it was hoped that this would happen sooner or later, it would not come about immediately. In the meantime, 'all reasonable steps should be taken to promote foreign demand for British exports'; in particular the embargo on new overseas issues in London should be relaxed. Phillips told the Chancellor that this argument was 'well worth reading'. He thought the unemployment estimate was not unduly pessimistic, and pointed out that he and his colleagues had already been advocating a reconsideration of the embargo policy on 'substantially the same lines'.[16]

During 1934 recovery slowed down. Since to the Committee this 'suggest[ed that] the beneficial effects of [the reduction in interest rates in 1932] . . . are gradually working themselves out', it put in another recommendation for relaxation of the embargo. This would improve the financial position of sterling area and other customers, whose governments would then be able 'to pursue a more liberal policy both in the field of foreign

businessmen in these industries. All the C.E.I. reports were circulated to the Cabinet, who discussed half of them.
* This is discussed fully below, pp. 134-45.

exchange and in that of industrial development'. It would probably benefit Britain's exports both by increasing consumption in these countries and by relaxing 'the pressure to export which has had such disastrous effects on those branches of our economy with which these exports compete'.[17]

The Treasury's argument for the same policy measure was on the following lines:

(1) the embargo was no longer needed to serve the purposes for which it had been imposed;

(2) 'world recovery [was] so much bound up with financial solvency and lower interest rates';

(3) increased prosperity abroad would mean more British exports, even though the connection between increased foreign lending and increased exports was not close.*

The embargo had been imposed in June 1932 to ensure the success of the conversion operation by keeping competitors out of the London capital market. At that time the ban covered *all* new issues. By the beginning of 1933 it had been narrowed to new foreign issues and some types of Empire issues (optional conversions). By the end of 1933 the important conversion operations of the British and some Dominion Governments had been carried out; the sterling exchange did not need protection (in fact it was threatening to become too strong) and exports had stagnated. Hopkins, Phillips, and Fisher therefore tried to persuade the Chancellor to do away with the embargo on foreign issues. To maintain 'a much more elastic control', all foreign issues should pass through a committee which would if necessary give preference to loans whose proceeds were likely to be spent in Britain.†

Chamberlain, however, was not in favour of relaxation, and the Governor of the Bank was not enthusiastic. According to his biographer, Norman 'disliked [the embargo] though ready in the circumstances to have it enforced by legislation if necessary'.[18] The Treasury memoranda show that the idea of legislation was the Governor's, and that the Treasury regarded Norman as 'the most uncompromising advocate' of the embargo.[19] One reason for the Governor's attitude was that he saw the choice as between 'a complete embargo . . . and complete freedom'.[20] Phillips conceded that control could not be complete while transactions in existing securities were allowed, but

---

* This was a significant shift, as the Treasury officials realised, from the neoclassical view of the 1920s which appears in, e.g., the report of the C.C.R. Committee on Overseas Loans. (See Moggridge, *British Monetary Policy 1924–1931*, pp. 217–18). It implied that the full-employment assumption that characterised the notorious 'Treasury view' of the 1920s had been dropped.

† T. 175/84, Fisher, Hopkins, and Phillips to Chancellor, 30 November 1933; T. 175/84, Note by Hopkins, 16 October 1934; see also T. 160/533/F 13296/01, Hopkins to Fisher and Fergusson, 6 February 1933; and T. 175/84, Phillips to Hopkins, 7 June 1933. The Treasury officials recognised that the effect of foreign lending in keeping the exchanges down would be reduced if the lending led to increased British exports.

control was not extended to such transactions as the Governor desired, simply because it was much easier to control new issues.[21] The Governor's other reason for wishing to extend control to transactions in existing securities by means of legislation was the danger of speculative movements of capital.* Chamberlain's reasons for continuing the embargo were in part at least political.[22] After the Capital Issues Committee had been set up in 1936, the Treasury managed to persuade Chamberlain's successor as Chancellor, Sir John Simon, to permit some relaxation in 1938, for the reasons given earlier. Chamberlain and Norman were still not enthusiastic.[23]

It is doubtful whether the removal or relaxation of the embargo would have had any effect in increasing overseas lending. Later experience with controls on international capital movements tends to suggest they are not very effective, and the low level of foreign lending during this period may well have been due to investors' pessimism rather than to the far from complete embargo on overseas loans.[24]

Unlike the embargo recommendation, the Committee's next suggestion for promoting exports, stabilisation of the sterling exchange, did not accord with the Treasury's views. It was made in May 1935, when domestic activity had recovered from the slight setback observed in 1934, but when the outlook for external trade was still discouraging. The Committee feared that these poor prospects might worsen if the gold bloc countries abandoned their present exchange rates, as seemed bound to happen sooner or later. When this happened the U.K. should cooperate in an attempt to secure stable exchanges, by setting a tentative gold parity, though this would have to be variable so as to prevent any subordination of internal credit policy to exchange requirements.[25]

Henderson did not approve of this proposal. He told Stamp that it belonged to 'the category of eccentric currency proposals, which we ought to be careful not to overdo'; he also criticised it as both 'hypothetical', that is irrelevant to current conditions, and 'dubious on merits'.[26] Phillips (and Hopkins) agreed with Henderson. In June 1935 Phillips, referring the Chancellor to an article by Henderson in the *Lloyds Bank Review*, pointed out that 'We have far more to lose, and are more likely to lose, from a setback in our internal recovery than we are likely to gain in the field of foreign trade.' Even temporary stabilisation, while 'definitely refusing to commit ourselves to any change in our existing credit policy', was out of the question. Current exchange rates were out of equilibrium; there were dangers of speculative movements of funds; and furthermore:

* T. 160/533/F 13296/02, Hopkins to Chancellor, 15 July 1933; T. 175/84, Fisher *et al.* to Chancellor, 30 November 1933. Norman also, in 1932, advocated some form (unspecified) of control over all new issues (in order to prevent speculation) because the 'traditional warning signals' (an adverse movement of the exchanges on the gold standard) were absent (T. 160/533/F 13296/01, Waterfield to Fisher, 10 November 1932; Fisher to Hopkins and Fergusson, 'Capital Embargo', 11 November 1932; Phillips to Hopkins, 15 November 1932; see also Clay, *Lord Norman*, pp. 459-60, 464-5).

The country has, in the last two or three years, benefited enormously from the liberal credit policy pursued by the Bank of England ... Having had to deal pretty closely with the people at the Bank for a long time past, I am of opinion that once a definite exchange figure is named ... their management of credit will be likely to become decidedly less liberal than at present.[27]

On these grounds Britain stayed off the gold standard for the rest of the 1930s.

The Keynes–Henderson plan and the World Economic Conference of 1933

One of the Committee's proposals that attracted a great deal of serious consideration within the Treasury was the Keynes–Henderson plan for an international note issue, advocated most persuasively in the Committee's Fourth Report, of July 1932.

The origins of the plan

Given the internationalist bias of the most important members of the Committee, it is not surprising that they adopted the plan which Henderson originally put to the government as a proposal for the Lausanne Conference on reparations held in June–July 1932. Keynes had since the summer of 1931 been emphasising the benefits that could be gained by bold international cooperative action.[28] In its First Report the Committee had mentioned the need for 'plans for useful international action' to raise world prices and revive world trade; and in its Second and Third Reports it had dwelt at length upon the need to restart the flow of international lending presently dried up by fears of insolvency. However, the Committee did not make any detailed policy suggestions for the forthcoming Lausanne and Ottawa conferences because it decided that 'no advantage would be served ... in view of the fact that it would be necessary for the Government to reach decisions on questions of principle in regard to these conferences in the near future'. When the Lausanne Conference ended with an agreement to abolish reparations and a decision to ask the League of Nations to call a World Conference 'to decide upon the measures to solve the other economic and financial difficulties which are responsible for, and may prolong, the present world crisis', the Committee took the opportunity to propose Henderson's plan as a major part of the government's programme for this conference.*

---

* The conference eventually took place in London in June–July 1933, before which there had been discussions in Washington between American and British Treasury representatives and between Roosevelt and MacDonald in the spring of 1933. During the winter a preparatory committee of experts met in Geneva to prepare an agenda for the conference. The members were nominated by various governments, the Bank for International Settlements, and the League of Nations, and included Leith-Ross and Phillips. On the preparation and proceedings of the conference, see Foreign Relations of the United States: 1933, Vol. I (1950), pp. 452–762; H. Feis, 1933: Characters in Crisis (1966), Chs. 19–20; S. V. O. Clarke, The Reconstruction of the International Monetary System: The Attempts of 1922 and 1933 (1973), Ch. III; H. V. Hodson, Slump and Recovery 1929–1937 (1938), Ch. VI; and C. P. Kindleberger, The World in Depression 1929–1939 (1973), Ch. 9.

Henderson first showed his plan to Hopkins before Lausanne, in May 1932, when he had asked him: 'Would you look at the enclosed? Don't trouble to tell me it isn't practical politics. Assuming that it was, is there anything wrong with it?' The enclosed was 'A Monetary Proposal for Lausanne' suggesting that the Bank for International Settlements should issue notes which would be the equivalent of gold, thereby providing interest-free loans to governments who could use their new-found 'gold' to pay off external debts and/or carry out expansionary domestic policies. The conditions surrounding the note issue would be the adoption of a fixed parity, the removal of exchange restrictions, and the agreement to repay advances as prices rose towards their 1928 level. On any outstanding advances in excess of a country's current quota, interest should be paid at 5 per cent. The initial allotment to governments would be on the basis of some economic criterion, for example 50 per cent of the gold value of the country's exports in 1928, and the total issue would exceed the aggregate of such quotas by 5 per cent to strengthen the Bank's reserves.[29] The total issue would be about £1,000m gold.[30]

Hopkins passed Henderson's plan to Phillips, who was impressed: he saw it as 'a scientific attempt to widen the basis of credit in the world' by providing more credit and distributing it to potential users, namely governments short of cash. But he did not think it was practical politics.[31] Henderson replied to this that he would 'not be surprised if American opinion changed so rapidly in the next few months as to be ready to consider things that are certainly impracticable now'. At the cost of weakening its effectiveness, the scheme could be modified to meet American and French objections; for example, the interest-free advances could be distributed on the basis of existing gold reserves.[32]

Henderson's plan received more consideration during the discussions in Whitehall on the economic and monetary questions that might be raised at Lausanne. Leith-Ross thought the slender chances of acceptance would be destroyed if the proposal were launched at Lausanne, where 'as a matter of tactics . . . [he] suggested the British Government . . . take a strong line in demanding international action to raise the level of world prices without producing any specific plans'. While the conference was in progress, Keynes wrote to MacDonald that he was 'very strongly in favour' of the plan, which was 'exactly what the situation requires'. Henderson then wrote another memorandum on the plan for the Committee on Economic Information, who adopted it as the second half of its Fourth Report.[33]

A month later, MacDonald set up an Economic Advisory Council Committee on International Economic Policy, which included several members of the Committee on Economic Information, to 'advise him personally as to the points to which British policy [at the World Economic Conference] should be specifically directed'. At its first meeting this committee decided to look at the 'constructive proposals' in the Committee's Fourth Report, and included in its first report a version of the Henderson plan written by Blackett, Keynes, and Henderson. Under this scheme only governments or central banks of countries needing help would receive advances, at a gilt-edged rate of interest, subject to more or less the same conditions as before.[34]

For once, the Treasury made known some of its views on the plan to the Economic Advisory Council. In August 1932 Stamp told the Committee on Economic Information that discouraging 'individual official criticisms [of the Fourth Report] had been made to the powers that be'. Nevertheless, at a meeting at 10 Downing Street in September MacDonald assured the Committee on International Economic Policy that 'it was not his intention that their advice should simply be left on one side after criticisms had been passed upon it by the Departments'; he would see what could be done to give the committee an opportunity of 'ascertaining and replying to' departmental criticisms. As a result, 'in the exceptional circumstances . . . of the present case', the Chancellor gave the committee copies of a Treasury memorandum on the committee's first report and of a report by Leith-Ross and Phillips on the work of the Preparatory Committee for the World Economic Conference. After reading these the committee decided to recommend the more ambitious plan in the Fourth Report of the Committee on Economic Information, because it 'underst[ood] the Treasury have no criticisms to offer from the technical or economic standpoints but agree[d] there would be much to be said for . . . [the plan] if other important countries could be persuaded to accept it'. It also thought the Treasury overestimated the difficulty of acceptance.[35] Since it is known that the Treasury suggested a watered-down version of the Keynes–Henderson plan to the Americans in April 1933,[36] it is necessary to look more closely at the Treasury's words and deeds.

The Treasury's reactions to the plan

The aim of the Treasury's cheap money policy was to bring about a rise in U.K. prices. The importance of the World Economic Conference to the Treasury was that 'it enable[d] a plea to be made for international action with a view to raising wholesale commodity prices'. This was necessary because

Unless such an increase of prices occurs, the problems will remain, becoming more pressing as time passes . . . Failure to obtain agreement on monetary policy at the World Conference would . . . mean . . . that the financial deadlock caused by the low level of prices in each country . . . would be solved haphazard by a disorderly depreciation of currencies, involving widespread defaults or repudiation of debts and incalculable social and political repercussions.[37]

The difficulty facing the British government with respect to the conference was that if Britain advocated an international reflationary scheme France and the other countries still on the gold standard would not accept it, but since these countries were bound to take the opportunity to demand that

Britain return to the gold standard the government needed some positive counter-suggestion. The problem was compounded by the fact that the British government would not countenance participation in an international programme of public works.[38]

The Treasury's first reaction to the Henderson plan was that it was *too* impracticable to put forward. It told the Committee on International Economic Policy: 'If the U.K. could dictate conditions to the world at large, there would have been much to be said for these proposals . . . But . . . we shall find it difficult enough to obtain even a sympathetic hearing. The extreme novelty of the proposals is against them.' The Treasury officials therefore looked for 'a simpler and less ambitious plan dealing only with the existing stock of gold', which might be more acceptable to the French, and hence more likely to be discussed at the conference. They did not favour the plan put forward by the Committee on International Economic Policy in its first report because the changes weakened the effectiveness of Henderson's plan too much.[39] After discussion between Phillips, Leith-Ross, Hawtrey, Niemeyer (now at the Bank), and Kisch (Financial Adviser to the India Office), they came up with the 'Kisch Plan'.[40] Kisch described the purpose of his plan as:

A. The enlargement and redistribution of the gold basis of credit by international action so as to fortify the Banks of Issue in the debtor countries and enable the withdrawal of exchange restrictions, the discharge of debt services and the resumption of normal trading.
B. The safeguarding so far as possible against the recurrence of a similar gold mal-distribution in the future.

The governments of countries with surplus gold stocks would borrow gold from their central banks and use it to subscribe to an International Credit Corporation, which might be a subsidiary of the Bank for International Settlements or under its control. The new corporation would lend the gold at a low rate of interest to the governments of debtor countries, who would in turn sell it to their central banks, thus reducing the governments' indebtedness and improving the central banks' reserve positions. The effect 'would be to place purchasing power at the disposal of the debtor countries . . . so that they could again restart normal relations with the creditor countries'. The consequence would be 'a rise in gold and sterling prices'. Kisch did not spell out how this would come about. The plan was also weak on guarantees for creditors against loss by default, but 'this would be a detail which could without doubt be adjusted if the general idea should prove acceptable'.[41] The Kisch plan was thought to be a reasonable substitute for Henderson's because it would increase the effective world stock of gold by redistributing it, and yet would not involve creating a new currency. It also bore a superficial resemblance to a Monetary Normalisation Fund that had been suggested at the 1932 Stresa Conference on the difficulties of Central and Eastern European countries – a conference which had been chaired by Bonnet, the

French Minister of Finance.* Phillips also asked Henderson for his opinion; he was 'in favour of it [Kisch's plan] as might have been expected', but pointed out its weaknesses.† The other members of the Economic Advisory Council committees were not informed of its existence.[42]

By the end of 1932 Phillips had formulated 'his view of the objectives [the British government] should place before the Conference as antecedent to any question of our returning to the gold standard'. The objectives were:

(a) the maintenance and extension of the cheap money policy;
(b) far reaching practical reforms in the working of the gold standard, and especially in the ... [practice] of the Bank of France ...
(c) if possible some constructive proposal for securing that the reforms ... actually lead to a redistribution of the existing congested gold supplies in favour of the debtor nations whose supplies are exhausted.[43]

The Bank was asked for its views, and Phillips's comments on them are illuminating:

the Bank's [own] proposals come to (i) inability to stabilise; (ii) cheap and abundant money; (iii) a few frills [a general agreement to suspend sinking funds for a time].

On this basis the monetary side ... of the Conference ... will be completely nugatory. The discussions will be confined to a demand from gold countries for everyone to stabilise on gold and a politely worded refusal from non-gold countries to do this ...

We feel that it would be much more useful, if practicable, to get people's minds working on another range of ideas ... [in particular] the Kisch plan ...

It is clear that the scheme would not be acceptable to France and the United States at present, but it would get people's minds off the controversy of gold versus non-gold and direct them to the real point that debtor countries must be helped or they cannot continue to trade and that the help must come out of the clot of gold in Paris and New York.‡

* T. 172/1814, Phillips to Hopkins, 16 December 1932, and 'Prospects for the World Economic Conference', December 1932; F.O. 371/17304, Brief to Ministers for Bonnet's visit to Britain in March 1933. The Kisch plan also to some extent resembled the Kindersley plan discussed by the Bank and the Treasury in 1931, which envisaged the setting up of an International Credit Corporation to raise money from the public, particularly in America and France, and lend it as ten-year advances to governments, public authorities, or mortgage banks in other countries. It would be a private institution, subscribed to by leading banks in America, Britain, and France, and hence not under the control of the Bank for International Settlements. Like the later scheme, it was intended to redistribute gold from the United States and France. (T. 160/398/F 12377, Leith-Ross to Hopkins and Chancellor, 2 February 1931; T. 177/19, Resumé of different plans for an international financial institution, 20 December 1932).
† T. 188/56, Phillips to Kisch, Leith-Ross, and Hawtrey, 8 December 1932. One of Henderson's objections related to the role of Britain. Kisch had suggested that the U.K. could promise to return to gold once world prices had risen, remove the embargo on overseas loans, or actually contribute to the pool. Henderson pointed out it was 'illogical' for Britain to lend at all in a scheme intended to redistribute gold stocks.
‡ T. 172/1814, Phillips, 'World Economic Conference', 10 December 1932. Niemeyer was the only supporter of the scheme in the Bank. The Bank's other advisers dismissed both the Henderson and the Kisch plans as impracticable and were 'prepared to go rather materially farther than ... [the Treasury] ... in giving qualified undertakings as to stabilisation' (T. 172/1814, Hopkins to Chancellor, 12 December 1932; Phillips, 'World Economic Conference' 10 December 1932).

In line with this, and with an earlier suggestion that the Henderson plan should be discussed at the Preparatory Committee of Experts,[44] the subject of an International Credit Institute was raised at the second meeting in January. The resulting agenda for the conference mentioned the possibility of such a scheme. Although couched in vague terms, this was 'the first occasion on which any such suggestion . . . figured in an international document'.[45]

The next stage in the Treasury's preparation for the conference was inter-Treasury discussion. When Bonnet visited London in March the Treasury decided that since 'the critical test of our plan will be the attitude of the U.S.', it would be 'a waste of time . . . to discuss it with the French at this stage'.* It is hard to tell how optimistic the Treasury was about its plan at this time. At the end of the month, when commenting on the Committee on International Economic Policy's second report, Phillips did not seem very optimistic:

In the case of France, the whole mentality of the country must change before it accepts the Bank of International Settlements as the controller of world financial policy. In the case of the U.S.A. there is the objection that the Federal Reserve Bank is *not* a member of the Bank of International Settlements, and is *not* specially friendly to that body . . . An international note issuing authority is not the simple conception it might appear.†

However, Roosevelt's coming to power in the United States might open out new possibilities:

The real and only point is, *How would the present U.S.A. government regard the plan?* We are in complete ignorance at present.

If President Roosevelt showed signs of favouring an international note issue in preference to an international loan plan, then we ought to go for it.[46]

When economic discussions between the British and American Treasuries began at the end of March, the British representatives waited for a suitable opportunity to mention their plan. On 3 April the discussion turned on action to be taken to raise prices. Feis (Economic Adviser to the State Department) thought Keynes's proposal for an international note issue was unlikely to command general acceptance and was therefore impracticable. He favoured simultaneous action by several countries to initiate large public

---

* F.O. 371/17304, Leith-Ross to Vansittart, Brief prepared for ministers in connection with Bonnet's visit, 16 March 1933. Chamberlain did, however, mention the Henderson plan to Bonnet on 17 March, the day after he had seen Keynes in connection with 'The Means to Prosperity' which had been published in *The Times* on 13–16 March (F.O. 371/17304, Notes of meeting between Chamberlain and Bonnet, 17 March 1933; Keynes Papers, Keynes to Kahn, 20 March 1933).

Keynes's version of the plan in 'The Means to Prosperity' differed from Henderson's in that it suggested that no individual country's quota should exceed $450m (out of an aggregate of $5,000m) and that the governors of the international monetary institution should be elected by the participating governments.

† The protracted negotiations over the Keynes plan for a Clearing Union and the White Plan in 1942–4, which eventually resulted in the International Monetary Fund and the International Bank for Reconstruction and Development, amply demonstrate the truth of this last remark.

works schemes, and action to reduce trade restrictions. Lindsay (the British Ambassador in Washington) cabled home that he would like to know the government's attitude to such schemes; the Treasury replied that it found the public works idea 'alarming'.[47] The question of international action also came up in the discussions on exchange stabilisation. On 5 April Warburg (consultant to Roosevelt on monetary policy) stated that the U.S. authorities wished to encourage the resumption of foreign lending, but were 'not . . . favourably disposed to extension of international credits to debtor countries except to strengthen central bank reserves when other factors of disequilibrium had been removed'; they would insist on financial action being accompanied by action to remove trade barriers. Lindsay cabled the Treasury: 'Can we usefully put forward specific schemes for international financial action at this stage?'[48] It was at this point that Chamberlain gave the Treasury authority to mention the Kisch plan, an outline of which was sent on 13 April.[49] According to Leith-Ross,

the Americans said flatly that it would be impossible to get Congress to agree to any participation by the U.S. in such a scheme, and in any case they thought it premature to discuss it as, in their view, the resumption of foreign lending ought not to be encouraged until the existing structure of indebtedness has been reorganised.[50]

The Treasury told the Cabinet in May that the Keynes–Henderson plan proposed in the second report of the Committee on International Economic Policy was now 'back history'. 'President Roosevelt and the "brain trust" would not support . . . [it because] they see no chance of acceptance as is necessary to make it work.'[51]

Since by this time America had gone off gold, the Committee on Economic Information suggested a new possibility for the conference, namely an all-round devaluation on a *de facto* basis. In accordance with the attitude adopted by Keynes in 'The Means to Prosperity', the members thought that the risks to Britain involved in a *de facto* return to the gold standard were worth taking in the interests of world economic stability.[52] The Treasury officials thought this suggestion was 'on sound lines', but they could not see how in the midst of the current uncertainties an all-round devaluation could be discussed publicly yet. Instead, they wanted to begin with an agreement with the Americans by which the sterling–dollar exchange would be kept within fixed limits.[53] The negotiations on this which took place in Washington and London were eventually torpedoed by Roosevelt's 'bombshell' on 3 July.[54]

Until the President's message, the Treasury, in spite of the discouragement received in Washington, had not given up hope of airing the Kisch plan at the conference. The Keynes plan was raised (by the Treasury) at the Cabinet committee on the conference on 18 May, when ministers were told that since the U.S. would oppose the plan, its chances were negligible. Although the officials had learnt in Washington that a plan for an international credit institution would also encounter considerable difficulties, the Treasury believed 'this *is* one of the few really hopeful possibilities of securing rapid world recovery and the attempt to persuade the Americans should . . . be made'.[55] The committee agreed that the Keynes plan should not be raised. Prompted by the Chancellor, and backed by MacDonald, the committee agreed that the Kisch plan should be produced at an appropriate moment during the conference. The briefs for the British delegation therefore included a copy of the Kisch plan.[56] Roosevelt's message on U.S. monetary policy shattered the conference. As a result, the Treasury's plan never saw the light of day. The gold standard countries renounced the idea of international cooperation and formed the gold bloc; the Treasury reluctantly gave up hope of putting forward its plan.[57]

The Keynes–Henderson plan has attracted considerable attention because of its resemblance to the schemes discussed before the founding of the International Monetary Fund.[58] As Debenham later remarked, 'Henderson's initiative has to be judged by whether the remedy was appropriate when he made it.'[59] It was clearly appropriate in that if it could have been adopted in its strongest version by all economically important countries it would have improved the international economic situation. But this begs the question. A large part of the world economy's troubles in the 1930s was that there was little or no wish for international economic cooperation: 'It is fruitless to speculate about how the conference might have turned out if the United States negotiators had been able to offer war-debt cancellation, exchange stabilisation, tariff reduction and support for an international monetary fund . . . [for] even if the American delegation had been in a better negotiating position, there is considerable doubt about how far major countries abroad would have supported such a cooperative approach.'[60] The Treasury officials, for all the 'realism' that induced them to dilute Henderson's proposal, seem to have shared the Committee's premature optimism.

When Keynes put forward his plan for an International Clearing Union in 1941 the Treasury was found once more to share his optimism. In fact, Keynes thought he 'received more encouragement for this from all quarters in Whitehall than for anything I have ever suggested'.[61] Ironically, his only opponent in the Treasury was Henderson, who was by this time chronically pessimistic about the post-war world and critical of most bold policies.[62]

The Committee on Economic Information and budgetary policy 1932–5

The Committee and the Treasury both regarded budgetary policy as complementary to the cheap money policy, but they differed over what constituted an appropriate supporting budgetary policy. After concentrating on international economic problems in its first three surveys, the Committee turned to domestic economic policy in its report of November 1932. The previous report had described the solution that the Committee favoured, but since 'no speedy improvement in the international sphere [could] be expected', the Committee considered 'certain aspects of the internal economic position of Great Britain'. 'Certain aspects' covered three elements of the National Government's economy policy: the principle of the balanced budget, the curtailment of public works programmes, and the unemployment benefit and pay-cuts. These were criticised as deflationary. Although they may have been necessary during the financial crisis, confidence at home and abroad in the British financial position was now restored, and with some signs of recovery the time had come to back up the cheap money policy with a more liberal budgetary policy. The Committee advocated the cessation of the discouragement of local authority public works programmes, borrowing for the unemployment fund, and suspension of the sinking fund. The report ended with mention of the possibility of a national appeal to encourage 'wise spending' (consumers' expenditure on domestic equipment and home redecoration) and an appendix on that subject by Henderson. It also stressed the common ground between the members, while admitting the different emphases they placed on considerations of sound finance.[63] In January 1933 MacDonald invited the Committee to 10 Downing Street to discuss the unemployment problem. At MacDonald's request, the Committee followed this up with a letter to him on 'Financial Policy, February 1933'. This elaborated the reasons for the timing of its proposals and was later discussed by the Cabinet.[64]

Official comments on the proposals were of two kinds:

(i) public works were in general an inadequate remedy for unemployment; and

(ii) what could or should be done was already being done.

The aim of the Treasury's budgetary policy in the early 1930s was to create confidence. One reason was that cheap money would not achieve much if entrepreneurs were pessimistic about future prospects.[65] Furthermore, 'A general expectation that trade will be bad and prices will fall further is a powerful factor in causing bad trade and low prices. When people think trade will improve and prices rise . . . conditions tend to improve.'[66] Another reason was that any hint of an inflationary policy might prejudice the use of sterling as 'a great medium of international exchange'.[67]

When Chamberlain became Chancellor of the Exchequer, he

made it his definite aim, in dealing with national finance, to build up the resources of the nation until they were in an unassailable position. He had also wanted to demonstrate the strengthening of the national resources by progressive remissions in successive Budgets . . . It had been almost an essential of that policy that his first Budget should be an unpopular one. His second Budget had been a little better, and . . . his third would be better still. To complete the policy it was important to avoid an anticlimax in the case of his fourth Budget by making all the concessions and remissions in the third Budget.[68]

This implied that the economy cuts and tax increases of September 1931 could not be revoked until a surplus had been achieved. In April 1934

Chamberlain restored unemployment benefit by the full amount of the 1931 cut, increased the pay of civil servants by 50 per cent of the cut, and reduced the standard rate of income tax by 6d; the following year he restored the rest of the salary cuts and made further reductions in taxation.[69]

The maintenance of confidence was the Treasury's main justification for avoiding budget deficits in 1932-5. Another argument used was that deficits were unnecessary because they would bring about the desired rise in prices only insofar as they were financed by creating credit, something that could be done better (without the deleterious effects on confidence and without increasing the national debt) by cheap money.[70]

Against public works as a means of promoting recovery they had a long list of objections, theoretical and practical.

If they do *not* involve reflation, they simply divert money from normal trade to abnormal relief works. If they do involve reflation, it is far better that the additional credit should be used for normal trade and not for hot-house schemes. Relief works have always been found to be exceedingly expensive; they take a very long time to organise; and when they come to an end, they create fresh unemployment.[71]

However, the practical arguments were regarded as decisive:

the answer [to the question of public works] is purely empiric but quite conclusive. We have tried this policy ... for ... ten years or more ... and ... we have never at any moment succeeded in touching more than the fringe of the problem of unemployment then existing. Rightly or wrongly the borrowing of large sums for public works has come to depress the community as a wasteful process ... and it certainly could not at the present time make any but the most negligible impression upon the figures of unemployment with which we are now contending.[72]

The Treasury's comments on the Committee's proposals concentrated on the public works issue. Hopkins made three points:

(i) He was doubtful of the Committee's assumption that the lower turning-point of the depression had been reached, 'considering the rocks that lie ahead', in particular the impending collapse in America.

(ii) He did not think the government could persuade local authorities to increase their capital expenditure: 'There is no ban on capital works as such [under the 1931 economy measures] ... Probably one of the troubles is that [authorities] are very slow to propose expenditure which [they] could reasonably afford.'

(iii) The Cabinet Committee on Trade and Employment was already considering schemes that would need Exchequer assistance, such as railway electrification and the manufacture of petrol from coal, and an appeal for 'wise spending'. The Chancellor was also considering spending more on roads and public buildings.[73] Hopkins was well aware of Chamberlain's budgetary aims; he had helped to prepare a forecast of the 1935 budget position in order to indicate the scope that Chamberlain would have for reducing taxes or increasing expenditure in 1932-5.[74] The Cabinet was accordingly informed that the Committee's letter on financial policy was 'based on a misapprehension of policy . . . and . . . some of the assumptions as affecting the economic future were not borne out by the latest information at the disposal of the government'.[75]

The Committee on Economic Information's proposal that the government borrow for the Unemployment Fund was also made by Professor Henry Clay in November 1932 in the Report of the Royal Commission on Unemployment Insurance. The Treasury ruled it out because of 'the effect it would have on opinion abroad'.[76] The emergency measures of September 1931, according to which the Exchequer was responsible for transitional benefit, remained in force until the National Government agreed on the Unemployment Act of 1934, which set up the Unemployment Assistance Board. The Committee's sinking fund proposal, however, was 'much less open to . . . objection'.[77] The Treasury had already given up the attempt of the 1920s to reduce the size of the debt (though not the desire to fund as much of it as possible). In September 1931 it had suspended the non-contractual sinking fund; thereafter, once interest rates had been reduced, it made little statutory provision for redemption, and thus had little scope for further reduction.*

While Chamberlain was quite sure of the form budgetary policy should take, MacDonald seems to have had lingering doubts about the economy measures. He set up a sub-committee of the Economic Advisory Council to advise him personally 'on the question of the effects on trade activity and national prosperity of the economy policy in recent months, and as to whether and what safeguards and limitations are needed, or whether any expansion would be desirable'. The members were Stamp (chairman), Blackett, Simon, Robbins, and Henderson (secretary). They first met on 1 February 1932; their report was one of the few Council reports that MacDonald did not circulate. The memoranda and the report make a strange contrast to the reports of the Committee on Economic Information. The committee was anxious to stress that recent wage and salary cuts affecting public servants did not entail any reduction of general purchasing power, merely a redistribution in favour of the tax-payer. The policy of balanced budgets with provision for debt repayment was the right way to maintain confidence; if there was any scope for relaxation it should be used to ease the burden of taxes as a means of reviving business confidence and the level of private activity.

In this connection we deprecate the point of view which conceives the relief of direct taxation, as compared with the relief of indirect taxation, or the relief of other sufferers

---

* T. 171/309, Hopkins to Fergusson, 22 April 1933, and Note by Phillips, undated; T. 160/760/F 14596, 'Sinking Funds Account', 2 March 1938. Some of the budget surpluses were used to retire debt, but only once, in 1934, did this reach the magnitude of the years 1925–31 (Pember and Boyle, *British Government Securities in the Twentieth Century* (1950), pp. 522–6).

from the economy policy of last autumn, as primarily a question of the equitable apportionment of benefits among different classes of the community.

Hence their recommendation that the cuts should be maintained. In view of the improvement in Britain's competitive position as a result of devaluation, however, no further cuts or any general wage reductions were necessary for the time being. Similarly, since no net increase in purchasing power would result from restoring unemployment benefits to their old level, it was better to ease the tax burden on the community at large. In any event, 'a generous and easy system of unemployment relief is apt to make for a rigidity of the economic structure'.

On public works the committee considered that in general the policy of curtailment of new capital expenditure on roads should be maintained. Loan-financed projects of a semi- or non-remunerative kind were probably not diverting funds from the private sector under existing circumstances, but the future tax or interest burden on the budget should not be lost sight of. On balance it would be unwise to reverse the current policy, though there might be some scope for state encouragement of public utility schemes 'which approximate at all closely to remunerative industrial enterprises'. Finally, the committee suggested there was some danger that hospitals, universities, and schools might have been unduly influenced by a sense of public duty into making unnecessary cutbacks in capital development. It would also be unfortunate if individuals made 'drastic and hastily conceived economies, such as the dismissal of domestic servants, which their financial position does not require'. This did not mean, however, that public encouragement should be given to private spending. Since 'the disposition to save is not something that can be turned on and off at will like a tap, it would in our judgment be a mistake to do anything calculated to weaken the habit of thrift, especially in the wage-earning classes and others where the incentive to save has been built up as a slow social process'. When trade and business investment recovered, 'we shall have need of all of our available savings to satisfy the requirements of ordinary industrial developments at home and abroad'.[78]

It would be hard to imagine a more atavistic document – and not simply judged on post-*General Theory* standards.[79] Presumably it served to reassure MacDonald in accepting Chamberlain's orthodox policies.

The National Government's unemployment policy

Like its predecessors, the National Government, in its first two years of office, set up unemployment committees. The first of these, meeting in December 1931 and January 1932, reviewed the effects of past public works schemes and concluded that 'considered merely as a means of providing employment', they had been 'unduly burdensome in relation to the very limited results obtained'. In future, 'the main trend of Government unemployment policy will . . . [pass] into the international and fiscal fields'. The remaining unemployed would have to be assisted by unemployment benefit or by retraining schemes. While the committee recommended the maintenance of the current restrictive road policy, it also recommended the extension of the 1929 Development (Loan Guarantees and Grants) Act for three years, and an examination of possible measures to assist industry. The Cabinet was advised to appoint a standing committee 'to watch developments, to co-ordinate departmental policy and to submit recommendations for further State action as may from time to time seem desirable'.[80] But the standing committee, which met only three times, came to negative conclusions on the schemes it considered (for example, assistance to unemployed allotment holders, land drainage, and land settlement); it also recommended that the 1929 Development Act should be allowed to lapse.[81]

In September 1932 MacDonald appointed a Cabinet Committee on Unemployment to consider relief measures other than the dole. This met several times in October and November and discussed the questions of training, recreation, and provision of allotments for the unemployed.[82]

MacDonald also set up a Committee on Trade and Employment in November 1932, which he apparently intended as a continuation of the fight against unemployment begun by the Economic Advisory Council and the Labour Government's Unemployment Committee. A few industrialists and others were recruited to advise and comment on schemes for reducing unemployment. After discussion among potential members of the committee, which included Henderson and Clay, the Prime Minister's idea materialised as a panel of businessmen advisers and a Cabinet committee.* These bodies did not achieve much, partly because the scope of their work was circumscribed from the beginning.

Nothing must be done to suggest – either at home or abroad – that we lack courage, and that we have reverted to the non-economy policy that proved so disastrous to our home and foreign credit position . . .
There is no question of adopting grandiose schemes for roads or public relief works.[83]

The panel met only three times, the Cabinet committee little more. They did, however, discuss both 'wise spending' and public works schemes, and at the first meeting of the panel MacDonald explained the government's unemployment policy.

The idea that the unemployed constituted a single block of nearly 3,000,000 persons must be abandoned. The unemployed really fell into . . . those persons who could, on a

* Prem. 1/126, MacDonald to Sir Harold Bellman, Sir Andrew Duncan and Lord Weir, 28 October 1932; Clay to MacDonald, 29 October 1932; Weir to MacDonald, 31 October 1932; MacDonald to Weir, 2 November 1932; Minutes of a conference of 8 November 1932; Horace Wilson to MacDonald, 8 November 1932; Henderson and Wilson, 'Committee on Trade & Employment', 8 November 1932; Wilson to MacDonald, 9 November 1932. The members of the panel were: Lord Weir, Sir Andrew Duncan, Sir Harold Bellman, Sir Alan Anderson, Sir Hugo Hirst, Sir Alexander Walker, J. J. Mallon, Sir Horace Wilson, Henderson and Howorth (secretaries).

return of industry to normal conditions, be absorbed in trade and industry; and ...
those persons who, so far as could be foreseen at present, could not be absorbed on any
revival of trade that could reasonably be anticipated ...

The consideration of the problem of the [surplus] workers ... would be entrusted to
a Cabinet Committee of Ministers, who would keep in close touch with the National
Council of Social Service which was engaged on the preparation on a national basis of
a comprehensive plan for the development of training centres for the unemployed, and
the organisation of schemes to provide them with useful occupation ...

The revival of trade and industry must ... depend upon world conditions and upon
our national policy in the light of those conditions. In the meantime, it was desirable
that the various schemes of industrial development (raising perhaps some question of
Government assistance or co-operation) which have been considered in the past, should
be reviewed afresh in the light of today's economic conditions. Examples were – coal
hydrogenation, railway electrification, other electrical development, twenty-ton
waggons ...[84]

The panel's discussion of the suggested topics was either negative or
inconclusive. It did, however, favour sending a letter to the building societies
under the Prime Minister's signature to say that the government approved
of their scheme to lend money for house improvements, repairs, and
maintenance. Sir Harold Bellman, Chairman of the Abbey Road Society,
who first raised the issue on the panel, suggested the money should be lent
at 5 per cent. The Cabinet committee agreed to the letter subject to the
Treasury's stipulation that it contain no hint of approving a rate of interest
as high as 5 per cent.[85] At the committee's next meeting Horace Wilson and
Henderson raised the Committee on Economic Information's suggestion of
an appeal for 'wise spending'. As Henderson knew, the Prime Minister had
been interested in the idea; but his colleagues did not share his enthusiasm.
The Chancellor reported the Treasury's current attitude to the proposal,
which was that such an appeal was unnecessary because it 'in no way helped
the export trade, and merely encouraged the home trade that was already
protected'.[86]

With respect to public works, the Cabinet Committee on Trade and
Employment provided Chamberlain with an opportunity to reiterate the
Treasury's sound financial principles. At the same time, however, he
announced that he was prepared to undertake some expenditure on roads
and public buildings. This was not entirely in accordance with his principles
but could be justified on grounds of cheapness. The committee agreed, with
the proviso that 'care should be taken to avoid any implication that there
had been a change of policy'.[87] Later in the year the Cabinet was told that
the road programmes suspended in September 1931 were being completed.[88] In other words, there *had* been a change in policy.*

---

* Once signs of recovery had been noted, the committee ceased to meet. MacDonald tried to
revive it in February 1934 because 'in his view the Government after two years of office had
accomplished very successfully the first part of their task. There remained one large problem –
namely that of the permanently unemployed', but he was unsuccessful. The panel met, for the
third and last time, in February 1934, when the industrialists indicated that they thought the
government's policy had been successful. Stamp also attended this meeting; he was less com-

The development of the Treasury's views on public works, 1932–5

Keynes first published his 'The Means to Prosperity' in *The Times* on 13–16 March 1933. As soon as the first article appeared Chamberlain asked his Treasury officials for their reply. Keynes advocated public works on a large scale, using the multiplier to argue that the saving to the budget (by reducing unemployment benefit payments and increasing tax revenue) was greater than commonly supposed; he urged the raising of a £60m loan to finance the expenditure, and the remission of £50m taxation at the expense of the sinking fund.* Chamberlain particularly wanted comments on 'the questions of reducing taxation by suspending the sinking fund, borrowing where reasonable and especially borrowing for the cost of new roads and part of the dole which could well be spread'.[89]

The first thing that exercised the civil servants was an attempt to disprove Keynes's estimates of the potential saving to the budget of loan-financed public works. Other arguments mentioned were the length of time public works took to get into operation, and the undesirability of unbalancing the budget.[90] Although Phillips did not accept the multiplier, he objected to these arguments:

The one gilt edged argument in this collection is *delay*. Keynes' whole point is the urgency of immediate action, whereas we know perfectly well that public works don't get started in a year and don't get in full working order for three years. While I agree with the other detailed criticisms, we must not be too sure that arguments along these lines are going to get us through. Where I differ personally from Keynes is that I do not accept his first step, namely, his allegation that expenditure on public works will put 6,000 new men directly into employment. Once you grant him that, then, though you may whittle down his arguments, you cannot get rid of them. After all, what he is saying is that here is a course of action that would be simply magnificent for the nation and which is very cheap because it has such favourable reactions on the Budget. Even if he is proved to have over-estimated the savings to the Budget, that by itself does not prove that his policy is a bad one.

I think the detailed criticism . . . is a little unfair to Keynes, because he quite frankly admits that the savings to the Budget may be delayed.[91]

Accordingly, the next version of the Treasury memorandum began by stating that the best criticism for the Chancellor to use was the long delay inevitable in any public works scheme.

Phillips thought that 'Mr. Keynes' theory is right only if there are large unused savings and if they can be attracted into investment by issuing

placent, being 'disappointed at the very large amount of unemployment which might have to be dealt with. The figure he had in mind was more like 1m. or 1½m.' (Cab. 27/502, Committee on Trade and Employment, 8th, 9th, and 10th meetings, 20 July 1933, 1 and 7 February 1934; Cab. 27/503, Panel on Trade and Employment 3rd meeting, 5 February 1934).

* He also advocated the Henderson plan for an international note issue as a proposal for the World Economic Conference; see above, pp. 114–21. He did not elaborate the multiplier in *The Times* but in the *New Statesman* on 1 April. He sent both articles to the Treasury and included them both in the American edition of *The Means to Prosperity*. The latter is reprinted in the *Collected Writings*, Vol. IX.

gilt edged stock without raising the long-term rate of interest' and that this was conclusive against large-scale adoption of Keynes's ideas. But he also thought there were useful policy suggestions in the articles:

It cannot be reasonably argued that such relatively small matters as the Cunarder etc. ought to be subjected to severe economic analysis. If desired we could also investigate possibilities as to a temporary renewal of some form of modest housing subsidy or some form of assistance to a National Housing Corporation in the borrowing of its money. So far as it goes a limited programme of borrowing for roads and bridges could be quickly got going in populous districts, though this involves a definite reversal of policy as compared with recent times.

Alternative positive action was 'a plan to give financial encouragement to industrial undertakings which were willing to use their reserves or borrow new money for capital renewals and extensions immediately', and a relaxation of the embargo on new overseas issues so as to encourage British exports.[92]

Phillips asked Henderson for his observations on the draft of his memorandum, adding 'I expect you won't like it'. Henderson did not like it, because of its incorrect assumption that Keynes's argument assumed the existence of vast idle bank deposits.[93] He agreed with Phillips that the delay involved made large-scale public works impracticable, and that the adverse effect on the balance of payments made international reflation preferable to exclusively domestic reflation. He continued:

I'm afraid that there is an unpleasantly large measure of truth in the above, and that it does constitute a real limiting factor. I don't think Keynes would disagree. This is, in effect, the point of his last article. But I ask you to observe –

(1) that his limiting factor applies to a revival of internal trade activity, however brought about, just as much as to one coming from an ordinary accession of business confidence and optimism as to one stimulated by public works or the remission of taxation;

(2) that though a limiting factor it is *not* an absolutely debarring one. A considerable internal trade improvement would not worsen the balance of trade more than we could well afford, particularly when it is borne in mind that an increase of British imports of raw materials and food would stimulate improvement in the primary producing countries, and would raise our receipts from overseas investments. World recovery can indeed only be brought about, if the stronger financial countries lead the way, and we belong to this category[;]

(3) that this is not, therefore, a valid objection to Keynes's suggestions, or any others, for promoting internal recovery, provided their application is kept within reasonable limits.

Those of Phillips's arguments which were valid against a large-scale public works scheme had 'no force at all as applied to a reversal of public works policy from one of extreme contraction to the degree of expansion that is administratively feasible'. Nor did they affect Keynes's other proposals for borrowing for the Unemployment Fund and suspending the sinking fund.*

* Keynes Papers, Henderson to Phillips, 16 March 1933. Henderson had earlier told Keynes that 'of course I'm entirely in favour of reversing the engines as regards public works programmes ... [but] I don't like the approach of the Kahn calculations'. He also thought, as usual, that Keynes underestimated the administrative difficulties and adverse effects on confidence of

Henderson's criticisms caused Phillips to admit that 'his [Keynes's] argument is no doubt valid . . . for a moderate expenditure'. In his next draft he also mentioned the adverse psychological effects of unbalanced budgets.[94]

Chamberlain received the several versions of the Treasury memorandum, and a memorandum from the Inland Revenue. Acting on his own initiative, Henderson also pointed out to Chamberlain the adverse effects on confidence, and hence on economic activity, that the U.S. Government's deficits had had.[95] In a speech to the House of Commons on 22 March Chamberlain used the final Treasury memorandum, which incorporated material from the previous memoranda and therefore mentioned the matter of delay, the dubiousness of Keynes's calculations of the savings to the budget, and the disagreeable consequences (especially on opinion abroad) of an unbalanced budget.[96] Chamberlain also summoned Keynes to see him on 16 March: 'Can it be', said Keynes, 'that the walls of Jericho are flickering?'[97]

The answer to Keynes's question seems to be 'Yes, but not yet tumbling.' The policy of the government in 1933 was to consider giving assistance to schemes which were 'well thought out and justified on their merits'.[98] Schemes which could be justified as 'revenue-producing or . . . of public import' were assisted; this applied to the construction of the Cunard liner *Queen Mary*, new telephone exchanges, and the extension of London's Underground railways.* By the beginning of 1935, however, Phillips and Hopkins had come to believe that public works could play a role similar to that suggested by the Committee on Economic Information. After a discussion between senior Treasury officials, Fergusson, the Chancellor's Secretary, told Chamberlain that he 'perhaps ought to know that . . . the opinion was expressed . . . [particularly by Phillips and also by Hopkins] that there was a need for stimulating capital expenditure', not only to provide transport and other services in growing prosperous parts of the country but also 'on general economic grounds'. These grounds were, according to Hopkins, that 'the stage now reached in the general recovery is one at which an expansion of public borrowing would be useful for keeping up the impetus'. Phillips elaborated: 'The argument for public works is that the government intervention on a limited scale may do something to accelerate recovery. Apart from certain industries such as house-building and the iron and steel industry the response to cheap money has lagged a little.' Public works would 'necessarily involve some burden to the State which otherwise it might hope to escape', but material costs were probably cheaper now than they would be in future, and 'the [real] question is whether a certain measure of help now . . . would secure an earlier revival of prosperity'. Public

---

large-scale public works, and concluded: 'Speaking generally . . . I am very much off the idea of public works as a major constructive remedy for our present troubles.' (Henderson Papers Box 8, Henderson to Keynes, 28 February 1933).

* Chamberlain's diary shows that he favoured assisting Cunard to build the *Queen Mary* for reasons other than employment (Feiling, *Life of Neville Chamberlain*, p. 235; see also pp. 241–2).

works should also be used in the depressed areas to compensate for the permanent decline in their exports. Hopkins and Fisher therefore recommended that the government encourage and help the local authorities to raise loans and undertake public works, up to a total of about £60m.[99]

When the Cabinet committee examining Lloyd George's 'New Deal' asked the Treasury for a list of potential public works schemes, the Treasury prefaced it with a statement of the general considerations that should be taken into account. On the one hand, 'the employment value of public works has been found in the past to be disappointing' because of the magnitude and location of the unemployment and the inevitable delays in any project. On the other hand, cheap money, which was 'the natural means of reviving investment activity and, therefore, of combating unemployment within the limits allowed by the world situation', was also subject to a lag, so that 'anything that the Government could do – without discouraging private enterprise – would be useful at the present juncture'. The document also mentioned the multiplier. This seems to have been regarded as a possibly true, but as yet unconfirmed theory, rather than one that was definitely false.* Thus, while the Treasury's 1935 view, like Henderson's, did not involve acceptance of the multiplier theory, neither was it the notorious 'Treasury view' of 1929–30 nor the position of 1932–3.

The figures of government expenditure in the 1930s show that the central government's current expenditure and its loans and grants to local authorities, as well as the local authorities' current expenditure and investment, all increased markedly in 1935. Most of this was due to the housing programme, which was already under way at the beginning of 1935. However, there was also some expansion in government expenditure for investment in other fields, for example suburban railways.[100] (The figures for the next two years are affected by the rearmament programme.)

One development of the mid-thirties with which the Committee on Economic Information was not concerned was the special areas legislation of 1935 and 1937. The Treasury officials were involved in these matters, but while they were not opposed to increased public expenditure and the establishment of government factories in the depressed areas, they apparently shared the Committee's macroeconomic bias.[101]

The Treasury's ideas on the role of budgetary policy changed further after 1935. Before considering this change, and the advice which the Committee on Economic Information was giving at that time, it is useful to consider one of the Committee's 1934 reports that has not so far been mentioned. This, the Committee's Thirteenth Report, records its views on the long-

---

* Cab. 27/583, General Purposes Committee 2nd meeting, 5 February 1935; Cab. 27/584, 'Public Works', Memorandum by Treasury, 20 February 1935; see also the Cabinet committee's report, which was drafted by an official sub-committee under Hopkins, Cab. 24/254, C.P. 46(35), General Purposes Committee, Report, 1 March 1935.

The Cabinet seems generally to have regarded a list of potential public works as useful political ammunition rather than anything else (Cab. 27/583, 2nd meeting of G.P. Committee).

term prospects of Britain's export trade and on the appropriate commercial and agricultural policies that should be pursued in the light of these prospects. Given that it was both commissioned and much discussed by the government, it also provides an opportunity to take stock of the position the Committee had come to assume in Whitehall in 1934-5, after three years of work.

Trade policy 1934

By late 1933 the government found itself with the problem of what to do about British agriculture in the context of the Ottawa and other trade agreements made since 1932.[102] These had resulted in some agricultural protection, notably import quotas on meat, butter, and bacon. Under the Wheat Act of 1932, there was also a 'levy-subsidy' scheme for wheat, whereby British growers received a subsidy out of the proceeds of a levy on wheat imports. The Minister of Agriculture, Walter Elliot, wanted to extend 'levy-subsidies' to other foodstuffs. This raised a question of principle: did the change in Britain's international position over the last couple of decades, and/or the change in her commercial policy since 1931, imply that Britain, who had to a large extent relied on imported food in the past, should now protect and develop her agriculture? If so, how far and by what means? Several ministers wanted the question of principle examined.[103]

The Committee on Economic Information was, therefore, asked to undertake an inquiry into 'the co-ordination of different agricultural and industrial considerations in formulating trade policy'. It was arranged that when completed the report would be examined by an inter-departmental committee under Leith-Ross.* The Committee began its inquiry in June 1934 by asking each member to write a short note on the factors which should be borne in mind in the preparation of the report. In the light of these they decided to write the report on the lines suggested by Henderson in his first and subsequent notes. This meant that the report (i) dwelt on the past and likely trends in Britain's export trade and on the implication of the slowing down in population growth for Britain's future import needs, (ii) argued that in the light of these factors a small amount of agricultural protection, at least in times of depressed world agricultural prices, would be desirable,

---

* Cab. 58/17, C.E.I. 35th meeting, 19 June 1934; Cab. 23/79, Cabinet 30(34)6, 25 July 1934.
 It is possible that some members of the C.E.I., in particular Henderson and Leith-Ross, and perhaps Keynes, made the suggestion that their Committee was the appropriate body to undertake the inquiry. These three were all in favour of a levy-subsidy scheme. Henderson had been contemplating 'a special committee on agricultural policy' before the request was made to Stamp, and Leith-Ross was very active in both the preparation of the report and its subsequent official discussion. Keynes paid a visit to the Ministry of Agriculture in March 1934, but on the other hand Cole later mentioned 'Keynes' view that the problem is too difficult for the Committee to tackle'. (Cab. 58/19, Memoranda by Henderson, Leith-Ross, and Keynes, 28 and 29 June and 3 July 1934; Henderson Papers Box 1, Debenham to Henderson, 21 June 1934; Keynes Papers, Appointment book for 1934; Cab. 58/19, Memorandum by Cole, 27 June 1934).

and (iii) concluded by indicating a preference for levy-subsidies rather than quotas for the commodities protected. The Committee thought that there was little scope for increasing employment by increasing domestic agricultural production. To absorb the unemployed, exports would have to be fostered, preferably in new lines, to take account of the industrialisation of former customers for Britain's old staples. The Committee also thought that the possible benefits from depreciation and the tariff were largely exhausted, so that further *industrial* protection was not desirable.*

The Committee intended 'to formulate as clearly as possible certain broad principles which, in our judgment, have a vital bearing upon our commercial policy', and to leave the application of the principles to officials. This took place through Leith-Ross's committee and the Cabinet's Produce Markets Supply Committee. Professor Drummond has described fully these developments and their consequences. Very briefly, the government had already decided that it wished to extend the levy-subsidy scheme to meat and had opened lengthy and ultimately unsuccessful negotiations with the Dominions for this purpose. In the meantime Leith-Ross's committee endorsed the principles of the Committee on Economic Information report, and recommended their application to bacon as well as to meat. The Produce Markets Supply Committee discussed both reports in December. At Baldwin's suggestion it concentrated initially on the general principles and discussed the progress and prospects of the negotiations. Little action ensued, because as far as immediate practical application of the levy-subsidy idea was concerned, 'nothing need be done because nothing could be' until the Dominions (and the Argentine) agreed.[104]

The report enhanced the Committee's prestige among ministers. It was generally regarded as clear and illuminating on the very important matters it discussed. Partly for this reason the Treasury considered publishing it as a reply to Lloyd George's 'New Deal', given his emphasis on developing British agriculture. Since, however, it 'would [not] pin down that particular Proteus' (Phillips's description of the Lloyd George plan) and would create an awkward precedent, it was thought preferable that ministers should use the arguments in their speeches.[105] By this time the Cabinet was regularly discussing the Committee's reports circulated by MacDonald. When Bald-

---

* The report is reprinted below.

Keynes's contribution was mainly support of Henderson, but he also raised the possibility that there might in the short run be little or no conflict between industry and agriculture because of the widespread unemployment and the resulting distinction between measures to increase employment in the short run and measures to allocate resources optimally 'if we ever again have the good fortune of enjoying full employment', which he did not regard as particularly likely. (Cab. 58/19, Memoranda by Keynes, 3 July and 17 August 1934; Henderson Papers Box 1, Debenham to Henderson, 21 June 1934).

The C.E.I. report was much more to Keynes's taste than the report of the 1930 Committee on Agricultural Policy had been since it considered the very questions that Keynes had criticised the earlier committee for not asking, namely the long-run trends of agricultural prices and production and the future prospects for British agriculture (above, p. 39).

win replaced MacDonald as Prime Minister, in June 1935, the procedure changed somewhat; in particular the contact with the Treasury was increased. This was probably on Chamberlain's initiative, and it resulted in Phillips's joining and playing an active role in the work of the Committee.*

Recession and the measures to combat it

The most important, and certainly the most influential, reports of the Committee on Economic Information were those submitted in 1935 and 1937 which forecast a recession in 1937 or 1938 and recommended measures to avoid or at least mitigate it.

Early in 1935 Sir William Beveridge, who was chairman of the Unemployment Insurance Statutory Committee that had been set up under the 1934 Unemployment Act to advise from time to time on the solvency of the insurance scheme, wanted expert advice on the probable trend of unemployment over the next few years in order to assess whether he could safely increase benefits or reduce contributions out of the surplus he was accumulating. Beveridge's committee was in the position, apparently contrary to the government's intentions, that if it recommended that the Fund should distribute a certain amount to insured persons, the Minister of Labour was obliged to distribute the whole of that sum and had discretion only over the method, for example by increasing benefits rather than by reducing contributions.[106] In February 1935 Stamp told the Committee on Economic Information that the Treasury had privately informed him that it thought a 'small committee of Cambridge economists' should advise Beveridge's committee on the probable trend of unemployment over the next few years, and had asked him if the Committee on Economic Information might be able to do this. The Committee thought it would be 'impossible . . . to submit definite estimates, but . . . they might be able to make a helpful contribution by outlining the various considerations which ought to be borne in mind by any authority called upon to prepare an estimate on this subject'. At the next meeting Stamp reported that he had been discussing the question with the Prime Minister and the Treasury. The current suggestion was that the Committee should be asked to forecast the probable trend of unemployment on a number of given assumptions, and should add to its members Professors A. L. Bowley, L. Robbins, D. H. Robertson, and a paid assistant, to carry out the detailed work of making the necessary calculations on the agreed assumptions.

In April Beveridge explained his problem to the Committee. He said that he had initially asked the London and Cambridge Economic Service because

---

* J. H. Jones, *Josiah Stamp, Public Servant*, pp. 302–3, 325–6.
   Officials had already been made full members of the Committees on Economic Information and on Scientific Research in May 1934 (Cab. 58/25, 8th meeting of Committee on Scientific Research, 11 May 1934).

he wanted 'the minds of Bowley and Robbins and Dennis Robertson . . . [and] also . . . Hubert Henderson . . . on the subject'. When he had told the Prime Minister that he wanted some outside advice, the Prime Minister said that 'if it meant spending money it had better be done through you [the Committee]'. Since the task was primarily statistical (involving 'not . . . above a quarter of an hour's honest work for a genuine economist', according to Keynes), the Committee set up a small sub-committee, of Henderson, Bowley, Robertson, and David Caradog Jones, to prepare the report, which the full Committee would consider in October.[107]

In the meantime the Committee prepared three reports. The first of these, the Committee's Sixteenth Report on 'Statistics of Population and their relevance to economic change', recommended that population censuses should be taken every five years beginning in 1936, and that the ages of parents should be entered on birth certificates. The Committee were concerned about the deflationary consequences of the decline in the rate of growth of the population, and thought that more information should be collected in order to assess the likely trends. It seems that Henderson was the most alarmed by the prospects: he suggested the subject, helped to write the report, and went to see the Registrar-General in order to try to secure approval of the recommendations. Although the Registrar-General saw no objection to the second recommendation, the Cabinet had already rejected the Minister of Health's proposal for a census in 1936 on the grounds of cost.*

The Committee's Seventeenth Report discussed exchange rate policy,[108] and then in June the Committee decided its next report should pay 'special attention . . . to the prospects of the building industry, the course of costs in that industry, and the possibility of a slackening of demand in the near future in the industry'. This reflected increasing fears, in and out of Whitehall, that the present recovery might not go much further and would cease entirely when the building boom ended.[109] Henderson outlined the causes for apprehension to the Trend of Unemployment Committee. First of all, 'recoveries do not proceed for ever . . . Sooner or later, something occurs to cause a setback.' The present recovery, now three years old, was slowing down so that not much more reduction of unemployment could be expected before the next depression began. Furthermore, the present recovery depended on the housebuilding boom, which could not continue indefinitely at its present rate.[110]

* C.E.I. 48th–51st meetings, 14 February–14 May 1935; C.E.I. 16th Report, 2 April 1935; Cab. 23/81, Cabinet 4(35)9, 16 January 1935.

    A couple of years later the Cabinet agreed to introduce a Bill providing for orders in Council 'which may prescribe particulars, to be obtained confidentially for statistical purposes only, on the occasion of registration of births, deaths, stillbirths and marriages'. This was suggested by the Minister of Health, now Kingsley Wood, 'in view of the importance of the population and birth-rate problems and the urgent need for improved "fertility" statistics'. (Cab. 23/89, Cabinet 37(37)14, 13 October 1937, and Cab. 23/90A, Cabinet 39(37)23, 27 October 1937).

The Eighteenth Report was Debenham's work: the Committee made only a few alterations in his draft, which Keynes thought 'quite excellent'.[111] It first described the course and causes of recovery up to 1935. Then, looking ahead, it warned that though the immediate prospects were quite promising, 'no prediction can be made with greater confidence than that the present rate of housebuilding cannot be maintained', and 'there is a grave danger that in 1937 or thereabouts this country may be faced with a crisis of the same magnitude as the last, but with one serious disadvantage in addition, namely, the saturation of that field of demand, which is most quickly responsive to a reduction in the rate of interest'. The next depression would 'call for at least as rigorous an insistence on . . . [cheap money] as was necessary in 1932'. The government should begin to give priority to public works schemes that would provide their maximum employment in 1938-40.[112]

Starting from these economic assumptions, the members of the Sub-Committee on the Trend of Unemployment predicted an average unemployment percentage of $15\frac{1}{2}$-16 over the years 1936-45. They proceeded in three stages. The first was to examine the course of unemployment over past trade cycles, where they observed that 'in every case the percentage of unemployment in the third year following a year of maximum unemployment was generally considerably lower than the average percentage of unemployment in the following decade'. Secondly, they estimated how much of the present unemployment fell into each of three categories: normal minimum unemployment (the sum of seasonal, frictional, and other temporary unemployment, which 'would continue to exist under the most satisfactory conditions of trade'); cyclical unemployment; and unemployment representing a geographical or occupational maladjustment of labour.[113] To estimate normal minimum unemployment, they took as a starting-point the unemployment percentage that prevailed in the more prosperous areas of Great Britain in May 1929, that is before the world slump. The figure arrived at was about 6 per cent or about 160,000 insured persons. As a independent check upon this result they also attempted to estimate separately the components of normal minimum unemployment. As a measure of unemployment due to maladjustments they took the unemployment that would remain in other parts of the country when unemployment in the southern divisions was reduced to its normal minimum. This turned out to be 800,000-900,000 insured persons. The remaining unemployment would, therefore, be cyclical. Thirdly, they assessed the probable demand for housing over the next few years and compared it with the present rate of housebuilding. At that rate of supply the estimated demand would be satisfied by the end of 1938.* This led them to expect a fall-off in housebuilding in 1937. They then calculated the effect of a fall-off in building, to

---

* Both the C.E.I. (in its 18th Report) and the sub-committee based their estimate of housing demand on the Registrar-General's estimate in the 1931 census. According to Marian Bowley, that method was 'obviously sensible' (*Housing and the State*, pp. 10-11).

one-third or one-quarter of its present rate, on unemployment, estimating the repercussions of a fall of this magnitude on other employment by looking at the repercussions of the fall in numbers employed in the export industries in 1929–32. They forecast that unemployment would reach a peak of 20 per cent in 1940. The analysis 'suggest[ed] as a reasonable working hypothesis':

(i) The unemployment percentage is likely to continue to fall for a period of one, two or three years until a trade setback occurs; but in view of the heavy concentration of unemployment in the northern areas and in Wales, the reduction of unemployment in this period will not be very large, and is unlikely to exceed a figure of about 2 per cent.
(ii) A setback to trade is likely to occur between 1936 and 1938, entailing a large upward movement of the unemployment figures. This depression is, however, unlikely to carry the unemployment percentage to so high a level as that reached in 1932 . . .
(iii) After this depression a renewed process of recovery may be expected, and before this recovery is exhausted, the unemployment percentage may be carried to an appreciably lower minimum than is likely to be reached in the next two or three years.

This hypothesis implied an average unemployment percentage for the next ten years of $15\frac{1}{2}$–16.[114]

The full Committee endorsed its sub-committee's conclusions and sent the report on to the Prime Minister, the Chancellor, and Beveridge's committee. During the discussion of the report, Keynes indicated that he was 'less optimistic than the sub-committee in respect of the last years of the period . . . attach[ing] greater importance to the exhaustion of investment opportunities than to the draining off of the surplus labour in the depressed areas'. Phillips thought that the sub-committee was too pessimistic, at least for the first few years, because a decline in housing might be compensated by increased exports as American recovery progressed, and/or by increased investment in sectors other than housing.[115]

The year 1936 witnessed several events relevant to this narrative. The government embarked on a sizeable five-year rearmament programme; the gold bloc countries finally devalued in September, and the American, British, and French Treasuries entered into the 'Tripartite Agreement' and announced their intention to cooperate in exchange rate policy; recovery spread throughout the world, with rising world commodity prices being helped on their way by speculation; recovery speeded up in Britain.[116] To economists the year is also notable for the publication of Keynes's *General Theory*.

So much has been written about the *General Theory* that it would be foolish to attempt anything profound and original here. We have described the theory of Keynes's *Treatise* at some length earlier because many of his recommendations to the Economic Advisory Council were based on that analysis. But Keynes's 'thinking never stood still';[117] the development of his views towards the *General Theory* began soon after he had completed the

Treatise and appeared in his policy advice from 1932 onwards.[118] In 'The Means to Prosperity' in 1933 he could give a rationale for public works policies based on a component of his new theory, the consumption–income relationship embodied in the multiplier.[119] By 1935 he was explaining to Salter that 'my own belief today is that neither the real remedy nor the power of persuading people to adopt it will come except from a more fundamental diagnosis of the underlying situation and a wide-spread understanding of this diagnosis and conviction of its correctness'.* The *General Theory* provided a large part of this more fundamental diagnosis. For expositional simplicity, which was perhaps natural in a world with flexible exchange rates, it was cast in terms of a closed economy.

One way of summarising the *General Theory*'s attack on 'classical' economic theory is to say that whereas the latter assumed either that the economy would be at full employment in the absence of wage and other non-monetary rigidities, and/or that interest rates would always 'naturally' move in the appropriate direction to encourage investment to absorb all the available full-employment savings, Keynes pointed out that the economic system was not self-adjusting.[120] As Meade has recently put it, 'Keynes's intellectual revolution was to shift economists from thinking normally in terms of a model of reality in which a dog called *savings* wagged his tail labelled *investment* to thinking in terms of a model in which a dog called *investment* wagged his tail labelled *savings*.'[121] If savings is determined by income, as Keynes like most Marshallians assumed, then if investment is deficient the level of national income will be below that required to produce full employment.

Keynes's major policy goal was still stability of the economy at a high level of employment; but the perspective on the instruments and the difficulties of achieving this goal reflected five years of thought plus the experience of the slump. Given that investment was the motive force of the system,† employment policy had to regulate investment. An appropriate monetary policy directed at long-term interest rates, as in the *Treatise*, would provide the right long-term environment. In contrast to the *Treatise*, however, where monetary policy was expected to do *all* the work, it might not, given the state of entrepreneurial expectations, provide the solution to short-term instabilities. For that, fiscal regulation might be necessary, particularly if the monetary authorities found it difficult or inexpedient to operate in long-

* Keynes Papers, Keynes to Salter, 10 July 1935. He did not, therefore, sign the foreword to 'The Next Five Years'. On this publication, see H. Macmillan, *Winds of Change 1914–1939* (1966), Ch. 12.

On Keynes's attitude see also 'Poverty and Plenty: Is the Economic System Self-adjusting?', *Listener*, 21 November 1934 (*Collected Writings*, Vol. XIII, pp. 485–92), where he distinguished his theoretical presumptions from those of Henderson, Brand, and Robbins.

† The accumulation of capital was also necessary to bring about the 'Economic Possibilities for our Grandchildren', i.e. a state of affairs in which the economic problem would no longer dominate people's lives. See also Keynes to Wedgwood, July 1943, quoted in D. E. Moggridge, *Keynes* (1976), pp. 127–8.

term securities markets rather than relying on Bank rate. Open-market purchases of Treasury bills or other short-term securities could only affect *long* rates indirectly, and it was long-term rates – very much subject to 'the state of the news' – that affected the bulk of investment. Added to this view of the world was the concept of liquidity preference. The public's desire to hold balanced portfolios of financial and other assets was a function of their expectations of the future and the desire to be liquid in the face of uncertainty – which were not completely under the control of the authorities. Hence if the authorities wanted to achieve a 'high'-employment level of aggregate demand, they would have to take into account the portfolio balance of the public, their expectations, and the balance of public expenditure in relation to prospective private investment.

The Committee's February 1936 'Survey' included a description of an apparently Keynesian theory of the trade cycle in a discussion of recovery policies in the U.S. and Germany. It stressed the causal role of fluctuations in investment, which induced the fluctuations in consumption and employment, and the increased desire for liquidity in times of crisis and depression. Since 'depressions are characterised by a reduction in the yield obtainable from the investment of capital in productive assets below that obtainable on securities providing a fixed money income', effective remedies must satisfy the increased desire for liquidity (to prevent interest rates from rising) and keep up consumption (to keep up the demand for the products and hence the profitability of capital goods). The report mentioned two forms of 'effective intervention' by the government and the monetary authorities: the 'orthodox remedy' of cheap money (which satisfied the increased preference for short-term assets) and deficit budgeting (which supported the level of consumption). It did not mention any more direct control of investment.[122] But a year later when the Committee suggested a policy for the U.K. recession forecast for 1937, it strongly recommended that the government use the investment under its control to compensate for fluctuations in private investment.

Meanwhile the Committee prepared surveys in June and December which concentrated on the events preceding and following the devaluation of the franc. Its pessimism of 1935 was somewhat reduced by the announcement of the rearmament programme, which might offset the effects of the end of the housing boom, and by the improved trade prospects after the gold bloc devaluation. It pointed out that to take full advantage of the new opportunities Britain might have to relax the policy of protection and the Ottawa Agreements, because 'full recovery, both in the Empire and the rest of the world, cannot be expected without some resumption of trade along its old channels'.[123] In October the Committee members had thought of giving consideration to 'the danger that the undesirable features usually associated with a boom might soon make their appearance' in the U.K., but in their subsequent report they confined themselves to mentioning the possibility that rising raw material prices might push up the cost of living.[124] In December, however, they decided their next report should 'deal primarily with the implications of the present expansion of activity in the investment industries, and the financial and other measures which could now be taken to mitigate the consequences to industry which might be anticipated should this activity decline'. In January (1937) they became more specific. The report should suggest counter-cyclical public investment, the possibilities of 'meeting exceptional demands from abroad' and of meeting defence expenditure out of revenue, and the avoidance of any rise in long-term interest rates.[125]

Keynes was at this time publicly advocating these measures in *The Times*.[126] The Committee strongly recommended all of them in its Twenty-second Report, despite Robertson's objections to Keynes's recommendations on monetary policy. These objections obliged Stamp to add to the customary preamble ('as usual, the report represents the general views of the Committee, without attempting to express the different shades of opinion held by individual members') a statement that Robertson dissociated himself from paragraphs 11 and 23–6.[127] Robertson explained his objections to these paragraphs as follows:

The general effect . . . seems to me calculated to produce (1) an exaggerated expectation of the extent to which it is possible, in a community still far from wholly authoritarian, to control the course of activity without permitting some reaction of interest, short and long, to conditions of enhanced demand for loans; (2) an exaggerated view of the objections to permitting such reaction.

The argument seems to be 'There are (i) some things we don't want at all, (ii) others which we want but can be postponed. A rise in the rate of interest will, it is true, check the production of class (i) but, by leading to an expectation of a further rise, will actually stimulate the production of class (ii). Hence it must be avoided.'

I am very doubtful . . . whether the argument about class (ii) is sound. If it is *not* sound, the *prima facie* argument that a rise in the rate of interest will check class (i) remains unshaken . . .

I feel that the whole argument . . . is exaggerated, and unduly influenced by peculiarities in the situation of 1929–32.[128]

The different views of Robertson and Keynes on monetary policy stemmed from their different theories of the causes of the trade cycle. Robertson made this clear to a wider audience in an article in September 1937. To Robertson 'the phenomena of boom and slump [were] not primarily a matter of interest rates at all, but of something much more deep-seated, namely of the inevitable discontinuity which attends the effort of man to achieve material progress'. In other words the cycle was caused largely by the inevitable bunching of new inventions and technological innovation. It seemed to him 'doubtful how much the most skilful monetary policy [could] be expected to do' in eliminating the cycle. What it could do, and should be allowed to do, was discourage speculative or otherwise undesirable investment during the boom. To Keynes, on the other hand, although the cycle was not a purely monetary phenomenon, it could be aggravated by monetary factors, in particular the behaviour of interest rates and liquidity preference. In a boom situation higher interest rates had to be 'avoid[ed] . . . as we would hell-fire', in order not to precipitate a slump. Robertson did not believe monetary policy was this powerful and could make much difference to the timing of the turning-point. What *was* necessary was 'to be thinking . . . of how to act . . . in the face of the [inevitable] fading out' of the boom; Robertson therefore wholeheartedly supported the proposals for counter-cyclical regulation of public works.[129] It seems that the airing of theoretical differences in front of the Treasury officials helped to make them aware of the fundamental issues at stake;[130] it certainly did not detract from the effectiveness of the report.

The Treasury officials approved and wanted immediate action. Since the Committee 'raise[d] in a definite manner questions of great importance', Phillips recommended the immediate appointment of inter-departmental committees to consider the practical possibilities for counter-cyclical public investment and to review tariff policy. The Committee's suggestion of some control over the use of iron and steel should also be examined. Hopkins, Fisher, and Leith-Ross rapidly agreed, and between them they eventually managed to persuade the Chancellor to set up two committees, one on Public Capital Expenditure, under Phillips, and the other on Trade Policy, under Leith-Ross.[131]

The report of Phillips's committee began by summarising the views of the Committee on Economic Information and setting out the principal practical difficulties of public works expenditure. It went on, however: 'These objections, which are formidable, do not . . . indicate that nothing can be done.' Public works other than on rearmament should be postponed now and speeded up later to 'serve the double purpose of assisting rearmament and . . . of alleviating a possible depression'. Although 'it is impossible to anticipate the date or extent of the next depression, it is certain that whenever it occurs the provision of a considerable amount of employment on work of real importance, which has been postponed on a definite plan, will be of real value'. The remainder of the report reviewed in detail the existing and proposed programmes of government capital expenditure and listed the schemes on which work should be postponed now and speeded up or expanded later; the proposals implied a reduction of £20m in annual capital expenditure in the boom followed by an increase of £50m in the slump.* The committee suggested that the Minister of Health should send a circular (of which it provided the draft) to local authorities inviting them to prepare a programme of the capital expenditure which they had in contem-

---

* These figures are a sizeable proportion of both combined Central Government and Public Authorities G.D.F.C.F., which was £132m in 1936 (Feinstein, *National Income*, Table 39), and the amount of public capital expenditure which the committee estimated was under the control of the government in 1936 (£250m). (The difference between the figures is due to the perennial problem of defining public investment.)

plation over the next six years; they were asked to set out the items in order of priority, and for the time being to request sanction only for the urgent items. It also recommended a standing committee to provide continuous review of the situation and inter-departmental cooperation, because 'the success or failure of the policy we have proposed must depend . . . on the speed with which it is possible to effect a transition from the phase of reduction of public capital expenditure to the phase of acceleration [and] this . . . will depend upon the extent to which the necessary preparations are carried out in the intervening years'.[132]

Unfortunately, as we have already noted, it had taken the Treasury officials some time to persuade Chamberlain to act. Phillips's committee was further delayed by Leith-Ross's various visits abroad. By the time Phillips's committee reported in August, recession was threatening to spread to Britain from the U.S.A. Once the recession was observed to have reached Britain in December,* the committee prepared a revised report, which advocated the preparation of additional public works schemes. It also noted the first signs of a decline in private housebuilding which led it to fear that a sharp decline could coincide with the end of the rearmament programme in two years' time.[133] The Minister of Health should therefore send out an immediate circular requesting local authorities to prepare a programme of building to be carried out in the next five years.[134]

The Chancellor (now Sir John Simon) put this suggestion to the Cabinet on 26 January 1938. Chamberlain (now Prime Minister) 'agreed with the Chancellor . . . that it would be foolish to take the line that nothing could be done in this matter as no-one would believe them' but thought 'the possibilities were limited'. Other ministers believed that the Cabinet should approve in principle. This view prevailed, and the circular was sent out in May 1938.† The circular may seem, especially given the long lags in decision-making, a pale reflection of the original proposals, but it was 'certainly a great advance on anything which had been done before. There is reason to believe that it caused many local authorities to draw up long-term programmes who had never dreamed of doing so before. Some even . . . gave some serious thought to the question of works which fell outside their normal programme.'[135] The Cabinet also agreed to the committee's other recommendations, but these were, of course, soon eclipsed by rearmament.[136]

Before turning to the action on the other Committee on Economic

---

* Contemporary economic commentators did not begin to judge that a British recession had begun until December (*Economist*, Commercial History and Review of 1937, 12 February 1938; C.E.I. 24th Report).

† Cab. 27/640, C.P. 6(38), 'Public Capital Expenditure, Memorandum by Chancellor covering reports by an inter-departmental committee', 20 January 1938; C.P. 7(38), 'Public Capital Expenditure, Memorandum by Minister of Health', 21 January 1938; Cab. 23/92, Cabinet 2(38)5, 26 January 1938; Cab. 27/640, 'Draft letter to local authorities, Note by Secretary [of Standing Committee]', 10 March 1938. The generally lukewarm reaction of ministers probably explains the delays in the process of acting on the Treasury's recommendations.

Information recommendations of February 1937 (on iron and steel rationing, monetary policy, debt management, and rearmament finance), it is interesting to look more closely at Phillips's views. The official policy of rearmament announced in March 1935 had been put into practice only slowly, its first noticeable effects being on the 1936 budget.[137] By the end of 1936, according to Phillips, '[the] need to rearm [was] already causing certain difficulties in connection with the Budget, the balance of payments, a shortage of certain kinds of skilled labour and of certain kinds of materials'. This meant 'serious attention [had to] . . . be drawn to the movements in the price level', which might necessitate a rise in Bank rate within the next two years and hence the end of cheap money. In order to avoid or at least postpone this, Phillips made several suggestions, which included the financing of rearmament as much as possible out of revenue, avoiding any increase in tariffs or quotas even though the balance of payments would worsen, and counter-cyclical regulation of public expenditure, which was soon to be advocated by the Committee on Economic Information. He summarised his reasons as follows:

There is no case for raising interest rates at the moment or perhaps for almost a year to come. But in the meanwhile the more we can deal with the possible dangers of rising prices and expanding activity by selective ad hoc measures the less need there will be of applying the harsh brake of a severe general credit contraction later.

But in any case one must expect some setback after the rearmament programme is completed and the building boom is over and it may not be too early to be thinking about the measures that will be needed to maintain the volume of economic activity and the money income of the country.[138]

Thus, while Phillips believed (like Robertson) that dear money should if necessary be applied to prevent a boom from getting out of hand,[139] and though he was influenced by the exigencies of rearmament finance, he was *thinking along the same lines* as the other members of the Committee.

One of the first of the Committee's recommendations that the Treasury officials looked into was iron and steel rationing, on which they consulted Horace Wilson, in April 1937. They decided that they 'should not attempt a system of control until other methods had proved inadequate and there was a general feeling in favour of control'. Regulation of public investment was 'a more immediate question' and would, if effective, help to relieve the steel shortage.[140]

The official Committee on Trade Policy met before the Committee on Public Capital Expenditure, partly because of backing from another quarter. In March Eden (Foreign Secretary) asked Chamberlain for a ministerial committee on tariff policy, giving two reasons for his request. Firstly, he thought 'we [could] no longer be certain of peace in our time' and he wondered if it was 'possible that the policy of 1931 should be modified in the circumstances of 1937' in order to try and relax international political tension by economic means. Secondly, 'many authoritative and independent persons have suggested for quite different reasons that the time has come to call a halt to, and if possible to moderate, both the development of the Ottawa principle and the progressive protection obtained by British industries in the U.K.'; he mentioned as authorities Keynes, the Committee on Economic Information in its Twenty-first Report, and Leith-Ross.* When Chamberlain sought his officials' advice on a reply to Eden, they reminded him that they had already suggested a committee on trade policy.[141]

The committee completed its report by 9 June in order to release Leith-Ross for a League of Nations Economic Committee meeting in Geneva. Like the Phillips committee it generally agreed with the views of the Committee on Economic Information and made several specific proposals.[142] Some of these were 'not practical issues at present', for example Britain's attitude to Germany if she devalued, and the resumption of trade negotiations with Japan.[143] The suggestion that the Import Duties Advisory Committee should be asked not to raise any tariffs and to undertake a review of existing ones met with opposition from the Board of Trade, in the form of what the Board itself described as its 'old unhelpful attitude, that we shall do more by the method of bi-lateral negotiations . . . than by one-sided acts of policy'.[144] The recommendation that Britain should make concessions to the Dominions if she concluded a trade agreement with the U.S.A. involved, of course, the negotiations with several countries already in progress. One outcome of these negotiations was the Anglo-American Trade Agreement, which was one of the many ways in which the Ottawa policy was more or less abandoned by 1939.[145] Obviously, in all of this the Committee on Economic Information was only a small voice amongst many more powerful ones.

The questions of financial policy involved only the Treasury. With respect to rearmament finance and the maintenance of cheap money its intention was largely to follow policies similar to those favoured by the Committee, but the practice depended very much on 'external' factors. The methods of financing rearmament were largely dictated by the amount needed, which rose increasingly rapidly as war drew nearer.[146] Although in 1936 Phillips had feared that cheap money would have to end if boom conditions continued, the recession of 1937-8 removed that threat. At the same time, however, the Treasury persisted in its long-standing objective of funding the national debt – a policy which tended to raise the long-term rate of interest. This continuance of funding operations, much criticised by Keynes, in Committee reports and elsewhere,[147] reflected the fact that the Treasury officials, as late as 1939, 'had no coherent theory of any relation between short and long rates'.[148] Because of this, they saw nothing wrong in retaining

---

* T. 188/175, Memorandum by Eden, 24 March 1937. At the request of the Prime Minister Leith-Ross had prepared a report on the balance of payments for the Cabinet in December 1936. He had argued that the country should not try to remedy the adverse balance of payments by attempting to reduce imports (Cab. 24/265, C.P. 339(36), Memorandum on the Balance of Payments by the Chief Economic Adviser to H.M. Government, 7 December 1936; Leith-Ross, Money Talks, pp. 228-9).

the 'funding complex' they had acquired in 1920 when the mass of short-term debt had seemed to threaten them with loss of control over the money supply and prices.[149] From an attempt Phillips made to explain the determination of interest rates to Chamberlain in July 1937,[150] it is clear that Phillips's thinking, like that of many economists of his time, was in a transitional stage. Some Keynesian criticisms of the classical theory, or at least of its policy prescriptions, had been accepted, but it was not recognised how far-reaching these criticisms were.

Accordingly, of the two other proposals of the Committee's Twenty-second Report, the Treasury examined the possibility of raising 'those branches of the stamp duties which would be especially felt by speculators', but disliked Keynes's suggestion that it issue more securities with a fixed redemption date in order to keep up the prices of the longer maturities. In fact, given the large amount of debt maturing in the next few years, which ruled out both new long-term and new short-term loans, the officials thought they would 'have to do what the Committee suggest on this occasion but it will be because we cannot help it not because it is right'.[151]

These developments within Whitehall were not disclosed to the Committee (except to Debenham, who was secretary to both the Phillips and Leith-Ross inter-departmental committees).[152] Phillips was always 'careful . . . not to impart indiscreet information to the Committee'.* Salter, who was one of the signatories of the Oxford economists' letter to *The Times* in June 1937, thought counter-cyclical regulation of public expenditure was 'still heresy in Whitehall', Henderson imagined Cabinet ministers had given up reading Committee on Economic Information reports, and Keynes was still complaining of the apparent prevalence of orthodoxy in Whitehall in 1939.† After the Twenty-second Report the Committee seemed to lose heart. Keynes was ill and did not attend for eighteen months. The next report, in November 1937, was, the members agreed, 'the most unsatisfactory report [they had] ever produced'. Keynes thought it was verbose, out of date, and confused – 'a really dreadful document'.[153] The Committee had chosen in July to discuss 'questions connected with the price level, the future of international trade, and the future of gold',[154] that is the issues raised by the 'gold problem' which had been much discussed in the first half of 1937. The high price of gold since the devaluation of the dollar in 1934 had encouraged increased world gold production and dishoarding. The only

---

* T. 160/771/F 19429, Phillips to Catterns, 29 November 1938. Whitehall's concern about secrecy induced Hemming to stop sending Committee papers to Salter when he was elected to Parliament in 1937. Salter protested, and the matter was referred to the Committee on the E.A.C., and apparently not raised in the C.E.I. again. Keynes Papers, Hemming to Salter, 30 June, Salter to Hemming, 6 July, Hemming to Salter, 8 July, and Salter to Hemming, 14 July 1937; C.E.I. 73rd meeting, 8 July 1937).

† Salter, *Memoirs of a Public Servant*, p. 253; Keynes Papers, Henderson to Keynes, 11 November 1937; Keynes, 'Democracy and Efficiency', *New Statesman*, 28 January 1939. Keynes was, however, aware that 'the Treasury, though a bit scared of up-to-date methods, have not settled convictions against them' (Keynes Papers L/39, Keynes to Scrimgeour, 3 August 1939).

major buyers for the greatly expanded supply coming on to the market, further increased in 1937 by Russian and French gold sales, were the British and American Treasuries. In April 1937 there were rumours that the U.S. might reduce the price of gold, which caused sharp drops on security and commodity markets in America and elsewhere.[155] The British Treasury was concerned because a fall in the price of gold would mean either a large loss on the holdings of the Exchange Equalisation Account, or an upward revaluation of sterling. On the other hand, if the price of gold were not altered, the two Treasuries would sooner or later find it impossible to persist in their policies of sterilising gold, and serious world inflation would develop.[156] The British authorities' views on what to do differed. The Governor of the Bank 'favour[ed] an immediate approach to the U.S. with a proposal that they should reduce their buying price [for gold] with a promise from us to conform to such a movement'.[157] Phillips and Hopkins favoured a reduction in the price of gold, but did not want to encourage it until British unemployment 'has been reduced as far as it will go and . . . rising prices give no adequate further stimulus to production . . . Even if this time may not be so far ahead it is certainly not yet.' Further, any such action must be undertaken only as part of a general agreement between all the major countries.[158] Leith-Ross still thought that the ultimate objective should be a return to the gold standard, and that Britain should join in international discussions on currency stabilisation.[159]

Some of these differences spread into the Committee's discussions. As Henderson explained to Keynes, there was not only 'a variety of issues that were never sharply defined in discussion . . . [and] about three or four distinct points of view', but also 'the real protagonists of adverse points of view include[d] Leith-Ross and Phillips, who are obviously in complete disagreement with one another, but who, after the manner of officials, do not attempt to expound their position clearly'.[160] At one stage in the lengthy process of drafting and redrafting, Leith-Ross insisted that the report should mention the advantages of returning to the gold standard; Phillips and Henderson objected. Stamp tried to compromise by including Phillips's objections; these rendered the report inconsistent, to which Henderson and Robertson objected. At yet another meeting the offending paragraphs were removed. The report was so inconclusive that Robertson 'doubt[ed] whether the most leisured and the most brilliant minister will be able to arrive at any clear idea of what the Committee's mind is on these important subjects'.[161]

Henderson was wrong in assuming that ministers no longer read Committee reports. The Prime Minister circulated this report to the Cabinet and asked the Treasury for its comments. Hopkins sent Chamberlain a note on the report written by Leith-Ross for the President of the Board of Trade, which 'says all that needs to be said about the nature of the report which is unusually inconclusive'. Since 'the latter part of Sir F. Leith-Ross's note [was] in effect a plea for stabilisation of sterling on gold', he also sent a note giving Phillips's and his own views on that subject. Chamberlain concluded: 'I find myself, so far as I can venture to express an opinion, in agreement with Sir R. Hopkins.'[162]

By this time, as Hopkins and Leith-Ross pointed out, the subjects of the report were no longer topical. Phillips had visited Washington in September and had learnt that Morgenthau (the Secretary of the U.S. Treasury) was not in favour of changing the price of gold.[163] By November, with the development of the recession in America, the problems of the world economy looked very different from those of early 1937.

In January 1938, in its next report, which was very much shorter than the previous one, the Committee discussed the American recession and its repercussions on the U.K. Since it still feared that housebuilding would soon fall off substantially, it expected the present recession to worsen in 1939 and 1940. In the first draft Debenham suggested two measures to avoid or mitigate this: increased public investment and credit expansion. Phillips then expanded this part of the report in three directions. He strengthened the argument for counter-cyclical public works, by emphasising the need for plans to be made immediately, an understandable move given the current activities of Phillips's committee and the imminent Cabinet discussion of its report;* he mentioned a third policy, namely promoting exports by lowering trade barriers and encouraging foreign lending;[164] and he expanded a paragraph advocating the building up of food stocks in Britain.†

The Committee initially intended its next report to contain an amplification of its recommendations on public works, and, in line with a suggestion by Keynes, a recommendation for improved statistical information on construction. Since it did not meet between January and May 1938, the Committee scrapped the original idea and reported on the economic situation in the U.S.A. instead.[165] The gap in the meetings may have been due to the discussions then taking place on the future of the Economic Advisory Council.[166] Stamp had earlier become very concerned about the

---

* Above, pp. 141–2. The advantage of C.E.I. reports in furthering Phillips's objective was that they would reach and be read by Neville Chamberlain.

† Cab. 58/22, Draft 24th Report; 81st meeting of C.E.I.; 24th Report, 4 January 1938. Several C.E.I. members advocated, in and out of Whitehall, the policy of stockpiling imported food and raw materials in order to reduce exchange difficulties in the event of war. After Keynes had advocated this in a lecture to the British Association in August 1938, Phillips, with the backing of Waley and of Cobbold of the Bank of England, urged the setting up of an inter-departmental committee. Though he succeeded in getting a committee, he did not then get much support from other government departments. (Keynes, 'The Policy of Government Storage of Foodstuffs and Raw Materials', *Economic Journal*, September 1938; T. 160/873/F 15814/1–3, Setting up, proceedings and report of Inter-departmental Committee on Exchange Difficulties and Essential Materials, November 1938–July 1939; see also Salter, *Memoirs of a Public Servant*, pp. 245–9, and Keynes Papers A/38, correspondence between Keynes and Salter and others).

Like the 'later version' of the Keynes–Henderson plan (the Clearing Union) a later version of this Keynes plan (an international commodity union) became official Treasury and Cabinet policy in 1942–3 (Keynes, *Collected Writings*, Vol. XXVI, forthcoming).

state of the Committee and had contacted Chamberlain. Apparently Chamberlain encouraged the Committee to remain in existence and to concern itself with the economic problems created by rearmament and the preparations for war.[167]

The economic problems of defence

The first and most obvious thing to be said about the effects of the greatly increased defence expenditure on the British economy in 1938 is that it put an end to the recession of 1937–8. Public works, albeit not of the kind advocated by the economists, did indeed combat the slump.[168] By the time the Committee on Economic Information came to discuss the effects of rearmament in October 1938, the turning-point was passed. By this time, too, the Munich crisis had occurred and the nation was preparing for war in earnest.

For the Committee's two reports on the economic problems of defence Keynes was back in action, and the analysis and policy recommendations of both reports owed much to him. The major points made in these reports and in Keynes's other writings at that time were that the fundamental problem of rearmament was one of the allocation of physical resources, rather than of public finance, and that higher interest rates would not help. When the Committee prepared the first of the two reports unemployment was still high; hence it was anxious that the government should not resort to deflationary monetary or fiscal measures in a misguided fear of the inflationary effect of its greatly increased expenditure. It recommended that competing demands for resources suitable for both rearmament and other purposes should be dealt with by means of a system of priorities for orders in the investment industries and the discouragement of consumption of particular goods such as motor cars by, for example, raising the horse-power tax. The report concentrated on the balance-of-payments problem. Increasing employment and production brought with them increased imports of goods needed specifically for rearmament, of raw materials, and of food and other consumption goods purchased out of the incomes generated by the increased production. At the same time exports were reduced by the fall in exports from industries producing armaments. Although Britain's gold reserves were large, most had been acquired since 1932, partly because of an inflow of short-term capital, whose holders might regard a persistently large balance-of-payments deficit as a reason for withdrawal. The balance on current account could be improved through the stimulation of exports by means of trade agreements and the reduction of imports by taxes on some consumption goods. Devaluation was rejected because the amount consistent with maintenance of the Tripartite Agreement would not achieve much. More immediately useful, however, would be measures to improve the capital account. Keynes suggested reimposition of the embargo on new overseas issues and a ban on the purchase of foreign securities by British residents, limitation of Empire borrowing in London, and borrowing by the Treasury in Canada by means of bills repayable in dollars. The aim was to finance the deficit and support the sterling exchange, without resorting to credit restriction and dear money.[169]

The Treasury men, with the exception of Leith-Ross, shared the Committee's view that they should not resort to deflationary measures; as unemployment was still high, the greatly increased loan expenditure did not threaten inflation. They also agreed about the seriousness of the balance-of-payments problem, and were apparently attracted by Keynes's suggestions. When Keynes first put them forward, Phillips showed them to Catterns at the Bank of England and reported the reaction to the Chancellor. The Bank's, and the Treasury's, attitude was that the sound ideas, in particular tightening up the policy on overseas loans, were already being carried out, while the issue of dollar bonds in Canada was open to the objection that they would be bought back by British investors.[170] With respect to the Committee's other suggestions, Hopkins successfully proposed to the Chancellor that in the 1939 budget income tax should not be raised, and that the tobacco and horsepower taxes should be substantially increased.[171]

By April Keynes and Phillips were agreed that government spending was reducing the 'abnormal unemployment' of the inter-war years.[172] The Committee's next report, in July, described current problems as 'the adequacy of the potential output of the industries most concerned with the production of supplies for the defence programme', and 'the possibility of a general excess of demand over supply'; both threatened inflation and a worsening of the balance-of-payments deficit. The Committee recommended the control of investment expenditure, limitation of dividends, investment of undistributed profits in government securities, stimulation of exports, and measures such as the building up of stocks of food and raw materials, to relieve the pressure on the balance of payments and on shipping which would occur in wartime. Sterling would have to be supported because once war came it would be essential to have adequate foreign exchange reserves to pay for imports of food and munitions. Exchange control would also have to be contemplated.[173] Both here and in a memorandum he sent to the Chancellor and to the Governor of the Bank, Keynes emphasised that the interest-rate weapon should not be used to restrict private investment. In his memorandum he pointed out there were other deterrents available which were both more discriminating and more effective, for example, control over new issues, a system of priorities, and taxation. Foreign lending could also be prevented by controls. The Committee's report pointed out that higher interest rates would not be very effective where firms normally financed investment out of undistributed profits; they would have most impact on the building industries and hence release few resources for export; they would also greatly increase the cost of government borrowing.[174]

The report included a 'brave pioneering effort' (Keynes's words) to quantify the magnitude of the problem by trying to estimate the excess of investment demand over capacity in 1939 and the supply of savings available to finance new investment. Debenham estimated that investment demand would exceed capacity by £75–170m in 1939 and that there would be a deficiency of up to £100m between the financial resources available for the purchase of investment goods and the financial resources required. The attempt to use these hastily constructed figures to support the Committee's proposals alarmed Keynes, who thought it 'wildly irresponsible . . . to feed Cabinet ministers with these guesses', and persuaded the Committee not to claim too much for them.*

According to Sayers, it was by means of the Committee's Twenty-seventh Report that the Prime Minister and the Chancellor 'receive[d] as the considered advice of the experts, outside and inside, this rejection of the interest rate weapon on the two grounds that it could not substantially help the mobilisation of the production effort and that it would be a nuisance from the point of view of government borrowing'.[175] The Chancellor had also received Keynes's memorandum in May.[176] Phillips had been quite sympathetic to Keynes's ideas then, although he did not accept the point that even when full employment was reached higher interest rates should be avoided, and did not believe that the Treasury could set the rate at which it borrowed. Like Hawtrey, who was less sympathetic to Keynes's arguments, he thought the feasible rate was 4 per cent.[177] However, by the autumn Phillips (and others) had come to believe that it was possible to finance the war on a 3 per cent basis. The Treasury officials had been discussing the terms of war-time borrowing since April. In July 1939 the Phillips Committee on Control of Saving and Investment, of which Robertson was a member at Phillips's request, considered Keynes's ideas on war-time and immediate pre-war borrowing. They discussed 'the questions of economic theory involved, and their relation to Treasury policy on borrowing on short- and long-term'. The resulting report suggested the possibility that the government could treat each sector of the market separately and tailor its borrowing to suit different types of investors.† In October Phillips suggested discussions with the Governor, who favoured a '3 per cent War'. All

---

* C.E.I. 27th Report; Keynes Papers, Keynes to Stamp, 1 July 1939; Cab. 58/22, Keynes to Debenham, 1 July 1939; 96th meeting of C.E.I., 4 July 1939; Keynes Papers, Stamp to Keynes, 5 July, and Keynes to Stamp, 25 July 1939.

    Stamp supported Keynes because in 1935 he had been chairman of a Treasury Committee on Savings (whose members were Phillips, Hawtrey, Clay, and Gregg) which had also tried to estimate the volume of savings and investment. Stamp told Keynes that it 'broke down finally because it could reach no useful conclusion' (Keynes Papers, Stamp to Keynes, 5 July 1939; see also T. 160/653/F 15470/01, Committee on Savings, Proceedings and Papers).

† T. 160/1289/F 19426/1–3, Minutes, memoranda and report of Committee on Control of Saving and Investment, April–August 1939. The report also pointed out that government borrowing from banks would not be inflationary insofar as it mopped up deposits held idle because of liquidity preference.

concerned regarded it as essential that the rate should not rise during the war as it had done, with such expensive consequences, during the first world war. The decision was taken on 26 October and the first war loan was offered at 3 per cent in March 1940.[178] It proved to be a comparative failure, but the authorities stuck to their principles for the rest of the war.[179]

Robertson was not the only member of the Committee on Economic Information called in to advise the Treasury in the summer of 1939. Phillips had been thinking of Henderson for his committee but it was decided that Henderson should join Stamp and Clay in preparing a 'survey of war plans in the economic and financial sphere'. The Stamp Survey was established on 30 June 1939 to 'undertake a review of the plans and proposals prepared by the various Departments for the purpose of keeping the country going during war'. After the outbreak of war it concentrated more and more on the formulation and coordination of economic policy and thus, according to Austin Robinson, 'contributed greatly both in detail and broad policy to the avoidance of major dislocations in the transition from peace to war'.[180] Furthermore, under the influence of the Stamp Survey and Keynes's *How to Pay for the War*, serious pioneering efforts in using quantitative methods in making economic policy, the development of national income and expenditure estimates got under way. The outcome was Kingsley Wood's Keynesian budget of April 1941. In December 1939 when the Survey was asked to prepare a periodic review of the country's balance-of-payments position and of changes in the manpower and materials positions for the Ministerial Committee on Economic Policy, additional economists were recruited as the Central Economic Information Service. A year later this body, initially in Robbins's words 'a sort of annex to the deliberations of the three wise men', was split into the Economic Section of the Cabinet Office and the Central Statistical Office. In the meantime, at the beginning of 1940 as one response to Keynes's *How to Pay for the War*, an official estimate of the national income by Bowley was presented to the Stamp Survey, who decided that a full financial survey was needed. By the second half of 1940 Meade and Stone (in the Central Economic Information Service) were preparing the first draft of part of the first Budget White Paper on National Income and Expenditure.[181]

An indispensable figure in these developments was Hopkins.[182] Although most of the changes in Treasury thinking and innovations in Treasury policy in the 1930s originated with Phillips, it was usually Hopkins who put the proposals to the Chancellor. Phillips was apparently somewhat uncommunicative in manner,[183] and it is possible that he would not have exerted as much influence on policy as he did without Hopkins's backing and powers of persuasion. Furthermore, it is known of Hopkins but not of Phillips that he became convinced of the utility of Keynesian ideas during the second world war. Phillips went to Washington as head of the British Treasury mission in 1940 and died in 1943. Very little is discoverable about his war-time views on British economic policy.* Hopkins, the defender of the 'Treasury view' in 1930, wholeheartedly supported Keynes's ideas from the autumn of 1940, in many respects fathered the 1944 Employment White Paper, read the *General Theory* twice, and used arguments and quotations from it in writing the report of the 1945 National Debt Enquiry, which laid the foundations of the post-war cheap-money policy.[184] The 'conversion' of the Treasury to Keynes's ideas on economic management was apparently complete.†

Note on the Committee on Scientific Research

The scientific work of the Committee of Civil Research and the Economic Advisory Council has been more or less completely ignored in this study; with respect to the first of these bodies we refer the interested reader to R. M. Macleod and E. K. Andrews, 'The Committee of Civil Research: Scientific Advice for Economic Development', *Minerva*, Summer 1969, and to the records of the scientific sub-committees.[1] Six new Economic Advisory Council sub-committees on scientific subjects were appointed, on the education and supply of biologists, the slaughtering of livestock, British representation at international scientific meetings, cattle diseases, protection of the fauna and flora of Asia, and nutrition in the Colonial Empire.[2] At the same time several sub-committees of the Committee of Civil Research were continuing their work, for example, the tsetse-fly committee, the locust control committee, and the committees on the mineral content of natural pastures, on a Severn River barrage, on dietetics, and on the fishing industry.

The scientific counterpart to the Committee on Economic Information was the Committee on Scientific Research. It produced several reports, two of which, on Science and Finance, may also be of some interest to economists. The Committee on Scientific Research began meeting in April 1932. MacDonald announced that he was 'anxious that like the Committee on Economic Information ... [the members] themselves should choose subjects for inquiry and should not leave the initiative to him'. One of the topics suggested at this first meeting was 'a comparison of the extent to which banks in this country and abroad possess organised means of scientific advice on problems raised by schemes submitted to them by firms requiring bank advances'; eighteen months later the committee produced its first report on 'the question of improving the contacts which at present exist [in Britain] between the world of science and finance'. There were two problems involved: firstly, the avoidance of company flotations based on unsound or dubious scientific claims, a phenomenon which had been quite common in the 1928 'new issue boom'; secondly, the difficulty of firms' obtaining finance to develop new scientific discoveries. The committee's suggestion was that banks and issuing houses should develop the habit of consulting freely with such bodies as the Royal Society, the Department of Scientific and Industrial Research, the Medical Research Council, and the Agricultural Research Council on the scientific merits of pro-

---

* What we do know is that Keynes and Phillips corresponded frequently and that Phillips worked closely with Keynes when he was in Washington (see *Collected Writings*, Vols. xxv–xxvi and Keynes papers L/P).

† The war-time Treasury included one persistent opponent of Keynes, namely Henderson. Whereas economists who had held theoretical views opposed to Keynes, such as Robbins, Hayek, and Robertson, welcomed and practically supported *How to Pay for the War* (see *Collected Writings*, Vol. xxii, Chs. 1, 2), Henderson was profoundly sceptical of almost all the ideas for improved economic management and a better post-war world that Keynes supported, with one or two exceptions such as family allowances (ibid. and Vol. xxvii).

posed new ventures. To encourage this the Treasury should, via the intermediaries of the chairman of the Committee of the London Clearing Banks and the Governor of the Bank of England, inform banks and issuing houses that the scientific bodies were available for such consultation.

This suggestion had earlier been agreed with the Treasury, who also discussed the idea with the Deputy Governor of the Bank. The Cabinet agreed in January 1934, but then 'a delay of a year supervened while the Royal Society assembled itself to decide that it was not a suitable body to fill the role assigned to it and the E.A.C. Committee re-assembled itself to decide that in the circumstances their original recommendation should stand subject to elimination of any reference to the Royal Society'. The committee made this recommendation in its third report. A further delay resulted from the difficulties caused for certain financial institutions by 'wild' speculation in the pepper market in 1935. Hopkins and Norman therefore 'held the matter up until pepper was forgotten' and the letters – to the chairman of the Stock Exchange as well as to the Governor and to the chairman of the Committee of the London Clearing Bankers – were finally sent in October 1935.[3]

The Committee on Scientific Research also prepared reports on the need for improved nutrition of the British people, pollution of the atmosphere by smoke, and the supply of quinine in the Empire. It met infrequently, perhaps partly because two of its members died. Although the body seems to have been regarded as valuable by many government officials it ceased to meet in March 1938.[4]

CHAPTER 6

CONCLUSIONS

We hope that this study of the Economic Advisory Council and its committees, together with the documents reprinted below, will enable a more balanced judgment to be made on the successes and failures of this pioneering advisory institution in a field which has been more closely cultivated since the second world war. Our own conclusions on specific episodes will be apparent by now, but it also seems useful to draw attention to some of the wider issues raised by the experience of the Economic Advisory Council.

In Chapter 2 we pointed out that the Council, as originally constituted, brought together two sets of ideas which had emerged in post-1918 discussions of economic policy formation. These we labelled 'technocratic' and 'representative' respectively. The conflation of these two sets of ideas was a major cause of the Council's failure. The representative principle was recognised in heavily diluted form: a mixture of businessmen and trade union leaders chosen by the Prime Minister was a token move in this direction. When combined with the more technocratic apparatus of an economic staff, it resulted in a body which was open to all the criticisms made by its more activist members at the time, especially by those who were led to expect that it would be an 'engine for action'. It did not come near to satisfying the proponents of a Council of Industry or National Economic Council capable of authoritative deliberation on questions of industrial relations and economic policy. Nor did it satisfy the aspirations of those who argued that Parliament, with its party squabbles, no longer provided an adequate arena for well-informed discussion of complex economic questions and consequently favoured the establishment of an industrial or vocational parliament, parallel with, though subordinate to, the existing Parliament.

During the immediate post-war period the vocational parliament idea was prevalent in socialist circles. The Webbs broached it in their *Constitution for a Socialist Commonwealth of Great Britain* in 1920; and it figured in the guild socialist literature, to which Cole was a prominent contributor, where industrial self-government went hand in hand with workers' control.[1] By the end of a decade in which economic problems dominated politics, the idea acquired support in circles which could not be said to have been influenced by socialist discussions. The Liberal Party showed an interest in the national council idea in its 'Yellow Book', and it appears from Layton's remarks cited earlier that some Liberals envisaged the Council as a constraining influence on government as much as an advisory body.[2] The popularity of the idea in circumstances in which clear majority government was difficult to achieve was not confined to the Liberals. The Conservative industrialist Sir Alfred Mond, initially an advocate of a League of Industrial Peace based on covenants and sanctions similar to those of the League of Nations, moved on to the view that Parliament should create an elaborate supreme Economic Council as a third chamber.[3] Another major convert to the idea of an economic sub-parliament was Winston Churchill, an ex-Chancellor of the Exchequer, who first raised the matter when the establishment of the Economic Advisory Council was announced in Parliament. He subsequently developed the theme in the Romanes Lecture in June 1930, when he proposed delegating economic issues to an assembly which could treat them properly 'as matters requiring high, cold, technical, and dispassionate or disinterested decision'.[4]

Although industrial parliaments no longer carry much conviction, governments, to judge from the succession of attempts to establish some control over wages, incomes, and prices in this and other countries since the second world war, have a continuing interest in securing the advice, consent, and cooperation of industrial and trade union leaders in carrying out their responsibilities in the field of economic management. In this respect the Economic Advisory Council, though a failure, deserves a small place in the history of a political and economic instrumentality which, with the possible exception of the National Economic Development Council, has yet to be successfully established.

The Economic Advisory Council deserves greater recognition as a technocratic innovation. Even during the brief life of the Council proper, the existence of a small full-time economic staff represented a considerable improvement on the previous state of affairs; it proved to be a permanent innovation. Nevertheless, the Council and its staff as a body failed to influence the economic policy of the second Labour Government, and the reasons for this are not hard to find. There were the defects in the Council's constitution which probably increased the likelihood of disagreement between members of the Council, particularly between the businessmen and the economists. There were also more important reasons for the government's lack of response to the economists' proposals than the cleavage within the Council and its constitutional inadequacies. During 1930 the government manoeuvred itself into a position where its policy options were determined by previous decisions, especially the commitment to remain on the gold standard. Here Snowden was the chief person responsible for the outcome. As Chancellor of the Exchequer at a time when the commitment to the gold standard left monetary policy in the hands of the Bank of England alone, and as a convinced free-trader and upholder of financial orthodoxy, Snowden was the most powerful member of the government on all economic questions. Many of the policy alternatives which emerged from the Council's discussions were ruled out *ab initio*, so that when the government was overwhelmed by the international financial crisis there was practically no leeway for action along different lines. Nevertheless, as is clear from the evidence presented in Chapter 4, both during and after the crisis the Prime Minister and the Treasury were anxious to have the advice of Keynes, Henderson, and Stamp, the Council's three most prominent economists. It seems justifiable to conclude, therefore, that in spite of the failure of the Council experiment the economists had established a claim to play an active advisory role by virtue of their special expertise in day-to-day policy-making. They continued to exercise this role throughout the 1930s through the medium of the Committee on Economic Information.

In Chapter 5 we showed how the new context created by the departure from the gold standard enabled the economists who served on the Committee on Economic Information to be more successful in making their views heard in the Treasury. Thus while Sir Arthur Salter was probably correct in saying that the recommendations of the Committee would have 'profoundly changed the policy of the time', and that they 'anticipated much that later became orthodox in Whitehall',[5] we would argue that he was wrong in thinking that the Committee was ineffective. Secrecy served more to conceal the successes than the failures of the experiment.

The reasons for the success of the Committee, especially when compared with the Council, relate both to the form and content of the advice offered. The fact that its proposals were framed within the context of the government's cheap money and exchange rate policy, which the Committee approved and wanted to see maintained, facilitated official discussion. Under the new régime not only were external constraints slackened, but the Treasury became responsible for every aspect of financial policy. The advice of the Committee went directly to the policy-makers who mattered. The smallness of the Committee, its composition almost entirely of economists and civil servants, and the relative constancy of its membership also helped to strengthen its position. In carrying out the single function of appraisal and advice, it was able to maintain a remarkably consistent viewpoint, and to achieve a high level of continuity and relevance.

In saying this we are denying the validity of Sir Frederick Leith-Ross's criticism of the Committee, namely that

The discussions at the meetings were lively and often controversial, but I do not think that any of the reports produced gave a clear and unqualified guidance to Ministers in regard to economic policy . . . The secretary . . . worked like a slave to secure agreement between the irreconcilable views of the members on the recommendations to be made.[6]

The only case to which this judgment could be applied is the Committee's Twenty-third Report of October 1937. On that occasion 'irreconcilable views' resulted in a highly unsatisfactory report. But the views in question were not those of the economists: the disagreement was between the two Treasury officials, one of whom was Leith-Ross. With one exception, the reports, as their introductions always made clear, 'represented the general views of the Committee without attempting to express the different shades of opinion held by individual members'. In the case of the exception, Robertson, disagreeing with Keynes's views on monetary policy, dissociated himself from six paragraphs.

The airing of differences of viewpoint in front of the Treasury members may even have been beneficial in changing the theoretical basis of the Treasury's views. The increasing interest shown by the Treasury in the Committee's deliberations was symbolised by the fact that two of its officials became full members. In this way the Committee avoided one of the criticisms legitimately levelled at the Council, namely that 'its work . . . was not effectively integrated with that of the departments affected [so that] it bore the appearance of an auxiliary engine not geared to the main shaft'.[7] It did not, however, avoid the problem of there being no effective 'minister in charge'.[8] The Committee could only be effective in influencing major policy decisions insofar as it managed to convince the Treasury officials, who in turn had to convince the Chancellor.*

This raises the still unresolved question of whether economic advisers should be concentrated in the Treasury or attached to another minister or department. There have been several attempts in this country to create a 'counterweight' to the Treasury's dominance, notably the Economic Section of the War Cabinet, the Department of Economic Affairs, and most recently Programme Analysis and Review (P.A.R.) and the Central Policy Review Staff (C.P.R.S.). The Economic Advisory Council may have been intended as such a counterweight; the Committee on Economic Information certainly retained a secretariat which was independent of the Treasury.† Its successor, the Economic Section of the War Cabinet, went a stage further in having its own minister, first Arthur Greenwood, and then the Lord President of the Council, Sir John Anderson. But when Anderson became Chancellor of the Exchequer in 1943 he retained ministerial responsibility for the Economic Section. Keynes regretted this at the time because: 'I think it would be a pity to upset the balance of power between the Chancellor and the President

---

* Chamberlain may have been willing to listen to unorthodox advice, but he rarely acted on it. He consistently denied, however, that the National Government was 'a safety-first government destitute of new ideas . . . in fact it is continually introducing changes of a really revolutionary character' (Feiling, *Life of Neville Chamberlain*, p. 229). It is possible that his reluctance to accept his official advisers' proposals on, say, public works in the later nineteen-thirties may have been due to a belief that the government was already being sufficiently radical already. Now that the Chamberlain papers have just been opened, it should be possible for scholars to answer such questions.

† In a letter to the authors Sir Austin Robinson has said that 'when he joined the same small staff in the Cabinet Office in 1939 there was still a strong tradition of independence from Treasury control over their thinking'.

of the Economic Committee . . . I have always thought it a mistake to link the Economic Section to the Treasury where they would either be too powerful or not powerful enough.'[9] The Economic Section was absorbed into the Treasury in 1947, when an Economic Planning Board was also set up. This body was the forerunner of the National Economic Development Council of 1961, and ultimately of the Department of Economic Affairs and the National Plan of 1965. Commenting on the outcome of this train of events, one recent study has concluded that 'what remained at the end of the 1960s was a strengthened Treasury, a Cabinet Office which had made itself a central administration, and the same sets of problems that led before to dissatisfaction with these official arrangements'.[10] The success or failure of the latest attempt to devise new arrangements, the C.P.R.S., will also depend on the attitude of the Treasury and/or the personalities of its members: P.A.R. was a successful innovation, but only at the cost of its being taken over by the Treasury.[11] Indeed, Treasury dominance in economic policy may be inevitable: it may be the case that 'if full benefit is to be derived from economic (or indeed other) advisers, it is no use putting them in a separate compartment from those who are engaged in the day-to-day work of administration in those fields in which advice is needed . . . Only so can advisers make their influence felt at the early stages when facts are being sorted out, theories are beginning to emerge and the first pointers to future policy are being formulated'.[12] The Treasury discussions of exchange policy in the winter of 1931–2 provide an example of advisers being of more use than might otherwise have been the case as a result of their views being officially considered at an early stage.[13] Keynes himself came to hold a similar view: in 1945 he wrote that 'with modern developments of policy, decisions on such matters [as public capital expenditure] have become so much a part of the Government's economic programme as a whole that they should not be dissociated from the Chancellor of the Exchequer as the responsible minister and his official department'.[14]

The experience of the Economic Advisory Council and the Committee on Economic Information shows that disagreements among economists did not prevent them from making definite policy recommendations. Nevertheless, there was a lack of consensus on fundamental matters of economic analysis during this period, the effects of which were compounded by differences of opinion over the appropriate advisory 'style' to be adopted. These are connected with some of the wider issues involved in the interpretation of the 'Keynesian revolution'. It is by now widely recognised that the consensus which formed around Keynes's ideas in the late 1930s and during the second world war was largely responsible for increasing the usefulness of economics and economists to governments. Since Keynes himself features so prominently in this study, it seems worth asking what light our findings shed on this aspect of the 'revolution'. We concentrate

on the role of Keynes vis-à-vis other economic advisers to the British government in the inter-war years.[15]

Chapter 2 showed that a case for employing economists in government
was articulated long before any of the positions which we now associate
with the name of Keynes were formulated. It belongs in fact to the immediate
post-1918 period of enthusiasm for 'scientific administration', which was
later to be reinforced by the persistence of economic problems of a radically
different character from those faced by pre-war governments. Keynes himself fully endorsed this movement. His faith in the 'scientific spirit' as opposed
to the 'sterility of the party attitude', aiming at compromise rather than
truth, is amply demonstrated in his claims on behalf of the Council before it
was created, and in his letter to the Prime Minister proposing the establishment of the Committee of Economists. While he was aware of the limitations
placed on action by habits and existing political interest groupings, he
regarded most economic problems as basically intellectual problems, sus-
ceptible to rational solution. His uniqueness as an adviser lay in combining
this with a mixture of realism, intellectual radicalism, and capacity for public
persuasion which prevented him from being either a visionary or a mere
technocrat concerned only with exploring the freedom set by the *status quo*.
But even if Keynes's claims on behalf of economics are understandable,
there is still need for some explanation as to why others accepted such claims
at sufficiently near face-value to advocate or acquiesce in the creation of a
body like the Economic Advisory Council. A possible explanation can be
found in the doctrine of 'salvation through science', which seems to have
commanded fairly widespread allegiance in the inter-war period. In its naive
form this manifested itself in a belief in the capacity of the expert to provide
technocratic solutions to most problems – solutions around which consensus
would develop if only prejudices could be set aside. To a modern reader the
confidence expressed during the inter-war period in the power of 'scientific'
methods and technology to solve Britain's problems and usher in a new
age is remarkable, not simply because we are more disillusioned but because
circumstances might have encouraged less optimistic attitudes.

During and after the first world war there was a marked increase in state
support and involvement in scientific research and its applications to industry,
chiefly through the Department of Scientific and Industrial Research and
its industrial research associations.[16] 'Rationalisation' was also in many
respects synonymous with 'salvation through science'. Since, however,
rationalisation also frequently entailed adverse effects on existing work
practices and employment prospects, trade union leaders such as Bevin
constantly drew attention to these effects, while at the same time defending
the record of the trade union movement on restrictive practices. What now
seems significant is that there should be so little evidence of retreat into
romantic anti-technology redoubts. The General Council of the T.U.C.
continually emphasised the positive role which trade unions could play in

fostering innovation and rationalisation.* The spokesmen for land settlements and a return to the simple delights of rural existence as a solution to the unemployment problem – Ramsay MacDonald, George Lansbury, and a section of the Liberals – were not associated with the trade union movement.

This may explain the apparent ease with which some of the faith in science and the benefits of technology could be transferred to the far more divisive terrain cultivated by economists.

Given the experimental character of the Economic Advisory Council, and some of the grandiose claims made on its behalf when it was founded, more serious scepticism might have been expected. One reason for the lack of scepticism may be that most politicians and laymen held a simplistic view of what economists had to offer. This led them to believe that economic problems would yield their secrets by a careful scrutiny of the 'facts'. Such naive empiricism can certainly be detected in the memorandum which preceded the establishment of the Committee of Civil Research in 1925: it spoke of 'most economic problems [being] at bottom statistical'.[17] A version of the technocratic fallacy also seems to lie behind Churchill's proposal for a chamber of economic experts, and it may have been the spread of this kind of thinking that led Harold Laski to issue a warning against the growing faith in government by expert under the title *The Limitations of the Expert*, in 1931.[18]

The proceedings of the Economic Advisory Council quickly revealed that more was at stake than 'statistics', just as the proceedings of the Committee of Economists revealed that more was at stake than questions of political evaluation and administrative expediency. When faced with the 'common-sense' solutions favoured by the businessmen on the Council, the economists tended to close ranks.[19] The counter-charge was that economists dealt in 'mere theory' as opposed to the wisdom of practical experience; it was most frequently made in cases where the advice of economists did not conform with decisions reached on other grounds. Thus although Churchill obliged his official advisers to produce counter-arguments to Keynes's criticisms of the gold standard policy before making the decision to return to gold in 1925, he dismissed Keynes as an 'academic theorist' in the parliamentary debate on the subject.[20] The introduction of the tariff in 1932 provides an example of the way in which politicians pursue the opposite tack when expert advice can be mobilised as a rationalisation for measures already decided on other grounds.[21]

---

* This was, for example, the theme of the presidential address given by George Hicks to the T.U.C. annual congress in 1928, which was one of the first moves towards the Mond–Turner talks. The speech ended on the following note: the new industrial order was characterised by 'vast changes in technology, in methods of management, enlargement of the scale of production, finance and organisation. Scientific research, psychological investigation, and enlightened common sense have been applied in working out the principles of a more efficient, economical and humane system of production.'

The economists working for the Economic Advisory Council displayed a self-consciousness about their role vis-à-vis businessmen and politicians which may reflect the novelty of the situation.[22] This self-consciousness did not lead them all to the same conclusion as to the proper attitude which the 'economist *qua* economist' should adopt towards the political world in which he found himself. Thus Pigou, who believed that economics should be judged ultimately by its practical results in terms of human welfare, combined this with a contempt for politicians which made him wary of compromising his intellectual position, and hence more reluctant than Keynes to commit himself firmly to specific policy measures, especially those like the tariff which required high standards of political conduct. Pigou was also prone to take refuge in the idea that as an academic economist he was more concerned to clarify issues than formulate solutions: economists were 'engineers, not engine-drivers'.[23] Robbins was not content to adopt Pigou's somewhat fatalistic stance, mentally shrugging his shoulders when faced with a clash between political expediency and what he regarded as the correct diagnosis; he went further in spelling out his views *qua* citizen on the political and moral dangers of nationalist solutions like the tariff. Although Keynes's opinions on politicians as a breed were probably not very different from those of Robbins and Pigou, he was consistently more optimistic about the prospects of overcoming prejudice by force of intellectual argument; and he entered into a variety of temporary alliances with politicians whom he hoped to mobilise in the cause of a particular 'right' solution. As the 1931 crisis approached and deepened, Henderson began to regard Keynes's intellectual solutions as moral evasions. With the options running out, Henderson was more inclined to believe that the common-sense position of the majority of businessmen and politicians might be the right one. He was certainly not the only person in 1931 speaking in terms of an uncontrollable sequence of events which would ensue from failure to carry through with economy measures. With his tendency to revert to moral and historical categories, he may have been misled by what can now be seen as false parallels with the inflationary collapse of the German mark after the first world war. Nevertheless, it is difficult not to conclude that in giving currency to such phrases as 'uncontrolled inflation', as he did in the drafts which he prepared for the official announcement of the departure from gold, Henderson's judgment as an economist was swayed by the political emotions of the moment.[24]

These differences of professional 'style' do not alone, however, explain why the revolution in policy-making should be associated with the name of Keynes. As several writers have pointed out, Keynes was by no means alone among economists in opposing such remedies as wage-cutting and advocating public works policies as a solution to unemployment.[25] This is borne out by the widespread agreement over the 'public works issue' in Britain where all the economists on the Committee of Economic Information, and many others, could unanimously advocate increased public expenditure to back up the cheap money policy in 1932–3 and to combat the forecast slump in and after 1935. In the later 1930s, moreover, some of the Treasury men came to join this consensus.[26]

Whether or not there was something that can be called a pre-Keynesian orthodoxy on policy matters within the economics profession, it is clear that it is not a mythical beast so far as most businessmen, bankers, civil servants, and political leaders were concerned. The evidence on official attitudes towards such issues as free trade, the gold standard, balanced budgets, debt redemption, and the 'Treasury view' which we have given earlier furnishes ample testimony to the existence of an orthodoxy. The evidence on business attitudes provided by the Committee on the Economic Outlook, and the proceedings of the Council generally, not only confirms that this orthodoxy was widely endorsed, but that it was coupled with a predominantly 'structural' or microeconomic approach to the problems of unemployment and depression. This focussed attention on the problems faced by particular industries in adjusting to their loss of competitiveness, and suggested that the only adequate solutions to Britain's difficulties lay in the elimination of excess capacity, the reduction of unit costs by means of rationalisation, and redeployment or reduction in the size of the work-force. There were, of course, heterodox critics within each of the major political parties, but they tended to concentrate on specific items within the 'orthodox' package – free trade, the 'Treasury view', and the gold standard. These critics did not succeed in changing the course of policy before 1931, or, with the exception of free trade, before the second world war.

Throughout the latter half of the 1930s Keynes acted consistently and prominently as one of the leaders of the opposition to orthodoxy in policy matters, supplying its critics with intellectual ammunition in the form of an alternative to the 'structural' diagnosis stressing the importance of monetary factors. However, since the Treasury officials were to some extent 'monetarists', partly because of Hawtrey but also because the quantity theory of money was an integral part of 'classical' economic theory, Keynes could not produce a really satisfactory alternative to the orthodox views until he had abandoned that theory. Keynes's ability to provide an alternative increased with his completion of the *Treatise on Money* but it only became really forceful when he argued on the basis provided by his *General Theory*. As far as economics as a discipline is concerned, the true significance of the *General Theory* undoubtedly lay in its theoretical innovations rather than in the relatively small proportion of pages devoted to policy questions.[27] At the same time, it was this book which provided an intellectual basis for the war-time and post-war commitment to full employment and aggregate economic management. In this respect our study does not greatly alter the story of the Keynesian policy revolution, which took place mainly in the 1940s.[28] On the other hand, our study suggests that the conclusion of, say, Blaug that 'the historical significance of Keynes is not that he advocated anything new in the way of economic policies but that he provided a coherent theory to justify the policy measures which orthodox economists also advocated but only as special measures given the circumstances of the time' needs some qualification.[29] In the first place, many 'orthodox' economists operated with models of the economy which allowed for the real-world existence of 'exceptions' likely to render the system incapable of achieving full employment automatically. This was certainly true of Henderson, Pigou, and Robertson when they joined Keynes in recommending bolder government policies. But the stance adopted by Robbins in the Committee of Economists is representative of other 'Austrians' at the London School of Economics and elsewhere;[30] and there is evidence that the civil servant 'economists' in the Treasury during the 1920s believed in the self-adjusting properties of the economic system.[31]

Furthermore, the agreement on public works policies between Keynes and, say, Pigou did not conceal major differences of emphasis on both theory and policy questions. Thus while Keynes moved from the *Treatise* to the *General Theory*, Pigou in his *Theory of Unemployment* (1933) returned to his normal long-run preoccupations and emphasised the 'neutrality' of monetary factors. This way of analysing post-war unemployment brought him back to the level of real wages as the nub of the problem.* Hence in 1935 we find him criticising the economy measures adopted in 1931, but maintaining that

It is possible to imagine an economy campaign of an entirely different character; one which seeks to counteract the slump by securing cuts in the rates of pay asked for by labour and capital in the hope of thereby causing more men to be employed. This policy, if it could be carried out, would, in my opinion, be a true antidote, within its limits, to slump conditions.[32]

It is not true that the theories held by, say, Pigou and Robertson on the one hand, and Keynes on the other, yielded the same policy conclusions with respect to monetary policy. Keynes's theory of the term structure of interest rates, which he first put forward in the *Treatise* and developed into the liquidity preference theory of the demand for money in the *General Theory*, has different implications for debt management from those derivable from the more 'classical' theory held by Robertson. Keynes and Robertson also had different theories of the trade cycle. Consequently they arrived at different recommendations concerning the use of monetary policy in the 1937–8 recession.[33] We do not, therefore, share the scepticism of Terence Hutchison, who has suggested that the theoretical disputes which

---

* Thus one of Pigou's major conclusions in *The Theory of Unemployment* was that the post-war level of unemployment could be attributed to the fact 'that the goal of long-run tendencies in recent times has been a wage level substantially above that proper to nil unemployment, and that a substantial part of post-war unemployment is attributable to that fact' (p. 256).

took place in the 1930s were largely irrelevant to the policy problems of the time.[34]

We have already indicated that the airing of theoretical differences in front of the Treasury officials on the Committee on Economic Information helped to make them more aware of the issues at stake. We would further suggest that Robertson became more influential as an adviser than Henderson during the 1930s precisely because he was able and prepared to discuss the theoretical issues raised by Keynes in formulating advice to the Treasury.* Although Hopkins described Henderson as 'incredibly able' in backing his appointment as Secretary to the Council in 1930,[35] Henderson's increasing disenchantment with economic theory rendered him less influential in the later part of the period. Furthermore, his pessimism concerning the efficacy of certain types of government economic policy was increasingly at odds with the Treasury's growing awareness of the need for macroeconomic management.

This awareness was one of the chief ways in which, according to Bridges, 'the scope of Treasury business in . . . [the] inter-war years . . . was affected by the economists'.[36] Mainly through its 'subsidiary', the Committee on Economic Information, the Economic Advisory Council ultimately proved its usefulness during the second world war, when the economist members of the Committee formed the nucleus of the government's economic staff. It was during this period that the ideas of economic management which they had been putting forward in the pre-war years were taken to their logical conclusion when the government accepted responsibility for maintaining adequate levels of aggregate demand and employment. Our final conclusion is, therefore, that Keynes was right in saying in 1942 that there were 'few passages in the history of controversy more valuable . . . than that which took place among economists in the ten years . . . before the war'.[37]

---

* See particularly the records of the Phillips Committee on Control of Saving and Investment in 1939 mentioned above pp. 150–1.

SELECTED REPORTS

*Reports of Committee on Economic Outlook, April and May 1930**

THE ECONOMIC OUTLOOK.

MEMORANDUM BY MR. H. D. HENDERSON.

I.—THE GENERAL BACKGROUND.

1.   UNTIL last autumn the centre of the British economic problem was the decline in the volume of our export trade, both absolutely and relatively to the foreign trade of the outside world. Several of our old-established exporting industries had lost an important fraction of their export business, and there were no export developments in newer trades of a comparable order of magnitude. This loss of export trade gave rise directly to the problem of "surplus labour" attaching to old-established industries like coal and cotton, and, indirectly, to various maladjustments which impeded the development of internal trade.

2.   Meanwhile, general business activity, both in Great Britain and throughout the world, was prejudiced by a steady deflationary trend resulting from something in the nature of a world scramble for gold following on the general return to gold standards. The fall in gold prices between 1924 and 1929 was heavy, the rate of fall exceeding that of the long deflationary period from the late 'seventies to the middle 'nineties. This necessarily acted as a brake upon the expansion of business and, in the case of Great Britain, increased the difficulty of absorbing the "surplus labour" of the distressed exporting industries in other expanding occupations. For some time, however, the buoyant condition of the American and European stock markets gave rise to repercussions immediately favourable to business activity, and no serious world depression made itself felt until the Wall Street collapse last autumn.

* P.R.O. Cab. 58/145, E.A.C. (E.O.) 4, 3 April, and E.A.C. (H.) 85, 2 May 1930.

II.—THE RECENT SET-BACK.

3. Since then a severe and world-wide trade depression has been super-imposed on our special national difficulties, and this constitutes the dominating fact in the immediate situation. Stimulated by the sense of impoverishment resulting from Stock Exchange losses, the "vicious circle" of reactions which characterises the typical trade depression is now in full play. With commodity prices moving downwards, purchasers have become increasingly reluctant to buy, until they feel sure that bottom has been reached. Thus the volume of business is further restricted, and this in turn accentuates the fall of prices. This condition in one market communicates itself to others, until practically every trade in practically every country is affected in some degree.

4. The fall in the prices of primary products during the last few months is of a most formidable character. Agricultural prices on the average were over 15 per cent. lower by the end of 1929 than at the end of 1928, and the fall has continued during the present year at an accentuated rate. Commodities like tin, spelter, lead and rubber, which are sensitive barometers of the trend of trade, have all fallen heavily in price. Freight rates, which constitute, perhaps, the most significant single indication of the activity of foreign trade, have fallen by nearly one-third in the course of the past year. This is a movement of the first order of magnitude comparable with the fluctuations which have ushered in the most severe depressions in economic history.

5. This fall in prices is bound to exercise prejudicial reactions for some time at least on business activity in industrial countries. We must expect a reduction in the purchasing power of agricultural communities, which will make itself felt in a diminished demand for industrial products. This consequence is already expressing itself in the additional difficulties with which our export trade is now confronted in some of its most important overseas markets. For example, the exchange difficulties in Australia, Argentine and Brazil are mainly attributable to the fall in the prices of primary products and to the adverse balance of payments which those countries have accordingly to face. The heavy discount at which the Argentine exchange now stands imposes a severe deterrent to exports to that country, while the difficulty of remitting money at all from Australia is, perhaps, a still more serious obstacle to trade. The decline of the Chinese exchange as the result of the fall in the price of silver creates a similar difficulty.

6. It is to be feared that these unsatisfactory developments have not as yet exerted their full depressing influence on British industry and employment. There is always a long time-lag between cause and effect in economic affairs. Employment at any particular time is dependent on the volume of orders placed some months previously; and the placing of orders takes some time in its turn to respond to an alteration in the business outlook. The prevailing

impression of business-men suggests that the present state of order-books is such that we must expect for some months ahead a further slackening of employment in the majority of trades.

III.—THE PROSPECT AHEAD.

7. When we look further ahead, the outlook is far more hopeful. A general trade depression, though for some time cumulative in its operation, sets forces in motion which ultimately effect a cure; notably cheap money. In the present case, money rates have fallen very rapidly. In Great Britain Bank Rate has been reduced by successive stages from $6\frac{1}{2}$ per cent. in October 1929 to the present figure of $3\frac{1}{2}$ per cent., and seems likely to reach 3 per cent. very shortly. We have not previously had Bank Rate below 4 per cent. since July 1923; and it has been well above 4 per cent. for most of the period. Already the low money rates now prevailing have exerted a definitely beneficial influence on the general business situation. Stock markets have begun to recover, and, what is more, new issues have been stimulated—a factor of considerable importance to industry since the volume of new capital issues gives some indication of the amount of development work of a capital nature which industry is likely to undertake in the near future. It seems not unlikely that wholesale commodity prices have now reached bottom.

8. Taking a long view, the possibility that cheap money rates may prevail at home and abroad for a considerable time opens out a more hopeful prospect than a mere recovery from the recent trade set-back. The fact that short money rates have been prevailingly high during recent years has entailed the consequence that the long-term rate of interest has been correspondingly high. If now money rates rule low for a sufficient length of time to create a general expectation that an era of cheaper money has been reached, the long-term rate of interest may be expected to fall substantially; and the stimulus which this might give to industrial activity and particularly to public utility development throughout the world might prove of the first importance. The differences made to the profitability of undertakings of a capital character by changes in the rate of interest is not, perhaps, sufficiently appreciated. If, for example, we suppose the rate of interest to fall from 5 per cent. to $2\frac{1}{2}$ per cent., the effect is to reduce by no less than one-half the annual cost (apart from upkeep) of a house or a commercial building costing a given sum of money. From this it will be clear that a big fall in the rate of interest would bring into the region of profitability a large range of capital enterprises which are hopelessly unprofitable now.

9. There are, indeed, grounds for thinking that an unduly, and in a sense an artificially, high rate of interest may have lain at the root of the unsatisfactory trade conditions of recent years. The rate of interest has been kept high by the prevailingly high level of short money rates; and short money rates have ruled high for reasons which have had little or nothing to

do with the state of industry or trade. In the United States, money was kept dear in order to check Wall Street speculation. In Great Britain money was kept dear in order to prevent the foreign exchanges from falling and gold from flowing out. Accordingly, the long-term rate of interest may have been kept by extraneous considerations of this character at a level considerably above its true level, considerably above, that is to say, the level at which the demand for savings would carry off the available supply. In this way a considerable portion of the world's potential savings may have failed to find its proper outlet in real investment, with the result that it has been wasted in maintaining unemployment and idle plant. If this be so, a big fall in the rate of interest may be what is required to correct a deep-seated maladjustment in the post-war economic system, from which many of our troubles spring.

IV.—THE MONETARY FACTOR.

10. To a slight extent the long-term rate of interest responds at once to a fall in money-rates such as has taken place in recent months. But the full effect of cheap money on the rate of interest cannot be realised until money rates have been low for some time and are expected to continue low. We have thus a further reason for expecting that, at the best a considerable interval will elapse before a substantial recovery of trade makes itself felt. But the question also arises: What are the chances of money remaining cheap for a long time to come? May not the same causes which were responsible for the high money rates of recent years reassert themselves the moment that trade begins to recover? May not a revival of Wall Street speculation induce the Federal Reserve authorities once more to put up their rates? May not this, coupled with a continuing tendency on the part of Continental Central Banks to enlarge their stores of gold, keep the sterling-exchange precarious, and compel a higher Bank Rate here than our own trade situation warrants? In this connexion the question of the adequacy of the world stocks of gold to sustain a full volume of world trade without a continually falling price-level is one of fundamental importance. There are some grounds for fearing that if the policies of certain central banks remain what they are now a steady downward trend of world prices will be inevitable, in which case business conditions generally may remain indefinitely under the shadow of depression. Certainly the monetary policies of the principal central banks of the world are a factor of the first importance. These are questions which would appear to come within the purview of the Macmillan Committee on Finance and Industry, so far as they are matters with which it is within the competence of this country to deal.

V.—THE IMMEDIATE OUTLOOK FOR EMPLOYMENT.

11. The above argument may be summarised as follows: On a long view, the situation contains more hopeful possibilities than have been apparent for many years past. But these possibilities are very far from being certainties, and depend for their realisation on the monetary policies pursued throughout the world. At the best, the immediate outlook for British industry and employment is not encouraging. It is possible that the fall in commodity prices may now have run its course, and that business confidence will soon recover. But there is usually a long interval between such developments and a revival of industrial activity.

12. In some trades, it is true, there is reason to hope for a speedier improvement. In cotton, for example, where merchants abroad have for some time past been allowing their stocks of piece-goods to run down in the expectation of lower prices, it is possible that the volume of business may show some recovery fairly soon after it is generally believed that bottom prices have been reached. Again, industries such as motor-cars and artificial silk, which have been held back by special uncertainties relating to the Budget, may go forward directly the Budget has been introduced. But, generally, it is to be feared that we have not yet seen the full effects on industrial activity of the slump in prices and the business recession which has already taken place. This certainly is the view suggested by past experience of general trade depressions.

13. Moreover, the present depression falls upon British industry at a time when it is in no condition to sustain such a trial. Many of our basic industries have been in a bad condition for several years past, and contain a large proportion of firms which have been losing money and have been carrying on with great difficulty. In such circumstances we must expect the general depression, which is now upon us, to knock out far more firms, and accordingly to intensify unemployment more severely than would be the case if it had succeeded a period of real prosperity. So far as unemployment is concerned we have also to bear in mind the fact that the measures of rationalisation which are in progress in several of our industries, while they should serve in the long run to improve our competitive position, are likely in the first instance to increase the displacement of labour.

14. There are accordingly grounds for serious apprehension as to the future course of unemployment, particularly during the remainder of the present year. And it becomes important to consider carefully and objectively every possible line of remedial policy.

VI.—REMEDIAL POLICIES.

15. The possibilities of remedial policy may be approached in the following way: There are four broad heads under which an increase of employment can be brought about:—

(a) An increase in the volume of exports.

(b) A diversion of home consumption from goods now imported to goods made or services rendered at home.

(c) An increase in the total volume of home consumption.

(d) An increase in the production of capital assets at home.

The above is an exhaustive catalogue. In no other ways whatever can employment be increased. It will be useful to consider each of these heads in turn.

(a) Export Possibilities.

16. The substantial decline in the volume of exports represents the most unsatisfactory feature of our post-war economic life; and public attention and public policy have accordingly been largely preoccupied with the problem of restoring our exporting position. Thus it is mainly upon the exporting industries that the movement towards rationalisation has been concentrated. In connection with some schemes of industrial reconstruction arrangements are made or advocated to enable the industries concerned to sell more cheaply abroad than at home, with a view to stimulating exports. It is on the ground of the necessities of the export trade that the high level of money wages in Great Britain, as compared with Continental countries, is called in question; and it is chiefly on the same ground that the need is urged for modifying business practices and trade union restrictions which impede industrial efficiency. It is primarily in order to promote British export trade that British Governments are urged by one school of thought to promote the objective laid down by the [1923] World Economic Conference of securing a general reduction of world tariffs by international agreement, and by another school to foster trade within the Empire by extensions of Imperial Preference or other schemes of Imperial co-operation.

17. The above enumeration practically covers the ground of the various alternative means open to us for increasing the volume of our exports. To most of these possibilities a considerable measure of attention is already being given. The Bank of England has set up a new organisation to promote the rationalisation of industry. Special inquiries are being conducted, under the auspices of the Economic Advisory Council, into the iron and steel and cotton industries. The broad question of Imperial Preference has recently been referred to a sub-committee of the Council. The general position and prospects of the export trade were exhaustively surveyed by the recent Balfour Committee on Industry and Trade. It would seem doubtful,

therefore, whether, at this stage, the Council could usefully take any further steps to explore the possibilities under this heading.

18.   There can be no question as to the supreme importance of promoting the export trade by every feasible and desirable means. An adequate volume of exports is vital to the British economy; and the continued erosion of the export trade which we still retain would place us before long in very serious difficulties. The decline in exports which has taken place since the war has not so far prejudiced our power to buy foodstuffs and raw materials, because we have been able to counter it by reducing correspondingly the amount of fresh investments which we make annually abroad. Before the war we used to export much more than we required to pay for our imports, and we used to invest abroad the proceeds of our "export surplus." Now we are exporting less and investing correspondingly less; but the process could not easily or prudently be carried much further; for, allowing for the change in the value of money, our capacity to invest abroad has already been cut down by about one-half. Moreover, this has entailed reactions detrimental to the rest of our economic life. The curtailment of our rate of foreign investment within the limits of our available "export surplus" does not come about automatically. It has to be enforced by the pressure of high money-rates relatively to those in foreign centres. Part of the responsibility for the high money-rates prevailing in Great Britain in recent years must, therefore, be laid at the door of the loss of export trade.

19.   But the importance of the export trade should not lead us to exaggerate the possibilities of securing a positive increase of employment under this head. In recent years we have been losing ground relatively to other competing countries in world markets. We have to fight against various adverse circumstances. The tide of demand has turned throughout the world against some of those industries in which we largely specialized. Some of our staple industries again have reached a stage of development at which it is possible for countries with a comparatively low level of skill and standard of living to carry them on almost as efficiently as ourselves. Such industries must therefore tend in the nature of things to pass more and more to such countries. We have lost most of the advantage which we derived in the Victorian era from the long start which we had as a manufacturing country; and we are faced in a steadily increasing degree with the competition of other countries as efficiently equipped as ourselves in respect of business management and technical skill. Moreover, the trend of tariffs throughout the world is still upwards, and will probably remain so for so long as the trend of world prices is downwards.

20.   In these circumstances we shall probably do well if—apart from sharing in any general world recovery from the recent set-back—we succeed in maintaining our export trade at the level of recent years, and adding to it a modest annual increment. The importance of the export trade remains fundamental; and it is necessary to consider carefully the reactions upon

exports of any proposal designed to stimulate domestic trade. But it would seem idle to look to the export trade to supply much positive contribution within any reasonable space of time to the problem of increasing employment.

(b) The Diversion of Home Consumption from Imports.

21. This is the Protectionist solution, and raises the large issue of Protection. Besides protective duties, there are, however, a variety of expedients by which the same object may be promoted in special cases. For example, arable farming might be assisted by requiring millers to use in their gristings not less than a defined percentage of British wheat. Pressure may be put on Government departments, local authorities and public utility concerns to buy goods of British origin, even when this means paying a higher price, *e.g.*, the recent proposal that the army should consume only British beef during certain months of the year. The encouragement of the railway companies to use steel sleepers in place of wooden sleepers comes under the same general category. Again, internal taxes may be so devised as to serve, in effect, a protectionist purpose. Our system of motor vehicle taxation is an instance of this. Finally, the machinery of an Import Board endowed with a statutory monopoly of the importation of a particular commodity may be so used as to give a preference to the home producer and thus to divert consumption from imported to home produce.

(c) The Stimulation of Total Consumption.

22. The total volume of home consumption varies considerably in accordance with the general state of business and trade activity, and for this reason any improvement effected under the other heads of the analysis would have a larger effect on employment than might appear at first sight. Thus a recovery in the export trade, or increased activity in home investment, would stimulate employment over the whole range of domestic trade. Moreover, any factor favourable to trade in general, such as cheap money, will increase employment under this heading. Apart from a general trade improvement, there are not many ways in which it would be possible to stimulate directly the total volume of home consumption. The possibility of developing the system of instalment buying, which has done so much in recent years to maintain a high volume of consumption in the United States, may, perhaps, be mentioned in this connection.

23. A much larger problem arises under this heading. The huge margin which exists between the prices obtained by the manufacturers or producers of staple commodities and the prices which the ultimate consumers pay is a phenomenon to which attention has been increasingly directed in recent years; and allegations are frequent that (*a*) the distributors secure an excessive

margin of profit relatively to producers, and (*b*) that the whole system of distribution, involving many intermediary stages, and at particular stages a large number of dealers with a comparatively small turnover, is wasteful and inefficient. In support of these allegations, it may be pointed out (*a*) that there is little doubt that in those trades which have been the subject of special adversity in recent years, the main brunt of the distress has fallen on the producer, leaving the distributor comparatively unscathed; and (*b*) that, while under the pressure of this economic adversity, the organisation of many industries has been drastically overhauled, there has been, speaking broadly, no similar concentration on improving the distributive system. There have been various *ad hoc* inquiries in recent years into the marketing of coal and foodstuffs; but the question arises as to whether a more systematic study of what may be called the rationalization of distribution may not now be desirable.

24. If the retail prices of consumable commodities could be reduced in this way, an increase in the total volume of home consumption might be expected to ensue. But obviously there is not here any possibility of speedy results.

(d) Development of Capital Assets at Home.

25. It remains to consider the possibilities open under the fourth heading. As has been argued above, a substantial fall in the world rate of interest as the result of cheap money ruling for a considerable period would probably exercise a powerful effect in stimulating capital expansions and new capital undertakings. But it is important to remember that the capital requirements of ordinary industry are normally not very large. By far the greater part of the real investment of the last century, and indeed of every epoch, was accounted for by buildings, transport and public utilities of various kinds, which have come increasingly of late within the domain of public policy. Public policy must, therefore, inevitably play a preponderant part in the determination of the volume of capital development.

26. The broad issue thus arises as to the extent to which the Government should, under present conditions, endeavour to promote home investment. In this connection the following points call for consideration:—

(*a*) The technical scope for an investment programme including (i) works directly executed by the State or local authorities, (ii) assistance by the State to works undertaken by public utility concerns or others.

(*b*) The cost which such a programme would impose on the Budget in relation to the offset it might secure by reducing unemployment and increasing the yield of revenue.

(*c*) The possible effects which it might have in retarding the fall in the rate of interest and thus retarding capital expansion in ordinary industry.

VII.—CONCLUSION.

27.   The principal questions which call for objective examination in the light of the foregoing analysis are the following, though many of them are, of course, covered by existing or recent inquiries:—

(a) The prospects of cheap money and a lower rate of interest, and the bearing thereon of monetary policy.

(b) The possibility of reducing costs of production by improved industrial efficiency or lower labour costs.

(c) The possibility of reducing distributive costs by a reconstruction of the existing distributive system.

(d) The possibilities of lower world tariffs or Imperial Preference.

(e) Protection, or other means of diverting consumption from imported goods.

(f) The question of home development.

Report by the Chairman (Mr. J. M. Keynes) and Mr. G. D. H. Cole.

1.   AT their first meeting . . . the Economic Advisory Council appointed a Committee with the following terms of reference:—

"To supervise the preparation of a memorandum indicating the principal heads of the investigation which should be embraced in a diagnosis of the underlying economic situation."

. . .

3.   At their second meeting . . . the Council agreed that the Committee should be invited to consider the question of an inquiry into the desirability of more extensive State action for the purpose of increasing employment by capital expenditure by loan or otherwise, such an inquiry to include the preparation of a statement of the nature and organisation of the work to which unemployed workers might most advantageously be set.

4.   We attach the memorandum . . . which has been prepared by Mr. H. D. Henderson.

5.   Apart from seasonal changes, we see no hope of an immediate material decrease in unemployment, but feel, on the other hand, that there is a serious risk of a further large increase in unemployment in (say) November, which is, in any case, a bad month seasonally. It is against a possible background such as this that we feel that the suggested alternative remedies should be studied immediately.

6.   It seems to us that, broadly speaking, there are, and can be, only three ways of increasing employment which it lies within our own power to promote, namely:—

(a) An increase of exports, whether by a reduction of wages or by an increase of efficiency so as to put costs of production on a more competitive level, or by inter-imperial arrangements.

(b) A decrease of imports by tariffs, bounties, Import Boards or other measures.

(c) An increase of home capital development, whether by private enterprise or by Government aid or initiative.

7. Events in the outside world, which would help, comprise—

(a) a general rise of world prices;
(b) a reduction of tariffs by foreign countries;
(c) a general revival in the volume of international trade and development.

8. It will be observed that each of these external aids is correlative to one of the internal aids.

9. The desirability of greater health and prosperity in the export trades is universally accepted. But to expect an increased efficiency in these trades sufficient to absorb within a moderate period of time the bulk of the persons now unemployed, both in these industries and in other industries, would be quite unreasonable. The value of British exports in 1929 was about £730,000,000. About 20 per cent. of this is represented by the value of imported raw materials, leaving a net production for export of £584,000,000. Making use of the census of production and subsequent data, the average net output per annual worker employed may be taken as about £245. We may therefore guess that somewhere about 2,400,000 workers were employed, directly or indirectly, in manufacturing for export in that year. (It would be interesting to have an accurate estimate as to what the number was.) On these assumptions the employment of another (say) 325,000 workers on producing directly or indirectly for export would therefore mean increasing our exports (at the present price level) by about £100,000,000. We know of no improvements in the export trades likely to materialise on this scale within this year or next. Yet the present number of the unemployed is in the neighbourhood of 1,650,000.

It is a further ground for not placing too much reliance on "rationalisation" in the export trades as a means of increasing employment, that many so-called "rationalising" schemes are primarily devised to enable industries to produce at a level below their present capacity without the surplus capacity evoking cut-throat competition, which involves all producers alike in losses. These plans are likely for the time being to increase profits, but they are not so likely to increase exports or employment.

10. The remaining possibilities seem to be tariffs, bounties, import control and the like, on the one hand, and a programme of home development on the other. As to the merits of these two policies, we express no opinion. But we see no third alternative, so far as the near future is concerned,

except a policy of inactivity in the hope of some favourable development turning up in the outside world.

11. As to what matters should be further inquired into, we think that the possible subjects of investigation fall into three groups:—

(a) Those measures the desirability of which has been a matter of general agreement for some time past, so that no question of doubt or controversy arises.
(b) Those matters which are already being inquired into.
(c) Those suggestions, the value of which still needs clearing up, because they are either novel or controversial.

12. We report that the chief questions in group (c)—though one or two of them may turn out to be in group (b)—are, in our opinion, the following:—

(I) Is there room for a material reduction of marketing and distribution costs of consumable commodities? In particular, could economies be expected from centralised marketing methods?
(II) Have the abnormalities of the present time any important bearing on the issue of Free Trade, treating this issue in a broad sense so as to cover proposals for tariffs, subsidies, Import Boards, inter-imperial arrangements, &c.?
(III) Would a large plan of home development materially reduce un-employment? If so, what part should the State play in such a plan and what test of usefulness or "economic productivity" should projects be expected to pass?
(IV) Is a long period of cheap money of vital importance? If so, what are the best means of securing this?

13. Of these questions, (I) was dealt with at the last meeting of the Council (E.A.C., 3rd Meeting, Conclusion 4). Question (IV) should probably be included in group (b) above, since it is presumably being considered by the Macmillan Committee. Question (III) may also overlap, to some extent, with the work of the Macmillan Committee, but is so urgent and important as to deserve an *ad hoc* Committee. Question (II) may overlap slightly with the work of the Empire Trade Committee, but also, in our opinion, deserves an *ad hoc* Committee.

14. Our recommendations are as follows:—

(a) That the staff should be asked to prepare reports on Questions (II) and (III).
(b) That Committees—consisting of members of the Economic Advisory Council—should consider the reports of the staff referred to in (b) above on Questions (II) and (III), and send them forward to the Economic Advisory Council with covering memoranda.

(c) That the personnel of the Committee on Question (II) should overlap with that of the Empire Trade, 1930, Committee, and that the personnel of the Committee on Question (III) should overlap with that of the Macmillan Committee.

15.   We suggest that, in the event of there being important differences of opinion on any Committee, its Chairman should be asked to encourage the presentation of more than one covering memorandum so as to secure clear-cut opinions, in preference to a colourless document embodying a compromise, for compromise comes more usefully at a later stage.

Report by Sir Arthur Balfour and Sir John Cadman.

1.   At the first meeting of the Economic Advisory Council, a Committee was appointed with the following terms of reference:—

"To supervise the preparation of a memorandum indicating the principal heads of the investigation which should be embraced in a diagnosis of the underlying economic situation."

and at the second meeting on March 13th further discussion took place, when the Committee were asked—

"To inquire into the desirability of more intensified State action for the purpose of increasing employment by capital expenditure on loans, or otherwise, and to prepare a statement of the nature of organised work to which unemployed workers might most usefully be set."

2.   We have conferred with our colleagues, as requested at the meeting of the Council, held on April 10th, and find that we approach these terms of reference from fundamentally different points of view.   In these circumstances, the best service we can render to the Council is to express our views in a separate document.

3.   We do not believe the situation is capable of solution by direct action of the State.

4.   Indications at the moment are lacking that the downward trend of British exports is likely to discontinue during 1930.

5.   In our opinion, the fundamental object of our inquiry is to discover the reasons for Great Britain's failure to secure her share of such improvement in world trade as is taking place.

6.   It seems clear that taxation of the volume which has been imposed in the past few years has gravely interfered with the surplus that remains in productive industry for rationalization, reconstruction, renewals, and maintenance and extension of sales organisations abroad.   It is also certain that the increase in local rates of the country from £79 millions in 1913–14 to £188 millions in 1929 is a direct charge on cost of production and has hampered export trade.

7. Urgent inquiry seems advisable into the effect upon unemployment and emigration of increased expenditure on social services. This inquiry should embrace—

(a) To what extent emigration has been retarded by (1) social services and (2) legislation and national policy both here and abroad.
(b) The extent to which unemployment has been increased or induced by social services and other forms of relief.

8. The real question to be faced is that of costs of production, more particularly in the basic industries of this country, which are not competitive with those of other industrial countries.

Some of the most serious factors in this connection are—

(a) The uneconomic wages paid to workers in sheltered industries which are not affected directly by competition from industries in other countries.
(b) The question of hours worked in this country in relation to those worked in other countries.
(c) An inquiry is urgent into whether production has increased *per capita* in relation to the money spent on social services and housing, &c., as a set-off against those expenditures. In this connection regard must also be paid to the increase of horse-power per head of persons employed.
(d) Demarcation as between trades and other factors tending to restrict output.

9. It is necessary to study the effect of uncertainty in industry. Changes in tariffs, together with high taxation and the other costs mentioned above, have undoubtedly deterred money from flowing into industry.

10. It seems certain that, if any great State-aided expenditure is proposed, it will deter private enterprise from entering into new ventures, or from extending those in which it is already engaged. The first essential at the present moment is stability and a dependable situation in which enterprise and energy can be used with reasonable chance of success.

11. There is real need for a condition of stability and confidence which will enable the employers and employed in each industry to face their problems and to make such adjustments as may be necessary to meet world competition.

12. One of the reasons for this country's inability to compete in the markets of the world is that we have never applied the American theory that heavy taxation, high standard of living and great expenditure on social services are economically practicable only if the rate of production per head increases proportionately. In actual practice, during recent years, artificial means have been responsible for decreases in the rate of production per head, and it seems to us that without a complete psychological change in

this respect the inferiority of this country in world competition will continue.

13. We have been forced more and more to occupy ourselves in the finer higher quality trades, and to withdraw from the bulk trades and basic industries. This tendency arises from an application of the theory that our greater skill and experience enable us to produce better quality goods. Gradually, however, our competitors have widened their invasion, and to-day we meet competition from other industrial countries, not only in the bulk trades and more ordinary lines of production, but also in the higher and better quality manufactures. The time has come, therefore, when we urgently need to revise our whole attitude towards production unless our decline is to continue steadily.

14. The effect upon agriculture of the foregoing considerations is to render that industry unable to achieve prosperity. It has to compete in wages, hours and conditions with the present uneconomic circumstances in other industries, and its purchases have, moreover, to be made in a market in which costs of production are artificially elevated.

15. Our conclusions, therefore, are—

(i) That until the whole tariff situation is clarified and removed from Politics, it will be impossible to place ourselves on a definite and competitive basis with the rest of the world.

(ii) That the policy of informal contacts which the Bank of England makes with the other central Banks of the world has been beneficial.

(iii) That each industry must examine its costs of production and endeavour to improve them by—

(a) consideration of labour costs, hours, industrial efficiency and overhead charges;

(b) examination of distributive costs.

(iv) That large State aided schemes which interfere with industrial enterprise should not be prosecuted.

(v) That continual additions of expenditure by Acts of Parliament at the present time are not warranted by the industrial situation and merely further handicap our competitive power.

(vi) There is need for a national investigation in regard to the waste and uneconomic use of imported food-stuffs and raw materials.

(vii) In our opinion, schemes submitted to the Committees should not—

(a) be a direct or indirect cause of inflation;

(b) directly or indirectly damage the National Credit;

(c) postpone the inevitable adjustment of cost of production in relation to world competition;

(d) discourage emigration;

(e) result in further taxation or local rates;

(*f*) be of merely a transient character, but of a productive nature; (*g*) tax food or raw materials.

*Report of Committee of Economists, October 1930**

II.—THE CAUSES OF THE PRESENT DEPRESSION.

(a) Great Britain and the World Slump.

5. The present depression of trade is one which Great Britain shares with most of the civilised world. Since the autumn of last year we have been in the grip of a downward fluctuation of trade which has engulfed almost every country, whether free trade or protectionist, agricultural or manufacturing, backward or forward in economic efficiency. To suppose that this catastrophe is due to the policy of particular Governments or the inefficiency of particular groups of producers would be to ignore obvious facts.

6. Nevertheless, there are certain peculiarities in the position of Great Britain which distinguish her difficulties from those of the rest of the world. Up to the eve of the great slump, speaking very broadly, the rest of the world was experiencing a period of prosperity. In America, indeed, trade was definitely booming. Elsewhere the main indices of activity were favourable. But in Great Britain, although some parts of the country—*e.g.*, London—and some trades, exhibited considerable prosperity, speaking generally we were suffering from serious malaise. It is important, however, not to exaggerate the dark side of the picture. Some industries were going ahead fairly rapidly. Real wages had risen considerably: between 1924 and 1928 average real wage-rates increased 6·5 per cent., and average real earnings per week increased 8·5 per cent.([1]) But when all this is taken into account, the general verdict must be that we were not doing nearly as well as we could have done. The total of unemployed had not sunk perceptibly below a million since 1924. Great areas in the North were stationary or declining. Our export trade as a whole showed disquieting symptoms of stagnation.

7. Before the advent of the great slump there was lack of adjustment in our position relatively to other countries.([2]) Since the slump began there is no reason to suppose that this condition has been remedied. In judging our present troubles we have to distinguish between the difficulties which we share with the rest of the world and those which are peculiar to our local want of adjustment. We examine first these local difficulties, since it is over these that we may hope to exercise most control.

---

* P.R.O., Cab. 58/151, E.A.C. (H.)127, 24 October 1930; also Cab. 24/216, C.P. 363(30).

([1]) London and Cambridge Economic Service: Article in April 1930 issue and subsequent figures.

([2]) See Appendix, Tables A, H and M.

(b) The Nature of the Domestic Difficulties of Great Britain.

8. The depression of trade in Great Britain since the war may be regarded as being the resultant of two sets of causes: (*a*) adversely changing external conditions, and (*b*) a lack of internal adaptability.

(i) *External Changes.*

9. The main changes in the broad external environment of British industry since the War are too well known to need extensive comment. Broadly speaking they may be classified as follows:—

(*a*) There have been changes in the conditions of demand for the products of various industries, due to the change from war to peace. During the War the industrial structure of this country suffered abnormal distortions. To meet the demands of war, many industries were distended to an extent which the demands of peace could not profitably sustain. At the end of the War, after the brief inflationary boom, these industries were plunged into depression. In the ten years that have elapsed considerable contraction has taken place, but it would be rash to assert that this process is by any means over.[3]

(*b*) Side by side with these abnormal changes of demand, but in their effects closely parallel with them, come certain general changes in world economic conditions. Of these the most important are (i) the development of the cotton industry in the East; (ii) the less favourable terms on which the agricultural areas of the world have succeeded in disposing of their products—a change which not only affects the volume of demand for the products of our export industries, but also carries with it an adverse movement of domestic agricultural prices; (iii) the spectacular decline that has taken place in the value of silver, which has had the effect of considerably intensifying the difficulties of our trade with the Far East; and (iv) the considerable substitution of oil for bunker coal and of hydro-electric power by countries formerly dependent on British coal.[4]

(*c*) Our difficulties in this respect have been aggravated by certain political misfortunes which have intensified the effects of changing demand. In some ways we have been definitely unlucky. It is conceivable that the occupation and evacuation of the Ruhr, with its disturbing effects on the coal trade, the currency disorders in France, Italy, Belgium and Germany, the General Strike and the troubles in India and China might have been averted by extraordinary pre-

[3] See Appendix, Tables D and F.
[4] See Appendix, Tables E and J.

181

science on the part of statesmen, but their main weight has fallen on those who were powerless to prevent them, and their cumulative effect has been felt by a society whose powers of rapid adaptation were already being strained to the utmost.

(d) The incidence of these changes was to some extent localised and particular. The fall in gold prices in general, and of sterling prices in particular, which took place between 1924 and 1929 had a wider influence. Opinions still differ sharply about the extent of the dislocation which was brought about by the restoration of the gold standard; but it is clear that, in so far as it raised the value of the pound, it increased the difficulties of the export industries. If gold prices in general had risen after that event, little difficulty would have been experienced. As it was, they continued to fall, thus accentuating the difficulties of readjustment.(5)

(e) Finally, there can be no doubt that we have suffered from the tariff policies of other countries.

(ii) *Internal Rigidities.*

10. Changes of the kind outlined above are bound to impose on *any* economic system the necessity of readjustment. They may even be the occasion of an inevitable and permanent loss. But the extent to which they actually damage any given system depends upon the ease with which it adapts itself to change and upon the flexibility with which it responds to the new conditions of demand, of price and production. Even with perfect flexibility, some loss may still be inevitable. But if flexibility is absent, the loss will be much more considerable.

11. Unfortunately there is reason to suppose that, in the period since the War, our capacity for rapid adaptation has been inadequate. This is due in part to adverse changes in the age compositions of the population. The proportion of the more active age-groups was drastically curtailed by the losses of the War; and consequently there is a shortage of men in the prime of life in important positions.

12. Lack of adaptability has also been due to the domination of false ideas. Since the War, a series of policies has been fashionable, each capable of ingenious defence in itself, but the whole tending cumulatively to industrial ossification and the diminution of the National Dividend. These tendencies show themselves in three ways:—

(i) In the first place they may be seen in the increase of rings and monopolistic combinations designed deliberately to restrict the volume of trade. This does not mean that large-scale rationalised production is necessarily bad or that all combinations are of a restrictive

(5) See Appendix, Table B.

nature. But it is clear that much that passes as legitimate and far-seeing industrial policy is in fact restrictive and anti-social. Examples of this type will readily occur to anyone familiar with the cotton trade or the various industries which provide the materials of housing.

(ii) Secondly, there has been a reluctance on the part of industry to recognise the existence of changed conditions, either on the side of technique or on the side of demand.

(iii) Thirdly, the persistence of restrictive rules and practices among trade unions has been very marked. These take two forms: (*a*) restrictions on entry to particular occupations and the demarcation of different occupations, and (*b*) restrictions on the conditions under which certain work can be done.

These restrictions involve craft loyalties and attachments to old customs which it would be wrong to undervalue, but it would be equally wrong to ignore their deleterious effects on production. If men are excluded from a particular occupation, they are either unemployed or are compelled to sell their labour for lower rates elsewhere. If employers are prevented from using the most up-to-date methods of production, the efficiency of industry suffers and the total available for distribution is diminished. If, in the last ten years, productivity has failed to increase at the rate it might otherwise have done, it would be wrong to absolve from responsibility such policies as result in one man working four looms when in other countries men work at least twice as many, or in a man taking four years to qualify as a building operative when he could certainly do so in one. Customs of this sort might have some justification in a society isolated from world competition. But in a world of rapid change, their persistence must lead to local stagnation and decay.

13. The internal paralysis from which society has been suffering since the War manifests itself in yet another way which, from the point of view of the causation of unemployment, is even more important. We refer to rigidities in the price and income structure.

14. It is clear that since the War there has been present in our price and income structure much greater rigidity of this sort than at any earlier period in our history. The rigidity of certain prices is well known; it is the obverse side of the policy of monopolistic restriction referred to above. The rigidity of wage-rates in certain sheltered industries is also well known. Before the War, if unemployment in any industry went beyond a certain point, it was in the interests of the trade unions to modify wage-rates. To-day, the existence of the unemployment insurance system, divorced as it has become from any actuarial basis, is tending to prevent these adjustments. Yet if such adjustments are not made, it is a matter of common experience that unemployment follows.

15. If in a single industry there were much unemployment, it would be fair to argue that wages in that industry were too high in the sense that if they were lower there would be less unemployment. But this argument cannot be extended in its simplest form to industry as a whole in the pre-slump period, for two reasons, viz.:—

(a) Although *some* wages may have been too high, in this sense, others may have been too low in the sense that if the restrictions which kept wages high in the one industry had been removed, those wages might have risen.

(b) Changes in wages have general reactions upon productivity in industry as a whole. And it may well have been that before the recent slump, if the rigidity of wages had been relaxed, the improvements in efficiency and the rate of progress thus made possible would almost immediately have created a situation where a greater volume of employment would have been secured without seriously impairing the average wage.

16. For it is quite clear that rigidity of wage-rates is capable of being a definite hindrance to change and to progress. The rate at which an industry can expand is, in part, a function of the rate of wages it has to pay. If, for example, the increase of wages in the building industry had been less, the rate of building would have been greater, the price of houses would have been less, the redistribution of the population would have taken place more rapidly and the general purchasing power of wages would have been greater.(6)

17. Moreover, when wages are kept rigid, there is a grave danger that the arrangement of industry which is thus brought about may be injurious to the interests of the working classes as a whole. Labour-saving machinery which, from the point of view of securing full employment for the total working population, is definitely *uneconomical*, may be introduced, and, at the same time, the full benefits of desirable rationalisation may be lost. There is a considerable consensus of opinion that the "technological" unemployment, of which much has been heard in Germany in recent years is due to these causes.

III.—THE FALL OF PRICES.

18. Between 1924 and September 1929 gold prices of staple commodities, as calculated in Dr. Bowley's special index number, fell in the United States by 4 per cent., in Sweden by 14 per cent. and in Holland by 14 per cent. In the United Kingdom over the same period, sterling prices of the same class of commodities, partly in consequence of the return to gold, fell 22 per cent. In the years which have since elapsed there has been a further

(6) See Appendix, Tables G, I, K and L.

catastrophic fall: between September 1929 and August 1930, dollar prices fell 21 per cent., Swedish prices 14 per cent., Dutch prices 17 per cent., and sterling prices 17 per cent. In the great depression of the eighteen-nineties, prices fell about 18 per cent. altogether, spread over a period of six years. Apart from the slump of 1921, when the fall was from an exceptional point reached so rapidly that it had not had time to affect established costs of production, there is no recorded case in recent economic history of so violent and rapid a collapse in the prices of staple commodities.(7)

19.   As against this very large fall in the wholesale prices of staple commodities (30 to 35 per cent. since 1924 in terms of sterling),(8) British money wage-rates have remained virtually unchanged. Between 1924 and September 1929 wages fell 1 per cent., whilst during the past year they have fallen by less than another 1 per cent.(9)

20.   It is not to be expected that the fall in the cost of living will be so great as the fall in the prices of staple commodities, since, by the time goods reach the consumer, a considerable part of the price represents home costs of one kind or another, including manufacturing, distribution and retailing costs, which do not fall so long as our own level of money wages is maintained, except at the expense of normal business returns. Actually, the cost of living fell 5 per cent. between 1924 and September 1929, and has fallen only a further 3½ per cent. during the past year.(10) It may be that the more recent of these figures does not yet reflect the full effect of the fall which has already occurred in staple commodities, owing to time lags, frictions, etc.

21.   We do not think it prudent to assume that there may not be a further fall of world prices. We should expect some recovery from the present exceptionally low level at a date which may be near at hand. But it is not certain that this rise of prices will go far enough to mend the situation or that it may not be followed by a further sagging tendency in the price-level continued over a long period. The existing international situation as it affects credit, rates of interest, the state of international confidence and the use of gold in bank reserves has not necessarily done its worst. For the same reasons that it has been producing a fall of prices hitherto, its mere continuance may provoke a further fall for some little time to come.

(a) Effects of Large Changes in the Value of Money.

22.   We would wish to affirm with all the emphasis at our command the disastrous consequences which are to be expected if this fear were to be fulfilled. All money settlements of every kind, upon which the stability and prosperity of modern life, organised as it is, so profoundly depend,

(7) See Appendix, Table B.
(8) Board of Trade and Sauerbeck Indexes.
(9) Dr. Bowley's Index: see also Appendix, Tables H and K.
(10) See Appendix, Table G.

would become hopelessly inappropriate—international settlements and national debts not less than money wages.[11]

23. Outstanding examples of this are the following:—

(a) The effective burden of inter-Governmental debts arising out of the war is very greatly increased. In the case of German reparations, for example, it is probable that the whole of the concessions made to Germany by the Young Plan, as compared with the Dawes Plan, have been obliterated by the fall in prices which has occurred subsequently. The safeguards against this very danger contained in the Dawes Plan were withdrawn under the Young Plan, and the payments under the Young Plan are already in serious jeopardy.

(b) The budgetary burden of internal National Debts is also greatly aggravated. It is not easy at this stage to calculate the amount of the increase, since the level of money incomes at home has not yet adjusted itself to the external price-level. But if this adjustment were made, the value of money incomes derived from interest on the National Debt would be increased by 30 per cent. as compared with 1924, and by 15 per cent. as compared with 1929, at the expense of the rest of the community.[12]

The same argument applies, of course, to all other forms of bonded debt expressed in terms of money. In the case of industry, the percentage of the gross receipts, reduced in terms of money, required to meet debenture and preference interest, not reduced in terms of money, is seriously increased.

(c) The same considerations apply to many other Government obligations, which are fixed in terms of money—even when the arrangements governing them are not so unalterable as those governing the National Debt—so long as no measures are taken by Parliament to alter them. This applies, for example, to all pensions, and, in particular, to unemployment relief. The latter was fixed in 1920 at 15s. for the single man, when the cost of living was particularly high. With the present cost of living, 9s. to-day has the same value as 15s. in August 1920. As a matter of fact the money value of unemployment benefits has been substantially increased since 1920, with the result that the real benefits to-day are at least double what was thought adequate in 1920.[13]

(d) Money wages and money incomes generally, other than business profits, which constitute the residue, also become seriously inappropriate to the new situation unless they are altered. In these cases, the obstacle to a change is for the most part neither law nor contract, but a strong social resistance to changes which, for the very

[11] See Appendix, Table C.
[12] See Notes 7, 8 and 9.
[13] Ministry of Labour Gazette.

reason that they would have to take place piecemeal and without any ordered plan, are likely to be open to charges of inequity and injustice. But it is the inevitable result of so many of the items of production-costs remaining fixed in terms of money that the residue which forms the inducement to the business man, and is of the order of only 17 per cent. of the whole, is reduced to vanishing point.[14]

24. The result of all this is that money costs interpreted in the widest sense are out of line with money prices. Consequently, producers lose money: they are unable to maintain their former labour forces; and unemployment ensues on a colossal scale.

(b) The Disparity between the Prices of Primary Products and Manufactured Goods.

25. The foregoing represent the maladjustments which arise if a fall in prices becomes evenly spread over commodities in general. For the time being, however, the outstanding feature of the economic situation is a disharmony of a different kind. The prices of primary commodities, *e.g.*, agricultural products and metals, have fallen very heavily, and are now on the average very little above, while many of them have fallen well below, the pre-war level. The prices of manufactured goods have not fallen in anything like the same degree. The result is an extreme disparity between the two sets of prices, which is quite incompatible with an active condition of world trade. So long as the industrial interests of the world attempt to charge anything like the prevailing prices for the manufactured goods they produce, while offering only the prevailing prices for primary products, it is clear that the primary producers will only be able to purchase a diminished quantity of manufactured goods. Until new markets for these goods are found or new types of goods produced instead of them—and this must take a considerable time—industrial unemployment on a large scale must prevail. Partly as a result of this, the prices of manufactured goods are likely to fall, under the pressure of competition between competing manufacturers and competing manufacturing countries. In all industrial countries there is bound to be a strong movement towards the reduction of costs by every available means, which will almost certainly include a lowering of salaries and wages. It is indeed evident that in many countries such a movement is already well under way.[15]

26. It may therefore prove that we are only now approaching the phase of the world depression which is really critical for an industrial country like Great Britain. If manufacturing costs of production are cut drastically

[14] Bowley and Stamp, "The National Income, 1924."
[15] See Appendix, Table J.

throughout the world, it will not be prudent, or indeed possible, for us to abstain from joining in the general movement. For if we do abstain, we shall run a serious danger of seeing our already precarious hold upon the export markets of the world weakened to a disastrous degree.

27. At the same time it is evident that an international price-cutting and wage-cutting contest is something to be looked forward to with great alarm and to be avoided if it is by any means possible. If other countries cut wages, the effect on the value of money throughout the world must be such that we shall be compelled to follow suit sooner or later. But it would be a far better way out for everyone if the route back towards equilibrium was not sought in this direction, but rather by raising the prices of staple commodities so as to make wage cuts less necessary. We think that the most strenuous effort should be made for international co-operation to this end, precisely because, failing such an effort, we fear that a wage-cutting campaign amongst the leading industrial countries is a real possibility and may prove a serious menace to social stability.

IV.—REMEDIES OF AN EXTERNAL CHARACTER.

28. It will be clear from the foregoing analysis that the future course of world prices is a matter of the very first importance for Great Britain. A speedy and sufficient recovery of world prices would go a long way towards providing a solution of our difficulties. On the other hand, if world prices fall further in the near future, or after a brief and partial recovery, resume a downward trend, the strain upon the economic system of Great Britain, as well as of many other countries, may become well-nigh intolerable.

29. We believe that monetary conditions play a dominating part in determining the course of world prices over a long period. In the circumstances which obtain to-day, monetary conditions depend upon the production of gold, its distribution among the different countries, and the prevailing practices of Central Banks relating to its use. The facts with regard to the supply of gold have recently been surveyed by a Committee appointed by the Economic and Financial Section of the League of Nations, and we do not propose to enter into the question in any detail. Our conclusions are:—

   (i) that on the whole and, having regard to the prevailing practices of certain foreign Central Banks, the facts are not such as to encourage optimism;

   (ii) that on the other hand there is no insufficiency in the total supply of gold, provided that it is used with reasonable economy, and with due regard to the needs of the world situation by Central Banks; and

   (iii) that accordingly the problem is one which turns upon the policies which Central Banks pursue, and upon the possibility of inducing them to act together with the object of securing a reasonable degree of stability, at an appropriate level, in the purchasing power of gold.

30. The matter is not one in which it is possible for any single country acting alone to accomplish much. Some influence we can exert, but a great deal more might be accomplished by the Federal Reserve System of the United States joining the Bank of England to take drastic action on a common plan. It is further perhaps permissible to hope that under the pressure of the world trade depression and the gradual extension of its detrimental reactions to countries which have not hitherto felt its effects in a severe degree, the psychological atmosphere may shortly become far more favourable than it is at present to more general co-operation among Central Banks, preferably through the agency of the Bank for International Settlements.

31. The most urgent need at present is of a different character from the measures which would have been required, prior to the recent fall of prices, to avoid an undue fluctuation in the level of prices. The difficulty at the moment is not a general scarcity of short-term credit for first-class borrowers. It arises, in the first place, because such borrowers are reluctant to enter upon new enterprise in an atmosphere of a falling price-level. It is due, in the second place, to the decline of the standing of many borrowers in the opinion of lenders, because the dislocations entailed by the world depression have given rise to widespread distrust of the stability of the financial and currency systems of several countries. Notable instances at the present time are most of the countries of South America, Australia, China and several of the countries of Central Europe.

32. The first obstacle to the revival of enterprise might be diminished by the favourable reaction, both on the willingness of lenders to convert short-term credit into long-term credit and on the willingness of borrowers to engage in new enterprise, that would follow joint action on the part of the Central Banks directed towards creating in the minds of financiers a strong conviction that the present easy terms for short-term credit are likely to continue for a long time to come.

33. A second objective of co-operation between Central Banks might be to allay and remove the distrust now felt towards the general credit of the group of countries that we have mentioned above, by forming a large joint pool for approved loans or in some other way. There is real danger, as matters are now tending, that the severity of the world depression may be increased and its duration prolonged by a renewal of the currency débâcles of the early post-war period. It would lie outside our province to pursue this matter in further detail since the whole question is of a difficult and delicate character in which international political complications and dangers play an important part; but we desire to record our conviction that the

chance of a speedy recovery in world trade will turn in large measure upon whether or not it is possible to restore a feeling of confidence in the financial stability of those many countries which are now the subject of distrust.

34. At the present time, the international situation is so disastrous, that the time may be approaching when some more far-reaching effort at international co-operation than has been considered hitherto may be imperatively demanded. The social and economic systems of many parts of the world are unable to support the present monetary chaos, without breakdown and civil dissension.

V.—WAYS OF RESTORING ELASTICITY TO THE ECONOMIC STRUCTURE OF GREAT BRITAIN.

35. Not much that this country acting alone can do in the economic sphere will materially accelerate world recovery. It is one of the inevitable consequences of our position in the world economy that, while our absence of prosperity may be of our own making, our prosperity must wait on world conditions. On the whole, we gain much more than we lose from the intimate nature of our international connections; and it is reasonable to accept this dependence as a not too exorbitant price for the benefits that it provides.

36. But, while the influence that we can exercise on the world is limited, it is clear that what action we take to meet our local difficulties must depend, in part, upon our estimate of the course of world conditions. If then we cannot rapidly reverse the external tendencies responsible for our local disequilibrium, it is the more incumbent upon us to do what we can to remove the local disabilities of adaptation.

37. No very satisfactory measures have yet been proposed for the direct control of rings and monopolies. But in the past this country has been backward in giving full publicity to the working of such bodies. The experience of the Board of Trade Committee on Trusts might well be reviewed. Business interests have nothing to lose from the maximum publicity, except possibly where international rivalries are involved.

38. No direct Government action, short of the introduction of methods of coercion, can do much to remove trade union restrictions. This is a matter for action by employers and workmen in the industries concerned. The demarcations and trade customs, which grew up in an environment when international competition was not so intense and when there was more slack in the productive machine, are now entirely inappropriate and inimical to the interests of the working classes as a whole. Cotton operatives, for instance, who resist the introduction of the eight loom system, may be safeguarding indeed their immediate interests, but they are only intensifying the difficulties of the industry. In such circumstances it is the general body of wage-earners who are necessarily the chief sufferers.

39. We are convinced that there are many ways in which the efficiency of the labour force could be increased without any change in its actual skill, in the sense of becoming more valuable to the employer and therefore more worth the existing wage, merely by the removal of artificial restrictions. We know that trade unions attach great importance to restrictive provisions, which have often been hardly won and sometimes represent a real contribution to the amenities of working conditions.

40. But if they would agree to reopen the whole question of restrictions all along the line and consider afresh with an open mind what it is really reasonable and desirable to enforce in the actual conditions of to-day in the interests of labour as a whole, and not merely of one union taken in isolation, there might be a surprising increase in the effective output of labour and, consequently, in the ability of the employer to offer increased employment at the existing wage.

41. It is, however, open to the Government to undertake a systematic reform of the whole system of unemployment insurance; and this is urgently required in the public interest. There is no doubt that this system, designed as it was with the most beneficent intentions, is now gravely abused. This system impedes mobility from industry to industry. It encourages the adoption of methods for meeting fundamental industrial change, such as short-time (appropriate only to short-time fluctuations), which tend to aggravate the disease it was intended to cure. It conduces to an artificial rigidity of wage-rates and it constitutes a definite tax on employment.

VI.—WAYS OF INCREASING INDUSTRIAL EFFICIENCY.

42. Under the head of industrial efficiency come measures designed to improve industrial organisation and technique. A vast amount of attention has been given in recent years to the problems of industrial reconstruction, with particular reference to the depressed staple industries; various official inquiries have been held resulting in many practical suggestions as to the lines along which improvement should be sought. We do not regard ourselves as qualified to offer any useful suggestions upon these matters, which are essentially of a technical character, though we are disposed to suggest that from the standpoint of the ultimate prosperity of British economic life the efficiency of industries which are expanding or are capable of expansion deserves to be regarded as of no less importance than the efficiency of industries which are encountering serious difficulties. It is clearly of vital importance that everything possible should be done to keep British industry efficient and up to date. But the main question which presents itself in the present inquiry is how far such measures can suffice as a remedy for the troubles analysed in the previous Sections. For the most part improvements in industrial methods and technique are being adopted, and are likely to be adopted, about as fast by our principal competitors as

by ourselves, and, so far as this is true, though it remains of cardinal importance that we should not lag behind, we are not likely to secure much positive amelioration of our competitive position under this head. Moreover, it is necessary to remember that many of the changes which are included to-day under the vague term "rationalisation" are not of a kind calculated to increase productivity or employment. It is, for example, an important purpose of many so-called rationalisation schemes to arrange an orderly contraction of output in a declining industry with a minimum of financial loss to the firms concerned. This is, speaking generally, a desirable objective, but it is not calculated to make any direct contribution to the problem of unemployment. A further consideration to be borne in mind is that in so far as improved industrial technique takes the form of the introduction of labour-saving machinery, which it is only profitable to introduce because wage-rates are uneconomically high, they will involve a temporary aggravation of unemployment, except to the extent that it is mitigated by a temporary stimulus to the industries manufacturing the labour-saving machinery.

43. Altogether, therefore, we are driven to the conclusion that industrial reconstruction cannot supply in itself a complete solution to our serious economic difficulties. We say this without wishing in the least to minimise the supreme importance to the economic well-being of Great Britain of pressing forward well-considered schemes of industrial reconstruction to the utmost in our power. In the difficult economic conditions which now confront us we can ill afford to carry the burden of remediable industrial inefficiency.

VII.—REDUCTIONS IN DOMESTIC MONEY WAGES.
(a) The Export Industries.

44. Throughout the last few years the money cost of production of British goods has been maintained at a level which has made it difficult for British industry to keep its hold upon the world markets. We are, indeed, very far from supposing that the whole blame for our exporting difficulties is attributable to excessive costs of production; nor do we take the view that the largest possible volume of exports should be the main objective of economic policy. Various circumstances, which have nothing to do with British money costs of production, such as those referred to in paragraph 9 (c) above, have exerted an adverse influence on British exports since the War. Moreover, even where a decline in our exports is attributable to the fact that we have been losing ground to competitors, it does not necessarily follow either that excessive costs were the essential cause of the decline or that the reduction of our costs (otherwise than by means of increased efficiency) is a desirable remedy. As industrialisation spreads throughout the world, industrial countries with a low standard of living naturally tend to displace older industrial countries like ourselves in those forms of manufacture

which do not call for a very high degree of skill or for highly trained technical staffs. Doubtless in such cases, if we were to cut wages progressively, as the new competition developed, we could hold on to a larger share of the world's trade for some time. But such a policy would be foolish and in the long run hopeless. It is better to let go those branches of trade which are marked out by technical circumstances as the natural field of newer industrial countries, and to seek compensation by concentrating more on other industries in which we have greater relative advantages.

45. The volume of our exports in 1929 was about 10 per cent. less than in 1913.[16] The largest part of this decline was probably attributable to causes of the type discussed above. Even so, the loss of export trade confronts us with awkward problems of readjustment, because some of the principal exporting industries which have been losing ground are highly localised industries whose workpeople cannot move easily to other occupations. But the problem so far is essentially one of readjustment, not of national decline. There is no strict necessity for us to maintain an export trade of the pre-war dimensions in order to purchase the foodstuffs and raw materials which we must obtain from abroad.

46. Unfortunately, even before the slump, there was reason to believe that the selling prices of British goods were above a properly competitive level not only in trades which we must expect to see pass in the course of time to new competitors, but over a wide range of trades which are pre-eminently proper to an advanced industrial nation. In the light of the world depression these misgivings are necessarily deepened. From 1925 to 1929 our total exports tended on the whole to increase, if only at a disappointing rate, and it had seemed reasonable to conclude that the danger of a further absolute decline was not serious. But the present depression reminds us that the years 1925–1929 were years of activity for world trade as a whole and suggests that, taking good years and bad years of world trade together, our total exports may be still declining not merely relatively to those of other countries but absolutely as well.

47. Although we do not consider that an export trade of the pre-war dimensions is an indispensable necessity for British economic life, the maintenance of an export trade upon a substantial scale is certainly essential to us. There are moreover no British products of which we have anything in the nature of a world monopoly and which we can therefore be sure of selling independently of the price we charge. The maintenance of a substantial export trade requires in the long run as an essential condition that our costs of production should be comparable with those of our competitors in world markets. We entertain grave doubts whether over the greater part of industry that condition is fulfilled to-day. Just as it takes a long time either for an individual business or for a country to establish a commanding

[16] Board of Trade Journal and information given in the Report of the Balfour Committee on Industry and Trade.

position in the markets of the world, so it takes a long time either for an individual business or a nation to lose that position once it has been established, but the process of decline if it gets to a certain point is apt to develop more rapidly in its later stages. In the situation revealed and aggravated by the world depression, the danger that we may see our export trade dwindle to a disastrous point, unless we can secure a substantial reduction of our money costs of production, is one we can no longer afford to disregard.

(b) Home Industries.

48. Nor is it only in the export industries that the wage situation is important. It is plain that, other things being equal, the quantity of employment in home industries could be increased if wage-earners there were prepared to accept lower money rates of wages. How large a percentage of wage-reduction, whether in general or in particular industries, would be required to evoke in the near future a given percentage increase in the volume of employment we have found ourselves unable to decide. Nevertheless, we must not under-estimate the advantages to employment generally which would ensue from wage-reductions in some of the more highly paid sheltered industries. Since such reductions would be likely to reduce the cost of living, they would make it easier to secure any unavoidable wage-reductions in other directions.

(c) Difficulties in the Way of Wage Reductions.

49. One of the great practical difficulties of attempting to improve employment by means of wage-reductions is the anomalous disparities which exist at present between wages in different occupations. It is in the unsheltered industries which have to sell their goods against foreign competition that the pressure towards wage-reductions will be strongest: but in many of those industries wages are already unduly low in comparison with wages in other occupations. On the other hand, the industries where wage-rates are highest relatively to the pre-war standard, and where wage-reductions would accordingly entail a lesser degree of hardship, are usually sheltered industries where the wage-earners' bargaining position is strong. Nevertheless, the case for wage-reduction on comparative grounds in some of those industries where the rates are out of line with wages elsewhere is so clear that we think an attempt at adjustment could be amicably made. But the friction and ill-will which must be aroused by any general movement towards lower wages will be greatly intensified if the wage-earners are singled out as the only class which is asked to make sacrifices. The recipients of salaries and of interest, and of fixed incomes generally, have benefited just as much as the wage-earners from the fall in the cost of living. So far as the case for wage-reductions rests on changes of price-level, we hold strongly

that no general appeal should be made by industry to its workpeople to accept lower wages without a proposal at the same time for a commensurate reduction in higher salaries and directors' fees.

50. It is desirable, however, to point out certain facts which are relevant to the problem. Since 1924, when the fall in the cost of living is taken into account, real wages in Great Britain have increased on the average by about 9 per cent.[17] Moreover, one of the principal reasons why the cost of living has not fallen so much as wholesale prices is precisely that money wages have not fallen appreciably. If money wages were now to fall, it would be reasonable to expect some offset to this in a reduction in the cost of living. So long as rents remain at their present level, the amount of this offset may be disappointing, but we would judge that it would be equivalent to not less than one-fifth of the reduction of wages. Thus if money wages were now to fall even by as much as 10 per cent. on the average, the result would be to leave real wages somewhat higher than they were in 1924, so long as the prices of primary products remain near their present level. In the face of continually falling prices, no country can prudently maintain the principle that money wage-rates are sacrosanct independently of their relation to real wage-rates.

51. To sum up—

(i) Existing money wage-rates cannot be regarded as sacrosanct in a world subject to violent changes in the value of money.

(ii) Certain wage adjustments in the downward direction, particularly in sheltered industries whose existing wages are out of line with wages in other comparable industries, are desirable now.

(iii) If world prices fail to recover to a materially higher level, general wage-cuts in this country (or their equivalent) will become inevitable, because the failure of the price-level to recover will probably mean that such wage-cuts have been made elsewhere.

(iv) But, on the other hand, as we have said in paragraph 27, it would be unwise for this country to lead the way with a general wage-cut or to encourage an incipient world movement in this direction.

(v) In view of the immense practical difficulties of any general reduction in money wages, every other remedy with any serious balance of argument in its favour should be tried first.

(vi) Furthermore, if a general wage-cut becomes inevitable, it is most desirable that it should be undertaken as part of a wider scheme for re-settling money incomes generally (including *rentier* incomes in particular), and not wages alone.

[17] See Appendix, Table H.

VIII.—SUBSIDIES TO WAGES.

52. The effect upon unemployment of a general subsidy to money wages is *primâ facie* the same as that of an equal proportionate reduction in money wage-rates. Should it prove possible by a low rate of subsidy to absorb a large number of the unemployed, it might happen that the whole cost of the subsidy would be off-set by the associated reduction in the amount of unemployment benefit.[18] In this event, if the wage-earning classes did not, in consequence of the subsidy, demand and secure higher rates of money wage, unemployment would be much reduced and no off-setting disadvantage would occur. It would, however, be highly optimistic to suppose either that a general wage subsidy at any given rate would in fact reduce the volume of unemployment sufficiently to pay for itself out of unemployment benefit, or that, if it did so, the wage-earners would refrain from demanding increased rates of wage. Hence in practice it is to be feared that this policy, if the subsidy were at all substantial, would involve a heavy additional charge on the Budget even when allowance is made for savings on the Unemployment Insurance Fund; and in the present state of the national finances there can be no doubt that this would have very unfavourable repercussions. Moreover, a general system of wage subsidies would appear to many persons as a plunge into the abyss: and business confidence might be so shaken that employment would suffer through that cause an indirect injury much greater than any direct gain that might fall to it. We are of opinion, therefore, that a policy of general wage subsidies is not one that ought to be adopted.

53. We therefore turn to proposals for a system of wage subsidies in respect, not of all wage-earners, but of additional wage-earners whom employers would undertake to engage with the help of the subsidy. On the assumption that an unemployed man costs the State one pound a week, to bring him into work by means of a subsidy would be a clear gain all round, so long as the required subsidy was anything less than a pound. Moreover, under this system there would be less prospect of wage-earners demanding a rise in money wages, and much less shock to business confidence than might be looked for with a general wage subsidy. The difficulties in the way of a scheme of this type are, however, very great:—

(*a*) In competitive industries it is well-nigh impossible to say for any length of time what is the number of employees actually additional to the number that would have been in employment without the subsidy.

(*b*) Moreover, the employers who are successfully marketing their product without the subsidy may rightly urge that the subsidy is really a bounty to the less efficient.

(*c*) If the increased output caused through the subsidy can only be marketed

[18] The present cost of unemployment benefit is now about $7\frac{1}{2}$ per cent. of the wages of the insured population.

at a lower price—as must often be the case—the unsubsidised businesses find their position and margin of profit actually worsened.

(*d*) Even if the number of additional employees at work were constant or determinable, they would not be necessarily continuously in the same businesses, since according to the fluctuations of the fortunes of different individual businesses the claim to be employing some of the surplus qualifying for subsidy would be shifting and indeterminate.

54. It may be that in particular cases these difficulties could be overcome and a workable scheme could be devised in which the disadvantages were at a minimum and the advantages to employment at a maximum. If and where this is so, it appears to the majority of us (Mr. Keynes, Professor Pigou and Sir Josiah Stamp) that the cases for wage subsidies in respect of *additional* employees at a rate less than the present rate of unemployment pay is a strong one. We have not investigated any particular proposals under this head. One of us, however (Mr. Henderson), is of opinion that it would be impossible to frame any scheme of subsidies which would not by its repercussions do more harm than good, and holds strongly that the path of subsidies to wages is one which should be avoided. If attempted in particular industries, subsidies would need to be so framed that their temporary character was emphasised; and provision would need to be made for their gradual abolition in such a way as not to create disturbance. Subsidies to wages in particular industries, as a permanent system, are, in our view, highly undesirable. Moreover, it must be remembered that any system of subsidies, whether general or particular, is difficult to administer without risk of abuse.

IX.—WAYS OF INCREASING BUSINESS CONFIDENCE.

55. An improvement in the state of business confidence would lead to greater readiness to hire labour for a future return. Business men would borrow more both on short term and on long. Indeed, an improved state of confidence would help employment in two ways; it would raise the terms on which borrowers would think it worth while to borrow, and it would lower the terms on which lenders would be ready to accommodate British enterprise. Thus, the money that people saved would be utilised in real investment; the price level might rise in some measure; activity in one field would stimulate activity in others. Once the movement started— unless subjected to some violent jar—it would advance under its own momentum. If the development of confidence in this country is not accompanied by a similar development elsewhere, then, in consequence of the relative rise in the price-level here, a tendency might be set up for gold to flow abroad. If this should happen it would, in our view, be vitally

important that the Bank of England should be prepared to suffer a substantial loss of gold rather than check the upward movement too soon by enforcing an advance in short money-rates.

56. The best means of restoring business confidence is a psychological problem on which the opinion of this Committee is not likely to be specially valuable. In the long run we do not see how business confidence is likely to be maintained otherwise than by an actual recovery of business profits. This means that, if business and employment improve for other reasons, the effect of this improvement on business confidence may be cumulative; which is, indeed, a part of the justification of emergency measures of a temporary character. For the effect of judicious emergency measures might be to improve business confidence, after which business confidence might take the place of the emergency measures as providing the necessary stimulus.

57. The ways of restoring business confidence which have been recommended in one quarter or another and seem to us to have some plausibility may be catalogued as follows, without our expressing any opinion as to the quantitative effects to be expected from them or as to their general desirability regarded merely as stimuli:—

(a) A solution of the Budget problem satisfactory to business sentiment—in particular, the avoidance of increased direct taxation, the avoidance of any serious reduction of the Sinking Fund and the avoidance of increased expenditure.

(b) A drastic reform of the system of Unemployment Insurance. It is widely felt that, if Parliament can suffer the present monstrous anomalies of the Dole—as they seem to be to a wide consensus of public opinion—without trying to do away with them, this must be symptomatic of a general unwholesomeness in the body politic. A far-reaching reform might cause a great revulsion of feeling as showing those fears to be groundless.

(c) A tariff on manufactured imports is recommended in some quarters partly on the ground that it would supply just the stimulus (or, as others would contend, the dope) which business needs after the depression caused by losses partly due to forces, such as the return to gold and the fall of world prices, beyond its own control. With the general question of a tariff we deal later.

(d) In general, any remedies which would improve the prospect of earning profits might also be classified as partly producing their results through their effect on business confidence.

X.—WAYS OF INCREASING HOME INVESTMENT.
(a) Cheap Credit.

58. The amount of home investment, and so the volume of employment, would be increased if the terms on which borrowers can be accommodated were made easier through a reduction in the rate of interest or an improvement of facilities in other ways.

59. The most general effect in this direction would be produced by a credit policy on the part of the Bank of England to make bank-credit as cheap and abundant as possible. The difficulty is, of course, that the Bank of England cannot, under gold-standard limitations, move far in this direction, unless other Central Banks do the same. Some of us consider that an important cause of existing unemployment is to be found in the fact that world conditions in combination with the requirements of the gold standard have enforced on the Bank of England in recent years a credit policy which has kept the volume of domestic investment below what it would otherwise have been.

60. In recent months short-term rates of interest have fallen to a low level. Probably we have not yet experienced the full benefits of this; for capital projects take a long time to mature and the amount of those actually afoot is still under the influence of the abnormally high rates of 1929. But it is particularly noticeable that, so far, the reduction of short-term rates of interest is only very slightly reflected in long-term rates—which are of much greater significance to borrowers for fixed investment.

61. We consider that a policy on the part of the Treasury and the banking system intended to bring down long-term rates of interest, even if it meant some raising of short-term rates, would be useful on balance as facilitating an increase of long-term investment.

(b) Regulation of Foreign Issues.

62. From time to time in recent years the higher rates of interest offered abroad as compared with those which domestic investments are able to yield have given rise to a pressure towards lending money abroad instead of at home. In such conditions, the effect of high world rates of interest under a gold standard has been to put the domestic rate above the rate at which enough new domestic investment can come into existence. If our exports were low enough in price and in sufficient demand abroad, great activity in the foreign loan market or in buying foreign investments would reflect itself to a practically equal extent in increased exports. But if this economic outlet is not available owing to the position of our export trade, then a state of disequilibrium is created, which, again, by increasing rates of home interest, accentuates the difficulty. The only method of restoring equilibrium so far adopted has been an embargo on foreign lending in London or a kind

of informal rationing of foreign borrowers, but this has hitherto been ineffective and open to objection in practice. The harm that arises when there is a difference between the capacity to lend abroad and the capacity to export, or because increased foreign lending cannot be reflected in diminished imports, might perhaps be mitigated by certain special measures. The control already exercised by the Bank of England over the rate of new foreign issues may operate to some slight extent to avoid exceptional pressure at inconvenient times. But it is easily evaded. Bonds issued on foreign markets find their way to the London market, without having paid British stamp duty and contrary to the wishes of those responsible for the regulation of the British market. We think that a distinction might be made between foreign bonds officially admitted to the British investment market (perhaps by the Treasury on the recommendation of the Bank of England) and those not so admitted, income derived from the latter being subject to a special income tax.

(c) Subsidies and Public Works.

63. The next possibility under the head of increasing home-investment is that of promoting useful schemes of capital development, either by pressing forward such work as lies within the direct control of the Government, or by the offer of State subsidies to local authorities and public utility companies. Under conditions of extensive unemployment such as prevail to-day, and have prevailed in lesser degree for some years, we are convinced that what we may term the policy of "public works" is, in principle, a sound policy for the State to pursue. We do not accept the view that the undertaking of such work must necessarily cause a mere diversion from other employment. On the contrary, we think it improbable that public works, which comply with the conditions which we detail below, involve during a trade depression any important degree of diversion from employment in ordinary industry. Apart from any such possible off-set, the effect of public works in increasing employment is, of course, not necessarily or even often confined to the number of workpeople directly engaged upon them. They entail an increased demand for the services of the industries which supply the materials used; and the increased purchasing power of the workers employed in these ways has further beneficial repercussions upon trade in general. There accrues, accordingly, an important saving to public funds in the shape of reduced expenditure on unemployment benefit, as well as some increase in the yield of the general revenue, which makes it good business, even from the standpoint of the Budget, to pay subsidies amounting to a considerable percentage of the cost of the work (say at least, one-third) provided that the effect of the subsidies is to secure that work is put in hand, which would not otherwise be undertaken.

64. We think it desirable to stress these considerations lest disillusionment

with the apparent results of the public works policy of recent years should encourage the belief that experience has demonstrated that a programme of public works is disadvantageous rather than advantageous to employment. No policy of public works can, of course, outweigh the effects of a world slump of the magnitude of the present one. But we are of opinion that unemployment would stand to-day at a decidedly higher level, if the Government a year ago had attempted to cut down road programmes and development work generally instead of pressing them forward.

65. On the other hand, it is important to recognise that public works can only be justified if certain conditions are fulfilled. In the first place, the works in question must really be of a useful and productive character. To undertake costly projects of no or only a negligible value merely for the sake of providing employment would be an absurdly wasteful proceeding. Indeed, inasmuch as the projects would necessarily consume a great deal of useful materials, this would be more wasteful than it would be to pay the unemployed full wages for doing nothing. Secondly, works which are to be of assistance in mitigating unemployment in times of bad trade, must be capable of being put into operation and carried out with speed. Unfortunately, however, the works for which there is the strongest case, from the point of view of their social and economic utility, are often of a kind which it is extremely difficult to get going quickly, while, on the other hand, the utility of projects which it is comparatively easy to set in hand without delay is often extremely dubious. Thirdly, the works must be of such a nature as not to create later on a difficult "demobilisation" problem. A programme of public works which consists mainly of heavy outdoor navvying work is exposed to a real weakness under this head. Such works necessarily employ a larger proportion of men of the lower age groups than the average industry. They are apt, moreover, to entail the undue stimulation of the demand for certain kinds of materials. Fourthly, as regards those works which are subsidised but not directly undertaken by the State, it is obviously important, but difficult in practice to ensure, that the subsidies are not paid for work which would have been undertaken in any case.

66. Finally, the scope and scale of the programme as a whole must be such as to commend itself as reasonable and sensible to public opinion. A hastily improvised programme of dubious projects, which was widely regarded as wasteful and profligate, and raised doubts as to the general soundness of the public finances, might have serious reactions, for example, on the rate of interest at which the Government could borrow. While, as we have said, we do not believe that employment created by public works need involve a diminution of resources devoted to private investment, it might easily do so, if it took a form which aroused apprehension as to the stability of the public credit.

67. The above conditions necessarily set limits to the extent to which it is possible to meet unemployment by the policy of public works.

XI.—TARIFFS.

68. We approach the expedient of Tariffs from the standpoint of economists who, at all times previous to the present emergency, have been strongly opposed to them. We accept, that is to say, the validity of the traditional Free Trade argument.

The central economic argument for Free Trade may be expressed as follows:—

69. In normal conditions, when there is no chronic abnormal unemployment, the effect of a tariff must mainly be to divert the productive forces of the community from one occupation to another, and not to increase their total activity. It has been usual to admit that special cases can be imagined (*e.g.*, infant industries or key industries) where there may be advantages in the deliberate diversion of production out of its "natural" channels by tariffs or otherwise. But as a rule there will be a strong presumption that tariffs of the kind which are imposed in practice will tend to divert production from the channels where we are relatively more efficient into channels where we are relatively less efficient; that is to say, the play of natural forces will be more successful in discovering the occupations in which we can employ ourselves most profitably, than any system of tariffs will be. This will be particularly the case as time goes by. A tariff is apt to be inelastic and not easily changed in accordance with changing circumstances. The older but less profitable industries will cry out successfully for protection which will enable them to retain productive forces which otherwise would be finding their way into newer and more profitable industries. Moreover, in so far as the productive forces of the country are occupied in protected trades where their relative efficiency is less than it is in certain other trades, the effect will be seen in a higher cost of living relatively to the money-wages, and consequently in a lower standard of life.

(a) Advantages of a Tariff.

70. The question we have to face to-day is the extent to which this historic argument is invalidated for the time being by (i) the existence of chronic large-scale unemployment, (ii) the doubt whether we can hope materially to expand or even to retain our present favourable balance of trade by means of a moderate cut in our money costs without a restriction of imports, (iii) the possibility that the effect of a tariff on the "terms of trade" might be greater in present circumstances than formerly, and (iv) whether the promotion of economic solidarity within the British Empire may not be a safeguard against the danger of economic isolation in the modern world.

(i) *Chronic Large-Scale Unemployment.*

71. Among economists this issue was, before the War, mainly discussed without reference to the possible effects of protective duties upon the volume of employment. The popular idea that since, subject to certain reservations, exports are the price paid for imports, it is impossible that these duties should increase employment as a whole, was indeed no part of the economist's stock in trade. It was always obvious that a contraction of imports might be balanced in part not by a contraction of exports, but by an expansion in our purchases of foreign securities; it was equally obvious that a contraction of imports might be equivalent to leaving abroad a larger part of the interest due on our existing foreign investments as further foreign investment. Even in so far as exports were contracted it would not follow that export industries must be contracted to an equivalent extent, since their efforts might be turned to satisfying the needs of new men brought into the protected home industry. But before the War, though, of course, unemployment existed and was sometimes large in amount, nearly all of it could be accounted for as a function of processes of adjustment to which any lasting system of fiscal duties was irrelevant. There was no large intractable mass of unemployment associated with dislocations between costs and world prices such as has existed ever since the post-armistice boom. No doubt, even before the War, a movable system of import duties, to be put on in bad times and removed in good, would have affected the employment situation favourably. But, in pre-war controversy, the protective tariff contemplated was intended to be permanent—tariffs to be imposed and removed at short intervals being never seriously debated; and there was at that time at any rate no unemployment of a sort relevant to, or capable of being appreciably affected by, this policy. For this reason the unemployment issue was often left on one side in tariff discussions. The situation is now fundamentally different. There is, and has been ever since the post-armistice boom, an enormous mass of, so to speak, chronic unemployment, associated with the dislocations discussed in earlier sections of this Report, much exceeding in amount and different in type from that which prevailed before the War. It is essential to inquire how far this new situation provides new arguments in favour of protective duties.

72. In present conditions the imposition of reasonably devised protective duties (though one of us (Professor Pigou) thinks that in practice it might not be easy to devise them) that should exclude a substantial portion of the imports that now compete with our home industries would, for some time to come, directly increase the aggregate volume of employment in this country, and by so doing would set up repercussions through the saving on the unemployment benefit and so on, that would, by indirect processes increase it still further. The gain would probably be associated with some increase in the cost of living and a corresponding reduction in real wages and

in the value of money incomes generally; but since a main alternative remedy for unemployment—a reduction of money wages—must also involve an equal or greater reduction of real wages, this consideration is not of great weight. The important question to decide is whether the direct effect, and therewith the indirect effects, of reasonably devised protective duties in increasing the aggregate volume of employment would be large or small. The answer to this question turns in great part upon the degree of adverse reaction which the contraction brought about in our imports is likely to produce on our export industries.

73. The majority of us (Mr. Keynes, Mr. Henderson and Sir Josiah Stamp) take the view that in present conditions the main part of the reduction of imports would be balanced for several years by increased sales to us of foreign securities. If we use surplus capacity now out of employment to make, under the protection of a tariff, an article which we now import, the relief to the foreign exchanges may enable the Bank of England to relax credit conditions, with the result that there may be an increase of foreign lending by this country; so that the fruits of the labour of the newly-employed surplus capacity go to increase the amount of the country's foreign wealth. Or, alternatively, the former imports may be partly replaced by imports of a different kind, namely, those which are needed to satisfy part of the increased consumption of the newly-employed workers. We return to these considerations below.

74. One of us (Professor Pigou) holds that the adverse reaction would after a short time be nearly commensurate with the original contraction of imports. His reasons are as follows. In so far as the price-level was raised here, our export industries would be directly handicapped; in so far as imports—or substitutes for them—excluded from our market were driven to seek an outlet elsewhere, these industries would be faced with stronger competition in neutral markets. Moreover, the effect of a reversion to protection on the part of this country might well, in the present international situation, lead to a rise in the tariffs of other countries and so to a still further handicap upon our exports. Yet again, in so far as either home or export industries use imported goods either as raw materials or machinery in their own work, these home industries will be *pro tanto* prejudiced. Professor Pigou, whilst agreeing that the present abnormal employment situation strengthens the case for protective import duties in some measure, is not prepared to admit that it strengthens it very much.

(ii) *The Maintenance of Foreign Investment on an Adequate Scale.*

75. If the view of the majority on this matter (paragraph 73), from which Professor Pigou dissents, is correct, the point is very important. For there is a further set of considerations, which formerly, perhaps, were of small practical significance, but may be of first-class importance to-day. We

believe that it is difficult or impossible at the present time for Great Britain to employ her productive resources to the best advantage without a somewhat large proportion of foreign investment to total savings. Great Britain is an old and relatively well-equipped country; and it is natural, therefore, that the outside world should be able to offer more openings capable of yielding a high rate of interest than can be found at home. But if the volume of savings which is thus attracted towards overseas is greater than our favourable foreign balance of trade, the Bank of England tends to lose gold, with the result that a credit disequilibrium is set up which is likely to have a most adverse effect on business profits and hence on employment. The only remedies are to be found either in an increase of home investment, the possibilities of stimulating which we have already explored, or in an increase of the favourable foreign balance. Some of us find the main reason of the present disequilibrium of profits and employment, not so much in an unduly high standard of life, as in the fact that the pressure of savings to find an outlet abroad is greater than the amount of foreign investment which corresponds to the balance of trade which we actually have at present.

76. Thus unless something occurs greatly to increase the relative attractions of home investment, a substantial increase of our favourable balance of trade may be a necessary ingredient in any complete solution.

77. Now the favourable balance of trade can be increased either by increasing our exports or by diminishing our imports. By reducing our costs, and particularly by cutting our wages costs, we can increase the volume of our exports. The difficulties of making sufficient headway along this line are: (1) the resistance of the workers to wage reductions; (2) the prospect that our foreign competitors are likely, at any rate for a time, to meet any cuts we may make by cuts of their own; and (3) the fact that the *value* of our exports, as distinct from the *volume*, will not be much increased unless the percentage increase in the volume of trade is decidedly greater than the percentage reduction of prices (*e.g.*, if by cutting our prices 10 per cent., we only increase the volume of our exports 10 per cent., the value of our exports is no greater than it was before). For a country situated as Great Britain is, it would be better to occupy our unemployed resources in making increased exports, so far as this is possible on satisfactory terms. But it seems obvious to some of us that, if we cannot overcome the difficulties of an adequate solution along these lines, it is better to occupy our unemployed resources in making goods to take the place of goods we now import than not to occupy them at all. For this is just as effective a way of increasing our power to make foreign investments and to augment employment as increasing our exports would be. Thus the question arises—and this is not merely a feature of the immediate crisis, but may face us for some time to come—whether, assuming that we have to find further employment, either on making exports or on making goods to replace imports, we should not

rely in part on the latter form of employment to supplement the, perhaps limited, opportunities for the former. At any rate, in deciding where lies the balance of advantage for or against a tariff, this, together with the existence of large unused capacity in plant, machinery and agriculture, is one of the factors which must be taken into consideration. With some of us, indeed, this has been the decisive factor in convincing us that the adoption of some kind of generalised tariff is, on the whole, advisable for such period as the economic equilibrium is out of gear owing to our wage-levels not having been adjusted to a rapidly reduced price-level.

78. It has been put to us—to give a concrete example—that, assuming we need an increase of £50 million in our favourable balance of trade, in order to make foreign investments in countries needing new capital out of British savings surplus to our own requirements, it might be to the national advantage and result in a higher standard of living, if we were to set about achieving this by facilitating the production at home of, for example, iron and steel products or pig- and poultry-products which we now import, rather than by trying to force out a larger volume of our older staple exports by competitive wage-cuts which might be met, for all we know, by almost equal cuts on the part of our competitors. It should be added that the argument for a tariff in such cases would be partly of the "infant industry" type, as well as of the type discussed above, inasmuch as the object would be to select industries which there seemed good hopes of our being able to foster and expand.

79. Moreover, this policy might also be to the advantage of the overseas countries which need our surplus savings for their further development. In other words, it is better in such circumstances for the rest of the world, as well as for us, that our surplus capacity should be used to create wealth than that it should lie idle; for this will have the indirect effect of releasing resources for the capital development of the overseas countries which most need them, as well as of adding correspondingly to the foreign investments of this country.

(iii) The Terms of Trade.

80. Economists have always recognised that, when a country imposes taxes upon imports—whether imports that compete with home products or others—it will in some measure turn the real terms of trade in its favour; that is to say, it will cause a unit of its export goods to buy somewhat more import goods than before; or, in more popular language, that in some measure it will make the foreigner pay its import duties. Before the War, for a number of reasons which it is not necessary to enumerate, it was, however, generally agreed that, so far as this country was concerned, the gain that could be looked for under this head was very small. It was likely, moreover, to evaporate as time went on, being an advantage which we could only snatch on a scale worth having if we took the foreigner by

surprise and before he had time to adapt himself to the new circumstances. In present conditions, in view of the large amount of surplus capacity in the iron and steel and some other industries abroad, it may be that a more substantial advantage might be won. Foreigners determined to sell in our markets might cut their price to match the duty. It must be observed, however, that, so far as they did this, the volume of imports would *not* be reduced, and, therefore, the advantages under the head of employment would be replaced by advantages to the Budget.

(iv) *Danger of Economic Isolation.*

81. Finally, it is necessary also to take account of a consideration of a vaguer character. The tendency since the War has been in the direction of an intensified economic nationalism, and, despite the counter-movement set on foot by the World Economic Conference of 1927 and the succeeding discussions at Geneva, that remains in practice the prevailing tendency. It is true that there is a growing realisation throughout Europe of the mischief caused by this tendency, but the signs are that this new mood, when it gains sufficient strength, will express itself rather in agreements between neighbouring groups of countries to grant one another preferential tariff concessions, to which the outside world is not admitted, than in a general reduction of tariff barriers. This, indeed, is the principle which underlies the present project of economic co-operation between the agrarian States of Europe and which also inspires the vaguer project of a United States of Europe.

82. If agreements of this kind materialise, it may be possible for Great Britain to secure for her trade the preferential terms accorded to each other by the participating States in consideration of the fact that we impose few duties upon their goods. On the other hand, there is a manifest danger, if such agreements are entered into in some quarters, whilst elsewhere the tariffs of other countries are becoming increasingly high, that we may find ourselves in a dangerous position of economic isolation. It may happen accordingly that our interests may best be safeguarded by cultivating closer economic relations with the Empire and seeking for an extension of inter-Imperial trade, even if it were to prove to be at the expense of some loss of trade with the outside world.

83. At the present moment the Dominions, largely as the result of the difficulties caused by the world depression, are in no mood to abate their policies of national protectionism, and we do not consider that an increase of preferences which takes the form of raising the duties against imports from outside the Empire without abating the tariffs against our goods, can offer very substantial advantages to British trade. We see no great probability therefore at the moment of entering into any fully satisfactory arrangements with the Dominions, though we write without knowledge as to what exact

arrangements the Dominions might be prepared to offer as the result of negotiations.

84. It is, however, fair to remember that the preferences already accorded to us by the Dominions without any important tariff *quid pro quo* are of very real advantage to us. Indeed, the more our difficulties in world markets increase, the more dependent do some of our staple industries such as textiles become on the preferential markets of the Dominions; and a withdrawal of all the preferences now granted to us by the Empire would undoubtedly be a serious blow to British trade.

85. In those circumstances, though we have no basis for an immediate proposal, we consider that the development of inter-Imperial preference may very likely become a wise economic policy for Great Britain, and this possibility weakens the presumption against using certain types of tariff just now as a means of temporary relief from our present difficulties.

(b) Objections to a Tariff.

86. On the other side of the account, there remain with unabated force certain arguments of a more general kind against a tariff, namely:—

(a) A tariff may be a means of snatching, at the expense of other countries, an advantage for ourselves which is not so great as the damage done to them; so that if everyone plays the same game, the world as a whole is worse off. The world would be richer under a system of general Free Trade than it is.

(b) Governments dependent upon popular elections are certain to impose protective duties, not on weak industries that may need them, but rather on strong industries that control numerous votes.

(c) Once duties have been imposed, vested interests are created; and it is difficult to remove them when the need for them disappears, without inflicting considerable incidental hardship.

(d) So long as the issue of Protection versus Free Trade divides political parties, duties are liable to be imposed or removed not on their merits but according to the exigency of party conflict, with the result that industrialists are never certain of their position and may be diverted from the task of tackling their proper problems to perpetual "lobbyings" in pursuit of fiscal favours. The more the prosperity of particular industries is made dependent upon Government action, the less likely it is that public affairs will be conducted with a single eye to the interests of the community as a whole.

87. Different persons will weigh up differently the balance of advantage or disadvantage resulting from courses of action which, while probably increasing employment in the immediate future, would also be open to these objections.

88. These issues are not strictly determinable on considerations of economic theory alone. They must largely depend on how long we expect the existing disequilibrium to last, how seriously we estimate the immediate social risks of a policy which looks to the more remote future for its reward, how seriously we regard the dangers of economic isolation if we reject any practicable appeal of the Dominions for closer economic co-operation, how great an actual diminution of the national wealth will ensue in the meantime if we do nothing, how much can be expected from alternative policies, and so forth; and, on the other hand, how much ultimate damage we might do to our economic strength by diverting our productive energies into channels which may not be the best in the long run, how much injury we may inflict on international ideals and the cause of peace and amity throughout the world, how far the British national character and political life are likely to prove exempt from the grosser evils of Protectionism.

(c) Conclusions.

89. When we come to the question of particular schemes, we think it important to distinguish sharply between two different types of tariff.

(i) Safeguarding.

90. We understand by safeguarding duties tariffs imposed primarily for protective purposes in favour of specially selected industries. We have already argued above that a theoretical case may exist for such duties, especially when an argument of the "infant industry" character is applicable. But in the actual conditions of Great Britain to-day, we think that it is difficult to find exceptional cases of this kind.

91. Apart from existing duties, there is no case amongst manufactures, which appears to us to deserve serious consideration, except a tariff on iron and steel and their products. In this case, the majority of us (Mr. Keynes, Mr. Henderson and Sir Josiah Stamp) are in favour of protective duties in the present grave emergency, subject to the strict condition that the industry should rationalise itself in accordance with an approved plan and that the tariff should be of a weight and scope appropriate, *not* to present conditions but to those which will exist after their reconstruction.

92. One of us (Professor Pigou) dissents from this proposal concerning iron and steel on the following grounds:—

(a) It would be impracticable to adopt this proposal without at the same time not merely granting drawbacks to export industries that use steel in their work, but also somehow compensating home industries that do this. From simple beginnings an elaborate and complicated system of duties or other compensatory arrangements would thus grow up.

(b) The condition for protection, *i.e.*, that the industry should undertake to rationalise itself, is not one that is capable of being enforced; for the industry is not an individual. It might even happen that, under the shelter of protection, inefficient firms would be maintained and the process of rationalisation actually impeded.

(c) A duty of this character, though imposed as a temporary measure, would prove in practice, when the circumstances, in respect of which the majority contemplate it, have disappeared, exceedingly difficult to remove.

(d) If it be the fact that, in view of the heavy losses which it has sustained, the industry is unable to raise the capital necessary to modernise its plant and so do without some form of Government assistance, methods of assistance other than those of a tariff are available.

93. In the case of agriculture, it has been put to us that pig-products and poultry-products offer an important field for replacing imports by home production, and the majority of us (Mr. Keynes, Mr. Henderson and Sir Josiah Stamp) think that the case should be seriously examined.

(ii) A Revenue Tariff.

94. A comparatively low tariff (say 10 per cent.) covering wide categories of imports without discrimination, either on manufactured goods or manufactured goods and food, and designed to mitigate the conditions of general disequilibrium now existing, rather than to favour particular industries, can be supported by arguments which are not applicable to safeguarding duties.

95. The majority of us (Mr. Keynes, Mr. Henderson and Sir Josiah Stamp) think that a sufficient case exists for such a tariff, having regard to the various considerations discussed above, to the Budgetary problem, any relief to which is obviously of great importance, and to the effect on business confidence in reviving energy and enterprise. We recommend that a general tariff of this kind, whether it was limited to manufactured goods or was of a wider character, should in any case be removed in the event of abnormal unemployment being clearly at an end, or of a substantial recovery of the price-level (say) to the 1925–28 standard. Whether it can be said in advance that the political constitution and psychology in this country at a future time will be such as to prevent these limits and conditions from being observed, we regard as a matter for political and not for economic judgment. It is not a question which can be answered negatively merely by an induction from economic history, since there is no precedent for a tariff introduced subject to such specific limitations as we prescribe.

96. We are of opinion that this tariff should be relaxed in favour of any of the Dominions that grants us a sufficient preference in exchange: and that we should allow complete freedom of import to any country which allows the same freedom to us.

97. One of us (Professor Pigou), while agreeing that the arguments for such a tariff are stronger than for safeguarding duties, nevertheless dissents from this proposal on the following grounds:—

The majority propose that a 10 per cent. general tariff should be imposed now and should be removed again when abnormal unemployment disappears or the price-level is restored. If there were any real prospect of this condition as to removal being adhered to, the objections to the proposal would not be very serious; though the knowledge that it is proposed to remove the duty when unemployment disappears could hardly fail to have a disturbing influence on business. But in practice it is very unlikely that the tariff would be removed when this depression ends. On the contrary, even if it were not raised much above 10 per cent. during the present depression, as in fact might easily happen, it would almost certainly be kept on afterwards; then, at the next depression, to meet that, the rates of duty would be increased; and so on cumulatively. The temporary tariff, little as it is desired by those proposing it, would become not merely a permanent, but an ever-expanding tariff. There is no instance in history of a tariff imposed to meet a depression and removed when good times returned.

XII.—METHODS OF ADJUSTING MONEY INCOMES GENERALLY.

98. We have attributed a major part of our present difficulties to the change in the value of money. In so far as this may require a compensating change in money wages, it would be easier to justify a general reduction of money wages which was accompanied by a change in other kinds of fixed or quasi-fixed money incomes. The case is, therefore, strong for trying to find some kind of general scheme which would affect a wide range of money incomes and would not be concentrated on particular categories. Moreover, a general scheme would avoid the difficulties and inequities of piecemeal settlements.

99. The advantages of the general schemes to be considered in this section can be classified as follows:—

(i) They would apply to a wide range of money incomes and not merely to money wages, and would therefore effect a more complete economic readjustment and would be more commendable to public opinion.

(ii) They would be likely to involve a less reduction in real wages than a reduction in money wages that would have an equal effect upon employment (rents being the most important item in this connection for the working class, but the relief to taxation being also of first-rate importance for the community as a whole).

(iii) They would (if they involved a rise in prices) be likely to provoke less social resistance than a reduction of money wages which involved the same reduction of real wages; inasmuch as for all sorts of human reasons men cling to the level of money wages which they have won for themselves, and will not readily believe promises of future compensating benefits from an increase in the purchasing power of money, even though these promises are well-founded.

(iv) They would effect their results automatically or by agreement over the whole field, instead of piecemeal by a series of separate conflicts, which are likely to result unequally in accordance with the bargaining strength of the different groups concerned; for, apart from special measures, there is no available means for bringing about a general reduction of wages except by a series of struggles industry by industry and district by district, the results of which would be unequal and unfair and the reductions perhaps greatest where they would be least useful or least justifiable. Indeed, a struggle of this kind would offer a prospect to which no one could look forward without misgiving.

100. It is for these reasons that a general rise in world prices (*i.e.*, a general fall in the value of money) would be the best of all remedies. Failing this, the most obvious method would be to alter the value of sterling in terms of gold, *i.e.*, to devaluate.

(a) Devaluation.

101. Prior to the return to the gold standard in 1925, the value of sterling had, in fact, been fluctuating in terms of gold within a somewhat wide range. It would have then been open to this country to fix the value of sterling at a different relation to gold from that which was actually chosen, and, in fact, the majority of us were in favour at that time of postponing the decision to fix the value of sterling at its pre-war parity.

102. It is, however, quite a different matter to-day to go back on the decision then made. We think that there would be grave objections to such a course, because of its reactions on our international credit, and none of us are prepared to recommend it at the present time. Nevertheless, we should not put out of our minds the possibility that it may conceivably become necessary in the future for a number of countries to join together in making drastic changes in an international currency system which is serving us so ill.

(b) Tariffs plus Bounties.

103. In view of the difficulty of raising world prices and the objections to devaluation, we have considered whether any alternative scheme is

possible which would have effects internally similar to those of a rise of world costs or of devaluation, and yet would be something which we ourselves could put into force without injury to the national credit.

104. The following is an outline of a scheme intended to be of this kind which has been laid before us, with some of the arguments which can be adduced in its support:—

(1) "The proposal is for a uniform tariff of, say, 10 per cent. on all imports whatsoever, including food, and a bounty of the same amount on all exports whatsoever.

(2) The effect of such an arrangement on international trade would be to restore substantially the conditions which would exist under Free Trade if world costs were to rise 10 per cent., or if domestic costs were to be reduced 10 per cent.; except that it is more favourable than the latter to our export trades and to trades which compete with imports, and would be therefore all the more helpful in increasing our foreign balance and the volume of our foreign investment.

(3) The effect at home would be similar to a rise of world costs, but different from a cut in domestic money costs, since the latter would leave *rentiers* and other recipients of fixed incomes to get the full benefit of the resulting fall in the cost of living. It would, therefore, be much fairer, since it would affect the value of all incomes, &c., fixed in terms of money, in the same kind of way, and would not discriminate against wage-earners.

(4) It would have, in effect, the same result as devaluation, *except that it would leave sterling international obligations unchanged in terms of gold.* There are, obviously, very great advantages in this from the point of view of the national credit. Moreover, since we are a creditor nation in terms of sterling, and our imports exceed our exports, there is actually a pecuniary benefit to us in leaving the gold value of sterling alone.

(5) It would diminish the real burden of the internal national debt as compared with wage reductions, since the service of the national debt would be a smaller percentage of the national income in terms of money than if money wages were to be reduced. Moreover, it would bring, on balance, a substantial sum into the Exchequer.

(6) It could be brought about by a single act of legislation, of a kind much less likely to be unpopular than reductions of money wages concentrated on the working classes, the position of all other recipients of money incomes being left untouched. At the same time, it would involve no interference with contract.

(7) Since the tariff or the bounty, as the case might be, would apply to *all* exports and *all* imports (ships for this purpose would have to be regarded as an export), no rebates or complications of any kind would be required. Imported raw materials would pay the tariff, but when they were worked up into exports they would get the money back in the shape of the bounty. The only point that could arise in the case of manufacture for export would

be the interest on the import duty paid during the period of manufacture, which might be met by some sort of deferred system of discharging the duty out of the subsequent proceeds of the bounty.

(8) It would tend to have an equalising effect as between sheltered and unsheltered industries, since it would be the unsheltered industries which would benefit directly and in the first instance.

(9) For various reasons such a scheme might be impracticable in its entirety; but it could be applied in part without losing all its advantages. Bounties on exports may sometimes be inconsistent with our commercial treaties or with the tariff arrangements of other countries. In this case it would be necessary to substitute for bounties a rebate equivalent to the duties paid on imported material, and further assistance to the export industries would have to take some other form. Or again, the fact that our imports exceed our exports, so that a balance of revenue would remain, would make it possible to free from the tariff some categories of goods which it was considered undesirable to tax. At the minimum such a scheme would dwindle into practically the equivalent of a 10 per cent. tariff on manufactured goods, part of the proceeds of which might be devoted to granting special reliefs from taxation to the export industries. For several of the arguments adduced above are partially applicable to a tariff not accompanied by a bounty.

(10) Such a scheme should be regarded primarily as a means of avoiding economic instability at home due to the violent change in world prices, the necessity for which might, one would hope, be temporary. In the event of a sufficient recovery in world prices, it should be gradually reduced and finally abolished."

105. As to the advantages of this scheme, we are equally divided. Two of us (Mr. Keynes and Sir Josiah Stamp) are much attracted by it. They recommended that its practical possibilities should be carefully explored. They prefer it, on principle, to a tariff, because it is free from the possibility of adverse repercussions on our export industries, and because, being more clearly an expedient to preserve equilibrium, it avoids some of the disadvantages of a protective tariff. The question of the feasibility of bounties or other means of assisting exports is one on which they find it difficult to pronounce before a concrete scheme has been worked out. In any event, as in the case of the 10 per cent. tariff above, it should be removed in the event of abnormal unemployment being clearly at an end or of a substantial recovery of the price-level (say) to the 1925–8 standard.

106. Two of us (Mr. Henderson and Professor Pigou) on the other hand are opposed to this proposal. A general scheme of bounties upon exports would, in their view, be immediately countered by action under anti-dumping clauses or otherwise on the part of other countries. All countries resent subsidies given by other countries to their exports as a particularly unfair form of competition; and the view that it is bad inter-

national conduct to resort to such practices has become widespread in recent years. If accordingly this country were to adopt the scheme proposed it would not only expose itself to retaliatory action; but would be generally regarded as having committed a serious offence against international economic comity. These considerations, to say nothing of the practical difficulties which the organisation and working of such a scheme would involve, lead them to conclude that the bounty element in it would need either to be abandoned altogether or to be so whittled down that its purpose was defeated. If, however, this element is excluded, the scheme becomes indistinguishable from that of the simple 10 per cent. tariff on imports, discussed above in paragraphs 94–97.

XIII.—SUMMARY OF CONCLUSIONS.

107. We summarise our principal conclusions as follows:—

(a) THE CAUSES OF THE PRESENT DEPRESSION.

An entirely new situation has been created by the present trade depression, which has been marked by the catastrophic fall in the prices of staple commodities. Between September 1929 and August 1930, dollar prices fell 21 per cent. and sterling prices 17 per cent. (paragraphs 5 and 18).

Although the greater part of the civilised world has also been engulfed in the present depression, there are certain peculiarities which distinguish the difficulties of Great Britain from those of the rest of the world. Up to the eve of the slump the rest of the world was, generally speaking, experiencing a period of prosperity; but for some years Great Britain had shown signs of serious malaise; during this period the total of unemployed in this country never fell below a million. Great areas in the North were stationary or declining. British export trade as a whole showed disquieting symptoms of stagnation (paragraph 6).

The depression of trade in Great Britain since the War may be regarded as the resultant of (a) adversely changing external conditions and (b) a lack of internal adaptability (paragraph 8).

The main changes in the broad external environment of British industry since the war are to be found in:—

(a) the altered conditions of demand for the products of certain industries due to the change from war to peace;

(b) general changes in world economic conditions, e.g., the development of the cotton industry in the Far East, the less favourable terms on which agricultural countries have been able to dispose of their products, the great fall in the price of silver, etc.

(c) political developments during the period, e.g., the occupation of the Ruhr, currency disorders in many European countries, troubles in India and China, etc.;

(d) the general fall in world gold-prices between 1924 and 1929 and dislocation in Great Britain caused by the return to the gold standard;

(e) the tariff policies of other countries (paragraph 9).

In the same period the capacity of Great Britain for rapid adaptation has
been insufficient to cope with the changing conditions with which it has
been confronted. This has been due to—

(a) the adverse changes (due to war losses) in the age composition of the
population (paragraphs 10 and 11):

(b) the increase of rings and monopolistic combinations designed deliberately to restrict the volume of trade (paragraph 12);

(c) the reluctance on the part of industry to recognise the existence of
changed conditions, either on the side of technique or on the side
of demand (paragraph 12);

(d) the persistence of restrictive rules and practices among trade unions
on (i) the entry to particular occupations and the demarcation of
different occupations, and on (ii) the conditions under which certain
work can be done (paragraph 12):

(e) the rigidity of wages (paragraph 14).

Rigidity of wage-rates may act as a definite hindrance to change and progress, as the rate at which industries can expand is, in part, a function of the
rate of wages it has to pay. Moreover, when wages are kept rigid, there is a
grave danger that the arrangement of industry which is thus brought about
may be injurious to the interests of the working classes as a whole (paragraphs
16 and 17).

(b) THE EFFECTS OF LARGE CHANGES IN THE VALUE OF MONEY.

In spite of the phenomenal fall in world gold prices in the last twelve
months (paragraph 18), it would be imprudent to assume that there may not
be a further fall. Some recovery may be anticipated at a fairly early date
from the present exceptionally low level, but it is not certain that this rise
may not be followed by a further sagging tendency in the price level continued over a long period (paragraph 21).

If this should happen, it is impossible to over-estimate the disastrous
consequences that may be expected. All money settlements of every kind,
upon which the stability and prosperity of modern life, organised as it is, so
profoundly depend, would become hopelessly inappropriate (paragraph 22).
If the large changes that have taken place in the last year in the value of
money remain unaltered or become aggravated, the following are outstanding examples of the results which will ensue:—

(a) a very great increase in the effective burden of inter-Governmental debts arising out of the war (paragraph 23);

(b) a great aggravation of the budgetary problem presented by internal national debts and all other Government obligations which are fixed in terms of money (*e.g.*, pensions, unemployment relief, &c.) (paragraph 23);

(c) a similar increase in the effective burden on industry of all forms of bonded debt (*e.g.*, debenture interest, &c.) (paragraph 23);

(d) a serious disequilibrium between money costs and money prices leading to business losses and a great increase in unemployment (paragraphs 23 and 24).

The foregoing represent the maladjustments which arise if a fall in prices becomes evenly spread over commodities in general. At the moment, the outstanding feature of the economic situation is an extreme disparity between the prices of primary products and manufactured goods, which is quite incompatible with an active condition of world trade. Until new markets are found for the manufactured goods which the primary producers are unable to purchase or new types of goods are produced instead of them, industrial unemployment on a large scale must prevail. In such circumstances under the pressure of competition, the prices of manufactured goods are likely to fall owing to the inevitable movement in industrial countries to reduce costs by every available means (including the reduction of salaries and wages (paragraph 25)).

This is the most critical phase of the world depression for an industrial country like Great Britain, since if manufacturing costs of production are cut drastically throughout the world, it will not be possible for this country to abstain from joining in the general movement (paragraph 26).

(c) REMEDIES OF AN EXTERNAL CHARACTER.

An adequate recovery of world prices would go a long way towards providing a solution of the present difficulties.. Monetary conditions, which play a dominating part in determining the course of world prices over a long period, depend upon the production of gold, its distribution among the different countries and its use by Central Banks. On this head our conclusions (paragraph 29) are:—

(i) the prevailing practice of certain foreign Central Banks are not such as to encourge optimism;

(ii) there is no insufficiency in the total supply of gold, provided that it is used by Central Banks with reasonable economy;

(iii) the problem turns upon the policies which Central Banks pursue, and upon the possibility of inducing them to act together.

The matter is not one in which it is possible for any single country acting alone to accomplish much. Some influence this country can exert; and more might be accomplished, for example, by the Federal Reserve System of the United States joining the Bank of England to take drastic action on a common plan (paragraph 30).

The difficulty at the moment is not a general scarcity of short-term credit for first-class borrowers; but is due, in the first place, to the reluctance of borrowers to enter upon new enterprise in an atmosphere of a falling price-level; and, in the second place, to the decline of the standing of many borrowers in the opinion of lenders owing to the widespread distrust of the stability of the financial and currency systems of a number of countries (paragraph 31). The revival of enterprise might be promoted by joint action on the part of the Central Banks directed towards creating a strong conviction that the present easy terms for short-term credit are likely to continue for a long time to come (paragraph 32). Central Banks might also allay the distrust now felt towards the general credit of certain countries by forming a large joint pool for approved loans or in some other way. It is of the first importance to restore a feeling of confidence in the financial stability of those many countries which are now the subject of distrust (paragraphs 33 and 34).

(d) WAYS OF RESTORING ELASTICITY TO THE ECONOMIC STRUCTURE OF GREAT BRITAIN.

No very satisfactory measures have yet been proposed for the control of rings and monopolies, but the experience of the Board of Trade Committee on Trusts might well be reviewed (paragraph 37).

As regards trade union restrictions no direct Government action is possible. The demarcations and trade customs are now inappropriate and inimical to the interests of the working classes as a whole. If the trade unions would agree to reopen the whole question, there might be a surprising increase in the ability of employers to offer increased employment at the existing wages (paragraphs 38–40).

We recommend that His Majesty's Government should forthwith undertake a systematic reform of the whole system of unemployment insurance, which is now gravely abused. It impedes mobility of labour, encourages the adoption of unsatisfactory methods of meeting industrial changes and conduces to an artificial rigidity of wage-rates (paragraph 41).

(e) WAYS OF INCREASING INDUSTRIAL EFFICIENCY.

Great attention has been devoted in recent years to measures designed to improve the industrial organisation and technique of the staple industries, but the efficiency of industries which are expanding or are capable of expansion is equally important. Improvements in industrial methods are being rapidly adopted by foreign countries and though it is of cardinal importance that Great Britain should not lag behind, little positive amelioration of the competitive position can be expected under this head. Moreover, in so far as "rationalisation" includes schemes for orderly contraction of output, it is likely to increase unemployment; and improved industrial technique which takes the form of the introduction of labour-saving machinery may also involve a temporary aggravation of unemployment (paragraph 42).

All well-considered schemes of industrial reconstruction should be pressed forward to the utmost, but they cannot by themselves provide a complete solution to the present economic difficulties (paragraph 43).

(f) REDUCTIONS IN DOMESTIC MONEY WAGES.

(i) Existing money wage-rates cannot be regarded as sacrosanct in a world subject to violent changes in the value of money.

(ii) Certain wage adjustments in the downward direction, particularly in sheltered industries whose existing wages are out of line with wages in other comparable industries, are desirable now.

(iii) If world prices fail to recover to a materially higher level, general wage-cuts in this country (or their equivalent) will become inevitable, because the failure of the price-level to recover will probably mean that such wage-cuts have been made in other countries.

(iv) But, on the other hand, it would be unwise for this country to lead the way with a general wage-cut or to encourage an incipient world movement in this direction.

(v) In view of the immense practical difficulties of any general reduction in money wages, every other remedy with any serious balance of argument in its favour should be tried first.

(vi) Furthermore, if a general wage-cut becomes inevitable, it is most desirable that it should be undertaken as part of a wider scheme for re-settling money incomes generally (including *rentier* incomes in particular), and not wages alone.

(g) SUBSIDIES TO WAGES.

The effect upon unemployment of a general subsidy to money wages is *primâ facie* the same as that of an equal proportionate reduction in money wage-rates. If it were possible by a low rate of subsidy to absorb a large number of the unemployed, it might happen that the whole cost of the subsidy would be off-set by the associated reduction in the amount of unemployment benefit. But it would be highly optimistic to suppose that a general wage subsidy at any given rate would, in fact, reduce the volume of unemployment to this extent. Hence it is to be feared that, if the subsidy were at all substantial, it would involve a heavy additional net charge on the Budget. In the circumstances, we are of opinion that a policy of general wage subsidies is not one that ought to be adopted (paragraph 52).

Wage subsidies in respect, not of all wage-earners, but of additional wage-earners, whom employers would undertake to engage with the help of the subsidy, are not open to the same objections. But the practical difficulties in devising schemes of this type are very great (paragraph 53). It may be that in particular cases these could be overcome and a workable scheme could be devised in which the disadvantages were at a minimum and the advantages to employment at a maximum. If and where this is so, it appears to the majority of us (Mr. Keynes, Professor Pigou and Sir Josiah Stamp) that the case for temporary wage subsidies in respect of *additional* employees at a rate less than the present rate of unemployment pay is a strong one. Mr. Henderson holds strongly that the path of subsidies should be avoided. But subsidies to wages in particular industries, as a permanent system, are highly undesirable (paragraph 54).

(h) WAYS OF INCREASING BUSINESS CONFIDENCE.

An improvement in the state of business confidence would lead to an increase of employment in home industries (paragraph 55).

In the long run business confidence is not likely to be maintained otherwise than by an actual recovery of business profits. Such a recovery might be secured by judicious emergency measures, after which business confidence might take the place of such measures as providing the necessary stimulus (paragraph 56).

The following measures would assist in the improvement of business confidence:—

(*a*) A solution of the Budget problem which avoided increased direct taxation;

(*b*) A drastic reform of the system of Unemployment Insurance (paragraph 57).

A tariff on manufactured imports is also recommended in some quarters under this head (paragraph 57).

(i) WAYS OF INCREASING HOME INVESTMENT.

The amount of home investment, and so the volume of employment, would be increased if the terms on which borrowers can be accommodated were made easier either through a reduction of the rate of interest or through Government stimulus, by means of subsidies or public works (paragraph 58).

(*a*) The Bank of England cannot, under gold-standard limitations, move far in the direction of making bank credit cheap and abundant unless other Central Banks do the same; a policy on the part of the Treasury and the banking system intended to bring down long-term rates of interest, even if it meant some raising of short-term rates, would be useful on balance as facilitating an increase of long-term investment (paragraph 59).

In recent months short-term rates of interest have fallen to a low level, but this reduction is only very slightly reflected in long-term rates—which are of much greater significance to borrowers for fixed investment (paragraph 60).

(b) The effect of high world rates of interest under a gold standard is to put the domestic rate above the rate at which enough new domestic investment can come into existence. Since the War, attempts have been made to restore equilibrium by imposing an embargo on foreign lending in London, and subsequently by the informal rationing of foreign borrowers, but these measures have hitherto proved ineffective. Bonds issued on foreign markets have found their way to the London market, without having paid British stamp duty and contrary to the wishes of those responsible for the regulation of the British market. In these circumstances, a distinction might be made between foreign bonds officially admitted to the British investment market (perhaps by the Treasury on the recommendation of the Bank of England) and those not so admitted, income derived from the latter being subject to a special income tax (paragraph 62).

(c) Under conditions of extensive unemployment such as prevail to-day, and have prevailed in lesser degree for some years, the policy of promoting useful schemes of capital development, either by pressing forward such work as lies within the direct control of the Government or by the offer of State subsidies to local authorities and public utility companies is a sound one for the State to pursue, since we do not accept the view that the undertaking of such work must necessarily cause a mere diversion from other employment (paragraph 63).

The saving to public funds in the shape of reduced expenditure on unemployment benefit must not be overlooked; but it is important to recognise that public works can only be justified if they are of a useful and productive character and are capable of being put into operation and carried out with speed. Considerations of this character necessarily set limits to the extent to which it is possible to meet unemployment by the policy of public works (paragraphs 64–67).

(j) TARIFFS.

We accept the validity of the traditional Free Trade argument that there is a strong presumption that tariffs of the kind which are imposed in practice tend to divert production from the channels where a country is relatively more efficient into channels where it is relatively less efficient (paragraphs 68 and 69).

(a) Advantages of a Tariff.

But the question to-day is the extent to which this historic argument is invalidated for the time being by (i) the existence of chronic large-scale unemployment, (ii) the doubt whether this country can hope materially to expand or even to retain her present favourable balance of trade by means of a moderate cut in money costs without a restriction of imports, (iii) the possibility that the effect of a tariff on the "terms of trade" might be greater in present circumstances than formerly, and (iv) whether the promotion of economic solidarity within the British Empire may not be a safeguard against the dangers of economic isolation in the modern world (paragraph 70).

> (i) Though unemployment before the War was sometimes large in amount, there was no large intractable mass of unemployment associated with dislocations between costs and world prices such as has existed ever since the post-armistice boom. The unemployment issue thus was often left on one side in tariff discussions. The situation is, however, now fundamentally different, and in present conditions the imposition of reasonably devised protective duties (though one of us (Professor Pigou) thinks that in practice it might not be easy to devise them) that should exclude a substantial portion of the imports that now compete with our home industries would, for some time to come, directly increase the aggregate volume of employment in this country, and by so doing would set up repercussions through the saving on the unemployment benefit and so on, that would, by indirect processes increase it still further. The gain would probably be associated with some increase in the cost of living and a corresponding reduction in real wages and in the value of money incomes generally; but since a main alternative remedy for unemployment—a reduction of money wages—must also involve an equal or greater reduction of real wages, this consideration is not of great weight (paragraphs 71 and 72).
>
> The important question to decide is whether the direct effect, and therewith the indirect effects, of reasonably devised protective duties in increasing the aggregate volume of employment would be large or small. The answer to this question turns in great part upon the degree of adverse reaction which the contraction brought about in our imports is likely to produce on our export industries. The majority (Mr. Keynes, Mr. Henderson and Sir Josiah Stamp) take the view that in present conditions the main part of the

reduction of imports would be balanced for several years by increased sales to us of foreign-held securities (paragraphs 72 and 73).

One of us (Professor Pigou) holds that the adverse reaction on exports would after a short time be nearly commensurate with the original contraction of imports (paragraph 74).

(ii) If the view of the majority in this matter is correct, the point is to-day a very important one. The majority believe that it is essential at the present time for Great Britain to devote a somewhat large proportion of her total savings to foreign investment (paragraph 75). The favourable balance of trade, which must be equal to the amount of foreign lending if the Bank of England is not to lose gold could be increased either by increasing exports or by diminishing imports. By reducing costs, and particularly by cutting wages costs, it is possible to increase the volume of exports, but there are great difficulties in making much headway along this line. It is therefore better to occupy our unemployed resources in making goods to take the place of goods now imported than not to occupy them at all. For this is just as effective a way of increasing foreign investment and augmenting employment as increasing exports would be (paragraph 77). Moreover, tariffs might also be to the advantage of the overseas countries which need our surplus savings for their further development (paragraph 79).

(iii) There is general agreement that, when a country imposes taxes upon imports, it will cause a unit of its export goods to buy somewhat more import goods than before, or, in more popular language, that in some measure it will make the foreigner pay its import duties. Before the War, it was generally agreed that, so far as Great Britain was concerned, the gain that could be looked for under this head was very small, but in present conditions, in view of the large amount of surplus capacity in the iron and steel and other industries abroad, it may be that a more substantial advantage might be won (paragraph 80).

(iv) The tendency since the War has been in the direction of intensified economic nationalism, which is seen in such projects as the movement of neighbouring groups of countries to grant one another preferential tariff concessions, to which the outside world is not admitted. If such agreements materialise, the interests of Great Britain may perhaps best be safeguarded by cultivating closer economic relations with the Empire. We consider that the development of inter-Imperial preferences may become a wise economic policy for this country (paragraphs 81 to 85).

(b) Objections to a Tariff.

Notwithstanding the foregoing advantages, there remain with unabated force certain arguments of a more general kind against a tariff, namely:—

(i) A tariff may enable a country to snatch for itself an advantage which is not so great as the damage which it inflicts on the world. The world would be richer under a system of general Free Trade than it is (paragraph 86).

(ii) Governments dependent upon popular elections are certain to impose protective duties, not on weak industries that may need them, but rather on strong industries that control numerous votes (paragraph 86).

(iii) Duties create vested industries, which it is difficult to remove later without inflicting considerable incidental hardship (paragraph 86).

(iv) So long as the issue of Protection *versus* Free Trade divides political parties, duties are liable to be imposed or removed not on their merits but according to the exigency of party conflict (paragraph 86).

(c) Conclusions.

We differ among ourselves in weighing up the balance of advantage or disadvantage resulting from courses of action which, while probably increasing employment in the immediate future, would also be open to the objections indicated above (paragraphs 87 and 88). In formulating our conclusions we think it important to distinguish sharply between two different types of tariff, viz., safeguarding and a revenue tariff (paragraph 89).

A theoretical case may exist for safeguarding duties, by which we understand tariffs imposed primarily for protective purposes in favour of specially selected industries, especially when an argument of the "infant industry" character is applicable. But in the actual conditions of Great Britain to-day, we think that it is difficult to find exceptional cases of this kind (paragraph 90).

Conclusions of Mr. Keynes, Mr. Henderson and Sir Josiah Stamp.

(i) Safeguarding.

Apart from existing duties, there is no case amongst manufactures which appears to us to deserve serious consideration, except a tariff on iron and steel and their products. In this case, we are in favour of protective duties in the present grave emergency, subject to the strict condition that the industry should rationalise itself in accordance with an approved plan, and that the tariff should be of a weight and scope appropriate, *not* to present conditions, but to those which will exist after their reconstruction (paragraph

91). In the case of agriculture, it has been put to us that pig-products and poultry-products offer an important field for replacing imports by home production, and we think that the case should be seriously examined (paragraph 93).

(ii) A Revenue Tariff.

Having regard to the various considerations discussed in the Report, to the Budgetary problem, and to the effect on business confidence, there exists a sufficient case for a comparatively low general tariff (say 10 per cent.) covering wide categories of imports without discrimination, either on manufactured goods or manufactured goods and food, designed to mitigate the conditions of general disequilibrium now existing, rather than to favour particular industries (paragraph 94).

We recommend—

(a) that such a tariff should in any case be removed in the event of abnormal unemployment being clearly at an end, or of a substantial recovery of the price-level (say) to the 1925–28 standard. (The possibility of these limits and conditions being observed we regard as a matter for political and not for economic judgment; there is no historical precedent for such a tariff as we envisage, and the question cannot therefore be answered negatively (paragraph 95);

(b) that the tariff should be relaxed in favour of any of the Dominions according to this country a sufficient preference in exchange, and that complete freedom of import should be accorded to any country which allows the same freedom to Great Britain (paragraph 96).

Dissent of Professor Pigou.

(i) Safeguarding.

Professor Pigou dissents from the conclusions of the majority concerning the protection of iron and steel on the following grounds:—

(a) it would be impracticable to protect iron and steel without at the same time not merely granting drawbacks to export industries that use steel in their work, but also somehow compensating home industries that do this. From simple beginnings an elaborate and complicated system of duties or other compensatory arrangements would thus grow up;

(b) the condition for protection, *i.e.*, that the industry should undertake to rationalise itself, is not one that is capable of being enforced; for "the industry" is not an individual. It might even happen that, under the shelter of protection, inefficient firms would be maintained and the process of rationalisation actually impeded;

(c) a duty of this character, though imposed as a temporary measure, would prove in practice, when the circumstances, in respect of which the majority contemplate it, have disappeared, exceedingly difficult to remove;

(d) if it be the fact that, in view of the heavy losses which it has sustained, the industry is unable to raise the capital necessary to modernise its plant and so do without some form of Government assistance, methods of assistance other than those of a tariff are available (paragraph 92).

(ii) A Revenue Tariff.

Professor Pigou, while agreeing that the arguments for such a tariff are stronger than for safeguarding duties, nevertheless dissents from the recommendation of the majority in favour of a low general tariff. His reasons are as follows. If there were any real prospect of a tariff once imposed being removed, as the majority suggest, when abnormal unemployment disappears or the price-level is restored, the objections to the proposal would not be very serious; though the knowledge that it is proposed to remove the duty when unemployment disappears could hardly fail to have a disturbing influence on business. But in practice it is very unlikely that the tariff would be removed when this depression ends. On the contrary, even if it were not raised much above 10 per cent. during the present depression, as in fact might easily happen, it would almost certainly be kept on afterwards; then, at the next depression, to meet that, the rates of duty would be increased; and so on cumulatively. The temporary tariff, little as it is desired by those proposing it, would become not merely a permanent, but an ever-expanding tariff. There is no instance in history of a tariff imposed to meet a depression and removed when good times returned (paragraph 97).

(k) METHODS OF ADJUSTING MONEY INCOMES GENERALLY.

The major part of the present difficulties is due to the change in the value of money. In so far as this may require a compensating change in money wages, it would be easier to justify a general reduction of money wages if accompanied by a change in other kinds of fixed or *quasi*-fixed money incomes. The case is, therefore, a strong one for trying to find some kind of general scheme which would affect a wide range of money incomes and would not be concentrated on particular categories. Moreover, a general scheme would avoid the difficulties and inequities of piecemeal settlements (paragraph 98). A general rise in world prices (*i.e.*, a general fall in the value of money) would be the best of all remedies. Failing this, the most obvious method would be to alter the value of sterling in terms of gold, *i.e.*, to devaluate (paragraph 100).

(i) Devaluation.

Whatever might have been possible in 1925 before the return to the gold standard, we should see grave objections to-day in reversing the decision then made; and none of us are prepared to recommend such a course at the present time. It may, however conceivable, be necessary in the future for a number of countries to join together in making drastic changes in an international currency system which is serving so ill (paragraphs 101 and 102).

(ii) Tariffs plus Bounties.

A proposal has been submitted to us for a uniform tariff of (say) 10 per cent. on all imports whatsoever, including food, and a bounty of the same amount on all exports whatsoever (paragraph 104).

On the advantages of this scheme we are equally divided, two of us (Mr. Keynes and Sir Josiah Stamp) being much attracted by the scheme, the practicable possibilities of which they recommend should be carefully explored. They prefer it, on principle, to a tariff (provided it were removed when the same conditions as those stipulated in the case of a tariff are fulfilled (paragraph 105)). The remaining two of us (Mr. Henderson and Professor Pigou) are opposed to this proposal since, in their view, a general scheme of bounties upon exports would be countered by foreign countries under anti-dumping clauses, etc. Moreover, such a scheme would be generally regarded as a serious offence against international economic comity (paragraph 106).

REPORT BY PROFESSOR L. ROBBINS.

1. INTRODUCTORY.

I have refrained from signing the Report for reasons which I set out below. (See especially paragraph 6 below.) I am, however, in substantial agreement with Sections I to VII, which represent what seems to me to be a true diagnosis of the causes of the present troubles, and which, in regard to international remedies and remedies designed to restore elasticity to industry and the wage system, indicate broadly the measures to which I myself attach importance. The remainder, however, appears to me to contemplate at disproportionate length measures which are neither desirable nor, in many cases, practicable, and I wish to dissociate myself altogether from the decision to frame this part of the Report on these lines. There are, moreover, certain matters about which I wish to make my own attitude explicit.

2. RINGS AND MONOPOLIES.

I attach much more importance than my colleagues to the proposal that action should be taken fully to investigate and bring to the public notice the operation of rings and monopolies. I do not anticipate an immediate effect on the employment position from the most energetic adoption of such measures, but I do not believe that it is expedient to ask the trade unions alone to revise their attitude toward restrictive practices, or to permit certain reductions of wages, unless, at the same time, steps are taken to expose and deal with monopolistic practices on the part of other sections of the community.

3. FOREIGN LENDING.

I should be definitely opposed to any measures which would, in my opinion, tend permanently to restrict the volume of our foreign lending. I am, therefore, not prepared to support the suggestion that, in certain circumstances, differential taxation should be imposed on incomes from certain kinds of foreign investment, for I believe that this would be the effect of such measures. To impose differential taxation on any form of foreign investment would be at one blow to inflict damage to the prestige of London as an international money market, and, at the same time, to repudiate all the laborious efforts which have been expended by the representatives of this country at Geneva to eliminate the anomalies of double taxation. The attitude of other Governments in restricting foreign investment is not infrequently made the subject of opprobious comment over here. If we wish to urge other people to good international behaviour, it is scarcely consistent, at such a time, to imitate precisely those elements in their policy which we are at present exhorting them to abandon.

4. PUBLIC WORKS, ETC.

As regards expenditure on Public Works, etc., I agree with my colleagues as to the nature of the criteria to which such measures should be submitted. I am less certain, however, that the effect of such measures as have already been put into operation has been wholly good; and I am more apprehensive that a continuance of this policy may definitely tend to delay the coming of recovery. Moreover, I am very dubious of the wisdom of the general policy of subsidising the rate of interest at which certain business enterprises can borrow. In exceptional circumstances, I can conceive a justification for this policy, but I believe that it is difficult to carry it far without grave danger of waste and maldistribution.

5. WAGE SUBSIDIES.

I am opposed to wage subsidies. In my view they are bound to cause unfairness and anomaly, and, in the present budgetary situation, to discuss them at length appears to me to be wholly superfluous.

6. TARIFFS.

As regards those sections of the Report which relate to tariffs and similar measures, I am in complete disagreement with the majority of my colleagues. I do not believe that the adoption of the measures there discussed would be expedient, *and I do not believe that the form of the discussion adequately represents the balance of the arguments involved.* My objections under this head may be summarised thus:—

As regards the general discussion of the arguments for and against tariffs, there are many propositions in the Report with which I am not in serious disagreement. The total effect I believe to be misleading. The impression which I imagine it will make on the mind of any lay reader is that the various arguments against Free Trade which it enumerates are to be regarded, and are regarded in fact by the majority of professional economists, as being of a degree of importance at least commensurate with the arguments against. This inference, I believe, would be wholly false. In the main, I believe it to be true to say that, in the past, the so-called exceptions to the general presumption in favour of Free Trade have been regarded by economists as academic playthings—interesting as illustrating remote analytical points, but, from the point of view of practice, completely insignificant—and there is no reason to suppose that this is not still the case. Some economists in this country, despairing of the rigidity of money wages, may have turned to Protection as a desperate expedient, but, in my opinion, it is questionable whether their verdict will be generally accepted.

The tariff is essentially an expedient for avoiding the effects of the rigidity of money wages, and its result must inevitably be to reduce real wages by raising prices. I agree with my colleagues that the rigidity of money wages is undesirable, and that, in the present emergency, some reduction of money wages may be necessary. But I do not believe that, if this cannot be achieved by calm and straight-forwarding reasoning, it is desirable that it should be attempted by indirect means. A tariff would tend to involve lower real wages. There should be no mistake about that.

But, while the tariff must thus be conceived as an expedient for avoiding the effects of wage rigidity, it is highly doubtful whether, even so, it is to be regarded as an effective expedient. A substantial proportion of the unemployed are in the export industries which are technically unprotectable. These industries will not be helped by Protection. On the contrary, they will be injured. And this for two reasons:—

(a) In the first place, they will be injured because, if we contract the volume of imports, we injure our foreign customers. It is not, strictly speaking, true that in the very short run our imports and exports necessarily expand and decline in exact correlation. But discovery of this simple fact, long known to all reputable economists, should not blind us to the solid core of truth in the old classical catchword. The Report suggests that the contraction would be met by an increase in foreign lending. I do not believe that this would necessarily follow. But, if it did, it would surely be an odd state of affairs in which we had to lend more abroad in order to enable customers to buy goods which we had prevented them from obtaining by the exchange of their own products!

(b) Secondly, and of even greater immediate importance, as far as the short run problems are concerned, protection would raise the costs of the export industries. If the tariff is general, raw material prices must be affected. If it is limited to manufactures, domestic prices would still be raised. And it must not be forgotten that many manufactured imports are the raw material of some of our main exporting industries. The tinplate industry of Wales, the shipbuilding industry generally, would be prejudiced by a tariff on imported steel.

Nor should we slur over the international repercussions of the adoption of a tariff policy by this country. A tariff is an affirmation of separatism, a refusal to co-operate, a declaration of rivalry. That twelve years after a war which devastated civilisation and threatened to destroy the goodly heritage of European culture, we should even be discussing such measures, is a sad reminder, not only that some men lose faith in a great ideal when it is not realised quickly, but that most are totally blind even to the most obvious considerations of material interest. The blow which would be struck to the movement for lower tariffs in the rest of the world by a decision on the part of this country to adopt a policy of Protectionism, would itself involve reactions sufficiently serious to counterbalance any possible benefits. Our position in the modern world is not such that we can afford to give the slightest encouragement or provocation to the forces which are continually at work making for higher tariffs elsewhere.

7. As regards the particular tariffs discussed in the Report, what I have said above indicates the nature of my objections to the 10 per cent. general tariff. If it is not accompanied by drawbacks, it at once hits the export trades. If it is, it creates glaring anomalies. A drawback on imported steel, for example, would be an incentive to use the foreign product. I have no belief that the tariff would be temporary, or would not lead at once to all the political abuses which elsewhere have accompanied the introduction of tariffs. We think too highly of ourselves if we suppose that it is an open

question whether we can escape these things. Those of us who do not mind corruption in public life may decide to pay this price for the problematic benefits: it is important that we should realise the nature of the price we are paying.

8. The "tariff bounty" proposal seems to me to be of academic interest only. Any tariff expert could destroy any belief in its practicability in five minutes. It is certain that it would be met by the immediate erection of anti-bounty duties by foreign Powers. If it becomes a system of tariffs plus drawbacks, it becomes administratively inconvenient.

9. As regards the special "safeguarding" duties proposed for iron and steel, and pig and poultry products, I am entirely unconvinced that any case has been presented. I agree with Professor Pigou's minute of dissent as regards iron and steel. If there is a special case for assistance to this industry, there are many ways of providing it other than by means of a tariff.

As regards pig-and-poultry products, the proposal seems to me even less desirable. There is no reason to suppose that the producers of these products are in extraordinary difficulties; there can be no shadow of justification for regarding the keeping of pigs or fowls as an infant industry. Moreover, here is a case where the repercussions on our export trade might be expected to be directly injurious. A substantial proportion of our pig-product imports come from Denmark. Denmark is a considerable buyer of English manufactures. If we cease to buy Danish bacon, is it to be supposed that the inhabitants of Denmark can continue to buy the same quantities of our manufactures? Perhaps it will be replied that we may lend them (or others) the money to do so. This does not seem to me the kind of reply which will appeal to the practical judgment.

There is, however, one argument which some might think to be in *favour* of the taxation of Danish pig-products. Our imports from Denmark are produced by poor but industrious peasants, owning their own land and having few available sources of alternative occupation. Circumstances of this sort provide one of the rare cases in which, *for a time*, it is actually possible to exact taxation from the foreigner. If we tax Danish bacon, it is conceivable that, *for a time*, we may raise some little revenue, not at the cost of the English consumer, but at the cost of the standard of life of the Danish peasant producer. To some of my fellow-countrymen this may appear desirable. To others it may appear mean and despicable.

APPENDIX.

STATISTICAL MATERIAL PREPARED BY THE STAFF OF THE ECONOMIC ADVISORY COUNCIL.

Table A.—Index Figures of Industrial Production.

—	1924.	1925.	1929.	2nd Quarter, 1930.
Great Britain ...	100	101·1	111·8	103·4
U.S.A.	100	109	124	109

Sources: Board of Trade Journal, Federal Reserve Bulletin, London and Cambridge Economic Service (for 1925 figure).

Table B.—World Prices.

The following table shows movements of world prices and prices in certain countries, as given by Dr. Bowley's index designed for international comparisons. The base-year is 1925. The figures given for the months shown in 1928 and 1929 appear to have been maxima and those for 1927 minima. All prices have been reduced to gold, by reference to the rate of exchange.

—	1922.	1923.	1924.	1925.	Jan. 1927.	May 1928.	Sept. 1929.	Aug. 1930.
Britain	97	103	101	100	91	95	87	72
U.S.A.	88	99	98	100	88	100	94	74
Germany	...	...	98	100	95	105	96	87
France	112	105	103	100	101	105	96	87½
Sweden	100	101	100	100	91	94	86	75
Weighted average world prices ...	92·2	99·9	99·1	100·0	90·5	100·4	93·3	76·8

Table C.—Estimate of the National Income in Terms of Money.

THE following table gives estimate of the National Income in terms of money. The rise of money value of the national income between 1924 and 1928, in spite of the fall in commodity prices, was partly due to increased production and partly to the increasing relative importance of services (*e.g.*, retail distribution of which the price has not fallen).

From 1928 to 1929 it appears that there was a further considerable rise in both wages and profits.

(£ million.)

—	1911.	1924.	1928.
Wages*	770	1,600	1,720
Profits and Salaries*	583	1,295	} 1,925
"Unearned" interest from home Investment†	270	530	
Net proceeds of industry and trade	1,623	3,425	3,645
Net income from overseas	194	156	250
Net income from land and houses	171	222	255
Total *Social income*	1,988	3,803	4,150
Transfer Payments made out of above.			
National Debt interest (internal‡)	16	268	277
Health and unemployment benefits	16	67	69
War and services pensions	9	89	78
Old Age and Widows' pensions	10	24	40
Poor relief...	14	32	32
Revenue raised for making the above and other Payments.			
Direct taxation (excluding P.O. and Road Fund)	84	494	493
Indirect taxation (Customs and Excise)	72	235	253
Rates	73	160	188
Wages as % of net proceeds of industry and trade ...	47·5	46·7	47·1

* Before deduction of insurance contributions.
† Excluding National Debt interest.
‡ External payments are deducted from the receipts from overseas investment.

Sources: Bowley and Stamp, *The National Income,* 1924. Brought up to date with *Report of His Majesty's Commissioners of Customs and Excise,* 1929, *Ministry of Labour Wage Enquiry* (*Gazette,* October–December, 1929), and monthly estimate of insured persons at work.

Table D.—Exports as a Percentage of Production.

The following table shows the diminishing importance of the export trade relatively to our whole national economy. Distinction is drawn between workers in manufacture and workers in all occupations (the latter includes building retail trade and so forth).

—	Workers Manufacturing for Export as a Percentage of all *Manufacturing* Workers.	Workers for Export as a Percentage of the Whole Occupied Population.
1907	44·5	...
1924	39·4	29·6
1929	38·4	27·4
1930 (2nd quarter) ...	33·8	23·5

Sources: Flux, A. W. National Income, Journal, Royal Statistical Society, 1929, Part 1, and calculations by method indicated in memorandum prepared for the Economic Advisory Council in May 1930 (Council Paper E.A.C. (H.) 91).

The following table gives the figures on which Table D is based:—

(000's).	Workers Employed by Export Trades.		Total Engaged in Mining and Manufacture.	Total Engaged in Building Distribution Services, &c.
	(i) Manufacture.	(ii) Transport and Distribution.		
1907	2,465	300	5,550	3,700 approx.
1924	2,485	325	6,315	3,200
1929	2,445	350	6,375	3,815
1930 (2nd Quarter)	2,000	285	5,905	3,915

Table E.—Value of certain Commodities Exported.

—	1913.	1924.	1929.	1930 (on basis of first nine months).
Coal	50·7	72·1	48·6	46·6
Iron and steel ...	50·5	74·5	68·0	54·0
Cotton	126·4	199·2	135·4	95·2
Wool	35·6	67·8	52·9	38·8
Machinery	33·8	44·8	54·4	48·0
All exports	525·3	801·0	729·6	588·1

Sources: Statement of Trade and Navigation.

Volume of British Exports (1924 = 100).

1913	120 (approx.)
1924	100
1929	108·3
1930 (2nd Quarter)	87·4

Sources: Board of Trade Journal and Report of Balfour Committee on Industry and Trade.

Table F.—Unemployment in Export Industries.

The following table shows the extent of the concentration of workers in the old staple industries.

Sources: Ministry of Labour Gazette. Calculations carried back to 1911 from information in Census 1921 and 1911, Census of Production 1924, and information in Balfour report, by method given in the Journal, Royal Statistical Society, 1929, Part I.

(Figures in Thousands.)

—	Numbers Seeking Employment.				Numbers Unemployed.		
	1911.	1921.	1924.	1929.	June 1924.	June 1929.	August 1930.
Coal	1,038	1,201	1,229	1,075	60	204	253
Iron and Steel	192	262	308	284	50	50	96
Engineering and Shipbuilding	718	1,039	994	932	184	110	203
Cotton	550	527	555	555	87	76	258
Wool	228	227	253	239	16	34	64
All Insured Industries ...	10,430	11,000	11,327	12,094	1,085	1,164	2,119

Table G.—Retail Prices.

—	July 1914.	July 1924.	July 1929.	Aug. 1930.
Food	100	162	149	144
Rent	100	147	153	153
Clothing	100	225	215–220	210
Fuel and light ...	100	185	170	170
General	100	170	161	157

Source: Ministry of Labour Gazette.

Table H.—Real Wage and Productivity Changes since 1924.

The following table examines in detail the factors relating to the rise in real wages since 1924. It will be seen that, on the whole, physical volume of output per head has risen faster than real wages, which have been held back by the fact that retail prices have fallen more slowly than wholesale. There has been some rise in the ratio of wage-costs to proceeds. The figures in the Table refer to manufacture and mining.

Sources: Board of Trade Index of Production.

Employment estimated by method given in Journal, Royal Statistical Society, 1929, Part I.

Real wages from Professor Bowley's index and Ministry of Labour Cost of Living Index.

Selling value of manufactured goods from average values of British exports.

Year	Persons Employed (000's).			Output Index.			Output per head.			Real Wages.	Index of Selling Value Manufactured Goods.	Index of Margin between Manufactured Goods and Raw Materials.	Money Value of Net Output per Man.	Money Wages.
	Manufacture.	Mining.	Distribution Transport, Building Services.	Manufacture.	Mining.	General.	Manufacture.	Mining.	General.					
1924	5,220	1,093	3,229	100	100	100	100	100	100	100	100	100	100	100
1927	5,470	840	3,693	109·3	95·0	106·8	104·3	123·8	106·8	105	86·5	86·0	91·7	100·7
1928	5,463	771	3,767	109·4	89·2	105·5	104·5	126·4	106·8	105	86·3	86·8	92·6	99·7
1929	5,547	829	3,815	115·1	96·8	111·8	108·2	126·3	110·7	106	84·0	86·8	96·1	99·1
1930 (1st quarter)	5,316	861	3,835	113·2	102·0	110·9	111·2	131·3	113·2	107	82·0	86·0	97·5	98·7
1930 (2nd quarter)	5,145	758	3,845	107·5	87·4	103·4	109·3	126·1	110·4	110	80·5	85·8	95·8	98·3

Money value of net output from above index of selling prices and Sauer-beck index for raw materials, assuming 30 per cent. of selling value represented by raw materials in 1924 (*vide* Flux, National Income, Royal Statistical Society, November 1928).

Table I.—Wages in certain Industries.

The following table gives comparisons between wage rates in different industries together with other relevant information, such as the rate of growth of the industry and the existing margin of unemployment. Absolute comparisons are attempted. Relative changes since 1914 are difficult to ascertain, partly because there have been considerable changes in the relative importance of industries since then, partly because (as was pointed out by the Royal Commission on the Coal Industry, 1925) the year 1914 was the climax of a series of exceptional years during which there had been a remarkable rise in wages in the exporting industries relatively to wages in general.

For all industries for which comparable information is available figures are given showing the rate of growth of the industry, the margin of unemployment in June 1929 (*i.e.*, at the climax of seasonal activity) and average wage rates for skilled and unskilled workers. Where there is only one recorded wage rate for the whole industry (under some such title as "day workers") this figure is given separately in the third column as "uniform rate." Except for one or two industries which are highly localized (*e.g.*, cutlery), the figures given are the average of rates in three representative areas; *i.e.*, Greater London, the Lancashire-Staffordshire industrial district, and South-Western England, as representing a predominantly rural area with scattered industrial centres. *The figures given refer only to time rates for adult male workers.* This accounts for the exclusion of such industries as cotton and coal, where most of the work is done on piece rates.

—	Expansion, 1923–29.	Unemployment %, June 1929.	Wages (s. per Week, 1929).			Number insured, July 1929.
			Skilled.	Unskilled.	Uniform Rate.	
I.—*Industries expanding at a greater rate than Insured Population.*						000's.
Silk and artificial silk	+103·4	8·7	60	42	...	73·9
Heating and ventilating apparatus ...	+ 61·1	4·7	72	52	...	8·7
Musical instruments	+ 49·9	8·0	78	55	...	28·4
Electrical wiring and contracting ...	+ 44·4	7·7	79	?	...	16·6
Paint, varnish, &c.	+ 44·2	4·1	...	...	52	18·9
Brick and tile	+ 41·4	8·7	...	...	52	82·0

Table I. (*cont.*)

—	Expansion, 1923–29.	Unemployment %, June 1929.	Wages (s. per Week, 1929).			Number insured, July 1929.
			Skilled.	Unskilled.	Uniform Rate.	
						000's
Electrical engineering	+ 41·2	4·6	65	?	...	84·4
Stone quarrying	+ 39·6	8·2	65	49	...	42·7
Distributive trades	+ 36·4	5·7	64	54	...	1,679·0
Wall-paper	+ 35·9	3·5	77	45	...	6·2
Public works contracting	+ 34·0	18·6	65	55	...	164·4
Furniture	+ 33·1	6·0	74	57	...	120·3
Electrical cables	+ 31·6	5·0	55	49	...	94·0
Laundry	+ 28·9	3·6	...	...	60	135·0
Road transport	+ 25·8	11·3	66	58	...	182·6
Constructional engineering ...	+ 24·6	10·5	75	68	...	28·2
Cement	+ 23·8	5·7	...	...	47	19·5
Building	+ 21·2	8·6	73	55	...	826·0
Hosiery	+ 19·7	5·9	...	...	45	105·8
Brush and broom	+ 18·2	11·1	...	...	44	10·2
Rubber	+ 17·4	7·0	...	...	42	65·3
Printing	+ 17·4	4·0	100	63	...	253·6
Cutlery and tools	+ 14·7	14·0	76	57	...	33·5
Seamen	+ 12·8	15·5	67	41	...	141·4
Railway wagon	+ 10·8	8·6	60	45	...	54·2
Drink...	+ 10·8	6·4	76	62	...	108·5
General ironfounding	+ 10·5	9·5	61	43	...	88·8
Tailoring	+ 8·6	4·4	98	45	...	199·4
Grain milling	+ 8·5	7·0	69	53	...	29·5
II.—*Industries Declining*						
Boot and shoe	− 2·1	13·6	...	...	57	135·2
Wire	− 2·9	8·8	86	53	...	22·3
Docks	− 4·9	31·8	...	...	64	171·2
Baking	− 8·0	6·4	72	63	...	144·8
General engineering	− 8·6	8·8	63	42	...	586·7
Leather goods	− 9·0	7·2	65	46	...	26·0
Brass goods	− 10·9	7·8	70	56	...	28·1
Dressmaking...	− 11·1	2·8	...	...	48	103·4
Wood-working	− 12·5	9·3	50	35	...	23·2
Bolts, screws, nails, &c. ...	− 12·7	9·3	56	41	...	25·4
Lace	− 16·3	9·7	70	46	...	16·9
Coke ovens	− 16·3	12·8	54	44	...	12·0
Ship-building	− 21·5	22·7	64	48	...	204·5
Carriage and cart	− 30·9	7·4	73	47	...	18·9

Sources: Standard Time Rates and Hours of Labour, *August* 1929 (Ministry of Labour); and *Labour Gazette,* July and November 1929.

Table J.—Relative Price Movements.

(1924 = 100.)

—	Food (Sauerbeck).	Raw Materials (Sauerbeck).	Average Prices of British Imports (Board of Trade).	Average Prices of British Exports (Board of Trade).
1924	100·0	100·0	100·0	100·0
1925	97·8	97·0	100·1	97·3
1926	91·6	91·2	91·6	91·7
1927	88·0	88·1	87·6	86·5
1928	88·5	85·4	88·6	86·3
1929—				
January–March	86·0	85·6	86·5	84·8
April–June	84·0	80·7	86·6	83·2
July–September	84·5	80·0	86·5	84·5
October–December ...	81·2	76·7	85·2	83·7
1930—				
January–March	78·5	73·0	81·0	82·0
April–June	74·0	68·3	76·5	80·5

Table K.—Employment, Output per Head, &c., in Main Industrial Groups, 1924–1929.

The following table examines in further detail the rise in productivity per head since 1924. Current value of net output is calculated for each group of industries on the assumption that net output is proportional to gross output.

Sources: Board of Trade Index of Production. Employment calculated from annual figures published by Ministry of Labour. Output per head from above two. Selling prices from average value of exports (except for coal and iron and steel where Board of Trade price indexes are used directly).

	Volume of Employment. (Thousands.)				Physical Volume of Output. 1924 = 100.				Output per Worker. 1924 = 100.			
	1924.	1927.	1928.	1929.	1924.	1927.	1928.	1929.	1924.	1927.	1928.	1929.
Coal mining	1,093	840	771	829	100·0	94·0	89·0	96·4	100·0	122·4	126·2	127·1
Iron and steel	245·0	235·8	227·5	231·5	100·0	110·0	102·3	114·0	100·0	114·3	110·2	120·6
Engineering and shipbuilding (including motors and electrical trades)	1,158	1,118	1,206	1,243	100·0	115·2	113·1	120·9	100·0	112·2	115·7	115·6
Textiles	1,088	1,155	1,138	1,130	100·0	101·6	99·9	98·5	100·0	94·7	95·5	94·8
Food, drink and tobacco ...	476·6	497·5	496·3	498·3	100·0	99·7	101·9	106·0	100·0	95·5	97·8	101·4
Leather and boots ...	179·1	180·8	165·6	165·0	100·0	107·7	102·0	98·5	100·0	106·7	110·4	106·9
Chemicals and allied trades	183·8	192·7	202·9	205·3	100·0	105·2	110·3	112·5	100·0	100·4	99·9	100·8
All industry	6,324	6,338	6,242	6,359	100·0	106·8	105·5	111·6	100·0	106·6	106·9	111·1

	Index of Selling Prices, 1924 = 100.				Output per Worker. (£ per annum at Current Prices.)				Annual Earnings. (Average per Worker.)	
	1924.	1927.	1928.	1929.	1924.	1927.	1928.	1929.	1924.	1928.
Coal mining	100·0	86·1	75·5	90·0	175	185	171	186	123	97
Iron and steel	100·0	84·3	78·7	77·5	226	219	197	211	153·1	151·1
Engineering and shipbuilding (including motors and electrical trades)	100·0	96·0	96·1	94·1	214	231	238	232	131·3	135·5
Textiles	100·0	79·5	84·4	81·7	178	136	144	138	84·7	84·8
Food, drink and tobacco ...	100·0	86·8	88·9	81·9	371	306	323	308	105·3	105·5
Leather and boots ...	100·0	99·8	117·2	109·4	190	200	245	222	115·7	111·7
Chemicals and allied trades	100·0	89·8	85·0	82·1	380	342	321	314	131·5	135·5
All industry	100·0	87·2	86·7	85·0	218	204	203	206	120	117

Table L.—Earnings and Productivity in Certain Industries, 1907–1924.

The following table is designed primarily to show for certain important industries the rise in *money* wages since pre-war days as compared with the *money* value of net output per head. The division of the proceeds of industry between wages and profits is thus shown directly without the necessity of calculating "real" wages and "physical" productivity per head.

Sources: Census of Production Preliminary Reports. Earnings and Hours Enquiries, 1907, 1924, 1928. Selling prices index calculated from Census of Production Reports.

	Net Output per Person Employed (£ per Annum).		Average Annual Earnings (£ per Annum).			Average Weekly Hours.		Earnings as Per Cent. of Net Output.		Selling Prices (1907 = 100).
	1907.	1924.	1906.	1924.	1928.	1906.	1924.	1906-7.	1924.	1924.
Coal	127	175	86	123	97	8 per shift	7 per shift	68	70	211
Iron and steel ...	115	218	82	155	153	54·5	44·8	71	71	158
Engineering ...	109	199	68	123	129	53·0	47·0	62	62	
Shipbuilding ...	98	164	71	131	130	52·9	47·0	73	80	137
Motor and cycle...	109	226	68	144	153	53·4	47·0	62	69	90
Cotton	79	159	48	93	93	55·5	47·9	61	58	251
Wool	71	187	40	102	99	55·6	48·0	56	55	280
Silk and artificial silk	55	255	34	99	103	54·5	48·0	62	39	
Hosiery	61	159	39	88	94	33·9	47·6	64	65	258
Textile finishing ...	109	251	55	126	125	55·7	48·0	51	50	268
Clothing	62	151	35	70	72	51·7	46·2	56	46	256
Boot and shoe ...	71	170	47	115	110	53·6	47·8	66	68	179
Grain milling ...	178	341	61	139	138	58·1	46·7	34	41	158
Baking	104	254	54	119	116	55·5	48·6	52	47	167
Brewing	325	685	63	136	135	54·9	47·9	19	20	213
Tobacco	155	617	35	108	116	49·6	47·1	23	18	295
Brick	78	209	56	126	126	55·4	48·5	72	60	
Pottery	68	156	48	98	97	52·5	46·9	71	63	
Chemicals	183	369	63	134	139	54·7	48·1	34	36	178
Rubber	124	247	52	112	114	55·0	47·7	42	45	
Printing	108	294	59	151	154	51·5	47·3	55	51	
Furniture	85	196	63	129	133	53·1	46·7	74	66	
Laundry	55	136	33	78	...	54·0	47·0	60	58	
Building	84	205	68	147	147	53·2	45·3	81	72	
Gas	205	272	78	152	158	52·6	48·5	38	56	
Water	411	509	70	146	149	55·1	47·5	17	29	
Electricity	249	472	74	163	170	51·9	47·3	30	34	
All industry (manufacture and mining)	100	220	52	120	117	54	47·1	52	55	193

Table M.—Physical Volume of Output per Head, 1907 & 1924.

The following table gives the results of a calculation designed to secure some measure of changes in the net output of industry expressed in an unchanging money standard. The materials of industry and the final produce of industry are obtained free of duplication and correctors applied to the 1924 figures in accordance with the rise in prices of raw materials and finished goods respectively. By subtraction the "real" net output is obtained.

—	Value 1907. (£ million.)	Value 1921. (£ million.)	Prices 1924. (1907 = 100.)	1924 at 1907 Values.
Final product ...	1,139	2,478	190	1,304
Materials	464	848	175	484
Net output ...	675	1,630	...	820

This shows a rise of $21\frac{1}{2}$ per cent. of "real" aggregate net output as against a rise of $10\frac{1}{2}$ per cent. in the number of workers between 1907 and 1924. But there are no statistical data as to the increase of capital which has assisted in bringing this about and which needs to be remunerated out of the product.

Sources: Reports of Census of Production 1907 and 1924. Value of raw materials in 1924 from Flux loc. cit. Prices of finished goods calculated from average values in Census of Production.

First Report of Committee on Economic Information,
September 1931[*]

THE BALANCE OF
INTERNATIONAL PAYMENTS.

I.—INTRODUCTORY.

1. On the 14th September, 1931, we were instructed by the Prime Minister to prepare a report on the balance of international payments. For the purpose of carrying out these instructions, we have prepared for our own guidance the following terms of reference:—

(a) To prepare an estimate under the ordinary headings of the change in the balance of international payments for the year 1931, in order to obtain a view of the current and anticipated strain upon the exchanges.

(b) To enumerate the factors at home and abroad affecting each item and to attempt to estimate the probable rate of deterioration.

(c) To prepare a broad statement of possible remedies.

* P.R.O. Cab. 58/30, E.A.C. (S.C.) 1, 25 September 1931; also Cab. 24/223, C.P. 242 (31).

2.   We have been greatly assisted in our inquiry by the Board of Trade, and, in particular, by Mr. A. W. Flux, C.B., and Mr. H. Leak of that Department, who have attended each of our meetings when this question has been under consideration.   Our Chairman has also received in confidence from the Chairmen of a number of important Companies trading abroad information regarding the change in earnings in 1931, the broad effect of which is to confirm the estimates put before us by the Board of Trade.

II.—ESTIMATED BALANCE OF INTERNATIONAL PAYMENTS.

3.   The latest published official estimate of the balance of trade is that which appeared in the Board of Trade Journal in February last.   On that occasion the Board of Trade gave the following estimate for the years 1928, 1929 and 1930:—

TABLE I.

Estimated Balances of Income and Expenditure in the Transactions (other than the Lending and Repayment of Capital) between the United Kingdom and All Other Countries, 1928, 1929 and 1930.

(In Million £'s.)

Particulars.	1928.	1929.	1930.
Excess of imports of merchandise and bullion	358	366	392
Estimated excess of Government receipts from overseas*	15	24	21
Estimated net national shipping income†	130	130	105
Estimated net income from overseas investments	270	270	235
Estimated net receipts from short interest and commissions	65	65	55
Estimated net receipts from other sources	15	15	15
Total ...	495	504	431
Estimated total credit balance on items specified above	137	138	39

* Including some items on loan accounts.
† Including disbursements by foreign ships in British ports.

4.   In the following paragraphs we examine the Board of Trade estimate under each of the headings indicated above and give an estimate for the year 1931.   It is important to observe that these estimates were prepared prior to the suspension of gold payments which took place during our inquiry, and that no allowance has been made in them for the effect of the depreciation of sterling, which we deal with separately in Section III.

(a) Excess of Imports of Merchandise.

5. The excess of imports over exports of merchandise for the first eight months of this year was practically the same (£246 million) as in the corresponding period of last year. The average monthly excess of imports over exports of merchandise is normally rather greater in the latter part of the year than in January–August, owing mainly to the seasonal increase in the quantity of grain imported in the autumn. The price of wheat and other grain is, however, this year very much lower than it was a year ago, and has decreased more than import prices generally. If this low price continues, it will improve the prospect of having a smaller visible adverse trade balance than last year.

6. If, as may be assumed, the excess of imports over exports is not greater this year than it was last year, *i.e.*, £386 million, it should be noted that owing to price changes the excess of imports will represent a larger volume of goods in 1931 than it did in 1930.

7. Since the first half of 1930 the fall in the average value of goods imported into and exported from the United Kingdom has been 20·6 and 11·4 per cent. respectively. Thus, if this country had imported and exported the same quantity of goods this year as last, the excess of imports over exports in 1931 would have been £246 million instead of the £386 million referred to above. (We have assumed that the price changes of the first half-year apply to the whole year.) For the first six months of this year as compared with 1930 there was a reduction of 25 per cent. in the aggregate quantity of goods exported and a small reduction in the aggregate quantity of goods imported. For some purposes, however, an aggregate figure of imports is misleading. In the following table we give index numbers of the volume of imports in the first half of this year and of the two preceding years, based on the corresponding period of the year 1924:—

TABLE II.

Index Numbers of the Volume of Imports in the First Half-year in
1929 *to* 1931.

1924 = 100.

January–June.	Food, drink, and tobacco.	Raw materials and articles mainly un-manufactured.	Articles wholly or mainly manufactured.	Total.
1929	104·2	114·4	138·4	115·4
1930	102·9	106·0	144·1	113·5
1931	108·9	95·4	133·7	110·2

It will be seen from the above figures that, in spite of a reduction this year in the aggregate quantity of imports as compared with 1929, there has actually been an increase in the quantity of food, drink and tobacco imported. This increase would be still greater if tobacco were excluded. Imports of raw materials have naturally declined with the decline of the export trade. Excluding goods required as raw material for manufactures exported, the total volume of goods imported is probably greater in the current year than in 1930.

(b) *Estimated Excess of Government Receipts from Overseas.**

8. Last year Government receipts from Overseas exceeded expenditure by about £21 million. This year these receipts have been substantially affected by the Hoover plan, but only a part of the burden of that plan, which amounts to £11 million, will come into the calendar year of 1931. Of the deficit on this account, it is estimated that £5 million will come into the calendar year, leaving £6 million as a deficit in respect of payments in the first quarter of 1932. It would, in our view, be reasonable to estimate an excess of Government receipts from Overseas as a whole at about £15 million for the year 1931. Of these receipts, £10 million may be put for the first half year and £5 million for the second.

(c) *Estimated Net National Shipping Income.*†

9. Freight rates have not shown any substantial change since the beginning of 1930, the average for the first eight months of this year exceeding that for the corresponding period of last year by less than 5 per cent. Time charter rates have declined to a considerable extent, and there has also been a substantial reduction in the amount of shipping in employment. Further, passenger traffic has fallen off greatly this year, and passengers' fares have been reduced.

10. As will be seen from the table in paragraph 3 above, the Board of Trade estimated the net national shipping income for 1930 at £105 million. On the assumption that there is no substantial change in freight rates during the remainder of the year and no material change in the number of vessels in employment, the national shipping income for 1931 may be estimated at about £85 million. It is possible that the national income from this source may be slightly smaller in the second half of this year than it was in the first owing to the decrease in the number of vessels in employment. We estimate the figures for the first and second half of the year at £44 million and £41 million respectively.

---

* Under this heading are included some items on loan accounts.

† Under this heading is included disbursements by foreign ships in British ports.

(d) *Estimated Net Income from Overseas Investments.*

11. As will be seen from the table given in paragraph 3 above, the net income from overseas investments, *i.e.*, the gross receipts in this country from investments abroad less payments to persons resident outside the United Kingdom in respect of investments in the United Kingdom, was estimated by the Board of Trade as £270 million for the year 1929. The Board of Trade arrived at this figure by working up a pre-war estimate of the amount of British capital invested abroad. It is mid-way between the figures arrived at by recent investigations carried out by Sir Robert Kindersley for the year 1927 (£285 million) and by the "Economist" for the year 1928 (£255 million). Sir Robert Kindersley has recently made a further estimate for the year 1929, the previous estimate having admittedly been made on an imperfect basis. It is necessary, therefore, to revise the published Board of Trade estimate of receipts from overseas investments in the year 1929.

12. Sir Robert Kindersley estimates the income received from British overseas investments in 1929 at £231 million. From this must be deducted a sum of about £15 million, representing payments made to non-residents in respect of investments in the United Kingdom. In the case of companies registered in this country and operating abroad, Sir Robert Kindersley's estimate only includes the dividends distributed. From the national point of view it is the gross receipts of the companies from abroad that have to be taken into account and it is necessary, therefore, to raise Sir Robert Kindersley's estimate in order to arrive at the total receipts remitted to this country. The gross receipts include head office expenses in this country and any sums that may have been added to the reserves in this country. The information available in regard to these points is by no means complete, but from inquiries which have been made it would appear that a sum of approximately £25 million should be added to the estimate for the year 1929 on this account. After account has been taken of a possibly inadequate allowance made by Sir Robert Kindersley for the income received in the United Kingdom in respect of investments not quoted in the official Stock Exchange list, the estimate for the year 1929 is raised to £240–£260 million. The reason that we have adopted a range is that there are a number of factors about which there is insufficient information to justify our making a firm estimate. The calculations would seem to indicate a figure rather towards the lower limit of the range, though other considerations would lend support to a somewhat higher figure.

13. As the result of the foregoing revision of the figure for 1929, it is necessary to reduce the Board of Trade figure of £235 million for 1930 to £210–£230 million.

14. For the year 1931, we have endeavoured to estimate (*a*) the income received in the first half of the year, and (*b*) the income likely to be received in the second half. In the first half-year, there was no serious default in

respect of the foreign and Dominion Government and Corporation stocks. Dividends from railways were substantially reduced, and dividends from mines, rubber, oil, tea, &c., were all less than in the previous year. In the case of rubber there was a substantial net loss.

15. In the case of British companies, it is, of course, remitted earnings from abroad and not dividends paid during the year which have to be brought into account, but the dividends paid assist in making an estimate as to the probable amount of the remitted earnings. Actual losses, if covered from reserves in this country, have also to be taken into account.

16. The bulk of the loan capital consists of Foreign and Dominion Government and Corporation stocks and some reduction in the receipts of interest on this account may be expected for the second half as compared with the first half of this year. So far, however, as can at present be estimated, this reduction is not likely to be very large. There is, however, the probability, if world conditions do not improve, of an increasing default in respect of these fixed interest securities next year.

17. We have made a number of inquiries in regard to the most substantial blocks of capital invested abroad, and we estimate that the net income from overseas investments for the first half of the year was probably about £90–£100 million, and that for the second half of the year it is likely to lie within the range £55–£75 million. For the calendar year 1931 we estimate the net income from overseas investments at between £145 million and £175 million. Taking the middle figures, this means a reduction of about £60 million as compared with 1930.

18. It is important to observe that the decline in our receipts from overseas investments generally would almost certainly be further accentuated if there were a complete suspension of fresh loans from London. It is probable, for example, that the payment of dividends due this year on Indian Government stocks was only made possible by the raising of some £16 million by loans in the London market this spring.

(e) *Estimated Net Receipts from Short Interest and Commissions.*

19. The Board of Trade estimate (see table in paragraph 3 above) of receipts in 1930 in respect of short interest and commissions was £55 million. It is extremely difficult to frame exact estimates of the changes in these receipts, but from such indications as are available in regard to the volume of trade this year as compared with last and in regard to the rates for short loans and acceptances in this country, we consider that, subject to the qualification in the following paragraph, the receipts under this heading may amount in 1931 to nearly £40 million. In view of the increased payments in respect of borrowings this autumn, the net receipts from the second half of the year may be expected to be about £5 million less than those in the first six months.

20. Actual receipts from acceptances may be expected this year to be about the same as in 1930. We have been responsibly informed that up to date this year there have been approximately £6 million of defaults in respect of acceptances. The general practice of financial houses is to set any such losses against the income received from acceptances, and if these losses are charged against income for the purposes of the balance of trade, the above estimate would require to be reduced by at least £6 million, and, possibly, by as much as £10 million, if allowance is made for further defaults during the remainder of this year. The date when the default occurs is, however, not the date when the balance of trade is affected by the loss, since the money is remitted abroad immediately following the acceptance. On the whole, we consider that these losses should be included in the revenue account, and we therefore estimate the net receipts in 1931 from short interest and commissions at about £30 million.

(f) *Estimated Net Receipts from Other Sources.*

21. In this category are included a number of miscellaneous payments and receipts, such as receipts from the sale of second-hand ships, tourist expenditure, emigrants' remittances, savings of returned migrants, and expenditure by foreign Governments on their Diplomatic and Consular Services in this country.

22. Receipts from the sale of second-hand ships were estimated some years since at about £4 million per annum, but this year the receipts on this account will be negligible. The expenditure of tourists in Great Britain is likely this year to show a large decline. The expenditure of British tourists abroad is not likely to have been affected to nearly the same extent. This year there has been a considerable increase in the number of migrants returning to this country, and a very large reduction in the number of emigrants.

23. For a number of years past the estimate for these miscellaneous items has been placed on a conservative basis at £15 million per annum. In the circumstances, we consider that some reduction may be expected this year and we are disposed to estimate receipts under this head for 1931 at £10 million.

(g) *Summary.*

24. In the following table we give a revised estimate of receipts and payments on revenue account for the year 1930, together with our estimates divided into half-yearly periods for the year 1931. In this table we have omitted the £5 million excess of imports over exports of bullion and specie in 1930, as movements of gold should be regarded as a balancing factor rather than as an item on revenue account:—

TABLE III.

Estimated Balance of Income and Expenditure in the Transactions (other than the Lending and Repayment of Capital) between the United Kingdom and All Other Countries 1930 and 1931.

(In million £'s.)

—	1930.	Jan.–June 1931.	July–Dec. 1931.	Jan.–Dec. 1931.
Excess of Imports over exports of merchandise ...	386	183	203	386
Estimated excess of Government receipts from overseas	21	10	5	15
Estimated net national shipping income	105	44	41	85
Estimated net income from overseas investments ...	210–230★	90–100	55–75	145–175
Estimated net receipts from short interest and commissions	55	18	12	30
Estimated net receipts from other sources	15	5	5	10
Total	406–426	167–177	118–138	285–315
Estimated total credit or debit balance on items specified above	+20 to +40	−6 to −16	−65 to −85	−71 to −101

★ Estimate revised in accordance with paragraphs 12 and 13.

25. We have included in our estimates nothing in respect of sums received from sinking funds and maturity payments of overseas loans held in this country. Sir Robert Kindersley estimated that for the year 1929 these receipts amounted to £48·5 million. It is probable that in the current year they will be substantially less. These sinking fund payments are, of course, not a receipt on revenue account, but a capital item; and against them it is necessary for us to make fresh loans on a fairly substantial scale as a condition of continuing to receive the interest on many of our investments. We think it better therefore to leave these sinking fund payments out of our calculations.

26. The estimated debit balance of international payments for the second half of this year is much larger than that for the first half. This is due in part to the normal increase in the excess of imports over exports of merchandise in the latter part of the year, but is mainly caused by the loss in income from our overseas investments. It is possible that the Board of Trade figures

both in this and in preceding years have erred on the side of caution and have omitted some favourable items, but even after making allowance for this possibility, it would seem that the net debit against this country is now running at a rate of not less than £2 million a week.★

27. It is worth emphasising that the deterioration in our trade balance is mainly due to the falling off in our income from overseas investments, which is occasioned by international causes, and very little to the worsening of the visible balance of trade. It is, of course, evident that over the last few weeks the exceptional pressure on the exchanges has been due to capital transactions. The unfavourable balance of trade, though it mounts up heavily in course of time, cannot be responsible over a short period (except indirectly in so far as it affects confidence and foreign sentiment) for the heavy drain of recent weeks.

III.—EFFECTS OF THE DEPRECIATION OF THE POUND.

28. The estimates given in the previous Section are those which we should have made prior to the depreciation of the sterling exchange. They relate, however, to the year 1931, three-quarters of which has already passed, so that, in view of the various time-lags involved, the effect of recent weeks on them cannot be very material. If we look further forward and consider the probable outcome of the year commencing October 1931, there are two important disturbing factors which have to be considered. The first of these is the risk that our invisible income from overseas investments may be still further diminished; and the second is the net result on our trade balance of the change in the gold value of sterling.

29. As regards the first of these factors, our income in 1930 from fixed-interest investments overseas has been estimated at about £105 million and the income from the variable investments at about £130 million. The latter sum has already been greatly reduced; but, so far, the reduction of the former has been quite small, so slight that in compiling our estimates we have reduced it by only £5 million for the current year, and we believe that even this modest reduction is on the safe side. Looking further forward, we believe that these receipts must be regarded as in the highest degree precarious unless there is a great change in the international position. The depreciation of sterling, however, in itself represents an important favourable influence in the right direction. For if sterling is depreciated by 25 per cent., this means that it is that much easier for the debtor countries to meet their sterling obligations. It is even possible that in the coming year our receipts in respect of these loans in terms of depreciated sterling may amount to more, when they are reconverted into gold at the lower exchange, than they would have been if we had attempted, with imperfect success, to exact

★ This, of course, is not a constant rate since the income from overseas investments is received at irregular intervals.

payment at the former gold parity. Whether this mitigation of the problem of the debtor countries will be sufficient without a rise in gold prices must be uncertain. The change of gold parity by ourselves, and by the other countries which are likely to follow our example at an early date, will indeed lead to a rise in prices in terms of the currencies thus affected, which should prove stimulating to trade. But it may well be necessary that *gold* prices should rise, before normal prosperity returns or debtor countries are able to meet their liabilities in a normal way.

30. As regards the effect of the fall in the sterling exchange on the other items of our international Balance Sheet, it is extremely difficult to make even an approximate estimate, especially at a time when the degree of the gold depreciation of sterling and the action of other countries in relation to their own currencies are still matters of conjecture. As regards imports and exports, a depreciation of (say) from 20 to 30 per cent. in the gold value of sterling must necessarily have a strong tendency to restrict the volume of imports and to increase the volume of exports, since its influence on imports is equivalent to that of a tariff, and its influence on exports, so long as sterling costs of production are unchanged, to that of export bounties. The restriction of imports will help at once to reduce the aggregate value of our imports as measured in gold. Indeed, the effect on imports may be more drastic at the outset than it will be later on. The bounty on exports, on the other hand, will serve to reduce the gold prices at which our exports are sold, so that until the volume of our exports is increased proportionately, the net effect will be to reduce the aggregate gold value of our exports. It may, therefore, be a considerable time before the balance of payments in respect of imports and exports is materially improved by the depreciation of the pound. Moreover, the instability of the exchanges which must be expected for some time will introduce a factor of uncertainty which will tend to delay the increase in the volume of exports. Ultimately, however, the depreciation of the pound will improve substantially the balance of payments in respect of imports and exports; but the extent of the improvement from this cause will depend, in part, on the policy pursued by other countries in respect of their own currencies.

31. As regards Government receipts and payments, there will be some increase reckoned in sterling, but a reduction reckoned in gold, in the overseas expenditure of the defence services (the total being £7 million in a full year), of the diplomatic services, &c.

32. The effect of our national shipping income will be similar to the effect on our exports, *i.e.*, it is likely to be favourable in the long run by improving the power of our shipowners to meet foreign competition.

33. As regards our income from overseas investments, we have already expressed the view that the diminution in the real burden to debtor countries of sterling loans may actually serve to maintain our receipts from such loans,

as measured in gold, at possibly even a higher level than would otherwise have been the case. As regards variable interest overseas investments, the effect on our receipts is likely to be favourable in so far as debtor countries allow their currencies to move with sterling. Nevertheless, even if there are no further defaults there will be a reduction of £25 million (assuming a depreciation of 25 per cent.) in the gold value (though not in the sterling value) of our receipts.

34. The value of our receipts from "short interest and commissions" is likely to be reduced, at any rate for the time being, by a diminished use of the sterling bill, which must be expected to result from the instability of sterling.

35. The main effect of the depreciation of the pound on the balance of payments will be that on merchandise imports and exports. Whatever uncertainty there may be regarding the net balance of the initial effects, ultimately the balance of payments should be materially improved. The extent of this improvement will, of course, depend on the eventual level at which sterling settles, and on the course pursued by other countries, as well as on many other factors at present unknown.

IV.—THE QUESTION OF REMEDIAL ACTION.

36. We conclude that it is in any case vital for the solvency of our trade balance that sterling should remain for the time being substantially below gold parity, and we are of the opinion that in existing circumstances a decline in the gold value of sterling by 25 per cent. would not be by any means excessive. At any rate it would, we think, be unwise from the point of view of the balance of trade to make artificial efforts to maintain the value of sterling except in the event of a serious further slump.

37. Our examination of the figures leads us to the conclusion that, even after allowing for all likely assistance from exchange depreciation, whether or not accompanied by a tariff, the problem still remains difficult of complete solution unless there is a recovery in world prices and a general revival of world trade. It is important, therefore, that we should not allow our minds to be occupied too exclusively by our domestic problems, but that we should be thinking out a comprehensive international policy.

38. Until lately our power of international initiative was paralysed by our anxiety to prevent, or provide for, foreign withdrawals of balances. But now that we have recovered greater freedom of action, we should consider most carefully how best to use it. Plans for useful international action are more possible to-day than they were a short time ago. It is probable that many other countries will be constrained to follow our example, whilst those countries which remain on the existing gold parity will bear the whole brunt of the competition of those countries which depart from it. France and the United States are likely to find themselves at no distant date with their export trade cut to pieces and their banking systems seriously

impaired. These factors might tend to make them more reasonable in their discussion of international remedies.

V.—SUMMARY OF CONCLUSIONS.

39. We summarise our conclusions as follows:—

(a) During the past year there has been a marked adverse change in the balance of international payments, with the result that there is a large and growing debit balance which we estimate is now running at a rate of not less than £2 million in a week.

(b) The adverse change in the balance of payments is mainly attributable to a large decline in our receipts from overseas investments. Up to the present this decline has not spread to any considerable extent to our fixed-interest investments. A large part of the income from these investments must be regarded, however, as in a high degree precarious, unless there is a great change in the international position.

(c) The outlook for the balance of payments has been materially altered by the depreciation of sterling, which will principally affect merchandise imports and exports. Whatever uncertainty there may be regarding the net balance of the initial effects, ultimately the balance of payments should be materially improved. The extent of this improvement will, of course, depend on the eventual level at which sterling settles, and on the course pursued by other countries, as well as on many other factors at present unknown.

(d) Even after allowing for all likely assistance from exchange depreciation, whether or not accompanied by a tariff, the problem still remains difficult of complete solution unless there is a recovery in world prices and a general revival of world trade. Plans for useful international action are more possible to-day than they were a short time ago. We should not allow our minds to be occupied too exclusively by our domestic problems, but should be thinking out a comprehensive international policy.

Committee on Financial Questions, Report on Sterling Policy,
March 1932*

I.—THE POSITION OF STERLING.

1. IT is only those who are in possession of the full facts as to the volume and nature of the foreign balances remaining in London who can judge whether and when the position of sterling is sufficiently strong to ensure that any policy adopted would not be upset by the recurrence of a large foreign drain.

* P.R.O. Cab. 58/169, E.A.C. (H.) 147, 9 March 1932.

2. Subject, however, to this reserve, we are of the opinion that the position of sterling is sufficiently secure to make it no longer unreasonable to consider long-term policy.

3. During the months that followed our departure from the gold standard, the withdrawal of foreign short-term balances from London continued on a substantial scale, and cast a considerable strain on the sterling exchanges. The depreciation of the pound which ensued stimulated, however, various capital movements in the opposite direction. The diminished use of the sterling bill entailed a large repayment of foreign short-term obligations to London. The premium obtainable for gold led to a large efflux of gold from the private hoards of India, amounting to over £40 millions by the beginning of March. In the earlier months there were also fairly considerable sales by British investors of American and other foreign securities. Assisted by these various movements, the Bank of England were able not only to meet the withdrawals of foreign balances without any serious break in sterling, but to accumulate sufficient foreign exchange as well as to repay the £50 millions Franco-American credit which fell due at the end of January. This achievement had the effect of reviving confidence throughout the world in the future of sterling, which was further strengthened by the reduction of Bank Rate in the middle of February. A "bull" movement in sterling has accordingly developed which has already made it possible to repay £43 millions of the £80 millions Treasury loan which falls due in September; and in the last few days the sterling exchanges have risen sharply.

4. In so far as this strength of sterling is attributable to purely speculative purchases, the probability of a reaction must be borne in mind. There remains also the possibility of a recurrence of withdrawals from London, in the event of serious financial trouble in Central Europe or elsewhere. We think it very unlikely, however, that these factors will give rise to any serious weakness in sterling. Moreover, the capital movements which have come to the aid of sterling in recent months, notably the Indian gold efflux, which seems likely to continue for a considerable time, serve to demonstrate the substantial and varied character of the capital resources upon which we can rely if sterling should temporarily be forced down at any time to an unduly low level. Thus the growing world confidence in the pound is based on solid considerations; and it seems probable that the balance of capital movements will continue to be towards rather than away from London.

5. Nor do we think it likely that the adverse balance of trade will prove an important factor of weakness in the sterling position. The depreciation of the pound has set at work forces tending to stimulate exports and (accentuated by tariffs) to check imports, which should serve to reduce materially the adverse trade balance which existed last autumn. The same forces, moreover, are tending to improve the trade balances of countries like

India, Australia and Argentina, which are closely linked with the British financial system. An improvement of the trade balance of these countries will contribute nearly as much to the strength of sterling as will a commensurate improvement in the balance of trade of Great Britain. On the other hand, the trade balances of the gold-absorbing countries, particularly France and the United States, have deteriorated markedly in the past year, and this deterioration is likely to proceed more rapidly in future as the result of the departure of so many countries from the gold standard. Since the value of sterling in terms of gold means in effect its value relatively to the franc and the dollar, and a few other currencies which are effectively on a gold basis, the deterioration of the trade balances of these countries will tend to strengthen sterling. While, therefore, under the present depressed conditions of world trade, the correction of the British trade balance may be gradual and for a considerable period incomplete, we should be surprised if this were to cast any serious strain on the sterling exchanges.

6. We take the view, therefore, that the pound is now reasonably well-assured against the dangers which it was natural to apprehend at the time of our departure from the gold standard. The present position of sterling is one of considerable underlying strength. Indeed, it is now probable that our monetary policy in the near future will be embarrassed by the return to London of foreign short-term balances of a precarious nature.

7. To avoid misapprehension, however, we feel it necessary to add that we take a grave view of the world economic situation. The fall of commodity prices, as measured in gold, has proceeded so far as to create throughout the world a widespread condition of latent financial insolvency, which is particularly serious in Central Europe, and which may at any time throw up to the surface overt catastrophes serving still further to depress business and numb new enterprise. Meanwhile, the system of international borrowing and lending, both long and short, upon which the development of international trade depends, has been brought almost to a standstill; and the processes of international commerce are further impeded, not only by higher tariffs, but by the more rigid obstacles of quota systems and exchange restrictions. The vicious circles, in short, set up by the depression, are in full swing throughout the world as a whole; and in these circumstances it is only a limited consolation that we can derive from the fact that there is no longer cause for misgiving in the weakness of our relative position.

8. In the light of the foregoing review of the tendencies that are at work, we make the following observations upon the questions of policy that present themselves.

II.—THE GOLD STANDARD.

9. If sterling continues to develop strength in the course of the next few months, the restoration of the pound to its former parity with gold may conceivably come once more to be regarded as a realizable aim; and we may

then expect that it will be urged in influential quarters that the restoration of the gold standard on the old basis should be made the objective of our policy. We are, however, strongly opposed to making this our objective. We are satisfied that at anything like the present level of gold prices, the former gold parity is substantially in excess of the appropriate value of the pound. Our industrial life has suffered serious disadvantages in the last few years from the attempt to maintain the pound at an excessive external value; and it would be a capital mistake to make this attempt a second time.

10. We go further. In our opinion it would be unwise to make it our governing aim to return to gold in the existing conditions, or any which seem likely to obtain in the near future, even on the basis of a new and lower parity; and we should regard it as unfortunate if the Government were to commit itself to the adoption of such a policy. In the last few years the gold standard has failed to fulfil one of the primary requisites of a sound monetary system, namely, the maintenance of a substantial stability in the level of prices. On the contrary, wholesale gold prices have fallen by about 33 per cent. in the last three years, and a fall of prices of this order of magnitude is immensely more prejudicial to trade than are the inconveniences of fluctuating foreign exchanges. We do not think it necessary to discuss the causes to which this result should be attributed. It is sufficient to say that under the conditions which now prevail, we can see no grounds for assurance that the gold standard will work more satisfactorily in the future than in the past. Until there can be some assurance on this point, it would be a mistake for us to tie ourselves to gold again.

11. In deprecating any commitment at this stage to a return to gold, we are further influenced by the following consideration. Several countries have already followed Great Britain in departing from the gold standard; and there is a considerable likelihood that several other countries will be compelled by circumstances to depart from it in the near future, unless meanwhile gold prices rise. Meanwhile the burden of the economic depression is accentuated in those countries which remain on gold, and is likely to be accentuated still further by each fresh departure. The prestige of the gold standard system in the eyes of world opinion is thus being steadily weakened; and as this prestige weakens, the advantages which we should derive from restoring our currency to a gold basis diminish, while if we keep our hands free, our influence is increased for securing the conditions of more satisfactory international monetary arrangements.

III.—THE STERLING AREA.

12. This brings us to the question of co-operating in the pursuit of a common policy with other countries which have also departed from gold. Several of these countries have so far linked their currencies with sterling, either formally, as is the case with a large part of the British Empire, or

informally, as is the case with the Scandinavian countries. There has thus come into existence a sterling group of countries which already covers an area of considerable importance; and, inasmuch as the countries which can be said to be effectively and securely upon the gold standard are comparatively few, it is a conceivable development that the sterling group may come to represent the predominant international system.

13. It is very desirable, in our opinion, that the majority of countries which are not at present upon a gold basis should be encouraged to link themselves to sterling as closely and definitely as possible. By this means trade secures the advantage of stable foreign exchanges within the sterling area; the utility of the sterling bill as an instrument of international commerce is enhanced; and sterling itself acquires a greater measure of stability and strength relatively to gold standard countries. It is not so clear that it would be equally to our advantage that the majority of countries which to-day remain on gold should abandon it for sterling. It so happens that the majority of countries which have already departed from gold are countries which produce primary commodities rather than manufactured articles, whose trade is therefore complementary rather than competitive with ours, whereas the countries which remain on gold include our principal industrial competitors. Our exporting industries have so far derived a very real advantage in international competition from the depreciation of the pound, and this advantage is not sensibly diminished by the fact that, for example, the Scandinavian currencies have undergone a corresponding depreciation. If, however, the currencies of countries like Germany, Czechoslovakia, Italy, Belgium, France, or the United States were to depreciate, there would be a substantial loss of the competitive advantage which we have derived in recent months. It is doubtful accordingly whether any such development would be on balance in our interests. On the other hand, if and as the depreciation of any of the above currencies were to occur, it would probably be desirable that they should be linked with sterling rather than left unanchored. Moreover, it might help to avert catastrophe in Central Europe if the embarrassed debtor countries there were to link up with sterling.

14. For the time being, our interests lie in the consolidation of the existing sterling group, rather than in the extension of its area. At present the adherence to sterling of many of the countries which are off gold is partial, provisional and precarious. The question therefore arises whether it would be possible to consolidate the sterling group, by negotiations with a view to the pursuit of a common policy; or, alternatively, whether we should aim at a common monetary policy for the British Empire.

IV.—EMPIRE CO-OPERATION.

15. In connection with all such projects of co-operation, one fundamental difficulty must be borne in mind. Any sound monetary system must be

administered by a central banking authority in a position of great power and prestige, able to control effectively the volume of currency and credit in the community over which the system operates. The note issue must either be in the hands of that authority, or governed by regulations of a character which do not deprive it of effective control of the volume of money. It would be chimerical to suppose that either Great Britain or the Dominions would agree to entrust the regulation of their internal credit systems to some newly-created institution representative of the Empire as a whole, or to abandon their rights of independent note issue. It would be even more chimerical to suppose that any such arrangements could be made between a larger group of countries. In these circumstances, a unitary monetary system, whether for the Empire as a whole, or for a wider sterling area, is impossible; and there remains only one form which the pursuit of a common policy can take, namely, that the Bank of England should control the value of sterling independently, by the same means that it employs to-day; and that the other countries should so regulate their monetary systems as to maintain their exchanges at a fixed parity with sterling. This, however, is the practice that prevails to-day, in so far as other countries adhere at all closely to sterling.

16. Thus the only means that is open to us for the consolidation of a sterling group or for the development of a common monetary policy for the Empire is to convince the countries concerned that the closest and most definite adherence to sterling is likely to be in their best interests.

17. For this purpose, the most essential condition is that other countries should have confidence in the future of sterling, should believe that it is likely to fulfil more satisfactorily than any other available alternative the functions of a standard of value. In the existing state of opinion, it is probable that a declaration of our intention to restore the pound to a gold basis at an appropriate parity at the earliest possible moment would do most to confirm confidence abroad in the reliability of sterling. As we have already indicated, we should deprecate such a declaration at this juncture. From the standpoint, however, of maintaining the cohesion of the sterling group, it is important to avoid any express declaration of an opposite character, such as would exclude the possibility of an eventual return to gold.

18. For the rest we think that a useful purpose would be served by the development of a practice of consultation between our financial authorities and those of other sterling countries, within the Empire and outside it, with the object of keeping the latter in touch with the course of our policy and of assuring them that, in shaping our policy, any special interests of theirs will be taken into consideration. Such consultation is particularly desirable in the case of the Dominions. It seems best, however, that it should develop naturally, and proceed at first, at all events, on an informal rather than a formal basis. For this reason we doubt whether any constructive proposal can emerge from the formal discussion of the question of Empire currency co-operation at the forthcoming Ottawa Conference. At present

there is a marked diversity of policy and opinion in regard to monetary matters between the different Dominions. South Africa still adheres to the gold standard, and the question of her continued adherence has become a leading party issue. Canada, though she is off gold, shows no signs of associating herself with sterling.

19. The course of sterling has, however, one important bearing on Imperial policy, which it may be useful to bear in mind in connection with the Ottawa Conference. The principal economic benefit which the Imperial connection has conferred upon the Dominions has been the provision of capital on cheap terms for the development of their resources. The facilities of the London capital market have been in past years at the disposal of the Dominions under exceptionally favourable conditions. The fact that trustees in this country are authorized to invest money in loans raised by Governments and public authorities in Empire countries but not in foreign countries has enabled the countries of the Empire to borrow large sums of money for development purposes at very much cheaper rates than could any foreign country, however strong its financial position. The benefit which the United Kingdom has conferred on other parts of the Empire in this way is very substantial.

20. As the result of the financial crisis and the weakness of sterling in recent months, the issue of new overseas loans, whether to the Empire or to foreign countries, has been brought virtually to a standstill. For the time being, accordingly, the Dominions are deprived of the facilities of the London capital market, and their economic difficulties are materially increased thereby. As sterling recovers in strength, it will become possible to permit a gradual resumption of overseas lending, though it will probably be desirable for a considerable time for our financial authorities to watch carefully the volume and the nature of the new overseas issues that are made. Any new overseas issue will be exposed to the objection of tending to weaken the sterling exchanges, but the extent of this weakness will depend in practice upon the degree to which the borrowing country uses the loan to buy goods from Great Britain. The governing consideration of ensuring the strength of sterling will make it desirable to direct the flow of our new overseas investment to countries which buy as largely as possible from us. It is desirable, therefore, that it should be recognized that the purchase of British goods is a natural and appropriate condition of the effective reopening of the benefits of the London capital market to Empire countries.

V.—THE STERLING PRICE-LEVEL.

21. We revert to the question of the general objective to which policy in regard to sterling should be directed. The governing consideration, in our opinion, should be to secure stability of sterling prices at a suitable level. Nothing is more important for the orderly development of economic life

than the avoidance of large price disturbances such as have occurred in recent years. The present level of sterling prices, however, is unduly low for satisfactory and remunerative trade, and some recovery of the price-level will be an inevitable feature of any trade improvement. It would be unwise, therefore, to attempt to stabilise sterling prices at their present level; such a course would mean in effect stabilising conditions of trade depression.

22. The question thus arises how far it would be desirable that sterling prices should rise. Here it is necessary to take account of various considerations, some of which are dependent on, but others independent of, the movement of gold prices in the outside world. We deal first with those which are independent of the movement of gold prices.

23. From the standpoint of trade, it seems desirable that sterling prices should rise enough to be compatible with a normal condition of profits and trade activity on the basis of the existing level of money wages and incomes. But a rise of prices, limited in accordance with this criterion, would do little to reduce the real burden of fixed money claims on the productive energies of the community, including in particular the real burden of the National Debt. Indeed, inasmuch as there have been cuts in the wages and salaries of considerable sections of the population during the course of the present depression, a recovery of prices to a point appropriate to the present level of money incomes would leave the real burden of the National Debt charge and other fixed money claims somewhat heavier than it was a few years ago. Now, even under the conditions prevailing before the present slump, the magnitude of the National Debt charge imposed a serious strain upon our financial system, entailing the maintenance of direct taxation at a level which was felt to be deterrent to business enterprise, and which led taxpayers to resort increasingly to various methods of tax avoidance. It is not easy to see how substantial tax relief can be afforded, unless the burden represented by the National Debt is by some means reduced. Now, therefore, that our enforced departure from the gold standard has restored to us freedom of choice in regard to our future monetary arrangements, it is clearly desirable that the reactions of our policy upon the real burden of the National Debt should be borne in mind.

24. For some years a marked disparity has existed between the wages of "sheltered" occupations and the wages of occupations which are subject to the pressure of foreign competition. It is desirable that this disparity should be corrected in some degree; and the changes consequent upon our departure from the gold standard are tending in fact to correct it. The correction of the disparity may, however, take either of two forms—(a) a reduction of the wages of the more highly paid sheltered occupations, or (b) an improvement in the wages of the depressed exporting industries. At present it is mainly the former tendency that is manifest; and this is the tendency which must necessarily prevail so long as the price-level remains as low as it is to-day. Having regard, however, to the desirability of lightening rather than in-

creasing the real burden of the National Debt, we consider that the rise of prices at which we should aim should be sufficient to permit of a readjustment of relative wages taking mainly the form of a levelling-up of wage-rates that are relatively low.

25. So far, however, we have been arguing without reference to the movement of gold prices in the outside world. The foregoing conclusions are, therefore, subject to the reservations contained in the succeeding paragraphs.

VI.—GOLD PRICES AND THE STERLING EXCHANGES.

26. At a given level of gold prices, a rise in the sterling price-level must in general be associated with a fall in the sterling exchanges (relatively to gold currencies) and *vice versâ*. The sharp rise in the sterling exchange which has occurred in the past few days makes likely accordingly a fall of sterling prices, although as has been argued above, the existing sterling price-level is too low for satisfactory trade conditions. It is true that a rise of sterling may stimulate some recovery of gold prices, just as its depreciation from gold parity may have contributed to the further fall of gold prices in recent months; and in this way a recovery of the pound might do something to relieve the acute difficulties of Central Europe, and improve the position in other gold standard countries. Unless, however, it is accompanied by other conditions favourable to trade, it will probably contribute more to lower sterling prices than to raise gold prices. A lowering of sterling prices would aggravate business depression not only in Great Britain but in those other countries as well which are regulating their currency upon a sterling basis.

27. For this reason, we regard it as important that the policy of cheaper money, initiated by the reduction of Bank Rate to 5 per cent. on the 18th February, should be carried progressively further. There is nothing in the condition of internal trade at the present time which makes the discouragement of a high Bank Rate appropriate. At the time of the departure from the gold standard, fears were naturally entertained that a substantial rise in internal prices might result, which might possibly threaten the development of a "vicious spiral" of rising prices, rising wages and progressive currency depreciation. So far, however, nothing has occurred to justify these fears. Although the exchange depreciation of sterling was about one-third for a considerable period, wholesale prices have risen by only about 8 per cent., the cost of living has increased by only 2 points, which corresponds roughly to the normal seasonal increase at this period of the year, and the tendency of money wages has continued downwards. Though some industries exposed to foreign competition have become more active as the result of the improvement in their competitive power, there has been an accentuation of depression in most sheltered trades. Broadly speaking our general conditions are still

marked by a deflationary rather than an inflationary trend. In these circumstances an increase in unemployment is a natural consequence.

28. These considerations derive added force from the growing strength of the sterling position. For in view of the possibility that is thereby opened out of a recovery of the pound, it has probably become more important to provide safeguards against an undue fall than against an undue rise of sterling prices. Cheaper money in London would be an influence in the direction of higher prices throughout the world generally. If a rising tendency of world prices could be initiated in this way, it is possible that the effect of a moderate recovery of the pound in raising gold prices might be important, and its effect in depressing sterling prices comparatively unimportant. The growing strength of sterling is, indeed, a phenomenon which, according to the use that is made of it, is capable either of seriously increasing our local difficulties or of contributing materially to world recovery.

29. Even, however, if accompanied by a rising tendency of gold prices, it is important that the rise of the sterling exchanges should not be allowed to proceed too far. The increase in gold prices is likely to be much more marked in the case of primary commodities than of industrial products; and our exporting industries are not, therefore, likely to find it possible to obtain appreciably higher gold prices in world markets for the goods which they produce. It will be necessary, therefore, for our exporting industries to retain a substantial part of the advantage in international competition which they have derived from the fall of the pound, if we are to avoid a recurrence of the unsatisfactory conditions of the latter part of the last decade. While, therefore, some improvement in the sterling exchanges is to be desired if gold prices rise substantially, the improvement ought not to be proportionate to the increase of gold prices as measured by the customary indices of wholesale prices.

30. The foregoing represent the general considerations by which, in our opinion, policy in regard to sterling should be guided. But in view of the uncertainties which attach to the future course of world trade and gold prices, we think that it would be at present premature to attempt the definite stabilisation of sterling whether upon a gold or any other basis.

*Fourth Report of Committee on Economic Information**

SURVEY OF THE ECONOMIC SITUATION, JULY 1932.

I.—Recent developments.

THE following are some of the principal economic events occurring since the preparation of the Committee's last report (Council Paper E.A.C. (S.C.) 3):—

---

* P.R.O. Cab. 58/30, E.A.C. (S.C.) 4, 20 July 1932; also Cab. 24/232, C.P. 273(32).

2. The outstanding economic events of recent months, are the agreement reached at the Lausanne Conference and the announcement by the British Government of the scheme for the conversion of the £2,000 millions of 5 per cent. War Loan. The boldness of the enterprise represented by the conversion scheme is evident, when it is remembered that the yield on long-date Government securities was rather over 4 per cent. as late as the 16th June, and was about £3 17s. 4d. on the day before the announcement of the offer, while the effective yield of the new security, allowing for the bonus of 1 per cent., is about £3 10s. 9d. The scheme, however, was universally acclaimed and elicited an immediate market response, all classes of Government securities rising sharply to prices representing yields in the neighbourhood of that on the new security, and the upward movement extending to Stock Exchange securities in general, including ordinary shares and foreign Government bonds.

3. This result is the more striking in view of the fact that the previously existing prices of British Government securities represented a substantial improvement in British Government credit, during the present year, unaccompanied by any similar improvement in the credit of foreign governments. The following table shows the respective prices of the 3 per cent. securities of the British, French and Dutch Governments at different dates during the past twelve months:—

TABLE I.

Prices of Government securities.

	Great Britain. 3 per cent. Local Loans.	France. 3 per cent. Perpetual Rentes.	Holland. 3 per cent. Dutch, 1898.
1931—			
July 15	66½	86·95	80¼
September 15 ...	66	89·40	83¾
September 30 ...	59¾	83·80	66½
October 15	62	83·75	71¾
1932—			
June 30	77⅝	73·55	71½
July 2	83	74·50	71¾
July 7	84	76·50	75½
July 20	...	...	...

4. The launching of the conversion scheme on the 30th June was preceded by the reduction of Bank rate to 2 per cent. on the previous day. The short-term rates of interest had already fallen to levels only equalled in 1894 and 1895. In spite of the attractions of non-assented War Loan as a short-term investment new Treasury bills (which were issued at an average rate of 15s. 0·19d. per cent. a fortnight ago) were issued this week at an

average rate of only 17s. 2·38d. per cent. The values of all classes of shares have improved as a result of the conversion scheme. Industrial shares which had been stable throughout June at levels rather above the low point reached at the end of May rose sharply, the *Financial News* share index rising from 51·2 at the end of May to 54·0 at the end of June, and to 60·7 on the 8th July. On the other hand the sterling exchange fell. Though the conversion offer contributed towards this, there were other influences at work. During the first half of June this fluctuated between 3·66 and 3·70. On the cessation of the drain on New York mentioned subsequently, it fell to between 3·60 and 3·62. Recently there has been a further fall as low as 3·54.

5. Employment in Great Britain has continued to decline, falling from 9,484,000 in April to 9,402,000 in May, and again to 9,394,000 in June. At the end of that month the total figure of unemployment was 2,770,000. The position, moreover, is more serious than this aggregate. For while there has been a marked decrease in unemployment among women in the last ten months (due, in part, to the effects of the means test), there has been a serious and progressive increase in unemployment among men. Between March and June there occurred in coal mining an increase in unemployment much heavier than is usual at this time of year. There has been some seasonal improvement in building and public works contracting, in distributing, and in other services, but not so much as is normal.

6. There are other indications of a slackening of industrial activity. For example, the receipts of the railways from goods traffic showed the following declines as compared with 1931:—

	Per cent.
1st to 8th weeks	− 7·5
9th to 16th weeks	− 8·3
17th to 24th weeks	−11·2

Similarly the index of the consumption of electricity published by the *Economist*, which is corrected for seasonal variation and normal increase, fell sharply in May to the level of last September, after having ruled at a substantially higher level from October to April.

7. The foreign trade returns for June continue to show a smaller adverse balance of trade than has been usual in recent years. For the last five years, the adverse balance of trade for the first half-year has been as follows:—

	£ million.
1928	183
1929	185
1930	188
1931	183
1932	144

8. The improvement of £39 millions as compared with 1931 is the result of a decrease of £58 millions in imports (of which £43 millions was in manufactured goods, particularly textiles, apparel and manufactures of metal) partially offset by a decrease of £19 millions in exports and re-exports.

9. The fall in commodity prices has continued. During the six weeks from the 4th May to the 29th June, British prices as measured by the *Economist* index number, have fallen by 5·7 per cent. Prices have also fallen in France and the United States, but in a lesser degree. In recent weeks prices in the United States have risen somewhat.

TABLE 2.

Wholesale commodity prices.

(September 18, 1931 = 100.)

Date.	United Kingdom. (*Economist* indices.) Complete index (sterling).	Primary products (sterling).	Index of sterling-dollar exchange.	U.S.A. (Irving Fisher).	France. Statistique général.
May 4	103·3	106·5	75·6	89·3	96·8
May 18	102·6	105·9	75·6	88·6	95·1
June 1	100·2	101·0	75·7	87·3	94·0
June 15	97·8	99·7	75·3	86·0	92·7
June 29	97·4	99·3	74·1	86·4	91·5
July 13	97·5	101·3	72·9	87·3	...

10. The drain of gold from New York during May and the first half of June reached enormous proportions. In the middle of June this movement came to an abrupt end, partly because foreign deposits in New York had been reduced to the lowest convenient point, partly because domestic confidence was restored by the passing of the Tax Bill, and the rejection of the Soldiers' Bonus Bill. The Federal Reserve Banks continued their purchases of Government securities throughout the period, but only on a scale sufficient to maintain the surplus reserves of the member banks at a figure that was substantially unchanged. The principal changes in the balance sheet of the Federal Reserve Banks since the 7th April (when the vigorous open market policy was initiated) and the 14th July were as follows:—

TABLE 3.

Principal assets and liabilities of the Federal Reserve Banks.

(In millions of dollars.)

—	April 7.	May 26.	June 16.	July 7.	July 14.
Gold	3,032*	2,857	2,561†	2,578	2,588
Bills discounted	635†	471	496	500	516
Bills bought	58	38	66	77	62
Government securities ...	885†	1,525	1,692	1,801	1,821
Total resources	5,380†	5,635	5,635	5,732*	5,769
Notes in circulation ...	2,562	2,532†	2,576	2,868*	2,836
Member bank deposits ...	1,952†	2,214*	2,101	1,953	2,014
Other deposits	68	106	97	82	102

* Maximum.   † Minimum.

During recent weeks there have been considerable increases in the notes in circulation, which, so far as it goes, supports the suggestion that hoarding may again be becoming common in the United States. As a result, the previous increase in member bank deposits has been almost wiped out.

11. At the beginning of June the formation of a pool to undertake the purchase of bonds was announced. Its capital was fixed at $100 million, and was subscribed by a number of banks. The anticipation of its operations caused a rise in the price of bonds. This was not wholly maintained when it became clear that no dramatic intervention in the market was intended.

12. The prices of American stocks have been in the neighbourhood of the low point reached at the end of May, and have shown no strength. Commodity prices have recovered slightly from the low point reached in the middle of June, and the general tendency to rise has been maintained in recent weeks. In the middle of June there were some indications of increased business activity. More recently, however, there seems to have been a further fall.

13. Production in France is at present at a very low level, the index compiled by the Statistique générale showing a decline of 34 per cent. in April in comparison with the high point reached in 1930. This evidence of a decline in production is borne out by the reduction recorded in employment up to the end of April. In May, on the other hand, there was a slight increase in employment and figures for unemployment show a decrease throughout June. Movements in the French unemployment figures are unreliable as an indication of changes in the level of business activity, as they take no account of the repatriation of foreign workers, which has recently been taking place on a very considerable scale. But making allowance for this, there is no longer the rapid deterioration in the French economic position that was noticeable in the first quarter of this year.

14. One of the main factors in the decline in French production has been the fall in both the value and volume of exports. Compared with 1929 the volume of exports in the first quarter of 1932 was smaller by nearly 40 per cent., while their value has fallen by 56 per cent. The decline in values for the two months April and May compared with 1929 was 62 per cent.

15. French imports have, since the autumn of last year, been systematically reduced by a system of quotas. The volume of imports in the first quarter of 1932 is 24 per cent. less than in the second quarter of 1931, in which quarter imports reached their peak. The severity of the quota restrictions has, however, been relaxed lately in the case of certain important commodities, and there are signs that the process may be carried further.

16. Wholesale prices in France showed a tendency to rise in the first three months of this year, partly as a result of the restriction of imports, and partly in view of a more hopeful sentiment. Since March, however, there has been a further fall, prices at the end of June being at their lowest point since stabilisation.

17. Though the Bank of France's gold holdings continue to increase, this increase is at present more than balanced by the decrease in its holdings of foreign exchange. Since the beginning of May the total of gold and foreign exchange has been reduced by more than a milliard francs.

18. The volume of world trade continues to decline. The following table gives particulars for the four principal trading nations:—

TABLE 4.

Comparison of the trade of the four principal trading nations for the first five months of 1932 and 1931.

(Figures in millions of dollars.)

	1932. Imports.	1931. Imports.	Decline per cent.
United Kingdom	1,088*	1,698	36
U.S.A.	637	936	32
Germany	481	860	44
France	496	755	34
Total	2,702	4,249	36
	Exports.	Exports.	
United Kingdom	656*	968	32
U.S.A.	727	1,130	36
Germany	603	1,012	40
France	333	536	38
Total	2,319	3,646	36

Table 4 (*cont.*)

			Balance.	Balance.
United Kingdom	...	...	− 432*	− 730
U.S.A.	...	...	+ 90	+194
Germany	...	...	+122	+152
France	...	...	− 163	−219
Total	...	...	− 383	− 603

* The pound is taken at its average value for 1932, namely, 3·60 dollars.

19. Although the French visible balance of trade has improved relatively to 1931, this improvement was confined to the first quarter of the year. In April and May the adverse balance was nearly the same as last year. The German visible balance of trade has been favourable for the first five months of this year to the extent of R.M. 465 millions, in addition to which there have been reparation deliveries amounting to R.M. 52 millions. This represents a favourable visible balance at the rate of R.M. 1,200 millions per year. Together with her credit balance on invisible account, this is about sufficient to meet the interest and amortisation charge on the external debts. But the present favourable visible balance is based on a reduction of imports to a monthly level of R.M. 400 millions, as compared with over R.M. 1,000 millions in 1929, which has probably entailed drawing on internal stocks of raw materials.

20. In South America there has been a widespread outbreak of political disorders, including revolutions, civil conflicts and the rupture of diplomatic relations between neighbouring States. In some countries decrees have been passed forbidding the acceptance of deposits expressed in terms of foreign currencies. In Argentina there is a serious shortage of foreign exchange, despite a much improved trade balance.

21. The Japanese exchange has shown continuous weakness being at present quoted at 1s. 6½d. This is leading to complaints in the Indian market. The exchange deterioration is probably due to the continued unfavourable balance of trade. The figures for the first five months of this year and last year are as follows:—

TABLE 5.

Japanese foreign trade for first five months, 1931 and 1932.

(In millions of yen.)

				1932.	1931.
Imports	...	...	...	700	577
Exports	...	...	...	438	468
Balance	...	...		− 262	− 108

On the other hand, it is to be noted that the Japanese have repaid in full the £8 million sterling loan of the South Manchurian Railway which recently fell due. The weakening of the exchange may have been due in part to the accumulation of sterling for this purpose.

II.—Lausanne and the Conversion scheme.

22. The agreement at Lausanne is the most hopeful development which has occurred since the depression began. The system of large-scale Reparations has been one of the main elements of fundamental instability in the post-war economic system, and has thus contributed in a very large degree both to the occurrence of the world economic depression and to the international financial crisis which has followed from it. As long as the Reparations problem remained unsolved, it served to block the road to any constructive international policy, and threatened to aggravate the situation further at any time by provoking a default which might have had far-reaching consequences, both financial and political. Assuming that the Lausanne Agreement is accepted by the peoples concerned, and is made effective by an amicable writing down of other war debt claims, it is fair to say that an indispensable preliminary step to world recovery has now been taken.

23. The agreement has had a marked effect in raising the prices not merely of German Bonds, but of Central European bonds generally. This implies a strengthening of international confidence which, as we shall later argue, is an essential condition of world improvement. It may prove, however, that the beneficial reactions of the agreement taken by itself will be comparatively limited. Germany has not been paying Reparations for some time past, and no one has supposed that she was likely to be called upon to pay them for a long time to come. Other factors than Reparations enter into the distrust of the financial position of Germany and Central Europe, however much Reparations may be responsible in the last analysis. These factors are not only financial but also, in part, political, including the growing internal political instability of Germany and the many sources of friction in international affairs. It seems unlikely, therefore, that the Lausanne agreement will suffice to remove this distrust. For this purpose constructive policies of international co-operation are probably essential. The main significance of the Lausanne agreement is that it clears the way for them. We deal with the opportunities that are thus opened up in a later section of our report.

24. In a different sphere, the British conversion scheme may also exert important repercussions on the general economic situation. As we have already pointed out, it is only in Great Britain that the trend of yields on Government securities has been downwards in the past twelve months. In countries with positions as strong as those of France and Holland, the prices of Government securities have been falling. Thus the general world tendency

has been that at a time when the power of capital to earn a return has been steadily declining, lenders, apprehensive of the security of even the most gilt-edged investments have been reluctant to lend unless compensated against risk by higher interest rates.

25. Before world trade can recover it is essential that this tendency should first be reversed, and the British Conversion scheme, if it achieves a marked success, may prove a decisive factor in reversing it. If the credit of the British Government can be established securely on a basis of not much more than $3\frac{1}{2}$ per cent., it seems not unlikely that investors in other countries will take a more favourable view of the securities of their own Governments, and that less money will accordingly be hoarded or kept in a very liquid form. In this way the conversion scheme, if it succeeds, may give an impetus towards lower interest rates not merely in Great Britain but in the world generally.

26. From the national standpoint it is obvious that a successful conversion scheme will be of great value both in directly relieving the budgetary position and in confirming confidence in the capacity of Great Britain to surmount her economic difficulties.

27. The immediate response of the Stock markets and of public opinion to the announcement of the conversion scheme has been all that could be desired. None the less, it would be premature as yet to attempt to judge whether the scheme will be successful. The essential criterion of success in our judgment is not the degree to which holdings of 5 per cent. War Loan are converted. There would be nothing to regret in a response which left a moderate percentage of the War Loan unconverted. This would, indeed, in our judgment be preferable in some ways to a complete conversion. In view of the prospect of conversion and the limits that existed to the possibility of capital depreciation, War Loan had for some time past assumed the character, in the eyes of financial institutions, of a semi-short-term security. The investment needs of some of the present holders of War Loan might, therefore, be best met by a new short-dated security which could be issued at a low rate of interest. On the other hand, it is important that the new War Loan should not fall to a substantial discount when the process of conversion is complete. There is, we think, a certain danger that some of the financial institutions which have been persuaded on public grounds to convert holdings of War Loan which they have hitherto regarded as a semi-short security, may endeavour to sell part of the new $3\frac{1}{2}$ per cent. Loan at an early date, thus tending to depress its price. The success of the conversion, from the standpoint of its bearing upon British Government credit and long-term rates of interest generally, cannot be said to be assured until the extent of this danger can be gauged in the light of experience.

28. The foreign exchanges represent another possible source of danger to the success of the conversion scheme. The announcement of the scheme has been followed by a general rise in the prices of British securities of a gilt-

edged character to figures at which they give low yields as compared with those which can be obtained on comparable foreign securities. Foreign holders of British securities may be tempted in these circumstances to sell them and to invest the proceeds in their own countries, and their disposition to do so will be increased in so far as the idea gains ground that the British conversion scheme marks a turning-point towards a lower level of interest rates in the world. A movement of this kind would throw some strain upon the sterling exchanges, and this strain might be greatly increased if British investors were to decide on any considerable scale that the present was a favourable time to sell some of their British securities and invest, say, in American fixed interest securities. It is important to appreciate that in this connection, as in so many others, we have to reckon with the cumulative nature of economic tendencies. A slight weakening of sterling arising from the causes mentioned, by altering prevailing ideas as to the future course of sterling, might stimulate a much larger movement.

29. For these reasons it will be some months before the success of the conversion scheme in the widest sense can be regarded as definitely established. In the meantime, the response which it has so far secured is an encouraging factor. The development of the international situation is likely to remain, however, the decisive factor in determining the course of British trade; and we turn, therefore, to examine this situation at some length.

III.—The International Financial Crisis.

30. It is generally recognised that an acute international financial crisis has been the dominating feature of the development of the world depression in the past year. It may be doubted, however, whether the full significance and implication of this phenomenon are generally appreciated.

31. The financial crisis is international, not merely in scope but in character. Its essential aspect, that is to say, is not the fact that something in the nature of an international financial crisis, or at least a widespread condition of financial apprehensiveness, exists in every country at the present time. The vital point is that the crisis is primarily one of international financial relations. The soundness, not so much of financial concerns, but of whole countries, has aroused distrust. There has followed a "run" upon those countries by the outside world, which has driven them in effect to close their doors. Distrust has then spread to other countries, believed to be heavily involved in their failure. The "run" has been transferred to them until they too have been forced to do something analogous to closing their doors. This has been the central theme of the financial story of the past twelve months—an international financial crisis, analogous to the old-fashioned financial crisis in the successive waves of distrust which it has entailed, but with the distrust directed against the whole economy of countries rather than the solvency of financial institutions.

32. An international financial crisis of this character is an essentially new phenomenon. It has happened, of course, in past depressions that countries, such as those of South America, have got into financial difficulties, that their Governments have defaulted on their external loans, that their currencies have depreciated, that their troubles have had widespread repercussions in depressing world trade as a whole, and in losses to investors in countries like Great Britain. But, in the first place, these losses were mainly a matter of the depreciation of long-term investments; there was comparatively little international short-term money to be lost or frozen. Secondly, the repercussions never entailed a serious "run" upon any important financial centre, or any distrust of its soundness. The parallel in the internal sphere to previous international financial troubles would be the bankruptcy of a number of industrial firms of some but not outstanding importance, entailing the loss by investors of the capital subscribed and some loss to the banks, but no real shock to the stability of the financial structure. In the past twelve months, on the other hand, we have witnessed a phenomenon analogous to the failure of some important banks.

33. In the light of our present experience, it seems possible that the stability of the pre-war international financial system was really more precarious than was ever realised, and it is perhaps surprising, in view of the many serious disturbances that have marked the course of international politics, that no crisis of the present character should have occurred before. It is worth recalling that the central theme of Bagehot's *Lombard Street*, that classic description of the London money market, was the latent danger of a run upon London, and the inadequacy of the then Bank Reserve as a safeguard against this danger. After pointing out that as a sequel to the Franco-German war—"London has become the sole great settling-house of exchange transactions in Europe, instead of being formerly one of two," and that foreign deposits in London had greatly increased, Bagehot continues as follows:—

"And this foreign deposit is evidently of a delicate and peculiar nature. It depends on the good opinion of foreigners, and that opinion may diminish or may change into a bad opinion. After the panic of 1866, especially after the suspension of Peel's Act (which many foreigners confound with a suspension of cash payments), a large amount of foreign money was withdrawn from London. And we may reasonably presume that in proportion as we augment the deposits of cash by foreigners in London, we augment both the chances and the disasters of a 'run' upon England.

"And if that run should happen, the bullion to meet it must be taken from the Bank. . . . .

"In consequence, all our credit system depends on the Bank of England for its security. On the wisdom of the directors of that one joint-stock company, it depends whether *England shall be solvent or insolvent*."

The italics are Bagehot's own, and they form one of the rare examples of the use of italics in the book. They may be taken as an indication of the genuine apprehensiveness of one of the shrewdest judges of financial affairs, that what happened in 1931 might have happened even sixty years ago.

34. In fact, however, the City of London passed safely through all the vicissitudes of the pre-war period, and each fresh world crisis appeared to demonstrate the strength of her position. The culminating demonstration was supplied on the outbreak of the Great War, when despite the fact that Great Britain was a belligerent, all the foreign exchanges moved strongly in her favour, owing to the fact that London's short-term claims greatly exceeded her short-term obligations. Nor was it merely that London succeeded in difficult times in maintaining her own solvency. She used to assist in maintaining solvency elsewhere by large shipments of gold to centres of financial crisis, drawing gold in her turn from centres which were not affected. The familiar descriptions of London as the world's banker indicate, that is to say, a real and important function which, until the present crisis, London never failed to discharge.

35. It is of the essence of the present world difficulties that it became impossible for London to continue to discharge that vital function, and that no other centre has been willing and able to discharge it. The developments of the post-war period had added new elements of danger, largely unperceived until the crisis arose, to the stability of the international financial structure. The large scale of Germany's borrowings from abroad since 1926, and in particular the large extent to which those borrowings took a short-term form, made natural a "run" upon Germany, when the severity of the world depression had become pronounced. The resulting failure of Germany to meet her immediate obligations meant the failure of a country far more important economically than had ever failed before, and entailed inevitable embarrassment in every financial centre. In the circumstances it was only to be expected that there should be demands on London, as the world's banker; but, owing to other post-war developments, the demand which London was liable to meet had become enormous. Largely as the sequel to the flight of capital from many European countries during the post-war inflation period, many banks on the Continent had accumulated large balances in London, which they had been persuaded to leave there in the name of international co-operation for the more economical use of gold. The "deposits of cash by foreigners in London" had thus been "augmented" to a larger order of magnitude than had sufficed to arouse the apprehensions of Bagehot. With other factors to accentuate distrust of the soundness of the British position, a "run" was directed upon London which she was unable to sustain.

36. From a purely national standpoint, the enforced departure of Great Britain from the gold standard has had many advantages. It has given a

much needed relief to our exporting industries whose competitive position in world markets was becoming desperate. It has served to maintain our local economic system for some months from further deterioration despite the deepening of the world depression. It has conferred similar advantages upon other countries which have linked their currencies with sterling. But it has also increased the consciousness of the instability of international financial relations. The psychological effect in the outside world of the fall of sterling was profound. No one has been able to feel quite confident since it happened of the security of any currency in the world; and this general lack of confidence serves to render precarious even currencies like the dollar which are impregnable against a purely external drain. This makes it impossible for the United States, and perhaps for any single country to step into the breach and to discharge the functions of a world banker by advancing money to embarrassed countries.

37. There thus exists to-day a condition of international financial distrust which reacts upon international trade in essentially the same way as an internal financial crisis reacts upon internal trade. Every country is in the position that either there has been a run upon it which it has failed to sustain or that there may at any moment come a run upon it including a flight from it by its own citizens. There may be waves of renewed confidence in particular currencies, as there has been in sterling in recent months, but no reliance can be placed in such changes of sentiment. To each country, therefore, a favourable balance of payments appears a vital necessity, just as a liquid position is essential to each financial concern in an internal crisis. If it has not got a favourable balance it must seek to create one; if it already has one it feels bound to do all it can to preserve it and to strengthen it. In these circumstances every country is reluctant to buy more than it can help from other countries, or to lend to them more than it can help; and the import prohibitions, quota schemes and the restrictions on exchange dealings which are helping to cripple international trade are the natural consequence. Huskisson declared with reference to the financial panic of 1825 that the country was within twenty-four hours of a state of barter. The reduction of international trade to a state of barter is equally inherent in a breakdown of the international financial system.

IV.—The Possibilities of constructive action.

38. In the light of the above analysis, we regard a revival of confidence in international financial relations as the fundamental condition of world recovery. Failing a growth of confidence in this sphere, we doubt if it will be possible to avoid a further deterioration in the position of international trade, and it is probably idle to hope that any particular country can secure a material improvement in its domestic economic life so long as the international position continues to degenerate. For this reason, we attach great

importance to the Lausanne agreement, and to the possibilities of further action which it opens out.

39. There may be a better prospect now or in the near future, than there has been hitherto, that deliberate efforts to bring about a recovery may be aided rather than thwarted by the normal development of the credit cycle itself. In the earlier phases of a cyclical depression, opinion is only too ready to expect the downward movement to be reversed in due course by the unaided operation of natural forces; whereas after the depression has continued for some time, all hope of such a reversal rapidly ebbs away. A point has now been reached, in our opinion, when it may be necessary to remind the world that a part of our economic troubles is due to the operation of the same kind of forces as have brought about slumps in the past. For to the extent that this is the case, the mere lapse of time will, for a variety of reasons, tend to bring a remedy. The depression on this occasion is, indeed, so violent and prolonged and its causes so complex and powerful that there may be good reason to fear lest the economic and financial system may lose its resiliency before the turn comes; and it would, therefore, be most imprudent to rely on natural forces or to relax our deliberate efforts at appeasement and stimulus. But this should not lead us to overlook the fact that a point will come, and may be near at hand, when the underlying conditions will begin to work with, rather than against, concerted plans for recovery.

40. The Lausanne agreement has already had an appreciable effect in strengthening international confidence. It would be unwise, indeed, as we have already indicated, to build large hopes on the settlement of Reparations taken by itself. The conference, however, also passed a resolution setting up a committee to consider the measures required for the restoration of the countries of central and eastern Europe and a resolution inviting the League of Nations to convoke a world conference on monetary and economic problems.

41. A scheme by which the stronger countries would co-operate in the reconstruction of the embarrassed countries of central and south-eastern Europe would contribute greatly to the restoration of international financial confidence, and so to the re-establishment of normal trading conditions. In the meantime, the announcement that such a scheme is even being contemplated should exercise a useful steadying influence. There are, however, obvious difficulties in the way of providing international assistance by means of loans to debtor countries. For it is highly probable, in view of the present position of the debtor countries, that any loans made to them will represent a case of throwing good money after bad, while on the other hand creditor countries are likely in present circumstances to be reluctant to endanger the liquidity of their international position by making loans on any substantial scale which will probably be frozen assets. Nor, indeed, would the support of particular groups of debtor countries prove an adequate remedy to the disorganisation of trade which affects the whole world.

42. To overcome these wider difficulties, it may be important, therefore,

to have recourse to constructive international action in the monetary sphere. A clue to the type of action which might be effective may be found by pursuing further the analogy of the old-fashioned internal financial crisis. In London, during the nineteenth century, a technique for allaying incipient financial panics was evolved, as the result of the teachings of experience. The cardinal principles of this technique were twofold:—

(i) That, at a time of crisis, the Bank of England should lend, not less freely, but more freely, to all borrowers who could offer security that was normally sound.

(ii) In order to make the above possible, that the Bank of England should be authorised, in case of need to issue additional notes.

43. Both the above principles were invoked in the solution of every serious financial panic in the last century. At the time of panic of 1825, which was perhaps the most serious of all, the note-issue of the Bank of England was not yet subject to any quantitative limitation; but it had been the practice of the Bank until that time to issue notes only against the security of Exchequer Bills. "We found," wrote Sir Robert Peel to the Duke of Wellington, "that the Bank had the power to lend money on deposit of goods. . . . . We advised the Bank to take the whole affair into their own hands at once, to issue their notes on the security of goods. . . . . They reluctantly consented, and rescued us from a very embarrassing predicament." Having agreed to this course, the Bank acted with decision. According to the account of Mr. Harman, "we lent money by every possible means, and in modes which we had never adopted before; we took in stock on security, we purchased Exchequer Bills, we made advances on Exchequer Bills, we not only discounted outright, but we made advances on deposits of bills of Exchange to an immense amount—in short, by every possible means consistent with the safety of the Bank." In this way the panic which, according to Huskisson, threatened to reduce the country to a state of barter, was allayed. But, of course, the Bank could not have lent with this freedom but for its power to issue notes which were legal tender. Indeed deposit-banking being then in its infancy, its advances were made for the most part in the form of notes.

44. In 1844 the Bank Act was passed which limited the fiduciary note issue of the Bank. In subsequent financial panics, however, a temporary increase in the note issue was made possible by the expedient of the "crisis letter," i.e., a letter from the Prime Minister and Chancellor of the Exchequer authorising the Bank to issue notes in excess of the legal limits and promising to obtain from Parliament the necessary indemnity. With this authority behind them, the Bank did not hesitate to lend on a scale sufficient to arrest the panic. As the century wore on, the knowledge that the Bank Act would be suspended in case of need, and that, as a consequence, harassed debtors

with good security to offer would be able to obtain advances from the Bank, sufficed to prevent panics from arising.

5. The question thus arises whether similar principles could be applied in the solution of our present international difficulties. It would be much easier to organise effective international assistance to embarrassed countries, if some means could be found of securing at least a temporary increase in the supply of the means of payment available for the discharge of international obligations, which would also serve as a safe basis for internal credit expansions. Just as a temporary increase in the supply of internal legal tender is an appropriate and essential instrument for allaying an internal financial panic, so, it may be suggested, is a temporary increase in the supply of international legal tender an appropriate and, it may prove, an essential instrument for remedying an international financial crisis. The same fundamental justification exists in both cases. A supply of internal legal tender, which may be fully adequate for the needs of the public under normal conditions of confidence, may be wholly inadequate when confidence is badly shaken and everyone in endeavouring to obtain payment of what is due to him. Similarly, a world supply of monetary gold which may be fully adequate for the needs of international trade under normal conditions of confidence may be quite inadequate under conditions of international distrust and disequilibrium such as now prevail.

6. An increase in the supply of international means of payment could be secured in a variety of ways. An international agreement to remonetise silver would, for example, have this effect. This, however, is not a proposal which we favour. The annual output of silver is not very large in relation to that of gold, and there is no reason to think that the value of the silver likely to be forthcoming from other sources would be large enough to form a substantial addition to the metallic reserves of the world's currency systems. Moreover, bimetallism, if adopted at all, would have to be adopted as a permanent change. It is therefore essentially inappropriate as a remedy for a temporary crisis; and it would do nothing to bring the supply of international means of payment under deliberate control. Finally, it would be as difficult to secure the necessary international agreement for the remonetisation of silver, as for a more constructive plan.

7. A more hopeful line of approach would be to develop the functions of the Bank for International Settlements. It might be agreed, for example, that the various Central Banks should deposit a minimum percentage of their gold reserves with the Bank for International Settlements, while agreeing to count these deposits as part of their reserves for reserve ratio requirements. The Bank for International Settlements would then be enabled, on a metallic basis, to compensate the effects of any immobilisation, sterilisation, or hoarding of gold by making advances to Central Banks, thus assisting the restoration of the international financial position. Such a conception of the functions of the Bank for International Settlements is not novel. We under-

stand that it was present in the original discussions which preceded its establishment.

48. A more powerful effect would be produced if the Bank for International Settlements were authorised to issue notes up to some definite maximum which the various Governments of the world would agree to accept as the equivalent of gold. A great variety of schemes for international reconstruction might be evolved on the basis of this principle. On the assumption that the situation may call for a large and far-reaching remedy, the following may be put forward as an example:—

(a) The Bank for International Settlements might make advances, at a very low rate of interest, or possibly free of interest, to the various Governments of the world, up to an aggregate sum of say £1,000 millions gold, this sum being distributed among them in accordance with some agreed criterion of economic importance (see paragraph 50 below). The advances could be made subject to appropriate conditions, such as the removal of restrictions on exchange dealings.

(b) To enable it to do so, the Bank for International Settlements would be authorised to issue International Certificates, declared to be the equivalent of so many grains of gold, and accepted as such by the various Governments up to the amount of the advances made.

(c) If and when the gold price level of commodities rose substantially, the advances would be gradually recalled and the issue of Certificates reduced correspondingly. It would be the object of the Bank for International Settlements, in determining the proportion of the advances to be recalled at any time, to prevent an undue rise of prices, without precipitating a recurrence of depression by an over-drastic curtailment. If any Government was unable to make immediate repayment of any sum when called upon to do so, the advance of this sum might be extended at a comparatively high rate of interest.

9. If a practicable scheme could be evolved on some such lines as these, there could be little doubt as to its helpfulness in breaking through the present international economic difficulties. It would put the debtor countries into a position to meet their international obligations; it would thus make possible the abandonment of restrictions on exchange dealings, and contribute generally to "unfreeze" the international position. At the same time, it would facilitate credit expansion in the creditor countries, and would make it easier for their Governments to increase internal purchasing power by reducing taxation, by stimulating capital expenditure, or in other ways. The fulfilment of these various purposes need not be seriously impeded by the obligation which would rest on the Governments to repay the advances in the event of a substantial rise in prices. It is the fall of prices that is mainly responsible for the present financial difficulties of Governments and debtor

countries; and it is reasonable to assume that, on the basis (say) of 1928 prices, the financial position of Governments generally would be greatly improved, and that the majority of debtor countries would be able to meet their obligations.

50. The central difficulty which would be raised by the attempt to formulate a practicable scheme along the above lines would be that of selecting a satisfactory criterion for the distribution of the advances among the various Governments. The criterion of the volume of foreign trade might be objected to by large countries as unduly favourable to small ones. The criterion of gold reserves, which would from some points of view be the most logical and appropriate, would be open to objection as unduly favourable to those countries which had contributed to the present world difficulties by accumulating large idle gold reserves. This objection might be largely met by taking as the criterion not the gold reserve which any country actually possessed, but the minimum reserve of gold or *devisen* required by its laws on some given date as the basis for the volume of currency and credit then existing. Probably the most acceptable criterion would be a complex one, which might include foreign trade and legal gold reserve minima and possibly other elements as well. The task of securing international agreement for any criterion would obviously be difficult; but it is so much to the interest of all countries to avoid a further intensification of the world depression that it should be easier to overcome this difficulty to-day than it would be in ordinary times.

51. Another point that would require careful consideration would be the possibility of default on the part of some Government either in respect of the interest due on the advance made to it or in respect of the capital when called upon to repay. Apart from some special provision, the latter would entail the consequence of the technical insolvency of the issue department of the Bank for International Settlements; and it might mean that a portion of the Certificates would continue indefinitely in existence, even though prices had risen sufficiently to make desirable their complete cancellation. This possibility might be provided against in various ways, *e.g.*, by the deposit of bonds by the Governments participating in the scheme as security for the advances received. Moreover, if a low rate of interest were charged on all the advances made, it would be appropriate to provide that the sums so received should constitute a special guarantee fund. The scheme would thus assume the character of mutual insurance.

52. Any scheme of the above type would require an alteration of the statutes of the Bank for International Settlements, and would raise further questions of practical detail into which we do not enter at this stage. We are convinced, however, that the scheme which we have outlined is technically and economically sound, and requires only the support of a sufficient number of important countries to be put into effect. But we are quite prepared to find initial scepticism on the part of particular countries which

will only be overcome by the developing psychology of an even more desperate international situation.

53. Some of the objects which the above scheme is designed to fulfil might be secured by combining schemes of financial assistance to embarrassed countries with concerted policies of credit expansion on the part of the stronger creditor countries. But though it might be easier to obtain agreement for such a policy when stated in general terms, it would probably prove in practice at least equally difficult to secure the simultaneous adoption of the measures necessary to carry even such a limited policy into effect on a scale adequate to the needs of the situation.

54. We are of opinion, therefore, that the possibility of using the medium of the Bank for International Settlements to secure a temporary increase in the international means of payment should form an important subject of discussion at the forthcoming international monetary and economic Conference. In the meantime, we recommend that the matter should be made the subject of a systematic inquiry, in which we should be prepared, if desired, to co-operate.

Fifth Report of Committee on Economic Information,
November 1932, Sections III and IV*

III.—Trade activity and financial policy.

24. To sum up our observations on sterling: we think that the future course of the exchanges must be regarded as a matter of great uncertainty, so long as the question of the December debt payment to the United States remains unsettled. But there is nothing in the exchange position to give grounds for any fundamental uneasiness. No sufficient reason remains for permitting exchange considerations to dominate our internal financial policy. Indeed, in the stage which we have now reached, minor modifications of our internal financial policy, which are not calculated to prejudice the psychological situation, would not exert any important influence on the exchanges.

25. On the other hand, our financial policy may exert in various ways an important influence on the state of trade activity. We think, therefore, that the time has come when certain aspects of our financial policy should be reviewed in the light of their bearing on the trade situation to-day.

26. The financial policy adopted last year in response to the widespread distrust of the British position had three main aspects, which it is important from the standpoint of our present argument to distinguish from one another. In the first place, it entailed the principle of a balanced budget, *i.e.*, the raising of revenue sufficient to defray all government expenditure, and the application of this principle to include expenditure on items such as

---

* P.R.O. Cab. 58/30, E.A.C. (S.C.) 5, 22 November 1932; also Cab. 24/235, C.P. 422(32).

unemployment benefit, and roads, which our previous financial arrangements had permitted to be met by borrowing. Secondly, it entailed a curtailment of programmes of public works, undertaken by the municipalities but stimulated and subsidised by the central government, the expenditure on which is met by borrowing, but which throws a burden on the local and national budgets of future years. Thirdly, it entailed reductions in current expenditure, cuts in unemployment benefit, in the pay of teachers, police, the fighting services, &c., designed to diminish the amount of taxation which it is necessary to raise in order to cover expenditure.

27.   The last of these features of our present financial policy gives rise to no question relevant to the activity of trade. In so far as the state pays out smaller sums by way of wages, salaries and benefits, but, on the other hand, takes away correspondingly smaller sums from the public by way of taxation, there is no net reduction in the aggregate purchasing power of the community, and no clear presumption that trade will be affected on balance in one direction rather than the other, provided that those who are relieved are as ready, and as able, to spend as those who suffer the cuts. The other two features of our financial policy raise, however, different considerations.

(a) Public works.

28.   The curtailment of public works programmes which are normally financed by means of loan involves a diminution in the sums paid out by public authorities without any corresponding diminution in the sums extracted from the public in the form of taxation. Except, therefore, in so far as it stimulates the undertaking of capital enterprises by ordinary industry, the curtailment of public works programmes serves to diminish the aggregate purchasing power of the community, and has an influence prejudicial to trade activity. It is possible that the curtailment of public works programmes during the last year may have contributed something to the establishment of the lower interest rates which now prevail and, theoretically, no doubt, lower interest rates should tend to encourage capital expenditure by industrial firms and by the public generally. This encouragement by itself, is insufficient under present conditions to stimulate capital expenditure on any considerable scale. Business men can hardly be expected to venture substantial sums of money on new plant merely because they can borrow the money for the purpose cheaply, so long as trade conditions are as unprofitable as they are to-day. Until, therefore, some means is found of increasing the volume of purchases by the consuming public, industry is unlikely to be stimulated to capital expenditure on any appreciable scale by lower interest rates. Moreover, even if this difficulty could be overcome, the amount which industry would be likely to expend on fixed capital would probably be of a much smaller magnitude than that involved in the reduction of public works programmes.

29. Moreover, even if it be allowed that the curtailment of public works has played an appreciable part in the past year in establishing lower rates of interest, its utility for this purpose must now be regarded as exhausted. We have already established a disparity between the rates of interest prevailing in London and those prevailing in other centres at least as great as we can hope to sustain. In these circumstances, we cannot hope to push the rate of interest still lower by curtailing public works programmes still further. Conversely, there is no reason to suppose that a relaxation of the policy of slowing down public works would react materially on interest rates at the present time. Thus, under present conditions, there are no compensating advantages to trade and employment to set against the disadvantages of the policy of curtailment.

30. The question of public works raises, however, other issues of a controversial character. In so far as they are not financially remunerative they throw a burden on the future budgets of the state and the local authorities. Throughout the post-war period the policy of pushing forward public works schemes in the interests of employment has been pursued on so large a scale that the annual burden which falls to-day on the national and local budgets in respect of the public works of preceding years is already substantial. Widespread misgivings have accordingly been aroused as to the financial soundness of a practice which thus entails a cumulative increase in budgetary burdens; and many local authorities, which include those districts in which unemployment is most serious, are to-day in a financial position in which they cannot prudently afford to incur further liabilities for the future. Moreover, the large amount of public work that has been done in the post-war period has necessarily served to diminish the opportunities remaining for schemes possessing a high degree of financial remunerativeness or quasi-commercial utility. We differ among ourselves as to the precise weight which should be attached to these considerations at the present juncture.

31. We are agreed that a point has now been reached when it is undesirable to discourage, on general financial grounds, local authorities whose financial security is not in question from undertaking work which they themselves desire to undertake without any subsidy from the Exchequer. We are further agreed that it is undesirable under present conditions to seek to hold up the completion of public works on which a large amount of money has already been spent, and the ultimate completion of which is clearly desirable. Work that must, in any case, be done one day should not be slowed down now. We regard it as important that these principles should be observed, particularly in view of the reports which we understand will shortly be published, urging fresh economy in local expenditure. Apart from works undertaken by public authorities, there are various schemes of industrial development, such as railway electrification and the hydrogenation of coal, which raise some question of government assistance or co-operation.

The fall in the rate of interest should make an important difference to the economic feasibility of such projects, and we are of opinion that it is desirable that they should now be re-examined with this point in mind. Where such schemes approximate to the character of economic propositions, we regard it as desirable that they should be pressed forward.

(b) Budgetary equilibrium.

32. We pass to the first of the three aspects of our present financial policy, that, namely, of the balanced budget. The question is one of considerable delicacy in view of the history of the past few years. The impression arising in 1931 from the publication of the May report of an enormous and rapidly-growing budget deficit was an important contributory cause of the distrust of sterling. The psychological conventions that go to make up general confidence are still attached to the maintenance of the principle of budgetary equilibrium, without reference to underlying economic issues involved.

33. There are, however, good grounds in our judgment for reconsidering the manner in which this principle has been applied. The revenue and expenditure of the modern state account for so large a proportion of the national income that the balance between what the state draws in on the one hand and pays out on the other is necessarily an important factor in determining the aggregate purchasing power of the consuming public. For the state to draw in more than has been customary by means of taxation, and to pay out less than has been customary in expenditure, is necessarily a deflationary influence, adverse to trade activity; and, though considerations of confidence may at times compel recourse to such a policy, it should not be carried further in a time of depression than considerations of confidence really justify.

(c) Unemployment insurance finance.

34. A very important item in our present public expenditure is unemployment benefit. It would be natural to expect, as one of the advantages of having placed unemployment relief on an insurance basis, with a fund separate from the ordinary Exchequer, that the fluctuations of unemployment expenditure would provide an automatic and legitimate corrective to the ups and downs of trade. If, as was the original idea, the unemployment insurance fund accumulated reserves in years when unemployment was comparatively low, and dissipated them in years when it was exceptionally high, a useful set-off would be provided to the decline in purchasing-power arising from a depression, which would help, when other influences were favourable, to promote recovery. Unfortunately, the history of the unemployment insurance fund has been such that it has tended to produce the opposite result. Under the influence of over-optimistic ideas as to the

future course of unemployment, its finances were so arranged that its expenditure tended to exceed its revenue during the years of good world trade. When the world depression began, accordingly, the unemployment insurance fund, so far from having accumulated reserves, was already loaded with a substantial debt. In the early phases of the depression, this debt grew rapidly, and eventually exceeded £100 millions. The spectacle of this growing debt contributed largely to the impression of radical financial unsoundness which prevailed in the summer of 1931. Accordingly, an integral feature of the financial policy subsequently pursued was the cessation of borrowing by the unemployment insurance fund. Thus, we are now endeavouring to defray out of current revenue at the bottom of a depression of unprecedented severity the whole expenditure on relieving a volume of unemployment which now approaches 3 millions. Expenditure on such essentially capital purposes as new road construction and the building of new Employment Exchanges is also being defrayed out of revenue, an arrangement which entails the postponement under present financial conditions of work which is urgently required. At the same time, the national budget includes a substantial provision for the sinking fund.

35. This is to go further than in our judgment is required by considerations of sound finance or by considerations of maintaining confidence. No other country attempts to-day to balance its budget in the same strict sense that we are attempting. Every other country makes provision for borrowing to meet various forms of expenditure which are regarded as abnormal. Whatever the course of employment in the immediate future may prove to be, it may be taken as reasonably certain that unemployment will fall in due course to a substantially lower level than prevails to-day, and we ought not, in our judgment, to be deterred by the past history of unjustifiably optimistic estimates to refrain from acting on this assumption. The present difficulties of the world are aggravated in various ways by the disposition of governments of many countries, in their anxiety to avoid the repetition of past and proven mistakes, to rush in to no less serious mistakes of an opposite character. To insist under present conditions on continuing to defray from current taxation the whole of our expenditure on our present unemployment, would be an excess of austerity, for which past excesses of extravagance provide no adequate justification.

36. An opportunity for reconsidering our financial policy in this respect arises in view of the publication of the report of the Royal Commission on Unemployment Insurance, and of the reconstruction of the insurance system which will presumably follow. We think it desirable that an integral feature of any such reconstruction should be to secure a balancing of revenue and expenditure on the basis of an unemployment figure high by the standards of the past, but substantially lower than that prevailing to-day, and to permit a renewal of borrowing for excess expenditure during the remainder of the depression. We do not believe that the adoption of such

a policy would serve to weaken confidence in the soundness of our national finances, while, on the other hand, it would be of material assistance to the trade position. Views very similar to these are expressed by Mr. Henry Clay in a note appended by him to the report of the Royal Commission.

(d) *The sinking fund.*

37. For similar reasons, we are of opinion that it is inexpedient to maintain a substantial sinking fund in the budget at the present time. The sinking fund means that the state is abstracting more than it is spending from the incomes of the public; and this serves necessarily to check the volume of consumption and consequently of trade activity. In this way it may serve rather to weaken than to strengthen confidence. We are satisfied that if by suspending the sinking fund, in whole or in part, it became possible to reduce taxation in the next budget, the psychological, as well as the directly economic, results would be advantageous, particularly if the reduction took a form calculated to encourage development and enterprise. The rise in the price of government securities has entailed an automatic suspension of the contractual sinking fund requirements, which would supply additional justification for a modification of sinking fund policy. The case for such a modification becomes still stronger, if a renewal of borrowing for the unemployment insurance fund is regarded as impracticable. We think it is also desirable that arrangements should be made to permit borrowing for purposes of a capital character so that urgently needed work which would be helpful to the industrial situation should not be postponed merely on account of budgetary exigencies.

(e) *Concluding observations.*

38. In making the above suggestions, we are affected by the consideration that, in order to secure a trade improvement, it is important that as many as possible of the influences on which trade activity depends should be working simultaneously in the direction of recovery. It is of little use, for example, for the state to endeavour to stimulate trade by public works or in other ways, if the prevailing monetary conditions are such as to necessitate a restricted volume of credit. Conversely, easy money conditions are apt to be ineffective if other influences such as the state of business confidence or the financial policy of the state are adverse to trade activity. We have now reached a stage when many of the conditions on which recovery depends have been established; easy money conditions prevail in the chief financial centres, the essentials of internal financial confidence have been restored, the supplies of stocks in the principal commodity markets are consistent with recovery. The most important condition which is still lacking is an easing of the difficulties of international trade and an improvement in the sphere of

international financial relations. But so far as Great Britain is concerned, we are of opinion that some modification of our present internal financial policy will also be required.

IV.—Private spending.

39. A further question seems to us worthy of consideration in this connection. The actions of the members of the public in their capacity as consumers represent a factor of great importance. It is only when the consuming public begins to increase its purchases that we can hope for a genuine trade recovery. With this consideration in mind, appeals have often been addressed to the public for "wise spending" in the interests of trade and employment. The discussion which such appeals are arousing in the press at the present moment is an indication of the influence which they might exert if they were cast in a form and backed by an authority which carried conviction. At present they encounter certain obvious resistances in the minds of the great majority of people, who with diminished incomes and a fear that their incomes may be diminished further in the near future, cannot reconcile the idea of spending freely on miscellaneous items of current expenditure with deep-seated feelings of wise conduct.

40. It is possible, however, that such appeals might be given a form and a direction which would overcome this difficulty. It is possible, for example, that a considerable response might be secured if the appeals were concentrated on expenditure of a durable nature, such as, for example, domestic equipment and the reconditioning of property. The question of an organised national appeal for expenditure of a character calculated to be of enduring benefit to the individuals undertaking it, and accompanied if possible by arrangements with the industries chiefly concerned for specially reduced prices, seems to us worthy of examination. Possible lines on which such an appeal might be based are elaborated in an independent memorandum which has been submitted to us and which we think of sufficient interest to attach as an appendix to our report. Inasmuch as such an appeal would require a considerable period of preparation, we suggest that the possibility is one which might advantageously be explored without delay.

*Sixth Report of Committee on Economic Information**

FINANCIAL POLICY, FEBRUARY 1933.

The Committee desire to elaborate in the form of a letter to you the views on trade activity and financial policy which we expressed in section III of our fifth report. We do so because we are unanimous in attaching great importance to the question at the present juncture. Whatever differences

* P.R.O. Cab. 58/30, E.A.C. (S.C.) 6, 9 February 1933; also Cab. 24/238, C.P. 34 (33).

there may be between us in our views on the wisdom of the policy that was pursued in regard to such matters as public works in the years preceding the financial crisis, or the canons which should govern policy in regard to national and local expenditure in normal circumstances, we are united in holding strongly that in the circumstances which exist to-day there is an overwhelming case and an urgent need for a modification of our present financial policy in the directions which we have indicated in our fifth report. In order to bring out clearly the considerations which carry decisive weight in our minds in regard to this issue, we think it desirable to distinguish the present phase of the problem from other phases, even though this means dealing with matters upon which there are certain differences of opinion among ourselves.

2. The period from the stabilization of European currencies in the middle 'twenties until the beginning of the depression in 1929 was a period of good world trade. The period represented, that is to say, the upward phase of the ordinary cycle of fluctuations of business activity; and the heavy unemployment which existed in Great Britain during those years was not attributable to trade depression in the ordinary sense, but to special national difficulties. The essence of these difficulties was the loss of overseas markets by many exporting industries, arising from a variety of causes, including the return to the gold standard at a parity which left British costs of production unduly high for successful competition in world markets.

3. The beginning of the world depression in 1929 coincided with an intensified effort to stimulate schemes of public work. If the depression had been a comparatively mild one in the outside world, it is possible that the public works might have played an important part in diminishing the force of its impact on Great Britain, and possibly in promoting an early recovery. But the depression was in fact far too severe to be held in check by such means; forces of cumulative deterioration were soon established which were bound to run their course before recovery was possible; and, so long as they were in operation, the undertaking of public works, though serving to diminish for the time being the numbers of the unemployed, was necessarily impotent to reverse the trend of trade. On the other hand, it contributed something to weaken the position of Great Britain at two vulnerable points, those, namely, of the soundness of the public finances and of the balance of trade, and may thus have impaired our power to sustain the ensuing financial crisis.

4. However this may be, when the financial crisis occurred in the summer of 1931, it became, in the opinion of most of us, imperative to pursue a policy which made the restoration of financial confidence the paramount consideration. It is never easy to assess the reality of a danger that has been averted; and we do not, therefore, attempt to discuss whether anything in the nature of a débâcle of sterling would have been a serious possibility, if a different financial policy had been pursued. It is sufficient to say that an essential

pre-requisite of the recovery of trade from the depths of a depression is always the establishment of a low level of short-term money rates and long-term interest rates; and this objective could not have been secured unless both the world of international finance and the home investing public had been reassured as to the determination of the British Government to put its own financial house in order.

5. It is, however, one of the dangers of a reorientation of financial policy, whether in the direction of increased expenditure or of economy, that the policy is apt to be continued, and indeed in its actual application to gain an increasing momentum, after the circumstances which rendered it appropriate have passed away. That in our judgment is the present position.

6. The change that has taken place in the past eighteen months in the economic circumstances that are relevant to financial policy is so radical as to amount to a complete transformation. Financial confidence has been re-established, and the credit of the British Government stands higher to-day than that of any other Government. By the conversion scheme of last summer, Great Britain has taken the lead in the movement towards lower interest rates throughout the world. A very large improvement has been effected in the figures of the balance of trade; and beneath the vicissitudes connected with such factors as the American debt situation, sterling has developed an underlying strength which seems likely to continue and may even prove embarrassing. The competitive position of our industries in world markets has been greatly improved by the lower value of the pound. Thus those arguments for economy which rested on special weaknesses of our national position have now entirely lost their force. Great Britain is once more in the unquestioned position of a strong financial country.

7. But that is not all. We have now reached a phase of the world depression when the underlying economic conditions, which until recent months were adverse, may be helpful to the possibility of gradual recovery. The decline in consumption is no longer tending in general to outstrip the decline in production. The business world is no longer dominated by the fear of impending catastrophes which must exert far-reaching repercussions. In Great Britain, there are already signs that the ease of money and lower interest rates are beginning to stimulate certain classes of constructional activity.

8. Now, therefore, is the time when, in accordance with the traditional precepts of trade cycle theory, it would be most useful to apply the stimulus of increased development activity by public authorities. For, while in the early phases of depression a moderate expenditure on public works may prove an essentially futile resistance to the strength of the forces of deterioration, a comparatively modest expenditure, representing a net addition to the demand for goods and services, may suffice at such a juncture as the present to enable the forces of recuperation to gain the upper hand.

9. Yet it is precisely at this juncture that the economy policy is operating at its maximum effect. In the national budget we are attempting to defray

out of current revenue various types of expenditure which were previously met by borrowing. The policy of discouraging the development activities of local authorities naturally produces an increasing effect for a considerable time, since old schemes are gradually completed and new schemes are not commenced. The capital expenditure of local authorities is thus undergoing a continuous reduction big enough to be a material factor in the general state of trade. Indeed, we believe that it will be found upon detailed and specific inquiry that in the decline in the aggregate volume of bank advances in the past year the repayment of advances by local and other public authorities is the most conspicuous category. The operation of sinking funds for past loans on the one hand, coupled with the diminution of fresh borrowing on the other, is producing a state of affairs where at the bottom of the depression the net indebtedness of local authorities is in some areas actually falling. A further reduction in the expenditure of local authorities must be expected as a consequence of the new housing policy set out in the Housing Bill. We offer no opinion on the merits of this policy, but it is important to bear in mind that the expenditure of local authorities on housing during the next year or more will almost certainly show a big reduction on the figures of recent years.

10.   So far, therefore, from supplying a positive stimulus to trade recovery, the effect of the present policy in regard to national and local expenditure is to contribute a definitely adverse influence to the trade situation. Indeed, the main reason for doubting whether the present year will witness an important forward trade movement in Great Britain is the possibility that the diminished volume of activity by public authorities may counterbalance the effects of increased constructional activity in other fields. At the critical phase of the trade depression which we have now reached this is an extremely unfortunate state of things; and there is a strong case for a modification of policy which would permit a larger volume of capital expenditure by public authorities.

11.   Moreover, in the circumstances which exist to-day a considerable expansion of development activity might be permitted, we believe, without entailing any net addition, indeed with some actual relief, to budgetary burdens. The cost of maintaining unemployment represents, it must always be remembered, a heavy charge upon public funds. The undertaking of any work which absorbs in employment workers who would otherwise have drawn unemployment pay or poor relief entails, therefore, a saving of public expenditure under these headings; while the public finances further benefit in such indirect ways as the income-tax collected on the profits of the contractors and the customs or excise on the dutiable commodities purchased by the workers from their wages. Such gains are much larger than is generally appreciated, and in times like the present, when there is an abundant supply of capital available for investment, so that no possibility exists that the public work may divert capital from industrial use, we believe

that these gains suffice to outweigh any direct charge upon public funds except in the case of work the greater part of which must be borne by Exchequer subsidies. But much development work is being disallowed or discouraged at the present time in regard to which there is no question of any subsidy from the Exchequer; and in such cases the national finances would undoubtedly benefit if the work were to be put in hand. It is important to appreciate vividly that whenever a local authority is discouraged from applying for loan sanction for a scheme for which it asks for no Exchequer subsidy, a substantial burden in the forms of increased expenditure and loss of revenue equivalent to not less than one-quarter, and perhaps to one-half, of the cost of the scheme in question is thereby imposed upon the national finances.

12. It was in the light of these considerations that we urged in our Fifth Report that "a point has now been reached when it is undesirable to discourage, on general financial grounds, local authorities whose financial security is not in question from undertaking work which they themselves desire to undertake without any subsidy from the Exchequer." It is impossible to estimate with any precision the amount of work which is now held in abeyance, but which might be put in hand if this principle were acted on. But we think it well to observe that the extent of the work in question cannot be gauged by a reference to the figures of the actual applications for loan sanction that have been refused, for the impression prevails widely that it is contrary to the policy of the Government to countenance schemes of capital expenditure at the present time for which no plea of special urgency can be advanced, and this impression deters local authorities from bringing their projects to the stage of a formal application.

13. In the case of works the cost of which must be defrayed wholly or largely by the Exchequer, the most urgent need is a modification of the rigid embargo on borrowing which, we understand, prevails to-day. We urged in our Fifth Report that "it is undesirable under present conditions to seek to hold up the completion of public works on which a large amount of money has already been spent, and the ultimate completion of which is clearly desirable." An obvious example of work of this character is furnished by some of the unfinished by-passes round congested urban areas. No one questions that they should one day be completed. The difficulty in completing them is that under the financial rules which obtain the cost of their completion must be defrayed from the annual revenue of the Road Fund, which has no margin to spare, or else from the revenue raised by national taxation. The obvious objections to any further increase of taxation at the present time are so cogent that this limitation constitutes a powerful obstacle to the completion of even the most urgently needed by-passes. Thus the present arrangements entail the paradox that the completion of thoroughly desirable public work has to wait on an easing of the budgetary position, which means in effect waiting on a recovery of trade, although it is

precisely when trade is at its worst that it would be most advantageous to undertake it. It is for this reason that we urged in our fifth report "that arrangements should be made to permit borrowing for purposes of a capital character so that urgently needed work which would be helpful to the industrial situation should not be postponed merely on account of budgetary exigencies."

14. We desire to make it clear that the views we have expressed can be accepted without prejudice to the question of the considerations which should govern long-term policy in regard to national and local expenditure. We do not discuss how far the lower birthrate, which is the outstanding social phenomenon of the present century, may make it desirable to pursue a more cautious financial policy in certain respects than was customary in the past. But considerations of this character do not weaken the force of our present argument. Our essential contention is that, just as the restoration of financial confidence was made the governing consideration in our financial policy eighteen months ago, the restoration of trade activity should be made the governing consideration at the present time. If this principle is accepted, we are satisfied that it can be applied in ways which will neither endanger the renewed confidence in the financial stability of the country, nor conflict with the requirements of a far-sighted policy for the future. Finally, we cannot too strongly press our views as to the gravity of proceeding on the present lines without modification.

Thirteenth Report of Committee on Economic Information,
October 1934*

THE CO-ORDINATION OF TRADE POLICY.

1. Introductory.

THE economic development of Great Britain in the Victorian age was based in a peculiar degree on overseas trade and overseas investment. The heavy industries, coal, iron and steel, engineering and ship building, textile industries, such as cotton and wool, and such services as shipping and finance, all depended largely, and some preponderantly, on export and international trade; and these were the activities which expanded most rapidly, and which came to be regarded as the characteristic expressions of our economic life. So much was this so, that the growth of industries catering primarily for the home market bore the appearance of being a mere by-product of the growth of our overseas trade. Although in the last few decades before the war the competition of other industrial countries was becoming a subject of increasing concern, the volume of our overseas trade continued to expand right up to the war.

2. The development of our export trade was closely associated with

* P.R.O. Cab. 58/30, E.A.C. (S.C.) 15, 23 October 1934; also Cab. 24/251, C.P. 284(34).

overseas investment and emigration. A substantial part of the annual savings of the British public was invested in the development of the productive resources of remote continents, especially of the countries of the new world; and the flow of capital to the new world went hand in hand with migration on a large scale from Great Britain and other European countries. The economic intercourse which was thus developed was mutually advantageous in a high degree. It enabled the new countries to obtain both the capital equipment which was essential to the development of their resources, and the industrial products which were essential for maintaining their people in civilised conditions, neither of which they could have supplied for themselves economically or on a sufficient scale. Equally, it enabled Great Britain to obtain abundant supplies of food for her growing population and abundant supplies of raw materials for her growing manufactures, which she could not have produced at home at any reasonable cost. Again, in the nineteenth century, the migration of capital and population was advantageous to everyone concerned. The migrants who settled overseas and the savings that were invested in the development of new countries both earned, as a rule, a higher reward than they could have obtained if they had stayed at home, and their movement enabled the labour and capital which did remain at home to earn a higher reward also.

3. The process of developing the new world with the capital, population and industrial products of the old was indeed one of the outstanding features of the economic life of the Victorian age. In this process, Great Britain played, on the side of the old world, the leading part, having for a considerable period no serious competition, and it was to this fact that the rapidity of her economic progress was largely attributable. The growth of British export trade was not, of course, confined to the new world, but extended to every market. It was, however, in the trade with young and rapidly growing countries that the advantages of an international division of labour were most conspicuous.

4. The rapid growth of overseas trade was associated with the pursuit by Great Britain of a free trade policy. For a considerable period after the repeal of the corn laws, the wisdom of this policy was not seriously questioned; for, owing to our industrial pre-eminence, practically no British industry, as distinct from agriculture, suffered seriously from foreign competition in the home market. As other countries became formidable industrial competitors, while showing no disposition to imitate our free trade example, the wisdom of this policy came to be the subject of acute internal controversy. But the vital importance to Great Britain of a large and developing overseas trade was not called in question. Pre-war fiscal controversy was concerned largely with the best means of promoting this objective in a world of growing tariffs.

5. The position which our overseas trade had reached before the war was as follows: Our imports, for the average of the four pre-war years 1910–13,

amounted, after deducting re-exports, to £611 millions per annum. Our exports of commodities for the same period amounted to £474 millions per annum, leaving a visible import surplus of £137 millions. But our exports of services (*i.e.*, the net receipts due to us in respect of shipping freights, financial commissions, &c.) had reached an annual figure of appreciably over £100 millions. Thus our exports of goods and services together nearly sufficed to pay for our imports. In addition, we received a large annual income, as interest, dividends, &c., upon our overseas investments, amounting to about £200 millions. This gave us a large credit balance of not much short of £200 millions, available and used for fresh overseas investment. These figures relate, of course, to a period of active world trade. In the difficult years of the nineties, the average margin available for fresh overseas investment was for a long time less than £30 millions, and our foreign lending was upon a very reduced scale. In effect, the variations in our volume of overseas lending served as an adjusting factor in our balance of payments. In a period of world depression, the consequential decline in our exports and shipping receipts went hand in hand with a diminished flow of fresh overseas investment, so that our imports of food-stuffs were maintained without disturbance. Conversely, in times of good world trade, the favourable balance of payments accruing from a rapid expansion of our exports was adjusted without disturbance by an increase in overseas lending.

6.   In the post-war decade our exports were seriously curtailed. Although owing to the rise in prices, their value was larger than before the war, their volume according to the Board of Trade estimate, never reached more than about 83 per cent. (in the best year, 1929) of the pre-war volume. Moreover, although in the last half of the decade, international trade was growing fairly rapidly in the world as a whole, the degree of resilience displayed by British exports was comparatively disappointing. The unemployment of the post-war period was mainly attributable to the loss of export trade which was concentrated on the old-established industries such as coal and cotton. Meanwhile, the volume of our imports rose to a higher level than before the war and continued to grow steadily. Accordingly, our balance of trade became more adverse, despite the fact that the "terms of trade" moved in our favour, *i.e.*, that the prices of the goods we exported rose more than the price of our imports. The following was the position for the average of the years 1925–29:—

	£ millions.
Retained imports	1,124
Exports	727
Visible adverse balance	397
Net receipts from services (shipping, finance, Government receipts, &c.)	213
Net income from overseas investments	250

This left a credit balance available for fresh overseas investment of well under £100 millions on the average, as compared with nearly £200 millions before the war, despite the fall which had taken place in the value of money. This might have been an adequate margin if the period had been one of stagnant world trade with comparatively small demands from overseas upon the British capital market. In fact, however, world trade expanded during these years, and international lending assumed abnormally large dimensions. In these circumstances, with the machinery of the City of London equipped for lending on the larger pre-war scale, there was a prevailing tendency for our overseas loans to exceed the credit margin available for the purpose, the balance being rectified for the time being by what was in effect short-term borrowing, represented by the accumulation of foreign short-term balances in London. This caused a latent weakness in our exchange position which assumed serious importance in the ensuing slump.

7. The slump led quickly to a further serious fall in the volume of British exports, and also in our receipts from services such as shipping and finance. Our imports though they declined largely in value owing to the fall in prices fell comparatively little in volume; and before long our adverse balance of trade grew to such dimensions that a serious debit balance on international account was substituted for the credit balance which we had hitherto enjoyed. The following figures give the picture for the years of the depression:—

Table 1.

The balance of payments.

(£ *millions*)

—	1930.	1931.	1932.	1933.
Retained imports	966	806	658	637
Exports	579	397	371	372
Visible adverse balance	386	408	287	264
Net receipts from services, &c.... ...	194	134	86	105
Net income from overseas investments	220	170	145	155
Credit (+) or debit (−) balance (apart from gold movements)	+ 28	− 104	− 56	− 4

8. The adverse balance of payments was an important factor in the circumstances which led to the fall of the pound in 1931; and to rectify it became for a considerable period the leading preoccupation of our economic policy. This preoccupation supplied the final impulse to the abandonment of the policy of Free Trade, which had already been qualified in the post-war

decade, for example, by the McKenna and Safeguarding duties, and by small concessions of imperial preference. Various other considerations, however, contributed to the same result. The difficulties experienced in balancing the Budget despite very high rates of direct taxation, strengthened the argument against neglecting the revenue to be obtained from the extended system of import duties. Foreign competition was making serious inroads into the home markets of a growing range of British industries, giving rise to much unemployment which could be prevented by the adoption of protection. The difficulties experienced by British industries in holding their own in world markets strengthened the attraction of the idea of securing our position in Empire markets by developing the system of imperial preference. The growing complexity and subdivision of the tariff schedules of the other countries strengthened the possibility that we might be able to secure more favourable tariff treatment for our exports, if we had tariffs of our own to bargain with, than by relying solely on the most-favoured-nation clause. Finally, the tremendous fall in the world prices of many commodities made it evident that important sections of our economic life might be threatened with ruin if they were left entirely at the mercy of abnormal and unregulated competition from abroad. This consideration applied especially to agriculture; and its importance grew in the period following the abandonment of the Free Trade system. This gave rise to the idea of controlling imports in the interests of order and stability, an idea which derived support from the growing popularity of the slogan of "planning."

9. Thus the commercial policy which has been evolved in the last three years has been directed to the promotion of the following distinct objectives:—

(1) The improvement of our balance of trade.
(2) Revenue.
(3) The increase of employment by securing the home production of goods previously imported.
(4) Economic co-operation within the Empire.
(5) The strengthening of our position for bargaining with other countries for the reduction of their tariffs and other restrictions upon British goods.
(6) Safeguarding the stability of British industry and agriculture against the vicissitudes of world fluctuations.

10. Starting as we did from an essentially free trade position, there was for a time no serious conflict between these various objectives. But there are obvious possibilities of conflict when the measures adopted for one or other of these purposes are pushed beyond a certain point. The object of this report is to consider these possible conflicts, and to suggest the principles which should govern policy in reconciling them. In attempting this task,

we think it desirable to confine ourselves, so far as possible, to considerations of the broadest and most general character. We do not attempt to pass judgment upon the merits of the detailed measures which have been adopted in different fields; and we have therefore obtained no information from those responsible for the conduct of such measures. We regard it as our function to formulate as clearly as possible certain broad principles which, in our judgment, have a vital bearing upon the problems of commercial policy, and to indicate the criteria which should be used in applying them to particular cases, leaving it to others to work our their application.

2. The changing international background.

11. In order to view the problems that arise in their true perspective, it is desirable in the first place to appreciate certain fundamentally important changes which are taking place in the conditions which constitute the background of international trade. Everyone is aware that the forces of economic nationalism are in the ascendant throughout the world; and that a tendency prevails, seriously intensified for the time being by the circumstances of the depression, towards the heightening of tariff barriers and the creation of fresh obstacles to international trade. Equally familiar is the fact that the position of semi-monopoly as an exporter of industrial goods which Great Britain enjoyed in the early Victorian period has disappeared, and also the likelihood that the competition to which our industries are exposed in world markets is likely to become increasingly severe as the process of industrialization spreads throughout the world. But, to appreciate the full significance of these tendencies, it is necessary to take account of another change, more fundamental in character and of the broadest secular significance.

12. This is the fall in birth-rates which has occurred in the past two generations in Great Britain and other western countries, and is spreading rapidly throughout the western world. Already this has served to reduce the annual growth of population in Great Britain to a low figure. The flow of migration from Great Britain to the countries of the new world had also largely declined even before the world slump began. The check to emigration up to the present is mainly attributable to other causes than the decline in the British birth-rate. But the trend of our population figures makes it difficult to suppose that the pre-war process of large-scale migration would revive, even if the other obstacles were overcome.

13. For the fact that the aggregate population of Great Britain is still upon the increase obscures recognition of the virtually inevitable prospect that it will decline before long with considerable rapidity. This statement, it should be observed, does not rest upon any assumption that the average size of families will be still further restricted, though it seems possible that this may occur. The factor of age composition interposes a long time-lag between the establishment of fertility rates, incapable of maintaining the

population, and the actual decline of aggregate numbers. The number of children born in Great Britain still slightly exceeds the number of persons who die, because the aged persons, of whom the latter is largely composed, were born in days when our births were still far below their maximum annual total, which was reached about the turn of the century. But the number of babies born each year is already less than the number of persons of, say, between thirty and thirty-one years of age; so that even if none of the former were to die in the meantime, there will necessarily be fewer persons of the latter age in thirty years' time than there are to-day. In other and technical language, the gross reproduction rate of Great Britain is actually below unity. Still more so the net reproduction rate, which takes account of the probable mortality. The position may be expressed by saying that, for every four adults now alive in a particular age-group, we can only expect three a generation hence from the children now being born.

14. It may be useful to indicate the striking nature of the impending decline of our population, by reproducing part of a calculation in a recent number of the *Sociological Review*.★ This calculation yields the following result:—

Table 2.

Estimated future population of Great Britain.

(In hundreds.)

Ages.	1931.	1936.	1941.	1946.	1951.	1956.	1966.	1976.
0–15	10,840,6	10,067,1	8,791,3	7,610,7	6,621,2	5,917,9	5,048,2	4,106,1
15–45	21,052,6	21,356,5	21,633,0	21,221,4	20,219,4	18,693,8	15,261,4	11,962,2
45–65	9,730,0	10,080,7	10,288,9	10,550,4	11,061,3	11,688,0	11,953,0	10,914,7
65+	3,210,3	3,639,8	4,126,6	4,507,6	4,770,0	4,893,9	5,259,1	5,728,9
Total	... 44,833,5	45,144,1	44,839,8	43,890,1	42,671,9	41,193,6	37,521,7	32,711,9

Thus, according to this calculation, our population is likely to fall by more than a quarter in little more than forty years from now, and, indeed, the population under 45 by more than a half. Indeed, only a decided and early reversal of the present trend towards smaller families can prevent a very substantial decline.

15. This phenomenon is by no means peculiar to Great Britain. While the fall of the birth-rate has gone somewhat further in Great Britain and the net reproduction rate has sunk somewhat lower than perhaps in any other country, the position is broadly the same throughout practically the whole of western civilisation. The following table is taken from Kuczynski's *The Balance of Births and Deaths.*

★ See Leybourne, G. C., April 1934, the *Sociological Review* **26** (2): 130–138. The estimates of population in this paper are made on the assumptions that: (*a*) fertility rates will continue to decline till 1944 and then stabilise; (*b*) mortality rates will remain as at present; (*c*) there is no migration.

Table 3.

Net reproduction rate in western and northern Europe.

Country.	1925.	1926.	1927.
Denmark	1·19	1·10	1·03
England and Wales ...	1·05	0·88	0·82
Finland	1·15	1·09	...
France	0·94	0·94	0·91
Germany	0·94	0·89	0·83
Sweden	...	0·95	...

Thus the reproduction rates of Germany, France, and Sweden, like our own, had fallen, by 1927 or earlier, below unity, *i.e.*, below the level that would suffice to reproduce the existing population. Since the fall of birth-rates has continued steadily since 1927, it is probable that the same is now true of Denmark and Finland. The position in the United States and throughout the British Dominions (apart from the French-speaking section of Canada) is not materially different. Even in countries like Italy, where the net reproduction rate still remains well above unity, it is falling with a rapidity which suggests that this condition may prove short-lived. In contrast, there is no clear sign that any similar tendencies have begun as yet to affect the East; while in Japan the population is increasing at a rate comparable with that of Great Britain in the Victorian age, and is certain to continue to increase rapidly for a considerable period to come.

16. We are thus faced, in the fall of the birth-rate in western countries, with a phenomenon of secular importance and of international scope, the consequences of which are as yet only in an early stage of their development. In connection with almost every branch of policy, it is important to adjust our minds to the repercussions which this fundamental change is certain to exert. It may serve in many ways to increase the possibilities of a higher standard of living. But in this report, we are concerned only with the bearing of the decline of population upon the future of international trade and international economic life.

17. In the first place, we must expect that the further extension of the international division of labour between the old world and the new, along the lines of exchanging the industrial products of the former for the primary products of the latter, which played, as was indicated in paragraphs 1–3, a central part in our development in the Victorian era, will in future be greatly retarded. With our population already virtually stationary and destined shortly to decline, the market which Great Britain provides for primary products from overseas cannot continue to show that capacity for steady and rapid expansion which the newer countries, and in particular the Dominions, have hitherto taken for granted as the basis of all their projects for development. It is true that the consumptive power per head of the British

people may be expected to grow, with the improvement in the standard of living which will come from further technological progress. But as people become better-off, they usually spend only a small part of their additional incomes upon articles of food, while the increase in their consumption of commodities of any kind is usually less in proportion than the increase in their consumption of services, which create a relatively small demand for raw materials. Until our population begins actually to decline, the growth in incomes per head may be expected, of course, to keep our aggregate consumption of primary products upon the increase; and this increase may well be considerable in the years that lie immediately ahead as we recover from the world depression.

18. Apart, however, from the ups and downs associated with trade fluctuations, the rate of increase in the British consumption of primary products will almost certainly prove from now on, far smaller than it used to be, and may disappear altogether a couple of decades hence. Much the same may be expected to hold true of the consumption of western industrial countries as a whole. It is, of course, possible that a largely increased consumption of primary products might come from the populations of the Far East, particularly if conditions were established which permitted the development of a higher and more varied standard of life among eastern peoples. Subject, however, to this possibility, the outlook which confronts the newer countries as regard the markets for their primary products is unpromising. Meanwhile, the progress of agricultural technique is steadily reducing the number of persons required to produce a given volume of primary products; so that the newer countries are likely to find it increasingly difficult to maintain the number of their people engaged in primary production. Furthermore, the trend of population in Western Europe makes it extremely unlikely that large-scale emigration to the new world will revive. Moreover, with low birth-rates of their own in many cases, with immigration curtailed, and with difficult problems of economic adjustment to face, the new countries are unlikely to provide attractive outlets for the investment of capital from overseas on anything approaching the pre-war scale.

19. Secondly, the revolutionary change in the population outlook, however advantageous it may prove in other ways, gives reason to fear that disturbances of world prices may in future be more serious and more prolonged than they used to be. A temporary condition of over-production of certain commodities occurred often enough in the last century, and might give rise to serious setback, trouble and loss. But when the trend of population was strongly upwards and when accordingly the number of persons throughout the world, who constituted the effective market for each particular commodity, was increasing rapidly from year to year, the condition of over-production was necessarily transient. Demand was soon raised by its strong secular growth until it caught up with productive capacity, and this helped to set limits to the fall in prices which the temporary state of

over-production entailed. But there is no similar inevitable relief from the side of demand when the number of consumers is stationary or declining. The demand for a particular commodity may or may not possess a secular growth, according as it is a commodity upon which people, as they become better off, spend a large or a small portion of the increase in their incomes. If there is no considerable upward trend of demand, equilibrium can only be restored, once a condition of over production has been reached, by the permanent curtailment of productive capacity. But this is always an extremely difficult process, and in many cases, notably in that of primary products, an extremely slow one. For, as the present depression has illustrated, the producers of primary commodities are apt, when their selling prices have fallen disastrously, to endeavour desperately to increase their incomes by increasing the volume of their production.

20. This consideration serves to emphasise the sixth of the objectives which we enumerated in paragraph 9, that, namely, of securing a measure of stability to established economic interests in face of the vicissitudes of world markets. At first sight this has the appearance of an exceptional and short-period necessity, attributable to a quite abnormal economic crisis. But it may well prove that crises of comparable severity will recur frequently in future; so that it may be desirable that we should evolve permanent arrangements for dealing with such emergencies as they occur.

3. The export trade.

21. It follows from the analysis of the preceding section that the future outlook for our export trade is far from promising. For the time being, it is faced with all the difficulties resulting from the multiplication of trade obstacles throughout the world, with the result that the volume of our exports in 1933 was only 64 per cent. of the volume of 1929 and only 53 per cent. of the volume of 1913. While there has been a slight recovery in our export volume in the past year, it has been very slight, in marked contrast with the substantial degree of recovery that has been effected in our domestic trade.

22. Nor perhaps is the outlook very much brighter when we look somewhat further ahead. Owing to the depression, the volume of world trade has sunk well below the level which may be anticipated in a period of greater activity, and even if, as seems probable, there is no very speedy or substantial relaxation of the trade obstacles which have been set up in the last few years, the volume of world trade will expand as activity revives. British exporters, however, may not share in this increase to its full extent. For our competitive position, *vis-à-vis* other industrial countries, has been perhaps exceptionally favourable in recent years, owing to the fact that sterling has fallen while many of our principal competitors in Europe have remained on gold. It is possible that these countries may in the comparatively near future decide on devaluation, with the result that another obstacle would be thrown in the

way of our exports to them, while competition in neutral markets would be intensified. Thus against the recovery in the volume of international trade which may be expected to ensue from an improvement in the world situation, we have to set a disappearance of the comparatively favourable competitive position which we enjoy at present.

23. Most of the difficulties which hampered our staple export trades in the last decade still remain. The demand for British coal has been permanently reduced by the development of competing coal fields and competing sources of power. Many textile industries are already suffering from the competition of Asiatic producers, and this is likely to be soon extended into fields which have hitherto escaped. Moreover, behind these detailed facts there lie the broad considerations which were dealt with in the preceding section, namely, that we have lost the position of quasi-monopoly as an industrial exporter which we enjoyed in the nineteenth century, and that the process of extending the division of labour between the new world and the old is approaching a phase of exhaustion. These considerations cloud especially the outlook for the old-established exporting industries.

24. British economic life has adapted itself to the heavy loss of export trade with a degree of success that would have been deemed incredible before the loss occurred. In pre-war days, it would have been regarded as out of the question that Great Britain, with her dependence on imported food, with the pride of place in her industrial life attaching to such industries as coal and cotton, with her pre-eminence in shipping, with the City of London largely concerned with the finance of international trade, could lose not far short of one-half of her export trade and remain a prosperous country. Yet, in fact, since 1913 we have succeeded in maintaining a standard of life, which is probably to-day, upon the whole, about as high as it has ever been, and, in absorbing in employment the greater part of the annual increase, which up to date has been substantial, in the population of working age. Indeed, heavy as our unemployment is, we stand out once more to-day, despite our loss of export markets, as clearly the most prosperous of the principal countries of the world.

25. This experience has given rise not unnaturally to a disposition to question whether the development of exports is so important or even so desirable as used to be assumed. We think it well, therefore, to consider objectively how far the interests of Britain are really dependent on international trade, taking account first of the reasons that can be urged on the side of scepticism.

26. The progress of science, it is sometimes argued, and the spreading of industrial methods and aptitudes throughout the world, are tending more and more to reduce the advantages of international specialisation. Increasingly, international trade, if unimpeded by tariff or other obstacles, takes the form of the importation by one country of goods which it could produce at home almost as efficiently, and perhaps, after a brief interval,

quite as efficiently as the country from which it obtains them, in exchange for goods for the production of which it has again no very marked or inherent superiority. The mutual benefit derived from such exchanges is inconsiderable; the curtailment of international trade of this character need entail, therefore, no very serious loss.

27. On the other hand, the argument proceeds, it may entail a substantial gain under the heading of stability. For the conduct of international trade is exposed to the perpetual menace of disturbance. In proportion as a country engages in foreign trade, it hazards the fortunes of its industries, the employment of its workpeople, the general stability of its economic life, on the conditions and the policies pursued in other countries. It may be seriously injured, for example, by the sudden raising of tariffs or by an exchange crisis in some country abroad. The more extended is its international trade, the more vulnerable does it become to vicissitudes over which it can have no control.

28. Again, it is argued that, in so far as the export trade of a country is attributable to the making of foreign loans or investments, the trade may prove to be bad business for the country as a whole, if the borrowers subsequently default or the investments prove unprofitable. Upon this point, it should be observed that, contrary perhaps to the prevailing impression, the experience of the present slump affords little ground for anticipating such a result. Hitherto defaults on foreign loans have reached only small proportions, and the investors who placed their money abroad have probably on the average suffered no greater diminution of income than they would have done had they invested it at home.

29. There is in our judgement a considerable measure of force in these arguments. It would, we believe, be bad policy to subordinate every other consideration to the pursuit of the goal of the maximum possible volume of export trade. Our essential interests can probably be adequately secured by a volume of exports materially smaller in relation to our total production than we were accustomed to maintain in pre-war days.

30. But there are various reasons why we are convinced that the maintenance of a large-scale export trade is vital to our national prosperity. In the first place, large imports of food-stuffs and raw materials are essential to us, unless we are ready to accept a much lower standard of living. Nor can we expect to continue to obtain these food-stuffs and raw materials indefinitely at the low prices which have prevailed in recent years. In paragraph 7 above, there are set out the Board of Trade figures of the balance of payments for the years of the depression. These figures show that even in 1933 we had a small debit balance on international income account despite the facts that the prices of the goods we import have fallen much more than those of the goods we export and that our imports of such manufactured goods as we could easily produce at home have been drastically curtailed by protective measures. Moreover, it remains true that many

countries need the assistance of foreign capital for their development, and that Great Britain has a large annual volume of savings from which this need could be satisfied with advantage to this country. For this and other reasons, it is desirable to contemplate a resumption of overseas investment as more normal conditions return, though doubtless on a much smaller scale than formerly. For this purpose, we shall need to maintain a credit margin on the balance of payments. Accordingly, a substantial recovery in the volume of British exports is likely to prove essential in the long run, if we are to avoid exchange difficulties.

31. Secondly, as the result of our development in the nineteenth century, our economic life is still specialised in a large degree in occupations connected with export. Many of the industries which are most dependent on export are highly localised in character, so that to transfer their workpeople to other occupations represents a task of peculiar difficulty. Considerable progress was in fact made in the twenties in developing compensatory avenues of employment, as is indicated by the figures in table 5 below. But the obstinate continuance of large-scale unemployment during this period, and the emergence of the phenomenon of the distressed areas, show how formidable will be our problems of adjustment, if the exports of the staple exporting industries should fail to display any resilience as the depression passes away.

32. Moreover, for many of the occupations which are associated with export and international trade, we are peculiarly well-fitted by reason partly of long-established organisation and partly of inherent advantage. Our geographical position as an island at the door of Europe, with excellent harbours, and with abundant coal-supplies located near the coast, remains an asset of substantial value for international trade in general, and makes natural and appropriate our long-established pre-eminence in shipping and shipbuilding. The prestige of London as an international financial centre represents the result of the evolution of centuries, in which our assured political stability and the advantages of our national character have played an essential part. Our political position as the centre of a world-wide Empire supplies us in important markets with a valuable measure of good-will. These are all advantages which we should endeavour to utilise and exploit. Great Britain is the last country which could wisely pursue a policy looking in the direction of self-sufficiency or autarky.

33. For these various reasons we conclude that a revival of British exports is, subject to the qualifications of paragraph 29, of vital importance to British economic life. We turn to consider what conditions may be necessary, as regards our commercial and agricultural policy, to secure this object against the background of the unfavourable circumstances indicated in paragraphs 21–23. We do not discuss the influence which policy in other fields, such as monetary and financial affairs, might exert upon exports.

34. In the first place, important though their interests are, it would be a

mistake to envisage the problem exclusively in terms of the older staple types of exports. In these cases, the higher standard of life which the British people enjoy, as compared with most of their industrial rivals, serves necessarily as a competitive handicap, which is especially serious in industries in which we have no very decided technical superiority. The longer that an industry has been established the more apt is its technique to become stabilised and capable of effective imitation by countries at an early stage of industrial development where labour costs rule low. It is essential, therefore, if we are to maintain the vitality of our export trade, that we should keep in the van of new developments, so as to obtain compensation in fresh lines of trade for the old lines that we lose to lower-wage competitors. For this purpose, the higher standard of living which we enjoy is an advantage. The larger purchasing-power of our population supplies a more promising market for the development of new varieties of goods; and the country which first produces a commodity on a considerable scale for its home population, acquires for subsequent export purposes the advantage of the first start over its competitors.

35. It should be our aim to utilise this potential advantage in the development of our export trade. Our progress in this respect in the twenties was perhaps somewhat disappointing. We may recall the words of the Economic Mission to the Argentine in 1929:—

"The decrease in the British percentage and increase in the American has been caused not so much by the displacement of old trades as by the development of new trades, in which we have taken an insignificant share." ★   ★   ★   ★   ★   ★

"The large Argentine demand is for the new commodities of commerce and we do not supply them. Either we do not make them or we do not market them; at least not on the scale worthy of our position as an industrial and exporting nation. Yet this demand absorbs the fresh purchasing power and diverts a large portion of the old. The average Argentine household thinks more now in terms of motor cars, gramophones and radio sets than of Irish linen, Sheffield cutlery and English china and glass. The expenditure on new luxuries has diverted money which would otherwise have gone to the staple trades. The rapid increase in United States trade in the Argentine market is particularly marked in the new industries—motor cars and accessories, films and cinematograph goods, electrical appliances, radio apparatus, typewriters, cash registers and office appliances, sewing machines, domestic refrigerators, gramophones, new types of agricultural and road-making machinery, oil-well plant and supplies."

American exports to all countries of goods mentioned in the last sentence of the above quotation accounted in 1929 for nearly 40 per cent. of their exports of finished manufactures or for nearly £200 millions, of which motor cars and accessories amounted to £124 millions.

36. In the case of many of these commodities, American costs of production are far lower than our own. The predominance of American exporters in these fields was due to causes which contributed greatly to English industrial predominance in the nineteenth century. America has been, as England was then, the most prosperous nation in the world. Commodities, the demand for which in other countries is confined to the more well-to-do classes, are there in use among a very much larger section of the community, and are more cheaply produced upon a much larger scale than is possible elsewhere. If the people of Great Britain are permanently to enjoy a standard of comfort not greatly below that prevailing in the United States, it must be by taking every opportunity to obtain a fuller share of foreign markets in these new luxuries, so soon as demand in this country has developed sufficiently to support a reasonably efficient industry. For in a large measure the remuneration of British labour, in terms of the goods which must necessarily be imported from abroad, will depend on its power to produce at prices competitive with those of other advanced countries, commodities which the industrially less advanced nations are unable to produce cheaply. This consideration supplies an argument in favour of a commercial policy which would secure the development of the home manufacture of new varieties of goods which we are naturally well-fitted to produce.

37. Secondly, the events of recent years suggest that it may be desirable to concentrate mainly on the promotion of our export trade in markets which are not likely to subject it at any time to sudden and harassing disturbance. These are likely to be countries, our trade with which has a strongly complementary character. This supplies an argument in favour of cultivating friendly economic relations alike with the Dominions and with the Scandinavian and South American countries.

38. There remains a condition which is essential to the maintenance of an adequate export trade, namely, that our costs must be such as to enable our industries to hold their own against the competition of other countries. This brings us to the heart of the problem before us. We cannot and should not attempt to improve our general competitive position by lowering our standard of living. But we must endeavour to offset our comparatively high level of labour-costs by superior efficiency in production in our selling organisations, and in our distributive system generally. It is important, therefore, that the protective policy of this country should not be used to shield home producers from the necessity of emulating more efficient foreign producers and that continuing efforts should be made to increase the efficiency of our staple exporting industries by adequate organisation, both in production and marketing. Again, it is important that no expedient should be adopted for the support of agriculture which would cause a serious increase in the cost of living. With these considerations in mind, we turn to consider

the general bearing of our policy in regard to imports upon our exporting prospects.

4. The relation between imports and exports.

39. The relationship between a country's imports and its exports is not of so precise or rigid a kind that a given reduction in its imports must entail a precisely corresponding reduction in its exports, whether reckoned in volume or in value. There is, indeed, a precise quantitative relationship between the aggregate of the payments which a country makes abroad and the aggregate of the payments which it receives from abroad. But these payments include items arising from the movements of capital, and capital movements, both long-term and short-term, may undergo large variations. The account which we have given in section I of the changes which have occurred in the balance of payments is sufficient to show how widely the relation between imports and exports may vary. In the first post-war decade, our exports declined in volume by a large percentage while our imports increased in volume, and increased in value much more than did our exports. During the first years of the depression, our exports underwent a further sharp decline, while our imports diminished in a much smaller proportion. Since our departure from gold, our exports have been nearly maintained, while our imports have been largely curtailed. These changes have played a large part in the story of the fall of sterling from gold parity, and its subsequent recovery of underlying strength.

40. Nor is it only as a temporary matter that the relation between imports and exports may vary. In the short run a fall in imports, unaccompanied by a corresponding fall in exports, will serve to strengthen a country's exchange position. In the long run, it will serve to increase its margin for investment abroad, or to diminish its necessity to borrow abroad. It is, of course, essential that this increased margin should in fact be utilised for investment, and not allowed to accumulate in the form of gold or liquid balances abroad. Otherwise the maintenance of the level of exports would necessarily in time be endangered. In Great Britain we have seen the net annual rate of overseas investment vary within a generation from a figure of nearly £200 millions to a minus quantity. The range within which the relation between imports and exports can be altered is correspondingly large. We must, at the same time, also bear in mind that to an important extent overseas lending directly stimulates the demand for our exports.

41. It follows that, in such circumstances as existed in Great Britain in 1931, when the balance of payments was adverse, and when there was a large volume of unemployment both of labour and capital equipment, there is no necessary reason why the increased employment obtained by absorbing unemployed resources in producing at home goods previously imported should be balanced by a corresponding loss of employment in the exporting industries. There is, we think, no doubt that the increase in employment in

Great Britain since 1932 is largely attributable to the reduction of imports of manufactured goods, unaccompanied by a corresponding reduction of exports, which is attributable in turn partly to the fall of the pound and partly to protective measures. It should be added that the possibility of achieving this result rested largely on the fact that we had previously been a free trade country, importing a large quantity of goods which we could make almost equally cheaply at home. When a country excludes such goods in normal times by means of tariffs, its ability to obtain relief in times of depression is greatly diminished, as protectionist countries have had reason to learn.

42. Because, however, the relationship between imports and exports is not precise and rigid, it does not follow that measures taken to diminish imports are unlikely to affect exports at all. On the contrary, there are various ways in which protective measures tend to react adversely on exports; and the question whether this adverse effect is negligible, or important, depends on the circumstances of the particular case.

43. In so far as the measures adopted reduce the value of our imports, the reduced international purchasing power of the countries whose goods are excluded is likely to react prejudicially on our exports in general. If the countries which are adversely affected are in a weaker financial and exchange position than ourselves, the broad effect upon world conditions will be deflationary, and the reaction on exports may be correspondingly severe. Accordingly, greater weight attaches to this consideration now than it did in 1931, when we ourselves were in an especially weak exchange position. Again, the adverse reaction on exports will be increased if the adoption by us of protective measures causes other countries to raise tariffs or impose other obstacles upon the entry of our goods. It will also be increased in so far as the countries whose goods are excluded are good customers for British exports. Serious account must be taken of the latter considerations, in particular, in the case of our imports of primary products from the British Dominions and South American states.

44. We have indicated, in paragraphs 17 and 18 above, the serious difficulties which the revolutionary change in the population outlook creates for the countries, both within the Empire and outside, from whom our overseas supplies of food are mainly drawn. In most of these, the production of primary products, largely for export to the British market, is the dominating feature of their economic life. Most of them are new countries, with sparse populations, which have been accustomed to look forward to a rapid rate of development, and have equipped themselves with capital facilities and incurred financial obligations, on a scale which only the expectation of a rapid rate of development could justify. They had tacitly assumed that this development would be based largely, as it has been hitherto, on a steady increase in the export of primary products to the British market; and the mere prospect that the British demand for primary products may cease

to expand, let alone decline, which has been raised by the recent discussions of quantitative restrictions, has come to them accordingly as a disagreeable shock. To a large extent, of course, and as a long period matter, they have got to face this prospect as inevitable; for it has its roots not in British agricultural policy, but in our vital statistics. The rôle of supplier of food-stuffs to the industrial population of Great Britain no longer offers scope for unlimited expansion. The countries of the new world must adjust themselves to this inexorable fact, and they must pursue the development of new markets or seek another and more diversified basis for the continued development of their economic life.

45. If, however, we were to pursue in Great Britain a long-term policy of deliberately reducing imports of food-stuffs in order to develop agriculture at home, this problem of adjustment would be seriously aggravated. In these circumstances there would be a natural disposition in the food-producing countries to attribute to British policy a larger share of responsibility for their difficulties than would properly attach to it. Many of the countries in question are British Dominions, which, as such, have a special claim on Great Britain for a reasonable degree of considerateness for their vital interests. They are most of them countries which have been developed largely with the aid of British capital, and which normally purchase from Great Britain a large proportion of their imports. And they are precisely the countries with which in recent years we have seen the best hope of developing our export trade by commercial negotiations.

46. This consideration is reinforced when we pass to consider another way in which the reduction of imports may prejudice our export trade. The restrictions may serve to raise prices at home sufficiently to entail an increase in our costs of production, unless there is an off-setting reduction in the standard of living. So far as we can judge, the protection accorded to our manufacturing industries has not this effect in any material degree. But this danger is obviously greater if we endeavour by protective means to expand our home output of foodstuffs which enter largely into the cost of living, and which we are naturally less well fitted to produce.

47. The praises of the system of an international division of labour may have been sung too loudly and too indiscriminately in the nineteenth century. But the development of our trade with the New World on the principle of obtaining our necessary food-stuffs and raw materials partly as interest on the investment of our surplus capital resources and partly in exchange for our industrial products constitutes the classic example of the mutual advantages of international specialisation. To turn round now upon this whole development, and gratuitously to render functionless much of the organisation, equipment and personnel which is specialised overseas in primary production, with the corollary of rendering correspondingly functionless much of our industrial life which is specialised for export, to create or to aggravate a large-scale transfer problem for the new countries

at the expense of creating or aggravating a similar transfer problem for ourselves, would run counter to the whole idea of a rational development of the world's economy. The process of accomplishing this switch over would entail, both overseas and at home, a prolonged period of economic malaise, for every transfer problem of this sort operates as a generally depressing influence. It would, moreover, operate powerfully to destroy the intimacy and harmony of our relations with the overseas countries, and would be fraught with potentialities of the utmost gravity to the solidarity of the British Empire.

48. For these reasons, we conclude that a long-term policy designed to effect a progressive reduction of important food imports in the interests of British agriculture would be likely to cause a more than commensurate injury through its adverse reaction on other branches of British industry and on the standard of life.

5. Employment and agriculture.

49. We are now in a position to come more closely to grips with the chief issues of commercial and agricultural policy. We have already indicated our view that in the particular circumstances of recent years the protection accorded to British manufactures has served, in conjunction with the fall of the pound, to increase the volume of employment at home. But the possibilities of increasing employment by this means are now, in our judgment, speaking broadly, exhausted. We append to this report a table (appendix 2) which shows how drastically our principal imports of mainly manufactured goods have already been cut down. The following table represents an attempt to calculate for recent years the volume of employment (in terms of the number of workpeople) represented by our total home production and our production for export, and also the additional volume of employment which might be secured if the mainly manufactured goods at present imported could be manufactured at home without adverse repercussions:—

Table 4.

Employment in manufacture and mining in the United Kingdom.

	Year.	Estimated number of workpeople employed—		Potential volume of employment represented by imports.
		In production as a whole.	In production for export.	
	1929	5,871,000	1,659,000	573,000
	1930	5,408,000	1,325,000	550,000
	1931	4,825,000	1,001,000	550,000
	1932	4,788,000	1,028,000	312,000
	1933	5,050,000	1,040,000	315,000

* Persons employed in the manufacture of food, drink and tobacco are excluded from the table. The goods included for the purpose of calculating employment in foreign trade are those

50. This calculation is necessarily subject to a large margin of error; but it represents, we believe, the correct order of magnitude. On this basis the direct increase in the volume of employment that would result if we could secure that all the mainly manufactured goods which we still import were produced at home, without any adverse repercussion upon other interests, could not amount to more than about 300,000 workers. When we take account of the substantial measure of protection which our industries now enjoy, the strong consequent presumption that the manufactured goods which we still import could not be produced easily or cheaply at home, and of the extent to which it is true that the finished product of one industry is the raw material of another, it seems improbable that any further material gain to employment, and not unlikely that serious indirect loss, would result from an extension of industrial protection. Indeed, it is not unlikely that the degree of protection which is already afforded to many industries, while stimulating in its immediate effects, and perhaps necessary during a slump, may entail counterbalancing disadvantages which will prove increasingly serious as time goes on. It is perhaps too soon to attempt to measure how far this is so; and we therefore do not enumerate them in detail, though some of them are touched upon above and in paragraph 38. But we set out in appendix 1 a list of some of the statistical criteria which should be available to anyone attempting to weigh from the short period point of view the advantages or disadvantages of protection in particular instances.

51. There remains the question of agriculture. The argument of the preceding sections will have made sufficiently clear the reasons which lead us to formulate the following as the main principles which should guide our agricultural policy:—

(1) we should avoid measures calculated to raise materially the prices of essential foodstuffs to the British public above the level which would otherwise prevail or to entail a progressive reduction in the volume of our food imports;

(2) we should contrive, however, in times of severe depression of world agricultural prices, to secure reasonable prices for our farmers, sufficient to maintain financial solvency and to avert exhaustion of capital, impairment of equipment or curtailment of production.

52. The first of these principles, taken in conjunction with the impending decline in our population, obviously sets narrow limits to the extent to which we can hope to expand most forms of our home agricultural output. Indeed, in the case of many of the commodities which bulk most largely in our food imports, it would be, in our judgment, a mistaken policy to aim at an enlarged home production. For producing additional quantities of wheat Great Britain is at a natural disadvantage compared with the countries of the

covered by the following classes in the Board of Trade classification: For exports, Group II (classes A to D) and the whole of Group III; for imports, Group II (classes B and C) and the whole of Group III.

new world. For producing beet-sugar, again, Great Britain is at a disadvantage as compared with many continental countries, while beet-sugar is probably an uneconomic proposition relatively to cane. As regards both wheat and sugar, moreover, there is no tendency for imported supplies to deteriorate owing to transit and storage, and accordingly no advantage in respect of quality attaches to the home product.

53. In our judgment, such efforts as we make to expand agricultural output, as distinct from securing a reasonable degree of stability of prices for our existing output, should be concentrated on those agricultural commodities which can be produced with advantage to quality in areas adjacent to large consuming centres, or which we are otherwise especially well fitted to produce. These considerations apply to such commodities as fruit, milk, eggs, poultry and vegetables. These are also commodities of which an enlarged consumption would be especially desirable, from the standpoint of improving the dietary and, consequently, the physique of the population; it is largely to the stimulus of consumption that we must look to make a large output possible. But if the consumption of these commodities is to be stimulated, it is necessary that they should remain cheap. Again we should not lose sight in the case of agriculture of a general consideration which we stressed in connection with the exporting industries, namely, the importance of keeping in the van of new developments. Canning supplies an instance of a new development which is of great importance to agriculture for some products in some areas.

54. But when allowance has been made for such possibilities, the enlargement of agricultural output at which we can prudently aim remains very limited. It is, therefore, we fear, wholly illusory to suppose that agriculture can play the part which many would desire of supplying an opening for increased employment to compensate for the decline in the older exporting industries. Our experience in the last decade is pertinent in this connection. During this period, the numbers engaged in agriculture steadily declined,* although the volume of our agricultural output as a whole was fully maintained. Meanwhile, on the other hand, various other occupations showed a huge increase in the numbers of persons they employed; and the persistence of heavy unemployment in the chief exporting centres has perhaps served to blind us to the remarkable contribution which ordinary economic forces in fact made towards the solution of the transfer problem. The following table indicates what was accomplished between 1923 and 1933:—

* The number of persons recorded in the census as being engaged in agricultural occupations in Great Britain declined from 1,448,654 in 1921 to 1,352,967 in 1931. The number of persons *employed* on agricultural holdings of more than one acre have been as follows:—

Year.		Numbers employed.	Year			Numbers employed.
1929	...	... 888,000	1932	...	...	809,000
1930	...	... 857,000	1933	...	...	828,000
1931	...	... 829,000	1934	...	...	800,000

Table 5.

Estimated numbers of insured persons employed in the United Kingdom.*

(a) The principal industries which have expanded.

Industry.	June 1923.	June 1933.	Increase.
Distribution	1,159,000	1,766,900	607,900
Building	695,400	866,300	170,900
Hotels and restaurants	230,000	342,800	112,800
Electrical industries	129,800	207,600	77,800
Printing and paper trades	317,000	383,900	66,900
Motor vehicles	171,400	219,300	47,900
Food, drink, and tobacco	445,400	489,400	44,000
Laundries	99,200	140,200	41,000
Entertainments and sports	50,700	86,800	36,100
Professional services	102,300	134,900	32,600
Furniture	83,900	109,600	25,700
Clothing	404,000	426,700	22,700

(b) The principal industries which have contracted.

Industry.	June 1923.	June 1933.	Decrease.
Coal mining	1,176,000	639,300	536,700
Shipbuilding and marine engineering	211,200	89,200	122,000
General engineering	506,000	396,400	109,600
Iron, steel and non-ferrous metals ...	623,300	557,400	65,900
Cotton	439,000	374,300	64,700
Wool	240,900	198,100	42,800
Linen, hemp and jute	119,200	95,100	24,100
			Increase.
All industries	9,898,000	10,384,900	486,900

* The figures relate to persons between the ages of 16 and 64. The figures for 1923 represent an estimate for these age groups, based upon the actual number of persons of 16 and over in that year, and the proportion which employed persons between 16 and 64 bore to employed persons of 16 and over in each industry in 1927.

55. It will be observed that a large part of the increased employment of the past decade has been provided by the distributive trades, hotels and restaurants, and other services. It is natural that such a trend should arouse misgivings, since it is difficult to disabuse the mind of the instinctive impression that the more directly productive occupations have a superior dignity and usefulness, and even that a growth in the proportion of "non-producers" betokens something parasitic and unsound. As regards services generally, such apprehensions are, however, in our judgment unfounded, though there are grounds for believing that there is much waste in the organisation

of our distributive trades. Just as it is an inevitable feature of economic progress that a steadily diminishing proportion of the community should be engaged in the production of primary necessities like food, so, at the other end of the scale, it is inevitable that the proportion engaged in distribution, transport, and services should grow. Both tendencies represent the natural outcome of technical progress and a rising standard of life. It is to the further expansion of these occupations, together with the development of new and miscellaneous industrial occupations that we must continue to look for the solution of the transfer problem.

56. We turn to consider the second main principle formulated in paragraph 51, that, namely, of securing a reasonable minimum of prices for our farmers amid the vicissitudes of world fluctuation. This is an object which we think it is vital to secure. If no special steps had been taken for the assistance of agriculture during the present crisis, the collapse of world prices would have entailed widespread bankruptcy among large sections of British farmers, which would have left behind it a lasting detrimental effect upon the efficiency and prosperity of our domestic agriculture. It is an object, moreover, which, for reasons developed earlier, we think may prove of recurring importance; it is one which our position as a large importer of foodstuffs should make it comparatively easy for us to secure; but the task of securing it in detail bristles with difficulties, and it is desirable that careful thought should be given to the question of the methods which it is best to employ.

57. In the present crisis we have used, for a considerable number of commodities, the expedient of the quantitative limitation of imports. This expedient has been invoked partly to maintain prices, and partly to increase domestic production. From the standpoint of the British public, quantitative limitation is obviously an expensive method of securing the former purpose. For by this method the British consumers are required to pay higher prices not only for that part of the supply which is produced at home, but also for the part which is imported from abroad, although the public revenue derives no benefit as it does in the case of duties. In some degree, indeed, this has been the deliberate object of the use of the quota method. For it has been argued that it is in our interest, and in the interest of world recovery generally, to endeavour to maintain the purchasing power of primary producers overseas.

58. The measure of force which can be attributed to this argument in the peculiar circumstances of the crisis of recent years is reduced in so far as the benefit of the higher prices has not accrued to producers overseas, but has been intercepted by intermediate trading interests. In any case, it is impossible, we think, to justify on such grounds the continued adoption of a method which is so paradoxical and quixotic from the standpoint of British interests. The fact that we insist, as in effect we do under the quota system, on paying higher prices for foodstuffs we import than the producers overseas would be willing to accept is only of limited efficacy for raising the general world

prices of these commodities. For part of the supply which would normally come to Great Britain may be diverted to other markets, including the home markets of the supplying countries. Thus the foodstuffs affected may become materially dearer for the British consumer, while they are becoming cheaper for consumers overseas. The continuance of such a policy would be in glaring conflict with the principles on which our position as a large exporting country with a high standard of life has been built up. Doubtless this policy has helped to mitigate the unpleasant consequences, to the countries which supply us with food-stuffs, of a curtailment in the volume of their trade. In general, however, it would be wiser, in our judgment, to pursue a policy which would reassure these countries against the progressive diminution in the volume of trade, and to pay more regard to our own national interests so far as prices are concerned.

59. The possibility of assuring a reasonable price to the British farmer by methods which would be less burdensome to the British consumer is illustrated by the scheme that has been adopted in the case of wheat. By means of a comparatively small levy upon imports, British farmers have been able to secure for their wheat a reasonable price, far in excess of the ruling world price. The burden on the consumers has been negligible and has served merely to withhold from them part of the windfall benefit which they would otherwise have derived from abnormally low prices. The burden on the overseas exporters has been comparatively small, because our imports of wheat bear such a high relation to our home production, and the policy has proved comparatively unobjectionable to them because it is not associated with the prospect of a rigid limitation on, still less a progressive curtailment of, the *volume* of their exports.

60. The method of the wheat scheme would not, of course, be applicable to other commodities without considerable variations. Moreover, the method is open to the objection that it may lead to an undesired expansion of domestic output. The expansion in the production of wheat which has occurred is no doubt largely attributable to the substitution of wheat for other cereal crops which do not benefit from the subsidy. But there is obviously some danger that if the minimum price is originally fixed at too high a level having regard to the prices prevailing for other agricultural commodities, even a limitation of the maximum volume of production on which the subsidy is to be paid, such as is included in the wheat scheme, may not prevent a considerable increase in the production of the subsidised commodity. When an undesigned expansion of domestic output is thus brought about, the danger arises that the additional output will come to be regarded as part of our normal domestic production, with a claim to be preserved against overseas competition at the expense of the taxpayer and the consuming public. The admission of such a claim would be incompatible with the first of the two governing principles which we have formulated in paragraph 51. It is, therefore, important, in connection with any measures

that may be taken to maintain prices for the British farmer, to devise suitable safeguards against an undesired increase in supply, but care must equally be taken to avoid conferring a monopoly on existing producers.

61. The preceding paragraphs from paragraph 39 onwards have been primarily concerned with the effects of possible increases of restrictions of imports on the volume of our exports, since we understand that this is the question to which we were asked to direct our attention. We have not pursued in the same way the question of the effect on exports (*a*) of our future foreign exchange policy as affecting the future level of our domestic costs compared with costs abroad when expressed in a common unit, (*b*) of our future policy and inclinations towards foreign lending, (*c*) of the measure of recovery of world trade as a whole, and (*d*) of possible reductions of existing restrictions on imports both at home and abroad by means of negotiations. Lest, however, the particular aspect of the problem to which we have devoted our main attention should be seen out of its true perspective, we desire to add that the volume of our exports is likely to depend to a materially greater extent on the four other factors which we have mentioned than upon any future extension of restrictions on our imports, unless the latter were pushed to extremes.

6. Summary of principal conclusions.

62. We summarise our principal conclusions as follows:—

(1) The economic development of Great Britain in the Victorian age was based in a peculiar degree on overseas trade, the expansion of which was closely associated with overseas investment and emigration. The rapidity of her economic progress was largely attributable to the leading part which she played in the process of developing the new world with the capital, population and industrial products of the old (paragraphs 1–3).

(2) The fall in birth rates which has gone so far as to render almost inevitable a substantial decline in the population of Great Britain and other Western countries, is likely in future to change fundamentally the conditions which constitute the background of international trade. The market which Great Britain provides for primary products from overseas cannot continue to expand steadily and rapidly as it used to do. Disturbances in world prices may be more serious and prolonged than they used to be, particularly in the case of primary commodities, when the strong upward trend of demand, arising from growing numbers, can no longer be relied upon to afford relief to a condition of overproduction (paragraphs 4–20).

(3) The outlook for British export trade is far from promising. It appears doubtful whether there will be any very speedy and substantial relaxation of the trade obstacles which have been set up during the present crisis, while the comparatively favourable competitive position which we enjoy at present in world markets may disappear (paragraphs 21–23).

(4) The comparative success with which British economic life has adapted itself to the heavy loss of export trade which has occurred has given rise to a disposition to question whether the development of exports is so important or even so desirable as used to be assumed (paragraphs 24, 25).

(5) It would, we believe, be bad policy to subordinate every other consideration to the pursuit of the goal of the maximum possible volume of export. Our essential interests can probably be adequately secured by a volume of exports materially smaller in relation to total production than we were accustomed to maintain in pre-war days (paragraphs 26–29).

(6) But there are various reasons why we are convinced that the maintenance of a large-scale export trade is vital to our national prosperity. Large imports of food-stuffs and raw materials are essential to us, and we shall require in normal times a more favourable balance of payments than we have at present. Our economic life is still specialised in a large degree in occupations connected with export, for many of which we are peculiarly well fitted. Moreover, many of the industries which are most dependent on export are highly localised in character, so that to transfer their work-people to other occupations represents a task of peculiar difficulty (paragraphs 30–33).

(7) It would be a mistake to envisage the problem of the export trade exclusively in terms of the older staple types of exports. In all industries we should endeavour to keep in the van of new developments so as to obtain compensation in fresh lines of trade for the old lines that we lose to low-wage competitors. Our progress in this respect in the twenties was perhaps somewhat disappointing (paragraphs 34–36).

(8) It may be desirable to concentrate mainly on the promotion of our export trade in markets which are not likely to subject it to sudden and harassing disturbances. This supplies an argument in favour of cultivating friendly economic relations alike with the Dominions and with the Scandinavian and South American countries (paragraph 37).

(9) It is essential to the maintenance of an adequate export trade that our costs should be such as to enable our industries to hold their own against the competition of other countries, though we cannot and should not attempt to improve our competitive position by lowering our standard of living (paragraph 38).

(10) The relationship between a country's imports and its exports is not of so precise or rigid a kind that a given reduction in its imports must entail a precisely corresponding reduction in its exports, whether reckoned in volume or in value. But there are various ways in which protective measures tend to react adversely on exports; and the question whether this adverse effect is negligible or important depends on the circumstances of the particular case (paragraphs 39, 40).

(11) The countries, both within the Empire and outside, from whom our overseas supplies of food are mainly drawn, are already faced with a serious

problem of adjustment as the result of the impending decline in the British population. If we were to pursue a long-term policy of reducing imports of food-stuffs in order to develop home agriculture, this problem of adjustment would be seriously aggravated; and there would be a disposition in the food-producing countries to attribute to British policy a larger share of responsibility for their difficulties than would properly attach to it. Moreover, restrictions on food imports might serve to raise prices at home sufficiently to entail a rise in the cost of production through a rise in the cost of living (paragraphs 41–47).

(12) For these reasons, we conclude that a long-term policy designed to effect a progressive reduction of important food imports in the interests of British agriculture would be likely to cause a more than commensurate injury through its adverse reaction on other branches of British industry and on the standard of life (paragraph 48).

(13) We are of opinion that in the particular circumstances of recent years the protection accorded to British manufacturers has served, in conjunction with the fall of the pound, to increase the volume of employment at home. But the possibilities of increasing employment by this means are now, in our judgment, speaking broadly, exhausted. Indeed, it is not unlikely that the degree of protection which is already afforded to many industries, while stimulating in its immediate effects, may entail counterbalancing disadvantages which will prove increasingly serious as time goes on. It is perhaps too soon to attempt to measure how far this is so (paragraphs 49, 50).

(14) We suggest the following as the main principles which should guide our agricultural policy:—

(a) we should avoid measures calculated to raise materially the prices of essential foodstuffs to the British public above the level which would otherwise prevail, or to entail a progressive reduction in the volume of our food imports;

(b) we should contrive, however, in times of severe depression of world agricultural prices, to secure reasonable prices for our farmers, sufficient to maintain financial solvency and to avert exhaustion of capital, impairment of equipment or curtailment of production (paragraph 51).

(15) The first of these principles, taken in conjunction with the impending decline in our population, obviously sets narrow limits to the extent to which we can hope to expand most forms of our home agricultural output. In our judgment such efforts as we make to expand agricultural output, as distinct from securing a reasonable degree of stability of prices for our existing output, should be concentrated on such commodities as fruit, milk, eggs, poultry and vegetables, which can be produced with advantage to

quality in areas adjacent to large consuming centres, or which we are other-wise well-fitted to produce (paragraphs 52–55).

(16) As regards the second principle, we have relied largely during the present crisis on the expedient of the quantitative limitation of imports. This is an expensive method from the standpoint of the public. The possi-bility of a less expensive method is indicated by the wheat scheme, though the method there employed would not be applicable to other commodities without considerable variations (paragraphs 56–59).

(17) It is desirable that careful thought should be given to the question how the principle of maintaining a reasonable minimum of prices for British farmers can best be applied. In connection with any measures taken for the purpose, it will be important to devise suitable safeguards against an undesirable increase in supply, but care must equally be taken to avoid conferring a monopoly on existing producers (paragraph 60).

Eighteenth Report of Committee on Economic Information,
*July 1935**

THE ECONOMIC OUTLOOK FOR THE NEXT FEW YEARS.

I.—Introductory.

1. It is our intention in the present report to consider the economic scene from a rather different angle from that which we usually choose when preparing our periodic surveys. We are generally concerned with the events of the immediate past and the prospects for the immediate future. The outlook in this respect, however, continues to be dominated by the uncertain financial prospects in the industrial countries of western Europe, prospects which we have discussed at some length in our recent reports. We turn, therefore, to the consideration of more fundamental tendencies, and the part which they may be expected to play in determining the course of economic events in Great Britain over the next few years. In particular, we wish to examine the situation in regard to house building, which may be expected to have a very important effect in determining the present period of comparatively good trade.

II.—Retrospect.

2. We may begin our survey with a brief retrospect of the events lead-ing up to the recent depression and the present recovery. Most periods of bad trade in the past have been the consequence of an over rapid develop-ment in some sphere or other of economic life; and the depression which began in 1929 was no exception to this rule. But in the boom years preceding

---

* P.R.O. Cab. 58/30, E.A.C. (S.C.) 21, 20 July 1935; also Cab. 24/256, C.P. 157(35).

the depression Great Britain had for a number of reasons shared only to a limited extent in the surrounding activity. The chief centres of expansion had been in the United States, where there had been an unprecedented expansion of constructional activity, in central and western Europe, where the damage and disorganisation caused by the war were being made good with the assistance of loans from this country and the United States, and in the countries producing primary products which also, for the first time since the war began, found the capital markets of England and America open to them, and who proceeded to borrow on a lavish scale. In all these countries borrowers were prepared to pay very high rates of interest, which naturally reacted on the rates charged to borrowers in Great Britain. Moreover, as we now know, large liquid liabilities had accumulated in London as the result of the depreciation of continental currencies, and, as was apparent at the time, the expansion of British exports was hampered by the rise of new competitors and by changes in the nature of demand. This gave rise to a pressure on the exchanges which prevented the monetary authorities in London, hampered as they then were by the necessity of preserving the gold reserves against foreign drains, from pursuing a policy which would have made money available for development at home, at the rates of interest at which alone this development would have been possible. Throughout this period Britain's exporting industries, although they were suffering from underlying difficulties which gave them a definitely depressed appearance, were supported by the general stimulus to international trade provided by the enormous scale upon which international lending was then being undertaken. At the same time the industries dependent on home development, although they appeared to be in a comparatively prosperous condition, were prevented from expanding adequately by the high interest rates then prevailing.

3. In 1930 the market for foreign loans collapsed, partly as a result of the financial catastrophe in the United States in the previous year, partly as a result of the accumulating evidence of over-borrowing on the part of the countries which had previously been in the market. And as a consequence of this collapse international trade underwent a severe contraction, especially that branch of it which depended on the absorption of manufactured goods by countries specialised in the production of raw materials. The brunt of this contraction was borne by Great Britain, whose exporting industries were handicapped by the unduly high value of the pound, and whose free market, as it then was, provided a convenient outlet for the output of other industrial countries which could no longer find ready purchasers in the less industrialised parts of the world. The growth of competitive imports and the falling off of exports were primarily responsible for the deterioration of our industrial position in the years 1930 and 1931.

4. Nor at this time could the situation be alleviated by an expansion of internal capital development. For the slump had the effect of aggravating

the exchange difficulties from which Great Britain was suffering, and thus prevented any substantial reduction in the level of interest rates. It has always been the habit of the primary producing countries who finance their exports through London, to maintain substantial sterling assets as a reserve against the contingency of a period of bad trade. When the slump came they naturally drew upon these reserves. Sterling was, therefore, subject to pressure from three directions, first by reason of the excessive importation of manufactured goods into Great Britain from the continent and from America; secondly by reason of the withdrawal of balances by countries of what we should now call the sterling area to pay off debts incurred in dollars, francs, and other currencies; and finally, as the difficulties of Great Britain's position became increasingly manifest by the growing nervousness of holders of the liquid claims on London, which, as we have already remarked, were a legacy of the continental post-war depreciations. In these circumstances, the primary preoccupation of our monetary authorities was inevitably with the external stability of the currency, and the possibility of promoting recovery by stimulating internal activity through lowered interest rates had to be neglected. Indeed, the attempts which were then made to stimulate internal activity directly by a considerable programme of public expenditure, though mitigating the severity of unemployment, could only in the circumstances of the time add to difficulties of the exchange situation.

5. It was only after the crisis of 1931 that Great Britain was in a position to adopt a policy which brought with it any hope of a real recovery. From our present point of view two developments which have occurred since the crisis are of especial importance, first the consolidation, in fact if not in name, of the "sterling area"; secondly, the inauguration of a persistent policy of cheap money, both these developments being greatly assisted by the re-establishment of our national finances upon a satisfactory basis. As their consequence, we have seen on the one hand the growth of an area in which international trade has been able to develop on a comparatively secure footing, only hampered in a minor degree by currency and other restrictions; and, on the other hand, a marked revival of internal activity. Against these advantages of the divorce of the pound from gold, we must set the very severe dislocation of international trade with countries not on the sterling standard, a dislocation which was materially aggravated by the subsequent devaluation of the dollar.

III.—The home market for consumers' goods.

6. With these considerations in mind we may turn to the examination of the actual course of employment in the last six years, and we may take as a starting point a table of figures which we first compiled for the purpose of our fourteenth report, showing the composition of the demand for labour in insured industries, under certain broad headings, since the beginning of the

TABLE I.

Analysis of employment among insured workers in the United Kingdom in the period 1929–1935.

(Figures in thousands.)

| Year. | Total employment. (a) | Total labour required to produce goods and services consumed in the United Kingdom. | | | | | | Total (a−g). (d) | Extent to which United Kingdom labour required to produce goods consumed in the United Kingdom was less than the total in column (d) as a result of the import of competitive goods from abroad. (e) | Labour directly employed in the production of goods exported from the United Kingdom. (f) | Net external demand for labour. (f−e) (g) |
| | | Investment goods. | | | Consumption goods and services. | | | | | | |
		Building and building materials.	Iron and steel and engineering.	Total. (b)	Manufactured goods.	Direct services.	Total. (c)				
1929	10,884	1,295	1,019	2,314	3,905	3,596	7,501	9,815	550	1,619	1,069
1930	10,472	1,290	971	2,261	3,801	3,641	7,442	9,703	532	1,301	769
1931	10,040	1,282	860	2,142	3,762	3,703	7,465	9,607	545	978	433
1932	9,999	1,181	761	1,942	3,595	3,761	7,356	9,298	304	1,005	701
1933	10,329	1,249	792	2,041	3,740	3,841	7,581	9,622	301	1,008	707
1934	10,802	1,382	912	2,294	3,839	3,949	7,788	10,082	357	1,077	720
1935 ... ... (first quarter)	10,836	1,425	916	2,341	3,760	3,968	7,728	10,069	369	1,136	767

depression. In that report we suggested that it would be unwise to place too great reliance on these figures. In bringing them up to date we have been forced to make the assumption that the rate of recruitment in each group of industries since July 1934, which is the last date for which figures of the insured persons attached to each industry are available, was the same as in the period from July 1933 to July 1934. In fact, however, there can be little doubt that this is not the case, and that in the building industries in particular, a higher rate of recruitment has prevailed. Moreover, the estimates of employment lost and gained through foreign trade are based on variations in the volume of imports and exports, and take no account of changes in the productivity of labour, though the statistics suggest that this has recently increased materially. It is probable, therefore, that the contribution of foreign trade to the sum of employment is somewhat exaggerated.

7. In our fourteenth report we drew attention to the main changes in the composition of employment since 1929, namely, the increase in the numbers required to produce goods currently consumed in Great Britain, and the falling off in the net demand for labour in foreign trade. The question which concerns us at present is whether, as more normal conditions establish themselves, the first of these changes in the distribution of productive resources is likely to be maintained. This is a question of considerable importance to the prospects of employment in the next few years. Many branches of capital producing industries are still depressed considerably below the level of activity prevailing in 1929. As the general improvement continues, these industries may be expected to absorb more labour into employment. If the proportion of labour required for the production of goods and services for home consumption is maintained, an improvement in employment in the capital producing industries entails an equal proportionate improvement in total employment. If, however, this proportion shows a tendency to slip back to the level of 1929, the prospects of an improvement in total employment are less bright. Expressed in percentages of total employment, the demand for labour to produce goods and services for the home market in the last six years has been as follows:—

TABLE 2.

Percentage of total employment in the United Kingdom devoted to production for the home market in insured industries.

—	1929.	1930.	1931.	1932.	1933.	1934.
Labour required to produce goods and services consumed in the home market as a percentage of total labour employed	66·1	71·1	71·8	73·6	73·4	72·1
of which manufactures represent	35·9	36·3	36·2	36·0	36·2	35·5
and services represent	30·2	34·8	35·6	37·6	37·2	36·6

8. What then are the causes which have brought about this great improvement in internal trade? There are, we suppose, two principal explanations. First, the great improvement which the slump caused in the terms on which British exports can be exchanged for British imports has resulted in a considerable fall in the cost of living of British working class families. The average wages of a man in full employment are to-day in the neighbourhood of 95 per cent. of the wages obtained in 1929; and there is no reason to suppose that at the moment earnings are diminished by the prevalence of short-time to a greater extent than in that year.* But the prices of foodstuffs have fallen by approximately 20 per cent. since that time. Thus, assuming that food expenditure accounted for approximately 50 per cent. of total expenditure in 1929, and that the ordinary working man maintains to-day the same standard as previously, he must have available for expenditure on other items £55 for every £50 he spent in 1929, an increase of 10 per cent. If account is taken of the fact that quite £20 of the £50 available in 1929 must have been spent on rent, and probably is still so spent, the increase in income available for expenditure on items other than food and rent becomes even more impressive. Thus a substantial part of the increase in employment for home consumption must have been accounted for by greater expenditure by the working classes on goods and services produced at home, as a result of the improvement which has occurred in the level of real wages.

9. Secondly, as the result of the slump and its consequences there has been a re-distribution of incomes favourable to an increase in expenditure. Moreover, the fall in the rate of interest has materially reduced the incentive to save amongst those persons who formerly were in the habit of saving. To some extent, this is a phenomenon normally associated with the onset of a severe depression. There are a large number of corporate bodies and the like whose receipts are immediately affected by a depression but whose payments must remain substantially unchanged. We may instance not only the Government itself and the Unemployment Insurance Fund, but also public companies whose dividends are declared on the results of a past year's working. The recovery from the last depression, however, has been marked by a more permanent readjustment which has prevented a return to the position that obtained at the outset of the depression. The great fall which has occurred in the rate of interest, and in the earnings of companies, has affected especially the incomes of those members of the community who are normally in the habit of making substantial savings. This fall in incomes naturally has had a less than proportionate effect upon their expenditure; for few people are prepared to reduce their standard of life in order to maintain their rate of saving, especially at a time when they see the general value

---

* This was not the case in the worst year of the slump. Investigations carried out by the Ministry of Labour in 1927 and 1931 suggest that at that time earnings may have been reduced by the incidence of short-time by about 2 per cent.

of their estates increasing as the result of a general rise in the value of securities. Moreover, the fact that the incomes of the saving classes have been reduced by the establishment of lower interest rates more than have been the incomes of the rest of the community insures that a larger proportion of the total national income of the community shall be expended on current consumption.

10. In our last report we gave reasons for holding that in default of an improvement in investment activity or in the export trade an improvement in the demand for products for home consumption requires fundamental readjustments to take place. We have just described how in the period 1929–34 such readjustments were effected by a substantial fall in the comparative costs of British imports, and by a substantial fall in the rate of interest and in the normal level of industrial profits. It is therefore not surprising to find that in spite of a reduction in the numbers employed in investment activity and in foreign trade from approximately 3,400,000 in 1929 to 3,000,000 in 1934, there was a substantial rise in the numbers employed in satisfying the demand for the home consumption market from approximately 7,500,000 in 1929 to 7,800,000 in 1934. Now, however, these readjustments seem to have been completed, and in future we can only look for an expansion in internal consumption demand, as activity expands in the field of home investment and foreign trade. For this reason the future course of employment is now very much dependent on the course of activity in these industries, and the greater part of the remainder of this report is devoted to an examination of their prospects.

11. We cannot, however, assume that in future every increase in home investment and export trade will be associated with a proportionate improvement in the home consumption market. For reasons which we also gave in our last report further increases in activity are likely to be associated with the emergence of higher profits in particular industries and there may thus be a tendency for the general level of industrial profits to expand more rapidly than output, even though there is no rise in the general rate of interest. This in turn, by the converse process of reasoning to that employed in paragraph 9 above, will tend to diminish the proportion of current incomes expended on current consumption. Moreover, in the sphere of foreign trade the forces depressing the prices of British imports have for some time ceased to operate; and in future we may see a contrary trend. An expansion of British foreign trade is likely to be associated with an increase in the prices of British imports, and a consequent reduction in the surplus of wages which the working classes have available for expenditure on the products of home industry. We must assume therefore that in future the demand for labour in industries catering for the home consumption market will be less resilient than that in other industries.

12. We do not wish to leave the subject of home consumption demand without calling attention to a very remarkable change which has taken place

in its composition, namely, the great increase in the importance of the service group of industries. It will be observed from the table in paragraph 6 that the numbers employed in these industries increased throughout the depression, even when employment in every other sphere was declining. By 1934 employment within this group had increased by 350,000 in comparison with 1929, though employment in manufacturing for the home consumption market was still 65,000 lower than in 1929. In some respects the figures given present an incomplete picture. There has probably been some shift in the nature of industrial status in these industries. There are possibly fewer persons working on their own account and more as the employees of others. The figures, moreover, refer to employment between the ages of 16 and 64, and take no account of the employment of juveniles of the ages of 14 and 15. It so happens, however, that juvenile labour is to a very large extent concentrated in the distributive trades, which are included in the service group. Moreover, there have been important changes in the numbers of juveniles of 14 and 15 years of age available for employment since 1929. In that year the juveniles available were those who had been born in the years 1914 and 1915, before the birth rate had been materially affected by the war. They must have numbered approximately 930,000. By the end of 1932, in which year the shortage of births in the war was having its full effect, these numbers had fallen to 736,000.* By the end of 1934, on the other hand, the post-war increase in births was making itself felt and the numbers available for employment had risen again to 922,000, and by the end of this year it is estimated that their numbers will reach 1,049,000. The effect of a decline in juvenile labour at a time when the demand for labour in general was very slack must have been that many boys and girls of 16 who would normally have found more lucrative occupations remained on for an extra year in the distributive trades. Similarly, an improved demand for labour coincided with an increase in the supply of juvenile labour, and it is reasonable to suppose that boys and girls of 16 are now leaving the distributive trades in exceptionally large numbers. Thus, though the actual increase in employment in the service group of industries between 1929 and 1934 is probably correctly given by the figures in table 1, the annual increases are possibly quite misleading. The increases in the years 1929–32 may have been smaller, and the increase in the year 1934 much larger than appears at first sight.

13. The relative increase in the numbers employed in the service industries no doubt reflects a very real alteration in popular tastes and habits. It is, indeed, a matter of common observation that increased facilities for transport and entertainment are absorbing a larger share of the ordinary man's expenditure. But quite apart from changes in taste, the distribution of employment between manufacture and services has probably been affected in some degree by the considerable improvement in productive technique

* See the *Ministry of Labour Gazette* October 1934, p. 348.

which appears to have occurred recently in manufacturing industry as a whole. This is brought out in the following table, in which employment production and productivity per head in manufacturing industries are shown at quarterly intervals since 1929.

TABLE 3.

Indices of employment, production, and productivity per head in manufacturing and mining industries in the United Kingdom in the period 1929–34, by quarters.

(Year 1929 = 100.)
(Normal seasonal variations have been allowed for.)

Year and quarter.		Employ- ment.	Produc- tion.	Produc- tivity.	Year and quarter.		Employ- ment.	Produc- tion.	Produc- tivity.
1929	I	98·7	97·4	98·7	1932	I	85·7	83·8	97·8
	II	100·5	100·4	99·9		II	84·2	84·5	100·4
	III	101·2	102·5	101·3		III	83·4	81·2	97·4
	IV	99·4	99·9	100·5		IV	84·4	83·2	98·6
1930	I	97·3	98·0	100·8	1933	I	84·5	83·5	98·8
	II	94·3	92·4	98·0		II	86·5	86·7	100·2
	III	91·3	92·3	101·1		III	89·2	89·7	100·6
	IV	87·0	86·5	99·4		IV	90·1	92·0	102·1
1931	I	85·3	83·4	97·8	1934	I	90·7	97·8	107·8
	II	85·3	82·6	96·9		II	92·1	98·9	107·4
	III	83·5	82·8	99·2		III	92·5	98·4	106·4
	IV	85·0	85·2	100·2		IV	92·1	101·6	110·3

NOTE.—It should be observed that an increase in productivity per head does not necessarily increase the fund available for the payment of wages. In the first place this fund may be diminished by a reduction in prices at which goods are sold. Secondly, an increase in productivity is likely to be associated with an increase in the capital employed in industry, an increase which must involve higher interest payments.

14. It will be observed that in the opening stages of the depression productivity per head showed a tendency to decline, presumably as a result of short-time working. In 1934, however, there appears to have been a very important improvement, productivity per head rising to a level nearly 8 per cent. higher than that prevailing in 1929. Thus, although the actual numbers employed in manufacture for the home consumption market showed a decline between 1929 and 1934, there is reason to suppose that the actual volume of goods sold in this market showed a substantial increase.

IV.—Home investment.

15. Home investment comprises a number of fields of activity each subject to rather different influences. We may distinguish (i) replacements of plant, (ii) extensions of plant and new factory building, (iii) public works contracting, (iv) repairs to houses, and (v) new house building. Activity

directed towards the maintenance and extension of industrial plant and buildings must be primarily affected by the state of demand for industrial goods and the possibility of earning normal profits in industry. It must also be influenced by the liquid position of industrial enterprises, and by the possibility of raising capital freely in the new issue market. Public works contracting is largely, but not exclusively, dependent on public policy. House repairs are a fairly constant factor, which must be expected to move in much the same manner as expenditure on consumption goods. House building depends on the possibility of building houses at a price which, having regard to the current level of interest rates, can be let at the prevailing rents. Thus, though activity in each of these groups is likely to be influenced in some degree by changes in the rate of interest, the extent of their response to such changes may vary considerably.

16. The figures in table 1 indicate that by the beginning of 1935 the employment afforded by home investment activity somewhat exceeded that afforded in the same field in 1929. There has been, however, a very considerable change in the contribution to this total made by each of the groups which we have distinguished. Building has expanded, but engineering activity is still somewhat lower than before the slump. Moreover, within the field of building, the building of dwelling houses has shown a very large increase, whereas other kinds of building are still considerably below the level of 1929. We may attempt to make a more detailed examination of the available statistical material. The census of production of 1930 indicated that the building of new dwelling houses accounted for rather less than one-third of the value of the gross output of the building industry in that year; it may therefore be taken to have employed approximately 417,000 men. On this basis we may estimate the numbers of men employed on the building of dwelling houses from 1929 to 1934. We must, however, make some allowance for the increase in productivity per head in 1934, mainly occurring in the industries producing building materials; and also for the fact that the houses built have tended lately to be of a smaller average size, employing a smaller number of workpeople. Making a reasonable allowance for these factors in the light of the information available, we may calculate the numbers employed in the construction of new dwelling houses as follows:—

TABLE 4.

Employment in house building and other forms of building in the United Kingdom.

—	Numbers of new houses built in England and Wales.		Estimated employment in building new dwelling houses in the United Kingdom.	Employment in other forms of building activity in the United Kingdom.
	Completed in the year ending 31st March of the following year.	Estimated to have been constructed in the course of the calendar year.		
1929	201,000	200,000	469,000	826,000
1930	184,000	178,000	417,000	873,000
1931	201,000	199,000	466,000	816,000
1932	200,000	200,000	469,000	712,000
1933	269,000	256,000	600,000	649,000
1934	328,000	324,000	700,000	682,000

The figures in the last column receive some confirmation from the figures of the value of building plans passed for buildings other than dwelling houses. These plans are, of course, passed before the building is actually begun. If we relate the building plans passed in one year to the employment in the following year, we find a reasonable degree of correspondence, as may be seen in the following table, in which both sets of figures are reduced to percentages of the 1929 figure.

TABLE 5.

Building plans passed, and estimated employment for buildings other than dwelling houses.

1929 = 100.

—	1929.	1930.	1931.	1932.	1933.	1934.
Building plans passed in the preceding year	100·0	105·4	101·1	82·4	71·1	78·0
Estimated employment	100·0	105·7	98·8	86·2	78·6	82·6

Building plans approved for building other than dwelling houses showed a marked expansion in 1934, rising to 96 per cent. of the 1929 level, and we may therefore anticipate a considerable increase of employment in this field in 1935.

17. As a result of this examination we may estimate that the position of employment in investment industries for the home market to-day compares as follows with the position in 1929:—

TABLE 6.

Employment in the investment industries in the United Kingdom in 1929 and 1935.

—	1929.	1935.	Increase or decrease.
Construction of new dwelling houses	470,000	730,000	increase 260,000
Construction and repairs of other buildings and works	825,000	720,000	decrease 105,000
Iron and steel production and engineering ...	1,020,000	920,000	decrease 100,000
Total	2,315,000	2,370,000	increase 55,000

Obviously, the prospects for further expansion are very much greater in the case of the two latter groups, which are still comparatively depressed, than in the case of house building the activity of which is now on an unprecedented scale. But within these fields we cannot but suggest that the prospects are comparatively good. In our last report we suggested that recovery in this country has now reached a point where the productive capacity of certain industries is beginning to be severely taxed. Demands for new plant and building are likely to come in increasing quantities from these industries; and as recovery proceeds more and more industries are likely to be brought within this class. Thus, the recovery in the engineering trades, which up till now has been largely based on more confident replacement programmes in industry in general, is likely now to be supplemented by programmes of expansion in the more favoured industries. This recovery should also embrace the building of new factories. Indeed, a substantial indication of such a development is contained in recent figures for building plans passed. Provided always that the demand for new houses shows no tendency to decline we may look for a continued expansion in employment in home investment. As far as the engineering trades are concerned, the low level of employment compared with 1929 suggests that there are adequate facilities available for meeting this demand. The building industries, however, are in a quite different position. Employment is already well in excess of the 1929 level, and it is quite possible that schemes for expansion may be held up by the difficulty of securing adequate building labour, especially in those areas which are at present expanding most rapidly.

V.—Housing.

18. We have qualified our expectations of an improvement in employment in the demand for labour for home investment by the proviso that there should be no tendency for the demand for new houses to fall off. At

the moment, indeed, there is no sign of this. The statistics of building plans passed continue to forecast an increasing output. But in the long run no prediction can be made with greater confidence than that the present rate of house building cannot be maintained. Indeed, this is obvious when we consider that if houses continued to be built at the present rate, the total number of houses would be doubled in thirty years, or, alternatively, that the maximum number of houses which our present population could require would be entirely replaced in forty years. It is a very badly built house which does not last twice that time. Just as at one time an expansion of house building offered the greatest hope for Great Britain's recovery from depression, so to-day the possibility of a decline of house building must be one of the major sources of anxiety as to the continuation of the present recovery.

19. There have been many attempts to estimate the probable extent of housing demand. They are, however, largely vitiated from our present point of view by the fact that they have been undertaken with the object of determining the minimum number of houses required to establish a particular standard of housing accommodation based on some assessment of absolute needs. We need hardly point out that this is quite a different object from that which we have in mind, namely, the determination of the number of houses for which the present population, with its great diversity of incomes, is prepared to pay a rent high enough to make house building profitable, building costs and rates of interest being what they are to-day. The problem of overcrowding is of a quite different character. So long as house space can command a price, families whose means are for any reason inadequate must be expected to be economical in their use of it. The building boom will come to an end, because it is no longer profitable to build houses, long before rents have fallen to such a point that the poorest families can afford the standard of housing which social considerations make desirable.

20. The most authoritative survey of the housing requirements of the decade 1931–41 is contained in the Registrar-General's report* on housing published in connection with the census of 1931. The relevant argument of this report may be summarised as follows. The number of private families enumerated at each census up to and including 1911 has a fairly constant relation to various indices derived from the population statistics, based on such figures as the number of married women and the number of widows and widowers. In the decade 1911 to 1921, however, the increase in the number of private families was very much less than these indices would suggest as likely. This is evidence that at the date of the 1921 census the number of private families was reduced by an exceptional cause, namely, by persons who would normally have wished to live separately being forced to live together by reason of the shortage of housing accommodation. By 1931, however, the number of private families had expanded by an amount

* Stationery Office Publication 70–125–0–31 of 1935.

sufficient to make good the deficiency at the previous census. It may therefore be inferred that the state-assisted building effort in the decade 1921–31
had made good the housing shortage caused by the war, and the pre-war
standard of housing accommodation had been re-established. Nevertheless,
evidence of a continued housing shortage still remained in the shape of an
unduly low proportion of vacant premises, judged by pre-war experience.
In the decade 1931–41 the number of private families may be expected, on
the basis of the indices already referred to, to expand by 917,000 or by 9
per cent.; and on the basis of the existing relation between houses and private
families this should call for 771,000 new houses. To this increase, which is
necessary to maintain the pre-war standard of housing, certain additions are
required in order to obtain a total of the houses which must be built within
the decade 1931–1941. These additions may be tabulated as follows:—

(a) To make good demolitions and losses from the encroach-
     ment of industrial and commercial areas, less the
     additions to housing accommodation resulting from
     the conversion of large houses into flats   100,000
(b) Slum clearance schemes   300,000
(c) To restore the proportion of vacant premises to its pre-
     war figure   200,000
(d) To diminish overcrowding especially among sharing
     families   300,000

                                                                  —————
                                                                  900,000

These additions, together with the 800,000 houses necessary to provide for
the increase that would occur in the number of private families in the decade
1931–1941 on the assumption that in this respect social habits remain the
same, bring the total number of houses which must be built in that decade
to 1,700,000. And this is the estimate given by the Registrar-General.

21. It may be observed at once that not all this increase in requirements
will have already become effective. The natural increase in private families
since the date of the census was probably not much more than 400,000,
requiring perhaps 350,000 houses to contain them. The slum clearance
schemes have so far only resulted in the closure of about 40,000 houses.
Thus on the above estimate the total number of new houses which could
have been disposed of between the census date and to-day, even if the whole
improvement in housing accommodation anticipated for the decade had
been concentrated in its first four years, would be no more than a million.
In fact, however, a million new houses have already been built since the date
of the census. And yet it would be impossible to assert that vacant houses
are to-day available in the same numbers as before the war. We may,
therefore, assert that the Registrar-General's estimate is too low. There

must have been some factor at work causing an abnormal increase in the demand for houses.

22. The explanation is almost certainly that the number of families has been growing more rapidly than the indices derived from population indices would suggest. The extent to which people associate together to form a family is determined in part by natural convenience, in part by economic considerations. Very few people live alone by preference. On the other hand, people tend to live together to a greater extent than they would be led to by purely personal considerations because by so doing they effect a saving in rent, and in other items of expenditure, such as heating and lighting, and in a less degree in food, and are thus able to improve their standard of living in other directions. In so far as the cost of the above items of expenditure diminishes, the relative advantage of living together also diminishes and private families tend to disintegrate. The effect of recent social legislation has been to improve the status of a large number of older people who would probably prefer to live by themselves, by the provision of various kinds of state pensions. The number of families as defined in the census is thus an elastic factor, capable of considerable expansion. But there is clearly a limit to this expansion, and though it is difficult to measure it with any precision, we doubt, however, whether this factor by itself could in any circumstances increase the demand for houses by as much as 10 per cent. above the pre-war standard. Yet if the present rate of house building is maintained, by 1938, not only will this position be reached, but the normal number of vacant premises will also have been restored, and enough houses been built to replace those demolished under the slum clearance schemes.

23. In these circumstances it is extremely unlikely that the building of new houses can possibly continue at its present rate for as long as three years, and indeed we should expect that there will be a substantial decline in building activity in many areas before the end of 1936 and that this will have become general before the end of 1937. Moreover the decline, when it sets in, will be very considerable. House building might easily be reduced from its present level of 330,000 a year, to a level at which it no more than satisfies the demand for houses to supply the needs of the natural increase in private families and to replace normal demolition, *i.e.*, to a level of approximately 90,000 houses a year. In terms of employment, there might be a falling off in the demand for labour, direct or indirectly employed in the building industry, of the order of half a million men. To some extent it may be possible to mitigate this decline by further developments of housing policy, a question to which we revert later in this report (paragraph 45).

24. In considering the significance of this figure, it must be borne in mind that an adverse movement in foreign trade which had the effect of reducing employment, at its worst by 600,000 men, was responsible for the unprecedented slump of 1929–32. Thus there is a grave danger than in 1937 or thereabouts this country may be faced with a crisis of the same magnitude

as the last, but with one serious disadvantage in addition, namely, the saturation of that field of demand, which is most quickly responsive to a reduction in the rate of interest. In the final sections of this report we turn to consider the methods by which this prospective crisis may be best overcome, and the steps which it will be necessary to take in the meantime to insure that this country is in a position to take them.

VI.—Overseas trade.

25. British export trade has shown a quite considerable improvement since the bottom of the depression, and the volume of competitive imports which have been received into this country has expanded by only a moderate amount since the imposition of the tariff. Thus, the net employment in foreign trade has expanded since 1932 in proportion with the expansion of total employment. But the character of our export trade has undergone certain modifications. In the first place, there has been a change in the importance of different markets. This is illustrated by the following table:—

TABLE 7.

The direction of British exports in the first quarter of the years 1929, 1932, and 1935.

	1929.		1932.		1935.	
	£000's.	Per cent. of total.	£000's.	Per cent. of total.	£000's.	Per cent. of total.
British countries	81,662	45·3	40,469	43·8	48,738	46·2
Foreign countries now within the sterling area*	20,747	11·5	11,474	12·4	16,757	15·9
Other foreign countries ...	78,759	43·2	40,388	43·8	40,003	37·9
Total	180,172	100·0	92,331	100·0	105,498	100·0

* Finland, Sweden, Norway, Denmark, Portugal, Egypt, Iraq, Iran, Siam, and the Argentine.

26. Exports to British countries, and to countries within the sterling area, have expanded considerably since 1932, whereas exports to other foreign countries have remained stationary. In part this must be attributed to the advantageous agreements which it has been possible to conclude with the countries of the first two groups, particularly with Denmark and the Argentine. But other factors of great importance in stimulating this trade have been the close financial co-operation between these countries and ourselves, and the diffusion of the benefits of cheap money throughout the sterling area.

27. In addition to this change in the direction of trade, a further important change appears to be taking place in the character of the goods we export. The export of capital goods is apparently becoming more important and the export of goods for consumption less important. Normally speaking, the export of capital goods can be expected to decline more than other classes of goods in times of depression, and to expand more than other classes of goods in times of recovery. For depression is always most severe in the market for capital goods. The last depression, however, was marked by particularly heavy losses of markets by the textile manufacturing industries, partly as a result of Japanese competition, but mainly as a result of the increasing development of these industries in our overseas markets. As a consequence, the relative importance of exports of capital goods was maintained in the first two years of the depression and only showed a comparatively small decline in the years 1932 and 1933. In 1934 capital goods had practically regained the same relative importance as they held in 1929, and in 1935 we have seen a much more rapid expansion in their export than in the export of goods for current consumption. The following tables illustrate this point.

TABLE 8.

Exports of the produce and manufactures of the United Kingdom in the years 1929 to 1934.

(£s millions.)

—	1929.	1930.	1931.	1932.	1933.	1394.
Total exports	729·3	570·8	390·6	365·0	367·9	396.1
Exports of capital goods*	185·8	161·2	100·5	84·1	85·8	100·1
Exports of other goods ...	545·5	409·6	290·1	280·9	282·1	296·0
Capital goods exported as a percentage of the total	25·5	28·3	25·7	23·0	23·4	25·3

* Exports in Class III, Groups C, F, G and R.

TABLE 9.

Exports of the produce and manufactures of the United Kingdom in the first five months of 1934 and 1935.

—	1934.	1935.	Increase per cent.
	£s millions.	£s millions.	
Total exports	157·6	173·6	10·2
Exports of capital goods	37·9	46·7	23·2
Exports of other goods	119·7	126·9	6·0
Capital goods exported as a percentage of the total	24·0	26·9	...

The exceptional increase in the percentage of exports of capital goods in the year 1930 was almost entirely attributable to the maintenance of the level of exports of vehicles and ships in that year, goods which had no doubt been ordered in the year 1929 or earlier, but which, owing to their long period of construction, were only delivered after the slump had begun.

28. We may further inquire in what quarters the export of British capital goods is expanding most rapidly. The following table indicates that again it is the British countries and, as far as it is possible to judge, the foreign countries of the sterling area which are responsible for the greater part of the increase; though it also appears that even in other foreign countries an expansion is taking place.

TABLE 10.

Exports of British capital goods in the years 1929 to 1935.

—	1929.	1930.	1931.	1932.	1933.	1934.	1935*.
British countries.							
Dominions and India							
£s millions	76·3	59·3	37·1	31·3	35·4	44·5	56·0
Per cent. of 1929 ...	100·0	78·0	49·0	41·0	46·0	58·0	74·0
Colonial Empire—							
£s millions	18·5	17·0	11·5	8·8	10·1	11·4	14·5
Per cent. of 1929 ...	100·0	92·0	62·0	48·0	55·0	62·0	79·0
Foreign countries.							
£s millions	91·0	84·9	52·0	44·0	40·3	44·2	53·1
Per cent. of 1929 ...	100·0	83·0	57·0	48·0	44·0	49·0	58·0

* Estimate based on the increase in the first 5 months.

In the case of foreign countries it seems likely, on the basis of the information available, that about half of the increase between 1934 and 1935 is attributable to the countries in the sterling area.

29. Judged in the light of the tendencies which have made themselves apparent in the last few years, we may conclude that the prospects of British exporting industries are to-day more dependent than hitherto on the course of recovery within the British Empire and the foreign countries belonging to the sterling area than before the slump; and that the export of capital goods is gaining in importance relatively to the export of goods for current consumption. We do not believe that these tendencies will prove transitory. On the one hand, financial considerations and general policy are likely to maintain the economic interdependence of the members of the British Empire and other nations of the sterling group. On the other, the trend of policy in the overseas countries will no doubt continue to be in the direction of greater industrialisation; and in that event, though they will cease to be

such convenient markets for our textiles, clothing, and the like, they should be able to absorb increasing quantities of the products of our iron and steel and engineering industries.

30. In one respect the present condition of the Overseas Empire is just the reverse of that in Great Britain. The outstanding feature of the economic life of the raw material producing countries of the Empire is still the great reduction in internal purchasing power that has followed the decline in the prices of their exports relative to those of their imports. This has affected not only the volume of their imports, but also the volume of production of their own industries, where they exist. In Australia, for example, employment among trades unionists, which in 1929 amounted to nearly 400,000, fell below 300,000 during 1932, and is still less than 350,000. In cases where exports largely consist of foodstuffs for the United Kingdom market, their volume has shown a substantial increase; but where they consist of raw materials and are dependent on the volume of world industrial production, they are generally well below the 1929 level. In general, the degree of prosperity prevailing throughout the Empire remains lower than before the depression, though the rise which has occurred in raw material prices, expressed in sterling, and in the price of gold since the beginning of 1932, has been great enough to eliminate the worst of the difficulties encountered during the slump.

31. This generalisation, however, does not apply to South Africa, the price of whose principal product, gold, has risen far above that of 1929. In her case industry and agriculture are benefiting from the increased internal demand; foreign capital is freely available for development; and a substantial boom in house building appears to be proceeding.

32. Though all parts of the Empire are equally interested in the sterling prices of raw materials, their degree of economic development is in other respects extremely different. The Colonial Empire is almost entirely without manufacturing industries, and its demand for manufactured imports thus bears a simple relation to the prices it obtains for its exports. Apart from this all-important factor, the prospects of colonial trade are influenced by (i) the accumulation of unsold stocks of manufactured goods within each colony; and (ii) the degree of development expenditure undertaken by the colonial administrations. Over the years 1930–1933 imports into the colonies considerably exceeded the value of their exports, and though this excess was no doubt in part financed by drawing on accumulated funds in London, in part it took the form of the piling up of stocks in the colonies. The more satisfactory experience of 1934 appears to have had the effect of reducing these supplies, and the outlook for exporters to the Colonial Empire is so much the more favourable. Capital development in the Colonial Empire is largely dependent on the needs of the local exporting industries; and though the financial position of colonial administrations has improved enormously as the result of the rise of stock prices in London, no very great extension

of development can be expected until international trade in raw materials has regained and surpassed the 1929 level.

33. The Dominions present a far more complicated picture. Their financial organisation is much more elaborate; their economic interests are much more diverse. In every case there is a substantial manufacturing interest which it is the declared policy of every Dominion Government to foster, and which in fact was expanding rapidly up to the year 1929. This development and the effect of the slump on it may be judged from the following figures of employment in manufacturing industry in the Dominions:—

TABLE 11.

Persons employed in manufacturing industry in certain British Dominions.

(in thousands.)

	Canada.	Australia.	New Zealand.	Union of South Africa.
1925	544	428	...	158
1927	619	452	79	171
1929	694	450	81	189
1930	644	419	83	190
1931	557	339	80	...
1932	495	337	69	...
1933	...	371	69	...

34. The principal effects of the decline in food and raw material prices on the economic life of the Dominions were: first, the fact that the existing structure of internal indebtedness weighed with unlooked for severity upon those engaged in primary production; secondly, the difficulties that arose in the raising of further loans in the London market brought to an abrupt close the programmes of government financed expenditure on development; thirdly, the purchasing power available in the internal market was very seriously reduced, with disastrous repercussions on the development of manufacturing industry. These difficulties have, in most cases, by now been mastered. The weight of debt was attacked in many ways. In Australia and New Zealand the position of agricultural debtors was eased by the devaluation of the currency to 80 per cent. of its previous sterling value. In Australia, there was also the part voluntary, part compulsory, scaling down of interest charges in 1931. In New Zealand mortgage interest rates were scaled down to the capacity of the borrower to pay by the institution of a system of land courts. And in general the law took the unfortunate debtor under its protection. Financial conditions have now been very much eased throughout the Dominions and a condition of great financial liquidity now prevails, at any rate in New Zealand, Australia, and South Africa, though in the case of the two former this has only been possible at the expense of slowing down the normal rate of expansion. House building, for example, has very

greatly diminished in both these Dominions, though there has been a considerable recovery since 1932.

35.   Perhaps the most impressive instance of readjustment which the slump has seen is the disappearance of the Australian adverse balance of payments. The figures tell their own tale and deserve to be quoted. They are as follows:—

TABLE 12.

The estimated Australian balance of payments.

(thousands of £s. sterling.)

				Adverse balance.	Favourable balance.
1928–29	...	...	...	41,661	...
1929–30	...	...	...	71,616	...
1930–31	...	...	...	15,626	...
1931–32	...	...	...	...	6,360
1932–33	...	...	...	3,790	...

When we recollect the profound changes in economic conditions which were required to produce an improvement of £100 millions in the British balance of payments, the extent of this achievement in a population of less than a sixth of our numbers can be properly appreciated.

36.   Since 1931 Australia has been forced to finance her development out of her own resources, and it has only been possible to effect this as a result of the very small demand there has been in every field of investment activity. The gradual improvement in conditions since 1932 is, however, increasing the demand for capital, and since the beginning of this year interest rates have been rising.   It is now again cheaper for the Australian government to borrow in London rather than internally, and if the Australian recovery is to proceed, it is very probable that such borrowing will be necessary.

37.   It also seems likely that the gradual expansion in domestic demand will carry manufacturing industry in the Dominions back to the level of 1929.   We have already seen that there has been a considerable revival in the demand for capital goods, especially for machinery, from the Dominions, though, except in the case of South Africa, this still is a long way below the level of 1929.   In considering the future prospects of demand from this quarter, we must bear in mind the very great readjustments which there have been in relative manufacturing costs in Great Britain and the Dominions since 1929.   In Australia, for example, average wages* have been reduced from 101s. 2d. in 1929 to 81s. 10d. in September 1934, a reduction of 20 per cent.   In Great Britain wages have fallen by less than 5 per cent. Moreover, the Australian pound has been devalued by 20 per cent. of its sterling value.   As a consequence a large number of industries which in 1929

* Adult males only.

were only just able to maintain themselves with the help of the high Australian tariff must by now have become definitely competitive. It follows that any revival of internal Australian demand will be met to a large extent by increased production in Australia itself. Great Britain's trade will benefit only indirectly as a result of the increased demand for capital goods. But though in the long run this may be a factor tending to diminish Great Britain's exports, in the short run it may have favourable results. For the value of the equipment of a factory is likely to exceed the value of its current output. This tendency is likely to be true, though in a less degree, in other Dominions besides Australia.

38. The broad result of this examination of the position within the British Empire is that there is a good prospect of a continued improvement in British export trade in that direction, but that this improvement so far as the Dominions are concerned is likely to be largely confined to the products of the engineering and iron and steel trades. That is to say, we expect to see in the future a continuation of the trends which we have already observed in our exports during the last few years.

39. We are interested in the Empire not merely as traders, but as bankers as well. The stability of sterling and the maintenance of low money rates can be materially affected by events and policy in Australia, South Africa, and elsewhere. This, indeed, is one of the major lessons of the last depression. It was not so much the fact that Great Britain had by that time developed a serious adverse balance of payments which led to the exchange crisis of 1931. Far more important was the cumulative effect of many years of borrowing by the Empire as a whole. The effect of the return to the gold standard on the British balance of trade was not very great. The effect on the balance of trade of the whole Empire was much greater. The following table shows the balance of trade between British countries and foreign countries on the one hand, and of Great Britain with all countries, British and foreign, on the other.

TABLE 13.

The adverse balance of commodity trade of the British Empire and of the United Kingdom in the years 1924 to 1933.

(£ millions.)

—	1924.	1925.	1926.	1927.	1928.	1929.	1930.	1931.	1932.	1933.
Adverse balance of commodity trade between British countries and foreign countries ...	193	160	374	341	301	367	403	378	226	175
Adverse balance of commodity trade of the United Kingdom ...	337	393	463	386	352	382	386	407	286	258

Throughout the period of 1927–29 Great Britain considered in isolation had a favourable balance of payments large enough to meet the loans for abroad raised in the London market. But it is highly probable that the Empire as a whole was becoming increasingly indebted to foreign countries.

VII.—The outlook for the next few years.

40. So far as the immediate prospects are concerned, the conclusions to which we have come in the foregoing examination of the economic outlook are on the whole reassuring. There is room, we believe, for further expansion in the investment industries. Shipbuilding, for example, improvement of which is long overdue, shows signs of increased activity. Our exports should continue to increase. We should also expect to see a continued increase in demand in the home market for goods and services for current consumption. This, however, may be at a diminishing rate, especially as the rate of production for this market may be adversely affected by the fact that hitherto it has been stimulated by the rapid increase in the demand for working capital which is normally associated with a period of recovery. As the rate of recovery slows down, the effect of this favourable factor will *pro tanto* diminish. Though it is perhaps unwise to commit ourselves to a numerical estimate, our impression is that employment among insured persons within the age groups 16 to 64, might expand through these causes by not more at the outside than 250,000 persons a year, and that only so long as house building shows no serious recession. Though this is a comparatively high rate of increase judged by historical precedents, it must be observed that it will not be great enough to effect any substantial diminution in the numbers of the unemployed. During the next few years the numbers of persons over 16 years of age needing employment will expand very rapidly, because in these years the abnormally large numbers of children born just after the war will be reaching the age of 16.

41. As regards the prospects for a longer period, however, our conclusions are less favourable. The whole fabric of our present prosperity is threatened by the likelihood of a decline culminating possibly in a virtual collapse of activity in the construction of new dwelling houses. Other forces of expansion may be strong enough to maintain or even slightly to increase the level of general activity for a little time after a recession in house building begins. If the recession in house building were to culminate in a collapse, it would be such an important factor making for a contraction of trade, that a major depression would be almost bound to accompany it. We may predict with confidence that before the end of 1938 Great Britain will again be faced with the problem of dealing with an apparently inevitable increase in unemployment.

42. Whether or not this country is in a position to deal satisfactorily with the new crisis when it develops will depend in a large degree on the

policy pursued in the intervening years. The only satisfactory compensation for such a serious decline in the level of home investment as must, failing any large extension in the field of public capital development, be associated with the prospective falling off in house building would be an expansion in one of the two other main forms of economic activity, namely, production for consumption in the home market, and production for export. The first will require a major redistribution of the use of incomes as between saving and spending. The second will largely depend on events outside the control of this country, but it will be possible to promote it by a liberal commercial policy, and, so long as sterling retains its independent position as an international currency, it may be possible to assist it by appropriate financial measures.

43. Thus the situation which will arise when the next crisis occurs will continue to call for at least as rigorous an insistence on the policy of making money cheap in times of depression as was necessary in 1932. It is therefore essential that the general financial position of Great Britain at that time shall be such as to make the application of this policy possible. This must be fully borne in mind in considering any change in Britain's monetary policy. It would be disastrous if the free development of Britain's monetary policy were to be hampered by exchange difficulties such as we experienced in 1930 and 1931. It would also be highly unfortunate if Great Britain's national finances were to be in a suspect condition when the need for possibly rather unorthodox remedies makes itself felt. Great Britain, in 1938, must not find itself in the same difficulties as in 1930.

44. In this connection an important point of policy arises with regard to a possible stabilisation of the pound in relation to the dollar and the franc. If in 1938 there should be no rigid link between the pound and these currencies, and if sterling remained the international currency of a group of countries prepared to accept Britain's financial leadership with confidence, it would be possible to pursue a policy of cheap money, even though only small reserves of other currencies were available. If, however, by that time the pound were rigidly linked with gold, Great Britain would need to be in a position to lose considerable quantities of gold and foreign assets in the pursuit of its policy. We do not propose to pursue this part of the subject, as this would lead to a discussion of the larger question of the conditions necessary for stabilisation, with which we are not concerned in this report.

45. A final word must be said regarding the policy to be pursued by the government with the object of directly stimulating large schemes of home investment. The effectiveness of such intervention on the volume of employment depends very largely on the economic conditions prevailing at the time when they begin to affect the demand for labour. If this occurs at a time when the capital producing industries are fairly fully employed, the net effect on government investment on employment in the investment industries may be very much less than the numbers actually employed on

the government scheme. If, however, the demand is felt at a time when investment in general is depressed, it should have important repercussions, not only in those industries, but also in the industries supplying consumers' goods. In considering important schemes for home investment, preference should be given to those which will mature in the years 1938, 1939 and 1940. This principle is of special force in the field of housing policy. It would not be appropriate to stimulate the housing activities of local authorities at the present time, when house building is being carried on under private enterprise to an extent which cannot be maintained for long. On the other hand, it will afford considerable relief to the building industry if in the period of comparative depression that must inevitably follow the present boom local authorities are in a position to undertake a substantial programme of slum clearance and of providing houses for those classes of the population which are not in a position to pay the rents now demanded for houses built by private enterprise. Although, however, the time for action has not yet arrived, it is highly desirable that the necessary steps should now be taken to make possible the immediate application of this policy as soon as the depression makes itself felt.

Twenty-second Report of Committee on Economic Information,
February 1937*

ECONOMIC POLICY AND THE MAINTENANCE OF TRADE ACTIVITY.

IN most of the reports which we have submitted in the last few years we have paid greater attention to the analysis of the economic situation than to the discussion of general questions of economic policy. In this report, however, we shall be more concerned with policy than diagnosis, because in our opinion a stage in the development of economic activity has been reached when it is desirable that policy should be influenced by the possibility that events may later take an unfavourable course. We are far from suggesting any immediate worsening in the economic situation. The probability is, rather, that the present improvement will continue at least throughout the present year. If, however, the forces now at work are allowed to develop without control, there is a danger that they may produce a situation in which a substantial decline in activity will be very hard to avoid.

2. We would begin by emphasising that the dangers which we anticipate proceed from a different quarter from those which produced the depression of 1930 to 1932. That depression was characterised by a great falling off in the demand for British goods from abroad. Partly because there had been no unjustifiable expansion of activity in the investment industries in this

---

* P.R.O. Cab. 58/30, E.A.C. (S.C.) 26, 19 February 1937; also Cab. 24/268, C.P. 77(37).

country, and partly because the policy of the then Government was directed towards the maintenance of capital construction at home, there was in the United Kingdom between 1929 and 1931, only a very moderate decline in the domestic demand for the products of the investment industries. In 1932, indeed, there was a substantial decline in this demand; but it was in the main the result of a change in Government policy, induced by the critical condition of the sterling exchange.

3. The danger before us is that the present level of home investment activity will not be maintained as the economic situation develops. It may roughly be estimated that home expenditure on durable goods is to-day one-third greater than in 1929. Up to 1929 the level of home investment was adversely affected by the peculiar difficulties of Great Britain's economic position, and, in view of our present improved circumstances, a material increase in the absorption of investment goods is justifiable. Nevertheless, past experience confirms, what economic theory suggests, that in periods of general activity the demand for investment goods is apt to exceed that which it is easy to maintain, and that it is prudent, therefore, to anticipate a decline in demand within this field as a point of temporary saturation is approached in certain directions.

4. We have argued in previous reports that demand for British goods for export and home demand in the investment industries are of peculiar importance in determining the general level of British economic activity. The demand for British goods for current consumption in Great Britain is unlikely, in general, to vary substantially, so long as the home demand for investment goods, on the one hand, and for British goods for export, on the other, show no material alteration. But demand in these two last categories may vary substantially, without there having been any previous change in the level of demand for consumption in Great Britain. Moreover, because of the general interdependence of all forms of economic activity, an advance or recession in one branch is likely to communicate itself to others and thus to give rise to changes in the level of employment out of all proportion to that directly due to the original cause.

5. We have discussed in previous reports the future demand for new dwelling houses—a very important branch of the output of the investment industries. The conclusions to which we came were that it was extremely improbable that the present rate of construction would be prolonged beyond the end of 1938, that a recession in the course of 1937 was likely, and that the decline in output would eventually reach very serious proportions. The fact that the value of building plans approved for new dwelling houses has now for several months shown a marked falling off in comparison with the preceding year, suggests that the opportunities for profitable investment in this field are approaching exhaustion. During the last few years, however, an increasing share of the total value of building plans passed by local authorities has been taken by buildings other than dwelling houses, and

although it is likely that the building of new dwellings will decline in the course of this year, the present indications are that the total activity of the building industries will be maintained for the present.

6. Even in 1934, the output of the investment industries was probably substantially in excess of their output in 1929. But this increase was entirely due to the great expansion in house building. In 1935 the output of the investment industries continued to advance, though the output of new houses remained stationary; and in 1936 this advance was accelerated. We can attribute the continued expansion in the last two years to two causes; first to the demand for new plant and equipment as opportunities for the modernisation and expansion of our industries presented themselves under the stimulus of a reviving home demand; and secondly, to the demand arising from the rearmament programme. Direct rearmament expenditure is not in the same category as other purchases of investment goods; but expenditure on industrial equipment, whether induced by the expansion of consumers' demand, or by the new demand arising from the rearmament expenditure, is exposed, though in a lesser degree, to the same risks which we have noticed in connection with house building, the risk that in time a point of saturation will be reached.

7. In the case of houses it is possible to make some kind of estimate of the rate at which the supply of houses is approaching the point of saturation, because there are adequate statistics of the number of houses in existence, of the number of new houses built, and of the factors upon which depend the number of families, which, in turn, determines the demand for houses. In the case of industrial capital, the problem cannot be reduced to such simple terms. A review of the available facts, however, leads us to the conclusion that investment in industrial plant to-day is on a materially greater scale than in 1929. Though we cannot say with certainty that in every instance the present level of investment will not be maintained, in some cases, notably in the case of iron and steel, there are indications that even to-day the productive capacity of the industry is being expanded to a point at which difficulty may be found in utilising existing equipment, except in the quite abnormal conditions of demand which we are now experiencing. In general, we feel justified in assuming that the present industrial demand for the products of the investment industries is of a character which exposes it to the risk of a setback, even though consumers' demand for the products of industry is maintained, and of a substantial reduction in the event of any falling off in the demand of ultimate consumers.

8. The consequences to be apprehended from a falling off in the demand for the products of the investment industries are of two kinds. The first is a reduction in the level of incomes currently earned which, in turn, create the demand for the products of the consumption industries. The second is the appearance of a surplus of labour and productive resources in the investment industries which can only be absorbed with difficulty into other industries.

These consequences could most satisfactorily be avoided by arranging, if it were possible, that the flow of demand for the products of the investment industries should be as regular as possible from one year to the next. This leads us to the first aspect of economic policy which we believe should be seriously considered to-day.

9. We can no longer anticipate that the stimulus to economic activity generally associated with an increase in investment will make any substantial impression on the remaining volume of unemployment. If unemployment is to be further reduced, either there must be a qualitative change in the nature of demand, such, for example, as might occur if the exports of those industries which are not especially active at present, *e.g.*, cotton, could be stimulated, or special steps must be taken to increase the demand for labour in the areas where unemployment is the consequence of geographical maldistribution of the population. One of the reasons why unemployment diminished much more rapidly in 1936 than in 1935, was that the revival of the demand for heavy engineering products, induced by the rearmament programme and the increase in industrial investment, led to increased activity in districts, particularly in the north eastern area, where the under employment of existing resources was particularly marked. In the same way, any material expansion in the demand for our older staple exports would now have a much more marked effect upon total employment, than a similar but more widely diversified increase in demand. Furthermore, even in the case of those districts which used to rely on coalmining, the introduction of new industries, although they might depend for the bulk of their specialised labour force on immigration from more fortunate areas, would, by reason of the unused capacity of the ancillary industries in these districts, such as building, transport and distribution, probably prove helpful to employment as a whole.

10. Apart from the special areas the postponement of such investment activity as is not of an urgent character would, on balance, prove beneficial to the average level of employment over a period of years. For to-day, an attempt to increase investment expenditure would react rather on the level of profits earned by industry than on the total volume of employment; whereas later, should the total amount of investment activity fall below the minimum compatible with conditions of good trade, the undertaking of the investment projects now postponed would react favourably upon the general level of employment.

11. Our first recommendation is therefore that the government should take what steps are possible to postpone work upon investment projects which are not of an urgent character. Given time, the rate of investment activity can be reduced by increasing the long-term rates of interest; and if the influence of the government was used to accelerate a rise in these rates an immediate impression could, no doubt, be made on the activity of the investment industries. But we doubt whether action upon these lines would

produce the exact effect which is required to-day. We do not wish to see a reduction in the total expenditure upon investment projects over, say, the next five years, for our fear is rather that in the latter part of this period expenditure of this kind may be seriously deficient. Yet it is not unlikely that a substantial portion of the projects which might be postponed to-day as a result of a rise in interest rates would in the event turn out to be abandoned for good. Moreover, because of the inevitable lag between the initiation of a project and the full development of expenditure upon it, a rise in interest rates to-day might be exerting its greatest effect some time hence when the whole situation may have been profoundly modified. Finally, the influence of an immediate rise in interest rates on projects which could be postponed—projects, that is to say, which are not required to meet the exceptional demand created by conditions of exceptionally good trade— may be the reverse of that intended. For a rise in long-term rates of interest might produce an expectation of a further rise in the next few years; with the result that it would seem wiser to advance rather than retard the effective date of projects of this kind. Quite apart, therefore, from the considerations which we put forward later in paragraph 25, we should not feel that reliance upon efforts to raise long-term interest rates in order to bring about that selective and discriminating postponement of investment projects which we desire, would be justified, and, therefore, we do not advocate that course.

12. There remains the possibility of direct intervention in those spheres of investment activity over which the government exercises some degree of control. The most obvious of these are expenditure upon road improvements, railway electrification, slum clearance and other state assisted housing schemes, telephone and telegraph development, and in a lesser degree other expenditure on quasi-public services, such as docks, electricity and gas, water supplies, tramways and the like. We must exclude in present circumstances expenditure on defence, although in more normal times it would be highly desirable that heavy capital expenditure on the defence services should be undertaken when other forms of investment activity were at a low ebb. Even so there remains a substantial body of investment under some sort of Government control, which may be used in some degree as a makeweight to promote the stability of investment activity between good years and bad. There are, of course, well known difficulties in the execution of this policy. To an important extent expenditure under the headings which we have enumerated is required because of an expansion of demand arising from causes over which the Government has little control. The increase in telephone traffic, for example, is naturally fastest when trade activity is expanding; and except in so far as facilities have been over expanded in the previous depression, it is impossible to curtail expenditure during the subsequent boom. Furthermore, a very substantial part of the capital expenditure of local authorities and public utility companies is required to extend normal facilities to new housing estates, and is dependent on the rate of

house building. It cannot be anticipated without risk or postponed without injustice. Thus even if the government had complete control over the pace of development in the services enumerated its use of its powers to prevent undue fluctuations in the level of investment activity would be circumscribed within comparatively narrow limits.

13. Moreover, the control which the Government can exercise over the rate of capital expenditure is at present very far from complete. For example, in the case of capital expenditure undertaken by local authorities under powers already conferred upon them it is confined to the duty of giving or withholding authorisation for the local authority to raise money by way of loan and to the power of promising or refusing grants from public funds. Once the grant has been promised and the authorisation given the matter passes out of the direct control of the central government, though, of course, the latter may still influence local authorities by its advice. Yet the time which elapses between the granting of the authorisation and the beginning of expenditure varies considerably. In some cases the beginning of work may actually anticipate the authorisation by a week or so; in others it may not occur until three or even four years later. The machinery of control over the capital expenditure of local authorities is not designed to secure the co-operation of these authorities in the important work of using this expenditure as a make-weight to balance the fluctuations of other investment activity. It is a matter for consideration whether the powers of the central government in this respect should not be extended. In so far as co-operation is achieved to-day, it is on a purely voluntary basis, in response to circular letters which have been sent out from time to time explaining the Government's policy in this respect. Moreover, the willingness of local authorities to co-operate with the Government by postponing investment projects to-day may be materially affected by their desire to undertake capital expenditure at a time when the costs of borrowing are low. The effect of an appeal to local authorities would therefore be very much greater if it were reinforced by action on the part of the financial institutions most concerned with the issue of loans to local authorities. Since the conversion operation the order and rate of public issues by larger local authorities has been subject to generally accepted guidance amounting to unofficial regulation by the Governor of the Bank, and this degree of regulation might possibly be extended so long as the present investment situation persists. Furthermore, those smaller local authorities who are dependent for their finance on the Local Loans Fund, may even more easily be influenced by the wishes of the government.

14. The fact that the practical effect of a policy designed to retard, for the time being, the rate of public and semi-public expenditure is likely to be of only moderate dimensions, is a substantial argument in favour of the view that it can be adopted without risk. The last thing that could be required of such a policy is that it should be so effective as to precipitate just

those dangers which are to be feared from a decline in the present rate of industrial and private capital expenditure. Nevertheless it may be felt that more radical measures are required. In that event we would suggest that advantage might be taken of the present position of the iron and steel industry. There are very few capital works of any importance which can be undertaken without supplies of iron and steel, and it follows that control of the iron and steel output carries with it the power to delay constructional projects of a postponable character. At the moment there is a serious shortage of iron and steel and the delivery date quoted for new orders has already been pushed forward to a point at which serious embarrassment is likely to be experienced by consumers. Nevertheless the present and prospective capacity would probably be adequate to supply our average requirements over a period of years, if only it could be arranged that these requirements should come forward in a steady flow. A system under which the distribution of iron and steel was subjected to some form of rationing might contribute to this end, and without causing undue disturbance to employment or overseas trade might prevent too wide a gap developing between the enhanced capacity of the industry and demand under more normal conditions. Any such expedient would mean a new departure of policy raising important issues of principle, and could obviously only be adopted after every aspect of the problem had been carefully considered. We are so convinced, however, that fluctuations in iron and steel production are likely to play an important part in the ups and downs of trade activity that we recommend that the question should be thoroughly examined at an early date.

15. In making these proposals for the postponement, where possible, of capital works other than defence works, undertaken by public and quasi-public bodies, we would wish to exclude specifically from the scope of this policy works undertaken, or likely to give rise to substantial expenditure, in areas where unemployment still remains exceptionally high. Indeed, we think that as far as these areas are concerned, an extension rather than a contraction of public works expenditure is still required.

16. We cannot expect that the reserve of investment projects likely to become available through a policy of postponement during what remains of the natural life of the present recovery, is likely to be great enough to bridge the gap in investment activity which must be expected to occur between the time when the industrial demand for capital begins to show signs of falling off, and the time when it revives again. For it must be remembered that this decline in industrial investment will probably coincide with a more serious and more permanent falling off in housebuilding activity. This leads us to our second recommendation, namely, that the same public authorities who are urged to reduce their capital expenditure to-day should be encouraged to prepare plans for a considerable extension of their capital expenditure to become fully effective when the need arises.

17. The regulation of the capital expenditure of public authorities is not

the only step which can be taken to even out the fluctuations of trade activity between good years and bad. Changes in the level of imports and exports are in some measure comparable with changes in the level of home investment because they alter the relationship between the incomes earned in Great Britain and the expenditure on consumption in Great Britain. Thus trade policy cannot be wholly independent of the degree of activity in the investment industries at home. When this is low the reaction of increased importation on the level of home employment is much more likely to be serious than when it is high; and under the conditions likely to prevail in the current year we do not anticipate that any adverse repercussions on the level of employment are likely to result from a readiness to accept increased imports, even if only a small improvement in export demand should follow. But this is an extremely pessimistic assumption, and we should expect that a material proportion of any increase in our imports would be balanced by an increase in our exports which would create a demand for employment in just those quarters which are to-day in a position to meet it. Furthermore, in so far as the exceptional demand now arising from our domestic situation falls upon foreign suppliers, the consequences to home producers of a subsequent reduction in this demand are likely to be less severe, and thus a willingness to accept increased imports to-day is likely on the whole to promote stability in the level of domestic activity. In practice, of course, the effectiveness of such measures as a stabilising influence on domestic trade is considerably reduced by the fact that they are apt to be pursued by all countries at the same time, and, in consequence, to result in unnecessarily wide fluctuations in the volume of international trade, rather than stability of trade within the domestic field. Moreover, the level of tariffs through which effect can be given to such a policy cannot be raised or lowered without regard to the long period interests of the industries concerned. Nevertheless, our third recommendation is that for the time being we should acquiesce in the growth of our imports, even though this may result in a temporarily unfavourable balance of payments, especially in respect of imports coming from countries which are important potential markets for the products of our older exporting industries.

18. The recommendations which we have made hitherto have been directed towards the maintenance of stability in the field of investment. If that could be achieved, we believe that the problems in the monetary sphere, which have hitherto played such a prominent part in the history of the fluctuations of trade, would prove capable of comparatively simple solutions. But we must recognise that it is highly improbable that even the fullest practicable use of all the means open to the Government of operating directly on the level of investment activity, short of a radical modification of the pace of rearmament, would be sufficient to avoid either an extension of activity in the investment industries in the near future, or a serious diminution in this activity later on. In any event, the present level of invest-

ment activity is proving to be great enough to bring about a rising tendency in British costs, which, superimposed on rising prices for imported raw materials, has already substantially affected the level of wholesale prices.

19. Some degree of instability of prices must probably be accepted as a necessary consequence of the ups and downs of trade. But fluctuations in price beyond this point have generally been regarded as likely to aggravate the amplitude of fluctuations in employment. For they encourage any tendency which may otherwise exist for business men to abstain from investment in times of falling prices and to invest to excess in times of rising prices. Moreover, a belief that prices will rise is apt to lead to an undue eagerness to enter into contracts of indebtedness on insufficient security, which, when this belief is replaced by its contrary, are only too readily determined; with the result that the market for capital goods when prices are falling is unduly depressed by anticipations of widespread insolvency. For these reasons the prevention of any undue fluctuations of prices must be an important element in any policy designed to limit the fluctuations of trade.

20. There are a number of measures which, by general agreement, exercise a restraining influence on rising prices. The first of these is the traditional remedy of a balanced budget. The rearmament programme is one of the reasons for the present strong demand experienced by the investment industries, and it is perhaps impossible to prevent this demand from having an effect upon the prices charged by these industries. But the reaction of this demand upon the general price level will depend in a large measure upon the steps taken to finance it. If it is financed by way of loan the increased incomes of those it benefits largely represent an addition to the potential demand for other goods, and must tend to raise the general price level. If it is financed out of revenue, the increase in the aggregate of expenditure on other goods will be substantially smaller, and the effect will be to avoid (at any rate in part) the rise in the general price level which would otherwise occur. We believe, therefore, that as large a proportion as possible of the increased expenditure due to rearmament should be met by an increase in taxation.

21. Secondly, all possible steps should be taken to prevent the development of unjustifiable speculative activity. This calls more for action on the part of the financial community than on the part of the Government itself. But speculative activity takes so many forms and may so easily escape notice that it may be desirable for the Government to take measures designed to reduce the general level of speculative activity, for example, through an increase in those branches of the stamp duties which would be especially felt by speculators.

22. Finally, there is the question of monetary action. The changes which have taken place since 1931 have profoundly modified the connection which used to exist between short-term interest rates and the supply of

money. Moreover, the fact that to-day the Treasury is responsible for a much larger proportion of the demand for short-term money than used to be the case must influence the willingness of the Government to see rates raised against it in the market. In these circumstances it may be much more possible and desirable for the financial authorities to exercise adequate control over the supply of credit without recourse to the manipulations of short-term interest rates which are traditionally associated with this objective. In any event there is at present a wide divergence between Bank rate and market rate, so that a considerable stiffening of rates may occur within the money market before any change in Bank rate is called for. Although it is probable that, because of its importance as an indication of the views of the authorities and the influence it exerts conventionally on borrowers and lenders outside the immediate circle of the money market, a change in Bank rate is a step of far greater general significance than any change in market rates, it is not a question which requires immediate attention. We may, therefore, limit our discussion to the effects of the quantitative regulation of the basis of credit, however this may be effected, without attempting to anticipate the precise changes in market rates which may be entailed hereby, or to determine the extent to which the short-term rate of interest may be obsolete, or weakened, as an essential means of control—a question upon which, in such an untried area, opinions must certainly differ in degree.

23. The basis of credit may be increased, maintained at its present level, or restricted. We regard the last of these courses, which might be expected to carry with it an increase in Bank rate, as appropriate only in circumstances in which there is a pressing danger of a serious rise in prices. This we should define as a state in which it was plain that rises in wages were being demanded, and granted, on the ground that prices had risen, and rises in prices were occurring because wages had risen. In such circumstances there can be no end to an ever accelerating rise in the price level except through the use of the strongest financial measures.

24. We hope, however, that no emergency of this nature will arise. In that event the policy pursued should not be made to hinge upon its effect on the cost of short-term money to private borrowers. For we believe that within reasonable limits this may fluctuate without any material repercussions on the general business situation. We attach far greater importance to the effect of credit policy on long-term interest rates, as expressed by the yield on Government securities. We do not all estimate alike the extent to which in the circumstances of a boom new money created by financial action can be directed to the support of the gilt-edged market. We are, however, only concerned to point out that the criterion of policy in this field should be whether, in fact, the creation of new credit proves to be a factor supporting the gilt-edged market on the one hand, or on the other hand a stimulus to speculative activity. In the first case it may be persisted in, in the other it must be avoided.

25. We attach importance to the maintenance of a level of gilt-edged security prices not far removed from that which prevailed last year, because we believe that long-term considerations will require in future rates of interest lower rather than higher than those which then prevailed. The principal ground for our belief is that the cessation of the growth of population will carry with it a great falling off in the demand for new capital as the century proceeds. The prospective decline in the demand for new dwelling houses which we have discussed in previous reports is but one instance of the effect of the failure of the population to expand on the opportunities for new investment. This prospect carries with it certain important practical consequences. Psychological considerations play an important part in determining the speed with which the rate of interest is adapted to that required by economic considerations. As a result of the very rapid fall in the long-term rate of interest between 1932 and 1935 it is probable that the public would not, in the long run, resist very strongly a further fall in these rates from about 3 per cent. to, say, $2\frac{1}{2}$ per cent. provided that general economic conditions justified such a fall. If, however, there should now be a serious rise in long-term interest rates, the public reaction in a future situation which called for a second substantial fall in interest rates might be entirely different. The memory that on the last occasion interest rates rose again after their fall might give rise to very serious feelings of distrust as to the permanence of any fall that might then be sought; and the adjustment of economic life to the new situation might be greatly delayed.

26. Credit policy, however, is not the only means by which the gilt-edged market may be supported. At the moment a very large part of the Government debt has either no fixed redemption date, or a very distant one. It is therefore very vulnerable to alterations in the market view of the long-term outlook for interest rates. If our view of these prospects is correct, the Government could support its longer term issues through the offer of securities having a fixed redemption date, so far as the present programme of maturities permits, without increased charge for the moment—for the market would probably absorb such issues at materially lower yields than those now obtainable in irredeemable issues—and without risk of increased charges in the future. In this way it is possible that the gilt-edged market might be adequately supported without any intervention through increasing the basis of credit, a form of intervention which in present circumstances we should prefer, if possible, to avoid.

ECONOMIC ADVISORY COUNCIL COMMITTEES AND REPORTS

This list omits the scientific committees of the Economic Advisory Council. When a report was circulated to the Cabinet, the C.P. number is given. 'Reference' numbers are to pages in this book.

Committee	Members	Terms of reference	Proceedings	Reports	Reference
Economic Advisory Council (appointed 27 Jan. 1930)	J. R. MacDonald (Prime Minister) P. Snowden (Chancellor of the Exchequer) J. H. Thomas (Lord Privy Seal) W. Graham (President of Board of Trade) Noel Buxton (Minister of Agriculture) Sir Arthur Balfour E. Bevin W. R. Blair Sir John Cadman W. M. Citrine G. D. H. Cole Ernest Debenham Sir Andrew Duncan Sir Daniel Hall Sir William Hardy J. M. Keynes Sir Alfred Lewis Sir William McLintock Sir Josiah Stamp R. H. Tawney	To advise H.M. Government in economic matters To make continuous study of developments in trade and industry and in the use of national and imperial resources, of the effect of legislation and fiscal policy at home and abroad, and of all aspects of national, imperial and international economy with a bearing on the prosperity of the country	14 meetings: 17 Feb. 1930–16 Apr. 1931, 15 Jan. 1932. Cab. 58/2, 10–12, 14		20–5, 29–30, 33–6, 39–43, 73–7, 80–1, 86, 90, 107

Committee	Members	Terms of reference	Proceedings	Reports	Reference
Committee on Channel Tunnel (appointed 5 Apr. 1929)	E. R. Peacock (*Chairman*) Lord Ebbisham Sir Clement Hindley Sir Frederick Lewis Sir Henry Strakosch *Secretaries:* T. Jones A. F. Hemming	To examine and report on the economic aspects of proposals for the construction of a Channel Tunnel or other new form of cross-channel communication	35 meetings: 12 Apr. 1929–26 Feb. 1930. Cab. 58/121–6	First Interim Report, 20 Aug. 1929; Report, 28 Feb. 1930; C.P. 72 (30), published as Cmd. 3513	35–6
Committee on Iron and Steel Industry (appointed 26 July 1929)	Lord Sankey (*Chairman*) Thomas Shaw Cecil L. Budd C. T. Cramp Sir William Plender *Secretaries:* A. F. Hemming W. Palmer (Board of Trade)	To consider and report upon the present condition and prospects of the iron and steel industries, and to make recommendations as to any action which may appear desirable and practicable in order to improve the position of those industries in the markets of the world	30 meetings: 31 July 1929–27 May 1930. Cab. 58/127–31	Report, 30 May 1930; C.P. 189 (30) and C.P. 278 (31)	19–20, 46, 99
Committee on Cotton Industry (appointed 1 Aug. 1929)	J. R. Clynes (*Chairman*) A. V. Alexander Sir Alan Anderson Joseph Jones Sir William McLintock *Secretaries:* A. F. Hemming H. J. Hutchinson (Board of Trade)	To consider and report upon the present condition and prospects of the cotton industry, and to make recommendations as to any action which may appear desirable and practicable in order to improve the position of the industry in the markets of the world	25 meetings: 2 Aug. 1929–3 June 1930. Cab. 58/132–5	Report, 4 June 1930; C.P. 203 (30)	19–20, 46, 99

355

Committee	Members	Terms of reference	Proceedings	Reports	Reference
Committee on the Economic Outlook, 1930 (appointed 17 Feb. 1930)	J. M. Keynes (*Chairman*) Sir Arthur Balfour Sir John Cadman W. M. Citrine/E. Bevin G. D. H. Cole *Secretary:* H. D. Henderson	To supervise the preparation of a memorandum indicating the principal heads of the investigation . . . which should be embraced in a diagnosis of the underlying situation	3 meetings: 21 Mar.–1 May 1930. Cab. 58/145	Report, 4 Apr. 1930; two Reports, 2 May 1930	33–5, 165–80
Committee on Empire Trade (appointed 17 Feb. 1930)	Sir Arthur Balfour (*Chairman*) W. R. Blair Col. David Carnegie *Secretaries:* H. D. Henderson A. E. Overton (Board of Trade)	To prepare for the consideration of the Council a memorandum dealing with the nature of Empire trade, the actual effect of tariff preferences and the future trade relations between this country and the Dominions, having regard to the position of Great Britain *vis-à-vis* the Continent of Europe, and to the proposals that had been suggested by the French for a European Zollverein	4 meetings: 4 Mar.–5 June 1930. Cab. 58/149	Report, 12 June 1930; C.P. 228 (30)	33, 37–8
Committee on Unemployment Statistics (appointed 17 Feb. 1930)	Sir William McLintock (*Chairman*) E. Bevin Sir Horace Wilson *Secretaries:* H. D. Henderson A. Reeder (Ministry of Labour) Colin Clark	To examine the published returns relating to the number of persons recorded as unemployed and to suggest methods for the regular presentation of the figures in such a way as to avoid misunderstandings, whether at home or abroad, on the extent and nature of the present unemployment problem	2 meetings: 26 Mar., 2 Apr. 1930. Cab. 58/146	Report, 7 April 1930; C.P. 126 (30)	33, 37

Committee	Members	Terms of reference	Proceedings	Reports	Reference
Committee on Channel Tunnel Policy (appointed 13 Mar. 1930)	Sir Andrew Duncan (*Chairman*) E. Bevin Sir John Cadman J. M. Keynes Sir Alfred Lewis G. C. Upcott *Secretary:* A. F. Hemming	To prepare recommendations for submission to H.M. Government for the action to be taken on the following questions arising out of the report of the Channel Tunnel Committee:— (i) if, on the publication of the Report of the Channel Tunnel Committee, sufficient evidence were forthcoming to satisfy H.M. Government that the funds required for the construction of the British section of the Tunnel would be provided by private enterprise, should H.M. Government *so far as regards economic grounds* give their approval of the construction of the tunnel; (ii) if it appeared that the required financial support would not be forthcoming to enable the Tunnel to be built by private enterprise, was the evidence of the Report regarding the advantages of a Channel Tunnel to the country as a whole sufficient to justify H.M. Government either (a) itself constructing the Tunnel or (b) giving financial assistance to enable it to be constructed	2 meetings: 17, 25 Mar. 1930. Cab. 58/144	Report, 14 Apr. 1930; C.P. 114 (30)	35–6

Committee	Members	Terms of reference	Proceedings	Reports	Reference
Committee on Agricultural Policy (appointed 10 Apr. 1930)	E. D. Simon (*Chairman*) Sir Alan Anderson John Beard W. C. D. Dampier-Whetham E. R. Debenham Sir Daniel Hall R. H. Tawney Sir Matthew Wallace *Secretaries:* A. F. Hemming R. R. Enfield (Ministry of Agriculture)	To consider generally what is likely to happen under a continuance of the existing policy for agriculture, and in particular, to consider the following questions:- (a) Will the decline continue in production from the land and in employment on the land? (b) Is such a decline consistent with national economy or national safety?	9 meetings: 13 May–7 July 1930. Cab. 58/156–7	Report, 7 July 1930; C.P. 244 (30) and C.P. 279 (31)	33, 36, 39
Committee on Marketing and Distribution (appointed 10 Apr. 1930)	Sir Gilbert Garnsey (*Chairman*) Mrs E. Barton R. A. Burrows Sir John Cadman G. D. H. Cole W. Fraser W. Gallacher J. Hallsworth Prof. D. H. Macgregor Miss W. Nettlefold *Secretaries:* H. V. Hodson C. K. Hobson (Board of Trade)	To examine and report on the present system of marketing and distributing consumable commodities, in the light of the widening spread between the cost of living index and the wholesale price level; and to initiate special investigations to ascertain what economies might be effected in particular trades by reorganisation	6 meetings: 5 June 1930–8 Jan. 1931. Cab. 58/152–3	Report, 8 Jan. 1931	33–7

Committee	Members	Terms of reference	Proceedings	Reports	Reference
Committee on the Revision of the Cost-of-Living Index Number (appointed 8 May 1930)	Sir Andrew Duncan (*Chairman*) Prof. A. L. Bowley Miss Lynda Grier Prof. F. Hall R. T. Jones Sir Ralph L. Wedgwood *Secretaries:* H. D. Henderson J. Hilton (Ministry of Labour)	To consider: (*a*) whether there should be a new cost of living inquiry; (*b*) what should be the principles and methods by which it should be governed; (*c*) how a new series of index numbers could be constructed in the light of the data obtained from such an inquiry	5 meetings: 4 July–19 Dec. 1930. Cab. 58/147	Report, 26 Jan. 1931; C.P. 44 (31) and C.P. 16 (36)	36–7
Committee on Empire Migration (appointed 19 June 1930)	Viscount Astor (*Chairman*) Prof. A. M. Carr-Saunders G. D. H. Cole Captain L. F. Ellis Christopher Turnor *Secretaries:* A. F. Hemming W. J. Garnett (Overseas Settlement Department)	To consider the question of migration from the U.K. to overseas parts of the Empire in its economic aspects:– (*a*) in the immediate future, and (*b*) over a longer period, and to advise whether Government action to stimulate such migration is economically or otherwise desirable	20 meetings: 22 July 1930–22 June 1931. Cab. 58/163	Interim Report, 1 Oct. 1930; C.P. 329 (30); Final Report, July 1931; C.P. 297 (31), published as Cmd. 4075	33, 36–9, 96n
Committee of Economists (appointed 24 July 1930)	J. M. Keynes (*Chairman*) H. D. Henderson A. C. Pigou L. Robbins Sir Josiah Stamp *Secretaries:* A. F. Hemming R. F. Kahn	To review the present economic condition of Great Britain, to examine the causes which are responsible for it and to indicate the conditions of recovery	13 meetings: 10 Sept.–23 Oct. 1930. Cab. 58/150–1	Report, 24 Oct. 1930; C.P. 363 (30) and C.P. 234 (31)	40–1, 46–79

Committee	Members	Terms of reference	Proceedings	Reports	Reference
Committee on the Chinese Situation (appointed 24 July 1930)	W. Graham (*Chairman*) Sir Charles Addis Sir Arthur Balfour Hugh Dalton J. M. Keynes Archibald Rose *Secretaries:* A. F. Hemming T. G. Jenkins (Board of Trade)	To prepare an appreciation of the Chinese situation and to submit recommendations as to possible steps which could be taken to develop British trade in the Far East	4 meetings: 6 Oct.–18 Dec. 1930. Cab. 58/155	Report, 29 Dec. 1930; C.P. 8 (31)	41–2, 75
Committee on Unemployment Benefit (appointed 24 July 1930)	G. D. H. Cole (*Chairman*) Sir John Cadman Sir Sydney Chapman H. D. Henderson *Secretaries:* H. V. Hodson H. C. Emmerson (Ministry of Labour)	To examine the figures of unemployment benefit and their significance, and to indicate the abuses which have grown up in the system and to submit recommendations for their removal	4 meetings: 1 Oct.–5 Nov. 1930. Cab. 58/154	Report, 5 Nov. 1930; C.P. 426 (30)	42, 45
Committee on New Industrial Development (appointed 12 Mar. 1931)	J. H. Thomas (*Chairman*) Major Attlee Sir Andrew Duncan Sir William Hardy Sir Alfred Lewis Sir Holberry Mensforth James Morton *Secretaries:* H. D. Henderson A. F. Hemming	To examine the facts and arguments put forward in support of representations which H.M. Government have received to the following effect, viz.:– That the promotion of new industrial development in this country as a means of providing additional employment would be facilitated by the establishment of a central organisation, independent of existing	8 meetings: 23 Apr. 1931–25 May 1932. Cab. 58/167–8	Report, 28 June 1932; C.P. 279 (32), published 31 Aug. 1932 as H.M.S.O. publication 63–76, 1932	83

Committee	Members	Terms of reference	Proceedings	Reports	Reference
		Government and private organisations, whose function it would be:- (*a*) to draw up programmes of research into the practical application in industry of ideas, inventions or processes at present underdeveloped in this country and so far as existing agencies are concerned likely to remain undeveloped; (*b*) to institute the necessary research either by utilising existing facilities or by providing special facilities *ad hoc*; (*c*) to arrange, as and when the results of the research so undertaken warrant that course, for further tests on an industrial scale in order to establish the economic possibilities of the idea, invention or process; (*d*) to undertake, in proper cases, the further negotiations and arrangements necessary to secure the fullest application in the national interest of any results obtained; and to report:- (i) whether the establishment of such an organisation is desirable in the national interest, and, if so,			

Committee	Members	Terms of reference	Proceedings	Reports	Reference
		(ii) what form its constitution should take; (iii) what its relation should be to the state on the one hand and to private enterprise on the other; (iv) generally on the case for action on these or other lines			
Committee on Economic Information (appointed 14 July 1931)	Sir Josiah Stamp (*Chairman*) W. M. Citrine (1931–3) G. D. H. Cole J. M. Keynes Sir Alfred Lewis Sir Arthur Salter (1932–9) E. D. Simon (1932–6) D. H. Robertson (1936–9) Sir Sydney Chapman (Feb. 1932 only) Sir Frederick Leith-Ross (1932–9) Sir Frederick Phillips (1935–9) *Secretaries:* H. D. Henderson (1931–4) P. K. Debenham (1934–9) A. F. Hemming (1931–9)	To supervise the preparation of monthly reports to the Economic Advisory Council on the economic situation and to advise as to the continuous study of economic development	96 meetings: 15 Sept. 1931–10 July 1939. Cab. 58/17–23, 30	27 Reports: 1. The Balance of International Payments, 25 Sept. 1931; C.P. 242 (31) and C.P. 271 (31) 2. Survey of the Economic Situation, Mar. 1932; C.P. 96 (32) 3. Survey of the Economic Situation, May 1932; C.P. 161 (32)	83n, 94, 96–7, 114, 243–54 109–10, 114 114

Committee	Members	Terms of reference	Proceedings	Reports	Reference
				4. Survey of the Economic Situation, July 1932; C.P. 273 (32)	110, 114–21, 263–81
				5. Survey of the Economic Situation, Nov. 1932; C.P. 422 (32)	121–4, 126–7, 281–7
				6. Financial Policy, Feb. 1933; C.P. 34 (33)	122–4, 287–92
				7. The American Situation and the World Economic Conference, May 1933; C.P. 131 (33)	120
				8. Survey of the Economic Situation, July 1933; C.P. 202 (33)	
				9. Survey of the Economic Situation, 1933, 24 Oct. 1933; C.P. 254 (33)	110–11

Committee	Members	Terms of reference	Proceedings	Reports	Reference
				10. Survey of the Economic Situation, Jan. 1934; C.P. 20 (34)	
				11. Survey of the Economic Situation, Mar. 1934; C.P. 107 (34)	111–13
				12. Survey of the Economic Situation, July 1934; C.P. 206 (34)	
				13. The Coordination of Trade Policy, 23 Oct. 1934; C.P. 284 (34)	132–4, 292–319
				14. Survey of the Economic Situation, Dec. 1934 C.P. 299 (34)	111–13
				15. Survey of the Economic Situation, Feb. 1935; C.P. 48 (35)	

Committee	Members	Terms of reference	Proceedings	Reports	Reference
				16. Statistics of Population and their relevance to economic change, 2 Apr. 1935; C.P. 94 (35)	135
				17. Survey of the Economic Situation May 1935; C.P. 118 (35)	113–14, 135
				18. The Economic Outlook for the next few years, 29 July 1935; C.P. 157 (35)	136, 319–43
				19. Survey of the Economic Situation, Feb. 1936; C.P. 50 (36)	139
				20. Survey of the Economic Situation, June 1936; C.P. 173 (36)	139
				21. Survey of the Economic Situation, Dec. 1936; C.P. 341 (36)	139–40

Committee	Members	Terms of reference	Proceedings	Reports	Reference
				22. Economic Policy and the Maintenance of Trade Activity, 19 Feb. 1937; C.P. 77 (37)	140–5, 343–53
				23. Survey of the Economic Situation, Oct. 1937; C.P. 287 (37)	145–7
				24. Survey of the Economic Situation, Dec. 1937; C.P. 4 (38)	148
				25. Survey of the Economic Situation, June 1938; C.P. 169 (38)	147
				26. Problems of Rearmament, Dec. 1938; C.P. 296 (38)	148–9
				27. Defence Expenditure and the Economic and Financial Problems	149–51

Committee	Members	Terms of reference	Proceedings	Reports	Reference
				connected therewith, 20 July 1939; C.P. 167 (39)	
Committee on Scientific Research (appointed 14 July 1931)	Sir Daniel Hall (*Chairman*) Sir John Cadman Sir William Hardy Sir Frederick Hopkins Sir Charles Sherrington Lord Rutherford (1934–7) Julian Huxley (1934–8) Sir Charles Martin (1934–8) Sir Frank Smith Dr E. Mellanby Sir William Dampier (1932–7) Dr E. J. Butler (1937–8) *Secretaries:* H. D. Henderson A. F. Hemming D. Rickett	To advise the Economic Advisory Council as to the bearings of the reports of its scientific committees and generally as to the discharge of its functions in their scientific aspects	17 meetings: 21 Apr. 1932–14 Mar. 1938. Cab. 58/25–30	5 Reports: 1. Science and Finance, 29 Nov. 1933; C.P. 309 (33) 2. The need for improved nutrition of the people of Great Britain, 30 June 1934; C.P. 185 (34) 3. Science and Finance, 22 Nov. 1934 4. Atmospheric Pollution, 14 May 1937; C.P. 32 (38)	83n, 134n, 152–3

Committee	Members	Terms of reference	Proceedings	Reports	Reference
				5. Consumption and supply of cinchona alklaoids [quinine] in the Empire, Jan. 1938; C.P. 33 (38)	
Committee on Problems of Rationalisation (appointed 11 Aug. 1931)	Sir Matthew Nathan (*Chairman*) Sir William Beveridge C. T. Cramp J. J. Mallon Sir David Milne-Watson E. D. Simon *Secretaries:* A. F. Hemming W. Palmer (Board of Trade)	To review the working of large-scale industrial organisation, and particularly of the rationalisation schemes which have been effected since the war, in this and other countries; to examine in particular the light which their experience throws (1) on the difficulties of controlling large units effectively and on the limits that may thereby be set to the scale of organisation that is advantageous, (2) on the problems of the supply and selection of higher personnel capable of directing large business organisations effectively, and (3) on the problem of determining the optimum expenditure on labour-saving plant, having regard to the costliness of high overhead charges in periods of slack trade; to consider what lessons emerge of sufficiently general application to be of use in connection with further schemes of rationalisation	40 meetings: 22 Sept. 1931–21 June 1932. Cab. 58/175–80		83

Committee	Members	Terms of reference	Proceedings	Reports	Reference
Prime Minister's Advisory Committee on Financial Questions (appointed 19 Sept. 1931)	J. R. MacDonald (*Chairman*) R. H. Brand W. Layton R. McKenna Lord Macmillan Sir Josiah Stamp Sir Arthur Salter J. M. Keynes *Secretary:* H. D. Henderson	No formal terms of reference. In September 1931 MacDonald asked for 'an agenda of the financial problems from both the domestic and international standpoint that ought to be considered during the next few months with an elucidation of the issues raised'. In January 1932 MacDonald asked for an 'opinion as to whether ... the time was approaching when a definite policy should be pursued in regard to sterling, and if so, as to what the nature of that policy should be; in particular whether we should aim at a concerted policy for the Empire or perhaps for a larger group of countries which might be willing to adhere to sterling'	12 meetings: 22 Sept. 1931–9 Mar. 1932. Cab. 58/169	Report on Sterling Policy, 9 Mar. 1932	94, 100–1, 254–63
Committee on Limits of Economy Policy (appointed 12 Feb. 1932)	Sir Josiah Stamp (*Chairman*) B. Blackett Sir Woodman Burbidge L. Robbins E. D. Simon *Secretary:* H. D. Henderson	To advise [the Prime Minister] personally on the question of the effects of trade activity and national prosperity of the economy policy of recent months, and as to whether and what safeguards and limitations are needed, or whether any expansion would be desirable	3 meetings: 19 Feb.–18 Mar. 1932. Cab. 58/182	Report, 18 Mar. 1932	124–5

Committee	Members	Terms of reference	Proceedings	Reports	Reference
Committee on International Economic Policy (appointed Aug. 1932)	Sir Charles Addis (*Chairman*) Lord Astor B. Blackett Lord Essendon J. M. Keynes W. Layton Sir Arthur Salter Sir Josiah Stamp *Secretaries:* H. D. Henderson A. F. Hemming	To consider the programme of subjects to be discussed at the forthcoming international Monetary and Economic Conference and to advise [the Prime Minister] personally as to points to which British policy should be specially directed	9 meetings: 3 Aug. 1932–28 Mar. 1933. Cab. 58/183	First Report, 11 Oct. 1932; C.P. 361 (32); Second Report, 6 Apr. 1933; C.P. 100 (33)	115–21
Sub-committee [of Committee on Economic Information] on the Trend of Unemployment (appointed Apr. 1935)	H. D. Henderson (*Chairman*) Prof. A. L. Bowley D. Caradog Jones D. H. Robertson *Secretaries:* A. F. Hemming P. K. Debenham	To advise on the probable minimum level of unemployment in the decade 1936–1945 on the assumption that it will be a period of generally good trade, and to submit any observations which might emerge in the course of the inquiry regarding the probable maximum level of unemployment in the same period	11 meetings: 23 May–4 Dec. 1935. Cab. 58/24	Report, 4 Dec. 1935	134–7

DRAMATIS PERSONAE

Addis, Sir Charles – Manager, Hongkong and Shanghai Bank, 1905–21; Director, Bank of England, 1918–32; member, Committee on Chinese Situation, 1930; Vice-Chairman, Bank for International Settlements, 1929–32; Chairman, Committee on International Economic Policy, 1932–3.

Addison, Dr C. (later Lord) – Minister of Agriculture, 1930–1.

Alexander, A. V. (later Lord) – First Lord of the Admiralty, 1929–31, 1940–6; member, Committee on Cotton Industry, 1929–30.

Allen, Reginald Clifford (Lord Allen of Hurtwood) – Chairman and Treasurer, Independent Labour Party, 1922–6.

Amery, L. S. – Secretary of State for the Colonies, 1924–9; Secretary of State for Dominion Affairs, 1925–9.

Anderson, Sir Alan – Director, Anderson Green & Co., managers of the Orient Line; Director, Bank of England, 1918–46; member, Committee on Cotton Industry, 1929–30; member, Committee on Agricultural Policy, 1930; member, Panel on Trade and Employment, 1932–4.

Anderson, Sir John (later Lord Waverley) – Permanent Secretary, Home Office, 1922–32; Governor of Bengal, 1932–7; Lord President of the Council, 1940–3; Chancellor of the Exchequer, 1943–5.

Astor, Viscount – Parliamentary Secretary to Ministry of Health, 1919–21; a British delegate to League of Nations Assembly, 1931; Chairman of Directors of *The Observer*; Chairman, Committee on Empire Migration, 1930–1; member, Committee on International Economic Policy, 1932–3.

Attlee, Clement (later Lord) – Chancellor of Duchy of Lancaster, 1930–1; Postmaster-General, 1931; Leader of Labour Party, 1935–45; Prime Minister, 1945–51; member, Committee on New Industrial Development, 1931–2.

Baldwin, Stanley (later Lord) – Prime Minister, 1923–4, 1924–9, 1935–7; Lord President of the Council, 1931–5.

Balfour, Lord – Prime Minister, 1902–5; Lord President of the Council, 1925–9.

Balfour, Sir Arthur (later Lord Riverdale) – Master Cutler of Sheffield, 1911–12; Managing Director, Arthur Balfour & Co. Ltd; member, Coal Industry Commission, 1919; member, Advisory Council for Scientific and Industrial Research, 1916, 1929, 1933, 1935 and Chairman, 1937–46; Chairman, Committee on Industry and Trade, 1924–9; member, Economic Advisory Council; member, Committee on Economic Outlook, 1930; Chairman, Committee on Empire Trade, 1930; member, Committee on Chinese Situation, 1930.

Beard, John – Official, Agricultural Section, Transport and General Workers' Union; member, Committee on Agricultural Policy, 1930.

Bellman, Sir Harold – Chairman and Managing Director, Abbey Road Building Society; Chairman, Building Societies Association, 1933–7; member, Panel on Trade and Employment, 1932–4.

Beveridge, Sir William (later Lord) – In Board of Trade, 1908–16; Second Secretary, Ministry of Food, 1916–18; Director, London School of Economics, 1919–37;

Master of University College, Oxford, 1937–45; Chairman, Unemployment Insurance Statutory Committee, 1934–44; member, Committee on Problems of Rationalisation, 1931–2.

Bevin, Ernest – General Secretary, Transport and General Workers' Union, 1921–40; member, General Council, T.U.C., 1925–40; member, Committee on Finance and Industry, 1930–1; member, Economic Advisory Council; member, Committee on Economic Outlook, 1930; member, Committee on Unemployment Statistics, 1930; member, Committee on Channel Tunnel Policy, 1930.

Blackett, Sir Basil – Controller of Finance, Treasury, 1919–22; Finance Member of Executive Council of Governor-General of India, 1922–8; Director, Bank of England, 1929–35; member, Committee on Limits of Economy Policy, 1932; member, Committee on International Economic Policy, 1932–3.

Blair, W. R. – Director, Cooperative Wholesale Society, Cooperative Insurance Society, and Irish Agricultural Wholesale Society; member, Economic Advisory Council; member, Committee on Empire Trade, 1930

Bondfield, Margaret – Minister of Labour, 1929–31.

Bowley, Professor A. L. – Professor of Statistics in the University of London, 1919–36; member, Committee on Revision of Cost-of-Living Index Number, 1930; member, Committee on Trend of Unemployment, 1935.

Bradbury, Lord (formerly Sir John Bradbury) – Joint Permanent Secretary, Treasury, 1913–19; principal British delegate to Reparation Commission, 1919–25; member, Committee on Finance and Industry, 1930–1.

Brand, R. H. (later Lord) – Director, Lazard Bros. & Co., merchant bankers; member, Committee on Finance and Industry, 1930–1; member, Advisory Committee on Financial Questions, 1931–2.

Brown, Ernest – Minister of Labour, 1935–40.

Brown, Sir William – Permanent Secretary, Board of Trade, 1937–40.

Bruce-Gardner, Sir Charles – Chairman, Iron and Steel Industrial Research Council, 1929–30; Industrial Adviser to Bank of England, 1930–8.

Budd, Sir Cecil – Chairman, London Metal Exchange 1928–30; Director, British Metal Corporation Ltd; member, Committee on Iron and Steel Industry, 1929–30.

Butler, Dr E. J. – Secretary, Agricultural Research Council, 1935–41; member, Committee on Scientific Research, 1937–8.

Burbidge, Sir Richard Woodman – General Manager, Harrods Ltd, 1927–35, Managing Director, 1935–45; member, Committee on Limits of Economy Policy, 1932.

Burrows, R. A. (later Sir Richard) – Chairman, Lanes Associated Collieries and Manchester Collieries, Ltd; member, Committee on Marketing and Distribution, 1930–1.

Buxton, Noel – Minister of Agriculture, 1929–30.

Cadman, Sir John (later Lord) – Professor of Mining and Petroleum Technology, Birmingham University, 1908–20; Chairman, Anglo-Persian Oil Co. and Iraq Petroleum Co.; Director, Suez Canal Co.; member, Industrial Transference Board, 1928; member, Economic Advisory Council; member, Committee on Economic Outlook, 1930; member, Committee on Channel Tunnel Policy, 1930; member, Committee on Marketing and Distribution, 1930–1; member, Committee on Unemployment Benefit, 1930; member, Committee on Scientific Research, 1932–8.

Carnegie, Colonel David – Civil and ordnance engineer; Ordnance Adviser to Canadian Government, 1915–19; member, Committee on Empire Trade, 1930.

Carr-Saunders, Professor A. M. (later Sir Alexander) – Charles Booth Professor of Social Science, Liverpool University, 1932–7; member, Committee on Empire Migration, 1930–1.

Catterns, B. G. – Chief Cashier, Bank of England, 1929–34; Deputy Governor, 1936–45.

Chamberlain, Austen – Chancellor of the Exchequer, 1903–6, 1919–21.

Chamberlain, Neville – Minister of Health, 1923, 1924–9, 1931; Chancellor of the Exchequer, 1923–4, 1931–7; Prime Minister, 1937–40.

Chapman, Sir Sydney – Permanent Secretary, Board of Trade, 1920–7; Chief Economic Adviser to H.M. Government, 1930–2; member, Committee on Unemployment Benefit, 1930.

Churchill, Winston – Chancellor of the Exchequer, 1924–9.

Citrine, W. M. (later Lord) – General Secretary, Trades Union Congress, 1926–46; member, Economic Advisory Council; member, Committee on Economic Outlook, 1930; member, Committee on Economic Information, 1931–3.

Clark, Colin – Staff of Economic Advisory Council, 1930–1; University Lecturer in Statistics, University of Cambridge, 1931–7; Visiting Lecturer in Australian universities, 1937–8; Under-Secretary of State for Labour and Industry, Queensland, 1938–52; Director of Institute for Research in Agricultural Economics, Oxford, 1953–69.

Clay, Professor Henry (later Sir) – Jevons Professor of Political Economy, Manchester, 1922–7; Professor of Social Economics in the University of Manchester, 1927–30; Economic Adviser to Bank of England, 1930–44; Warden of Nuffield College, Oxford, 1944–54; member, Royal Commission on Unemployment Insurance, 1931.

Clynes, J. R. – Secretary of State, Home Office, 1929–31; Chairman, Committee on Cotton Industry, 1929–30.

Cobbold, C. F. (later Lord) – Entered Bank of England as Adviser, 1933; Governor, 1949–61.

Cole, G. D. H. – Fellow of University College, Oxford, and University Reader in Economics, 1925–44; member, Economic Advisory Council; Chairman, Committee on Unemployment Benefit, 1930; member, Committee on Economic Outlook, 1930; member, Committee on Marketing and Distribution, 1930; member, Committee on Empire Migration, 1930–1; member, Committee on Economic Information, 1931–9.

Cramp, C. T. – General Secretary, National Union of Railwaymen, 1920–33; member, Committee on Industry and Trade, 1924–8; member, Committee on Iron and Steel Industry, 1929–30; member, Committee on Problems of Rationalisation, 1931–2.

Cunliffe-Lister, Sir Philip (formerly Lloyd-Graeme, later Lord Swinton) – President of Board of Trade, 1924–9 and 1931; Colonial Secretary, 1932–5; Secretary of State for Air, 1935–8.

D'Abernon, Lord – British Ambassador at Berlin, 1920–6.

Dalton, Hugh – Reader in Commerce/Economics, University of London, 1920–36; Parliamentary Under-Secretary, Foreign Office, 1929–31; Chancellor of the Exchequer, 1945–7; member, Committee on Chinese Situation, 1930.

Dampier-Whetham, W. C. D. (later Sir William Cecil Dampier) – Secretary, Agricultural Research Council, 1931–5; member, Central Agricultural Wages Board, 1925–42; member, Committee on Agricultural Policy, 1930; member, Committee on Scientific Research, 1932–7.

Debenham, Sir Ernest – Director, Lloyds Bank and Royal Exchange Assurance Corporation; formerly (before 1930) of Debenham and Freebody; member, Economic Advisory Council; member, Committee on Agricultural Policy, 1930.

Debenham, P. K. (later Sir Piers) – Staff of Economic Advisory Council, 1930–9; Assistant Secretary, 1934–9; offices of War Cabinet, 1939–41.

Dobb, Maurice – Fellow of Trinity College, Cambridge, since 1924; Reader in Economics, University of Cambridge, 1959–67.

Duff, Sir Patrick – Private Secretary to successive Prime Ministers, 1923–33; Secretary, Ministry of Works, 1933–41.

Duncan, Sir Andrew – Coal Controller, 1919–20; Vice-President, Shipbuilding Employers' Federation, 1920–7; Chairman, Central Electricity Board, 1927–35; Chairman, Executive Committee, Iron and Steel Federation, 1935–40; Director, Bank of England, 1929–40; President of Board of Trade, 1940 and 1941; Minister of Supply, 1940–1 and 1942–5; member, Economic Advisory Council; Chairman, Committee on Channel Tunnel Policy, 1930; Chairman, Committee on Revision of Cost-of-Living Index Number, 1930; member, Committee on New Industrial Development, 1931–2; member, Panel on Trade and Employment, 1932–4.

Eady, W. (later Sir Wilfrid) – Principal Assistant, Ministry of Labour, 1929–34; Joint Second Secretary, Treasury, 1942.

Ebbisham, Lord (formerly George Rowland Blades) – Chairman, Blades, East and Blades Ltd; President, Federation of British Industries, 1928–9; member, Channel Tunnel Committee, 1929.

Eden, Sir Anthony (later Lord Avon) – Secretary of State for Foreign Affairs, 1935–8, 1940–5, 1951–5; Prime Minister, 1955–7.

Elliot, Walter – Financial Secretary, Treasury, 1931–2; Minister of Agriculture, 1932–6.

Ellis, Captain L. F. – General Secretary, National Council of Social Service; Associate Warden of Toynbee Hall; member, Committee on Empire Migration, 1930.

Esher, Lord (Reginald Brett) – Liberal M.P. 1880–5; permanent member, Committee of Imperial Defence, until death in 1930.

Essendon, Lord (Sir Frederick Lewis) – Chairman, Furness Withy & Co. Ltd and other associated shipping and insurance companies; Director, Barclays Bank; member, Shipping Control Committee, 1916; member, Committee on Channel Tunnel, 1929; member, Committee on International Economic Policy, 1932–3.

Fergusson, J. D. (later Sir Donald) – Private Secretary to successive Chancellors of the Exchequer, 1920–36; Permanent Secretary, Ministry of Agriculture and Fisheries, 1936–45.

Fisher, Sir Warren – Permanent Secretary, Treasury and official Head of Civil Service, 1919–39.

Flux, Sir Alfred William – Professor of Political Economy, McGill University, 1901–8; Assistant Secretary, Statistics Department, Board of Trade, 1918–32; sometime President, Royal Statistical Society; member, League of Nations Committee of Statistical Experts.

Forber, E. R. (later Sir Edward) – Chairman, Board of Customs and Excise, 1930–4; Chairman, Board of Inland Revenue, 1934–8.

Fraser, W. (later Sir William) – Chairman, Anglo-Iranian Oil Co. Ltd; Director, Burma Oil Co. Ltd, Iraq Petroleum Co. Ltd, and Great Western Railway Co.; Petroleum Adviser to War Office from 1935; member, Committee on Marketing and Distribution, 1930–1.

Gallacher, W. – Director, Scottish Cooperative Wholesale Society, 1912–43; member, Committee on Marketing and Distribution, 1930.

Garnsey, Sir Gilbert – Senior partner, Price Waterhouse & Co., chartered accountants; Chairman, Committee on Marketing and Distribution, 1930.

Gilbert, B. W. (later Sir Bernard) – Entered Treasury 1914; Joint Second Secretary 1944.

Gilmour, Sir John – Minister of Agriculture, 1931–2; Secretary of State, Home Office, 1932–5.

Graham, W. – President of Board of Trade, 1929–31; Chairman, Committee on Chinese Situation, 1930.

Gregg, C. J. (later Sir Cornelius) – Director, Statistics and Intelligence Department, Board of Inland Revenue; Chairman, Board of Inland Revenue, 1942.

Gregory, Sir Theodore – Cassel Professor of Economics in the University of London, 1927–37; member, Committee on Finance and Industry, 1930–1.

Grier, Lynda – Acting Head, Economics Department, Leeds University, 1915–19; Principal, Lady Margaret Hall, Oxford, 1925–45; member, Committee on Revision of Cost-of-Living Index Number, 1930.

Grigg, P. J. (later Sir James) – Principal Private Secretary to successive Chancellors of the Exchequer, 1921–30; Chairman, Board of Inland Revenue, 1930–4.

Haldane, Lord – Lord Chancellor, 1912–15 and 1924.

Hall, Sir Daniel – Director, John Innes Horticultural Institution; Chief Scientific Adviser to Ministry of Agriculture; member, Economic Advisory Council; member, Committee on Agricultural Policy, 1930; Chairman, Committee on Scientific Research, 1931–8.

Hallsworth, J. (later Sir Joseph) – Secretary General, National Union of Distributive and Allied Workers, 1916–47; member, General Council, T.U.C., 1926–47; member, British representation, International Labour Conference, Geneva, 1927–37; member, Committee on Marketing and Distribution, 1930.

Hankey, Sir Maurice – Secretary to Cabinet, 1919–38.

Hardy, Sir William – Director of Food Investigation, Department of Scientific and Industrial Research; member, Economic Advisory Council; member, Committee on New Industrial Development, 1931–2; member, Committee on Scientific Research, 1931–4.

Harrison, George L. – Governor, Federal Reserve Bank of New York, 1928–36.

Hartshorn, Vernon – Lord Privy Seal, 1930–1.

Harvey, Sir Ernest – Deputy Governor, Bank of England, 1929–36.

Hawtrey, R. G. (later Sir Ralph) – Director of Financial Enquiries, Treasury, 1919–45; Price Professor of International Economics, Royal Institute of International Affairs, 1947–52.

Hayek, Professor F. A. von – Lecturer in Economics, University of Vienna, 1929–31; Tooke Professor of Economic Science and Statistics in the University of London, 1931–50.

Hemming, A. F. – Assistant Secretary, Committee of Civil Research, 1925–30; Joint Secretary, Economic Advisory Council, 1930–4; Secretary, 1934–9; Administrative Head, Central Economic Information Service, 1939–40, and Central Statistical Office, 1941.

Henderson, H. D. (later Sir Hubert) – Secretary, Cotton Control Board, 1917–19; Lecturer in Economics, University of Cambridge, 1919–23; Editor, *The Nation & Athenaeum*, 1923–30; Joint Secretary, Economic Advisory Council, 1930–4; member, Committee on Economic Information, 1931–9; Fellow, All Souls College, Oxford, 1934–51; member, Stamp Survey, 1939–40; Economic Adviser, Treasury, 1939–44; Drummond Professor of Political Economy, University of Oxford, 1945–51.

Hilton, John – Director of Statistics, Ministry of Labour, 1919–31; Montagu Burton Professor of Industrial Relations, University of Cambridge, 1931–7.

Hilton Young, Edward (Lord Kennet) – Minister of Health, 1931–5; Chairman, Treasury Capital Issues Committee from 1935.

Hindley, Sir Clement – Chief Commissioner of Railways, Railway Board, India, 1922–8; member, Committee on Channel Tunnel, 1929.

Hirst, Sir Hugo – Member, Board of Trade Advisory Council, 1922–5, 1929–32, and 1936–9; member, Panel on Trade and Employment, 1932–4.

Hoare, Sir Samuel (later Lord Templewood) – Secretary of State for India, 1931–5.

Hobson, J. A. – Writer; Lecturer in English Literature and Economics for the Oxford University Extension Delegacy and the London Society for the Extension of University Teaching, 1887–97.

Hodson, H. V. – Fellow of All Souls College, Oxford, 1928–35; Staff of Economic Advisory Council, 1930–1; Assistant Editor, *The Round Table*, 1931, Editor, 1934–9; Assistant Editor, *The Sunday Times*, 1946–50, Editor, 1950–61.

Hopkins, Sir Frederick Gowland – Professor of Biochemistry, University of Cambridge, 1914–43; member, Medical Research Council until 1930; member, Committee on Scientific Research, 1931–8.

Hopkins, Sir Richard V. N. – Chairman, Board of Inland Revenue, 1922–7; Controller of Finance and Supply Services, Treasury, 1927–8; Second Secretary, 1928–42; Permanent Secretary, 1942–5.

Howorth, Sir Rupert – Deputy Secretary to Cabinet, 1930–42.

Hurst, Sir Alfred – Adviser and Personal Assistant to Chairman of Import Duties Advisory Committee, 1932–9.

Huxley, Julian – Biologist and writer; Professor of Zoology, Kings College, London, 1925–7; Secretary, Zoological Society of London, 1935–42; member, Committee on Scientific Research, 1934–8.

Jewkes, John – Professor of Social Economics, University of Manchester, 1936–46; Jevons Professor of Political Economy, 1946–8; Professor of Economic Organisation, University of Oxford, 1948–69; Director, Economic Section, War Cabinet Secretariat, 1941.

Johnston, T. – Parliamentary Under-Secretary for Scotland, 1929–31; Lord Privy Seal, 1931.

Jones, David Caradog – Sometime Reader in Social Statistics, University of Liverpool; Director, Social Survey of Merseyside, 1934; member, Committee on Trend of Unemployment, 1935.

Jones, Joseph – General Secretary, Yorkshire Miners Association, 1923–38; member, Executive Committee of Labour Party, 1926–31; member, Committee on Cotton Industry, 1929–30.

Jones, R. T. – Member, General Council, Trades Union Congress, 1921–33; member, Committee on Revision of Cost-of-Living Index Number, 1930–1.

Jones, Thomas – Deputy Secretary to the Cabinet, 1919–30; Secretary, Committee of Civil Research, 1925–30; Secretary, Economic Advisory Council, 1930; Secretary, Pilgrim Trust, 1930–45.

Kahn, R. F. (later Lord Kahn) – Fellow of King's College, Cambridge, from 1931; temporary civil servant in various government departments, 1939–46; Professor of Economics, University of Cambridge, 1951–72; Assistant Secretary, Committee of Economists, 1930.

Kennet, Lord – *see* Hilton Young, Edward.

Keynes, John Maynard (later Lord) – Fellow, King's College, Cambridge, 1909–46; Treasury, 1914–19 and 1940–6; member, Committee on Finance and Industry, 1929–31; member, Economic Advisory Council; Chairman, Committee on Economic Outlook, 1930, Committee of Economists; member, Committees on Channel Tunnel Policy, on Chinese Situation, on Economic Information, on Financial Questions, and on International Economic Policy.

Kindersley, Sir Robert (later Lord) – Director, Bank of England, 1914–46; Governor, Hudson's Bay Co., 1916–25; President, National Savings Committee, 1920–46; senior British representative, Dawes Committee of Reparation Commission, 1924.

Kisch, Sir Cecil – Secretary, Financial Department, India Office, 1921–33.

Lansbury, George – First Commissioner of Works, 1929–31; Leader of Labour Party, 1931–5.

Larke, Sir William – Director, British Iron and Steel Federation, 1922–46.

Layton, Sir Walter (Lord Layton) – University Lecturer in Economics, University of Cambridge, 1921; Editor, *The Economist*, 1922–38; Director, Economic and Financial Section, League of Nations; member, Advisory Committee on Financial Questions, 1931–2; member, Committee on International Economic Policy, 1932–3.

Leith-Ross, Sir Frederick – Deputy Controller of Finance, Treasury, 1925–32; Chief Economic Adviser to H.M. Government, 1932–46; member, Committee on Economic Information, 1932–9.

Lewis, Sir Alfred – Director and Chief General Manager, National Provincial Bank; Director, Bank of British West Africa; member, Economic Advisory Council; member, Committee on Channel Tunnel Policy, 1930; member, Committee on New Industrial Development, 1931–2; member, Committee on Economic Information, 1931–9.

Lewis, Sir Frederick – *see* Essendon, Lord.

Lindsay, Kenneth – Research Fellow, Toynbee Hall, 1923–6; Director, Voluntary Migration Societies, Dominions Office, 1929–31; General Secretary, Political and Economic Planning, 1931–5.

Lindsay, Sir Ronald – British Ambassador at Washington, 1930–9.

Lloyd, E. M. H. – Assistant Secretary, Empire Marketing Board, 1926–33; Secretary, Market Supply Committee, 1933–6; Assistant Director, Food (Defence Plans) Department, 1936–9; F.A.O., United Nations, 1946–7.

Lloyd George, David – Prime Minister, 1916–22; Leader of Liberal Party, 1926–31.

Loveday, A. – Lecturer in Economics, University of Cambridge, 1913–15; League of Nations Secretariat, 1919; Director, Financial and Economic Section, League of Nations Secretariat, 1931–9.

MacDonald, James Ramsay – Prime Minister, 1924, 1929–35; Lord President of Council, 1935–7.

Macgregor, Professor D. H. – Drummond Professor of Political Economy, University of Oxford, 1922–45; member, Committee on Marketing and Distribution, 1930.

McKenna, Reginald – Chancellor of the Exchequer, 1915–16; Chairman, Midland Bank, 1919–43; member, Committee on Finance and Industry, 1929–31; member, Advisory Committee on Financial Questions, 1931–2.

Maclean, Sir Donald – President of Board of Education, 1931–2.

McLintock, Sir William – Senior partner, Thomson, McLintock & Co. of Glasgow, chartered accountants; member, Committee on Cotton Industry, 1929–30; member, Economic Advisory Council; Chairman, Committee on Unemployment Statistics, 1930.

Macmillan, Lord – Lord of Appeal in Ordinary, 1930–9; Chairman, Committee on Finance and Industry, 1929–31; member, Advisory Committee on Financial Questions, 1931–2.

Macmillan, Harold – Conservative M.P. 1924–9, 1931–64; Prime Minister, 1957–63.

Mallon, J. J. – Warden of Toynbee Hall; member, Whitley Committee and numerous other reconstruction committees, 1917–20; member, Committee on Problems of Rationalisation, 1931–2; member, Panel on Trade and Employment, 1932–4.

Martin, Sir Charles – Director, Lister Institute of Preventive Medicine, 1903–30; Chief of Animal Nutrition, Australian Council for Scientific and Industrial Research, 1931–3; member, Committee on Scientific Research, 1934–8.

May, Sir George (later Lord) – Secretary, Prudential Assurance Co.; Chairman, Committee on National Expenditure, 1931; Chairman, Import Duties Advisory Committee, 1932–9.

Meade, J. E. – Fellow and Lecturer in Economics, Hertford College, Oxford, 1930–7; Member, Economic Section, League of Nations, Geneva, 1938–40; Economic Assistant (1940–5) and Director (1946–7), Economic Section, Cabinet Offices; Professor of Commerce, London School of Economics, 1947–57; Professor of Political Economy, University of Cambridge, 1957–68.

Mellanby, Dr E. (later Sir Edward) – Member, Medical Research Council, 1931–3, Secretary, 1933–9; member, Committee on Scientific Research, 1932–9.

Mensforth, Sir Holberry – Director, Tredegar Iron and Coal Co. Ltd; Director-General of Factories, War Office, 1920–6; member, Committee on New Industrial Development, 1931–2.

Milne-Watson, Sir David – President, British Gas Federation; member, Department of Scientific and Industrial Research; member, Committee on Problems of Rationalisation, 1931–2.

Mond, Sir Alfred (Lord Melchett) – Minister of Health, 1921–2; Chairman, Imperial Chemical Industries; Joint Chairman, Conference on Industrial Reorganisation and Industrial Relations, 1928.

Morrison, Herbert – Minister of Transport, 1929–31.

Morton, Sir James – Founder, Scottish Dyes Ltd; member, Dyestuffs Industry Development Committee, 1921–34; member, Committee on New Industrial Development, 1931–2.

Mosley, Sir Oswald – Chancellor of Duchy of Lancaster, 1929–30.

Nathan, Sir Matthew – Chairman, Board of Inland Revenue, 1911–14; Governor of Queensland, 1920–6; Chairman of two committees of Committee of Civil Research, 1927–30; Chairman, Committee on Problems of Rationalisation, 1931–2.

Niemeyer, Sir Otto – Controller of Finance, Treasury, 1922–7; joined Bank of England in 1927, Director, 1938–52.

Norman, Montagu (later Lord) – Governor, Bank of England, 1920–44.

Overton, A. E. (later Sir Arnold) – Entered Board of Trade in 1919; Permanent Secretary, 1941–5.

Peacock, E. R. (later Sir Edward) – Director, Baring Bros.; Director, Bank of England, 1921–4 and 1929–46; Chairman, Committee on Channel Tunnel, 1929–30.

Phillips, Sir Frederick – Assistant Secretary, Treasury, 1919–27; Principal Assistant Secretary, 1927–31; Deputy Controller, 1931; Under-Secretary, 1932–9; Joint Third Secretary, 1939–42; head, Treasury mission in Washington, 1940–3; member, Committee on Economic Information, 1935–9.

Pigou, A. C. – Professor of Political Economy, University of Cambridge, 1908–44; member, Committee of Economists, 1930.

Plant, Professor A. (later Sir Arnold) – Cassel Professor of Commerce in the University of London, 1930–65.

Plender, Sir William (later Lord) – Senior partner, Deloitte Plender Griffiths and Co., chartered accountants; Chairman, National Board for Coal Industry, 1921–5; member, Committee on Iron and Steel Industry, 1929–30; member, Committee on National Expenditure, 1931.

Pugh, Arthur (later Sir) – General Secretary, Iron and Steel Trades Confederation, and British Iron, Steel and Kindred Trades Association, 1917–36.

Reading, Lord – Secretary of State for Foreign Affairs, 1931.

Reeder, A. – Secretary, Unemployment Insurance Statutory Committee, 1935–9.

Rickett, D. H. F. (later Sir Denis) – Fellow of All Souls College, Oxford, 1929–49; Staff of Economic Advisory Council, 1931–9; Offices of War Cabinet, 1939–47; Treasury, 1947; Second Secretary, 1960–8.

Robbins, L. C. (later Lord) – Professor of Economics, London School of Economics, 1929–61; Director, Economic Section, War Cabinet Offices, 1941–5; member, Committee of Economists, 1930; member, Committee on Limits of Economy Policy, 1932.

Robertson, D. H. (later Sir Dennis) – Fellow of Trinity College, Cambridge, 1914–38, 1944–63; Reader in Economics, University of Cambridge, 1930–8; Cassel Professor of Economics in the University of London, 1939–44; an adviser at Treasury, 1939–44; Professor of Political Economy, University of Cambridge, 1944–57; member, Committee on Trend of Unemployment, 1935; member, Committee on Economic Information, 1936–9.

Robinson, E. A. G. (later Sir Austin) – University Lecturer in Economics, Cambridge, 1929–49; War Cabinet Offices, 1939–42; Economic Adviser, Ministry of Production, 1942–5; Professor of Economics, University of Cambridge, 1950–65.

Rose, C. Archibald – Commercial attaché, Shanghai, 1915, Peking, 1917; sometime Consul at Chungking, Chefoo and Ningpo, Hangchow; member, Committee on Chinese Situation, 1930.

Rowan, T. L. – Assistant Private Secretary to Chancellor of the Exchequer, 1933–7.

Rowe, J. W. F. – Lecturer in Economics, University of Cambridge, 1932–60; Fellow, Pembroke College, Cambridge, since 1934.

Runciman, Walter (later Lord) – President of Board of Trade, 1914–16 and 1931–7.

Rutherford, Lord – Cavendish Professor of Experimental Physics and Director of Cavendish Laboratory, University of Cambridge, 1919–37; member, Committee on Scientific Research, 1934–7.

Salter, Sir Arthur (later Lord) – Transport Department, Admiralty, 1904; Assistant Secretary, National Health Insurance Commission, 1913; Director, Ship Requisitioning, 1917; Director, Economic and Finance Section, League of Nations, 1919–20 and 1922–31; General Secretary, Reparation Commission, 1920–2; missions to India (1930), China (1931 and 1933); Gladstone Professor of Political Theory and Institutions, University of Oxford, 1934–44; M.P. (Independent) for Oxford University, 1937–50; head, British Merchant Shipping Mission, Washington, 1941–3; Chancellor of the Duchy of Lancaster, 1945; member, Advisory Committee on Financial Questions, 1931–2; member, Committee on Economic Information, 1932–9.

Samuel, Sir Herbert (later Lord) – Home Secretary, 1916 and 1931–2.

Sankey, Lord – Chairman, Coal Industry Commission, 1919; Lord Chancellor, 1929–35; Chairman, Committee on Iron and Steel Industry, 1929–30.

Schwartz, G. L. – Secretary, London and Cambridge Economic Service, 1923; Cassel Lecturer in the University of London, 1929; Editor, *Banker's Magazine*, 1945–54; Deputy City Editor, *The Sunday Times*, 1944–61; writer of the *Sunday Times* economics column, 1961–71.

Shaw, T. – Secretary of State for War, 1929–31; member, Committee on Iron and Steel Industry, 1929–30.

Sherrington, Sir Charles Scott – Brown Professor of Pathology, University of London; member, Medical Research Council; member, Committee on Scientific Research, 1931–8.

Simon, E. D. (Baron Simon of Wythenshawe) – M.P. (Liberal), 1929–31; Chairman, Committee on Agricultural Policy, 1930; member, Committee on Problems of Rationalisation, 1931–2; member, Committee on Economic Information, 1932–6.

Simon, Sir John (later Lord Simon) – Secretary of State for Foreign Affairs, 1931–5; Home Secretary, 1935–7; Chancellor of the Exchequer, 1937–40.

Sinclair, Sir Archibald – Chief Liberal Whip, 1930–1; Secretary of State for Scotland, 1931–2; Leader, Liberal Party, 1935–45.

Sloan, P. A. – Undergraduate, Clare College, Cambridge, 1926–9; Assistant Lecturer, University College of N. Wales, Bangor, 1931–3; lived and worked in the U.S.S.R., 1933–8.

Smith, Sir Frank – Secretary, Department of Scientific and Industrial Research, 1929–39; Secretary, Royal Society, 1929–38; member, Committee on Scientific Research, 1931–8.

Smith, Sir Hubert Llewellyn – Permanent Secretary, Board of Trade, 1907–19; Chief Economic Adviser to H.M. Government, 1919–27; Director, New Survey of London Life and Labour, 1928–35.

Snowden, Philip (later Lord) – Chancellor of the Exchequer, 1924, 1929–31; Lord Privy Seal, 1931–2.

Stamp, Sir Josiah (later Lord) – Entered Civil Service 1896; Assistant Secretary, Board of Trade, 1916–19; Chairman, London, Midland and Scottish Railway, 1926–41; Director, Bank of England, 1928–41; British representative, Dawes Committee, Reparation Commission, 1924; member, Committee on National Debt and Taxation, 1924; President, Royal Statistical Society 1930–2; member, Economic Advisory Council; member, Committee of Economists, 1930; Chairman, Committee on Economic Information, 1931–9; member, Advisory Committee on Financial Questions, 1931–2; member, Committee on Limits of Economy Policy, 1932; member, Committee on International Economic Policy, 1932–3.

Stewart, Sir Kenneth – Director, Manchester Chamber of Commerce in 1930.

Stone, J. R. N. – Offices of the War Cabinet and Central Statistical Office, 1940–5; Director, Department of Applied Economics, University of Cambridge, 1945–55; Leake Professor of Finance and Accounting, University of Cambridge, since 1955.

Strakosch, Sir Henry – South African banker; member, Financial Committee, League of Nations, 1920–37; member, Committee on Channel Tunnel, 1929–30.

Tawney, R. H. – Reader in Economic History, University of London, 1921–31, Professor, 1931–49; member, Consultative Committee, Board of Education, 1912–31; member, Coal Industry Commission, 1919; member, Economic Advisory Council; member, Committee on Agricultural Policy, 1930.

Thomas, J. H. – Lord Privy Seal, 1929–30; Secretary of State for the Dominions, 1930–5; Secretary of State for the Colonies, 1935–6.

Turnor, Christopher – Patron of seven livings; writer of books, articles, and pamphlets on the subjects of land and emigration; member, Committee on Empire Migration, 1930–1.

Upcott, G. C. (later Sir Charles) – Deputy Controller of Supply Services, Treasury, 1921–31; member, Committee on Channel Tunnel Policy, 1930.

Vansittart, Sir Robert (later Lord) – Permanent Secretary, Foreign Office, 1930–8.

Waley, S. D. (later Sir David) – Assistant Secretary, Treasury, 1924–31; Principal Assistant Secretary, 1931–9.

Walker, Sir Alexander – Chairman, John Walker & Son, whisky distillers; member, Panel on Trade and Employment, 1932–4.

Wallace, Sir Matthew – President, Scottish Chamber of Agriculture; member, Committee on Agricultural Policy, 1930.

Waterfield, A. P. (later Sir Percival) – Principal Assistant Secretary, Treasury, 1934–9.

Watson, Sir Alfred – Government Actuary, 1917; Chief Actuary to the National Health Insurance Joint Committee, 1921–9; President, Institute of Actuaries, 1920–2.

Wedgwood, Josiah – Secretary and then Director, Rural Industries Bureau, 1922–6; economic research work, 1926–8; Chairman and Managing Director, Josiah Wedgwood & Sons Ltd, potters, from 1930; Director, Bank of England, 1942–6.

Wedgwood, Sir Ralph L. – Chief General Manager, London and North-Eastern Railway, 1923–39; President, National Confederation of Employers' Organisations, 1930–1; member, Committee on Revision of Cost-of-Living Index Number, 1930.

Weir, Lord – Managing director, G. & J. Weir Engineering of Glasgow; Director-General of Aircraft Production, 1918; Secretary of State for Air, 1918; Director-General of Explosives, Ministry of Supply, 1939; member, Panel on Trade and Employment, 1932–4.

Wilson, Sir Horace J. – Permanent Secretary, Ministry of Labour, 1921–30; Chief Industrial Adviser to H.M. Government, 1930–9; Permanent Secretary, Treasury, 1939–42; member, Committee on Unemployment Statistics, 1930.

Wood, Sir Kingsley – Postmaster-General, 1931–5; Minister of Health, 1935–8; Chancellor of the Exchequer, 1940–3.

Woods, J. H. (later Sir John) – Entered Treasury, 1920; Principal Assistant Secretary, 1940–3; Permanent Secretary, Board of Trade, 1945.

NOTES

Chapter 1. Introduction

1 Treasury minute relating to the establishment of the Economic Advisory Council, Cmd. 3478, 27 January 1930.

2 See, for example, C. L. Mowat, *Britain between the Wars 1918–1940* (1955), p. 359; A. J. P. Taylor, *English History 1914–1945* (Penguin edn, 1970), p. 409; A. Bullock, *The Life and Times of Ernest Bevin*, Vol. I (1960), pp. 436–9; Sir John Anderson, *The Organisation of Economic Studies in relation to the Problems of Government*, Stamp Memorial Lecture, 1947; Lord (then Sir Edward) Bridges, *Treasury Control*, Stamp Memorial Lecture, 1950; and D. N. Chester and F. M. G. Willson, *The Organisation of British Central Government 1914–1964* (1968), p. 323.

3 Sir Richard Hopkins in D. N. Chester (ed.), *Lessons of the British War Economy* (1951), p. 3.

4 A. J. Salter, *Memoirs of a Public Servant* (1961), p. 230.

Chapter 2. Origins and background

1 *The Organisation of Economic Studies in relation to the Problems of Government*, Stamp Memorial Lecture, 1947, p. 5.

2 Keynes's work at the Treasury during this period is covered in *The Collected Writings of John Maynard Keynes*, Vol. XVI, ed. E. Johnson (1972).

3 See J. H. Jones, *Josiah Stamp, Public Servant* (1964).

4 *The Organisation of Economic Studies in relation to the Problems of Government*, pp. 6–7.

5 Llewellyn Smith's evidence to the Haldane Committee can be found in the Reconstruction Papers of Beatrice Webb held at the British Library of Political and Economic Science, L.S.E. See also H. L. Smith, *The Board of Trade* (1928), pp. 217–18, 234; J. Anderson, *The Organisation of Economic Studies in relation to the Problems of Government*; and D. N. Chester and F. M. G. Willson, *The Organisation of British Central Government*, pp. 294–6, 321–4.

6 Committee on the Machinery of Government, *Report*, 1918, Cd. 9230.

7 For a general account of the work of the Ministry of Reconstruction see P. B. Johnson, *Land Fit for Heroes: The Planning of British Reconstruction 1916–1919* (1968).

8 Chester and Willson, *The Organisation of British Central Government*, pp. 295–6.

9 Smith, *The Board of Trade*, pp. 239–41.

10 F. W. Leith-Ross, *Money Talks: Fifty Years of International Finance* (1968), pp. 145–7.

11 *Report on the Collection and Presentation of Official Statistics* prepared by a committee appointed by the Cabinet (1921). The original petition is included as an appendix to the report. Among the signatories were A. L. Bowley, A. C. Pigou, J. Stamp, and J. M. Keynes. During his period in the civil service Keynes had taken an interest in this matter (*Collected Writings*, Vol. XV, ed. E. Johnson (1972), pp. 11–12).

12 Above, pp. 15–16.

13 See, for example, Baldwin speech at Bradford as reported in *The Times*, 30 November 1923; Lord Salisbury letters to *The Times*, 18 and 19 March 1924; MacDonald

letter to *The Economist*, 22 March 1924; and Sir Leo Chiozza Money letter to *The Times*, 1 April 1924.

14 T. Jones, *Whitehall Diary*, Vol. I: *1916–1925* (1969), pp. 263–4. For evidence of similar thinking see Oswald Mosley, John Strachey and Allen Young, *Revolution by Reason* (1925).

15 T. Jones, *Whitehall Diary*, Vol. I, pp. 281–4; see also his comments on Clifford Allen's ideas on pp. 263–4, and Haldane, *Autobiography* (1929), pp. 331–4. Esher kept the issue before the public eye in a series of letters to *The Times* (15 January, 26 May, and 21 June 1924).

16 Cab. 23/48, Cabinets 39(24)18, 41(24)4, 43(24)3, 2, 15, and 22 July 1924.

17 Cab. 24/172, C.P. 366(24), 'Foresight and Co-ordination in Economic Enquiry', June 1924.

18 The memorandum cites the references given in n13 above as evidence of bi-partisan interest in the problem.

19 See pp. 159–60 above.

20 T. Jones, *Whitehall Diary*, Vol. I, p. 317; and B. Webb, *Diaries, 1924–32*, ed. M. Cole (1956), p. 142.

21 R. M. Macleod and E. K. Andrews, 'The Committee of Civil Research: Scientific Advice for Economic Development', *Minerva*, Summer 1969.

22 Ibid. pp. 682–3. Balfour's earlier interest in economic questions, as evidenced by his *Economic Notes on Insular Free Trade* (1903), seems not to have persisted into later years.

23 Cab. 23/50, Cabinet 27(25)12, 28 May 1925.

24 D. E. Moggridge, *British Monetary Policy 1924–1931*, p. 208. On the relations between Amery and the Treasury see also I. M. Drummond, *Imperial Economic Policy 1917–1939*, pp. 127–32.

25 Cab. 58/9, C.C.R. Overseas Loans Sub-Committee, Report.

26 T. Jones, *Whitehall Diary*, Vol. I, p. 318.

27 The minutes can be found in Niemeyer's papers (T. 176/17).

28 K. Middlemas and J. Barnes, *Baldwin: A Biography* (1969), p. 311; Cab. 23/50, Cabinet 30(25)4, 22 June 1925.

29 Prem. 1/70, T. Jones to MacDonald, 'The Committee of Civil Research', 29 November 1929.

30 T. Jones, *Whitehall Diary*, Vol. I, p. 319.

31 Ibid., Vol. I, p. 318 and Vol. II, p. 63. The chairman was Sir Arthur Balfour, later a member of the E.A.C.

32 W. M. Citrine, *Men and Work* (1964), esp. Chs. 13 and 14; and A. Bullock, *The Life and Times of Ernest Bevin*, Vol. I, pp. 287–90, 347–8, 386–7.

33 A detailed account of the background to the talks is given in R. Charles, *The Development of Industrial Relations in Britain*, Part IV.

34 Citrine, *Men and Work*, pp. 136–8, 242–3; Bullock, *Bevin*, pp. 265–7.

35 *House of Commons Debates*, Vol. 183, 4 May 1925, cc. 681–4.

36 For a fuller account of policy debate in the period see D. Winch, *Economics and Policy*, Chs. 4–6.

37 *Memoranda on Certain Proposals relating to Unemployment*, 1929, Cmd. 3331. On the Treasury view, see above, p. 27.

38 'The Treasury Contribution to the White Paper', *Nation & Athenaeum*, 18 May 1929.

39 Liberal Industrial Inquiry, *Britain's Industrial Future* (1928), Ch. X. The following chapter was devoted to the case for improving official statistics.

40 Ibid. pp. 222–5.

41 *Labour and the Nation* (1929), p. 21.

42 Cab. 27/389, 3rd meeting of D.U.(29) Committee, 27 June 1929, statement by Thomas: see also 1st meeting, 11 June 1929.

43 The most complete and accurate account of the Labour Government's economic policies is W. H. Janeway, 'The Economic Policy of the Second Labour Government, 1929–31', unpublished Cambridge University Ph.D. thesis, 1971. For published accounts, see R. Skidelsky, *Politicians and the Slump: The Labour Government of 1929–1931* (1967); T. Jones, *Whitehall Diary*, Vol. II: *1926–30* (1969), and B. Donoughue and G. W. Jones, *Herbert Morrison: Portrait of a Politician* (1973), Chs. 10 and 11. The C.C.R. committees on Iron and Steel and on Cotton became E.A.C. committees in 1930.

44 Cab. 27/397, N.S. (29)1, 'National Road Schemes, memorandum by Chancellor of Duchy of Lancaster', 11 September 1929.

45 Prem. 1/70, P.M.C.13, Clay, 'Economic General Staff', 14 December 1929.

46 Prem. 1/70, P.M.C.10, Keynes, 'Economic General Staff', 10 December 1929.

47 Prem. 1/70, P.M.C.7, Cole, 'Economic General Staff', undated.

48 T. Jones, *Whitehall Diary*, Vol. II, p. 219.

49 Prem. 1/70, Hankey, 'Economic General Staff', 14 December 1929.

50 Prem. 1/70, P.M.C.5, Fisher, 'Economic General Staff', 3 December 1929. Lord Weir supported Fisher (Prem. 1/70, P.M.C.6, Weir, 'Economic General Staff', 5 December 1929).

51 Prem. 1/70, P.M.C.9, Hobson, 'Economic General Staff', undated.

52 Prem. 1/70, P.M.C.12, Layton, 'Economic General Staff', undated; *Britain's Industrial Future*, pp. 222–5, 468–71.

53 T. Jones, *Whitehall Diary*, Vol. II, p. 220.

54 Ibid. p. 222.

55 Ibid. pp. 223, 227.

56 On MacDonald's motives see R. Bassett, *Nineteen Thirty-one: Political Crisis* (1958), and D. Winch, *Economics and Policy* (1972 edn), pp. 153–4.

57 Treasury minute relating to the establishment of the Economic Advisory Council, Cmd. 3478, 27 January 1930.

58 Prem. 1/70, Tom Jones, 'Economic General Staff', and covering letter to Mac-Donald, 14 December 1929.

59 Ibid., Prem. 1/70, Jones to MacDonald, 18 December 1929. Rumours of Cole's appointment appeared in *The Times*, 23 January 1930.

60 Keynes Papers NS/12, Keynes to Henderson, 6 January 1930; T. Jones, *Whitehall Diary*, Vol. II, p. 245. Sloan had received a first-class degree in economics at Cambridge in 1929.

61 Keynes Papers NS/12, Keynes to Henderson, 6 January 1930.

62 Treasury minute relating to the establishment of the E.A.C.

63 On the reasons for the Bank rate rise, see Moggridge, *British Monetary Policy 1924–1931*, pp. 138–9, 163–4.

64 Labour Party, *Report of 29th Annual Conference, 1929*, p. 230.

65 Above, pp. 29, 34.

66 Committee on Finance and Industry, *Minutes of Evidence*, Q. 7512 (Harvey, 2 July 1930), QQ. 3317–47, 3389–3493 (Norman, 26 March 1930); see also Henry Clay, *Lord Norman* (1957), pp. 160–71 and Ch. VIII; and D. Williams, 'Montagu Norman and Banking Policy in the Nineteen Twenties', *Yorkshire Bulletin of Economic and Social Research*, July 1959.

67 R. G. Hawtrey, 'Public Expenditure and the Demand for Labour', *Economica*, March 1925; S. K. Howson, *Domestic Monetary Management in Britain 1919–38*, pp. 12–13, 27–9, 40–3, 140–1; T. 175/26, Hawtrey, 'Floating Debt and Business Conditions', April 1930; 'Debt Policy and Unemployment', 29 June 1929; 'Debt Policy and Unemployment, II', 5 July 1929; T. 175/26 and T. 175/46, Hopkins, 'Notes for Evidence, Conversion Loan and Paying-off Treasury Bills', undated but May or June 1929; Hopkins, 'Gold Standard and Rationalisation', undated; T. 175/46, Hopkins, 'Plentiful

Credit and Cheap Money', undated; Committee on Finance and Industry, *Minutes of Evidence*, QQ. 5429–33, 5561–5701, 16 and 22 May 1930.

68 Above, pp. 18, 28, 44.

69 Above, pp. 44, 77, 82–3.

70 Cab. 24/209, C.P. 31(30), Mosley, 'Unemployment Policy', 16 January 1930. Mosley sent this memorandum to MacDonald on 23 January 1930, having shown it to at least Lansbury, Johnston, and Keynes (Cab. 24/209, C.P. 31(30), Mosley to MacDonald, 23 January; C.P. 32(30), Lansbury, 'Unemployment Policy', 24 January; C.P. 33(30), Johnston, 'Unemployment Policy', 24 January; Keynes Papers M/3, Mosley to Keynes, 16 January 1930).

71 Cab. 23/63, Cabinet 6(30)1, 3 February 1930; T. 175/42, 'Sir O. Mosley on Unemployment Policy', 1 February 1930; T. 175/42 and Cab. 27/413, U.P.C. (30)2, draft memoranda prepared for basis of report, April 1930; Cab. 24/211, C.P. 134(30), Unemployment Policy Committee, Report, 1 May 1930. The Treasury memorandum was primarily the work of Leith-Ross with assistance from his colleagues (T. 175/42, Leith-Ross to Grigg, 8 March 1930, and Fisher to Leith-Ross, 10 March 1930). The quotation is in fact from the first draft (1 February 1930).

72 The minutes of the six meetings are in Cab. 27/437. A livelier record is in T. Jones, *Whitehall Diary*, Vol. II, pp. 256–65.

73 *Daily Express*, 23 May 1930, cited by Skidelsky, *Politicians and the Slump*, p. 214.

74 Cab. 27/437, Conference of Ministers, 6th meeting, 4 June 1930; Cab. 23/64, Cabinet 31(30)1, 4 June 1930; Cab. 27/438, Panel of Ministers on Unemployment, 1st meeting, 16 June 1930. The minutes and memoranda of the Panel, which met fortnightly until May 1931, are in Cab. 27/438, 439, and 440.

Chapter 3. The Council and the slump

1 D. C. Corner, 'Exports and the British Trade Cycle: 1929', *Manchester School*, May 1956; E. H. Phelps Brown and G. L. S. Shackle, 'British Economic Fluctuations, 1924–38', *Oxford Economic Papers*, May 1939.

2 Moggridge, *British Monetary Policy 1924–1931*, pp. 153–5.

3 Howson, *Domestic Monetary Management in Britain 1919–38*, pp. 111–12.

4 T. 172/1690, Snowden to Churchill, 23 January 1930; see also Viscount Snowden, *An Autobiography* (1934), Vol. II: *1919–1934*, pp. 847–50.

5 B. Mallett and C. O. George, *British Budgets, Third Series, 1921–1933* (1933), pp. 282–7; T. 172/1684, Grigg to Snowden, 18 October 1929; T. 175/40, Hopkins to Snowden, 21 October 1929, and Phillips, 'Treatment of Budget Deficits', 3 January 1930.

6 See above, pp. 41, 44, 77, 82–3.

7 Cab. 58/11, E.A.C. (H) 106, Keynes, 'The State of Trade', 21 July 1930.

8 Prem. 1/70, P.M.C.2, Keynes, 'The Industrial Situation'.

9 T. Jones, *Whitehall Diary*, Vol. II, p. 225; Prem. 1/70, P.M.C.1, Lord Weir, 'The Industrial Situation', 5 December 1929.

10 Prem. 1/70, Snowden to MacDonald, 8 December 1929.

11 The minutes of the Council meetings are in Cab. 58/2.

12 Cab. 58/2, E.A.C. 4th meeting, 8 May 1930.

13 Cab. 58/10, E.A.C. (H) 83, 'Economic Outlook 1930, Note on Committee's Report by the Chancellor of the Exchequer', 8 April 1930.

14 Cab. 58/145, E.A.C. (H) 81, Committee on Economic Outlook, 1930, Report, 4 April 1930; E.A.C. (H) 85, Report by Chairman and Cole and Report by Balfour and Cadman, 2 May 1930. The reports are reprinted above.

15 Cab. 58/2, E.A.C. 3rd and 4th meetings, 13 March and 10 April 1930; Cab. 58/10, E.A.C. (H) 76, Committee on Channel Tunnel, Report, 5 March 1930, and E.A.C.

(H) 80, Committee on Channel Tunnel Policy, Report, 25 March 1930; Cab. 23/63, Cabinets 15(30)16 and 23(30)5, 12 March and 15 April 1930; Cab. 23/64, Cabinet 31(30)6, 4 June 1930.

16 Cab. 24/212, C.P. 184(30), 'The Channel Tunnel, Note by Prime Minister', 30 May 1930; Keynes Papers, MacDonald to Keynes, 17 March 1930; Cab. 58/144, Channel Tunnel Policy Committee, 2nd meeting, and Report, 25 March. From MacDonald's letter it appears that Keynes raised the question of nationalisation at the Council's March meeting.

17 Cab. 24/216, C.P. 390(30), Lansbury, 'Unemployment Policy'; Drummond, *British Economic Policy and the Empire*, pp. 85–6; Cab. 58/6, Committee on Empire Migration, Interim Report, 1 October 1930; Cab. 24/215, C.P. 343(30), Memorandum by Secretary of State for Dominion Affairs; Cab. 23/65, Cabinet meeting of 15 October 1930; Drummond, *Imperial Economic Policy 1917–1939*, pp. 131–2; Cab. 58/6, Committee on Empire Migration, Final Report, 11 July 1931. The committee's final report was published as Cmd. 4075.

18 Janeway, 'The Economic Policy of the Second Labour Government, 1929–31', pp. 135–40; Cab. 23/63, Cabinet 14(30)1, 11 March 1930; Cab. 58/10, Committee on Agricultural Policy, Report, 7 July 1930; Cab. 23/64, Cabinets 41(30)6, 42(30)2, 43(30)1 and 45(30)1, 16, 18, 22, and 28 July 1930; Cab. 24/213, C.P. 250(30), Snowden, 'Agricultural Policy', 17 July 1930. A statutory home wheat quota would oblige British millers to use a certain proportion of home-grown wheat in their flour, while import boards meant government agencies for the import and distribution of basic foodstuffs and raw materials. On these issues see particularly Drummond, *Imperial Economic Policy 1917–1939*, pp. 145–69.

19 Cab. 58/11, E.A.C. (H) 107, 'Report of Committee on Agricultural Policy, Comments by Keynes', July 1930.

20 The first three of these are: MacDonald Papers 1/208, Henderson, 'The Economic Outlook', 12 March; 'Unemployment at Home and Abroad', 29 March; and 'Note on the Economic Situation', 7 May 1930. From May onwards the E.A.C. staff sent reports on the economic situation to the Council (Cab. 58/14, E.A.C. (S) 1–4, 6–9, 5 May, 8 September, 24 October, and 9 December 1930, 9 February, 10 March, 13 April, and 21 July 1931).

21 MacDonald Papers 1/209, Henderson to MacDonald, 30 June 1930.

22 Cab. 58/2, E.A.C. 7th meeting, 10 July 1930.

23 Cab. 58/10, E.A.C. (H) 98 Revise, 8 July 1930.

24 Cab. 58/11, E.A.C. (H) 113, 'The State of Trade', 22 July 1930.

25 Cab. 58/11, E.A.C. (H) 120, 'The State of Trade', 13 August 1930.

26 On the details of the Unemployment Insurance and Poor Law provisions, see B. B. Gilbert, *British Social Policy 1914–1939* (1970).

27 Cab. 58/11, E.A.C. (H) 121, 'The Present Economic Position', 8 September 1930. The earlier statement quoted comes from the minutes of the Council's 8th meeting.

28 Above, pp. 28–9; Janeway, 'The Economic Policy of the Second Labour Government, 1929–31', pp. 46–56; Donoughue and Jones, *Herbert Morrison*, pp. 156–7; Cab. 27/437, Minutes of conferences of ministers, 13 May–4 June 1930; Cab. 27/438, 1st–4th meetings of Panel of Ministers, June 1930; T. 161/557/S 34462/4, Note by Grigg, undated; Statement of the Principal Measures taken by H.M. Government in connection with Unemployment, Cmd. 3746, December 1930. On the preparation of the White Paper, in which Henderson was involved, see T. 175/43, Henderson to Hopkins, 4 December 1930; MacDonald Papers 1/216, Henderson to MacDonald, 9 December 1930.

29 Cab. 24/438, 5th meeting of Panel, 5 July 1930, and 'Note of Proceedings at a Conference of Heads of Departments in regard to the unemployment situation',

9 July 1930; MacDonald Papers 1/197 and 1/198, MacDonald to Attlee and Anderson, 12 July 1930; Cab. 23/64, Cabinet 38(30)8, 9 July 1930; Cab. 23/90B, Hankey, 'Report to Cabinet of meeting with Lloyd George', 19 September 1930.

30   Cab. 27/438, 'Note of Proceedings at a Conference of Heads of Departments . . .', 9 July 1930; T. 161/557/S 34462/4, Hopkins to Grigg, 23 June 1930; MacDonald Papers 1/198, Anderson to MacDonald, 18 July 1930.

31   Above, p. 27; Cab. 27/439, U.P. (30)7, 'Note on the extent to which the cost of an expanded programme of national development can appropriately and usefully be met by state borrowing', 5 July 1930.

32   Cab. 24/214, C.P. 283(30), Attlee, 'The Problems of British Industry', 29 July 1930; T. 175/38 and T. 175/41, Leith-Ross, 'Note on the memorandum by the Chancellor of the Duchy of Lancaster entitled "The Problems of British Industry"', 6 August 1930. Cabinet discussion of Attlee's memorandum did not take place until December 1930 (above, pp. 77–9).

33   Cab. 58/11, Committee on Unemployment Benefit, Report, 5 November 1930; Cab. 23/66, Cabinet 9(31)6, 21 January 1931. The E.A.C. committee began its work with a visit to Germany to investigate unemployment benefits there. The report of that mission was presented to Parliament in November 1930. (Cab. 58/154, Minutes, memoranda and report of Committee on Unemployment Benefit, October–November 1930).

34   Cab. 23/65, Cabinet 61(30)4, 17 October 1930.

35   Henderson Papers, Keynes to Henderson, 5 June 1930; Cab. 58/10, E.A.C. (H) 88, Committee on Iron and Steel Industry, Report, 30 May 1930; Janeway, 'The Economic Policy of the Second Labour Government', pp. 110–11; Clay, Lord Norman, pp. 318–32. On the report, see also D. Burn, The Economic History of Steelmaking, 1867–1939: A Study in Competition (1940), pp. 436–41. Although the E.A.C. Iron and Steel Report was not published, its details leaked out, as also happened with several other E.A.C. reports at this time.

36   Cab. 23/64, Cabinets 31(30)9, 34(30)3, 38(30)7, 39(30)3, 40(30)2, 46(30)4, 4 and 25 June, 9, 10, 11, and 30 July 1930; Cab. 23/66, Cabinets 16(31)9, 24(31)3, 26(31)7, 27(31)7, 40(31)16, 4 March, 22 and 29 April, 6 May and 30 July 1931; T. 172/1772, Fergusson to Chancellor, 1 May 1931, Snowden to MacDonald, May 1931, and 'Note of a meeting between the Chancellor of the Exchequer, the President of the Board of Trade and the Governor of the Bank of England on the 11th May on the subject of the iron and steel industry'; Janeway, 'The Economic Policy of the Second Labour Government', pp. 118–22. The E.A.C. representatives at the Prime Minister's conference were J. H. Thomas, Cole, Duncan, and Lewis.

37   Cab. 58/10, E.A.C. (H) 89, Committee on Cotton Industry, Report, 4 June 1930; Janeway, 'The Economic Policy of the Second Labour Government', pp. 124–8. The earlier attempts involved both Montagu Norman and Keynes (Clay, Lord Norman, pp. 332–6; R. F. Harrod, The Life of John Maynard Keynes (1951), pp. 379–86).

38   Keynes Papers EA/1, Keynes to MacDonald, 10 July, and Pigou to Keynes, August 1930.

39   Previous treatments of the committee's proceedings can be found in Harrod, Life of John Maynard Keynes, pp. 426–7; Skidelsky, Politicians and the Slump, pp. 203–15; and L. C. Robbins, Autobiography of an Economist (1971), pp. 150–6.

40   Skidelsky is wrong, therefore, in treating Pigou's Macmillan evidence as though it was specially commissioned by Keynes for the Committee of Economists (see Politicians and the Slump, pp. 207–9).

41   Keynes Papers L/30, Keynes to Norman, 22 May 1930.

42   Keynes Papers EA/4, 'Relation between Primary and Secondary Employment' (undated, unsigned).

43   Above, pp. 59 and 69.

44   Cab. 58/150, E.A.C. (E) 7, 'Draft Heads for Discussion', 6 September.

45 Cab. 58/150, E.A.C. (E) 8, 'Questionnaire Prepared by the Chairman', 15 September.

46 J. H. Jones, *Josiah Stamp, Public Servant*, p. 300; and Webb, *Diaries 1924–32*, 14 October 1930.

47 On the shift from the *Tract* to the *Treatise*, see *Collected Writings*, Vol. xiii, Ch.2.

48 For an account of the development of Keynes's policy views which lays particular emphasis on this 'special case' see D. E. Moggridge and S. K. Howson, 'Keynes on Monetary Policy, 1910–46', *Oxford Economic Papers*, July 1974, pp. 226–47.

49 Cab. 58/11, E.A.C. (H) 106, 'The State of Trade', 21 July 1930; *Treatise*, Vol. ii (*Collected Writings*, Vol. vi), p. 345.

50 *Treatise*, Vol. ii, pp. 346–7; Cab. 58/11, E.A.C. (H) 106, 'The State of Trade'.

51 'The State of Trade'.

52 *Treatise*, Vol. ii, p. 165.

53 *Treatise*, Vol. i, p. 314; also Vol. ii, pp. 276, 278–9.

54 *Treatise*, Vol. i, pp. 243–6, Vol. ii, pp. 164–5, 314–15.

55 *Treatise*, Vol. ii, pp. 132–5, 185–6.

56 Keynes Papers L/30, Keynes to Norman, 22 May 1930.

57 *Collected Writings*, Vol. xiii, p. 195.

58 'The Economic Consequences of Mr. Churchill', *Collected Writings*, Vol. ix, pp. 207–30.

59 Cab. 58/11, E.A.C. (H) 106, 'The State of Trade'.

60 Ibid.

61 Cab. 58/2, E.A.C. 9th meeting, 7 November 1930.

62 'The Question of High Wages', *Political Quarterly*, January 1930, pp. 110–24.

63 Keynes Papers EA/1, Keynes to Henderson, 6 June 1930.

64 Committee on Finance and Industry, Unpublished Minutes, 28 February 1930, and *Report*, Cmd. 3897, Addendum 1, paras. 12–25.

65 Above, pp. 57–8.

66 For instance, in *The Means to Prosperity* (1933) (*Collected Writings*, Vol. ix, pp. 335–66).

67 Keynes Papers 1/30, Keynes to Norman, 22 May; *Treatise*, Vol. ii, pp. 285–96; Cab. 58/11, E.A.C. (H) 106, 'The State of Trade'.

68 Cab. 58/150, 'Answers by Robbins to Questionnaire prepared by Chairman'.

69 Cab. 58/151, E.A.C. (E) 24, 'A proposal for tariffs plus bounties', 26 September 1930.

70 Cab. 58/150, E.A.C. (E) 15, and *Collected Writings*, Vol. xiii, pp. 178–200.

71 Cab. 58/151, E.A.C. (H) 26, Pigou, 'Primary and Secondary Employment'; Keynes Papers EA/4, Pigou, 'Investment, Savings, Prices and Employment', and 'Business Losses', and Keynes, 'An Additional Way of Increasing Employment', all 27 September 1930.

72 Cab. 58/150, E.A.C. (H) 13, 'Answers by Robbins to Questionnaire prepared by the Chairman'.

73 Cab. 58/150, E.A.C. (H) 13, 'Answers by Robbins to Questionnaire'; see also *Autobiography of an Economist*, pp. 150–6.

74 *Autobiography of an Economist*, p. 154.

75 Cab. 58/150, Committee of Economists, Minutes of 3rd–9th meetings, 26 September–16 October 1930.

76 Cab. 58/150, 11th and 12th meetings, 19 and 22 September 1930; Robbins, *Autobiography*, p. 151; Keynes Papers EA/1, Keynes to Hemming, 22 September 1930; Lord Kahn to authors.

77 Cab. 58/150, 13th meeting, 23 October; Robbins, *Autobiography*, pp. 151–2; Keynes Papers EA/1, Hemming to Keynes, 27 October 1930. Lord Ebbisham's note of dissent from the report of the Channel Tunnel Committee was not regarded as a precedent because Ebbisham had also signed the report.

78 See references in footnote on p. 63 above.

79 Cab. 58/150, E.A.C. (E) 15, and *Collected Writings*, Vol. XIII, p. 180.

80 Cab. 58/150, E.A.C. (E) 12, 'Answers by Pigou to Questionnaire prepared by Chairman'. He made the same point in his evidence to the Macmillan Committee (*Minutes*, Q. 6151).

81 'Wage Policy and Unemployment', *Economic Journal*, September 1927.

82 *Minutes of Evidence*, Q. 6658; see also the note on remedies reprinted at the end of Pigou's evidence.

83 Cab. 58/150, E.A.C. (E) 12, 'Answers by Pigou to Questionnaire prepared by Chairman'.

84 Keynes Papers EA/1, Henderson to Keynes, 12 March 1930.

85 Cab. 24/212, C.P. 196(30), Henderson to Tom Jones, 3 June, and Henderson, 'Industrial Reconstruction Scheme', 30 May 1930; T. Jones, *Whitehall Diary*, Vol. II, p. 263. Henderson also sent copies to Horace Wilson, Hopkins, Chapman, and Hawtrey (B.T. 56/19/C.I.A./990/4, Henderson to Wilson, 30 May 1930). For official comments on Henderson's ideas, see B.T. 56/19/C.I.A./990/4, Eady to Horace Wilson and Wilson to Eady, 15 May, Eady to Henderson, 16 May, and Eady to Wilson, 27 May 1930.

86 Keynes Papers EA/1, Henderson to Keynes, 30 May 1930.

87 Keynes Papers EA/1, Keynes to Henderson, 3 June 1930.

88 Keynes Papers EA/1, Henderson to Keynes, 5 June 1930.

89 Keynes Papers EA/1, Keynes to Henderson, 6 June 1930.

90 Cab. 58/150, E.A.C. (E) 9, 'Answers by Henderson to Chairman's Questionnaire'. The final section of this memorandum is reprinted in H. D. Henderson, *The Inter-War Years and Other Papers*, ed. H. Clay (1955), pp. 66–70.

91 Cab. 58/151, E.A.C. (E) 28, Keynes, 'VIII. Remedies of Class C', 6 October; Keynes Papers EA/4, Henderson, 'Investment and Interest Rates', 7 October; Cab. 58/151, E.A.C. (E) 38, Keynes, 'Ways of Increasing Home Investment (Remedies of Class F)', 13 October, E.A.C. (E) 53, Henderson, 'Home Investment', 18 October; Cab. 58/150, 10th and 11th meetings, 18 and 19 October; Cab. 58/151, E.A.C. (E) 31, Second Revise, Draft Report, 16 October, and E.A.C. (E) 58, Draft Report, 20 October; and discussions with Lord Kahn.

92 Cab. 58/151, E.A.C. (E) 40, 'The Drift of the Draft Report', 13 October 1930.

93 Committee on Finance and Industry, *Report*, Appendix VI; Keynes Papers L/31, Clark to Keynes, 16 January 1931, Keynes to Daniel Macmillan, 2 December 1931; Keynes Papers MC/2, Clark to Keynes, 28 April and 5 May 1931; Clark, 'Statistical Studies of the Present Economic Position of Great Britain', *Economic Journal*, September 1931. The tables published in the Macmillan Report were tables D, H, K, L, and M of the Economists' Report.

94 *The General Theory of Employment, Interest and Money* (*Collected Writings*, Vol. VII), p. vi.

95 Cab. 23/65, Cabinet 54(30)5, 19 September 1930.

96 Cab. 23/65, Cabinets 56(30)2 and 61(30)4, 25 September and 17 October 1930.

97 Cab. 27/435, Minutes of Committee on Trade Policy, 1–11 December 1930.

98 Keynes Papers A/31, Keynes to MacDonald, 9 March, Ethel Snowden to Keynes, 7 March, and Keynes to Alexander, 17 March 1931.

99 T. 175/52, Fergusson to Forber, 4 March, Forber, 'Some Notes on Revenue Tariffs', 26 March 1931; T. 171/286, Fergusson to Chancellor, April 1931; Mallett and George, *British Budgets 1921–1933*, pp. 323–7.

100 See above, p. 82.

101 Cab. 58/14, E.A.C. (S) 2, 4, 6, 'The Economic Situation', Reports by the Staff, 8 September and 9 December 1930 and 9 February 1931; Cab. 58/2, E.A.C. 11th meeting, 12 February 1931.

Chapter 4. Economic advice during the crisis

1 Above, pp. 31, 78–9, 105.

2 Howson, *Domestic Monetary Management in Britain 1919–38*, pp. 69–71; T. 171/287, Hopkins to Snowden, 10 October 1930, and Fergusson to Snowden, 19 March 1931; Mallett and George, *British Budgets, 1921–1933*, pp. 318–27.

3 T. 171/287, Notes by Snowden of suggestions, undated; Fisher to Snowden and Fergusson to Snowden, 6 February 1931; T. 171/288, Grigg to Snowden, 17 August 1931.

4 Above, pp. 45–6.

5 Above, pp. 66–7; MacDonald Papers 1/171, Henderson to MacDonald, 'The Development of New Industries', 21 August 1930 (reprinted in *The Inter-War Years and Other Papers*, pp. 61–5); MacDonald Papers 1/175, Henderson to MacDonald, 4 November 1930; Cab. 58/14, E.A.C. (S) 5, Henderson, 'National Industrial Planning', 24 January 1931; Cab. 58/12, E.A.C. (H) 142, Henderson, 'Suggested Inquiry into Certain Problems connected with Rationalisation', 28 May 1931. Of the last memorandum there are drafts dated 27 March and 22 April in B.T. 56/44/C.I.A./1912.

6 Cab. 27/438, Panel of Ministers 24th meeting, 6 March; Cab. 58/2, E.A.C. 12th meeting, 12 March; Cab. 27/439, U.P. (30)65 and Cab. 58/12, E.A.C. (H) 141, 'Note by the Secretariat on a Proposal for stimulating new industrial development', 23 February 1931; Cab. 58/167, Committee on New Industrial Development, Minutes, memoranda and report, April 1931–June 1932.

7 Cab. 27/451, T.S.C. (31)2, 'Provisional list of Heads for discussion. Memorandum by Colin Clark', 11 May 1931; see also Clark's article, 'Statistical Studies of the Present Economic Position of Great Britain', *Economic Journal*, September 1931.

8 Cab. 27/451, Minutes and memoranda of Trade Survey Committee, 27 April–21 July 1931.

9 On the development of the crisis, see Clay, *Lord Norman*, pp. 375–97; S. V. O. Clarke, *Central Bank Cooperation 1924–1931* (1967), Ch. 8; Moggridge, *British Monetary Policy 1924–1931*, pp. 193–6, and 'The 1931 Financial Crisis: A New View', *The Banker*, August 1970; D. Williams, 'The 1931 Financial Crisis', *Yorkshire Bulletin of Economic and Social Research*, November 1963; and T. 175/70, Hawtrey, 'The Financial Crisis of 1931', 11 July 1932.

10 Cab. 23/67, Cabinet 36(31)3, 1 July 1931.

11 Committee on Finance and Industry, *Report*, paras. 255–7.

12 Keynes Papers L/31, MacDonald to Keynes, 2 August 1931.

13 Above, pp. 66–9.

14 Keynes Papers EA/1, Henderson to Keynes, 14 February 1931.

15 MacDonald Papers 1/19F, Henderson to MacDonald, 'The Economy Issue', 7 August 1931 (reprinted in *The Inter-War Years*, pp. 71–7).

16 Cab. 58/2, E.A.C. (H) 145, Balfour, 'The Economic Situation', 31 July 1931, circulated by MacDonald to the E.A.C. on 7 August.

17 Keynes Papers L/31 and MacDonald Papers 1/19F, Keynes to MacDonald, 5 August 1931.

18 'Some Consequences of the Economy Report', *New Statesman & Nation*, 15 August 1931, reprinted in *Essays in Persuasion* (*Collected Writings*, Vol. IX), pp. 141–5.

19 Keynes Papers, Keynes to Kahn, 13 August 1931.

20 MacDonald Papers 1/19F, Harvey to Snowden, 6 August 1931, and Snowden to MacDonald, 7 August 1931.

21 Janeway, 'The Economic Policy of the Second Labour Government, 1929–31', p. 264; MacDonald Papers 1/19F, Henderson to MacDonald, 11 August 1931.

22 Snowden's statement is not in the papers of the committee (Cab. 27/454) but in T. 171/288, N.E. (31)2, Forecast of Budget Position in 1931 and 1932, Note by Chancel-

lor, undated. The committee's report is C.P. 203(31) (in Cab. 27/454 and Cab. 24/222). Another source of information about the committee is the Graham memorandum used by Bassett, *Nineteen Thirty-one: Political Crisis*, Ch. 5, and Skidelsky, *Politicians and the Slump*, pp. 396–9. On the Treasury's discussion of new taxes, see T. 171/288, Memorandum by Fisher, Hopkins, and Grigg, 18 August 1931. It included another look at the tax on rentier incomes discussed in February (above, p. 83).

23   Cab. 23/67, Cabinets 41(31) and 43(31)F, 19 and 21 August 1931.
24   Clay, *Lord Norman*, pp. 387, 390.
25   Feiling, *Neville Chamberlain*, p. 192; MacDonald Papers 1/19F, 'Meeting of the General Council sub-committee and the Cabinet sub-committee...20th August 1931 ...'
26   Cab. 23/67, Cabinets 44(31)1 and 45(31), 22 August 1931.
27   Clay, *Lord Norman*, p. 392. The cable is in the MacDonald Papers 1/19F, and is reproduced in Clay, pp. 391–2.
28   Cab. 23/67, Cabinet 46(31), and Prem. 1/96, Note headed 'Division'.
29   Cab. 27/456, C.P. 208(31).
30   Mallett and George, *British Budgets, 1921–1933*, pp. 363–73; T. 171/288, 'Budget Position', undated.
31   'Notes on the Situation', *New Statesman & Nation*, 27 August 1931.
32   Keynes Papers, Keynes's notes for his speech.
33   Ibid. and 'The Budget', *New Statesman & Nation*, 19 September 1931, reprinted in *Essays in Persuasion (Collected Writings*, Vol. IX), pp. 145–9.
34   MacDonald Papers 1/19F, 'Notes on the Economy Issue', 27 August 1931.
35   Cab. 27/462, T. 172/1746, and MacDonald Papers 1/180, 'The Balance of Payments', 18 September 1931.
36   Prem. 1/97, Letters from the Prime Minister to his colleagues, 10 September 1931; Cab. 58/17, Committee on Economic Information 1st meeting, 15 September 1931.
37   Prem. 1/97, Duff, 'Notes of a meeting on 18 September 1931', 26 September 1931; see also Roskill, *Hankey: Man of Secrets*, Vol. II, pp. 558–9. MacDonald's suggestion resulted in the Prime Minister's Advisory Committee on Financial Questions, on which see above, pp. 100–1.
38   Leith-Ross, *Money Talks*, p. 140. Keynes also made his case for exchange controls in the Committee on Economic Information (Cab. 58/18, E.A.C. (E) 4, 'The Balance of International Payments, Draft Report, Draft Concluding paragraphs prepared by Mr. J. M. Keynes', 28 September 1931).
39   Prem. 1/97, 'Note by H. D. Henderson, approved by Treasury emphasising vital value now of measures already taken to balance the budget, 20 September 1931, Note for oral issue by the P.M. to Editors this evening'; see also 'Henderson's draft for broadcast (for C. of E. on 21.9.30)', in same file.
40   Snowden, *An Autobiography*, Vol. II, pp. 1055, 1063, 1067.
41   W. A. Brown, jun., *The International Gold Standard Reinterpreted* (1940), Vol. II, p. 1092.
42   *My Political Life* (1953), Vol. III, p. 22; see also Lord Swinton, *I Remember* (1949), pp. 37–8; and Feiling, *Neville Chamberlain*, pp. 177–8, 181.
43   Feiling, *Neville Chamberlain*, p. 201.
44   Cab. 24/225, C.P. 311(31), 'Cabinet Policy and Work', 7 December 1931. The first item on MacDonald's list was the currency question, on which see above, pp. 101–5. Henderson's memorandum is, presumably, 'Notes on the Balance of Payments', 21 January 1932, MacDonald Papers 1/180.
45   Cab. 23/69, Cabinet 88(31)4, 11 December 1931. The other members were Samuel, Simon, Thomas, Cunliffe-Lister, Hilton Young, Runciman, Snowden, and Gilmour.
46   Drummond, *Imperial Economic Policy 1917–1939*, p. 177. Runciman had been a guest

at the April 1930 Tuesday Club meeting when Keynes attacked the case for free trade (Minute Book of Tuesday Club).

47 T. 172/1768, Memoranda by Chamberlain and Phillips, 28 December 1931.

48 T. 172/1768, Samuel to Chamberlain, 30 December 1931; Cab. 27/467, Committee on the Balance of Trade 4th meeting, 13 January 1932.

49 T. 172/1768, Fergusson to Chamberlain, 1 January 1932.

50 Cab. 24/227, C.P. 32(32), Committee on the Balance of Trade, Memorandum by Home Secretary, 19 January 1932.

51 Cab. 24/227, C.P. 31(32), Committee on the Balance of Trade, Memorandum of Dissent by Lord Privy Seal, 18 January 1932; see also Cab. 24/227, C.P. 25(32), Committee on the Balance of Trade, Report, 18 January 1932.

52 Cab. 23/70, Cabinets 5(32), 6(32) and 7(32), 21–2 January 1932; Snowden, *An Autobiography*, Vol. II, pp. 1009–12; Feiling, *Neville Chamberlain*, pp. 203–4. The dissenters were Samuel, Snowden, Sinclair, and Maclean.

53 Feiling, *Neville Chamberlain*, p. 203.

54 T. 172/1772, Note by Chamberlain, 15 October 1932; Import Duties Advisory Committee to Treasury, 13 October 1932; T. 172/1773, Hurst, 'Summary of negotiations with the iron and steel industry', February 1933; Cab. 24/239, C.P. 88(33), Reorganisation of the iron and steel industry, Memorandum by Chancellor, 31 March 1933; Cab. 23/75, Cabinet 23(33)7, 5 April 1933; Iron and Steel Reorganisation Scheme, Correspondence between the National Committee for the Iron and Steel Industry and the Import Duties Advisory Committee, March and April 1933; T. 172/1773, Hurst, 'The Reorganisation of the Iron and Steel Industry', 31 October 1933; Fergusson to Chamberlain, 1 November 1933; Hurst to Fergusson, 23 January 1934. See also 'The Iron and Steel Industry', in British Association, *Britain in Depression* (1935), pp. 261–79; D. Burn, *The Economic History of Steelmaking, 1867–1939*, Ch. XVI.

55 D. S. Landes, *The Unbound Prometheus: Technological Change and Industrial Development in Western Europe from 1750 to the Present* (1969), pp. 475, 477; Burn, *The Economic History of Steelmaking*, p. 450n; R. S. Sayers, *A History of Economic Change in England 1880–1939* (1967), p. 85. The tariff's role in recovery generally can be summed up by saying that it helped but it did not initiate it (above, p. 106).

56 B.T. 55/51/R.C.I./1, Reorganisation of the cotton industry, June 1934–March 1936; Cab. 23/81, Cabinets 8(35)10, 14(35)5, and 49(35)8, 6 February, 13 March, and 27 November 1935; Cab. 24/253, C.P. 16(35), and Cab. 24/254, C.P. 50(35), 'Cotton Spinning Redundancy Scheme', Memoranda by President of Board of Trade, 21 January and 7 March 1935; B.T. 55/51/R.C.I./1, Horace Wilson, 'The Cotton Spinning Industry Act and "After"', July 1936. See also 'The Cotton Industry' in British Association, *Britain in Recovery* (1938), pp. 441–59.

57 'The Cotton Industry' in British Association, *Britain in Recovery*, pp. 441–59; Cab. 23/90A, Cabinet 47(37)10, 15 December 1937; Cab. 24/273, C.P. 304(37), Reorganisation of the Cotton Industry, Memorandum by President of Board of Trade, 10 December 1937; Cab. 23/93, Cabinet 26(38)7, 25 May 1938; Cab. 24/277, C.P. 120(38), Reorganisation of the Cotton Industry, Memorandum by President of Board of Trade, 20 May 1938; Cab. 23/96, Cabinet 60(38)14, 21 December 1938; Cab. 24/281, C.P. 292(38), 'Cotton Industry Bill', Memorandum by President of Board of Trade, 16 December 1938; Cab. 23/97, Cabinet 10(39)9, 8 March 1939.

58 Burn, *The Economic History of Steelmaking*, p. 485.

59 Above, p. 94.

60 Cab. 58/169, E.A.C. Committee on Financial Questions 1st meeting, 22 September 1931.

61 Prem. 1/97, Henderson to MacDonald, 20 September 1931.

62 Cab. 58/169, Henderson, 'The Problems arising from the suspension of gold payments', 24 and 25 September 1931.

63 Cab. 58/169, E.A.C. Committee on Financial Questions 4th meeting, 29 September 1931. A copy of the minutes can be found in T. Jones, *A Diary with Letters 1931–1950*, pp. 12–13.

64 See above, pp. 102–4.

65 Cab. 58/169, E.A.C. Committee on Financial Questions 8th meeting, 18 January 1932.

66 Cab. 58/169, 'Prime Minister's Advisory Financial Committee, Draft Statement of Views', 5 February, and 'Supplementary Draft Paragraphs', 10 February 1932.

67 Cab. 58/169, 'Note by the Secretary', 1 March 1932.

68 Cab. 58/169, E.A.C. Committee on Financial Questions, Report on Sterling Policy, 9 March 1932; reprinted above.

69 Cab. 23/69, Cabinet 74(31)3, 10 November 1931.

70 T. 175/56, Hawtrey, 'Pegging the Pound I', 28 September; T. 188/29, Hawtrey, 'Pegging the Pound II', 2 October; T. 175/56, Henderson to Hopkins, 6 October; T. 188/29, Henderson, 'Comments on Mr. Hawtrey's Memorandum, Pegging the Pound II', 6 October 1931; see also P. K. Debenham, 'The Economic Advisory Council and the Great Depression', *Oxford Economic Papers*, 1953 (Supplement), p. 39. Hawtrey's views reached the Prime Minister in a memorandum passed on by Clifford Allen (MacDonald Papers 1/19G, Clifford Allen to MacDonald, 4 December 1931, and 1/19G and 6/80, Hawtrey, 'Monetary Policy', undated).

71 T. 188/28, Leith-Ross to Henderson, 9 October, and Leith-Ross to Keynes, 16 October 1931. Leith-Ross referred to Keynes's article in the *Sunday Express* of 27 September 1931 (reprinted in *Essays in Persuasion* (*Collected Writings*, Vol. IX), pp. 245–9).

72 T. 188/28, Henderson to Leith-Ross, and Henderson, 'International Co-operation and the Gold Standard', 16 October 1931.

73 *Collected Writings*, Vol. VI, pp. 189–367, and Vol. IV, pp. 189–91.

74 Cab. 58/169 and T. 188/48, Keynes, 'Notes on the Currency Question', 16 November 1931.

75 Keynes Papers, Henderson to Keynes, 24 November 1931.

76 T. 175/57, Hopkins, 'Note on Mr. Keynes' Memorandum of 16 November', and Hopkins to Fergusson, 15 December 1931; above, p. 101.

77 The drafts are scattered among Treasury files, T. 175/56, 57, 58, and 64: see Howson, *Domestic Monetary Management in Britain 1919–38*, Appendix 4.

78 T. 175/57, Hopkins, 'The Present Position of the Pound', 12 January 1932; T. 175/57, Phillips, 'The Present Position of the Pound', 24 February 1932; and T. 175/58, Phillips to Henderson, 26 February 1932.

79 T. 188/48, Phillips to Leith-Ross, 31 March 1932; and T. 175/57, Memorandum by Phillips, 5 March 1932.

80 On these measures, see Howson, *Domestic Monetary Management in Britain*, pp. 86–9.

81 On Ottawa, see I. M. Drummond, *Imperial Economic Policy 1917–1939*, Chs. 5, 6.

Chapter 5. *The Committee on Economic Information 1932–9*

1 Howson, *Domestic Monetary Management in Britain 1919–38*, Chs. 5, 6; see also E. Nevin, *The Mechanism of Cheap Money: A Study of British Monetary Policy 1931–1939* (1955); R. A. MacIntosh, 'A Note on Cheap Money and the British Housing Boom', *Economic Journal*, March 1951; H. Bellman, 'The Building Trades', in British Association, *Britain in Recovery*; C. H. Feinstein, *Domestic Capital Formation in the United Kingdom 1920–1938* (1965), pp. 41–3. For a contrary view, see H. W. Richardson, *Economic Recovery in Britain 1932–39* (1967).

2 On the 'New Deal' and Swedish economic policy in the 1930s, and the debate over the nature of these policies, see H. Stein, *The Fiscal Revolution in America* (1969), Chs.

3–7; E. C. Brown, 'Fiscal Policy in the 'Thirties, a Reappraisal', *American Economic Review*, December 1956; Winch, *Economics and Policy*, Ch. 11, and 'The Keynesian Revolution in Sweden', *Journal of Political Economy*, April 1966; B. Gustaffson, 'A Perennial of Doctrinal History: Keynes and "the Stockholm School"', *Economy and History*, 1973.

3 Cab. 58/2, E.A.C. 14th meeting, 15 January 1932.

4 After a report on the history of the C.C.R. and the E.A.C. by Hemming in 1937, an official committee on the E.A.C. recommended that the Council should be remodelled on the lines laid down for the C.C.R. in 1925 and should resume that title (Cab. 58/16, Minutes, Memoranda and Report of Committee on the E.A.C., 1938).

5 Cab. 58/8, Henderson and Hemming, 'The Organisation of the Council', 14 July 1931.

6 Cab. 58/8, Note by Henderson and Hemming, 15 January 1932.

7 Cab. 58/17, C.E.I. 5th meeting, 18 February 1932. All the C.E.I. reports are in Cab. 58/30, and all its minutes in Cab. 58/17, so that these file numbers will not usually be given in the rest of this chapter.

8 On the common attitude of Salter, Stamp, and Keynes to the problems posed by the world slump, see their contributions to the Halley Stewart Lecture 1931, in December 1931–February 1932, published as *The World's Economic Crisis and the Way of Escape* (1932). See also Salter, *Recovery: The Second Effort* (1933). On Henderson, see *The Inter-War Years and Other Papers*, pp. 91–106, and Debenham, 'The Economic Advisory Council and the Great Depression', *Oxford Economic Papers*, 1953 (Supplement).

9 Salter, *Slave of the Lamp*, pp. 87–8.

10 On how the Treasury operates, see S. Brittan, *The Treasury under the Tories 1951–1964* (1964) and *Steering the Economy: The Role of the Treasury* (1971); H. Heclo and A. Wildavsky, *The Private Government of Public Money* (1974); H. Roseveare, *The Treasury: The Evolution of a British Institution* (1969), Chs. 8 and 9; and Lord Bridges, *The Treasury* (1964).

11 E. A. G. Robinson, Letter to the authors.

12 5th, 6th, and 8th Reports, November 1932, February and July 1933.

13 T. 188/72, Phillips, 'Recovery from the Trade Depression', 21 September 1933.

14 See, e.g., the 11th, 14th, and 18th Reports, March and December 1934 and July 1935.

15 T. 175/70, Phillips to Hopkins and Chancellor, 19 October 1932, and Hopkins to Chancellor, 20 October 1932; T. 172/1814, 'The level of prices as affected by monetary policy', Memorandum by Treasury, 29 September 1932; T. 175/17, Phillips, 'Notes on Cheap Money', 15 February 1933; T. 188/72, Phillips, 'Recovery from the Trade Depression', 21 September 1933; Leith-Ross, 'Money and Prices', September 1933; T. 175/93, Phillips, 'EAC – 12th Report', 27 July 1934.

16 C.E.I. 11th Report, March 1934; T. 175/93, Phillips, 'Eleventh Report of Committee on Economic Information', 17 April 1934; see also Note by Leith-Ross, 3 April 1934, in same file.

17 14th Report, December 1934.

18 Clay, *Lord Norman*, pp. 416–17.

19 T. 160/533/F 13296/01, Hopkins, 'Foreign Issues, Discussions with the Governor on the 9th February 1933', 10 February 1933; T. 175/84, Phillips to Hopkins, 7 June 1933; T. 160/533/F 13296/02, Hopkins to Chancellor, 15 July 1933.

20 T. 175/84, Phillips to Hopkins, 7 June 1933.

21 T. 160/533/F 13296/01, Phillips to Hopkins, 15 November 1932; Hopkins to Waterfield, 19 January 1933; T. 175/84, Phillips to Hopkins, 7 June 1933.

22 T. 160/533/F 13296/02, Fisher to Chancellor, 16 December 1933; Note by Chamberlain, 20 December 1933; T. 175/94, Phillips, 'The Kennet Committee and Investment Abroad', 17 November 1937.

23   T. 175/94, Phillips, 'The Kennet Committee and Investment Abroad', 17 November 1937; Hopkins to Fisher and Woods, 24 November 1937.

24   A. K. Cairncross, *Control of Long-term International Capital Movements* (1973); R. B. Stewart, 'Great Britain's Foreign Loan Policy', *Economica*, February 1938.

25   17th Report, May 1935.

26   Cab. 58/20, Henderson to Stamp, 13 May 1935.

27   T. 175/88, 'Relations with U.S.A.', 4 June 1935. See also Note by Hopkins, 4 June 1935. Phillips's memorandum used some notes by Stamp of his conversations on currency questions in the U.S. and Henderson's article to inform the Chancellor of the Treasury's views on stabilisation.

28   Above, pp. 88–9. Henderson's plan acquired its usual title when Keynes publicly advocated it in 'The Means to Prosperity' in March 1933.

29   T. 175/66, Henderson to Hopkins, 17 May 1932. The memorandum is reprinted in *The Inter-War Years*, pp. 103–6.

30   T. 175/66, Note by Phillips, May 1932, and Henderson, 'Monetary Discussions', 6 June 1932.

31   T. 175/66, Note by Phillips, May 1932.

32   T. 175/66, Henderson to Hopkins, 25 May 1932.

33   T. 175/58 and T. 175/66, Henderson, 'Monetary Discussions' and 'B.I.S. Note Issue, Illustrative Scheme', 6 June 1932; T. 175/66, 'Monetary Discussions at Lausanne', 7 June 1932. The latter memorandum includes the former memoranda with Leith-Ross's comments added. Keynes Papers A/32, Keynes to MacDonald, 21 June 1932.

34   Cab. 58/183, Committee on International Economic Policy 1st and 3rd meetings, 3 and 10 August 1932, and 1st Report, 11 October 1932.

35   Cab. 58/18, 'Comments received on the Fourth Report, Note by Chairman', 8 August 1932; Cab. 58/183, Committee on International Economic Policy 5th meeting, 14 September 1932; Note by Secretaries of E.A.C., 18 January 1933, and Committee on International Economic Policy, 2nd Report, 6 April 1933.

36   Kindleberger, *The World in Depression*, pp. 211–13; Clarke, *The Reconstruction of the International Monetary System*, pp. 21–2.

37   T. 172/1814, 'The level of prices as affected by monetary policy'. This memorandum was a joint effort by Hopkins, Phillips, and Waley for the Inter-departmental Committee on the World Economic Conference set up in July 1932 (T. 160/449/F 13017/06, Drafts of and correspondence on memorandum, September 1932; T. 160/447/F 13017/09/1, D.P.C. Committee 1st meeting, 29 July 1932).

38   T. 172/1814, 'The level of prices as affected by monetary policy'; T. 177/12, Hopkins to Norman, 24 October 1932; T. 175/70, Note by Phillips, 29 October 1932; T. 175/93, 'The foreign demand for the return of the U.K. to gold', October 1932; T. 172/1814, Phillips, 'World Economic Conference', 10 December 1932; T. 177/12, Phillips, 'Public Works as a method of raising price levels', 11 July 1933.

39   Cab. 58/183, 'The foreign demand for the return of the U.K. to gold', October 1932. This memorandum was written by Phillips and sent to and discussed at the Bank (T. 175/93, Draft by Phillips, 20 October 1932; T. 177/12, Hopkins to Norman, 24 October 1932; T. 175/70, Note by Phillips, 29 October 1932). The memorandum later went to the inter-departmental committee on the conference (T. 175/70, Hopkins to Chamberlain, and Note by Chamberlain, 31 October 1932).

40   T. 188/56, Kisch to Leith-Ross, 11 November 1932; Drafts of memorandum by Kisch; Phillips to Leith-Ross, 21 November 1932; and Phillips, 'Note on Kisch's memorandum of 11 November', 21 November 1932; T. 177/7, Kisch, 'The Gold Problem', 25 November 1932.

41   The criticisms were noted at the time by Phillips (T. 188/56, Phillips, 'Note on Kisch's memorandum of 11 November').

42   T. 175/93, Phillips to Hopkins, 27 March 1933.

43 T. 172/1814, Hopkins to Chancellor, 12 December 1932, and Phillips, 'Prospects for the World Conference'.

44 T. 172/1814, 'The level of prices as affected by monetary policy'; Cab. 58/183, 'The foreign demand for the return of the U.K. to gold'.

45 Cab. 58/183, Leith-Ross and Phillips, 'Report of the Second meeting of the Preparatory Committee for the World Economic Conference', 23 January 1932; League of Nations, Monetary and Economic Conference, Draft Annotated Agenda, pp. 22–3.

46 T. 175/93, Memorandum by Phillips, 27 March 1933; italics in original.

47 F.O. 371/17304, Telegram from Lindsay, 3 April 1933; Telegram to Lindsay, 5 April 1933.

48 F.O. 371/17304, Telegram from Lindsay, 5 April 1933.

49 T. 177/12, T. 175/70, and T. 188/78, Hopkins to Fergusson, 11 April 1933, and Note by Chamberlain, 11 April 1933; F.O. 371/17304, Telegram to Lindsay, 13 April 1933. The Treasury's *aide-mémoire* to the Prime Minister, who met Roosevelt later in the month, also included an outline of the Kisch plan (T. 175/17 and T. 188/78, Note by Phillips, 11 April 1933).

50 Cab. 29/142, Leith-Ross, 'Discussions at Washington on the Programme of the World Conference', 12 May 1933. Feis explained the objections a little more fully in a memorandum to his colleagues (*Foreign Relations of the U.S.: 1933*, Vol. I, pp. 574–5; see also Kindleberger, *The World in Depression*, p. 211).

51 T. 175/93, Phillips, 'C.P. (33) 100', 9 May 1933. This was a note for the Chancellor to use in Cabinet discussion of the report, which took place on 10 May (Cab. 23/76, Cabinet 34(33) 8, 10 May 1933).

52 Seventh Report, 'The American Situation and the World Economic Conference', 16 May 1933.

53 T. 175/93, Phillips, 'C.E.I. Sixth [sic] Report', 9 May 1933; T. 175/17, Phillips, 'The Question of Raising Prices', 15 May 1933.

54 Kindleberger, *The World in Depression*, pp. 217–20; Feis, *1933*, pp. 144–52, 182–7, 190–4, 211–34; *Foreign Relations of the U.S.: 1933*, Vol. I, pp. 619–94.

55 Cab. 29/140, M.E.C. (33) 8, Memorandum by Treasury, 'International Lending and Exchange Restrictions' (italics in original).

56 Cab. 29/140, Cabinet Committee on W.E.C. 4th meeting, 19 May 1933; Cab. 29/142 and T. 160/489/F 13017/021, 'Outlines of a Scheme for an International Credit Institution', June 1933. This was, as usual, Phillips's work (T. 160/489/F 13017/021, Waley to Phillips, and Note by Phillips, 2 June 1933). The briefs also included the Seventh Report of the C.E.I., mentioned above (p. 120).

57 Cab. 29/142, 19th, 21st and 22nd meetings of U.K., delegation, 3, 5, and 7 July 1933.

58 Harrod, *Life of John Maynard Keynes*, pp. 442–4; Kindleberger, *The World in Depression*, pp. 212–13. On the later schemes and their implementation, see K. Horsefield, *The International Monetary Fund 1945–1965* (1969), Vol. I, Chs. 1–5; R. N. Gardner, *Sterling–Dollar Diplomacy* (1956); Harrod, *Life of John Maynard Keynes*, Ch. XIII; and *Collected Writings of John Maynard Keynes*, Vol. XXV (ed. D. E. Moggridge, forthcoming).

59 'The Economic Advisory Council and the Great Depression', *Oxford Economic Papers*, 1953 (Supplement), p. 36.

60 Clarke, *The Reconstruction of the International Monetary System*, p. 29; see also pp. 21–2, 38–9.

61 Keynes to Norman, 19 December 1941, *Collected Writings*, Vol. XXV.

62 *Collected Writings*, Vols. XXV–XXVII.

63 C.E.I. 5th Report, November 1932, part of which is reprinted above.

64 C.E.I. 19th and 20th meetings, 26 and 31 January 1933; 6th Report, 'Financial Policy, February 1933', 9 February 1933 (reprinted above).

65 T. 172/1814, 'The level of prices as affected by monetary policy', Treasury memorandum, 29 September 1932.

66 T. 175/17, Phillips, Memorandum of 6 June 1932; see also T. 175/17, Phillips, 'Notes on Cheap Money', 15 February 1933; Phillips to Hopkins, 28 February 1933; and 'The Question of Raising Prices', 15 May 1933; T. 188/72, Leith-Ross, 'Money and Prices', September 1933.

67 T. 172/1814, 'The level of prices as affected by monetary policy', 29 September 1932.

68 Cab. 23/77, Cabinet 68(33)5, 6 December 1933.

69 B. E. V. Sabine, *British Budgets in Peace and War 1932–1945* (1970), pp. 36–7, 55–8.

70 See, e.g., T. 175/17, Phillips to Hopkins, 28 February 1933; Phillips and Hopkins to Chancellor, 'Mr. Keynes' First and Second Articles', 17 March 1933; Phillips, 'Mr. Keynes' Articles', 21 March 1933.

71 T. 172/1814, 'The level of prices as affected by monetary policy', 29 September 1932.

72 T. 175/70, Hopkins to Chancellor, 20 October 1932; see also T. 175/70, Phillips to Hopkins, 19 October 1932, and T. 188/72, Phillips, 'Recovery from the Trade Depression', 21 September 1933.

73 T. 175/93, Hopkins, 'C.E.I. 5th Report', 8 December 1932; Hopkins to Chancellor, 16 February 1933. On the Cabinet Committee, see above, pp. 126–7.

74 T. 175/64, Memorandum by Hopkins, 26 February 1933; T. 171/296, Hopkins to Chancellor, 11 March 1932; T. 175/59, Hopkins to Forber, 15 March 1932; T. 171/296 and T. 188/48, Hopkins, 'Speculative forecast of 1935 on the basis of "Old Moore's Almanack"', 21 March 1932.

75 Cab. 23/75, Cabinet 10(33)7, 22 February 1933.

76 T. 175/93, Hopkins, 'C.E.I. 5th Report', 8 December 1932.

77 Ibid.

78 Cab. 58/182, Committee on Limits of Economy Policy, Minutes, memoranda and report, February–March 1932.

79 Robbins, *Autobiography*, p. 153.

80 Cab. 27/468, Committee on Employment Policy, Report, 25 January 1932.

81 Cab. 23/70, Cabinet 11(32)6, 3 February 1932; Cab. 27/479, Employment Policy Committee meetings of 11 February, 18 April, and 9 June 1932, and reports, 21 April and 13 June 1932.

82 Cab. 27/490, Committee on Unemployment, Minutes and reports.

83 Prem. 1/126, Henderson and Wilson, 'Committee on Trade and Employment', 8 November 1932.

84 Cab. 27/503, Panel on Trade and Employment, meeting of 23 November 1932; see also Cab. 23/75, Cabinet 1(33)1, 19 January 1933.

85 Cab. 27/503, 2nd meeting of Panel, 1 December 1932; Bellman, 'Wise Spending', 30 November 1932; T. 160/1127/F 13040/1, Phillips to Hopkins, 3 December 1932; Cab. 27/502, Committee on Trade and Employment, 2nd meeting, 6 December 1932.

86 Cab. 27/502, Wilson and Henderson, 'Wise Spending', 14 December 1932; Committee on Trade and Employment 3rd meeting, 16 December 1932; Henderson Papers Box 1, Howorth to Henderson, 18 October 1932; Wilson to Henderson, 20 October 1932; Leith-Ross to Henderson, 22 October 1932; Duff to Henderson, 24 October 1932; MacDonald Papers 1/183, Cunliffe-Lister to MacDonald, 22 December 1932, and MacDonald to Cunliffe-Lister, 23 December 1932; T. 160/1127/F 13040/1, Note by Hopkins, 15 December 1932, and Phillips to Hopkins and Fergusson, 15 December 1932.

87 Cab. 27/502, 'Borrowing for Capital Expenditure by Government', Memorandum by Chancellor, 28 February 1933, and 6th meeting of Committee on Trade and Employment, 3 March 1933.

88 Cab. 23/75, Cabinet 36(33)9, 24 May 1933.

89 T. 175/17, Memorandum by Hopkins, 13 March 1933.

90 Ibid. and T. 175/17, Gilbert, 'The Means to Prosperity, Mr. Keynes' First Article, Treasury Note', 14 March 1933.

91 T. 175/17, Phillips, 'Gilbert on Keynes', 14 March 1933; see also T. 171/309, Hopkins to Fisher and Fergusson, 15 March 1933.

92 T. 175/17 and T. 171/309, 'Mr. Keynes' First & Second Articles'.

93 Keynes Papers, Phillips to Henderson, 15 March 1933. The Treasury had made the same assumption with respect to Keynes's *Treatise* position (T. 175/26, Leith-Ross, 'The Assumptions of Mr. Keynes', 27 March 1930).

94 T. 175/17, Phillips, 'Mr. Keynes' First and Second Articles', 17 March 1933.

95 T. 171/309, Hopkins to Fisher and Fergusson, 13 March 1933; 'The Means to Prosperity, Mr. Keynes' First Article, Treasury Note', 15 March 1933; 'Mr. Keynes' First & Second Articles', 'Mr. Keynes' Articles', 21 March 1933; 'Income Tax and Development Expenditure. Mr. Keynes: The Times 13 March 1933', Memorandum by Inland Revenue, 15 March 1933; Henderson, 'Suggested paragraphs for vote of censure debate'; Henderson to Fergusson, 15 March 1933; Fergusson to Chancellor, 16 March 1933; Note by Chamberlain, 16 March 1933; Fergusson to Henderson, 16 March 1933.

96 T. 175/17, 'Mr. Keynes' Articles', 21 March 1933; *House of Commons Debates*, Vol. 276, cc. 379–91.

97 Keynes Papers, Keynes to Kahn, 16 March 1933; see also Keynes to Kahn, 20 March 1933.

98 T. 188/72, Phillips, 'Recovery from the trade depression', 21 September 1933.

99 T. 172/1828, Fergusson to Chancellor, Hopkins to Chancellor, and Note by Phillips, 25 January 1935.

100 Feinstein, *National Income, Expenditure and Output of the U.K. 1855–1965* (1972), Tables 12, 13, 34, 39; M. Bowley, *Housing and the State 1919–1944* (1945), Chs. VII, VIII; Cab. 27/584, 'Public Works', Memorandum by the Treasury, 20 February 1935; R. F. Bretherton, F. A. Burchardt and R. S. G. Rutherford, *Public Investment and the Trade Cycle in Great Britain* (1941), pp. 211–14, 379–80; Cab. 27/640, Inter-departmental Committee on Public Capital Expenditure, Report, 13 August 1937.

101 See, e.g., T. 172/1828, Note by Phillips, 25 January 1935; Hopkins to Chancellor, Fisher, and Woods, 14 November 1936. On regional policy in the 1930s see G. McCrone, *Regional Policy in Britain* (1969), Ch. III; A. J. Brown, *The Framework of Regional Policy in Britain* (1972), pp. 281–5; D. E. Pitfield, 'Labour Migration and the Regional Problem in Britain 1920–1939', unpublished University of Stirling Ph.D. thesis, 1973, Chs. 6, 7.

102 On the problems stemming from Ottawa, see Drummond, *British Economic Policy and the Empire*, pp. 104–12, and *Imperial Economic Policy 1917–1939*, Ch. 7.

103 Drummond, *Imperial Economic Policy 1917–1939*, pp. 328, 368–9; Cab. 23/79, Cabinet 30(34)6, 25 July 1934; Feiling, *Life of Neville Chamberlain*, pp. 229–30; Henderson Papers Box 1, Debenham to Henderson, 21 June 1934.

104 Drummond, *Imperial Economic Policy 1917–1939*, pp. 327–72; Cab. 27/560, Minutes and memoranda of Produce Markets Supply Committee; Cab. 23/79, Cabinet 30(34)6, 25 July 1934 and Cab. 23/80, Cabinet 46(34)10, 12 December 1934; Cab. 24/251, C.P. 272(34), Report of Inter-departmental Committee on 13th Report of the Economic Advisory Committee on Economic Information, 3 December 1934; T. 188/101, Leith-Ross to Runciman, 'Co-ordination of Trade Policy', 6 December 1934.

105 Cab. 27/560, Produce Markets Supply Committee 13th meeting, 17 December 1934, especially comments by Baldwin and Elliot; T. 188/117, Leith-Ross to Hopkins and Chancellor, 21 January 1935; Phillips to Hopkins, 4 February 1935; Note by Fisher, 5 February 1935; Note by Chamberlain, 6 February 1935.

106 Lord Beveridge, *Power and Influence: An Autobiography* (1953), pp. 224–5.

107 49th, 50th, and 51st meetings of C.E.I.

108 See above, p. 113.

109 See e.g. T. 175/93, Phillips, 'E.A.C. – 12th Report', 27 July 1934; 'The Housing Boom – I', *Economist*, 26 October 1935.

110 Cab. 58/24, Henderson, 'Some Economic Factors', 27 June 1935.

111 Cab. 58/21, Keynes to Debenham, 18 July 1935.

112 The report is reprinted above.

113 The division was Henderson's.

114 Cab. 58/30, Henderson, Bowley, Caradog Jones, and Robertson, 'The Trend of Unemployment', 4 December 1935.

115 58th meeting of C.E.I., 11 December 1935; see also Cab. 58/21, Phillips, 'Housing in relation to other forms of capital expenditure', 19 December 1935 (a memorandum he circulated to the C.E.I. at one of the first meetings he attended).

116 See *The Economist*, Commercial History and Review of 1936; Hodson, *Slump and Recovery 1929–1937*, pp. 403–40; Kindleberger, *The World in Depression 1929–1939*, pp. 247–64.

117 J. E. Meade, 'The Keynesian Revolution', in Milo Keynes (ed.), *Essays on John Maynard Keynes* (1975), p. 182.

118 Above, p. 110.

119 Above, p. 128.

120 'Poverty and Plenty'; *General Theory*, esp. Chs. 3, 12–14, 18, 22.

121 Meade, in Milo Keynes (ed.), *Essays on John Maynard Keynes*, p. 182.

122 C.E.I. 19th Report, 10 February 1936.

123 21st Report, December 1936. On the trade-diverting effects of Ottawa, see Drummond, *British Economic Policy and the Empire*, pp. 18–24, and *Imperial Economic Policy 1917–1939*, Ch. 8.

124 66th meeting and 21st Report of C.E.I.

125 69th and 70th meetings of C.E.I.

126 'How to Avoid a Slump', 12–14 January 1937.

127 22nd Report, February 1937 (reprinted above); 72nd meeting of C.E.I. Keynes was in fact absent from the meeting at which Robertson raised his objections.

128 Cab. 58/22, 'Draft 22nd Report . . . Note by Mr. D. H. Robertson', 2 February 1937.

129 D. H. Robertson, 'The Trade Cycle – An Academic View', *Lloyds Bank Review*, September 1937, reprinted in *Essays in Money and Interest*, ed. J. Hicks (London, 1966), pp. 94–104; Keynes, 'A Monetary Theory of Production', *Collected Writings*, Vol. XIII, pp. 408–11; *General Theory*, Ch. 22; 'How to Avoid a Slump', *Times*, 12–14 January 1937; Robertson, 'Is Another Slump Coming?', *Listener*, 28 July 1937.

130 For further comment on this, see above, pp. 157, 163–4.

131 T. 177/38, Phillips, 'Report of the Economic Advisory Committee on the 1st March', Hopkins to Rowan, and Note by Fisher, 13 March 1937; T. 188/175, Leith-Ross to Hopkins, 9 and 14 April 1937; T. 177/38, Chamberlain to Minister of Health and other ministers, 19 May 1937. (The C.E.I. report, which was dated 22 February, was circulated to the Cabinet on 1 March.)

132 Cab. 27/640, Inter-departmental Committee on Public Capital Expenditure, Report, 14 August 1937.

133 On this forecast, see also T. 175/94, Hopkins to Fisher and Woods, 15 December 1937; T. 177/42, Phillips to Fisher and Chancellor, June 1938, and Note by Phillips, 27 June 1938.

134 Cab. 27/640, Addendum to Report of Committee on Public Capital Expenditure, 20 December 1937.

135 Bretherton, Burchardt, and Rutherford, *Public Investment and the Trade Cycle*, pp. 198–9.

136 Cab. 27/640, Cabinet Committee on Public Capital Expenditure, Explanatory Note.

137 T. 160/688/F 14996/1, Fisher to Chancellor, 'Defence ...', 2 December 1935, Phillips, 'General Note ... on methods of financing the Defence Programme', 29 November 1935, and Memorandum by Hopkins, 2 December 1935; Sabine, *British Budgets 1932–1945*, pp. 73, 79–80, 95.

138 T. 175/94, Phillips to Hopkins, 31 December 1936. On Phillips's views on the balance of payments, see also T. 177/24, Phillips to Hopkins, December 1936.

139 T. 175/94, Phillips to Hopkins, 31 December 1936.

140 T. 188/175, Hopkins to Fisher, 10 April, Note by Fisher, 12 April and Leith-Ross to Hopkins, 14 April 1937.

141 T. 188/175, Hopkins to Woods, 31 March 1937, Leith-Ross to Fisher and Woods, 2 April 1937, Fisher to Chancellor, 3 April, and Chamberlain to Eden, 7 April, Eden to Chamberlain, 10 April, and Chamberlain to other ministers, 4 May 1937.

142 T. 188/175, Committee on Trade Policy, Report, 4 June 1937. Leith-Ross's committee met daily for five days; Phillips's committee's six meetings in a month was the usual pace of official committees in the 1930s.

143 T. 188/176, Memorandum by Leith-Ross, 1 January 1938; see also Cab. 23/94, Cabinet 32(38)11, 13 July 1938.

144 T. 188/176, Leith-Ross to Hopkins, 4 January 1938, and Brown to Leith-Ross, 10 January 1938.

145 Drummond, *British Economic Policy and the Empire*, pp. 113–14, and *Imperial Economic Policy*, Ch. 8.

146 Howson, *Domestic Monetary Management in Britain*, pp. 120–6.

147 E.g. 12th, 15th, 18th, and 22nd C.E.I. Reports; speeches to National Mutual shareholders in 1934, 1935, 1936, and 1937, *Times*, 22 February 1934, 21 February 1935, 20 February 1936, and 25 February 1937.

148 R. S. Sayers, *Financial Policy 1939–45* (1956), pp. 156–7; Howson, *Domestic Monetary Management*, pp. 130–1.

149 Howson, *Domestic Monetary Management*, Ch. 2, and 'The Origins of Dear Money, 1919–20', *Economic History Review*, February 1974.

150 T. 175/95, Phillips to Chamberlain, 28 July 1937.

151 T. 177/38, Phillips, 'Report on the Economic Advisory Committee on the 1st March', 13 March 1937; see also T. 177/38, Hopkins to Rowan, 13 March 1937; and T. 172/1853, Phillips, 'Keynes on Defence Borrowing', 25 February 1937.

152 Debenham worked quite closely with Phillips over the next two years (see e.g. T. 160/878/F 16056, 'The Control of Prices in the event of war', and Henderson to Phillips, 12 October 1938, and Clay to Phillips, 14 October 1938).

153 Keynes Papers, Henderson to Keynes, 11 November, and Keynes to Henderson and Stamp, 7 November 1937.

154 73rd meeting of C.E.I., 8 July 1937.

155 Hodson, *Slump and Recovery*, pp. 440–2; Kindleberger, *The World in Depression*, pp. 264–9.

156 T. 177/39, Phillips, 'The Present and Future of Gold', 11 May 1937.

157 Ibid.; see also T. 177/39, Hopkins to Fisher and Chancellor, 25 May 1937, and Phillips, 'The Gold Question – views of the Governor', 24 May 1937.

158 T. 177/39, Hopkins to Fisher and Chancellor, 25 May 1937.

159 Ibid., and 'Note by Sir F. Leith-Ross. To be read as an addition to the end of Sir F. Phillips' note'; see also Cab. 58/22, Leith-Ross to Debenham, 29 September 1937; T. 160/770/F 15583, Leith-Ross to Brown and President of Board of Trade, 23 November 1937; T. 188/116, 'Personal views of Sir F. Leith-Ross on certain monetary aspects', 18 July 1935.

160 Keynes Papers, Henderson to Keynes, 11 November 1937; see also Stamp to Keynes, 11 November 1937.

161 73rd–78th meetings of C.E.I., 8 July–17 November 1937; Cab. 58–122, Drafts of

23rd Report; Cab. 58/22, Phillips and Henderson to Debenham, 30 October and 3 November, Note by Debenham, 3 November, Henderson to Debenham, 4 November, and Robertson to Debenham, 4 November 1937.

162   T. 160/770/F 15583, Howorth to Woods, 25 November; Hopkins to Fisher and Woods, 30 November; Leith-Ross to Brown and President of Board of Trade, 23 November; Hopkins to Fisher and Woods, 25 November; Note by Chamberlain, 2 December 1937.

163   T. 175/94, Phillips, 'Talk with Mr. Morgenthau on Gold', 25 September 1937; see also Kindleberger, *The World in Depression*, pp. 269–71.

164   See above, p. 113.

165   Cab. 58/22, Keynes to Debenham, 22 December 1937; 82nd–85th meetings of C.E.I.; 31 January, 6 and 24 May, and 2 June 1938; 25th Report, 27 June 1938.

166   Above, pp. 107, 394n4.

167   J. H. Jones, *Josiah Stamp, Public Servant*, pp. 302–3, 329.

168   Howson, *Domestic Monetary Management*, pp. 138–9; Bretherton, Burchardt, and Rutherford, *Public Investment and the Trade Cycle*, pp. 91–3.

169   87th–90th meetings of C.E.I., 25 October, 2 and 11 November, and 14 December 1938; Cab. 58/23, 'Paragraphs for draft 26th Report prepared by Mr. Keynes', 28 November 1938; 26th Report of C.E.I., 16 December 1938.

170   This argument seems to discount the possibility that the purchase of securities issued overseas could be prevented.

171   T. 175/104, Hopkins to Chancellor, 23 December 1938; Phillips, 'Economic Advisory Council Report on problems of rearmament', 21 December 1938; Leith-Ross, 'Twenty-Sixth E.A.C. Report', 22 December 1938; Cab. 58/23, 'Draft 26th Report, Note by Leith-Ross', 22 November 1938; T. 160/771/F 19429, Phillips to Catterns, 29 November 1938, and Catterns to Phillips, 9 December 1938; T. 175/104, 'Views of Treasury and Bank of England on suggestions made in paragraph 23 of Economic Advisory Committee Report of 16th December 1938'; T. 171/341, Note by Hopkins, 3 January 1939; Sabine, *British Budgets 1932–1945*, pp. 142–3. On the embargo, see also above, pp. 112–13.

172   Keynes, 'Crisis Finance', *Times*, 17 and 18 April 1939; T. 177/47, Phillips to Hopkins, 24 April 1939.

173   C.E.I. 27th Report, 20 July 1939. On stockpiling see above, p. 147.

174   Keynes Papers A/39, and T. 177/47, Keynes to Chancellor, 28 May 1939, Keynes to Norman, 28 May 1939, Keynes, 'Government Loan Policy and the Rate of Interest', 27 May 1939; see also Keynes, 'Borrowing by the State', *Times*, 24 and 25 July 1939; C.E.I. 91st–96th meetings, 3 May–4 July 1939; Keynes Papers, Keynes to Stamp, 1 July 1939; and C.E.I. 27th Report; Sayers, *Financial Policy 1939–45*, pp. 153–5.

175   *Financial Policy 1939–45*, p. 155.

176   Above, p. 149.

177   T. 177/47, Hawtrey to Phillips, 20 June 1939, and Hawtrey, 'Government Loan Policy and the Rate of Interest, Comments on Keynes's proposals'; Phillips to Hopkins, 24 April 1939.

178   T. 177/47, Phillips to Hopkins, 24 April, and Note by Hopkins, 25 April 1939; Hawtrey, 'War Borrowing'; Sayers, *Financial Policy 1939–45*, pp. 159–62; Clay, *Lord Norman*, p. 470. In the meantime there had been a not easily explicable episode, the rise in Bank rate to 4 per cent in August (see Sayers, *Financial Policy 1939–45*, pp. 156–9). By January 1940 Norman 'profess[ed] . . . to be a cheap money man and he agreed with . . . [Keynes's] suggestions' (including *How to Pay for the War*) (Keynes Papers, Kenneth Moore to Keynes, 9 January 1940).

179   Sayers, *Financial Policy 1939–45*, pp. 162, 197–210.

180   T. 160/1289/F 19426/1, Phillips to Hopkins, 4 June 1939, Horace Wilson to Phillips, 26 June 1939; T. 160/885/F 17545, Arrangements leading to Lord Stamp's

Survey, May and June 1939; Cab. 23/100, Cabinet meeting of 5 July 1939; Cab. 58/9, Stamp, 'The Work of the Survey in the first year of the war', 15 October 1940; E. A. G. Robinson, 'The Overall Allocation of Resources' in Chester (ed.), *Lessons of the British War Economy*, p. 38. Keynes did not enter the Treasury until June 1940 but as soon as war broke out Phillips consulted him on exchange control. He also, of course, gave the authorities much unsolicited advice. (*Collected Writings*, Vol. XXII, Chs. 1, 4).

181   J. R. N. Stone, 'The Use and Development of National Income and Expenditure Estimates' in Chester (ed.), *Lessons of the British War Economy*, pp. 83–7; Cab. 89/9, Stamp, 'The Work of the Survey in the first year of the war', October 1940; Cab. 89/27, The Income and Fiscal Potential of Great Britain: estimates of national income by Bowley; D. N. Chester, 'The Central Machinery for Economic Policy' in Chester (ed.), *Lessons of the British War Economy*, pp. 6–8; Robbins, *Autobiography of an Economist*, p. 169; Sayers, *Financial Policy 1939–45*, Chs. II, III; *Collected Writings of John Maynard Keynes*, Vol. XXII, Chs. 1, 2, 4. The first published version of *How to Pay for the War* was in *The Times* in November 1939; the pamphlet was published in February 1940 and is reprinted in *Collected Writings*, Vol. IX. The economists of the Central Economic Information Service included Meade, Stone, Robbins, Jewkes, and Austin Robinson.

182   Stone in Chester (ed.), *Lessons of the British War Economy*, p. 85.

183   See Keynes's obituary of Phillips in *The Times*, 13 August 1943, reprinted in *Essays in Biography* (*Collected Writings*, Vol. X), pp. 330–1.

184   Robbins, *Autobiography of an Economist*, pp. 186–8; Moggridge and Howson, 'Keynes on Monetary Policy, 1910–46', *Oxford Economic Papers*, July 1974. On Hopkins's central role in the Treasury, see also 'Sir Richard Hopkins', *Public Administration*, Summer 1956.

Note on the Committee on Scientific Research

1   The reports are in Cab. 58/4–5 and 9–12; the minutes and memoranda of the committees are in Cab. 58/31–120, 136–42; see also Cab. 58/8, EAC (G) 38, Hemming, 'Survey of the Development of the Functions of the Economic Advisory Council and its parent body the Committee of Civil Research', 25 July 1937.

2   The records are in Cab. 58/158–62, 170–4, 83–5, 184–92, 193–8, and 199–208.

3   Cab. 58/25, Committee on Scientific Research 1st meeting, 21 April 1932; Cab. 58/30, First Report, 'Science and Finance', 9 December 1933; Third Report, 'Science and Finance', 22 November 1934; T. 160/845/F 13727, Hopkins to Henderson, 21 November 1933; Phillips to Hopkins, 30 December 1933; Hopkins to Fisher and Chancellor, 11 October 1935; Hopkins to Norman, 18 October 1935. On the 1928 new issue boom see A. T. K. Grant, *A Study of the Capital Market in Britain 1919–1936* (1967), pp. 143–6, and R. A. Harris, 'A Re-analysis of the 1928 New Issue Boom', *Economic Journal*, September 1933; on the pepper scandal see Clay, *Lord Norman*, pp. 464–5.

4   Cab. 58/25, Minutes of Committee on Scientific Research; Cab. 58/16, Committee on the Economic Advisory Council, Report, 22 May 1938.

Chapter 6. Conclusions

1   See, e.g. G. D. H. Cole, *Industrial Self-Government* (1919) and H. J. Laski, *The State in the New Social Order* (1922).

2   Above, p. 23.

3   Lord Melchett, *Industry and Politics* (1927), pp. 63–5, 143–5, and *Modern Money* (1932), pp. 173–5, 205–13.

4   *House of Commons Debates*, Vol. 235, 20 February 1930, cc. 1–30; a by-election speech as reported in *The Times*, 19 March 1930; and *Parliamentary Government and the Economic Problem*, Romanes Lecture, London, 1930.

5 Above, p. 3.
6 Leith-Ross, *Money Talks*, p. 147.
7 Anderson, *The Organisation of Economic Studies in relation to the Problems of Government*, pp. 16–17.
8 Ibid.
9 Keynes Papers, Keynes to Eady, 3 October 1943.
10 Heclo and Wildavsky, *The Private Government of Public Money*, p. 270.
11 Ibid., Chs. 6, 7.
12 Bridges, *Treasury Control*, p. 14.
13 Above, pp. 101–5.
14 Keynes Papers, Keynes, 'The Concept of a Capital Budget', 21 June 1945.
15 Three recent studies of the relation between Keynes's theory and policy are Moggridge and Howson, 'Keynes on Monetary Policy, 1910–46', *Oxford Economic Papers*, July 1974; Moggridge, *Keynes* (1976); and D. Patinkin, 'On the Development of Keynes' Monetary Thought', *History of Political Economy*, Spring 1976.
16 R. S. Sayers, 'The Springs of Technical Progress in Britain 1919–39', *Economic Journal*, June 1950, pp. 279–80.
17 Above, pp. 10–11. It can also be found in the case for an economic general staff in the Liberal 'Yellow Book'.
18 Fabian Tract no. 235.
19 Above, pp. 34–5.
20 Moggridge, *The Return to Gold, 1925*, pp. 45–56, and *British Monetary Policy 1924–1931*, pp. 64–78 and Appendix 5.
21 Above, pp. 96–100.
22 See, for example, Henderson, 'The Background to the Problem', in *The Inter-War Years*, ed. H. Clay, p. 66.
23 *Theory of Unemployment*, p. v.
24 Above, p. 95.
25 For example, T. W. Hutchison, *Economics and Economic Policy in Britain 1946–1966* (1968), Appendix; Stein, *The Fiscal Revolution in America*, Ch. 8; and J. R. Davis, *The New Economics and the Old Economists* (1971).
26 Above, pp. 141–3.
27 The exact nature of these theoretical innovations is still the subject of debate. The challenge to the standard post-Keynesian interpretation of Keynes (of D. Patinkin, *Money, Interest, and Prices* (1956) and H. G. Johnson, 'The *General Theory* after Twenty-five Years', *American Economic Review*, May 1961) began with R. W. Clower, 'The Keynesian Counterrevolution: A Theoretical Appraisal', and F. H. Hahn, 'On Some Problems of Proving the Existence of Equilibrium in a Monetary Economy', both in F. H. Hahn and F. P. R. Brechling (eds.), *The Theory of Interest Rates* (1964). On the later developments see, for example, A. B. S. Leijonhufvud, *Of Keynesian Economics and the Economics of Keynes* (1968); R. Barro and H. Grossmann, 'A General Disequilibrium Model of Income and Employment', *American Economic Review*, March 1971; F. H. Hahn, 'Money and General Equilibrium', in G. C. Harcourt (ed.), *The Microeconomic Foundations of Macroeconomics* (forthcoming).
28 On the policy revolution, see Sayers, *Financial Policy 1939–45*, esp. Chs. 3–5; *The Collected Writings of John Maynard Keynes*, Vols. XXIII–XXVII, ed. D. E. Moggridge (forthcoming); Winch, *Economics and Policy*, Ch. 12; Stein, *The Fiscal Revolution in America*, Ch. 8.
29 M. Blaug, *The Cambridge Revolution* (1974), p. 73.
30 Above, pp. 60–3; Winch, *Economics and Policy* (1972 edn), pp. 197–202.
31 Howson, *Domestic Monetary Management in Britain 1919–38*, pp. 27–9, 91, 140–1.
32 *Economics in Practice* (1935), p. 51.
33 Above, pp. 140–1.

34 Hutchison, *Economics and Economic Policy in Britain 1946–1966*, Appendix, pp. 292–5.

35 Prem. 1/70, Jones to MacDonald, 18 December 1929.

36 *Treasury Control*, pp. 14–15; see also Howson, *Domestic Monetary Management in Britain 1919–38*, pp. 140–3.

37 Keynes Papers, Keynes to Durbin, 24 October 1942.

BIBLIOGRAPHY

Unpublished papers

Henderson Papers
Keynes Papers
MacDonald Papers
Public Record Office Papers. The call numbers and titles of the items used are:
  B.T. 55. Board of Trade, Records of departmental committees
    B.T. 55/51/R.C.I./1. Reorganisation of Cotton Industry 1932–6. Notes and memoranda preparatory to introduction of Cotton Spinning Industry Bill
  B.T. 56. Board of Trade. Chief Industrial Adviser
    B.T. 56/44/C.I.A./990/4. Economic Advisory Council – Memorandum by H. D. Henderson on scheme for industrial reconstruction
    B.T. 56/44/C.I.A./1912. Rationalisation. Memorandum for Economic Advisory Council by H. D. Henderson
  Cab. 23. Cabinet Office. Cabinet Conclusions
  Cab. 24. Cabinet Office. Cabinet Memoranda (C.P. Papers)
  Cab. 27. Cabinet Office. Cabinet Committees
    Cab. 27/378. Unemployment. Inter-departmental Committee. 1928
    Cab. 27/389 and 390. Unemployment. Inter-departmental Committee. 1929–30
    Cab. 27/397. Unemployment: National Schemes. 1929
    Cab. 27/413. Unemployment Policy. 1930
    Cab. 27/435. Trade Policy. 1930
    Cab. 27/437. Unemployment. Conference of Ministers. 1930
    Cab. 27/438, 439, and 440. Unemployment Policy. Panel of Ministers. 1930–1
    Cab. 27/451. Trade Survey. 1931
    Cab. 27/454. National Expenditure. 1931
    Cab. 27/456. Economy. 1931
    Cab. 27/462. Financial Situation. 1931
    Cab. 27/467. Balance of Trade. 1931
    Cab. 27/468. Employment Policy. 1931
    Cab. 27/479. Employment Policy. 1932
    Cab. 27/490. Unemployment. 1932
    Cab. 27/502. Trade and Employment. 1932–4
    Cab. 27/503. Trade and Employment. Panel. 1932–4
    Cab. 27/560. Produce Markets Supply Committee. 1933–4
    Cab. 27/583 and 584. General Purposes Committee. 1936
    Cab. 27/640. Public Capital Expenditure. 1937–8
  Cab. 29. International Conferences
    Cab. 29/140. Monetary and Economic Conference, London, 1933. Cabinet Committee
    Cab. 29/142. Monetary and Economic Conference, London, 1933. United Kingdom Delegation. Briefs, proceedings and memoranda
  Cab. 58. Committee of Civil Research and Economic Advisory Council
    Cab. 58/1. Minutes of Committee of Civil Research. 1925–8

Cab. 58/2. Minutes of Economic Advisory Council. 1930–2
Cab. 58/4, 5, 6, 8, 9, 10, 11, and 12. Committee of Civil Research and Economic Advisory Council Memoranda. 1925–39
Cab. 58/14. Memoranda by the Staff. 1930–5
Cab. 58/15. Notes on an Economic General Staff. 1929
Cab. 58/16. Memoranda of Committee on Economic Advisory Council. 1938
Cab. 58/17. Committee on Economic Information. Minutes. 1931–9
Cab. 58/18–23. Committee on Economic Information. Memoranda. 1931–9
Cab. 58/24. Sub-committee on Trend of Unemployment. Minutes and memoranda. 1935
Cab. 58/25. Committee on Scientific Research. Minutes. 1932–8
Cab. 58/26–9. Committee on Scientific Research. Memoranda. 1932–9
Cab. 58/30. Reports of the Standing Committees. 1931–9
Cab. 58/121–6. Channel Tunnel Committee. Minutes and memoranda. 1929–30
Cab. 58/127–31. Committee on Iron and Steel Industry. Minutes and memoranda. 1929–30
Cab. 58/132–5. Committee on Cotton Industry. Minutes and memoranda. 1929–30
Cab. 58/143. Conference on Iron and Steel Committee Report. 1930
Cab. 58/144. Committee on Channel Tunnel Policy. 1930
Cab. 58/145. Committee on Economic Outlook. 1930
Cab. 58/146. Committee on Unemployment Statistics. 1930
Cab. 58/147. Committee on Revision of Cost-of-Living Index Number. 1930
Cab. 58/149. Committee on Empire Trade. 1930
Cab. 58/150–1. Committee of Economists. Minutes and memoranda. 1930
Cab. 58/152–3. Committee on Marketing and Distribution. Minutes and memoranda. 1930
Cab. 58/154. Committee on Unemployment Benefit. 1930
Cab. 58/155. Committee on Chinese Situation. 1930
Cab. 58/156–7. Committee on Agricultural Policy. Minutes and memoranda. 1930
Cab. 58/163–6. Committee on Empire Migration. Minutes and memoranda. 1930–2
Cab. 58/167–8. Committee on New Industrial Development. 1931
Cab. 58/169. Committee on Financial Questions. 1931–2
Cab. 58/175–80. Committee on Problems of Rationalisation. Minutes and memoranda. 1931–2
Cab. 58/182. Committee on Limits of Economy Policy. 1932
Cab. 58/183. Committee on International Economic Policy. 1932–3
Cab. 89/9. Survey of Financial and Economic Plans. Papers. 1940–1
Cab. 89/27. Survey of Financial and Economic Plans. The income and fiscal potential of Great Britain: estimates of national income by Professor Bowley. 1940–1
F.O. 371. Foreign Office. General Correspondence
F.O. 371/17304, 17305, 17306. Western Department. 1933
Prem. 1. Prime Minister's Papers
Prem. 1/70. Proposal to set up Economic General Staff. 1929
Prem. 1/96. Financial Crisis of 1931: Diary of events up to the resignation of the Labour Government
Prem. 1/97. National Government measures in financial crisis including abandonment of the gold standard
Prem. 1/126. Government committee to consider steps to develop trade and employment. 1932
T. 160. Treasury. Finance Files
T. 160/398/F 12377. International Credit Corporation (Kindersley Plan)
T. 160/447/F 13017/09/1. World Monetary and Economic Conference. Interdepartmental Preparatory Committee

T. 160/449/F 13017/06. World Monetary and Economic Conference. Memoranda on price level as affected by monetary policy

T. 160/489/F 13017/021. World Monetary and Economic Conference. File of briefs

T. 160/533/F 13296/01 and 02. Restrictions on new capital issues. Memoranda of 1932–3

T. 160/633/F 15470/01. Committee on Savings 1935

T. 160/688/F 14996/1. Financing the Defence Programme: Papers leading up to the Defence Loans Bill 1937

T. 160/760/F 14596. Sinking Funds Account Memoranda 1931–8

T 160/770/F 15583. Economic policy in the light of changes in the economic situation and international political position since 1932; inter-departmental committee, 1937–8

T. 160/771/F 19429. E.A.C. Committee on Economic Information 26th Report: Problems of Rearmament

T. 160/845/F 13727. Report of Committee of E.A.C. on Scientific Research: 'Science and Finance'. 1933–9

T. 160/873/F 15814/1–3. Committee to consider mitigation of exchange difficulties in time of war by accumulation of stocks of essential commodities (including Keynes Plan)

T. 160/878/F 16056. Treasury views on Debenham's Memorandum on Armament Expenditure

T. 160/885/F 17545. Arrangements leading to Lord Stamp's Survey of War Plans in Economic and Financial Sphere

T. 160/951/F 14140/1. U.K. duties on iron and steel, 1935–9

T. 160/1127/F 13040/1. Economic situation: public and private spending

T. 160/1289/F 19426/1–3. Committee on Control of Savings and Investment, 1939

T. 161. Treasury. Supply Files

    T. 161/557/S 34462/1–4. Road Programmes. 1929–30

T. 162. Treasury. Establishment Files

    T. 162/472/E 23399. Economic Advisory Council. 1930–8

T. 171. Chancellor of the Exchequer's Office. Budget Papers

    T. 171/286. Budget 1931 (April): Customs and excise memoranda

    T. 171/287. Budget 1931 (April): Treasury memoranda

    T. 171/288. Budget 1931 (September): miscellaneous memoranda

    T. 171/296. Budget 1932: Treasury memoranda

    T. 171/309. Budget 1933: Treasury and revenue departments memoranda

    T. 171/341. Budget (1) 1939: proposals, Vol. 1

T. 172. Chancellor of the Exchequer's Office. Miscellaneous Papers

    T. 172/1684. Growth of Expenditure. 1929

    T. 172/1690. Correspondence with Mr Churchill re Finance during his term of office, and the new commitments of the Labour Government

    T. 172/1746. Cabinet Financial Situation Committee. 1931

    T. 172/1768. Balance of Trade Committee. 1931–2

    T. 172/1772–3. Iron and Steel Industry. 1931–3

    T. 172/1814. Preparatory Committee for World Monetary and Economic Conference

    T. 172/1828. Special and distressed areas. 1935–7

    T. 172/1853. Defence borrowing. 1937

T. 175. Treasury. Hopkins Papers

    T. 175/17. General monetary and financial policy. 1927–34

    T. 175/26. Memoranda on unemployment situation. 1928–30

    T. 175/38. Memoranda by the Chancellor of the Duchy of Lancaster and Major Attlee on the problems of British industry. 1930

T. 175/39. Unemployment: Mr Bevin's proposed charts. 1930

T. 175/40. Budget. 1930

T. 175/41. Sir O. Mosley's memoranda on the economic situation. 1930

T. 175/42. Sir Oswald Mosley's memoranda on retirement pensions and unemployment policy. 1930

T. 175/46. Bank for International Settlements: Gold Guarantee. 1930–2

T. 175/52. Miscellaneous correspondence on tariffs, etc. 1931

T. 175/56, 57, and 58. General financial policy. 1931–2

T. 175/59. Financial policy; at home and abroad. 1931–4

T. 175/64. Empire currency. 1932

T. 175/66. Mr Henderson's monetary proposal for the Lausanne Conference. 1932

T. 175/70. Suspension of gold standard, and general financial and monetary policy. 1932–3

T. 175/84. Monetary and financial policy. 1933–4

T. 175/93. Committee on Economic Information. 1935–9

T. 175/94. Financial Policy. 1936–7

T. 175/95. Bank of England: depreciation of securities held on behalf of H.M. Government

T. 175/104. General financial policy. 1938–9

T. 176. Treasury. Niemeyer Papers

T. 176/17. Embargo on overseas loans. 1925

T. 177. Treasury. Phillips Papers

T. 177/7. Gold problems (the Kisch Plan). 1932

T. 177/12. World economic and financial conference. 1932–3

T. 177/19. Résumé of different plans for the formation of an International Finance Corporation

T. 177/24. Balance of payments. 1935–6

T. 177/38. Economic Advisory Council. 1937

T. 177/39. World gold problems. 1937

T. 177/42. General Budgetary position. 1938

T. 177/47. Memorandum by J. M. Keynes on Government Loan Policy and the rate of interest. 1939

T. 188. Treasury. Leith-Ross Papers

T. 188/28. International Co-operation over the gold standard: 'Rules of the game' by H. D. Henderson

T. 188/29. 'Pegging the Pound': memorandum by R. G. Hawtrey and comments by H. D. Henderson

T. 188/48. Sterling: notes by Prime Minister's Advisory Committee on Financial Questions

T. 188/56. World Monetary and Economic Conference. Memoranda on various financial questions and problems

T. 188/72. International trade depression: U.K. recovery policy. 1933

T. 188/78. Monetary policy: memoranda for discussions with U.S. 1933–4

T. 188/101. Produce Markets Supply Committee: co-ordination of trade policy. 1934

T. 188/116. Exchange stabilisation. 1935

T. 188/117. The Lloyd George 'New Deal': proposals. 1935

T. 188/175 and 176. Trade Policy Committee. 1937

T. 200. Treasury. Committee on Finance and Industry

T. 200/4–6. Notes on discussions

Webb Reconstruction Papers

Serial publications

House of Commons Debates
The Economist
The Nation & Athenaeum
The New Statesman & Nation
The Times

Books, articles, and official reports

Allen, G. C., 'Advice from Economists – Forty-five Years Ago', *Three Banks Review*, June 1975
Amery, L. S., *My Political Life*, Vol. III: *The Unforgiving Years 1929–1940*, London, 1955
Anderson, Sir John, *The Organisation of Economic Studies in relation to the Problems of Government*, Stamp Memorial Lecture 1947, London, 1947
Balfour, Lord, *Economic Notes on Insular Free Trade*, London, 1903
Barro, R. and H. Grossman, 'A General Disequilibrium Model of Income and Employment', *American Economic Review*, March 1971
Bassett, R., *Nineteen Thirty-one: Political Crisis*, London, 1958
Beer, S. H., *Modern British Politics*, London, 1965
Beveridge, Lord, *Power and Influence: An Autobiography*, London, 1953
Blaug, M., *The Cambridge Revolution*, London, 1974.
Bowley, M., *Housing and the State 1919–1944*, London, 1945
Bretherton, R. F., F. A. Burchardt, and R. S. G. Rutherford, *Public Investment and the Trade Cycle in Great Britain*, Oxford, 1941
Bridges, Lord, *Treasury Control*, Stamp Memorial Lecture, 1950, London, 1950
The Treasury, London, 1964
British Association, *Britain in Depression*, London, 1935
Britain in Recovery, London, 1938
Brittan, S., *The Treasury under the Tories 1951–1964*, Harmondsworth, 1964
Steering the Economy: The Role of the Treasury, revised edition, Harmondsworth, 1971
Brown, A. J., *The Framework of Regional Policy in Britain*, Cambridge, 1972
Brown, E. C., 'Fiscal Policy in the 'Thirties, a Reappraisal', *American Economic Review*, December 1956
Brown, W. A. jun., *The International Gold Standard Reinterpreted*, 2 vols., Princeton, N.J., 1940
Bullock, A., *The Life and Times of Ernest Bevin*, Vol. I: *Trade Union Leader, 1881–1940*, London, 1960
Burn, D., *The Economic History of Steelmaking, 1867–1939: A Study in Competition*, Cambridge, 1940
Cairncross, Alec, *Control of Long-term International Capital Movements*, Washington, D.C., 1973
Carpenter, L. P., *G. D. H. Cole: An Intellectual Biography*, Cambridge, 1973
Charles, R., *The Development of Industrial Relations in Britain 1911–39*, London, 1973
Chester, D. N. (ed.), *Lessons of the British War Economy*, Cambridge, 1951
Chester, D. N. and F. M. G. Willson, *The Organisation of British Central Government 1914–1964*, London, 1968
Churchill, W. S., *Parliamentary Government and the Economic Problem*, Romanes Lecture, June 1930, London, 1930
Citrine, W. M., *Men and Work*, London, 1964
Clark, Colin, 'Statistical Studies of the Present Economic Position of Great Britain', *Economic Journal*, September 1931
The National Income 1924–1931, London, 1932
Clarke, S. V. O., *Central Bank Cooperation 1924–1931*, New York, 1967

The Reconstruction of the International Monetary System: The Attempts of 1922 and 1933, Princeton Studies in International Finance no. 33, Princeton, N.J., 1973

Clay, Henry, *Lord Norman*, London, 1957

Cole, G. D. H., *Industrial Self-government*, London, 1919

Cole, Margaret, *The Life of G. D. H. Cole*, London, 1971

Committee on Finance and Industry (Macmillan Committee), *Report*, Cmd. 3897, H.M.S.O., London, 1931

Minutes of Evidence, H.M.S.O., London, 1931

Committee on the Machinery of Government, *Report*, Cd. 9230, H.M.S.O., London, 1918

Committee on National Debt and Taxation (Colwyn Committee), *Minutes of Evidence*, H.M.S.O., London, 1927

Corner, D. C., 'Exports and the British Trade Cycle: 1929', *Manchester School*, May 1956

Davis, J. R., *The New Economics and the Old Economists*, Ames, Iowa, 1971

Debenham, P. K., 'The Economic Advisory Council and the Great Depression', *Oxford Economic Papers*, 1953, Supplement

Donoughue, B. and G. W. Jones, *Herbert Morrison: Portrait of a Politician*, London, 1973

Drummond, I. M., *British Economic Policy and the Empire, 1919–1939*, London, 1972

Imperial Economic Policy 1917–1939: Studies in Protection and Expansion, London, 1974

Feiling, K., *The Life of Neville Chamberlain*, London, 1946

Feinstein, C. H., *Domestic Capital Formation in the United Kingdom 1920–1938*, Cambridge, 1965

National Income, Expenditure and Output of the United Kingdom 1855–1965, Cambridge, 1972

Feis, H., *1933: Characters in Crisis*, Boston and Toronto, 1966

Foreign Relations of the United States: 1933, Vol. I, U.S. Government Printing Office, Washington, D.C., 1950

Gardner, R. N., *Sterling–Dollar Diplomacy*, London, 1956, and New York, 1969

Gilbert, B. B., *British Social Policy 1914–1939*, London, 1970

Grant, A. T. K., *A Study of the Capital Market in Post-war Britain*, London, 1937, reprinted as *A Study of the Capital Market in Britain 1919–1936*, London, 1967

Gustaffson, B., 'A Perennial of Doctrinal History: Keynes and "the Stockholm School"', *Economy and History*, 1973

Hahn, F. H., 'Money and General Equilibrium', in G. C. Harcourt (ed.), *The Microeconomic Foundations of Macroeconomics*, forthcoming

Hahn, F. H. and F. P. R. Brechling (eds.), *The Theory of Interest Rates*, London, 1964

Haldane, Lord, *Autobiography*, London, 1929

Halévy, E., *The Era of Tyrannies: Essays on Socialism and War*, London, 1967

Hancock, W. K. and M. M. Gowing, *British War Economy*, History of the Second World War, United Kingdom Civil Series, H.M.S.O., London, 1949

Harris, R. A., 'A Re-analysis of the 1928 New Issue Boom', *Economic Journal*, September 1933

Harrod, R. F., *The Life of John Maynard Keynes*, London, 1951

Hawtrey, R. G., 'Public Expenditure and the Demand for Labour', *Economica*, March 1925

Heclo, H. and A. Wildavsky, *The Private Government of Public Money*, London, 1974

Henderson, H. D., *The Inter-war Years and Other Papers*, ed. H. Clay, Oxford, 1955

Hicks, U. K., *The Finance of British Government 1920–1936*, Oxford, 1938

Hodson, H. V., *Slump and Recovery 1929–1937*, London, 1938

'Sir Richard Hopkins', *Public Administration*, Summer 1956

Horsefield, K. J., *The International Monetary Fund 1945–1965*, 3 vols., Washington, D.C., 1969

Howson, S. K., 'The Origins of Dear Money, 1919–20', *Economic History Review*, February 1974
  Domestic Monetary Management in Britain 1919–38, Cambridge, 1975
Hutchison, T. W., *Economics and Economic Policy in Britain 1946–1966*, London, 1968
Janeway, W. H., 'The Economic Policy of the Second Labour Government, 1929–31', unpublished Cambridge University Ph.D. thesis, 1971 (© William Hall Janeway 1971)
Johnson, H. G., 'The *General Theory* after Twenty-five Years', *American Economic Review*, May 1961
Johnson, P. B., *Land Fit for Heroes: The Planning of British Reconstruction 1916–1919*, Chicago, 1968
Jones, J. H., *Josiah Stamp, Public Servant: The Life of the First Baron Stamp of Shortlands*, London, 1964
Jones, Thomas, *A Diary with Letters 1931–1950*, London, 1954
  Whitehall Diary, 2 vols., ed. K. Middlemas, London, 1969
Kahn, R. F., *Selected Essays on Employment and Growth*, Cambridge, 1972
Keynes, J. M., 'The Question of High Wages', *Political Quarterly*, January 1930
  'A Note on the Long-term Rate of Interest in relation to the Conversion Scheme', *Economic Journal*, September 1932
  'How to Avoid a Slump', *The Times*, 12–14 January 1937
  The Collected Writings of John Maynard Keynes, ed. E. Johnson and D. E. Moggridge for the Royal Economic Society
    Vol. IV: *A Tract on Monetary Reform*, London, 1971
    Vols. V and VI: *A Treatise on Money*, London, 1971
    Vol. VII: *The General Theory of Employment, Interest and Money*, London, 1973
    Vol. IX: *Essays in Persuasion*, London, 1972
    Vol. X: *Essays in Biography*, London, 1972
    Vol. XIII: *The General Theory and After: Part I, Preparation*, ed. D. E. Moggridge, London, 1973
    Vol. XIV: *The General Theory and After: Part II, Defence and Development*, ed. D. E. Moggridge, London, 1973
    Vol. XV: *Activities 1906–1914: India and Cambridge*, ed. E. Johnson, London, 1971
    Vol. XVI: *Activities 1914–1919: The Treasury and Versailles*, ed. E. Johnson, London, 1971
    Vols. XXII–XXIV: *Activities: War Finance 1940–5*, ed. D. E. Moggridge, forthcoming
    Vols. XXV–XXVII: *Activities: Shaping the Post-war World, 1940–6*, ed. D. E. Moggridge, forthcoming
Keynes, Milo (ed.), *Essays on John Maynard Keynes*, Cambridge, 1975
Kindleberger, C. P., *The World in Depression 1929–1939*, London, 1973
Labour Party, *Labour and the Nation*, 1929
  Report of 29th Annual Conference, 1929
Landes, D. S., *The Unbound Prometheus: Technological Change and Industrial Development in Western Europe from 1750 to the Present*, Cambridge, 1969
Laski, H. J., *The State in the New Social Order*, London, 1922
  The Limitations of the Expert, Fabian Tract no. 235, London, 1931
Leijonhufvud, A. B. S., *Of Keynesian Economics and the Economics of Keynes*, New York and London, 1968
Leith-Ross, Frederick W., *Money Talks: Fifty Years of International Finance*, London, 1968
Liberal Industrial Inquiry, *Britain's Industrial Future*, London, 1928
Liberal Party, *We Can Conquer Unemployment*, London, 1929
  How to Tackle Unemployment, London, 1930
McCrone, G., *Regional Policy in Britain*, London, 1969

MacDougall, Donald, *Studies in Political Economy*, 2 vols., London, 1975

MacIntosh, R. A., 'A Note on Cheap Money and the British Housing Boom', *Economic Journal*, March 1951

Macleod, R. M. and E. K. Andrews, 'The Committee of Civil Research: Scientific Advice for Economic Development', *Minerva*, Summer 1969

Macmillan, Harold, *Winds of Change 1914–1939*, London, 1966

Mallett, B. and C. O. George, *British Budgets, Third Series, 1921–1933*, London, 1933

Melchett, Lord (Sir Alfred Mond), *Industry and Politics*, London, 1927

Modern Money, London, 1932

Memoranda by Ministers on Certain Proposals relating to Unemployment, Cmd. 3331, H.M.S.O., London, 1929

Middlemas, K. and J. Barnes, *Baldwin: A Biography*, London, 1969

Moggridge, D. E., *The Return to Gold, 1925: The Formulation of Economic Policy and Its Critics*, Cambridge, 1969

'The 1931 Financial Crisis – A New View', *The Banker*, August 1970

British Monetary Policy 1924–1931: The Norman Conquest of $4.86, Cambridge, 1972

'From the *Treatise* to The *General Theory*: An Exercise in Chronology', *History of Political Economy*, Spring 1973

Moggridge, D. E. (ed.), *Keynes: Aspects of the Man and His Work: The First Keynes Seminar Held at the University of Kent at Canterbury, 1972*, London, 1974

Keynes, London, 1976

Moggridge, D. E. and S. Howson, 'Keynes on Monetary Policy, 1910–46', *Oxford Economic Papers*, July 1974

Mosley, O., J. Strachey and A. Young, *Revolution by Reason*, London, 1925

Mowat, C. L., *Britain between the Wars 1918–1940*, London, 1955

Nevin, E., *The Mechanism of Cheap Money: A Study of British Monetary Policy 1931–1939*, Cardiff, 1955

Patinkin, D., *Money, Interest, and Prices*, New York, 1956; second edition, New York, 1965

'The Collected Writings of John Maynard Keynes: From the *Tract* to the *General Theory*', *Economic Journal*, June 1975

'On the Development of Keynes' Monetary Thought', *History of Political Economy*, Spring 1976

Pember and Boyle, *British Government Securities in the Twentieth Century*, privately printed, London, 1950

Phelps Brown, E. H. and G. L. S. Shackle, 'British Economic Fluctuations, 1924–38', *Oxford Economic Papers*, May 1939

Pigou, A. C., *Unemployment*, London, 1913

Industrial Fluctuations, London, 1927

'Wage Policy and Unemployment', *Economic Journal*, September 1927

Theory of Unemployment, London, 1933

Economics in Practice, London, 1935

Pitfield, D. E., 'Labour Migration and the Regional Problem in Britain 1920–1939', unpublished University of Stirling Ph.D. thesis, 1973

Report on the Collection and Presentation of Official Statistics, prepared by a committee appointed by the Cabinet, H.M.S.O., London, 1921

Richardson, H. W., *Economic Recovery in Britain 1932–39*, London, 1967

Robbins, L. C., *Autobiography of an Economist*, London, 1971

Robertson, D. H., 'Is Another Slump Coming?', *Listener*, 28 July 1937

'The Trade Cycle – An Academic View', *Lloyds Bank Review*, September 1937, reprinted in *Essays in Money and Interest*, ed. J. Hicks, London, 1966, pp. 94–104

Roseveare, H., *The Treasury: The Evolution of a British Institution*, London, 1969

Roskill, S., *Hankey: Man of Secrets*, Vol. II: *1919–1931*, London, 1972

Sabine, B. E. V., *British Budgets in Peace and War 1932–1945*, London, 1970

Salter, A. J., *Recovery: The Second Effort*, London, 1933

Memoirs of a Public Servant, London, 1961

Slave of the Lamp: A Public Servant's Notebook, London, 1967

Salter, A. J., J. Stamp, J. M. Keynes, B. Blackett, H. Clay, and W. Beveridge, *The World's Economic Crisis and the Way of Escape*, Halley Stewart Lecture 1931, London, 1932

Samuel, H., *Memoirs*, London, 1945

Sayers, R. S., 'The Springs of Technical Progress in Britain 1919–39', *Economic Journal*, June 1950

Financial Policy 1939–45, History of the Second World War, United Kingdom Civil Series, H.M.S.O., London, 1956

A History of Economic Change in England 1880–1939, Oxford, 1967

Schedvin, C. B., *Australia and the Great Depression*, Sydney, 1970

Shann, E. O. G. and D. B. Copland, *The Crisis in Australian Finance 1929 to 1931*, Sydney, 1931

The Australian Price Structure, 1932, Sydney, 1933

Skidelsky, R., *Politicians and the Slump: The Labour Government of 1929–1931*, London, 1967, and Harmondsworth, 1970

Oswald Mosley, London, 1975

Smith, H. L., *The Board of Trade*, London, 1928

Snowden, Viscount, *An Autobiography*, Vol. II: *1919–1934*, London, 1934

Stein, H., *The Fiscal Revolution in America*, Chicago and London, 1969

Stewart, R. B., 'Great Britain's Foreign Loan Policy', *Economica*, February 1938

Swinton, Lord, *I Remember*, London, 1949

Taylor, A. J. P., *English History 1914–1945*, London, 1965, and Harmondsworth, 1970

Templewood, Viscount, *Nine Troubled Years*, London, 1954

Webb, B., *Diaries 1919–24*, ed. M. Cole, London, 1952

Diaries 1924–32, ed. M. Cole, London, 1956

Williams, D., 'Montagu Norman and Banking Policy in the Nineteen Twenties', *Yorkshire Bulletin of Economic and Social Research*, July 1959

'The 1931 Financial Crisis', *Yorkshire Bulletin of Economic and Social Research*, November 1963

Winch, Donald, 'The Keynesian Revolution in Sweden', *Journal of Political Economy*, April 1966

Economics and Policy: A Historical Study, London, 1969: revised paperback edition, London, 1972

Young, G. M., *Stanley Baldwin*, London, 1952

INDEX